The Practice of Teaching

A Narrative and Case-Study Approach

Allen C. Ornstein
St. John's University

Richard T. Scarpaci
St. John's University

WAVELAND PRESS, INC.
Long Grove, Illinois

For information about this book, contact:
Waveland Press, Inc.
4180 IL Route 83, Suite 101
Long Grove, IL 60047-9580
(847) 634-0081
info@waveland.com
www.waveland.com

10-digit ISBN 1-57766-701-8
13-digit ISBN 978-1-57766-701-8

Printed in the United States of America

7   6   5   4   3   2   1

Contents

Instructional Elements   xi

Preface   xv

Part I
Perspectives on Effective Teaching Performance   1

1   Understanding the Effective Teacher   **3**

Reasons for Teaching   4

Keys to Effective Teaching   7
   The Learning Paradigm   7
   The Why, What, How, and Who of Teaching   9
   Effective Teaching Behaviors   11

Concepts of Learning   11
   Cognitive Structures and the Knowledge Base   12
   Learning How to Learn   13

Three Concepts of Learning   14
   Behaviorist Concept of Learning   14
   Constructivist Concept of Learning   18
   An Eclectic Approach to Learning   24

Teaching as an Art and a Science   25

Critical Thinking   27
   Strategies for Teaching Critical Thinking   29
   The IOSIE Method   29
   The Seminar Model   30
   Critical Thinking Research   32
   Types of Thinking   34

Defining Teaching Style   36
   Style and the Effective Teacher   37
   Determining Your Teaching Style   38
   Research on Teaching Style   41
   Teaching Style and Student Learning   43

A New Paradigm for Understanding Effective Teaching   45
   Empiricism vs. Radicalism   45
   Effective Teaching and the Hidden Curriculum   48

CONCLUSIONS 49   ■   KEY TERMS 50   ■   DISCUSSION QUESTIONS 50
MINI-CASES FROM THE FIELD 52   ■   FIELD EXPERIENCE ACTIVITIES 54
RECOMMENDED READING 54

Part II
The Practices and Technical Skills of Teaching   57

2   Instructional Objectives and Standards   **59**

Education Standards   60
   Defining Terms   62
   The Aims of Education   64
   Trends in Educational Goals   65

Objectives   70
   Program, Course, and Classroom Objectives   70
   Creating Goals, Objectives, Models, and Taxonomies   73
   Developing Goals (Tyler Model)   74
   Developing Objectives   78
   Taxonomy of Educational Objectives   79
   Establishing General and Specific Objectives   83
   Writing Your Own Goals and Objectives   92

Standards   95
   Standards and Practice   96
   The Current Status of Standards   100
   National Standards for Teachers   101
   Student Performance Standards   102
   Standards-Based Lesson Planning   104
   Best Practices   105

Theory into Practice   108
   General Objectives   108
   Precise Objectives   108

CONCLUSIONS 109   ■   KEY TERMS 109   ■   DISCUSSION QUESTIONS 110
MINI-CASES FROM THE FIELD 110   ■   FIELD EXPERIENCE ACTIVITIES 112
RECOMMENDED READING 113

3   Planning Instruction for Learning   **115**

Defining Curriculum   117

Teacher Planning   119

Planning by Level of Instruction   121
   Mental versus Formal Planning   123
   The Culturally Responsive Classroom   123

Courses of Study   125
  Unit Plans   126
  Lesson Plans   135
  Teaching Procedures: A Transmission View   145
  Teaching Methods: A Constructivist View   148
  Materials and Media   150
  Summaries   150
  Sample Lesson Plans   154
  Guidelines for Implementing Lesson Plans   160
Theory into Practice   164
  Unit Planning   164
  Lesson Planning   164
CONCLUSIONS 165   ■   KEY TERMS 165   ■   DISCUSSION QUESTIONS 166
MINI-CASES FROM THE FIELD 166   ■   FIELD EXPERIENCE ACTIVITIES 169
RECOMMENDED READING 169

4   Instructional Methods   **171**
Instructional Approach I: Practice and Drill   173
  Applications of Practice and Drill   173
  Implementing Practice and Drill   177
Instructional Approach II: Questioning   179
  Types of Questions   181
  Right Answers Count   186
  Asking Questions Correctly   187
Instructional Approach III: Selecting Direct
  or Indirect Instructional Practices   195
  Direct Instructional Practices   195
  Indirect Instructional Practices   197
  Instructional Practices Require Explanations of Content   201
Instructional Approach IV: Student-Centered Learning   204
  Problem Solving   204
  Students as Problem Solvers   205
  Students as Inquirers   210
Theory into Practice   212
CONCLUSIONS 213   ■   KEY TERMS 213   ■   DISCUSSION QUESTIONS 214
MINI-CASES FROM THE FIELD 214   ■   FIELD EXPERIENCE ACTIVITIES 216
RECOMMENDED READING 216

5   Instructional Resources   **219**
Selecting Instructional Resources   220
  Duplicating Materials   222
  Developing Materials   223
  Copying Materials   224

Presenting Instructional Materials   225
  Recognizing Field Dependent/Field Independent Learners   227
  Instruction with Textbooks   229
  Stereotyping in Textbooks   230
  Readability of Textbooks   233
  Electronic Reading Devices   235
  Cognitive Task Demands   239

Textbook and Pedagogical Aids   241
  Reading across the Content Areas   243
  Text Structure   249
  Guidelines for Using Textbooks   251
  Textbooks of the Future   251

Workbook Materials   253
  Disadvantages   253
  Advantages   254
  Guidelines for Using Workbooks   254
  Key Characteristics for Educational Software and Materials   255

Journals, Magazines, and Newspapers   256

Simulations, Games, and Technology   257
  Guidelines for Using Simulations, Games, and Technology   261

Theory into Practice   262

CONCLUSIONS 263 ■ KEY TERMS 264 ■ DISCUSSION QUESTIONS 264
MINI-CASES FROM THE FIELD 264 ■ FIELD EXPERIENCE ACTIVITIES 266
RECOMMENDED READING 267

6 Grouping for Instruction   269

Classroom Seating Arrangements   272
  Special Classroom Designs   273
  Factors to Consider in Classroom Designs   277

Whole-Group Instruction   278
  Class Size and Achievement   280
  Classroom Tasks   283
  Instructional Variables   286
  Guidelines for Teaching Whole Groups   287

Small-Group Instruction   288
  Ability Grouping   289
  Between-Class Ability Grouping   289
  Within-Class Ability Grouping   290
  Peer Tutoring   292
  Guidelines for Peer Tutoring   295
  Cooperative Learning   296
  Activities for Cooperative Learning Lessons   300
  Group Activities   303
  Group Techniques   304
  Guidelines for Group Activities   305

Individualizing Instruction for Enhanced Student Learning   308
  Individualized Instruction   308
  Mastery Instruction   311
Theory into Practice   316
  For Whole-Group Instruction   316
  For Small-Group Instruction   317
CONCLUSIONS 317   ■   KEY TERMS 318   ■   DISCUSSION QUESTIONS 318
MINI-CASES FROM THE FIELD 318   ■   FIELD EXPERIENCE ACTIVITIES 321
RECOMMENDED READING 321

7   Classroom Management and Discipline   **323**

Approaches to Classroom Management   325
  Assertive Approach: High Intervention Level   326
  Applied Science Approach (Instructional Practice):
    High Intervention Level   328
  Behavior Modification Approach: High Intervention Level   332
  Group Managerial Approach/Effective Momentum:
    Moderate Intervention   336
  Acceptance Approach/Logical Consequences:
    Moderate Intervention Level   341
  Success Approach/Choice Theory/Reality Therapy:
    Moderate Intervention   344
  Applying Glasser's Theories to Classroom Management   345
Implementing Alternative Approaches
  to Classroom Management   351
Guidelines for Using Punishment   357
Preventing Misbehaviors through
  Feedback, Trust, and Communication   359
  Building Self-Awareness through Feedback   359
  Developing and Maintaining Trust   360
  Communicating Effectively   361
Theory into Practice   366
CONCLUSIONS 367   ■   KEY TERMS 368   ■   DISCUSSION QUESTIONS 368
MINI-CASES FROM THE FIELD 368   ■   FIELD EXPERIENCE ACTIVITIES 371
RECOMMENDED READING 372

8   Academic Standards and Student Assessment   **373**

Standards   374
  The Significance of Standards   376
  Can Standards Make a Difference?   376
Evaluating Student Learning   377
  Criteria for Selecting Tests   377

Standardized and Nonstandardized Tests   380
    Norm-Referenced Tests   381
    Criterion-Referenced Tests   382
    Comparing Norm-Referenced and Criterion-Referenced Tests   383
    Types of Standardized Tests   386
    Questions to Consider in Selecting Tests   388

Teacher-Made Tests   389
    Differences between Short-Answer and Essay Tests   391
    Short-Answer Tests   393
    Multiple-Choice Questions   396
    Guidelines for Writing Multiple-Choice Questions   398
    Matching Questions   398
    Guidelines for Writing Matching Questions   399
    Completion Questions   399
    Guidelines for Writing Completion Questions   400
    True-False Questions   400
    True-False Questions: Pros and Cons   401
    Essay Questions   403
    Guidelines for Writing Essay Questions   406

Administering and Returning Tests   407
    Test-Taking Skills   408
    Test Routines   410
    Test Anxiety   413
    Returning Tests and Providing Feedback   414

Authentic Assessments   415
    Portfolios   415
    Performance-Based Assessment   417
    Project Work   418

The Purpose of Assessment   421

Theory into Practice   423

CONCLUSIONS 424   ■   KEY TERMS 425   ■   DISCUSSION QUESTIONS 425
MINI-CASES FROM THE FIELD 426   ■   FIELD EXPERIENCE ACTIVITIES 428
RECOMMENDED READING 429

9   Student Evaluation   431

Types of Evaluation   433
    Placement Evaluation   433
    Diagnostic Evaluation   435
    Formative Evaluation   435
    Summative Evaluation   436

Evaluation Methods and Approaches   437
    Specific Evaluation Techniques and Tools   438

Traditional and Standards-Based Grading   448

Standards-Based Grading   450
   Form of Grades   451
   Absolute Grade Standards   454
   Relative Grade Standards   455
   Combining and Weighting Data   456
   Contracting for Grades   456
   Mastery and Continuous Progress Grading   458
   Grading for Effort or Improvement   459

Records and Reports of Performance   460
   Report Cards   460
   Electronic Recordkeeping/Virtual Recordkeeping   461
   Cumulative Records   463
   Student Portfolios   464
   Guidelines for Grading Students and
     Reporting Student Progress   466

Communication with Parents   467
   Parent Conferences   468
   Letters to Parents   473
   Guidelines for Communicating with Parents   473

Accountability   474
   School Performance   477
   Student Performance   477
   Theory into Practice   478

CONCLUSIONS 479 ■ KEY TERMS 480 ■ DISCUSSION QUESTIONS 480
MINI-CASES FROM THE FIELD 480 ■ FIELD EXPERIENCE ACTIVITIES 483
RECOMMENDED READING 483

Part III
Preparing for Practice   485

10 Preparing for Practice   **487**

Reforming Teacher Education   488

Helping the Beginning Teacher   493
   Problems of Education Students and Beginning Teachers   493
   Teaching Inner-City and Culturally Diverse Students   496
   How Beginning Teachers (Novices) Teach   502
   Support from Colleagues   505
   Support from Other Beginning Teachers   507
   Guidelines for Improving Support for Beginning Teachers   508

Preparing Teachers for the Real Classroom   509
   Literate Critical Thinking   511
   IOSIE Method   512
   An Alternative: A Mentoring Model   513
   Self-Evaluation   514
   Reflection   515
   Guidelines for Self-Evaluation and Reflection   519

Supervision and Evaluation 521
   New Forms of Evaluation 523
   Authentic Evaluation 523
National Board Certification 525
Professional Associations and Activities 526
   Teacher Associations 526
   Advantages of Membership in Professional Organizations 527
   Professional Journals 528
   Meetings 528
   Coursework 529
   Researcher-Teacher Collaboration 530
Theory into Practice 534
CONCLUSIONS 536 ■ KEY TERMS 537 ■ DISCUSSION QUESTIONS 537
MINI-CASES FROM THE FIELD 537 ■ FIELD EXPERIENCE ACTIVITIES 540
RECOMMENDED READING 540

Endnotes 543
Name Index 578
Subject Index 581

Case Studies

Accountability and the Relationship between School and Student Performance, 475–476
Are Standards-Based Lesson Plans Necessary?, 140–141
Concept Formation, 208–210
Culturally Diverse Inner-City Students, 500–502
Defining an Effective Teacher, 46–48
Direct versus Indirect Instructional Strategies, 200–201
Grouping for Learning, 306–307
Helping the Beginning Teacher Prepare for a Job Interview, 532–533
Honor Roll Standards: Good or Bad?, 106–107
Learning with Textbooks, Trade Books, and Electronic Texts, 237–238
Lesson Planning, 152–153
Mastery Learning, 315–316
Parent-Teacher Conferences, 472–473
Preparing for Management Problems, 363–365
Questioning for Learning, 193–195
Reading in Content Areas, 248–249
Reasons for Teaching, 6–7
Standards versus Learning, 103–104
Teacher-Made Tests and Authentic Assessment, 419–421
Testing for Learning, 422–423
Twelve Beliefs that Lead to Effective Management Strategies, 349–351

Mini-Cases from the Field

A Constructivist Lesson Plan, 168–169
Ability Grouping versus Heterogeneous Grouping, 319–320
Acceptance Approach/Logical Consequences, 369–370
Accountability, 482–483
Administering a Standardized Test, 428
Aim of Education, 110
Are Objectives and Standards Necessary?, 110–111
Are Unit Plans Necessary?, 166–167
Are Workbooks Necessary?, 265–266
Assertive Approach, 368–369
Behavioral Modification Approach, 369
Communication with Parents, 482
Concepts of Learning, 52–53
Critical Thinking, 53
Direct Instructional Practices, 215
Do Standards Really Help?, 111
Evaluation Methods and Approaches, 481
Grouping for Instruction, 318

Guidelines for Using Punishment, 370–371
Homework as an Assessment Tool, 427
Implementing a Lesson Plan, 168
Indirect Instructional Practices and Child-Centered Learning, 215
Individualized Instruction, 320
IOSIE Method, 538–539
Is There a Correct Way to Plan a Lesson?, 167
Is There Really Such a Thing as Best Practices?, 111–112
Just What Is Curriculum?, 166
Keys to Effective Teaching, 52
Paper Textbooks or Electronic Reading Devices?, 264–265
Practice and Drill, 214
Preparing Teachers for the Real Classroom, 538
Questioning, 214–215
Reasons for Teaching, 52
Records and Reports of Performance, 481–482
Secrets for Success in the Practice of Teaching, 539–540
Selecting Instructional Materials, 264
Selecting Texts to Enhance Learning, 265
Simulations, Games, and Technology, 266
Small-Group Instruction, 319
Student-Centered Learning, 215–216
Success Approach/Choice Theory/Reality Therapy, 370
Supervision and Evaluation, 539
Support from Colleagues for Beginning Teachers, 537–538
Teacher Styles, Beliefs, and Characteristics, 53–54
Teaching Whole Groups, 318–319
Test Selection, 426–427
Types of Evaluation, 480–481
Types of Tests, 427–428
Using Standards, 426
What Is Standards-Based Lesson Design?, 112

Tips for Teachers

Advantages and Disadvantages of the Point System of Grading, 457
Alternative Assessment Criteria, 439
Appraising the Worth of a Textbook, 252
Components of Direct Instruction, 279
Directing a Parent Conference, 470
"Do's" in Asking Questions, 189–190
"Don'ts" in Asking Questions, 188–189
Enhancing Your Classroom Management Approach, 340
Enhancing Your Explanations, 196
Grouping Practices in Classrooms, 291
Improving Practice and Drill, 180
Improving Your Assessment Procedures, 382–383
Innovative Practices for Reporting Student Performance, 462
Key Words for the Taxonomy of Educational Objectives: Affective Domain, 88
Key Words for the Taxonomy of Educational Objectives: Cognitive Domain, 86–87

Key Words for the Taxonomy of Educational Objectives: Psychomotor Domain, 89
Learning Prescription, 441
Meaningful Methods for Cooperative Learning, 297
Organizing and Implementing Lesson Plans, 163
Organizing and Implementing Unit Plans, 129
Preparing Classroom Tests, 394
Selecting and Using Instructional Materials, 223
Stating Classroom Objectives, 94
Strategies for Managing Problem Students, 358
Strategies and Methods for Motivating Students, 10
Student Use of Textbook Aids, 241–242
Suggestions for Analyzing Preventive Measures, 365
Testwise Strategies, 408–409

Classic Professional Viewpoints*

Kathryn Kinnucan-Welsch, *Providing the Space and the Time for the Construction of Meaning,* 23
Robert J. Sternberg, *Critical Thinking in the Everyday World,* 28
E. Paul Torrance, *Be a Great Teacher!,* 49
Herbert J. Walberg, *Goal Setting,* 68
David R. Krathwohl, *Using the Taxonomy,* 82–83
Chester E. Finn, Jr., *State Academic Standards,* 98
Albert Shanker, *Lesson Plans and the Professional,* 136
Ralph W. Tyler, *Integrating Real-Life Experiences*, 160
Herbert M. Klieband, *The Persistence of Practice and Drill,* 174
Benjamin S. Bloom, *Methods for Teaching,* 211
Barak Rosenshine, *On Using Many Materials*, 227
Diane Ravitch, *Beyond the Textbook,* 239
Ernest R. Hilgard, *Psychology of Instruction,* 309
Anonymous, *On Being "Dumb,"* 311–312
Carolyn M. Evertson, *Effective Classroom Management,* 325
Sara Eisenhardt, *First-Day Procedures,* 333
Robert E. Yager, *Testing What We Intend to Teach*, 390
Bruce W. Tuckman, *Rules of Thumb for Taking a Short-Answer Test*, 395–396
Daniel L. Stufflebeam, *Reasons for Evaluation,* 434
Martin Haberman, *Evaluating Students in Schools,* 437
Julian C. Stanley, *Becoming a Teacher,* 520

*in order of appearance

Preface

Becoming a teacher is an extraordinarily complex venture. Some of what is needed for success is learned; some is attributable to who you are as an individual. This textbook argues for the *art* and *science* of teaching. The science of educational practice is growing; several chapters document what is now known. But you can know all that science and still be ineffective; and ironically, some individuals are relatively successful without knowing any of it. Such individuals may be good teachers, but they are not, at least in a technical sense, professionals. Professionals intentionally acquire a discrete body of specialized and theoretical knowledge (the type of knowledge that is now emerging about teaching), and they use that knowledge to help students learn.

This book is intended for any general methods or specialized methods class that seeks to show prospective teachers how to plan *what* to teach (objectives), how to determine *how* to teach (methods), how to reflect on what is taught (reflection), and how to assess whether students learned the requisite concepts (assessment).

As you begin your journey toward acquiring professional knowledge, you need to understand that successful teaching is predicated on several fundamental assumptions:

1. Teachers must possess thorough disciplinary knowledge.

2. Teachers must know the academic content standards for what they teach.

3. Teachers must know how learners learn in order to design meaningful instruction.

4. Teachers must know how to present content based on context and purpose.

Assumption 1 is fulfilled if you have a good general education. Assumption 2 is already addressed if you pursued disciplinary coursework in understanding and depth—that is, you earned a disciplinary major (or selected academic minors). Assumption 3 is fulfilled through educational psychology courses that emphasize work by people such as Jean Piaget, B. E Skinner, Edward Thorndike, and L. S. Vygotsky. Assumption 4 is the focus of this book. Specifically, this book focuses on *how* to teach: the process of communicating what you know in ways that help students construct knowledge.

Organization of This Text

The book is organized into three parts. Part I focuses on *Perspectives on Effective Teaching Performance*. Part II, *Practices and Technical Skills of Teaching*, breaks down the act of teaching into specific, discrete skills. Part III, *Professional Growth*, addresses issues related to ongoing professional development and suggests ways in which the skills necessary for the practice of teaching are part of both the art and science of what you do (or what any teacher does) in the classroom.

Features of This Text

The book is based on five fundamental elements, making it highly useful to a prospective teacher in today's schools. It is research based, example based, reflection based, expert based, and technology based.

Research

The book intentionally draws on the growing body of literature that shows that teachers really do make a difference in the achievement of students. In the 1960s, educators were told that family socioeconomic status was so important that teachers were "secondary." Today "value-added" research suggests that teachers do dramatically influence student achievement. What students *bring* to school (the socioeconomic capital of their families) does make a difference, but what *happens* to them once they are at school is just as important. That means that you as a teacher have just as much impact on a student's achievement as do the student's parents, and perhaps more so. What a responsibility *and* opportunity!

Example

One of the real problems with many methods texts is that they are heavy on theory and light on applications (examples). This text errs on the side of applications. Good teachers need theory, but that theory is meaningless if they do not know how to apply the knowledge. Many examples (tables, figures, charts, case studies, and analogs) are provided to make certain that what is described theoretically can be applied practically. Case Studies and Tips for Teachers help connect the theory and practice. In some instances, we even illustrate specifically within the cases the connections to teaching standards criteria and principles. This should enable you to see the theory-practice nexus more directly.

Reflection

During the 1990s the whole notion of reflecting-*in*-action and reflection-*on*-action became important professional dispositions that prospective teachers were expected to acquire. This text includes Questions for Reflection to help teachers think more deeply about some of the salient topics discussed. Once you start teaching you will need to learn how to reflect on what you are doing *as* you are doing it and to reflect on what you taught *after* you complete a lesson.

Expertise

Many individuals have shaped education in America. Many of their "voices" are part of this text—through Classic Professional Viewpoints. Their perspectives are extremely important and should help you see that many current educational issues are not new but are instead old problems that require new thinking.

Technology

The use of technology is increasingly prevalent for America's young people. Many of the pre-service teachers who read this text are accustomed to accessing websites to gather information about topics of interest. Throughout the text you will find Website information that will be helpful in enhancing your effectiveness.

To the Instructor

The Practice of Teaching is written for all who are interested in learning how to teach, improving their teaching, or teaching students how to learn. It will help prepare novice teachers for their new roles and provide seasoned teachers with new insights into *what* they are doing and *why* they are doing it.

The text focuses on the theory and practice of teaching. It attempts to blend theory with practice by reporting and analyzing important research and then presenting practical procedures and adaptive strategies for teachers to use. How do successful teachers start a lesson? How do they monitor classroom activities? How do they deal with disruptive students? How do they proceed with a student who doesn't know the answer? These are problems that teachers must deal with daily. The answers to these questions depend on how we apply to the classroom setting the theory we have learned in our coursework. Our hope is that you will be able to use this book to relate required teaching skills to defined and accepted teaching standards that will enhance your practice and your students' learning.

Prospective teachers and beginning teachers need to master theoretical concepts and principles and then *integrate* these concepts and principles into practice by developing specific methods and strategies that work on the job. The integration process, or the leap from theory to practice, is not easy. *The Practice of Teaching* helps by interweaving practical strategies and methods with research. Many theories and practices are presented with the understanding that readers can pick and choose the ones that fit their personality and philosophy. In each chapter, look for *Tips for Teachers* and *Case Studies*. These instructional aids are designed to help the reader apply the theory to practice.

The Practice of Teaching adopts a cognitive science approach, blending cognitive-developmental research with information-processing research. Consequently, a good deal of the subject matter is rooted in educational psychology, linguistics, and subject-related methods—and there is little that deals with the philosophy, history, or sociology of teaching.

Cognitive science focuses on how teachers teach and how learners learn, and it can be used to develop strategies that guide effective teaching and learning. This text presents research on how students process information, or what we call *learning strategies:* how to skim data, summarize information, take notes, do homework, read text material, take tests, and so forth. Existing research can also be used to teach students to think critically and creatively; to classify, infer, interpret, extrapolate, evaluate, and predict.

Research also exists to help identify effective teaching strategies. *The Practice of Teaching* uses cognitive science research to discuss how to teach by explaining, questioning, monitoring, and reviewing; how to diagnose, assess, and place students into groups for instruction; how to teach basic skills, concepts, and problem solving; how to manage the surface behavior of students on an individual and group basis; how to plan for instruction and utilize instructional technology; and how to use textbooks and improve instructional materials.

The new emphasis in cognitive science is concerned not so much with students' answers (though correct answers are clearly important), but rather with how students derive answers and what strategies teachers use to help students learn requisite material. This book informs teachers about research on how students process information and how teachers can modify their instruction to help students learn more effectively.

The many distinctive features of *The Practice of Teaching* include:

- Focus Points at the beginning of each chapter to help orient the reader, set the stage for what is to follow, and highlight the main ideas of the chapter
- Easy-to-read headings and subheadings that facilitate understanding and illustrate relationships among ideas
- Short descriptors and categories that help classify and conceptualize information
- Tables and charts organized as overviews that make learning more meaningful
- Research findings applied to classroom teaching
- *Classic Professional Viewpoints,* the perspectives of experts in the field, that highlight a major concept or principle and/or give advice for both the beginning and the experienced teacher
- *Case Studies* that illustrate some of the salient educational problems and help readers see the real-world nature of the problems
- *Questions for Reflection* that help readers critically reflect on the content
- Practical *Tips for Teachers* that give insights into teaching
- Conclusions that present itemized lists of facts pertinent to the subject-matter of each chapter

To the Student

The Practice of Teaching has five major purposes. The first is to help beginning teachers develop an understanding of what goes on in the classroom and what the job of teaching involves. Despite your familiarity with education from a student's point of view, you probably have limited experience with teaching from a teacher's point of view. And even if you are experienced, you can always integrate your own experiences about teaching with new information to achieve professional improvement and development.

A second purpose is to provide classroom teachers with concrete and realistic suggestions about ways of teaching—and how they can improve the teaching–learning process within their classrooms. Many teachers are unaware of their behaviors or the impact they have on students; others can sharpen their expertise in the methods and strategies that work with different students.

Another purpose is to apply theoretical and research-based data to teaching practices. Social scientists and educators have discovered many things about human behavior, and they have established many principles that can be translated into new practice in order to enhance student learning. Existing practices of the teacher can also be clarified and refined through an understanding of research. The idea is to convert "knowledge of teaching" into "knowledge of how to teach."

A fourth purpose is to show how teachers can make a difference and how they can have a positive influence on students. The data in this text suggest that teachers affect students, and that some teachers, because of their practices, have better results than others in terms of maximizing student success.

Finally, *The Practice of Teaching* deals with how teachers can teach students how to learn—with learning strategies that will increase students' chances for achievement and reduce the loss of human potential so pervasive in our society today. Understanding how to learn while developing a philosophical basis for one's decisions is the goal of the learner; helping students learn how to learn is the goal of the teacher. The extent to which students learn how to learn is influenced by how well the teacher can teach.

We are privileged that you are reading this textbook as part of your journey to become a teacher. Our hope is that your teaching journey is a long and fruitful one and that our text stimulates you to learn even more about what it means to be a classroom teacher.

Acknowledgments

Many people wrote the *Professional Viewpoints* features in *The Practice of Teaching*. They were kind enough to take time from their busy schedules to jot down some valuable advice or personal views about teachers and teaching. Their thoughts add a timely and unusual dimension to the text while providing useful information in an appealing manner. We appreciate their contributions to this text. And finally, I'd like to acknowledge Esther, who fulfills my life and has provided me with much needed understanding, support, and encouragement.

Allan C. Ornstein

I would like to acknowledge the support of the staff who worked with me in shaping the structure and content of this book. My work on this text is dedicated to my beautiful wife, Lucille Ann Scarpaci, without whose love and support it might never have been initiated and certainly would not have become a reality. In a world as troubled as ours, she has given me the strength to stand on principle and await the future with surety, enabling us to live our lives together with love and harmony.

Richard T. Scarpaci

Part I

Perspectives on Effective Teaching Performance

Part I examines teacher behaviors and explores how those behaviors influence your ability to teach and a student's desire to learn. As you will readily notice, the practice of teaching is incredibly dynamic. It demands a great deal of teachers, physically and emotionally, but it also can pay real psychological rewards.

In chapter 1 we explore the reasons for teaching, along with the concepts, ways of thinking, characteristics, styles, and behaviors that make an effective teacher. We also look at the keys to effective teaching, and basic concepts for learning within the framework of the art and science of teaching. We start with the art of teaching because it illustrates the incredible power and complexity of teaching, and we conclude with the growing body of scientific literature about teachers and teaching.

1

Understanding the Effective Teacher

> **FOCUS POINTS**
>
> 1. Realizing that there are many reasons for becoming a teacher, the most crucial reason being to educate future generations.
> 2. Identifying the keys to effective teaching and appreciating the contribution of both art and science to effective teaching.
> 3. Discovering the paradigms that dominate the practice of teaching.
> 4. Understanding the basic concepts of learning contained within the constructivist and behaviorist theories.
> 5. Identifying the critical thinking skills and strategies that facilitate true learning.
> 6. Understanding that teaching style involves one's beliefs, skills, and practices.
> 7. Realizing that it's not what you teach but what the student learns that counts.

OVERVIEW

This chapter asks you to consider why you want to teach and encourages you to honestly explore your own reasons. To paint a balanced picture of what teaching is, we begin with some general considerations about teachers. The object is *to describe teachers*, not just the teaching practices that those teachers use. Then we move on to more precise discussions about teaching. The heart of the chapter examines the art of teaching: Why is it that teachers with similar skills experience different levels of success? The answer lies in the nature of teaching as both a science and an art. Finally, the chapter examines how teaching influences student learning and creativity.

Reasons for Teaching

What are your motives for choosing a career in teaching? Those who are entering the teaching profession, and even those who are already teaching, should ask themselves this question. A motivation for many teachers is identification with adult models—parents and teachers—during childhood. Research indicates that women are influenced by their parents slightly more than by their teachers in their decisions to become teachers. Men are influenced by their teachers more than twice as often as by their parents.[1] The data suggest that parents encourage their daughters more than their sons to become teachers. Perhaps this is due to the wider range of professional choices that have been available for men in the past and the traditional view that teaching is a respected occupation for women but not for men.[2] Although job opportunities for women have increased in most fields, they still made up 80 percent of the public school teaching force, more than 80 percent of elementary teachers, and

45 percent of secondary teachers as of 2005. These percentages have not changed much since the mid-1960s.[3] In 2006, men accounted for less than one-fourth of all teachers.[3]

The situation is just as skewed when it comes to race and gender. Government data suggest that the teaching force lacks racial/ethnic diversity (88 percent white in 1972 and 91 percent in 2000) and is not gender balanced (31 percent male in 1961 and 26 percent in 2000).[4] The reason may be that male teachers feel a greater need to make more money, and teachers' salaries have lost ground during the recession.

Many have explored the idea that the choice of teaching as a career is based on early psychological factors. Wright and Tuska contend that teaching is rooted in the expression of early yearnings and fantasies.[5] Dan Lortie holds that early teaching models are internalized during childhood and triggered in adulthood.[6] Although these two investigations have different theoretical bases, both hold that, to a considerable extent, the decision to teach is based on experiences that predate formal teacher training and originate in one's childhood.

There are idealistic and practical motives for choosing a career in teaching. Ask why you are making this choice. Is it for love of children? A desire to impart specific content knowledge? An interest in and excitement about trying to change or serve society? Other less noble but still understandable reasons include job security, pension benefits, or the perception that preparing for teaching is relatively easy, compared with the training required by some other professions.[7]

It is essential to understand the importance of this career decision. Choosing teaching as a career affects your attitude and behavior toward your students. Whatever your reasons, it might be helpful to consider what has motivated your classmates, and others, to become teachers. Examine the five categories found in table 1.1 and determine which one best describes you. Then read Case Study 1.1 and see if it helps you focus your own ideas on why you have selected teaching as a professional vocation.

Table 1.1   Reasons for Deciding to Teach

Type	Description
The Crusader	seeks to change the system or society
The Content Specialist	wants to teach a specific content area
The Convert	starts another career but then "discovers that teaching is really a better career choice"
The Free Floater	is in teaching until a "real" career choice emerges
The Early Decider	knows from an early age that teaching is the right vocational choice

Source: Based on Carolyn Bogad's five categories of student teachers as described in Nathalie J. Gehrke, *On Being a Teacher* (West Lafayette, IN: Kappa Delta Pi, 1987).

The following case study presents various reasons for wanting to become a teacher. Read the case and see if you agree with the views of Anne Price, Cathy Kelly, or Bill Bradford regarding reasons for teaching.

Case Study 1.1
Reasons for Teaching

Bill Bradford had known Anne Price since the third grade. In all that time he had never known her to be stubborn or foolish regarding her future plans. She was a woman who knew what she wanted and knew how to get it. Her usual earnest approach had not prepared Bill for Anne's response to a simple question she was asked during recess. Cathy Kelly, Anne's best friend, had asked Anne why she wanted to become a teacher. Anne responded by saying there were many reasons, but the best was the vacation time and the short hours. Cathy exclaimed, "You must be kidding! Teaching is a profession that you enter for idealistic reasons such as love of children, or the desire to have an impact on our country's future, or wanting to change society in a meaningful way. It's sort of shallow and frivolous to say that what you're interested in has nothing to do with teaching. You sound awfully selfish to me."

At this juncture Bill interrupted and defended Anne by saying that being realistic was perfectly acceptable when choosing teaching as a profession. Nothing was wrong with being concerned about job security or pension benefits. These were sound, sensible motives for wanting to become a teacher. He further stated that it would be difficult to be idealistic without a realistic foundation. Remember, he told Cathy, we all have to eat and money does make the world go round.

Cathy looked at Bill and said, "I can't believe you're defending Anne. There are lots of reasons for choosing to become a teacher, and money and leisure time are not the right ones. Off the top of my head I can think of five sound and sincere reasons for wanting to teach. For one, you might want to change society for the better, as President Obama advocates. Or you might be interested in advancing knowledge in a specific content area, or you may have been born with a love for educating children. Some might even decide on this career change later in life or simply have an epiphany. Whatever reason you choose for wanting to become a teacher, none should ever be sanguine or materialistic."

Anne turned to Cathy and said, "What office are you running for? With you as a friend, who needs enemies? By the way, I do understand that a career decision is one of the most important choices one can make in life. Don't worry about my attitude! I am just a realist who knows where she is going. Children need to be taught how to behave and what is expected of them. My expectations are high. I know that anyone with low expectations will garner low results. What I'm telling you, Cathy, is that I intend to work hard for the benefit of the children in my classes. I don't think it's unreasonable to expect to be adequately compensated for hard work. My expectations are both high and achievable."

Cathy remarked to Anne, "That that was not what you said previously. It seems to me that you implied that your approach to children was based on your beliefs—and your beliefs seemed kind of shallow!"

Once again Bill interceded and said, "What you're really talking about is personality, and that's something we all have in abundance!"

Anne and Cathy both agreed that a teaching personality is probably a primary reason to want to teach and is the link to effective teaching that all effective teachers share in common.

Discussion Topics and Questions to Ponder

1. Who had the stronger argument for wanting to teach? Justify your answer.
2. Describe what Anne missed in her reasons for wanting to teach.
3. Compare the positions of Anne, Bill, and Cathy with regard to differences and similarities.
4. Table 1.1 (Reasons for Deciding to Teach) offers five reasons why one might want to become a teacher. Which one best describes yours? Explain your answer.
5. Whatever your reasons for wanting to teach, it might be helpful to examine your thoughts and feelings about those who have motivated you to want to become a teacher.

What would you do if . . . ?

1. You were asked to mediate the discussion.
2. Anne said, "Thanks for the input. I now know I was never meant to be a teacher."
3. Cathy changed her mind and supported Anne's position.

Questions for Reflection

On its Web page (http://www.teachforamerica.org/what-we-do/), Teach for America describes its mission as follows:

> Too often, where a child is born determines the quality of her education and life prospects. . . . Teach for America is building the movement to eliminate educational inequity by enlisting our nation's most promising future leaders in the effort.

Currently, there is great debate about this and other similar programs and whether they foster a long-term professional commitment to teaching. Do you think that such a commitment matters? Are teachers who plan to stay only a few years in teaching beneficial or detrimental to the profession of teaching? Explain your opinion. Can you find research support for your position?

Keys to Effective Teaching

Five keys to effective teaching must be mastered before you can call yourself a teacher (see box 1.1). These keys are simply a description of the proficiencies of an accomplished teacher. Management, method, mastery, expectations, and personality are the gears that turn the wheel for an effective teacher. Teachers adapt each key to their own unique personality type. As a key unlocks a door, these teaching keys can open the path to talented teaching. (These keys are discussed in further detail in the section below on effective teaching behaviors.) To arrive at this state one must embrace the learning paradigm.

The Learning Paradigm

The learning paradigm is opposite the traditional teacher-centered instructional paradigm in both mission and purpose. The conventional instructional para-

---

Box 1.1   Keys to Effective Teaching

1. *Personality* suited to positive interaction that engages learning
2. *Expectations* that all students will succeed
3. Ability to select *methods* related to how children learn
4. *Mastery* and proficiency in content area
5. Ability to *manage* the classroom effectively

Source: Adapted from Richard T. Scarpaci, *Resource Methods for Managing K–12 Instruction: A Case Study Approach* (Boston: Allyn & Bacon, 2009).

---

digm measures the efficiency of the teacher's instruction, while the innovative learning paradigm measures the learner's wisdom. Learning is not the transference of knowledge from teacher to student but rather is the construction and discovery of meaning by the learner. The mission and purpose of the **learning paradigm** clearly distinguish learning from instruction. An instructor offers courses; a teacher creates environments that leave no students behind. The reason for instruction is to deliver essential academic skills, while the purpose of teaching is to advance student comprehension. Therefore, while improving instructional practices aids students' skill development, focusing on learning helps students create knowledge.

Throughout the twentieth century an instructional model based on behaviorist learning theory was the strategy used for all instruction. The teacher was a transmitter of information in this version of teaching. *Behaviorism* regarded teaching as diagnostic proscriptive; the teacher analyzed student deficiencies and provided proscriptions to remedy deficits. This approach led teachers to rely on direct instruction as the primary pedagogical tool, and as a result the purpose of instruction became the enhancement and delivery of instruction.[8] Actual learning became a haphazard affair (as evidenced by numerous calls for school reform), compounded by the results of poorly designed standardized testing that left many students behind.

An alternative view highlights the role of the individual student in the learning process. This perspective is derived from the works of Jean Piaget and Lev Vygotsky, who asserted that in order to learn students must be socially engaged in the process of learning. Students must actively create their own knowledge based on their beliefs and experiences. This theory, known as *constructivism,* is in direct contrast to the well-developed teaching models based on behaviorism. It is a descriptive theory rather than a proscriptive one. The role of the teacher is that of a guide who leads students in their self-discovery of knowledge rather than the source of all wisdom and knowledge. These paradigms set the stage for understanding methods and instructional strategies. When teachers understand pedagogical beliefs such as behaviorism or constructivism, their effectiveness increases. When a teacher has clarity of thought and an understanding of instructional practices, student learning improves (see table 1.2).

Table 1.2   The Two Paradigms in American Classrooms

The Instructional Paradigm	*The Learning Paradigm*
Mission and Purposes	
• Provide/deliver instruction	• Produce learning
• Transfer knowledge from teacher to students	• Elicit students' discovery and construction of knowledge
• Offer courses and programs	• Create powerful learning environments
• Improve the quality of instruction	• Improve the quality of learning
• Achieve access for diverse students	• Achieve success for diverse students
Teaching/Learning Structures	
• Atomistic: parts more important than whole	• Holistic: whole more important than parts
• Time held constant; learning varies	• Learning held constant; time varies
• One teacher, one classroom	• Whatever learning experience works
• Covering material	• Defining specific learning objectives
• Private assessment	• Public assessment

Source: Adapted from Robert Barr and John Tagg, "From Teaching to Learning." *Change* (June 1995): 16.

The Why, What, How, and Who of Teaching

The paradigms outlined in table 1.2—mission/purpose and teaching/learning structures—help us understand the purposes of effective instructional practices by providing an answer for the "why" in teaching. The "what" and the "how" of teaching are readily understood. The teaching personality, the "who," is more often neglected. The "who" in teaching matters just as much as what we know and how we teach it. Great teaching is composed of more than just mastery of knowledge and method. It is fashioned out of spirit and personality, out of qualities inherent in all of us. Teaching is both an art and a science. Mere knowledge of content and method do not make an effective teacher. Personal characteristics and values are just as important, if not more so, than knowledge and method.

Effective teachers have a teaching personality that encourages commitment and enthusiasm and engages students in the learning process. Great teachers evidence a special type of personality that is defined and measured by students' social and academic achievements. No one is left behind when we believe all can succeed to the degree and level of their capabilities. When combined with perseverance and ingenuity, your teaching personality can lead you to mastery in teaching.

TIPS FOR TEACHERS 1.1

Strategies and Methods for Motivating Students

The teacher has the responsibility to help the learner feel and be successful. Students should not be bored but should be interested in their schoolwork. What follows are some basic applications of theories of motivation for producing learner success in school.

1. *Be sure students can fulfill their basic school needs.* Provide time to discuss academic and social expectations, responsibilities, and behaviors.

2. *Make sure the classroom is comfortable, orderly, and pleasant.* A student's sense of physical and psychological comfort is affected by such factors as room temperature, light, furniture arrangement, pictures and bulletin boards, and cleanliness.

3. *Help students perceive classroom tasks as valuable.* Learners are motivated when they believe the tasks they perform are relevant to their personal needs, interests, and goals.

4. *Be sure tasks are suitable for students' capability levels.* If the tasks are too difficult, students will quickly become frustrated and lose self-confidence. If the tasks are too easy, they will eventually become bored and lose interest in the work.

5. *Recognize that students have different levels of anxieties and need for advancement.* Some students need extra time, support, or help because they seem to be unmotivated. Most of this behavior is a defense mechanism brought on by previous failure, lack of stimulation, or poor self-esteem. Other students are reared in environments that result in stress and the need to excel.

6. *Help students take appropriate responsibility for their successes and failures.* Students need to be taught that they cannot excel in all activities and that if they do not adequately perform in one area they can improve with effort and also excel in other areas. Build on the strengths of students; work around (don't ignore) their weaknesses by providing support and encouragement.

7. *Help students set reasonable goals.* Encourage students to set realistic, short-term goals. Discuss the need for planning, practice, and persistence.

8. *Provide variety in learning activities.* Changes in instructional activities renew interest and help students pay attention. Younger students and low-achieving students need more variety to avoid boredom.

9. *Use novel and interactive instructional methods.* The idea is to get students to ask, "Why?" How come?" and "What will happen if I do *x, y,* or *z*?" The goal is to get students interested and then to think. Avoid too much "teacher talk"; it leads to a bored, passive audience.

10. *Use cooperative learning methods.* Get students to participate and work together. Have them work as a team so one student's success helps other students succeed. Cooperative learning reduces stress and anxiety, especially among low-achieving students.

11. *Monitor students' work; provide feedback.* Knowledge of results, notes on homework or written assignments, and even nods or verbal praise reinforce effort and provide students with recognition of achievement.

12. *Provide ways for improving.* Comments about skill performance and how to improve are important because they allow students to make corrections, avoid bad habits, and better understand content.

Effective Teaching Behaviors

Success in teaching is usually described in terms of five key elements that are common to effective teaching. There is no specific order of importance; each key is important in its own right. No single key could stand alone in defining or describing a teacher—each key must work in concert with the others. One's personality, however, acts as a unifying thread for all. *Teaching personality*, defined as a combination of character and values, espouses learning as the core for effective teaching. Positive *expectations* grow out of our understanding of learning, and our expectations determine the methods we will choose and the objectives we will set. The *methods* we select are expressions of our personalities, as are the instructional practices we implement. Perseverance and ingenuity are personal qualities essential to *mastery* of content. The final component, *management*, deals with the practicality of efficient class management and the teacher's role as a manager and purveyor of procedures. Again, personality plays a major role in choice of management techniques and strategies.

Effective teaching, then, is what happens when a teacher transforms expectations into understandable learning objectives that have been defined in terms of students' social and academic achievements. Students learn because teachers place a powerful emphasis on what students learn, not what instructors teach or promote. Clear lesson objectives facilitate student learning. Effective teaching also requires that the basic psychological needs of all learners are satisfied.[9] A master teacher is one who has developed a philosophical reservoir of knowledge pertaining to methodology, child development, psychological needs, subject-matter theories, brain theories, and intelligence theories. One's core educational philosophy is a synthesis of informational data. The effective teacher combines competency in practice with the understanding of theoretical knowledge about learning and human behavior. Her knowledge of content, combined with an understanding of instructional strategies, hones presentation skills. Content knowledge and methodology make up the "what" and "how" of teaching which, when combined, forms the teaching personality (the "who").

Reinhartz describes eight behaviors directly related to effective teaching. We can correlate these effective teaching behaviors to the five effective teaching keys. Even though correlation does not necessarily indicate causality, Reinhartz's eight behaviors (see box 1.2) do bolster intuitive evidence that the keys are a basis for good teaching.[10]

Concepts of Learning

The primary concept of learning in this text is not that the learner merely remains passive, reacts to stimuli, and waits for some reward. Here the learner is regarded as active and able to monitor and control cognitive activities. He or she acquires new information through assimilation and integrates it with previous information. Without this integration, new information would be lost to memory, and task performance dependent on the information would be unsuccessful.[11]

Box 1.2   Eight Behaviors for Effective Teaching

1. *Instructional clarity* is the result of focused lessons that engage students. This behavior relates to the keys with regard to method and personality. Teaching personality at times determines the method chosen to facilitate learning. Students normally respond well to teaching personalities they like. Instructional clarity is then easily achieved.

2. *Knowledge about content* is the result of perseverance and ingenuity, evidenced by the ability to structure and integrate concepts into curriculum. The effective teaching key for mastery of content knowledge is linked to this behavior.

3. *Establishment of learning expectations* is the result of understanding how children learn and creating attainable and measurable objectives. Instructional strategies based on clear objectives become achievable expectations.

4. *Variation in teaching* is the result of using strategies that promote opportunities for interactive learning, as opposed to passive learning. This behavior coincides with three keys: method (in the selection of approaches), management (in the ability to engage), and personality (in the ability to communicate).

5. *Utilization of resources* occurs when the teacher uses different instructional aids and materials during a lesson. This behavior links to the management key by using materials as motivational aids to focus attention, which also limits the opportunity for misbehavior.

6. *Knowledge of learning and development principles* means implementing appropriate learning strategies to meet student needs. Successful teachers implement effective teaching keys by means of traditional, progressive, and constructivist strategies.

7. *Communication with students on multiple levels* means a concentration on higher-order thinking skills. This type of behavior is enhanced by one's teaching personality.

8. *Enthusiasm* is infectious, and a teacher's passion for a subject inspires student participation. Personality is a prime key to creating enthusiastic learners.

Source: Adapted from J. Reinhartz and D. Beach, *Teaching and Learning in the Elementary Schools: Focus on Curriculum* (Columbus OH: Merrill, 1997).

Cognitive Structures and the Knowledge Base

When students want to identify, categorize, and process new information, they search their **cognitive structures**. If these cognitive structures are disorganized, unclear, or not fully age developed, students cannot learn—they cannot clearly identify, categorize, and assimilate new information. When based on previous learning, prior knowledge, and real-life experiences, new learning is meaningful to students, regardless of whether they are low- or high-achieving.

High-achieving students have a more expanded base of prior knowledge (in terms of in-depth knowledge and multiple forms of knowledge) than do low-achieving students.[12] This mature knowledge base permits learners to integrate important and/or complex information into existing cognitive structures. One of the premises grounding reform programs such as E. D. Hirsch's Core Knowledge (see www.coreknowledge.org) is that schools need to provide a content-rich curriculum so that students acquire the requisite background knowledge to handle increasingly complex cognitive tasks and then become better able to foster their own learning.

Those students who are capable of learning on their own are better able to (1) narrow, identify, or place information into preexisting categories; (2) sharpen prior information or distinguish from new information to avoid confusion or overlap; (3) tolerate or deal with ambiguous and unclear information without getting frustrated; and (4) assimilate existing schemata to interpret problematic situations.[13]

Learning How to Learn

A central idea of this text is that students construct their own cognitive frameworks and structures (i.e., they make their own sense of the world), and teachers guide that process using existing disciplinary frameworks. Teachers provide a structure for ideas that students then make personal sense of. The process of learning to learn assumes that students will use personal experiences to construct personal meanings and that the teacher has responsibility for shaping that process.

This view is a contentious one. Some would allow the "life of the mind" to permit students personal freedom in what and how content is learned. They see in standards (and standardized testing) a fixation that distracts students from genuine learning and from constructing their own meaning.[14] Others argue for an educational world that is academically proscribed—the same standards and assessments for all. We, however, rely on Aristotle's "golden mean" as a compromising balance. Students need some freedom to explore, but to be successful they also need to know things. Diversity does not demand total academic openness. "In a society stratified along racial and economic lines the absence of [state] standards guarantees that educational opportunities for students will be stratified according to where one lives and what one's background is."[15] Diversity requires common academic standards to offer a common benchmark for assessment and provide students with equal opportunity.

Learning-to-learn skills are basic thinking skills that are used in all content areas. Learning paradigm teachers foster learning-to-learn skills. Some of these skills are generic and can be taught in isolation as general strategies, without reference to content.[16] A good mathematical learner may not be as good in English or history, but that does not mean there is no transfer of learning skills from one subject to another. Different disciplines have their own principles, concepts, and methods that are distinguished from those of other disciplines.[17] What is learned in one area is not easily transferable to another area of learning because it is context based.[18]

Others believe generic learning skills can be taught to most students and transferred across subjects. Most learning skills can be incorporated into regular classroom activities or taught in a special course that incorporates cognitive processes that cut across subjects. Separate programs designed to teach thinking include Adler's Paideia Program, Feurestein's Instrumental Enrichment, Lipham's Philosophy for Children, and Pogrow's Higher-Order Thinking Skills (HOTS).[19]

Two basic concepts essential for understanding how we learn have been advanced by both behaviorist and constructivist psychologists. An eclectic view of teaching and learning best expressed in Jerome Bruner's early works still represents a commonly relied-upon third alternative. The path to understanding and learning is not necessarily straight. Bruner indicated that there were different approaches to learning, with distinctive forms of instruction that ranged from imitation to discovery and collaboration. These dissimilar eclectic approaches reflect differing beliefs and assumptions about learners. They imply that there might be more than one or two correct ways to understand the learning process.[20] We spotlight two basic approaches and one alternative.

Three Concepts of Learning

Behaviorists' view of teaching and learning is also called the *transmission approach*. It claims that children are blank slates who simply respond to stimuli. This traditional position holds that a teacher tells, shows, or demonstrates facts, knowledge, rules of action, and principles, which students then must practice to learn. Learning from this perspective is regarded as a process for measuring attainment of a fixed body of knowledge.

Constructivists' view of teaching and learning (or the *cognitive psychologist's approach*) is rooted in the concept that the construction of knowledge occurs in a sociocultural context, and it embodies an investigative style of learning. It advances the idea that children are self-regulating and may be influenced by environmental factors. Children essentially make their own decisions on how to behave and learn. Constructivism is a relativist view of knowledge with an emphasis on assessing higher-order thinking skills.

An *eclectic view* to learning has no specific theoretical rationale: It is comprised of individual strategies that have proved effective in the past. The practice has been described as a *cookbook approach* of "do's and don'ts" that have been used for ages by teachers. Goodlad describes an eclectic approach as a composite of strategies such as positive reinforcement, rewards, honor rolls, and special privileges—all taken from other approaches.[21]

Behaviorist Concept of Learning

From Aristotle to Watson, the historical references that led to behavioral psychology were essentially linear. From the time of the ancient Greeks through the Renaissance and the Victorian period, a clear line establishes the thought processes that led to behavioral psychology. The following five references are noted because they led to the founding of *behavioral psychology* and eventually behavior modification.

- Aristotle was the first to classify human behavior into categories that included sight, smell, hearing, appetite, and fashion.
- In the 1600s René Descartes viewed behavior as mechanical, and the body as a machine.

- In the 1800s Darwin proposed his theory of evolution and natural selection as an explanation of human behavior.
- In the early twentieth century Ivan Pavlov demonstrated behavior modification theory with his famous experiment that caused dogs to salivate when a bell was rung.
- In the early twentieth century John B. Watson was the first to formalize previous study into a field that he called "behavioral psychology."

Burrhus Frederic Skinner (1904–1990), the father of behavioral psychology, was a psychologist at Harvard University who claimed that our choices are determined by the environmental conditions under which we live. He found that a student's behavior could be controlled through a program of positive and negative reinforcement. His work led to the science of human behavior known as behavior modification that allows us to study and analyze human behavior. The controversy that surrounds Skinner developed because he told people they were not as important as they believed they were. He claimed that our minds were not our private preserve and that they could be controlled and shaped by science. His view was as controversial as that of Copernicus, who said the earth was not the center of the universe, and Darwin, who said the human body is the product of evolution and natural selection rather than intelligent design.

Skinner's contribution to the field was that he isolated behavior as its own entity, separate from all other aspects of life. He did this by disregarding the mind, soul, and human spirit. He explained that human behaviors were controlled by consequences and not by human will. Behaviors could be reinforced if a sufficiently strong reward was provided following the behavior. Behaviorists boast that they can modify behavior by either reinforcement or punishment and thus encourage learning. Rewards, according to Skinner, are whatever people desire as a result of their actions. This led to a theory called "Contingencies of Reinforcement," which is the result of situations, behavior, and consequences.[22]

The theoretical principles of behaviorism are prevalent in most learning environments. Any analysis of traditional teaching would evidence the powerful influence behaviorists have on learning. The concept of direct teaching (wherein a teacher transmits knowledge to students) is but one example. The use of exams to measure observable behavior of learning, the use of rewards and punishments in our school system, and the breakdown of the instruction process into "conditions of learning" are all examples of the impact behaviorists have had on education.

From a behaviorist perspective, computer-assisted instruction (CAI) is an effective way of learning. It uses the behaviorist approach of drill and practice to encourage learning new concepts and skills. Computer-generated questions act as the stimulus that elicits responses from students as well as providing rewards for correct answers. The "contingencies" of learning with computers are translated into different levels of the program. Rewarding the user for correct responses by allowing them to progress to a different level follows exactly the approach of operant conditioning. Educators have espoused CAI as an effective tool because it allows for self-paced instruction and liberates teachers from direct instruction, allowing them time to spend with those students with special needs.

In *Technology of Teaching* (1968) Skinner described examples of programmed instruction as part of his philosophy of education. Education was seen as a process whereby we arrange the educational environment to expedite learning. His teaching system consisted of lessons and rewards leading to self-control. Skinner claimed that positive reinforcement, not punishment, was the most effective consequence for any human response. This can be readily seen in the so-called correction strategies that behaviorists use to modify behavior. Reinforcement occurs when stimuli are used to reinforce behavior. Reinforcers can be used either for negative reinforcement (as in withdrawing stimuli for punishment) or for positive reinforcement (as when stimuli are used for rewards). An example of positive reinforcement is giving points for good behavior, while an example of negative reinforcement is taking points away for poor behavior. Some types of behavioral reinforcers appear in box 1.3. Skinner wrote,

> The application of operant conditioning to education is simple and direct. Teaching is the arrangement of contingencies of reinforcement under which students learn. They learn without teaching in their natural environments, but teachers arrange special contingencies which expedite learning, hastening the appearance of behavior which would otherwise be acquired slowly or making sure of the appearance of behavior which otherwise never occur.[23]

Skinner believed that more complex learning could be achieved by this process of contingencies and reinforcement ". . . through successive stages in the shaping process, the contingencies of reinforcement being changed progressively in the direction of the required behavior."[24] Remember that behavior modification is the name for the overall process, which derives from Skinner's work. Two key elements are behavior shaping and operant behavior. *Behavior shaping* is the systematic use of reinforcing stimuli to change one's behavior in a desired direction. *Operant behavior*, on the other hand, is any voluntary action that an individual performs. This simply means that any (operant) behavior can be reinforced negatively or positively by an outside force, the teacher.

The Neo-Skinnerian Model. Those who followed Skinner applied his principles to create a neo-Skinnerian model for reinforcement in the development of behavior modification. Their purpose was to create a model that could shape classroom behavior based on Skinner's principles for behavior shaping. The main strength of the neo-Skinnerian model is that behavior modification works, and works well.[25] It's simple to use and results are immediate. It accommodates most teachers' deep desire to preserve control while allowing students to experience success by obtaining rewards. Behavior standards are unvarying, consistent, and clear to all students. No time is wasted discussing rules and conduct. The model is well researched and works consistently for all ages. There is no doubt that behavior modification can encourage better student behavior and learning. Practically all teachers use it to some degree, but few follow it systematically because it is difficult to maintain.

A *behavior modification plan* is made up of essentially three steps: the first is analysis, to determine concerns and decide what the desired behaviors should be. The second step is to develop a plan and connect the desired behaviors you

Box 1.3   Types of Behavioral Reinforcers

- *Conditioned reinforcers* are strengthened by their relationship to another reinforcer—for example, verbal praise, material rewards, or special privileges granted for work well done,
- *Edible reinforcers* consist of items such as candy or other goodies. These reinforcers are not considered an appropriate reward today due to various state laws that prohibit their use.
- *Material reinforcers* are items such as physical objects and toys.
- *Activity reinforcers* such as recess, playtime, and field trips are commonly used to reward good work—for example, edible, material or activity reinforcers; candy, prizes or games).
- *Response-cost procedures* occur when a desirable stimulus is removed for some inappropriate behavior. The removal of playtime each time an infraction occurs is an example of response-cost procedures. The process of creating rules/rewards and punishments consists of making a rule, rewarding the rule followers, and punishing the rule breakers.
- *Time out* is the term used for a strategy in which a student is temporarily removed from the environment in which misbehavior is being reinforced. This usually takes the form of a "time-out seat" away from the rest of the students where a child is sent until he or she is ready to conform.
- *Punishment* should only be used as a last resort when positive approaches have failed. It can be used for "bad" behavior deemed as inappropriate and deserving of a punishment, such as a fistfight or any other violent act.
- *Extinction* is a strategy used to ignore inappropriate behavior until it disappears. It can be very effective when desired behaviors are also reinforced at the same time.

Source: Adapted from Richard T. Scarpaci, *Resource Methods for Managing K–12 Instruction: A Case Study Approach* (Boston: Allyn & Bacon, 2009), 24.

wish to accomplish with the reinforcers and consequences needed to achieve them. The third and final step is to implement the plan by correcting whatever it is that is causing the problem. This can be accomplished by reviewing and clarifying rules, describing and enforcing consequences, and teaching lessons that are as interesting as possible.

Unfortunately, there are weaknesses associated with behavior modification. It is too highly structured for most teachers to use on a constant basis. Many view its full application as being either analogous to bribing, overly calculating, or subversive to the exercise of free will. The problem for most is that if punishment is not included there is no way to deal with deliberate misbehavior. Results usually last as long as student interest in rewards is maintained. When rewards are terminated performance usually declines. Behavior modification ignores causes and solutions to problems; the human element is somehow missing. Children are not taught to govern their own behavior and develop responsibility for their actions, which should be inherent in a democratic society. To achieve desired behaviors through rewards devalues the intrinsic moral and ethical values of our society, allowing no opportunity to clarify emotions or develop the intellect, which is detrimental to a child's growth. Behavior modification, one could concede, is effective in immediate disciplinary actions but relatively weak in providing long-term solutions. It is, however, the key to the traditional views concerning understanding how children learn.

Behaviorist Learning Theory. Behaviorism has been described as an objectivist theory of learning, a form of direct instruction. Behaviorism seeks observable indicators that evidence learning is taking place. It is opposite the view of cognitive psychologists who equate learning with understanding the mental processes. Behaviorists say that they accept these mental processes but view them as unobservable indications of learning that focus on conditioning observable human behavior.

J. B. Watson, the father of behaviorism, defined learning as a sequence of stimulus-and-response actions in observable cause-and-effect relationships. The classical example of conditioning is Pavlov's experiment with the digestive process in animals. Pavlov noticed that a dog would salivate (response) upon hearing a bell ring. The dog learned to associate unconditional stimuli (normally feeding) with the neutral stimuli of a bell ringing. According to Skinner, voluntary or automatic behavior is either strengthened or weakened by the immediate presence of a reward or a punishment. The learning principle demonstrated by operant conditioning was that new learning occurs as a result of positive reinforcement, and old patterns are abandoned as a result of negative reinforcement.[26]

Constructivist Concept of Learning

Behaviorist and constructivist theories represent two alternative attempts to explain the same thing from distinctive perspectives. The acquisition of knowledge and the role of the teacher are viewed quite differently. Constructivist theory spotlights motivation and ability to construct meaning. Behaviorism is outdated and viewed as too teacher centered, emphasizing a process that matches skill objectives with test items and avoids meaningful learning. Behaviorists imply that knowledge is separate to the human mind and must be transferred to the learner by a teacher. This is fundamentally counter to the constructivist theory of learning that everyone has the ability to construct knowledge through a process of discovery and problem solving.

Constructivist theory is founded on the belief that students construct knowledge based on their schemata of existing personal beliefs. Compared to the traditional view of knowledge as fixed and independent of the learner, this constructivist idea is revolutionary. Constructivism from this perspective is a philosophical explanation about the nature of knowledge. Knowledge in the traditionalist view is thought to consist of a fixed number of truths that one accumulates. This logically leads to the traditional belief that the more facts one possesses the more knowledge one has. This view is in direct contrast to the constructivist view, which sees knowledge as tentative, subjective, and based on personal beliefs. Constructivists see knowledge as being based on working hypotheses, not on universal truths. Constructivists speculate that knowledge is fostered through interactions and not through the traditional concept of a transmission model.

The basis for constructivist theory is rooted in the works of many prominent educational theorists. Dewey, Montessori, Piaget, Bruner, Vygotsky, Maslow, Erickson, and Kohlberg each added a different dimension to a body of thought that came to be called constructivist. There is no clear line in its development except that it does initially stem from the ancients, who believed that one of the ways in which students learned was through a process they called active construction. Constructivist learning has emerged as a prominent approach to teaching. It represents a paradigm shift from education based on behaviorism to education based on cognitive theory. Fosnot summarized constructivist teaching practices by explaining that its epistemology assumes that learners construct their own knowledge based on interaction with their environment.[27] Learning is a personal act in which individuals create their own way to learning by establishing how, what, and when to learn. Learning is such a simple act that we do not question its occurrence—we are only concerned when it does not happen. Most see learning as a natural process, despite the many definitions and theories of learning that indicate its complexity.

Constructivist Learning Design. An understanding of learning and its applications are inherent in the work of G. W. Gagnon and M. Collay. They identify four epistemological assumptions consisting of the physical, symbolic, social, and theoretical construction of knowledge as the heart of what they refer to as constructivist learning. This theoretical process can be used as a guide for the constructivist teacher in preparing and reflecting on instructional exercises.[28] The steps for learners to construct knowledge are as follows:

- Learners who are involved in active learning are physically constructing knowledge.
- Learners who are making their own representations of action are symbolically constructing knowledge.
- Knowledge is socially constructed by learners who convey their meaning making to others.
- Learners who try to explain things they do not completely understand are theoretically constructing knowledge.

To be effective, teachers must develop situations for students to explain. Construct a road between what is already known and what you want your students to learn. Anticipate questions that students may ask, and answer without giving away an explanation. Encourage students to create a record of their thoughts in the form of a journal or a diary, and also encourage them to share it with classmates. The final step is to ask students for their reflections about what they learned. The rationale behind this learning design is to encourage students to think about focused objectives and outcomes (see box 1.4).

Different Constructivist Theories. Jean Piaget (1896–1980), a Swiss psychologist, saw human development as progressive stages of cognitive development. He described four stages, beginning in infancy and ending in adulthood. According to Piaget, we use the cognitive abilities we have at each stage to con-

---

Box 1.4   Design for Learning

1. The teacher plans and designs learning situations based on students' learning styles, interests, and needs.

2. The teacher designs a heterogeneous or homogeneous method for grouping students, taking available materials into consideration.

3. The teacher uses baseline data on what students already know to determine what he or she expects students to learn.

4. The teacher designs questions to appraise student understanding of concepts, skills, or attitudes to be learned.

5. The teacher arranges sessions where students share and evaluate each other's work.

6. Students are then asked to reflect about what they have learned. This is an internal process for self-assessment of individual student learning.

Source: Adapted from Richard T. Scarpaci, *Resource Methods for Managing K–12 Instruction: A Case Study Approach* (Boston: Allyn & Bacon, 2009), 26.

---

struct meaning drawn from our own environment.[29] There are two different ways to approach constructivist theories: the developmental and the environmental.

The *developmental theory* of cognition describes the structures of knowledge as pre-logical, concrete, and abstract operations. Piaget felt children learned to understand concepts through a series of stages. According to his stage theory, children move through a number of cognitive developmental stages before learning occurs, and concepts are internalized. *Environmental theory*, also called the *sociocultural theory* of cognition, alternatively states that children learn through an active involvement with their surroundings. There are two versions of constructivist theory as regards cognition: developmental and social constructivism.

- *Developmental constructivism,* the traditional view, claims that we learn by going from the concrete to the abstract, based on Piaget's theory of cognition.
- *Social constructivism* claims that knowledge is constructed by the individual in a sociocultural context.

Piaget believed that humans were different from animals at each stage of development. For education to be effective, it should be child centered, focused on the learner and learning, not on transmission. The aim of teaching was to facilitate learning, while encouraging students to create and verify truth. The art is in the science of selecting an aim, determining how to verify it, and finding a strategy to put it into operation.

Three unique processes—developmental, cognitive, and environmental—make up the way learning occurs. The developmental process deals with the physical growth of children. The cognitive process refers to the age at which mental activities such as learning, thinking, and remembering take place, while the environmental process sees knowledge constructed when the social milieu and the environment interact. This environmental process is described as a sociocultural theory of cognition.

The Adaptation Process Model.   Intelligence is the process of adaptation to one's environment. It can further be defined as the ability and capacity to be taught and acquire knowledge. Thinking, known as cognition, is a process related to intelligence and maturation that is impacted by one's environment. The term "schema" refers to any pattern of thinking one develops to understand the world by a process known as adaptation. The adaptive process consists of two items, *assimilation* (taking information and incorporating it with what you already know based on your experiences) and *accommodation*. Accommodation is defined as the process of taking in information and adding it to your existing body of knowledge *to create a new meaning*. The adaptation process says that the way you understand is to first collect data and unite it with your experiences, thereby giving data meaning (see figure 1.1).

Cognition itself refers to the diverse thinking processes of reflection, conceptualization, problem solving, and decision making. According to Piaget, there are four basic stages in cognitive development: sensorimotor, pre-operational, concrete operational, and formal operational (see box 1.5).

Social constructivists criticized Piaget for his individualistic approach to learning and disregard for acknowledged environmental factors. Whether we believe in the social constructivist version or Piaget's developmental version, the

Figure 1.1   **Adaptation Process Model**

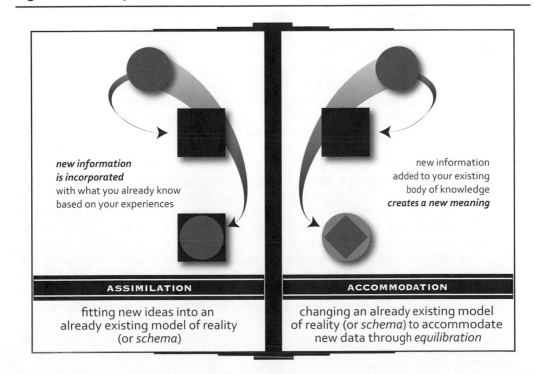

new information is incorporated with what you already know based on your experiences

new information added to your existing body of knowledge *creates a new meaning*

ASSIMILATION

fitting new ideas into an already existing model of reality (or *schema*)

ACCOMMODATION

changing an already existing model of reality (or *schema*) to accommodate new data through *equilibration*

Box 1.5   Piaget's Stages of Cognitive Development

Sensorimotor Stage (*birth to two years*)

At this stage infants experience the world through their senses and actions, such as looking, touching, and mouthing. Infants learn that objects exist even when they are not visible (object permanence). They begin to feel distress and anxiety when they see an unfamiliar face that does not fit their schema.

Pre-operational Stage (*two to six years*)

At this stage children are able to represent things with words and images but cannot reason with logic. They also acquire the ability to pretend and develop egocentrism.

Concrete Operational Stage (*seven to twelve years*)

Children think logically about concrete events, can grasp concrete analogies, and can perform arithmetical operations at this stage. The concept of conservation is perfected and children are able to understand mathematical transformations.

Formal Operational Stage (*twelve years to adult*)

During this stage teenagers develop the ability to think with symbols, as evidenced by the perfection of abstract and scientific reasoning. The potential for mature moral reasoning presents itself during this period.

theory still holds that children are the constructors of their own knowledge. Both cognitive and social development are necessary in order to become a contributing member of society. The real problem is to understand what the teaching practices that facilitate learning are. The argument can be termed *construction vs. instruction.* The form of constructivism is not the problem; rather, the problem is choosing between constructivist practice and traditional behaviorist teaching practices.

Constructivist Teaching Practices.   Constructivist classroom practice focuses on non-rote outcomes such as generalization, analysis, synthesis, and evaluation. Teacher empowerment, cooperative learning, performance assessment, product-oriented activities, and hands-on learning all fit the constructivist philosophy. Teachers are facilitators, not dispensers of knowledge. They encourage students to make their own meanings and accept diversity of opinions. Student construction of meaning is more important than teacher presentation. All children can learn in this model because we each construct our own knowledge. As progressive as these concepts are, they are not universally agreed upon. When Thomas Jefferson said, "All men are created equal," he was only referring to personal and political equality; he did not advocate social or economic (and certainly not academic) equality. Constructivist teaching practices (see box 1.6) require us to look at intelligence in a way different from traditional practice and to consider multiple intelligence and emotional intelligence. The constructivist approach to classroom practice is based on collaboration rather than the traditionalists' compliance. While traditionalists set goals and require compliance, constructivists insist on collaboration. Constructivist methodology consists of a four-step process of (1) identification, (2) solution, (3) implementation, and (4) evaluation. The assumption is that classroom practice needs to be reinvented using a collaborative approach (see box 1.7).

| classic professional viewpoint | **1.1** |

Providing the Space and the Time for the Construction of Meaning

Kathryn Kinnucan-Welsch

One of the aspects of teaching that I treasure most fondly is recalling those times that I was a participant in a powerful learning experience, the kind that offers a flash of insight—that "a-ha" that leaves one changed forever. I recall such a time some years ago when I was working with a group of teachers who were trying to bring a more student-centered, constructivist way of being to their classrooms. We were talking about questioning and how often teachers ask those questions that merely require students to "guess what's in the teacher's head." Each of us took a turn role-playing by asking questions that would encourage students to think deeply about a concept, to grapple with alternative explanations. It suddenly hit me: I was still asking my students in preservice education classes to give me the "right" answer, to please the teacher.

After that flash of insight, I brought to my graduate and undergraduate classes a fresh perspective on what it means to encourage students to construct their own meaning and a new understanding of the immense knowledge base required of all teachers. My goal for developing teachers is that they engage in constructing their own knowledge, both in the disciplines and in pedagogy, so that they may bring a more constructivist orientation to their own classrooms. We learn best when we are actively engaged in making sense of what we are trying to learn, something that is true for children as well as adults. In every classroom that means providing time for students to ponder, time to ask each other questions, time to explore possibilities. The way in which teachers provide students the opportunity to construct meaning will evolve *differently* in every classroom. How might it evolve in yours?

Box 1.6   Ten Constructivist Teaching Practices

- Encourage and accept student autonomy and initiative.
- Use raw data and primary sources, along with manipulatives and interactive or physical materials.
- Use cognitive terminology such as *classify, analyze, predict,* and *create* when framing tasks.
- Allow student response to drive lessons, shift instructional strategies, and alter content.
- Inquire about students' understandings of concepts before sharing your own understandings with your students.
- Encourage students to engage in dialogues with the teacher and others.
- Promote student inquiry by asking thoughtful, open-ended questions that allow students to question classmates.
- Engage students in experiences that might engender contradictions to the students' initial hypotheses and discussion.
- Provide time for students to construct relationships and create metaphors.
- Nurture curiosity by assisting students in making discoveries, introducing concepts, and applying them.

> ## Box 1.7   Key Constructivist Assumptions
>
> - Since we all construct our own knowledge, it follows that we all can learn.
> - Philosophy and instructional approach need not be consistent.
> - Teachers are guides, not sages.
> - Teachers create environments for students to obtain meanings.
> - Teachers accept diversity of opinion while not searching for "right" answers.
> - A constructivist class is an open system, not closed and judgmental.
> - Critical thinking is encouraged.
> - Constructivist teachers must set criteria and standards while not compromising the learning process.
> - Teachers address learning in daily activities that generate meaning through assessments.
> - Teachers create opportunities for students to explore big ideas.

How, then, do you implement a constructivist program? How do you assess students' learning? These two questions should be addressed prior to implementing a constructivist approach to teaching. Implementation of constructivist assumptions and practices are more difficult than just understanding concepts. Evaluation is difficult, since solutions differ and are not acceptable to all. There is little room for factual, objective tests. Essential to constructivist assumptions and practice is the use of reflection, self-evaluation, journals, projects, and other means of authentic assessment. A constructivist approach changes rules we are used to accepting. Teachers are no longer considered sages, but rather as guides who facilitate and create situations in which learning can occur. *Reductionism,* or looking for one right answer or absolute solution to a problem, is no longer the method to follow. A multiplicity of answers and views should be explored and discussed within the framework of established criteria and standards for solutions, without compromising the process. Critics still ask; "How can one evaluate answers if all construct their own solutions?" As difficult as this is to accomplish, constructivists believe it can be done through authentic assessment and by using big ideas to encourage learning and understanding. Teachers tend to appreciate the ideas and assumptions that lay the foundation for constructivist theory, but they shy away from using it in class. They claim, "It's not realistic." What they really mean is that it seems too difficult to use. But all good teaching takes effort and has varying degrees of difficulty, and constructivism contains many appropriate strategies necessary for effective teaching practices.

An Eclectic Approach to Learning

A review of the literature on learning theories demonstrates that it is practically impossible to tie learning and effective practice to one particular theory. A school environment does not necessarily reflect reality. Most learning models are presented as mental pictures that enable us to understand what we will never see. By modifying our ideas to accommodate for circumstances surrounding learning situations we can decide on appropriate instructional methods. To accomplish this we have to realize that some learning problems require highly prescriptive solutions, whereas others are more suited to learner control of the environment. The way we teach and learn from an eclectic perspective is based on commonsense processes: (1) know what you want to teach, (2) know the abilities of those in your class, (3) decide on the instructional model to use, and finally (4) assess student performance.

The major assumption in eclectic practice is that the teacher can solve managerial problems by applying specific "tried and true" prescriptions. The teacher's role is to react to each situation by following a set of simplistic remedies. Eclectic strategies, known also as cookbook remedies, are essentially a collage of standard teaching behaviors made up from other approaches and presented as absolutes. Some common examples are: (1) Always be consistent in enforcing rules, and (2) never play favorites when rewarding students.[30] Box 1.8 contains a list of effective teaching behaviors.

Box 1.8   Effective Teaching Behaviors

1. Effective teaching brings about intended learning outcomes.
2. Intention and achievement of goals are two dimensions related to effective teaching.
3. Effective teachers have a developed philosophy of education and understand the developmental stages. They also understand psychological needs and subject matter.
4. Effective teachers use brain and intelligence theories to understand how children learn.
5. Effective teachers are equally competent in theory and practice as well as in the art and science of teaching.

Source: Adapted from Richard T. Scarpaci, *Resource Methods for Managing K–12 Instruction: A Case Study Approach* (Boston: Allyn & Bacon, 2009).

Teaching as an Art and a Science

In the actions of gifted teachers we see the **art of teaching** and the **science of teaching**. Years ago, a researcher named Nate Gage argued for a better understanding of the scientific basis for the art of teaching. In reality, good teaching is neither exclusively art nor essentially science, but rather a combination of both. Good teachers do things well and conceptually know why they do them well—they have an explanation for what grounds their practices. Good teachers also know what goals they plan to achieve and how they will "move" students toward realizing those goals. Good teachers are centered on *student* learning, and such a focus demands that teachers think about both the art and the science of teaching.

If you focus on your behavior and not on what your students are learning, your effectiveness will be diminished. If you focus exclusively on students and not on the content or the methods, you are nothing more than a high-priced, well-educated babysitter.

A number of teacher movies draw attention to the power of effective teaching. *Stand and Deliver, Dangerous Minds,* and *Mr. Holland's Opus* are but a few of these films. Some of the movies capture the real lives of dynamic teachers (such as Jaime Escalante in *Stand and Deliver*); others are fictionalized depictions (for example, Robin Williams as John Keating in *Dead Poets' Society*). The movies offer a powerful lesson about the very nature of classroom teaching. In most of the popular teacher movies we can see a shift in how the teachers view the students. Indeed, what makes these movies emotionally engaging is that a pedagogical "shift" occurs before our eyes, and once the shift occurs, neither the teacher nor the students (nor the viewer) is the same. All are transformed.

Within American classrooms two paradigms dominate: one instructional and one learning (outlined in table 1.2).[31] The **instructional paradigm** encompasses what the teacher does in the classroom (i.e., how the teacher presents content material). The teacher considers the teaching act as relatively remote from the learner: "I taught Hamlet, but the students didn't learn it." Instructional-paradigm teachers (and administrators) talk in terms of technique and the quality of a technique: "He's a greater lecturer" or "She's fantastic with hands-on activities."

With the **learning paradigm** teachers focus on whether and how students learn. What matters to them is a student's learning, not their own behavior. Ted Sizer's exhibition-based learning falls into the learning paradigm because, in this approach, the teacher places attention on the student's ability to construct and represent content understandings.[32] Most teachers and a majority of administrators work within the instructional paradigm. While they may not consciously espouse this theory, it emerges as their theory-in-use. They and the larger community they serve (parents and a variety of significant others) want to see students looking busy and getting their work done—indeed, for years many state legislatures worried more about the hours allocated for instruction rather than the learning outcomes expected of students. Instructional-paradigm teachers focus on the tasks of teaching and often evidence a very high degree of skill in keeping students focused on worksheets, workbook pages, or the "odd-numbered problems on p. 54."

Far fewer teachers embrace the learning paradigm. Teachers who are oriented in this way function very differently in their roles as facilitators of learning. They are constantly "reading" the students to determine how to create a better atmosphere for student growth. Learning-paradigm teachers get outside themselves (personal performance) and get inside the minds of the *students:* How do *they* learn? How do *they* construct knowledge? How do *they* make sense of the world? How can I, as the teacher, participate in the learning process with my students?

Interestingly, research of the past decade may begin to nudge more teachers toward the learning paradigm. The value-added emphasis of researchers such as

William Sanders suggests that teachers make a real difference in student learning and that exposure to strong teachers for three years in a row makes a *dramatic* difference. Sanders' classic study concluded that fifth-grade math students who had three consecutive years of effective teachers scored in the eighty-third percentile, while students with three years of ineffective teachers scored in the twenty-ninth percentile.[33]

The value-added focus is central to a larger debate on accountability that argues the merits and problems of the idea (how much academic growth can be measured?).[34]

The learning-paradigm classroom is emotionally and intellectually demanding. The challenges for a teacher who seeks to foster a learner-centered classroom are numerous. The teacher needs more time to plan lessons, must expend more effort to determine how to reach the students, and can use less teacher control to force students to conform to his or her personal will. Given the fact that the average American teacher is at school for 7.6 hours per day and that he or she is teaching (or on duty) for most of that 7.6 hours, it is little wonder that the instructional paradigm dominates American education.[35] Harold Stevenson and James Stigler documented this reality several years ago, and there is no reason to believe that the circumstance has changed since then. Indeed, Stevenson and Stigler argue that some of the success of the Japanese is attributable to enhanced teacher planning time: Japanese teachers are at school in excess of nine hours per day, but they teach for less than four.[36]

The learning-paradigm teacher takes more personal risks and creates more administrative challenges. Most of the excellent teachers we know are not especially affable people. They are fighters. They fight for the students, and they are passionate about student learning. They do anything they have to do in order to make certain that students learn, even if it means confronting an administrator or tossing a disrespectful student out of the classroom.

The learning-paradigm school is a "messy" place. Because learning is such a personal endeavor, schools that really embrace this paradigm struggle to find ways in which to connect students with their environment. The curriculum for a learning-paradigm teacher is a guide, not a dictate; as a consequence the sequence of learning often conflicts with the prescribed learning sanctioned by the school. Learning is less linear and more nested in the students' experiences.

Critical Thinking

A necessary ingredient for the effective teacher is the ability to be a critical thinker and to teach critical thinking. A simple definition of critical thinking is *making reasoned judgments*. Reasoned means are arrived at by logical thinking, and judging consists of determining the degree to which a thing meets a standard, a rule, or other criteria.[37] Critical thinking can also be considered as the active use of formal logical procedures involving both cognitive processes and **metacognition** (the process of thinking about one's own thinking) to understand the world beyond its literal meaning.[38] Critical thinking deals with ideas that attempt to form new meanings; it requires background knowledge, the abil-

| classic professional viewpoint **1.2** | **Critical Thinking in the Everyday World** |

Robert J. Sternberg

Every teacher believes she teaches children to think. If she didn't, she would probably have followed a different career path. But the way we teach children to think in schools often has little to do with the everyday world, and, indeed, what works in school thinking may not work outside the classroom. For example, in the everyday world we need to recognize problems when faced with them; in school, teachers hand problems to students. In the everyday world, we have to figure out the exact nature of the problem confronting us at a given time: in school, teachers define problems for us. In the everyday world, problems are highly contextualized: A great deal of background information enters into our solutions to problems and influences the decisions we make—for example, the information needed to decide whether to buy a car, and, if so, what kind to buy, can't be compiled in a couple of sentences.

School problems, in contrast, are often decontextualized, with the result that children come to think that problems can be stated much more simply than is true outside academia. School problems are also well-structured so that there is usually a clear path to a solution. In contrast, everyday problems tend to be ill-structured with no clear path leading to an answer. Indeed, in everyday life usually there is not one right answer, quite unlike the multiple-choice and fill-in-the-blank tests we give. School also ill prepares us for working in groups, despite the fact that in the everyday world few problems are solved totally on one's own, without the need to talk to others about possible solutions. The bottom line is that to teach children to think, we need to do so in a way that prepares them for life outside of school—not just for life in the classroom, which may bear little resemblance to what goes on in the real world.

ity to draw on recognized information, and the ability to define objectives that regulate the critical thinking process.

Critical thinking is not making decisions or solving problems. It is not the same as reflective thinking, creative thinking, or conceptualization. These types of thinking have a purpose different from critical thinking. The word *critical* in critical thinking comes from *kriterion,* the Greek word for criterion, which means a benchmark for judging. Critical thinking is judging the reasonableness or soundness (logical validity) and truthfulness (accuracy) of statements.[39] Research has identified six essential elements of critical thinking (see box 1.9) that can be remembered when we think of the acronym SCARPO.

After all is said, critical thinking cannot be divorced from content. In fact, thinking is a way of learning content. Students should be taught to think logically, analyze and compare, and question and evaluate in all content areas. When skills are taught in isolation students only learn isolated skills with little relevance. Critical inquiry is an essential outcome of critical thinking. Skills should be taught in conjunction with subject matter while presenting students with real-life problems.

Box 1.9   Six Essential Elements of Critical Thinking

1. Critical thinkers are *skeptical*, questioning the accuracy, authenticity, and plausibility of what is presented. They are fair-minded, open-minded, respectful of evidence and reasoning, and they are willing to change their position when reason and evidence warrant (Paul and Elder, 2003).

2. Criteria for making judgments are the *conditions* that must be met. Critical thinking uses a variety of criteria—from values, standards, definitions, officially established requirements, precedents, and rules, to test results.

3. Critical thinking supports your proposition with an *argument* that provides evidence and reasoning.

4. *Reasoning* is the cement that holds an argument together. The term describes the process whereby we infer from facts and assumption (Lipman, 1991).

5. Your *opinion* or point of view is based on your experiences. You should gather information from many different sources with different points of view.

6. There are no general *procedures* for critical thinking. The approach involves asking questions and then making judgments based on specific criteria.

Source: Adapted from M. Lipman, *Thinking in Education* (Cambridge, UK: Cambridge University Press, 1991); R. W. Paul and L. Elder, *Critical Thinking Tools for Taking Charge of Your Learning and Your Life,* 2nd ed. (New York: Prentice-Hall, 2003).

Strategies for Teaching Critical Thinking

Critical thinking instruction is different from traditional instruction. In traditional instruction the teacher introduces materials and provides students with applications that they complete independently. Critical thinking instruction allows the teacher to provide a focus in the form of a question or problem. Working in cooperative groups, students attempt to solve the problem and report its findings back to the class. Each group is required to defend its solution. The teacher finally provides a summary and an opportunity to reflect on the various solutions presented.

The IOSIE Method

The IOSIE method (box 1.10) is a user-friendly, five-step process that helps us to identify and reflect on problems that teachers face in their everyday lives. The letters in the acronym IOSIE represent a mnemonic that can be used when analyzing any problem that requires reflection prior to solution. The method is a commonsense way of dealing with analysis that can be superimposed over most analytical, critical-thinking strategies. When a problem occurs, you must identify the cause and determine the objectives you wish to achieve by the solution you propose. You also must provide opportunity to evaluate and assess the results manifested by your implementation. This five-step method is basic to any analysis you might choose to employ.

Box 1.10   IOSIE Analysis Model

- The **I** represents the first step in the process, *identification* and assessment of the problem in all its aspects.

- The **O** stands for the *objectives* that you wish to achieve through your intervention. The first two are always the same: Facilitate learning and help the student to become an independent learner. Then prepare a list of both short-term and long-term objectives needed to resolve the identified problem.

- The **S** stands for the *solution*, which should be the result of the plan you put into effect to achieve your objectives.

- The **I** indicates the *implementation* of your plan and the procedures, personnel, materials and resources needed to implement your strategy.

- The acronym concludes with the letter **E** that stands for your *evaluation* and reflection on results.

Source: Adapted from Richard T. Scarpaci, *Resource Methods for Managing K–12 Instruction: A Case Study Approach* (Boston: Allyn & Bacon, 2009).

The process essentially focuses on improvement of critical thinking skills. Once you define and clearly identify the problem, you logically must make a plan to solve the problem. The solution should consist of both long- and short-term alternatives. After deciding on your plan, the next step is to implement it. The final step is your assessment related to whether or not you have achieved the established objectives. This step is crucial in determining the success of your proposal. If what you have decided upon has not worked, prepare another plan. At this juncture you may have to look at the problem from different perspectives.

To exercise critical thinking skills children can be asked to sort items, practice classification skills, discriminate between two or more items that are the same or different, write summaries, make predictions, explain events, solve problems, and brainstorm alternatives. The exercises should be developmentally appropriate. You would not have eighth graders building piles of blocks by color, but you might have them design an earthquake-proof structure as a project for a science class. See box 1.11 for suggestions on specific activities.

The Seminar Model

The seminar model is based on open-ended discussion questions about a text. A text may be a written document or photograph, a work of art, a map, a graphic math problem, an architectural drawing, or just about anything, as long as it is ambiguous and rich in ideas. Every seminar should be collaborative, intellectual, and open-ended. Regardless of the chosen text, seminars are carefully planned, formal classroom dialogues. Students must be actively engaged with an idea or an exercise that is immediately relevant to them as human beings. This will occur when students become involved in interactive, student-

---

Box 1.11   Examples for Developing Critical Thinking Skills

1. *Sorting Items.* Ask the children to perform the following tasks:
   a. Divide a list of foods into high- and low-calorie groups.
   b. Select a paragraph in the story you are reading that you consider the most interesting.
   c. Find the pairs of synonyms among the underlined words in the passage you are reading.

2. *Classify and sort.* Children can be given a group of words that they should classify and sort. Children make lists and decide on the categories. Ask children to list and classify adult occupations.

3. *Difference.* During language arts, have children identify and describe the difference between a colon and semicolon, fact and fiction, a joke and a tale, complete and incomplete sentences.

4. *Similarities.* Have children find similarities when comparing leaders and followers, or physical exercise and sleeping. Choose items that are unlike and ask for similarities, such as chocolates and kindness, horses and singing.

5. *Summaries.* Have children identify the main issues in a story in less than 30 words. Have children summarize the main ideas contained in their daily lessons.

6. *Predictions.* Have children write a new ending of a story they have read, a different ending than the author did. Ask children to consider what could happen if only female children were allowed to go to school.

7. *Explain events.* Ask children to relate factors that caused to the Great Depression and how these factors contributed to the economic crisis. Ask them what factors they believe made the Harry Potter stories so popular.

8. *Solve a problem.* Ask children to pick a real-life problem to solve, such as pollution, congestion in the city, or being late to return library books. Ask them to make a plan that will enable people to respect others.

9. *Brainstorm alternatives.* Group children and ask them to find an effective way to read their homework assignments, or to reduce bullying in the lunchroom, for example.

---

centered seminar dialogues that require reading, thinking, and speaking about and listening to ideas that are important to them.

The task of the seminar leader is threefold: (1) to ask questions that define the discussion, (2) to examine, and (3) to engage students. The teacher's role is that of a discussion facilitator who designs the seminar conditions and then gets out of the way so that students can participate. Specific tasks include the following teacher and student responsibilities:

Teacher Responsibilities

- Select an appropriate text and prepare open-ended questions.
- Coach students prior to the seminar, in order that they understand that they are expected to speak and listen with regard to the questions.

- Demonstrate good listening and note-taking skills during a seminar and pose genuine, provocative follow-up questions.
- Limit the amount of time the teacher speaks.
- Develop post-seminar procedures and activities that make the seminar dialogue relevant to children.

Student Responsibilities

- Invest the necessary time and energy in reading and studying the text in detail.
- Accept responsibility for improving their questioning, speaking and listening skills during a seminar.
- Consciously contribute to the seminar discussion by stating their own ideas and by actively listening to the ideas of others.
- Learn to agree and disagree with others in a thoughtful and respectful manner.
- Understand that the seminar is a part of the ongoing learning life of their classroom.
- Practice post-seminar writing as a way of articulating their increased understanding of the values and ideas gained from the text and dialogue.

Seminars utilize Socratic teaching methods in that open-ended questions are the focus of discussions and all discussions attempt to enhance students' critical thinking skills. Socratic teaching is teaching by questioning and by conducting discussions (seminars) of the answers elicited with the purpose of understanding, making insights, and increasing the knowledge base. Seminars should occur once or twice a week, depending on the book or materials to be read in advance. Seminars should be viewed as conversations with students, conducted by the teacher who acts as leader or moderator. The best seminars occur when issues and questions arise from great books.[40]

Critical Thinking Research

Critical thinking is a form of intelligence that can be taught. The leading proponents of this school are Matthew Lipman, Robert Sternberg, and Robert Ennis.[41] Lipman's program, although designed for elementary school grades, is applicable to all grades. He sought to develop the ability to use concepts, generalizations, cause-effect relationships, logical inferences, consistencies and contradictions, analogies, part-whole and whole-part connections, problem formulations, reversibility of logical statements, and applications of principles to real-life situations.[42]

In Lipman's program, children spend a considerable portion of their time thinking about thinking and about ways in which effective thinking differs from ineffective thinking. After reading a series of stories, children engage in classroom discussions and exercises that encourage them to adopt the thinking processes depicted in the stories.[43] Lipman's assumptions are that children are by nature interested in philosophical issues such as truth, fairness, and personal identity. He believes that children should learn to explore alternatives to their own viewpoints, consider evidence, make distinctions, and draw conclusions.

Lipman further distinguishes between ordinary thinking and critical thinking. Ordinary thinking is simple and lacks standards; **critical thinking** is more complex and is based on standards of objectivity, utility, or consistency. To be a critical thinker is to be an educated teacher. The goal is for educated teachers to help students move from ordinary to critical thinking, or (1) from guessing to estimating, (2) from preferring to evaluating, (3) from grouping to classifying, (4) from believing to assuming, (5) from inferring to inferring logically, (6) from associating concepts to grasping principles, (7) from noting relationships to noting relationships among relationships, (8) from supposing to hypothesizing, (9) from offering opinions without reasons to offering opinions with reasons, and (10) from making judgments without criteria to making judgments with criteria.[44]

Sternberg seeks to foster many of the same critical thinking skills but in a different way. He points to three categories of components of critical thinking: metacomponents (higher-order mental processes used to plan, monitor, and evaluate what one is doing); performance components (the actual steps one takes); and knowledge-acquisition components (processes used to relate old material to new material and to apply new material).[45] Sternberg does not specify how to teach these skills; he gives general guidelines for developing or selecting a program. He does suggest that when teachers use these skills their students process information more effectively.

Robert Ennis identifies thirteen attributes of critical thinkers. They tend to (1) be open-minded, (2) take a position (or change a position) when the evidence calls for it, (3) take into account the entire situation, (4) seek information, (5) seek precision in information, (6) deal in an orderly manner with parts of a complex whole, (7) look for options, (8) search for reasons, (9) seek a clear statement of the issue, (10) keep the original problem in mind, (11) use credible sources, (12) remain relevant to the point, and (13) be sensitive to the feelings and knowledge level of others.[46]

This approach is old-fashioned analysis and problem solving—something that good teachers have been doing for years. Teaching a person to think is like teaching someone to swing a golf club or cook a stew; it requires a holistic approach, not the structured efforts suggested by Lipman, Sternberg, and Ennis. "Trying to break thinking skills into discrete units may be helpful for diagnostic proposals," Sadler and Whimbey maintain, "but it does not seem . . . the right way in the teaching of such skills." Critical thinking is too complex to be divided into small steps or processes; teaching must involve "a student's total intellectual functioning, not . . . a set of narrowly defined skills."[47] Fred Newmann argues that explicitly teaching thinking is too reductionist—it pays too much attention to parts rather than the whole. The best way to teach thought is to ask students to explain their thinking, to require them to support their answers with evidence, and to ask them thought-provoking (Socratic) questions.[48] Formulating thinking into discrete skills or a special unit or course is artificial, while dividing thinking skills by subject matter is unwieldy and mechanistic.

Perhaps the major criticism of thinking-skills programs has been raised by Sternberg himself. He cautions that the kinds of critical thinking skills stressed in school and the way they are taught "inadequately [prepare] students for the kinds of problems they will face in everyday life."[49] Unintentionally, thinking-skills programs sometimes stress "right" answers instead of helping students decide and justify what to believe and do with regard to real-world problems.[50] Most problems and decisions in real life have social, economic, and psychological implications.

Types of Thinking

Creative thinking is enlarged in the term **creativity**, which has been used to describe at least three different kinds of human abilities: the process by which a symbolic domain is altered, innovative problem-solving abilities, and personal expression through the arts.[51] When researching the lives of highly creative people, Howard Gardner and Mihaly Csikszentmihalyi found creativity to be an ability to shape or change a worldview through one's ideas or works.[52] They discuss other applications of the terms *creative* and *creativity* from contemporary society, including a range of abilities from problem solving to personal artistic expression. They did not find these abilities in their research into highly creative people. Csikszentmihalyi points out that the terms *talent* and *genius*, synonyms often used to describe creative ability, are not apt descriptors for creative individuals. He did not find that these designations applied to the creative individuals interviewed. Instead, he found that creativity exists in its own domain and is governed by existing ideas that only change as a result of a person's culture or the time in which he or she lives.[53] Gardner and Csikszentmihalyi note that creativity functions within a system in which the domain, the gatekeepers of the domain, and the new idea or pattern identified by an individual interact to shape or change the domain. In addition to timing and culture, highly creative individuals are a product of what Gardner and Csikszentmihalyi call *personal creativity*, which resides in one's schema and can be shared and understood by others.

Tests are not an accurate measure of creativity; in fact, researchers have difficulty agreeing on what creativity is and who is creative. All children are potentially creative, yet because many parents and teachers impose so many restrictions on children's natural behaviors, children learn that creativity gets them into trouble and earns them disapproval. Parents often react negatively to children's inquisitiveness and "messing around." Teachers and parents impose rules of order, conformity, and "normalcy" to suit themselves, not the children.

There are many types of creativity—artistic, dramatic, scientific, athletic, and manual—yet we tend to use *creativity* as an all-encompassing term, limited in application to cognitive or intellectual behaviors. Educators tend to assess people's intelligence level based on their performance in one or two areas—predominantly linguistic or mathematical ability. As a teacher, your goal is not to assess how smart a student is, but rather to determine the various ways in which a student is smart and then use those ways to help that student learn how to learn. The undeveloped talents of many potentially creative children are lost because of our fixation on specific and limited kinds of knowledge.

Creative students are often puzzling to teachers. They are difficult to characterize, their novel answers are threatening, and their behavior often deviates from what is considered normal or proper. Curriculum specialists tend to ignore them in their plans, and teachers usually ignore them in their program and classroom assignments. Little money is earmarked to support special programs and personnel for them. Even if they recognize creativity, educators often lump "gifted" children together without distinguishing between intellectual and creative talents or between different types of creativity.

Sternberg distilled six attributes associated with creativity from a list of 131 characteristics he obtained from laypeople and professors in the arts, science, and business: (1) lack of conventionality, (2) intellectuality, (3) aesthetic taste and imagination, (4) decision-making skills and flexibility, (5) perspicacity (in questioning social norms), and (6) drive for accomplishment and recognition.[54] He also makes important distinctions among creativity, intelligence, and wisdom. Although they are mutually exclusive categories, they are interrelated constructs. Wisdom is more clearly associated with intelligence than is creativity, but it differs in its emphasis on mature judgment and use of experience in difficult situations. Creativity overlaps more with intelligence than it does with wisdom, but in creativity there is more emphasis on imagination and unconventional methods. In contrast, intelligence deals with more logical and analytical constructs.

Since the essence of creativity is novelty, we have no standard by which to judge it. In fact, Carl Rogers found that the more original the product, the more likely it is to be judged by contemporaries as foolish or evil![55] Individuals create because creating is self-satisfying and their action is self-actualizing. (This is the humanistic side of creativity, even though the process and intellect involved in creating are cognitive in nature).

Little agreement exists on a definition of creativity except that it represents a quality of mind associated with intelligence. The definition of creativity comes down to how new ideas have their origin. The creative processes are conscious and unconscious, observable and unrecognizable. Because unconscious and unrecognizable processes are difficult to deal with in the classroom, misunderstanding often arises between teachers and creative students.

Teachers generally require **reactive thinking** from their students; that is, they expect them to react to questions, exercises, or test items by giving a preferred answer. They tend to discourage **creative thinking**—that is, generating novel questions and answers. The reason is that teachers tend to be overreliant on teacher-centered strategies and underutilize inquiry-type models. This is the way most teachers were taught, and they feel uneasy about not having "right" answers. Some teachers do try to develop critical thinking in their students, but they need to go beyond reactive thinking and even beyond critical thinking to encourage learners to generate ideas on their own.

Society needs generative thinkers to plan, to make decisions, and to deal with social and technological problems. Teachers need to let students know that having one absolutely correct answer is not always possible, that depth of understanding is important, and that different activities require different abilities. Teachers must understand that nearly all students have the potential for creative thinking and a natural inclination to ask questions, but they need practice in order to do so. In order to stimulate creative thinking, teachers should encourage students to make inferences, to think intuitively, and to use inquiry-discovery teaching techniques. Three types of inferences have creative potential: (1) elaboration of characteristics, categories, or concepts (e.g., a student is told some of the objects in a category are "right" and some are "wrong," and the challenge is to identify the category); (2) elaboration of causality (e.g., What were the causes of World War I? Why did the compound turn into gas?); and (3) elaboration of background information (making inferences about possible effects of events, about facts from past events, or about facts in order to make decisions and solve problems).[56]

Intuitive thinking is a cognitive process that has been discouraged by traditional teaching, which relies on facts and rote. A good thinker, according to Jerome Bruner, is creative and has an intuitive grasp of subject matter. Intuition is part of the process of discovery; investigating hunches and playing with ideas can lead to new discoveries and additions to the storehouse of knowledge. The steps involved in intuitive thinking often cannot be differentiated or defined; according to Bruner, intuition involves cognitive maneuvers "based on implicit perception of the total problem. The thinker arrives at an answer, which may be right or wrong, with little, if any, awareness of the process by which he reached it."[57] Teachers must encourage students to make educated guesses, to follow hunches, and to make leaps in thinking. To instill fear of being wrong, or to discourage independent and/or innovative thinking on the basis that the student does not have the right answer, means to stifle creativity.

Defining Teaching Style

When we think about style in education we normally revert to various concepts related to learning styles and teaching styles. Style is the way teachers incorporate the distinctive characteristics of their personalities into their teaching behaviors, approaches, and strategies. A teacher's style clearly affects the way a classroom is run and the way in which learning takes place. Style is determined by a teacher's personality—for example, autocratic style and democratic style, which indicate both extremes on the spectrum of teacher control beliefs. One's life experiences and beliefs about how children learn also play a role in the selection of an appropriate style. One's style can be altered, intentionally or unintentionally—intentionally, as through the use of this book and the exercises within it, or through various life experiences. There are probably as many management styles as there are people; this is because most styles are not doctrinaire but instead are eclectic, resulting from a combination of beliefs and personality traits.[58]

It could be concluded that style encompasses personality type, patterns of behavior, type of performance, and attitude toward self and others. In a discussion on teaching style, Peterson defines style as how teachers utilize space in the classroom, as well as their choice of instructional activities and materials and their method of grouping students.[59] Her definition can be incorporated into our understanding of style. A basic assumption in understanding style is to look at the dichotomy created by two terms: process and product. Process is what a teacher does, and product is the result of that action. If the goal of classroom management style is to facilitate learning, maintain control, and teach students responsibility, then the process one uses can be judged by the end product.

The style one uses is directly related to one's own feelings and personality. The manner a teacher exhibits in the classroom can be seen as expressing the relationship between student and teacher. In a classic study (1943) three classifications were used—authoritarian, democratic, and laissez-faire—to describe group and individual social behavior. Lippitt and White[60] laid the groundwork for a formal classification of teachers' classroom behavior. They developed an instrument for describing the "social atmosphere" and quantifying the effects of group and individual behavior. Their results have been generalized in numerous research studies and textbooks on teaching. According to Lippitt and White, the authoritarian teacher directs and controls all the activities of the classroom. This style shares some characteristics with what is now called *direct instruction*. The democratic teacher encourages group participation and is willing to let students share in the decision-making process. This behavior is typical of what is now called the *indirect teacher*, a teacher who fosters and encourages cooperative group work and student participation. The laissez-faire style provides no goals and directions for group or individual behavior. It is frowned upon by most.

Style and the Effective Teacher

Emmer and colleagues[61] examined how differences in behavior management directly impact the effectiveness of teachers. Those teachers with less effective styles tended to issue general rather than specific criticisms to their classes. In cases where one individual disrupts the classroom, statements such as "We will wait until all are sitting properly before we continue with this lesson," or "Are we ready to behave now?" are examples of general criticisms. In each of the examples it would be much more appropriate to direct the criticism towards the one individual who is misbehaving. These researchers also found that ineffective teachers have difficulty in individualizing their instructional practices and issue vague directions with regard to classroom assignments. Focusing questions to the individual student's ability level, individualizing assignments, or allowing children to select their own work can alleviate this problem.

As a result of poor practices, ineffective teachers did little monitoring of students' work. The students' understanding of teacher expectations was limited. The most severe and egregious failure was that less effective teachers were shown to spend less time actually teaching than did effective teachers. When instructional time is limited because of the many distractions facing teachers, a poor end product is guaranteed. The best advice to teachers is to improve their time management skills and be as creative as possible in increasing instructional time. Effective teachers reinforce rules, model activities, and enforce good classroom monitoring techniques while acting promptly in curtailing misconduct.

Based on the descriptions of Kellough (2002), Emmer (1980), Peterson (1979), and Lippitt and White (1943) we see indications of specific teaching styles. You can determine what your own teaching style is through self-assessment centering on three characteristics: your beliefs, skills, and practices.

Beliefs.   When viewed from the perspective of style, beliefs can be generally related to one's convictions with regard to classroom management. The theoretical base for these beliefs usually refers to the level of control one feels most comfortable exercising in the classroom in order to create a successful learning environment. The level of control acceptable to a teacher is based primarily on his or her personality. Each of us must understand why we believe what we believe with regard to classroom learning. Beliefs can range from a behaviorist orientation to a guidance orientation. Those favoring a behaviorist approach tend to view the goal of classroom management as total teacher control, while those who are guidance oriented have beliefs that favor individual and group guidance (as opposed to control) approaches to classroom learning.

Skills.   The skills a teacher evidences are a clear indicator of his or her style. Each teacher brings to the classroom unique skills that can be improved through experience and specific instruction. These can be pedagogical skills that relate to how a class is taught, skill in using appropriate disciplinary measures, and the skills needed to physically set up a learning environment. Such skills are an integral part of one's teaching style. For example, a simple skill such as the use of appropriate tone in a teacher's voice can go a long way in establishing a good class climate, and a teacher's skill in determining the form of instruction for a particular lesson can determine the level of learning—or misbehavior—that occurs.

Practices.   Teaching style is also determined by the practices a teacher implements. For example, a physically well-organized classroom environment that provides ready access to supplies, features appropriately deployed furniture, and posts classroom rules is indicative of a teacher who is demonstrating good practices. Practices in the form of routines and procedures are well established in successfully operating classrooms. Practices that facilitate instructional transitions and orderly entrance and dismissal routines are indicative of well-run classrooms. Procedures in the well-run classroom will be evident in the smallest details, from rules for such mundane procedures as toileting, pencil sharpening, and classroom sanitation to essential rules for conduct and deportment. Disciplinary rules are posted or implied, as well as understood by every student. The teacher's expectations are clearly defined and comprehended by each child. A general consistency in management style is noted by the consistency in practice. Teachers who do not implement such positive practices invariably have less effective styles.

Determining Your Teaching Style

By now you should realize that individual style is directly related to one's personality, which governs one's beliefs, skills, and practices. We can assume that our teaching personality determines our needs, likes, and dislikes. The need to control classroom situations is clearly related to the practices a teacher would employ toward that end. Individual likes and dislikes, as well as unrealized bias, also relate to the selection of strategy used in a teacher's approach to class management. If these assumptions are correct, then it should be possible for us to understand our own teaching style through a process of self-reflection and analysis. Box 1.12 presents a set of twelve statements that relate to classroom managerial situations.

Box 1.12   Style, Personality, Beliefs, and Practices Inventory

Instructions: For each of the 12 items below, circle *a* or *b* to indicate the statement with which you identify the most. You must choose between the two statements for each item. Use the scoring key that follows to determine your teaching ideology.

1. *The following statement best reflects my own philosophy about classroom rules:*
   a. Students are immature and therefore limited in their functional abilities. They need adults to establish rules of classroom governance for them.
   b. The emotional needs of individual students must govern classroom management procedures, rather than a scripted, preestablished set of rules imposed indiscriminately on all.

2. *The following statement best reflects my own philosophy about assigned seating:*
   a. Teachers should assign seating during the first class session of a new school year. They need to assign each student his/her own desk, and students should be taught to take the space assigned to them.
   b. Students should be allowed to decide where they should sit. Students working in committees can decide through class meetings and discussions what rules they need to govern the operation of their classroom.

3. *The following statement best reflects my own philosophy about the sequence of classroom instruction:*
   a. Students should be given a choice of topics for class projects. Once they have chosen, their selection is final.
   b. The material students must learn and the tasks to be performed must be determined by the teacher, and the sequence of instruction must be followed.

4. *If classroom equipment and books are being misused, soiled, and at times destroyed, I would most likely:*
   a. Hold a class meeting, show the damaged books to the class, and ask them how they think this problem might be solved, including what action should be taken toward any student found to be misusing books.
   b. Physically remove or limit the number of books available and observe closely who is misusing them. Once the student(s) have been identified, explain how such actions affect other students, and express how you feel about the loss of the books.

5. *If two students of equal power and ability are in a rather loud verbal conflict over classroom supplies, I would:*
   a. Attempt to see that this situation does not get out of control by approaching the students and telling them the class rules while demanding that they desist, and promising a sanction if they do not.
   b. Avoid interfering in something that the students need to resolve themselves.

6. *If a student expresses a strong desire not to work with the group today, I would:*
   a. Permit this, feeling that this student has some emotional concerns related to the group experience.
   b. Raise this as an issue in a class meeting and ask for a discussion of the reasons and possible solutions from both the student and the group.

(continued)

7. *If the noise in class is at a disturbingly high level, I would:*
   a. Flick the lights to get everyone's attention, ask the students to be quiet, and later praise those who complied.
   b. Select those who are making the most noise, take them aside, and ask them to reflect on their behavior and how it affects others. Get an agreement from them to work quietly.

8. *During the first few days of class, I would:*
   a. Permit the students to test their ability to get along as a new group and make no predetermined rules until the students feel that rules are needed.
   b. Immediately establish class rules and fair consequences that I would apply if these rules were broken.

9. *If a student is frustrated by a classmate and has responded by swearing, I would:*
   a. Not reprimand the student but instead would encourage him to talk out what is bothering him.
   b. Confront the student and counsel him about the appropriateness of using good language.

10. *If a student disrupts class while I am trying to lecture, I would:*
    a. Ignore the disruption if possible and/or move the student to the back of the room as a consequence of this behavior.
    b. Express my feeling of discomfort to the student about being disrupted from my task.

11. *The following statement best reflects my philosophy on school rules:*
    a. Each student must realize that there are some school rules that need to be obeyed, and any student who breaks them will be punished in the same fair manner.
    b. Rules are never written in stone and can be renegotiated by the class, and sanctions will vary with each student.

12. *A student refuses to put away her work or materials after using them. I would most likely:*
    a. Express to the student how leaving things out of place will affect future activities in this space, and how frustrating this will be for everyone. I would then leave the materials where they are for the remainder of the day.
    b. Confront the student to reflect on her behavior, asking her to think about how the noncompliance affects others, and tell her that if she cannot follow the rules she will forfeit the use of materials in the future.

Scoring Key

Styles

1		2		3	
Least Teacher Control		*Relative Control*		*Most Teacher Control*	
Student Autonomy		**Confronting**		**Rules**	
Therapeutic		**Group Counseling**		**Strong Management**	
Listening, Relationship		**Leadership**		**Consequences**	
4b	1b	2b	4a	2a	1a
6a	5b	3a	6b	3b	5a
9a	8a	7b	9b	7a	8b
12a	10b	11b	12b	11a	10a

Source: Adapted from C. H. Wolfgang, *Solving Discipline Problems: Methods and Models for Today's Teachers* (Boston: Allyn & Bacon, 1999); Richard T. Scarpaci, *A Case Study Approach to Classroom Management* (Boston: Allyn & Bacon, 2007).

Your choice of response should provide an opportunity for you to assess your relative management style. Your beliefs should fall somewhere on a continuum from a style of least, to moderate, to most classroom management/control.

Teaching style encompasses a teacher's stance, pattern of behavior, mode of performance, and attitude toward self and others. Some would define teacher style in terms of how teachers utilize space in the classroom, their choice of instructional activities and materials, and their method of student grouping. Others might describe teacher style as an expression of a teacher's relationships with their students or simply how they carry out instruction, how they organize learning, or the classroom standards they implement.

Regardless of how you define teaching style, the notion of a pattern is central. Certain behaviors and methods are evident over time, even with different students and in different classroom situations. When you watch different teachers at work, including your college professors, you can sense that each one has a unique style of teaching, structuring the classroom, and delivering lessons. There is a purpose or rationale—a predictable teacher pattern—even in different classroom contexts. Novice teachers can modify aspects of their teaching style that have been dictated by their personality through their early teaching experiences and perceptions, and with appropriate training. As years pass, your own teaching style will become more ingrained and it will take a more powerful set of stimuli and more intense feedback to make changes. Teachers develop their own styles and teaching techniques based on their own physical and mental characteristics. If they are not genuinely themselves, students see through them and label them "phony." The social, psychological, and educational climates in the classroom and school also have something to do with determining teaching style. Nonetheless, no one should be locked into a "recommended style," regardless of conventional wisdom, contemporary history, or popular opinion. Teaching style is a matter of choice and comfort, and what works with one teacher may not work with another. Similarly, operational definitions of *good teachers* and *good teaching styles* vary among and within school districts. There is no ideal teaching style—and no educational institution (school or college) should impose one for all teachers to use with all students.

Research on Teaching Style

One of the most ambitious research studies on teaching style was conducted by Ned Flanders and his associates between 1954 and 1970. Flanders focused on developing an instrument for quantifying verbal communication in the classroom. His work dominated the way in which teaching behaviors were analyzed throughout the late 1970s and 1980s.[62] Every three seconds, observers sorted teacher talk into one of four categories of indirect behavior or one of three categories of direct behavior. Student talk was categorized as response or initiation, and there was a final category representing silence or occasions when the observer could not determine who was talking. Flanders found that as much as 80 percent of classroom time is generally consumed in teacher talk. The ten categories are shown in box 1.13.

Box 1.13   Flanders' Classroom Interaction Analysis Scale

Indirect Behavior

1. *Acceptance of feeling.* Accepts and clarifies the tone of feeling of the students in an unthreatening manner. Feelings may be positive or negative. Predicting or recalling feelings is included.

2. *Praise or encouragement.* Praises or encourages student action or behavior. Jokes to release tension, but not at the expense of another individual; nodding head or saying "Um hm?" or "Go on" are quick and easy ways to encourage students.

3. *Acceptance and use of student ideas.* Clarifies, builds on ideas suggested by students. As the teacher brings more of his or her own ideas into play, shift to category 5.

4. *Questioning.* Asks a question about content or procedure with the intent that a student will answer.

Direct Behavior

5. *Lecturing.* Gives facts or opinions about content or procedure; expresses his or her own ideas, asks rhetorical questions.

6. *Providing directions.* Gives instructions, commands, or orders with which students are expected to comply.

7. *Criticizing or justifying authority.* Makes statements intended to change student behavior from unacceptable to acceptable patterns; reprimands someone; states why the teacher is doing what he or she is doing; extreme self-reference.

Student Talk

8. *Response.* Students talk in response to teacher. Teacher initiates the contact or solicits student statements.

9. *Initiation.* Students initiate talk. If "calling on" a student is only to indicate who may talk next, the observer must decide whether the student wants to talk.

Silence

10. *Silence or confusion.* Pauses, short periods of silence, and periods of confusion in which communication cannot be understood by the observer.

Source: Adapted from Ned A. Flanders, *Teacher Influence, Pupil Attitudes, and Achievement* (Washington, DC: Government Printing Office, 1965), 20.

Flanders' indirect teacher tended to resemble Lippitt's and White's democratic teacher, and Flanders' direct teacher tended to exhibit behaviors similar to Lippitt's and White's authoritarian teacher. Flanders found that students in the indirect classrooms learned more and exhibited more constructive and independent attitudes than did students in the direct classrooms. All types of students in all types of subject classes learned more working with the indirect (more flexible) teachers. The ten categories in box 1.13 will help you answer the four questions below.

The following questions developed by Amidon and Flanders in the 1970s represented a possible direction for organizing and analyzing observations.

Forty years later, to what degree is this model still useful in describing what you have seen in classrooms? Does it help you understand student achievement?

1. What is the relationship of teacher talk to student talk? (This can be answered by comparing the total number of observations in categories 1 to 7 with those in categories 8 and 9.)

2. Is the teacher more direct or indirect? (This can be answered by comparing categories 1 to 4 [indirect] with categories 5 to 7 [direct].)

3. How much class time does the teacher spend lecturing? (This can be answered by comparing category 5 with the total number of observations in categories 1 to 4 and 6 to 7.)

4. Does the teacher ask divergent or convergent questions? This can be answered by comparing category 4 to categories 8 and 9.[63]

The data obtained from this system do not show when, why, or in what context teacher-student talk occurs, only how often particular types of interaction occur. Nonetheless, the system is useful for making teachers aware of their interaction behaviors in the classroom.

The research literature that does exist offers mixed reviews on whether teacher directness or indirectness actually makes a difference in student achievement. The Flanders system may help reveal the style of the teacher, but it does not suggest whether that style will produce a tangible achievement difference in students.

The Flanders system can be used to examine teacher-student verbal behaviors in any classroom, regardless of grade level or subject. Someone can observe the verbal behavior of a prospective, beginning, or even experienced teacher and categorize the teacher as direct or indirect.

Teaching Style and Student Learning

The analysis of teaching styles eventually leads to two questions: Is student learning affected by a teacher's use of different styles? Are different teaching strategies effective for different students? Clear empirical evidence to support an answer to either of these questions does not exist. Let us assume that the answer is "yes" in both cases. If the assumption is true, the aim is to match the appropriate teacher style and strategies with the appropriate group of students in order to achieve the best teaching–learning situation. Depending on one's particular philosophy, matching teacher style and student need is accomplished in one of several ways.

Herbert Thelen argued that teachers recognize four kinds of students: good, bad, indifferent, and maladjusted. Each teacher places different students in these categories; students considered teachable by one teacher may not be categorized as such by another. The proper fit between teacher and students results in the best kind of classroom or best group—the *teachable* group. Thelen contends that homogeneous grouping is essential for a group to become more teachable. A teacher in such a group accomplishes more with students than do teachers in groups where the range of ability and behavior is wide; moreover, it is easier to fit students and teachers in a homogeneous group. Any grouping that does not attempt to match students and teachers can have only "accidental success."[64]

Other researchers have addressed the problem of teachable groups and point out that effective teaching varies for students with different learning characteristics and socioeconomic backgrounds, as well as for different grade levels and subjects. For example, Donald Medley presents one of the most comprehensive reviews of 289 teacher process and product studies.[65] He concludes that effective teachers behave differently with different types of students. The most effective teachers of elementary school students from low socioeconomic backgrounds who may be low achieving (1) spend less time discussing matters unrelated to lesson content, (2) present structured and sequential learning activities, (3) permit little time for independent and small-group work, (4) initiate low-level and narrowly defined questions and are less likely to amplify or discuss student answers, (5) spend little time on and discourage student-initiated questions and comments, (6) provide less feedback on student-initiated questions, (7) engage in fewer rebukes, and (8) spend less time on discipline matters. The optimum type of instruction, questions, and management techniques tend to be completely different for middle-class students. Compare the much more recent analysis of teacher behaviors appropriate for lower-achieving students in box 1.14 with Medley's analysis.

Three things are important to note from Medley's review. First, his notion of modifying teaching strategies for different students is similar to Thelen's "fit" between teachers and students. Teachable students for one teacher may be quite different from those for another, and not all students are easy to teach or are teachable even under normal conditions. Some good teachers cannot successfully teach some types of problem students using approaches that they use with "nonproblem" students. Different students need different teaching techniques.

Second, Medley's description of effective teaching behaviors for students of low socioeconomic status does not resemble the current progressive model of instruction that many educators advocate (e.g., the use of inquiry approaches and self-discovery). Medley found that the least effective teachers with students of

---

Box 1.14   Teaching Lower-Achieving Students

- The teacher provides *active instruction* through a high level of teacher-led instruction. Unstructured time is avoided and high levels of teacher-student interaction are encouraged.

- The teacher *paces instruction* by breaking tasks into manageable segments, carefully assesses student learning, and then creates instructional sequences based on that learning.

- The teacher provides *remedial instruction* by recognizing the level of students' learning before proceeding further with instructional interventions.

- The teacher builds *positive attitudes* by finding ways for students to experience success as learners. Students are praised for real accomplishments and good work.

Source: Adapted from Carolyn Evertson, Edmund T. Emmer, and Murray E. Worsham, *Classroom Management for Elementary Teachers,* 5th ed. (Boston: Allyn & Bacon, 2000), 216–219.

low socioeconomic status were those who asked the most high-level and fewest low-level questions, whose students asked more questions and got more feedback, and who amplified or discussed student-initiated comments. Medley found that teachers who used more low-level questions and fewer high-level ones, whose students initiated fewer questions, and who tended not to discuss what students say, were the most effective. Unquestionably, Medley's ideas are threatening and open to criticism, since they can lead to tracking students by ability and restricting low socioeconomic-status students to limited cognitive experiences.[66]

It is important to point out that no one data source or methodology will sufficiently answer all critical educational questions. Multiple measures or indicators of instruction are needed to help capture a more comprehensive picture of what goes on in classrooms. Some new approaches are needed, such as (1) combining both qualitative and quantitative methods, (2) instruments based on "standards" of pedagogy, (3) comparisons between groups of students within the class, and (4) using instruments that assess authentic practices that relate to student gains on higher-level cognitive outcomes.[67]

Finally, Medley's ideas appear to be very much in line with teaching approaches that have been identified by current researchers as highly successful with low-achieving students, both at the elementary and secondary grade levels: basic skill, drill, time on task, feedback, competency, and mastery learning approaches. They coincide with instruction labeled *direct* and *explicit*.

Martin Haberman writes, *"Star teachers* conceive that their primary job is turning kids on to learning."[68] As a consequence, the star teacher begins to function in particular ways toward students. But just as important as those functions are the star teachers' attitudes toward students. For example, star teachers assume that problems are part of teaching. Some teachers become discouraged because they expect the "perfect" class. It does not exist! And teachers who persist in trying to "find" it will be disappointed. Star teachers emerge as stars because they work to transform problems into possibilities for all students. It sounds trite, but it is also true.

A New Paradigm for Understanding Effective Teaching

We have discussed the different ways in which teachers attempt to foster more critical inquiry in students. Some argue for imposing knowledge structures on students. Teachers possess knowledge and students need to absorb and be tested on that knowledge. Others suggest that it makes more sense for students to discover knowledge. Cognitive theorists argue that students construct (or make sense of) the information they receive in a way that makes personal sense to them.[69]

Empiricism vs. Radicalism

Constructivist ideas fall into different camps. Some are *empiricist oriented* and others are *radical*. **Empiricist-oriented constructivists** "believe that knowledge is anchored in the external environment and exists independently of the learner's cognitive activities, so they tend to speak about helping learners construct accurate concepts"; **radical constructivists** assert that "knowledge resides in the construction of learners."[70] The standards-based environment within which you will teach demands that students acquire certain understandings that reflect accurately what is known in the various disciplines. A middle ground between empiricist and radical constructionists are the dialectical constructivists, who argue that knowledge emerges from an interaction between the internal (cognitive) and the external (environmental) factors. For the dialectical constructivist, there are multiple ways to construct knowledge, but some are better than others and not all are defensible.[71]

A teacher's constructivist orientation is not an unimportant issue. The empiricist and dialectical constructivists are concerned with students' accurate representations of the realities they confront. The radical constructivists believe that the world is not really knowable because context changes what one knows. We contend that the key to constructivism, whether empiricist oriented or radical, is that good teachers go well beyond the transfer of knowledge. They know both how and when to transfer knowledge (i.e., a skill or process) and when to engage students in construction of knowledge. Such pedagogical knowledge entails use of both the science and the art of teaching. Examine Case Study 1.2 and attempt to construct an answer that allows you to understand the effective teacher.

The following case study presents a variety of views regarding the definition of an effective teacher. Read the case and see if you agree with Carl Hanson's, Jill Conway's, or Gale Kemp's beliefs regarding its true meaning.

Case Study 1.2
Defining an Effective Teacher

Carl Hanson had always wanted to be an effective teacher. He believed that effective teaching occurred when the teacher brought about intended learning outcomes that could be measured by a student's social and academic level of success, and when the psychological needs of all students are met. Unfortunately, these grandiose philosophical ideas had to be implemented in an urban inner-city high school that had a graduation rate of 28 percent—a school that was on the verge of being closed by the state education department. Less than 10 percent of the students at Carl's school spoke English as their primary language. Carl decided to survey his colleagues and find out what they considered a good definition of an effective teacher.

Jill Conway believed that above all, an effective teacher was a culturally responsive teacher—one who was validating, comprehensive, multidimensional, and transformative. "Effective teaching happens," said Jill, "when teachers use their cultural knowledge, prior experiences, and the performance styles of diverse students to make learning meaningful and appropriate." The idea, Jill felt, is to teach *to* and *through* the strengths of your students.

"Wait one minute!" Gale Kemp chimed in with a brief soliloquy on what an effective teacher really is able to do. Gale said that when she was in Teacher's College she had been taught that the keys to effective teaching were personality, expectations, methods, mastery, and management. Without these five elements you could never be effective as a teacher.

Hearing these divergent opinions, Carl said, "First, maybe we should find out what we can agree on. Can we agree that instructional clarity is a teaching behavior that students normally respond well to? What about being knowledgeable about your content area?"

Gale said, "That's what I meant by mastery: mastery of content."

Carl said, "Good, now we're getting somewhere. What about the establishment of learning expectations, and a knowledge of learning and development principles?" Gale agreed about the need for positive student expectations and knowledge of instructional methods. Carl said, "I guess that could also include variation in your teaching style and use of multiple resources, as well as highlighting the need for an effective teaching personality."

Jill, who had been quietly listening to Carl and Gale, nodded her head and said, "Could we sum up the definition by saying that effective teaching is indicated by appropriate use of technology, good classroom design, celebrating diversity, and cultural responsiveness focused on improved learning?"

"Jill, you've done it again. You've confused the issue of a definition with your obsession with cultural diversity," Gale interjected. "What about stressing the keys for effective teaching in a definition?" Carl said, "Maybe I was right all along when I said that effective teaching could be measured by your students' success."

Discussion Topics and Questions to Ponder

1. Which of the positions taken by Jill, Gale, and Carl is most quantifiable? Explain your answer.

2. What was wrong with Jill's definition?

3. Compare and contrast the keys to effective teaching with culturally responsive teaching (see the boxes below). Where are they similar, and where do they differ?

Culturally Responsive Teaching

- Acknowledging the legitimacy of the cultural heritages of different ethnic groups, both as legacies that affect students' dispositions, attitudes, and approaches to learning and as worthy content to be taught in the formal curriculum.

- Building bridges of meaningfulness between home and school experiences as well as between academic abstractions and lived socio-cultural realities.

- Using a wide variety of instructional strategies that are connected to different learning styles.

- Teaching students to know and praise their own and other cultural heritages.

- Incorporating multicultural information, resources, and materials in all the subjects and skills routinely taught in schools (Gay, 2000, p. 29).

Keys to Effective Teaching

1. *Personality* suited to positive interaction that engages learning
2. *Expectations* that all students will succeed
3. Ability to select *methods* related to how children learn
4. *Mastery* and proficiency in content area
5. Ability to *manage* the classroom effectively

4. Agree or disagree with the following statements. Justify your response.
   • Diversity is a positive force in a classroom setting.
   • You do not have to be culturally responsive to be an effective teacher.
5. Which of the three positions presented in the case study appeals to you? Explain your answer.

What would you do if . . . ?

1. Carl said to Gale that all culturally responsive teaching was communicating with students on multiple levels.
2. Gale said that enthusiasm is infectious and that personality is a prime key to creating enthusiastic learners.
3. No one agreed on a definition for effective teaching.

*G. Gay, *Culturally Responsive Teaching: Theory, Research, and Practice* (New York: Teachers College Press, 2000).

Effective Teaching and the Hidden Curriculum

Teachers become so preoccupied with teaching and learning that they fail to see how their daily actions contribute to the hidden messages of school—a phenomenon often called the *hidden curriculum*, "that which is taught implicitly, rather than explicitly, by the school experience."[72] These messages may be more powerful than any paradigm we adopt or critical thinking skills we encourage. Read carefully the words of one teacher and then consider how what you do with kids may supersede anything you ever intentionally plan:

> One year I was working with this boy who had been a D student all the way through. I could hardly keep him in his seat. He was just a rascally boy. He never stepped over the line completely, but he was a thorn in my side all year long. In the lab he would always do something offbeat. By the end of the year he was coming along in his work o.k. I didn't see him after that for two or three years. Then one day here was this young man coming down the hallway dressed in a smart business suit, and lo and behold, it was that fellow. I said, "Well, what have you been doing?" and he said, "I've been in the Marines and I came back to thank you."
>
> I said, "What for?" because I thought I'd never taught that boy any science.
>
> And he said, "It's not for the science. It's because you taught me to be honest and to say what I observed. That was really important to me. I'll carry that with me forever."[71]

classic professional viewpoint 1.3

Be a Great Teacher!

E. Paul Torrance

There are far too few great teachers, and society desperately needs them. Great teachers are great artists. Teaching is perhaps the greatest of the arts because the medium is the human mind and spirit.

My experience and research have made me aware of the importance of falling in love with what you are going to do—a dream, an image of the future. Positive images of the future are a powerful and magnetic force. These images draw us on and energize us, giving us the courage and will to take important initiatives and move forward to new solutions and achievements. To dream and to plan, to be curious about the future, and to wonder how much of it can be influenced by our efforts are important aspects of our being human.

There is considerable evidence that our future self-image is a powerful motivating force that determines what we are motivated to learn and achieve. In fact, a person's image of his or her future may be a better predictor of future attainment than of past performance.

I would encourage you to develop a future image of yourself as a great teacher—a new, positive, compelling, and exciting image. Then, fall in love with this image—your unique future self-image! You *can* become a great teacher—and that is a great thing!

CONCLUSIONS

- The kind of teacher you choose to be is based in part on your reasons for teaching.
- Teachers must provide motivating methods and materials for students by recognizing that each student is an individual with his or her own unique needs, abilities, and sense of self-esteem.
- Learning-paradigm teachers focus on what students do to construct their own knowledge. Such teachers focus on the essence of the teaching act, not on the "busyness" of the students.
- Students have different ways of thinking and learning, including but not limited to visual, auditory, and tactile processes.
- Students can be taught learning-to-learn skills, critical thinking skills, and creative thinking skills. The idea is for the teacher to move from teaching the facts and right answers to problem solving and creative thinking.
- Understanding how to be an effective teacher requires comprehending the keys to effective teaching and realizing that teaching is both an art and a science.
- Effective teachers must understand the basic concepts of learning contained within the constructivist and behaviorist theories.
- One's teaching style is derived from one's beliefs, skills, and practices.

KEY TERMS

art of teaching	critical thinking	learning paradigm
cognitive structures	empiricist-oriented	metacognition
constructivist theory	constructivists	radical constructivists
creative thinking	instructional paradigm	reactive thinking
creativity	intuitive thinking	science of teaching

DISCUSSION QUESTIONS

1. Why is it important to understand your own reasons for teaching?

2. Compare and contrast teacher characteristics and student learning variables. Clarify which characteristic of effective teachers correlates to which "key for effective teaching" (box 1.1). Provide an example for each.

> ### Characteristics of the Effective Teacher
> An effective teacher:
> - Is a good classroom manager.
> - Designs lessons to reach mastery.
> - Believes all can learn.
> - Uses new strategies to meet children's needs.
> - Has positive expectations that students will succeed.

3. Compare and contrast the characteristics of the effective teacher with the variables necessary for student learning.

> ### Variables Necessary for Student Learning
> - Classroom management
> - Learning processes taught (how to take notes, read text, work in groups, etc.)
> - A positive home environment and parental cooperation
> - Teacher and student interrelationship
> - What the teacher does in class
>
> (The least important factor is demographic data.)

4. Prepare a brief behavior modification plan that you could use to address the following situations:
   - Your class is disruptive upon entering the room.
   - Students claim that you give them too much homework and that it interferes with their other class assignments.

- A student informs you confidentially that a member of her class intends to cheat on your midterm.

5. Prepare a constructivist learning plan based on a constructivist learning design that you could use to address the following situations.

   - Your class is unruly upon returning from lunch and as a result loses, on average, ten minutes of instructional time each day.

   - Students claim they are not prepared to take your midterm examination because they have difficulty memorizing your notes.

   - A student comes to you and says he is having difficulty working in a cooperative group setting.

6. Write a brief explanation of each term, and compare and contrast their differences. Show how eclectic options can combine both behaviorist and constructivist terms. (See the example entry in the third column below.).

Behaviorism	Constructivism	Eclectic Options
Direct teaching	Indirect teaching	Use both direct and indirect teaching strategies based on the abilities and characteristics of my classes.
Objectivist	Pluralist/totalist	
Teacher-centered	Learner-centered	
Behavioral observations	Cognitive operations	
Focus on individual	Stress on group work	
Focus on one approach	Holistic in approach	

7. What teaching methods and approaches can be used to improve students' thinking skills?

8. What are the attributes of critical thinking and creative thinking? Which type of thinking is more important for students to develop in school?

9. Why do some claim that the three most important factors impacting teaching style are beliefs, skills, and practices?

10. Explain and discuss your reasons for agreeing or disagreeing with the learning paradigm.

Mini-Cases from the Field

Case One: Reasons for Teaching

Judy Jones, a newly hired first-grade teacher, was not sure whether she had chosen the right career. She had always wanted to be a teacher. Everyone told her it was an easy job with good hours and ample vacation time. But teaching was not turning out to be as easy as she had hoped. The children were giving her difficulty and seemed to ignore everything she told them to do. They did not listen, obey, or follow her directions. Judy's next-door neighbor Joan Finkelman, a very experienced veteran teacher, told Judy to just reflect on her reasons for wanting to become a teacher. Judy looked at Joan in bewilderment: How could reflection help her? When Judy became upset, Joan said, "Just think about it. That's all reflection really is."

1. Identify Judy's problem. Was it her class's behavior causing the problem, or the fact that Judy had not reflected on her choice of career? Explain and justify your answer.

2. What did Joan mean when she said that reflection is really just thinking?

3. Why is it important to reflect before acting?

4. How could Judy have used the instructional paradigm to her advantage?

5. How would you describe the appropriateness of Judy's reasons for wanting to become a teacher?

Case Two: Keys to Effective Teaching

Alex did not understand his principal's insistence that he learn the keys to effective teaching. He had been teaching for almost six months. During that time he had experienced a multitude of academic and behavioral problems. He felt his job required children to be quiet and to speak only when spoken to. What did personality, expectations, mastery, management, and methods have to do with his becoming an effective teacher? All Alex felt he needed to do was come to school on time, deliver his lesson, and maintain order.

1. It appears that Alex maybe confusing instruction with learning. How would you explain to Alex the purpose of teaching?

2. How would you describe Alex's beliefs regarding teaching?

3. Which of the keys does Alex seem to lack?

4. If you were to describe the keys, how would you explain personality?

5. How would you explain to Alex the "Why, What, How, and Who of Teaching"?

Case Three: Concepts of Learning

Roger Christiana had always wanted to become a teacher. Upon accomplishing his goal he was assigned to Dr. Maureen Quinlan's school, which had been recognized as one of the state's best schools. Dr. Quinlan insisted that every teacher articulate a well-defined concept of how children learn. This, she often stated, was the reason her school was so successful. When Roger's turn came to present his view at a staff conference, he simply stated that he felt children learned by doing and that he felt it was the responsibility of the teacher to construct meaning for the students. Students had to be trained, and good lessons were a stimulus for success.

1. Was Roger's understanding of constructivism correct? Explain your reasoning.

2. Is Roger's concept of learning clear and well defined? If so, how? If not, what is lacking in his conceptual definition?

3. Point out potential problems regarding his thoughts.

4. Does Roger have a right to his point of view, despite the fact that he appears not to understand the traditional definitions of the concepts he claims to espouse? Could the case be made that he is eclectic?

5. If you were given the same task as Roger, how would you have responded? Write a brief description that clarifies your concept of learning.

Case Four: Critical Thinking

Mary Hemming, a social studies teacher at Hartford Middle School, had been asked by her school's PTA president to speak at a parents meeting to explain how she would implement a critical-thinking program for their middle school. Mary wasn't really sure that she even favored a critical-thinking strategy as a necessary component in her school's curriculum, let alone knowing how to implement one.

1. Is a critical-thinking strategy a necessary component for a school's curriculum content?

2. Which of the critical-thinking strategies is least understood?

3. Compare the critical-thinking strategies and describe where there are overlaps.

4. Which of the following critical-thinking strategies could be considered most important for students: critical-thinking research, creative thinking, reactive thinking, or intuitive thinking?

5. Compare the arguments for and against a critical-thinking curriculum. Which position would you choose, and why would you choose it?

Case Five: Teacher Styles, Beliefs, and Characteristics

Frank Sussino had a style of teaching he considered well suited for the situation he found himself in. He was a former accountant who had always wanted to become a teacher. He believed he was a stern taskmaster and that student time on task would guarantee learning. He had just been hired at midsession to teach tenth-grade mathematics at Winfield High School. The prior teacher, Lucy Forbes, had taught for many years and had suddenly decided to retire and pursue a career in the theater. Before she left she advised Frank to "be creative." She had been loved by her students for her friendly, carefree approach to teaching. Her principal did not like her laissez-faire approach to the curriculum and claimed that her methods were responsible for her classes' problems with standardized tests. Consequently, Frank decided on a plan to improve his classes' test results.

1. How should the principal expect the class to behave when faced with Frank's taskmaster attitude?
2. From the brief description given, compare the teaching styles of Frank and Lucy.
3. What did Lucy Forbes mean when she told Frank to be creative?
4. If you were placed in Frank's situation, what would you do?
5. What do you think Frank had decided to do to improve test scores, and how do you think he was going to go about it?

FIELD EXPERIENCE ACTIVITIES

1. Observe two or three teachers at work in the classroom and try to describe how they motivate their students. How successful are they in doing so?
2. Make a list of the most common student behaviors that the teachers have to deal with.
3. Are the teachers you are observing learning- or instructional-paradigm teachers? Explain your answer.
4. Describe your own experiences with teachers. Which of your teachers have been learning-paradigm teachers? Which were instructional? Explain your answer.
5. Success in school is partially based on students' abilities to think critically. Identify the things that teachers you observed can do to foster critical thinking among students.

RECOMMENDED READING

Borich, Gary D. *Effective Teaching Methods: Research-Based Practice,* 7th ed. Upper Saddle River, NJ: Allyn & Bacon, 2010.
Provides effective, practical, research-based practices in an accessible, conversational style.
Burkett, Elinor. *Another Planet: A Year in the Life of a Suburban High School.* New York: Harper Collins, 2002.
A close examination of teacher and student lives in a suburban high school, illustrating the reality that schools are busy, complex places.
Chance, Paul. *The Teacher's Craft: The 10 Essential Skills of Effective Teaching* (Long Grove, IL: Waveland Press, 2008).
Commonsense, evidence-based principles to markedly improve student performance.
Educational Leadership 68, no. 4 (December 2010/January 2011).
An entire issue devoted to the effective educator.
Fried, Robert. *The Passionate Learner.* Boston: Beacon Press, 2001.
Offers a thoughtful description of how excellent teaching can be learned through practice and reflection.

Maran, Meredith. *Class Dismissed: A Year in the Life of an American High School, A Glimpse into the Heart of a Nation*. New York: St. Martin's Press, 2000.
  A poignant examination of life in one urban American high school that focuses on the lives of three high school seniors, illustrating implications both for how teachers teach and for how students learn.

Marzano, Robert J. *The Art and Science of Teaching: A Comprehensive Framework for Effective Instruction*. Alexandria, VA: ASCD, 2007.
  Balances the necessity of research-based data with the equally vital need to understand the strengths and weaknesses of individual students.

Ornstein, Allan C. *Teaching and Schooling in America: Pre- and Post-September 11*. Boston: Allyn & Bacon, 2005.
  Describes life and death, good and evil, peace and war, morality and immorality, equality and inequality.

Rose, Mike. *Possible Lives: The Promise of Public Education in America*. New York: Houghton Mifflin, 1995.
  A compilation of teacher stories taken from different social and economic contexts.

Sternberg, Robert J. *Understanding and Teaching the Intuitive Mind*. Mahwah, NJ: Erlbaum, 2001.
  Discusses the methods and findings of problem solving and intuitive thinking.

Part II

The Practices and Technical Skills of Teaching

In the eight chapters that make up this section, we explore the actions and technical skills needed to understand the practice of teaching by utilizing the arts and sciences. Our rationale is to focus on the artful practice of scientific teaching. We have attempted to provide a set of engaging activities and questions for you to reflect on. Narrative case studies are designed to prompt critical thinking about the issues addressed in each chapter. Their purpose is to help you develop a professional outlook and, subsequently, the practices and skills needed for effective teaching. To achieve success, you must completely develop, enhance, and understand the body of known knowledge that comprises the practice of teaching. This book provides some of that requisite knowledge and also attempts to provide a basis for learning the dispositions and performances essential for masterful teaching. There is no incompatibility between well articulated teaching standards and research-based teaching practices developed with the technical skills of teaching.

The 2002 No Child Left Behind legislation will leave no child untested and no teacher outside an accountability system, regardless of how it will be changed with future legislation. As a result, this section is designed to familiarize you with the guidelines for what to teach (the topic of chapter 2), how to teach the required content (discussed in chapters 3–7), and how to assess whether students have learned it (covered in chapters 8 and 9).

2

Instructional Objectives and Standards

OVERVIEW

The world that you are entering as a new teacher looks a bit different from that of the teachers who taught you. Their world was heavily oriented toward teachers' academic freedom, even in states with mandated curricula. In contrast, your world is one of clearly defined academic standards for students, and accountability for teachers and students relative to those standards. As a result of the No Child Left Behind legislation, you must become familiar with the guidelines for what to teach—the topic of this chapter.

Education Standards

Standards are the latest in a series of educational fads. The proponents of standards have largely been successful in shaping school policy throughout the United States. There are those who claim that standards based on high-stakes tests narrow the curriculum excessively, devalue teachers' professionalism, and alienate students from learning. Educators should question the meaning of national and local standards and the impact they have on the practice of teaching. Do teachers encourage low-level skill lessons in order to have students pass mindless tests? Are standards really the only way to monitor student achievement? Time will tell if standards have been used effectively as a foundation for educational reform. The types of standards are defined below.

1. *Academic/education standards* describe what students should know and be able to do in the core academic subjects at each grade level.
2. *Content/grade-level standards* describe basic agreement about the body of education knowledge that all students should know.
3. *Performance standards* describe what level of performance is good enough to describe students as advanced, proficient, below basic, or some other performance level.

Some educators question the rigor of the standards that all states now have in place. The American Federation of Teachers (AFT) is well known and much praised for its firm insistence on "coherent content standards" and has periodically appraised state standards for clarity, specificity, and classroom utility. In 2008 the AFT reviewed state standards in English, math, science, and social studies for all levels and found that only Virginia met their criteria for strong standards in all levels and subjects. Colorado, Illinois, Iowa, Montana, Nebraska, Pennsylvania, and Wisconsin had no strong standards, while other states were somewhere in between (see tables 2.1 and 2.2 for a list of states that have adopted standards). This unevenness in applying standards may have troublesome consequences for students or for school districts. It is important for you to remember that, regardless of what your state prescribes, what students learn depends on the choices that you, the teacher, make.

Table 2.1   Percentage of Strong Standards by State

0%	Colorado, Illinois, Iowa, Montana, Nebraska, Pennsylvania, Wisconsin
1–24%	Maine, New Hampshire, New Jersey, Rhode Island, Vermont, Wyoming
25–49%	Alaska, Idaho, Kansas, Kentucky, Minnesota, Nevada, Oregon, Washington
50–74%	Arizona, Connecticut, Delaware, Florida, Hawaii, Maryland, Massachusetts, Mississippi, Missouri, New Mexico, North Dakota, South Dakota, Texas, Utah
75–99%	Alabama, Arkansas, California, Georgia, Indiana, Louisiana, Michigan, New York, North Carolina, Ohio, Oklahoma, South Carolina, Tennessee, Washington, D.C., West Virginia
100%	Virginia

Source: American Federation of Teachers, AFL-CIO (AFT), *Sizing Up Standards 2008.* http://www.aft.org/pubs-reports/downloads/teachers/standards2008.pdf

Table 2.2   States with Strong Standards in Four Content Areas

English	Georgia, Indiana, New Mexico, New York, North Carolina, Tennessee, Virginia, Washington, D.C.
Mathematics	Alabama, Alaska, Arkansas, California, Delaware, Florida, Georgia, Hawaii, Idaho, Indiana, Louisiana, Maryland, Mississippi, New York, North Carolina, Ohio, Oklahoma, South Carolina, South Dakota, Texas, Utah, Virginia, Washington, D.C., West Virginia
Science	Alabama, Arkansas, California, Connecticut, Delaware, Georgia, Hawaii, Indiana, Louisiana, Maryland, Michigan, Mississippi, Missouri, North Carolina, Ohio, Oklahoma, South Carolina, South Dakota, Tennessee, Virginia, Washington, D.C., West Virginia
Social Studies	Massachusetts, Virginia

Source: American Federation of Teachers, AFL-CIO (AFT) *Sizing Up Standards 2008.* http://www.aft.org/pubs-reports/downloads/teachers/standards2008.pdf

Defining Terms

When figuring out what to teach, in addition to standards you will be guided by aims, goals, and objectives. Each of these tools will help you to focus your teaching and to plan units and lessons. You need to understand the purpose of each of these tools and how they can help you.

Aims. We use the term **aims** (or **purposes**) to refer to broad statements about the intent of education. Aims are descriptive, value-laden statements written by panels, commissions, or policy-making groups at a societal (or national) level. They express a philosophy of education, concepts of the social role of schools, and the needs of children and youth. In short, they are broad guides for translating the needs of society into educational policy. Aims are usually somewhat vague in terms of how they will be achieved, but they are clear in terms of their focus. One example of an aim is to prepare students for democratic citizenship (or, more briefly, citizenship preparation). But what does the phrase "prepare students for democratic citizenship" mean? What do we have in mind when we say "citizenship preparation"? If an aim has been clearly focused, we should easily be able to answer these questions.

Aims and learning outcomes for teaching contribute logical starting points for topic design. Expressing them involves the same process as describing the purpose and procedures for a research proposal. Once we are clear about *what* we want to achieve, we can then make decisions about *how* we will achieve it. *Statements of topic aims* are general statements that are formulated in clear language and express the nature and direction of the topic.

Aims are:

- significant and worthwhile,
- clear and unambiguous,
- attainable in terms of available facilities and resources, and
- achievable (through reasonable effort) by all students.

It is good educational practice to communicate to students what you are trying to achieve and what they should expect to gain. Aims are helpful for students, and they can help you to clarify your approach in your own mind.

Goals. Educators need to translate aims into statements that will describe what schools are expected to accomplish. These statements, called **goals**, are more focused than statements about the purpose of education. Goals make it possible to organize learning experiences in terms of what the state, school district, or school decides to stress on a systemwide basis. In effect, goals are statements that cut across subjects and grade levels to represent the entire school program. Although goals are more definite than aims, they are still nonbehavioral and therefore nonobservable and nonmeasurable. Goals provide direction for educators, but they do not specify achievement levels or proficiency levels. Examples of goals are "development of reading skills," "appreciation of art," and "understanding of mathematical/scientific concepts."

Goals are usually written by professional associations, state educational agencies, and local school districts, to be published as school and curriculum guidelines for what all students should accomplish over their entire school careers. Although goals are usually developed at the local or regional level, a more recent national movement proposes that one way of equalizing opportunity is to nationalize goals for education.[1] Core national standards have evolved from this movement. Because of the tremendous emphasis on assessment and accountability, teachers are increasingly required to use professional state and national goals, established by the learned societies or by state governments, to prescribe content to be covered.

Objectives.   Descriptions of what eventually is to take place at the classroom level are called **objectives**. They specify content and sometimes the proficiency level to be attained. Understanding why and how to use instructional objectives results in more effective teaching and testing. Using instructional objectives helps the teacher focus on what students should know at the end of the lesson plan or unit plan (a series of lessons related to a specific topic) and also helps students know what is expected of them. Instructional objectives help the teacher plan for teaching and organize instruction; they identify what to teach and when to teach it, thus serving as a map or guide for both teachers and students. Instructional objectives are stated in observable and measurable terms, and they clarify whether what we intended was achieved, or to what extent it was (or was not) achieved.

According to Hilda Taba, "The chief function of . . . objectives is to guide the making of . . . decisions on what to cover, what to emphasize, and what content to select, and what learning experiences to stress."[2] Because the possibilities of content, learning, and teaching are endless, teachers face the problem of selection: What content is most important? What learning activities are most appropriate? What unit plan is most effective? Objectives supply criteria for these decisions, "setting the scope and limits for what is to be taught and learned."[3]

Naturally, objectives should be consistent with the overriding goals of the school system, the state standards that may be in place, and the general educational aims of society. Each teacher, when planning for instruction, may contribute to these goals and aims in a different way. So how do goals and objectives relate? If the goal is development of reading skills, the objective may be to identify the main ideas of the author. If the goal is appreciation of art, the objective may be to recognize the paintings of major artists. If the goal is to understand scientific concepts, the objective may be to determine how hydrogen and oxygen change to water.

The relationship of aims, goals, and objectives is shown in figure 2.1—aims being the broadest and objectives being the most specific. Objectives can further be divided into program, course, unit, and lesson-plan objectives. Not all districts require this subdividing, but you should know how to do it just in case, and as a way to inform your own planning.

Figure 2.1   Relationship between Education Aims, Goals, and Objectives and the Appropriate Level of Implementation

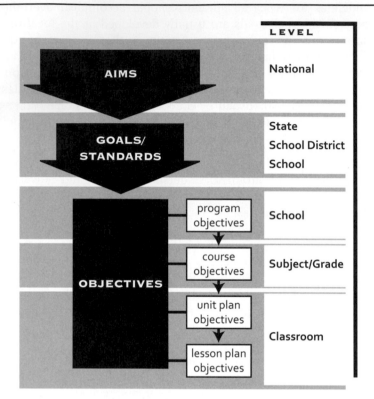

The Aims of Education

Aims are important statements that guide our schools and give educators direction. We will discuss them only briefly because they are not written by teachers. Perhaps the most widely accepted list of educational aims in the twentieth century was compiled by the Commission on the Reorganization of Secondary Education in 1918. Its influential bulletin was titled *Cardinal Principles of Secondary Education.* The seven principles, or aims, designated by the commission were (1) health, (2) command of the fundamentals, (3) worthy home membership, (4) vocational education, (5) civic education, (6) worthy use of leisure time, and (7) ethical character.[4]

The Commission's work was the first statement of educational aims that addressed the need to assimilate immigrant children and to educate an industrial workforce, reflecting events in the country at that period. The most important aspect of the document is that it emphasized the need to educate *all* students for "complete living," not only students headed for college and not only for developing cognitive abilities. It endorsed the concept of the whole child and the importance of meeting the various needs of a student, while it provided a common ground for teaching and enhancing American ideals and educating all citizens to function in a democratic society. These aims are still relevant for all levels of education and are still found today in one form or another in statements of educational aims.

For example, sixty-five years later in 1983, the report *A Nation at Risk* was compiled by a panel appointed by the US Department of Education. The report indicated that the well-being of the nation was being eroded by what they called a "rising tide of mediocrity." This mediocrity was linked to the foundations of our educational institutions and was seen as spilling over into the workplace and other sectors of society.[5] The report sought to upgrade the curriculum (i.e., command of the fundamentals) by improving basic skills for young children, improving textbook quality, increasing homework, strengthening high school graduation requirements, and raising college admission requirements. It also focused on parental training for children's early learning (overlapping with worthy home membership) and improving adult literacy and the knowledge base essential for a democratic and technological society (coinciding with civic education and vocational education).

We would argue that the No Child Left Behind (NCLB) legislation is one of those current essential aims of education. True, the NCLB has many definitions, but it's equally true that a lot of vagueness remains regarding *how* NCLB will be universally achieved. The devil is truly in the details of the NCLB legislative mandate because of the unevenness in testing mechanisms.

Trends in Educational Goals

Goals tend to reflect the developmental needs of children and youth. According to Peter Oliva, goals "are timeless, in the sense that no time is specified by which the goals must be reached," and at the same time they "are not permanent," in the sense that they "may be modified wherever necessary or desirable." Goals usually cut across subjects and grades and apply throughout the school. They do not delineate specific items of content or corresponding activities. Goals should be stated broadly enough "to be accepted at any level of the educational enterprise" but specifically enough to lead to desired outcomes.[6]

Increasingly, society is burdening the schools with roles and responsibilities that other agencies and institutions no longer do well or desire to do.[7] The schools are seen as ideal agents to solve the problems of the nation, community, and home. Many people and groups refuse to accept their own responsibility for helping children develop their capabilities and adjust to society. More and more, the schools are being told that they must educate and socialize all children, regardless of the quality of the initial input and support from home. As a result, schools are now attempting to accomplish too many things and are therefore not achieving many of them.

In preparing his classic 1979 *Study of Schooling,* John Goodlad surveyed the school goals that had been published by state and local boards of education across the country. From approximately 100 different statements of goals, he constructed twelve that represent the spirit of the total list (see box 2.1). He further defined each with subgoals and a rationale statement. The goals summarize what educators are expected to attend to and what they might be held accountable for.

Box 2.1   Major Goals of American Schools

1. *Mastery of basic skills or fundamental processes.* In our technological civilization, an individual's ability to participate in the activities of society depends on mastery of these fundamental processes.

2. *Career or vocational education.* An individual's personal satisfaction in life is significantly related to satisfaction with her or his job. Intelligent career decisions require knowledge of personal aptitudes and interests in relation to career possibilities.

3. *Intellectual development.* As civilization has become more complex, people have had to rely more heavily on their rational abilities. Full intellectual development of each member of society is necessary.

4. *Enculturation.* Studies that illuminate our relationship with the past yield insights into our society and its values; furthermore, these strengthen an individual's sense of belonging, identity, and direction for his or her own life.

5. *Interpersonal relations.* Schools should help all children understand, appreciate, and value persons belonging to social, cultural, and ethnic groups different from their own and to increase affiliation with and decrease alienation toward them.

6. *Autonomy.* Unless schools produce self-directed citizens, they have failed both society and the individual. As society becomes more complex, demands on individuals multiply. Schools help prepare children for a world of rapid change by developing in them the capacity to assume responsibility for their own needs.

7. *Citizenship.* Counteracting the present human ability to destroy humanity and the environment requires citizen involvement in the political and social life of this country. A democracy can survive only with the participation of its members.

8. *Creativity and aesthetic perception.* Abilities for creating new and meaningful things and appreciating the creations of other human beings are essential both for personal self-realization and for the benefit of society.

9. *Self-concept.* The self-concept of an individual serves as a reference point and feedback mechanism for personal goals and aspirations. Factors for a healthy self-concept can be provided by the school environment.

10. *Emotional and physical well-being.* Emotional stability and physical fitness are perceived as necessary conditions for attaining the other goals, but they are also worthy ends in themselves.

11. *Moral and ethical character.* Development of the judgment needed to evaluate events and phenomena as right or wrong and a commitment to truth, moral integrity, moral conduct, and a desire to strengthen the moral fabric of society are the values manifested by this goal.

12. *Self-realization.* Efforts to develop a better self contribute to the development of a better society.

Source: John I. Goodlad, *What Schools Are For* (Bloomington, IN: Phi Delta Kappa, 1994), 46–52. Reprinted with permission of Phi Delta Kappa International, www.pdkintl.org. All rights reserved.

Another set of goals that guided American education is the *President's Goals 2000.* These goals, proffered by former President Clinton, envision the ideal competitive American school and delineate what students should be able to accomplish. "Accountability starts with goals," said US Secretary of Education Arne Duncan ten years later.[8] He believed that with goals in place, everyone in the system knows what they are supposed to accomplish, and they can and will try to do it. "We need to be really tight on goals and have these common . . . standards that we're all aiming for, but then be much looser in how you let folks get there." Two big barriers stand in the way of using the approach to fix the education system: (1) Can government establish clear and ambitious goals for K–12 education? And (2) can educators become competent in the practices of improvement and innovation?

Most schools put more emphasis on cognitive and intellectual goals, especially at the secondary school level, while usually giving lip service to affective goals that relate to moral and ethical considerations. Elementary schools tend to address the needs of the whole child and provide more balance with cognitive, personal, and social growth and development. A number of schools are becoming increasingly concerned with and are formulating goals pertaining to social, multicultural, and global understanding, but the debate about how far schools should go in teaching affective goals—especially as they relate to moral and ethical considerations—is a topic of heated debate.[9]

When we formulate our goals, we might ask the following questions: To what extent should our schools emphasize the needs of society and the needs of the individual? Should schools emphasize excellence or equality? Should we put equal emphasis on academic, vocational, and general education? Should we put more emphasis on cognitive learning or on humanistic understanding? Which is more important—national commitment or personal conviction? Should we educate students to their own ability levels (recognizing that, for a few, this might mean only an eighth-grade education), or should we push students to achieve beyond their perceived aptitude and achievement levels? How should we apportion money to be spent on talented and gifted students, average students, and students with disabilities? How do we compare the payoffs to society and the obligations of society in educating different student populations? (See Classic Professional Viewpoint 2.1 for more insight into setting goals.)

These questions are tough and complicated. Not only do educators disagree about them, but wars have even been fought over them. The way we answer these questions both reflects and determines the kind of people we are. Most people in this country readily say they believe in democracy, but how they answer these questions determines what *democracy* means and how it affects and controls our lives. Trying to resolve these questions, at least in this country, ideally involves a balancing act that determines whether our moral and legal restraints overrule our political and economic considerations and whether the needs of the group can be placed in perspective with the rights of the individual.

Among the most forward-thinking examples of these endeavors is the effort of the Alameda Unified School District to outline a profile of graduates for the year 2004. The Alameda Graduate Profile identifies specific outcomes for gradu-

---

Goal Setting

Herbert J. Walberg

Part of my academic heritage came from Benjamin Bloom and his teacher, Ralph Tyler—both professors at the University of Chicago and among the most influential and eminent educational thinkers of the twentieth century. Writing on curriculum, Tyler identified goals, learning activities, and evaluation as the essential components of teaching. He argued that for efficient learning, goals should be clear; learning experiences should be carefully chosen to match the goals; and evaluation should be employed to assess the degree of goal attainment.

Bloom kept Tyler's portrait in his office, where I used to meet with him. As an educational psychologist, Bloom spent several decades working out ways of setting learning goals and finding the best conditions for their attainment. In what is referred to as "Bloom's taxonomy," he specified six levels of cognitive learning that encouraged educators to teach not merely factual knowledge but also analysis, synthesis, and other "higher thought processes." Through long-term research, Bloom tried to find the best conditions of goal attainment, not only in ordinary classrooms but also in sports, intellectual competitions, and the professions. His work extended Tyler's thinking by showing that setting challenging goals, investing effort and time, encouraging parents, being a friendly but demanding teacher, and providing timely and accurate feedback on progress are the common ingredients of success.

Bloom argued that, given such ideal conditions, any child can learn anything any other child can learn. Although this argument may claim too much, it had the useful consequence of challenging educators to seek higher standards for children's learning. Following Tyler and Bloom, subsequent research showed that extraordinarily accomplished adults set their own high standards and goals. Even young children, however, can learn how to set their own goals, concentrate their time on attaining them, and measure their progress.

---

ates, including particular personal qualities, work habits, and attitudes. The district outlines the "basics" that students need to know when they graduate (see box 2.2). These basics shape what and how teachers teach, and what and how students learn.

Many large school districts now have their goals and standards outlined for parents on locally developed websites. They may even have suggestions of ways for parents to develop their own children's potential. Two examples are the Academic Standards for Chicago Public Schools website and the California Standards for Public Schools website. These are illustrative of what districts throughout the country are doing. To see what the standards are for your state, visit the Achieve website (www.achieve.org). Achieve was created to help states analyze, develop, and implement high academic standards. One additional note on goals is appropriate: For the purposes of simplicity we treat goals and standards as equivalent. They are both ways in which educators attempt to define concisely what students must know and be able to demonstrate.

Box 2.2   New Basics: Alameda Unified School District

A. *Communication and Languages.* Has a functional command of the standard English language and communicates competently in at least one other language.

B. *Reading.* Understands, interprets, and appreciates written information in literature, in prose, and in documents and constructs meaning from a variety of materials.

C. *Writing.* Communicates thoughts, ideas, information, and messages responsibly, clearly, and eloquently in writing in a form that is grammatically correct.

D. *Arithmetic/Mathematics.* Performs basic computations and approaches practical problems by choosing appropriately from a variety of mathematical techniques. Communicates and thinks mathematically with confidence and enthusiasm.

E. *Listening.* Receives, attends to, interprets, and responds to verbal messages and other forms of communication.

F. *Speaking.* Organizes thoughts and communicates ideas, knowledge, and information through fluent, responsible speech.

G. *Historical, Social, and Global Awareness.* Knows how the American society, political systems, and economy function within a global context; understands and appreciates the diversity in America and in the world community; knows the general shape of world history and the specific history of the United States.

H. *Geography.* Applies locational skills and knowledge of geography to practical situations and current issues.

I. *Civics.* Understands the political institutions and processes, civil rights, and justice in a free society and participates as a responsible citizen in a democracy.

J. *Fitness and Health.* Applies nutritional, hygienic, and physical knowledge to maintain health; is free from substance abuse.

K. *Arts.* Develops appreciation of the arts and media as an expressive tool and a way to enrich life.

L. *Science.* Understands how things work and the underlying scientific principles; applies the scientific method to everyday life.

Source: Alameda Unified School District Graduate Profile, *Outcomes in the Year 2004 Profile* (Alameda, CA, 1998). http://alamedaclc.org/development/images/Graduate_Profile.pdf

Questions for Reflection

The emergence of the new national core standards will impact the art of teaching. Will they make teaching more difficult or easier for novice practitioners? Should the Common Core State Standards apply to all students in our nation? Go online (http://www.corestandards.org/the-standards) and research the new Common Core State Standards and compare to existing state standards. Are they really an improvement? Be aware that at present these standards exist presently in mathematics and language arts, as well as some specialized areas.

Objectives

When we move from goals and standards to instructional objectives, the role and responsibility of the teacher become evident. Objectives are behavioral in nature and are more precise than goals. Instructional objectives help the teacher focus on what students should know at the end of a lesson, unit, or course, and they also help students know what is expected of them. They help the teacher plan and organize instruction by identifying (with more specificity than standards) what is to be taught and when it is to be taught. Instructional objectives are stated in observable and measurable terms (outcomes, proficiencies, or competencies). Their specificity enables the teacher to determine whether what was intended was achieved, and to what extent.

Program, Course, and Classroom Objectives

Instructional objectives are formulated on three levels, with increasing specificity: program, course, and classroom. Objectives at the classroom level can further be divided into unit plan and lesson plan objectives.

Program objectives stem from the standards of the school and are written at the subject and grade level. Although they do not usually state specific content or competencies, they do focus on general content and behaviors. Like goals, they refer to the accomplishments of (and expectations for) all students, rather than those of individual students.[10]

Nearly every state and school district has an overview or set of program objectives at the subject and grade levels to facilitate teachers' understanding of what they should be teaching. In most cases these instructional objectives are formulated by curriculum committees made up of administrative, teacher, and community (or parent) groups.

Good curriculum development is never complete. As a new teacher you will find yourself in situations where the curriculum of the district will change over time and the burden is on you to know how to access and use the most recent standards in place for your field to design the learning experiences for your students.

Course objectives are derived from program objectives and are formulated at the subject or departmental level. They categorize and organize content and sometimes concepts, problems, or behaviors, but they do not specify the exact content to be examined or the exact instructional methods and materials to be used. Course objectives are stated in the form of topics, concepts, or general behaviors. The examples in Box 2.3 will help you distinguish among them.

Course objectives (as well as program objectives) help the teacher organize the content in terms of *scope* (topics, concepts, behaviors to be covered), *continuity* (recurring and continuing opportunities to teach important content and practice certain skills and tasks), *sequence* (cumulative development or successive treatment of topics, concepts, or behaviors that build upon preceding ones), and *integration* (relationships of content in one course to content in another course).[11]

Classroom objectives are usually formulated by the teacher. They divide course objectives into several units. In contrast, **unit plan objectives** are usually categorized into topics or concepts. Using two examples of course objectives taken from box 2.3, box 2.4 illustrates appropriate unit plan objectives for each.

Unit plan objectives usually encompass one to three weeks of instruction, organized in a sequence and corresponding to expectations for the entire class, not for particular individuals or groups. They are then further divided to create

---

Box 2.3   Stating Course Objectives

Stated as Topics (for American History)
 The Colonial Period
 The Revolutionary Period
 The Framing of the Constitution
 Manifest Destiny
 The Civil War Period
 The Reconstruction Period
 Industrialization and Colonialization
 Immigration and Nationalism
 World War I

As Concepts (for Science)
 Science and Knowledge
 Science and Method
 Science and Humanity
 Science and Environment
 Science, Products, and Technology
 Science and Space

As General Behaviors
 To develop critical thinking in . . .
 To increase understanding of . . .
 To have experience for . . .

Box 2.4   Stating Unit Plan Objectives

The Framing of the Constitution
 To understand the system of American government
 To identify characteristics of a democratic society
 To apply the principles of American government to classroom and school activities

Science and Method
 To organize inductive, deductive, and intuitive methods in answering question about
  a. the biological world
  b. the chemical world
  c. the physical world
 To organize scientific information according to
  a. logic
  b. explanations
  c. causal relations
  d. hypothesis
  e. projections
 To acquire the methods of
  a. inquiry
  b. experimentation
  c. problem solving
 To show interest in scientific hobbies or projects

lesson plan objectives, organized ideally around one day of instruction on a particular subject.

Unit plan objectives are sometimes called **general instructional objectives.** They should be specific enough to provide direction for instruction but not so specific that they restrict the teacher's selection of instructional methods, materials, and activities. Several different instructional techniques—lectures, discussions, demonstrations, laboratory work, textbook assignments, inquiry, cooperative learning—might be used to achieve the unit plan objectives.

Lesson plan objectives, sometimes called *specific instructional objectives*, further define the unit objectives by providing clear direction for teaching and testing. Instructional objectives at the lesson-plan level state (1) expected behaviors in terms of specific skills, tasks, or attitudes and (2) content. They may also state (3) outcomes or goals, sometimes called *standards*, in terms of level of achievement, proficiency, or competency and (4) conditions of mastery. There is currently debate on how detailed these objectives should be and whether too much specificity narrows a teacher's options. Lesson plan objectives are more specific than unit plan objectives. While lesson plan objectives may include outcomes and conditions for a specific instructional sequence, unit plan objectives do not. Whereas lesson plan objectives usually include specific methods, materials, or activities, unit plan objectives may or may not—and if they do, they are less specific. However, the two levels of objectives do have several characteristics in common. Such characteristics, as described by Taba, are listed in box 2.5. Taba presents historical grounding for the lesson planning process. Her classic approach suggests the timelessness of good planning—setting clear objectives that are understandable and relevant.

Box 2.5   Characteristics of Instructional Objectives at the Classroom Level

1. A statement of objectives should describe both the kind of behavior expected and the content or context to which that behavior applies.
2. Complex objectives need to be stated analytically and specifically enough so that there is no doubt as to the kind of behavior expected or what the behavior applies to.
3. Objectives should also be formulated so that clear distinctions are required among learners to attain different behaviors.
4. Objectives are developmental, representing roads to travel rather than terminal points.
5. Objectives should be realistic and should include only what can be translated into . . . classroom experience.
6. The scope of objectives should be broad enough to encompass all types of outcomes for which the school [or teacher] is responsible.

Source: Hilda Taba, *Curriculum Development: Theory and Practice* (New York: Harcourt Brace Jovanovich, 1962), 200–205.

To understand the kind of specificity involved in the two levels of classroom objectives, consider this unit plan objective, stated as a concept: "To gain understanding of graphs." Lesson plan objectives for this unit might read as follows:

1. To identify different types of graphs when using different types of data
2. To identify important terms of a graph
3. To implement practical application of graphs

Some educators would feel that these lesson plan objectives are not specific enough, since they lack outcomes and mastery level.[12] They might rewrite them in the following way:

1. All students will be required to identify which sets of data are best represented by a bar graph, line graph, and circle graph. Seventy-five percent of the class is expected to earn 75 percent or higher.

2. High-achieving students will be required to demonstrate understanding of five terms associated with graphs by (a) defining them and (b) supplying appropriate illustrations of each term. No more than one error will be permitted before moving to the next sequence of material.

3. All students will be required to read an annual corporate report and translate the narrative into at least three graphs to state the financial condition of the company in terms of (a) income, (b) operating cost, and (c) assets and liabilities. A panel of three students must unanimously agree that the graphs are accurate.

There is also an emerging technological sophistication with which learning objectives can be developed and assessed. Teachers are pulling goals from websites—both from other schools and from commercial sites—and then developing objectives and posting those on their own school websites for administrators to review. It's likely that you will begin teaching in such a situation, and you may be attending an institution that requires you to use one of the Internet-based resources to create and structure your lessons.

Creating Goals, Objectives, Models, and Taxonomies

In our discussion so far, we have been using several words—*aims, goals, objectives* or *standards*—that have subtle differences in meaning related to different levels of education (from national to classroom) and different levels of abstractness. At one end of the continuum are the value-laden abstract aims of society; at the other end are concrete objectives describing specific behaviors. Most teachers tend to favor the middle of the continuum, where goals and objectives are observable but not necessarily stated as clearly measurable or, if measurable, stated without proficiency levels. They may use such terms as *list, describe,* and *identify* in writing their classroom objectives. However, unless they are behaviorists or advocate outcome-based education, they may not always incorporate precise outcomes and conditions of mastery. There is no universal *right* way. What is right for you will likely be prescribed for you by your administrator.

Developing Goals (Tyler Model)

Ralph Tyler uses the term *purposes* when discussing what we call the goals of the school.[13] He believes that educators need to identify purposes (goals) by gathering data from three sources: learners, society, and subject specialists. Educators then filter their identified purposes (or goals) through two screens: philosophy and psychology. What results from the screening are more specific and agreed-upon objectives, or what he calls *instructional objectives* (see figure 2.2).

Figure 2.2   Tyler's Method for Formulating Objectives

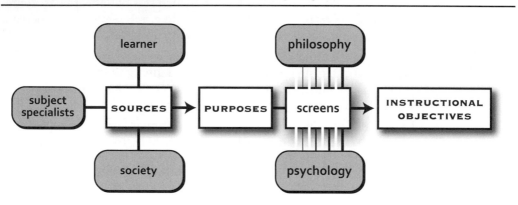

Even though Tyler uses the term *instructional objectives*, he is not advocating narrow behavioral objectives. For Tyler, objectives cannot be deduced from tiny bits of data or from only objective data. The formulation of objectives involves the intelligence, insight, values, and attitudes of people involved in making decisions. Wise choices cannot be made without the most complete data available, but judgments must still prevail. We now turn to Tyler's three sources from which to select goals, and two screens for refining goals into objectives.

Source 1, Studies of the Learners.   The responsibility of the school is to help students meet their needs and develop to their fullest potential. Studies that focus on educational needs of students provide a basis for the selection of goals for the school program. These studies distinguish between what the schools do and what other social institutions do, distinguish between what is done and what should be done, and identify or differentiate gaps between students of the particular school (or school district) and students elsewhere. It is possible to identify needs that are common to most students on a national, state, and local basis, as well as other needs that are common to all students in a school or to a certain group of students within a school or school district.

Source 2, Studies of Contemporary Society Outside of School.   Educators must be aware of the tremendous impact of the increasingly rapid rate of change, the explosion of knowledge, and the increasing complexity of technology in our lives, both currently and in the future. The trouble is that preparation for the future involves skills and knowledge that we may not fully understand today. As we analyze contemporary life, we need to study life at the community level in terms of needs, resources, and trends, as well as larger societal issues that extend to state, national, and international levels. For example, in preparing students for the world of work, we must look at local work conditions and opportunities; but since some students will move to other states or regions, conditions and opportunities must be considered elsewhere as well. Further, we live in a *global village*, one that is strongly interconnected: State, national, and international conditions eventually affect conditions at the community level.

Source 3, Suggestions from Subject Specialists.   Every subject area has professional associations that list goals and important knowledge in its field. Over the past several years, professional associations such as the National Council of Teachers of Mathematics and National Science Teachers Association have been increasingly active in defining what students need to know (see box 2.6). Some agencies are now creating materials that clearly illustrate for teachers the specific academic content standards for a state, the benchmarks and indicators by standards, and even the benchmarks and indicators by grade level (see, for example, www.battelleforkids.org).

Box 2.6   National Science Teachers Association's Sample Learning Goals for Students: Science Content Standards

Content Standard: K–12 Unifying Concepts and Processes
Content standard: As a result of activities in grades K–12, all students should develop understanding and abilities aligned with the following concepts and processes:
- Systems, order, and organization
- Evidence, models, and explanation
- Constancy, change, and measurement
- Evolution and equilibrium
- Form and function

Content Standards: K–4
Science as Inquiry
Content standard A: As a result of activities in grades K–4, all students should develop
- abilities necessary to do scientific inquiry.
- understanding about scientific inquiry.

Physical Science
Content standard B: As a result of the activities in grades K–4, all students should develop an understanding of
- properties of objects and materials.
- position and motion of objects.
- light, heat, electricity, and magnetism.

(continued)

Life Science
Content standard C: As a result of the activities in grades K–4, all students should develop an understanding of
- the characteristics of organisms.
- the life cycles of organisms.
- organisms and environments.

Earth and Space Science
Content standard D: As a result of the activities in grades K–4, all students should develop an understanding of
- properties of earth materials.
- objects in the sky.
- changes in earth and sky.

Science and Technology
Content standard E: As a result of the activities in grades K–4, all students should develop
- abilities of technological design.
- understanding about science and technology.
- abilities to distinguish between natural objects and objects made by humans.

Science in Personal and Social Perspectives
Content standard F: As a result of the activities in grades K–4, all students should develop an understanding of
- personal health.
- characteristics and changes in populations.
- types of resources.
- changes in environments.
- science and technology in local challenges.

History and Nature of Science
Content standard G: As a result of the activities in grades K–4, all students should develop an understanding of
- science as a human endeavor.

Note: These are selected standards that are not inclusive of all that is required.
Source: Lawrence F. Lowery (ed.), *NSTA Pathways to the Science Standards: Elementary School Edition*, 134. Copyright © 2001. Reprinted by permission of the National Science Teachers Association.

Screen 1, The Use of Philosophy.   Once purposes have been identified from studies of the learner, society, and subject areas, the educator must review and refine them in light of philosophy and psychology, or as Tyler says, filter them through two screens. As a school tries to outline its educational program, "the educational and social philosophy of the school can serve as the first screen."[14] We should be aware of the values and way of life we are trying to preserve and what aspect(s) of society we wish to improve. Goals should be consistent with the democratic values and ideals of our society, in all aspects of living. In this country education is anchored in the principles of democracy, and this overriding philosophy must be reflected in our school goals.

Screen 2, The Use of Psychology.   Goals must be in conformity with the psychology of learning—that is, the theories, concepts, and specific findings we accept. "A psychology of learning includes a unified formulation of the processes involved, such as how learning takes place, under what conditions, and what mechanisms and variables operate."[15] In formulating goals teachers need to consider how appropriate they are in terms of what is known about learning—whether the goals can be achieved, how they can be achieved, and what cost and time will be involved. Teachers should reject goals that conflict with their viewpoints about the psychology of learning or will compromise a student's potential for learning.

A great deal has occurred since Tyler first did his work in the early 1950s. Today, there is substantial controversy about how to use standards and specify goals and objectives. According to some critics of Tyler's work, there are simply so many different goals and objectives that teachers are forced to choose from among them, which limits teacher freedom. As a result, teachers are so focused on the prescribed curriculum that they fail to see the real needs of the learner. Wiggins and McTighe argue for establishing objectives, but they do so by carefully deciding what results they desire for students after reviewing national, state, and local standards. In essence, teachers must make choices. Some goals represent enduring understandings (i.e., the significant ideas that students need to explore and really "get inside of"), others are important to understand and do, and still others are worth being familiar with.[16] How do you determine what is worthy of and what requires understanding? Grant Wiggins offers four criteria or "filters" to answer the question:

1. To what extent does the idea, topic, or process represent a "big idea" having enduring value in the classroom?

2. To what extent does the idea, topic, or process reside at the heart of the discipline?

3. To what extent does the idea, topic, or process require "uncoverage" (i.e., ideas that often have student misconceptions associated with them and require more in-depth explanation)?

4. To what extent does the idea, topic, or process offer potential for engaging students?[17]

Wiggins and McTighe then recommend that teachers use standards to shape what is worthy and requiring of understanding. Table 2.3 depicts the process of using standards for determining what is worthy and then identifying learning experiences to teach that content. The important thing to note here is that teachers can start with standards/goals and move toward learning experiences, or they can decide on the desired results and then plan backwards, defining what evidence (of learning) they want and then what learning experiences they need to provide. Notice that in table 2.3 Wiggins and McTighe move from a focus on clear objectives (lesson design considerations or standards) to a process for how to teach students to achieve those learning goals (their "stage 3").

The reason we highlight Wiggins and McTighe's process is because of the current debate concerning constructivism. Chapter 1 briefly discussed constructivism and its several variations. In general, constructivism is a student-centered approach that focuses on helping students create and structure their own understandings and knowledge. Some critics of constructivism (e.g., Jeanne Chall)

Table 2.3   The Big Picture of a Lesson Design Approach

Key Design Question	Design Considerations	Filters (Design Criteria)	What the Final Design Accomplishes
Stage 1: What is worthy of/what requires understanding	National standards State standards District standards Regional topic opportunities Teacher expertise and interest	Enduring ideas Opportunities for authentic, discipline based work Uncoverage* Engaging	Unit framed around enduring understandings and essential questions
Stage 2: What is evidence of understanding?	Six facets of understanding Continuum of assessment types Research-based repertoire of learning and teaching strategies	Valid Reliable Sufficient Authentic work Feasible Student friendly	Unit anchored in credible and educationally vital evidence of the desired understandings
Stage 3: What learning experiences and teaching promote understanding, interest, and excellence?	Essential and enabling knowledge and a skill	Where is it going? Hook the students. Explore and equip. Rethink and revise. Exhibit and evaluate.	Coherent learning experiences and teaching that will evoke and develop the desired understandings, promote interest, and make excellent performance more likely

*Areas of student misunderstanding that require more explanation.
Source: Grant Wiggins and Jay McTighe, *Understanding by Design*, 2nd ed. (Alexandria, VA: ASCD, 2005), 34. Reprinted with permission. Learn more about ASCD at www.ascd.org

decry the use of student-centered approaches because they believe they compromise the quality of the learning environment; their argument is that the emphasis is on student centeredness at the expense of teacher-defined content.[18] Others argue that a form of constructivism and student-centered instruction is absolutely essential if students are truly going to learn how to learn.[19] In the next chapters we more fully explore how you can act in a way that informs your practice and also moves beyond this debate. Good teaching is not an either/or (teacher centeredness/student centeredness) matter. It is, instead, *what* and *how* oriented—what goals to choose and how to teach them successfully.

Developing Objectives

Objectives can be considered specific statements of a learner's behavior or outcomes that state the conditions of the behavior and set time limits. To achieve a goal a series of action steps are needed, and these become objectives. Performance objectives show what is expected, how it will be done, and what the standards are. They should be specific, measurable, attainable, results oriented, and able to be met within a specific time frame. Performance objectives indicate what students should be able to do at the end (as an outcome) of the program. They may refer to subject-specific concepts and skills, or attributes and abilities that are more general. Box 2.7 (SMART Objectives) provides an acronym that can be used as a guide to understanding how topic objectives are characterized. Some examples of topic objectives are as follows:

- Studying morals for five periods a week will result in 85 percent of the class passing the ethics examination.

- Motivational exercises employed in daily planning will encourage students to improve their weekly quiz scores.

- Direct reading instruction will be delivered in grades 3, 4, and 8 for three hours a day in order to improve achievement on standardized tests.

Box 2.7   SMART Objectives

S = Specific: detailed about particular aspects of expectations and describing the action and behaviors required for performance to achieve or exceed expectations. They should be clear and understandable.

M = Measurable, Meaningful: in language that is understandable to teachers and students as well as measurable for assessment.

A = Attainable, Appropriate: reasonable, appropriate to student skill level, and suitable for learners to attain and satisfy standards.

R = Results oriented, Realistic: focused on outcomes rather than tasks to be achieved within given practical period.

T = Time frame, Testable: some measure of testable progress/achievement made within a specific time frame.

Taxonomy of Educational Objectives

Another way of formulating instructional objectives is to categorize the desired behaviors and outcomes into a system analogous to the classification of books in a library, the chemical elements in a periodic table, or the divisions of the animal kingdom. Through this system of categorization, known as the **taxonomy of educational objectives,** standards for classifying objectives have been established, and educators are able to be more precise in their language. The taxonomy is rooted in Tyler's ideas that all words in a scientific system should be defined in terms of observable events and that educational objectives should be defined operationally in terms of performances or outcomes. This method of formulating objectives can be used for writing objectives at the program and course level. By adding specific content, the objectives can be used at the classroom level, including the lesson plan level.

The educational taxonomy calls for the classification of learning into three domains: cognitive, affective, and psychomotor. We discuss each domain in detail below.

Cognitive Domain. In the late 1950s, the *Taxonomy of Educational Objectives, Handbook I: Cognitive Domain* was developed by thirty-six researchers from various universities on a committee headed by Benjamin Bloom.[20] The **cognitive domain** includes objectives that are related to recall or recognition of knowledge and the development of higher intellectual skills and abilities.

1. *Knowledge.* This level includes objectives related to (a) knowledge of specifics, such as terminology and facts; (b) knowledge of ways and means of dealing with specifics, such as conventions, trends and sequences, classifications and categories, criteria, and methodologies; and (c) knowledge of universals and abstractions, such as principles, generations, theories, and structures (for example, to identify the capital of France).

2. *Comprehension.* Objectives at this level relate to (a) translation, (b) interpretation, and (c) extrapolation of materials. Example: to interpret a table showing the population density of the world.

3. *Application.* Objectives at this level relate to the use of abstractions in particular situations (for example, to predict the probable effect of a change in temperature on a chemical).

4. *Analysis.* Objectives relate to breaking a whole into parts and distinguishing (a) elements, (b) relationships, and (c) organizational principles (for example, to deduce facts from a hypothesis).

5. *Synthesis.* Objectives relate to putting parts together in a new form such as (a) a unique communication, (b) a plan of operation, and (c) a set of abstract relations (for example, to produce an original piece of art).

6. *Evaluation.* This is the highest level of complexity and includes objectives related to judging in terms of (a) internal evidence or logical consistency and (b) external evidence or consistency with facts developed elsewhere (for example, to recognize fallacies in an argument).

One point needs to be made about the cognitive domain. In discussing the cognitive domain, Bloom asserts that "many teachers . . . prize knowledge . . . because of the simplicity with which it can be taught or learned."[21] Quite frequently we stop with the knowledge category, because it is easy to teach and test. All we have to do is ask our students: "What are three products of Brazil?" or "What is the chemical formula for water?" Another reason we can fail to move beyond the cognitive domain is that we may equate knowledge with intelligence. This is illustrated by the tendency to think that people who recall trivial information on a television quiz show are of superior intelligence. However, it is not how much knowledge an individual possesses but what the individual can do with the knowledge that characterizes intelligence.

Affective Domain.   In the mid-1960s David Krathwohl and associates created the *Taxonomy of Educational Objectives, Handbook II: Affective Domain*. The **affective domain** is concerned with aims and objectives related to interests, attitudes, and feelings.[22]

1. *Receiving*. These objectives are indicative of the learner's sensitivity to the existence of stimuli and include (a) awareness, (b) willingness to receive, and (c) selective attention (for example, to identify musical instruments by their sound).

2. *Responding*. These include active attention to stimuli such as (a) acquiescence, (b) willing responses, and (c) feelings of satisfaction (for example, to contribute to group discussions by asking questions).

3. *Valuing*. These include objectives regarding beliefs and evaluations in the form of (a) acceptance, (b) preference, and (c) commitment (for example, to argue over an issue involving health care).

4. *Organization*. This level involves (a) conceptualization of values and (b) organization of a value system (for example, to organize a meeting concerning a neighborhood's housing integration plan).

5. *Characterization*. This is the level of greatest complexity and includes behavior related to (a) a generalized set of values and (b) a characterization or philosophy of life (for example, to demonstrate in front of a government building on behalf of a cause or idea).

Psychomotor Domain.   The original group of researchers never completed the description of the psychomotor domain, which deals with manipulative and motor skills. However, in the early 1970s Anita Harrow created a classification of psychomotor objectives that comes close to satisfying the intent of the original group.[23] The fact that it was published by the same company that published the original two taxonomies adds to the validity of this version of the **psychomotor domain.**

1. *Reflex movements*. Objectives relate to (a) segmental reflexes (involving one spinal segment) and (b) intersegmental reflexes (involving more than one spinal segment) (for example, to contract a muscle).

2. *Fundamental movements*. Objectives relate to (a) walking, (b) running, (c) jumping, (d) pushing, (e) pulling, and (f) manipulating (for example, to run a 100-yard dash).

3. *Perceptual abilities*. Objectives relate to (a) kinesthetic, (b) visual, (c) auditory, (d) tactile, and (e) coordination abilities (for example, to distinguish distant and close sounds).

4. *Physical abilities*. Objectives relate to (a) endurance, (b) strength, (c) flexibility, (d) agility, (e) reaction-response time, and (f) dexterity (for example, to do five sit-ups).

5. *Skilled movements*. Objectives relate to (a) games, (b) sports, (c) dances, and (d) the arts (for example, to dance the basic steps of the waltz).

6. *Nondiscursive communication.* Objectives relate to expressive movement through (a) posture, (b) gestures, (c) facial expressions, and (d) creative movements (for example, to act a part in a play).

Once we study the taxonomy, it becomes apparent that most teaching and testing we have been exposed to as students have stressed knowledge of facts, terms, conventions, classifications, categories, methods, and principles. As a teacher, you should not make the same mistake; rather, you should advance into other cognitive dimensions.

---

classic professional viewpoint 2.2

Using the Taxonomy

David R. Krathwohl

I have always been surprised at how timid many individuals seem to be about modifying the taxonomy frameworks. I thought some words of encouragement from one of the taxonomy authors might make everyone freer to use them in their own way. Not only will we not take offense at your modifying them, we are delighted to have you make the structures your own and invest some of your talent in their further development.

Unlike the ten commandments, which are said to have come down from heaven, the taxonomies are not set in stone! They are just frameworks to make easier such tasks as curriculum and test development. Use them as jumping-off places for modification; many people have. Look at how Christine McGuire changed the cognitive domain to better fit measuring the goals of medical education. She collapsed knowledge into two subcategories, expanded the application category (2.0, 3.0, and 4.0 below), and discarded the subcategories under evaluation and synthesis:

1.1   Items testing predominantly the recall of isolated information

1.2   Items testing recognition of meaning or implication

2.0   Generalization: Items requiring the student to select a relevant generalization to explain specific phenomena

3.0   Problem solving of a familiar type

3.1   Items requiring the student to make simple interpretations of data

3.2   Items requiring the student to apply a single principle or a standard combination of principles to a situation of a familiar type

4.0   Problem solving of an unfamiliar type

4.1   Items requiring the analysis of data

4.2   Items requiring the student to apply a unique combination of principles to solve a problem of a novel type

5.0   Evaluation: Items requiring the evaluation of a total situation

6.0   Synthesis: Items requiring synthesis of a variety of elements of knowledge into an original and meaningful whole*

The literature contains a variety of such adaptations of taxonomies. For example, all the chapter authors in Bloom, Hastings, and Madaus (specialists in art education, industrial arts, language arts, mathematics, pre-school, science, and social studies) struck off from ours to construct their own.** Consider these samples of their modifications of application:

- "functional application vs. expressive application"
- "solve routine problems, make comparisons, analyze data, and recognize patterns, isomorphisms, and symmetries"

These adaptations are a long way from the original framework aren't they? Many authors even blend affective and cognitive objectives in their structures.

Our experience suggests that the frameworks are most useful as you adapt them to fit your situation. Consider developing your own modifications or find one that fits your purposes.

*Christine McGuire, "A Process Approach to the Construction and Analysis of Medical Examinations," The Journal of Medical Education, vol. 38 (1963), 556–563.

**Benjamin S. Bloom, J. Thomas Hastings, and George E. Madaus, Handbook on Formative and Summative Evaluation of Student Learning (New York: McGraw-Hill, 1971).

Author's note: In 2001 David Krathwohl and Lorin Anderson revised Bloom's Taxonomy. This piece was written prior to the revision, but notice that Krathwohl suggests that teachers use the taxonomies "in their own way" and that he and others have now revised Bloom's work themselves. In essence, use the taxonomies to think about what students should learn and how you will have them learn it.

In 2001, Lorin Anderson and David Krathwohl significantly revised Bloom's Taxonomy. Because the vast majority of persons reading this book will be in programs that are implicitly or explicitly organized around the original structure, we have made a conscious decision to structure the domains in this textbook around the traditional framework, but we will rely on elements of the new framework as well. The new taxonomy has a *knowledge dimension* and a *cognitive process dimension*. The knowledge dimension focuses on factual, conceptual, procedural, and metacognitive knowledge. The metacognitive category is an especially significant addition because it focuses on the students' knowledge about cognition in general and personal cognition in particular. The categories in the cognitive process dimension are outlined in table 2.4. In the new taxonomy, the knowledge dimension is on one conceptual axis and the cognitive process is on another. Hence, for factual knowledge, teachers might identify learning objectives for cognitive processes involving remembering (table 2.4, item 1) or analyzing (item 4), or for procedural knowledge they might identify learning objectives for understanding (table 2.4, item 2) or creating (item 6). The old taxonomy included knowledge and cognitive process in one category. The original model described above is the taxonomy still used in most school districts.

Establishing General and Specific Objectives

The three domains of the taxonomy describe levels of complexity from the simple to the more advanced. Each level is built upon and assumes acquisition of skills of the previous level. One must have knowledge of facts, for example, before one can comprehend material. The taxonomy as a whole is a useful source for developing educational objectives and for categorizing and grouping existing sets of objectives. Perhaps the greatest difficulty in using it is deciding between adjacent categories, particularly if the objectives have not been clearly stated. To avoid becoming frustrated while categorizing objectives into appropriate categories, classroom teachers are advised to work in groups and share opinions. By studying and using the taxonomy they may eventually appreciate it as a valuable tool for identifying objectives and formulating test items.

Table 2.4   The Six Categories of the Cognitive Process Dimension and Related Cognitive Processes

Process Categories   Cognitive Processes and Examples

1. **Remember**—Retrieve relevant knowledge from long-term memory.

   Recognizing   (recognize the dates of important events in US history)

   Recalling   (recall the dates of important events in US history)

2. **Understand**—Construct meaning from instructional messages including oral, written, and graphic communications.

   Interpreting   (paraphrase important speeches and documents)

   Exemplifying   (give examples of various artistic painting styles)

   Classifying   (classify observed or described cases of mental disorders)

   Summarizing   (write a short summary of the events portrayed on videotapes)

   Inferring   (in learning a foreign language, infer grammatical principles from examples)

   Comparing   (compare historical events to contemporary situations)

   Explaining   (explain the causes of important eighteenth-century events in France)

3. **Apply**—Carry out or use a procedure in a given situation.

   Executing   (divide one whole number by another whole number)

   Implementing   (determine situations in which Newton's second law is appropriate)

4. **Analyze**—Break material into constituent parts and determine how parts relate to one another and to an overall structure or purpose.

   Differentiating   (distinguish between relevant and irrelevant numbers in a mathematical word problem)

   Organizing   (structure evidence in a historical description into evidence for or against a particular historical explanation)

   Attributing   (determine the point of view of the author of an essay in terms of his or her political perspective)

5. **Evaluate**—Make judgments based on criteria and standards.

   Checking   (determine whether a scientist's conclusions follow from observed data)

   Critiquing   (judge which of two methods is the best way to solve a given problem)

6. **Create**—Put elements together to form a coherent or functional whole, reorganize elements into a new pattern or structure.

   Generating   (generate hypotheses to account for an observed phenomenon)

   Planning   (plan a research paper on a given historical topic)

   Producing   (build habitats for certain species for certain purposes)

Source: Lorin W. Anderson and David R. Krathwohl, *A Taxonomy for Learning, Teaching and Assessing* (Boston: Allyn & Bacon, 2001), Table 3.3 "The Six Categories of the Cognitive Process Dimension and Related Cognitive Processes," 31. Copyright © 2001 by Addison Wesley Longman. Reprinted by permission of Pearson Education, Inc.

After you have decided you want to use the taxonomy and after you have determined what you want your students to learn, you might systematically review the major classifications of the various domains to make sure you are familiar with each classification. You might then ask the following questions when formulating objectives in the cognitive domain:

1. *Knowledge.* What specific facts do you want the students to learn? What trends and sequences should they know? What classifications, categories, and methods are important for them to learn? What general principles and theories should they learn?

2. *Comprehension.* What types of translation will students need to perform? What types of interpretation? What types of extrapolation?

3. *Application.* What will students be required to perform or do to show they can use the information in practical situations?

4. *Analysis.* What kinds of elements should students be able to analyze? What relationships? What organizational principles?

5. *Synthesis.* What kinds of communication should students be able to synthesize? What kinds of operation? What kinds of abstraction?

6. *Evaluation.* What kinds of evaluation should students be able to perform? Can they use internal evidence? Can they use external evidence?

When asking these questions and when formulating instructional objectives according to the taxonomy, keep in mind that the classifications represent a hierarchy. Before students can deal with analysis, they must be able to function at the three previous levels (knowledge, comprehension, and application). You should ask the same kinds of questions when writing objectives in the affective and psychomotor domains. Look at each level within the domain and ask what students are expected to achieve.

Tips for Teachers 2.1, 2.2, and 2.3 offer lists of key terms and direct objects that can be used as practical explanations for the cognitive, affective, and psychomotor domains, respectively. In all of these examples no specific content is described, which keeps them applicable to all subjects.

General Objectives (Gronlund's Model). Norman Gronlund developed a flexible way of formulating instructional objectives, whereby the teacher moves from a general objective to a series of specific learning outcomes, each related to the general objective. Gronlund's general objectives coincide with program (subject and grade) and course-level objectives, and his specific learning outcomes coincide with unit plan and lesson plan objectives. He recommends that teachers start with general objectives because learning is too complex to be described in terms of specific behaviors or specific outcomes, and because higher levels of thinking cannot be achieved by one specific behavior or outcome. Gronlund has prepared the following list of general objectives that can be used for almost any grade, subject, or course:

1. Knows basic terminology
2. Understands concepts and principles
3. Applies principles to new situations
4. Interprets charts and graphs

5. Demonstrates skill in critical thinking

6. Writes a well-organized theme

7. Appreciates poetry, art, literature, dance

8. Demonstrates scientific attitude

9. Evaluates the adequacy of an experiment[24]

TIPS FOR TEACHERS 2.1

Key Words for the Taxonomy of Educational Objectives: Cognitive Domain

Taxonomy Classification	Examples of Infinitives	Examples of Direct Objects
1. Knowledge	To define, to distinguish, to acquire, to identify, to recall, to recognize	Vocabulary terms, terminology, meaning(s), definitions, referents, elements, facts (sources, names, dates, events, persons, places, time periods), properties, examples, phenomena, forms, conventions, uses, rules, ways, devices, symbols, representations, styles, formats, actions, processes, developments, trends, causes, relationships, influences, types, features, classes, sets, arrangements, classifications, categories, criteria, methods, techniques, uses, procedures, structures, formulations
2. Comprehension	To translate, to transform, to illustrate, to prepare, to read, to represent, to change, to rephrase, to restate, to interpret, to rearrange, to differentiate, to distinguish, to make, to explain, to demonstrate, to estimate, to infer, to conclude, to predict, to determine, to extend, to interpolate	Meanings, samples, definitions, abstractions, representations, words, phrases, relevancies, relationships, essentials, aspects, qualifications. conclusions, methods, theories, abstractions, consequences, implications, factors, ramifications, meanings, corollaries, effects, probabilities
3. Application	To apply, to generalize, to relate, to choose, to develop, to organize, to use, to employ, to transfer, to restructure, to classify	Principles, laws, conclusions, effects, methods, theories, abstractions, situations, generalizations, processes, phenomena, procedures

4. Analysis	To distinguish, to detect, to identify, to classify, to discriminate, to recognize, to categorize, to analyze, to contrast, to compare, to distinguish, to deduce	Elements, hypotheses, conclusions, assumptions, arguments, particulars, relationships, interrelations, relevancies, themes, evidence, fallacies, cause-effects, consistencies, parts, ideas, assumptions, forms, patterns, purposes, points of view, techniques, biases, structures, themes, arrangements, organizations
5. Synthesis	To write, to tell, to relate, to produce, to transmit, to originate, to modify, to document, to propose, to plan, to design, to specify, to derive, to develop, to combine, to organize, to synthesize, to classify, to deduce, to develop, to formulate	Structures, patterns, products, performances, designs, work, communications, efforts, compositions, plans, objectives, specifications, operations, ways, solutions, means, phenomena, taxonomies, concepts, schemes, theories, relationships, abstractions, generalizations, hypotheses, discoveries
6. Evaluation	To judge, to argue, to validate, to assess, to decide, to consider, to compare, to contrast, to standardize, to appraise	Accuracies, consistencies, fallacies, reliability, flaws, errors, precision, exactness, ends, means, efficiency, economies, utility, alternatives, course of action, standards, theories, generalizations

Source: Newton S. Metfessel, William B. Michael, and Donald A. Kirsner, "Instrumentation of Bloom's and Krathwohl's Taxonomies for the Writing of Educational Objectives." *Psychology in the Schools* 6(3) (July 1969): 227–231. Reprinted by permission of John Wiley & Sons, Inc.

Note that the behavior (verb) in each statement is general enough to permit a host of specific learning outcomes. For each general objective there may be six or seven related specific outcomes that clarify what students will do to demonstrate achievement of the general objective.

The following two examples illustrate how to apply Gronlund's model and move students from general objectives to a series of related, intended learning outcomes. (Because Gronlund felt it important to keep specific learning outcomes content free, they are not really applicable to the lesson plan level, which should be content oriented.)

• *Understands the meaning of concepts*
1. Explains a concept in own words
2. Identifies the meaning of a concept in context
3. Differentiates between proper and improper instances of a concept
4. Distinguishes between two similar concepts on the basis of meaning
5. Uses a concept to explain an everyday event

TIPS FOR TEACHERS 2.2

Key Words for the Taxonomy of Educational Objectives: Affective Domain

Taxonomy Classification	Examples of Infinitives	Examples of Direct Objects
1. Receiving	To differentiate, to separate, to set apart, to share, to accumulate, to select, to combine, to accept, to select, to listen (for), to control	Sights, sounds, events, designs, arrangements, models, examples, shapes, sizes, meters, cadences, alternatives, answers, rhythms, nuances
2. Responding	To comply (with), to follow, to commend, to approve, to volunteer, to discuss, to practice, to play, to applaud, to acclaim, to augment	Directions, instructions, laws, policies, demonstrations, instruments, games, dramatic works, charades, speeches, plays, presentations, writings
3. Valuing	To increase measured proficiency in, to relinquish, to specify, to assist, to subsidize, to help, to support, to deny, to protest, to debate, to argue	Group memberships, artistic productions, musical productions, personal friendships, projects, viewpoints, arguments, deceptions, irrelevancies, abdications, irrationalities
4. Organization	To discuss, to theorize (on), to abstract, to compare, to balance, to organize, to define, to formulate	Parameters, codes, standards, goals, systems, approaches, criteria, limits
5. Characterization	To revise, to change, to complete, to require, to be rated high by peers in, to be rated high by superiors in, to avoid, to manage, to resolve, to resist	Plans, behaviors, methods, efforts, humanitarianism, ethics, integrity, maturity, extravagance(s), excesses, conflicts, exorbitancy/exorbitancies

Source: Newton S. Metfessel, William B. Michael, and Donald A. Kirsner, "Instrumentation of Bloom's and Krathwohl's Taxonomies for the Writing of Educational Objectives," *Psychology in the Schools* 6(3) (July 1969): 227–231. Reprinted by permission of John Wiley & Sons, Inc.

- *Demonstrates skill in critical thinking*
  1. Distinguishes between fact and opinion
  2. Distinguishes between relevant and irrelevant information
  3. Identifies fallacious reasoning in written material
  4. Identifies the limitations of given data
  5. Formulates valid conclusions from given data
  6. Identifies the assumptions underlying conclusions[25]

TIPS
FOR TEACHERS
2.3

Key Words for the Taxonomy of Educational Objectives: Psychomotor Domain

Taxonomy Classification	Examples of Infinitives	Examples of Direct Objects
1. Reflex movements	To flex, to stretch, to straighten, to extend, to inhibit, to lengthen, to shorten, to tense, to stiffen, to relax	Reflexes
2. Fundamental movements	To crawl, to creep, to slide, to walk, to run, to jump, to grasp, to reach, to tighten, to support, to handle	Changes location, moves in space while remaining in one place, moves extremities in coordinated fashion
3. Perceptual abilities	To catch, to bounce, to eat, to write, to balance, to bend, to draw from memory, to distinguish by touching, to explore	Discriminates visually, discriminates auditorially, discriminates kinesthetically, discriminates tactually, coordinates two or more perceptual abilities
4. Physical abilities	To endure, to improve, to increase, to stop, to start, to move precisely, to touch, to bend	Exerts tension, moves quickly, stops immediately, endures fatigue
5. Skilled movements	To waltz, to type, to play the piano, to plane, to file, to skate, to juggle, to paint, to dive, to fence, to golf, to change	Changes or modifies basic body movement patterns, uses a tool or implement in adaptive or skilled manner
6. Nondiscursive communication	To gesture, to stand, to sit, to express facially, to dance skillfully, to perform skillfully, to paint skillfully, to play skillfully	Moves expressively, moves interpretatively, communicates emotions, communicates aesthetically, expresses joy

Source: Adapted from Anita J. Harrow, *A Taxonomy of the Psychomotor Domain* (New York: McKay, 1972).

The teacher can add content to Gronlund's basic objectives. For example, an objective might be to identify three causes of World War I or to differentiate between a triangle and a rectangle. Gronlund maintains that once a teacher identifies content, there is a risk of writing too many objectives for each general objective or topic. For instance, instead of making the objective to identify the causes of World War I, as most teachers would do, Gronlund would say the objective is to identify important historical causes and events. In effect, he suggested that objectives should be stated in general terms beginning with phrases such as *to know, to understand, to apply, to evaluate*, or *to appreciate*. They then should be followed by specific behaviors that evidence the objectives' attainment. An example of this procedure would be, *To understand the causes of the Civil War by analyzing the economic, social, and political values of the North and the South.* According to Gronlund, the planning process consists of four steps:

1. Decide what and how a student should learn.
2. Decide the characteristics of the students in the class in order to meet needs.
3. Have knowledge of the discipline (subject) being taught.
4. Have knowledge of the methods needed to teach the subject.[26]

Box 2.8 highlights Gronlund's steps for setting instructional objectives—both general and specific. It can serve as a guide if you wish to adopt this method.

Specific Objectives (Mager's Model). Educators have used instructional or behavioral objectives for at least four decades. With the release of Robert Mager's (1962) text, *Preparing Instructional Objectives*, the use of objectives has become commonplace. Mager conceptualizes that the purpose of objectives is to assess student performance, not to direct practice. In what has been called the *outcomes approach*, objectives have three parts: (1) an observable behavior, (2) the conditions under which the behavior will occur, and (3) criteria for acceptable performance.

The reason the system is called an outcomes approach is that objectives specify student outcomes and/or how students will be evaluated, but not educational intent. Two examples of this approach would be, "Given six sentences, fifth graders will identify each that contains a metaphor," and "After reading four short stories, fifth graders will be able to identify the different genres." Some criticize Mager's approach because they say it does not identify the teacher's intent and that its primary emphasis is evaluation statements that specify student outcomes. Critics claim that a better way for describing an objective might be to answer two simple questions:

- What do I want my students to know?
- How will I know if my students understand?

Mager is more precise than Gronlund in his approach to formulating instructional objectives. His objectives have three components:

1. *Behavior* (or performance), which describes what the learner is expected to do (for example, to know, to use, to identify).

2. *Condition,* which describes under what circumstances or condition the performance is to occur (for example, given five sentences with adjectives . . . based on the statement . . .).

3. *Proficiency level* (or criterion), which states an acceptable standard, competency, or achievement level (for example: 80 percent, 9 out of 10, judged correct by the teacher).[27]

Since Mager is controversial in his approach to writing instructional objectives, it might be worthwhile to state some of the arguments for and against his approach. Some educators (including Tyler and Gronlund) claim that Mager's method produces an unmanageable number of objectives, leads to trivia, and wastes time. They also contend that the approach leads to teaching that focuses

---

Box 2.8   Steps for Stating General Instructional Objectives and Specific Learning Outcomes

Stating General Instructional Objectives

1. State each general objective as an intended learning outcome (i.e., pupils' terminal performance).

2. Begin each general objective with a verb (e.g., *knows, applies, interprets).*

3. State each general objective to include only one general learning outcome (e.g., not *knows and understands).*

4. State each general objective at the proper level of generality (i.e., it should encompass a readily definable domain of responses). Eight to twelve general objectives will usually suffice.

5. Keep each general objective sufficiently free of course content so that it can be used with various units of study.

6. State each general objective so that there is minimum overlap with other objectives.

Stating Specific Learning Outcomes

1. Beneath each general instructional objective, list a representative sample of specific learning outcomes that describes the terminal performance pupils are expected to demonstrate.

2. Begin each specific learning outcome with an action verb that specifies observable performance (e.g., *identifies, describes).* Check that each specific learning outcome is relevant to the general objective it describes.

3. Include a sufficient number of specific learning outcomes to adequately describe the performance of pupils who have attained the objective.

4. Keep the specific learning outcomes sufficiently free of course content so that the list can be used with various units of study.

5. Consult reference materials for the specific components of those complex outcomes that are difficult to define (e.g., critical thinking, scientific attitude, creativity).

6. Add a third level of specificity to the list of outcomes, if needed.

Source: Adapted from Norman E. Gronlund, *Measurement and Evaluation in Teaching,* 10th ed. (New York: Macmillan, 2008).

on low levels of cognitive and psychomotor objectives, emphasizes learning specific bits of information, and does not foster comprehension and whole learning.[28]

Mager and other educators argue that the approach does in fact clarify what teachers intend, what students are expected to do, and what to test to show evidence of learning.[29] It provides a structured method for arranging sequences of skills, tasks, or content; provides a guide for determining instructional methods and materials; and adds precision for constructing tests. Most teachers prefer a less specific approach, corresponding more to the methods of Gronlund.

Applying Mager's objectives approach could cause a teacher to write hundreds of objectives for each unit and course. If we selected his approach, we would first ask ourselves to identify or describe what the learner will be doing. Next we would identify or describe the conditions under which the behavior is to occur. Finally, we would state the performance criteria or achievement level we expect the learner to meet. Here are some examples. The behavior, condition, and proficiency level are identified.

1. Given six primary colors, students will be able to identify five. The behavior is *to identify,* the condition is *given six primary colors,* and the proficiency level is *five out of six.*

2. Based on the reading passage in chapter 7, students will compare the writing styles of Ernest Hemingway and John Steinbeck. Performance will be judged pass/fail by the teacher. The behavior is *to compare writing styles,* the condition is *after reading the passage in chapter 7,* and the proficiency level is *to pass* (a subjective judgment by the teacher).

3. From a required list of 10 words, students will correctly spell 9. The behavior is *to spell,* the condition is *a required list of words,* and the proficiency level is *90 percent* (9 out of 10).

4. From the foul line, students will make 6 out of 10 baskets. The behavior is *to throw a basketball,* the condition is *from the foul line,* and the proficiency level is *60 percent* (6 out of 10).

5. The student will be able to complete a 100-item multiple-choice examination on the topic of pollution, with 80 items answered correctly within 60 minutes. The behavior is *to complete an exam,* the condition is *60 minutes,* and the proficiency level is *80 percent* (80 out of 100).

Mager lists eight phrases he considers "fuzzy" that should be avoided in formulating objectives: to know, to understand, to appreciate, to grasp the significance of, to enjoy, to believe, to have faith in, and to internalize. He lists nine phrases that are open to fewer interpretations and are more appropriate to use: to write, to recite, to identify, to sort, to solve, to construct, to build, to compare, and to contrast.

Writing Your Own Goals and Objectives

The task of writing goals and objectives for a school district, school, program, or course usually falls to a school committee. Individual classroom teachers are typically responsible for developing unit plans or lesson plans. For example, in the state of Ohio there are 600 school districts, and each one has its own course of study from which each teacher creates personal lesson plans. Ohio is a local control state, but state standards shape what teachers teach, and state assessment measures are currently being used to determine whether students are learning requisite content. If you are a member of a district or school committee in any state, you should consult the following sources to make sure that your list corresponds to prescribed educational goals and objectives.

1. State standards (see www.achieve.org)
2. Community concerns voiced by state and local business organizations and special-interest groups
3. Parental concerns expressed in parental advisory committees, parent-teacher associations, and individual letters from parents
4. Professional literature on theories of learning and child development
5. Professional literature on student needs, assessments, and career choices[30]

Most published lists of objectives place primary emphasis on the cognitive domain; more limited attention is given to the affective and psychomotor domains. Lists of goals and objectives that have been published can be obtained from government agencies (e.g., state departments of education and regional educational agencies), professional agencies (e.g., the Association for Supervision and Curriculum Development, Phi Delta Kappa), publishing companies and businesses, universities, and school districts. Objectives published by the government and schools can be obtained free of charge and, as noted, are often posted on websites by school districts or by state education agencies. Professional organizations may charge a nominal fee.

In formulating classroom-level objectives—for either unit or lesson plans—keep in mind the following concerns or general rules. (See also Tips for Teachers 2.4.) Your objectives should:

- be related to the developmental needs and tasks of the learners, which in turn are related to the age and experiences of the students.
- be an outgrowth of diagnostic data (achievement, aptitude, personality, behavioral tests) and student records.
- be consistent with professional and subject-specialist opinions.
- be consistent with teaching and learning theories and procedures.
- build on student interests and strengths, not on adult interests and student weaknesses.
- relate to the whole child and several domains of learning, not to only one aspect of learning or solely to the cognitive domain.
- foster lower- and higher-order thinking skills to cover the range of levels in Bloom's taxonomy.
- be based on subject- and grade-level academic content standards.
- be flexible enough to keep pace with changing educational and social situations.

TIPS FOR TEACHERS 2.4

Stating Classroom Objectives

Theoretically sound and practical recommendations concerning the content and form of objectives are given here. These recommendations should help in the formulation of your own objectives at the unit plan and lesson plan level.

Content

1. Objectives should be appropriate in terms of the level of difficulty and prior learning experience of students.
2. Objectives should describe behaviors the teacher actually intends to act on in the classroom situation.
3. A useful objective will describe both the content and the cognitive process required for an appropriate student response.
4. The content of the objectives should be responsive to the needs of the individual and society.
5. A variety of types of knowledge should be expected, since most courses attempt to develop factual, conceptual, and procedural knowledge.

Form

1. Objectives should be stated in the form of expected student changes.
2. Objectives should be stated in behavioral or performance terms.
3. Objectives should be stated singly.
4. Objectives should be concise and trimmed of excessive verbiage.
5. Objectives should be grouped logically so they make sense in determining units of instruction for an evaluation.
6. The conditions under which the expected student behavior will be observed should be specified.
7. If possible, the objective should contain criteria for acceptable performance. Criteria might involve time limits or a minimum number of correct responses.

Source: Adapted from Allan C. Ornstein and Francis P. Hunkins, *Curriculum: Foundations, Principles and Issues,* 5th ed. (Boston: Allyn & Bacon, 2008); Grant Wiggins, *Educative Assessments* (San Francisco: Jossey-Bass, 1998).

No matter how carefully you plan your objectives, some unintended outcomes of instruction are likely. These outcomes may be desirable or undesirable, and most are likely to fall into the affective domain of attitudes, feelings, and motivation about learning. For example, as a result of a language arts lesson on a Tolstoy novel, some students may become more interested in reading novels on their own or be motivated to read more books by Tolstoy (or other Russian authors). However, other students may become bored with language arts or uninterested in reading novels. Even worse, teachers may fail to notice or may ignore such side effects, because they result more from the method than from the content of instruction and more from the teacher's behavior than from students' attitudes.

Teachers are always expected to show that they can create a meaningful lesson outline or guide. It is clear that as a teacher you are going to have to establish both general and specific objectives. At the present time, and in almost all states, teachers use the school district curriculum guides to establish specific learning objectives. This will change in the future with the new National Core Standards. E. D. Hirsch, Jr., and others have argued for nationalizing the curriculum. Hirsch contends that a nationalized curriculum better accommodates itself to a mobile student population—and American students are mobile.[31] The nationalizing idea will eventually take hold, and standards (and even national testing) will influence what you as a teacher might actually do when you enter the classroom.

Standards

Master teachers exhibit at least three common traits: (1) they possess good organization and planning skills, (2) they communicate their instructional objectives effectively to their students, and (3) they have high expectations for their students.[32] Effective teachers have also mastered the keys to effective teaching (box 1.1 in chapter 1). Researchers, however, would be hard pressed to state specific aims, goals, and objectives that would be shared by all. That is exactly what national and state standards are expected to do. Teachers have been given the responsibility to incorporate these aims, instructional goals, and objectives into their teaching. Let's briefly review the definitions of aims, goals, and objectives. You'll recall that an *aim* is a broad statement of very general outcomes leading to *goals* that are more narrowly defined statements of outcomes, and finally to *objectives*, which are specific statements of a learner's behavior. The curriculum your students are expected to master will be based on the aims, goals, and objectives spelled out in federal, state, and local governmental documents or a national core curriculum.

The underlying assumption of standards-based reform is that all students are capable of meeting high expectations. Student achievement data in the United States show long-standing gaps in performance. Expectations in our schools have varied widely, and expectations for economically disadvantaged and minority students generally have been lower than for other students. Many view standards as a foundation to build excellence and equity in our nation's public education system.

The standards movement began under President George H. W. Bush in 1991 at an educational summit that included state governors, but strangely no educators were present. A US Department of Education document titled *America 2000: An Education Strategy* resulted from the conference in 1991. The manuscript contained goals for restructuring schools and a strategy for the United States to regain its academic leadership among all other nations. The document became law on March 31, 1994 as *Goals 2000: Educate America Act* under President Clinton, who said the act was in effect, "reinventing education." The goals of the act were focused on our nation regaining world educational leadership. The strategy was directed at higher standards and new forms of assessments. Box 2.9 briefly lists the eight main educational goals approved by congress in 1994.

Box 2.9   National Education Goals 2000

- All children in America will start school ready to learn.
- The high school graduation rate will increase to at least 90 percent.
- American students will leave grades 4, 8, and 12 having demonstrated competency in challenging subject matter, including English, mathematics, science, history, and geography; and every school in America will ensure that all students learn to use their minds well, so that they may be prepared for responsible citizenship, further learning, and productive employment in our modern economy.
- The nation's teaching force will have access to programs for professional development.
- US students will be first in the world in science and mathematics achievement.
- Every adult American will be literate and will possess the knowledge and skills necessary to compete in a global economy and to exercise the rights and responsibilities of citizenship.
- Every school in America will be free of drugs and violence and will offer a safe, disciplined environment conducive to learning.
- Every school will promote parental involvement and participation to promote the social, emotional, and academic growth of children.

Source: America 2000: An Education Strategy (US Department of Education, 1991). (Enacted into law on March 31, 1994, as *Goals 2000: Educate America Act.*)

It is apparent that *Goals 2000* has not been achieved and may never be achieved for everyone. Because of *Goals 2000*, each state attempted to adopt laws related to the federal goals that would make them eligible for federal funding. New York State's plan to achieve the goals set in federal law took the form of a compact that filtered down to the local level and established the strategic objectives in box 2.10. As of this writing, this compact has not been achieved.

One example of a document framed by a local authority, in this case by New York City, is the Curriculum Frameworks, created to realize the goals and the aims of the state and federal acts. The Frameworks is an assemblage of strategies believed to be essential in preparing children to become good citizens. The purpose was to establish a set of expectations for all, while allowing for flexibility. Schools were allowed latitude to employ different teaching strategies focused on achieving expectations outlined in the Frameworks. Box 2.11 lists six key principles found in the Frameworks.

Standards and Practice

To understand how we use standards in daily practice we must first understand what standards are. An *educational standard* is a statement that depicts what students should know or be able to do because of the teaching and learning they experienced—for example, a standard expressed in terms of knowledge or performance in a specific content area, such as "Children in grades K to 8 must read 25 books in various genres each school year."

Developmental standards focus on the levels of development exhibited by individual students. They are expressed in terms of age appropriateness. They highlight changes in the developing child with regard to personality traits, learning style, and family background. The purpose of these standards is to aid teachers in preparing age-appropriate lessons and activities.

Box 2.10   New Compact for Learning

- All children will come to school ready to learn.
- All children will read, write, compute, and use the thinking skills they need to continue learning by the time they are in the 4th grade or its equivalent.
- At least 90 percent of all young people will earn a high school diploma by age 21.
- All high school graduates will be prepared for college, work or both.
- All high school graduates will demonstrate proficiency in English and another language, mathematics, the natural sciences, and technology; in history and other social sciences; and in the arts and other humanities. (Standards will be developed.)
- All students will acquire the skills, knowledge, and attitudes needed for employment and effective citizenship.
- All children will demonstrate commitment to the core values of our democratic society and knowledge of the history and culture of the major groups that comprise American society and the world.
- Students of both genders and all socioeconomic and racial/ethnic backgrounds will show similar achievement on state assessment measures.

Source: State Education Department (March, 1991), *A New Compact for Learning: Improving Public Elementary, Middle, and Secondary Education Results in the 1990s* (Albany, NY: State Education Department).

Box 2.11   Key Principles of New York's Curriculum Frameworks

- All children are capable of learning and contributing to society.
- Parents and caregivers are children's first teachers.
- All students, including those with special needs, should be challenged to fulfill their utmost potential.
- Limited English Proficient (LEP) students must receive parallel instructional programs and be provided with equal access to quality programs.
- Schools need to reflect an education that is multicultural.
- Schools can make a difference in students' lives.

Source: State Education Department (March, 1991), *A New Compact for Learning: Improving Public Elementary, Middle, and Secondary Education Results in the 1990s* (Albany, NY: State Education Department).

State Academic Standards

Chester E. Finn, Jr.

State standards can be both a help and hindrance to teachers striving to develop an effective curriculum and pedagogy for their students. They help by setting subject-matter parameters; delineating the knowledge and skills that the state deems essential; and providing scaffolding on which district, school, and teacher can construct their own version of what students will actually study. They hinder by narrowing the curriculum to an unfortunate degree or—paradoxically—inflating it to absurd proportions, by establishing divisions that make it harder to bridge disciplines, by insisting on "coverage" of material that may be unrealistic or inappropriate in actual class settings, and occasionally by creating sequences that don't work for practitioners—yet must be honored because of the tests that accompany the standards.

Still, state standards are a fact of life in most places, and teachers ignore them at their (and their students') peril, particularly where assessments and accountability mechanisms are keyed to them. It's best to view them as the skeleton of the curriculum and then work at supplying the flesh, the nerves, and the blood supply. This can actually be a blessing to teachers, who need not fret too much about deciding what knowledge and skills to impart and can instead concentrate on the sequence, materials, and instructional methods most apt to succeed with their students.

This becomes far more difficult, of course, if the state did a mediocre job of developing its academic standards—and one is bound by them regardless. Unfortunately, this worrisome situation exists in many parts of the country—or at least it did in 1997, when the Thomas B. Fordham Foundation undertook an appraisal of state standards in the five key subjects of English, math, science, history, and geography.

Our reviewers were generally dismayed by the vapidity and shoddiness of much that they found. The typical state's "grade" on the quality of its academic standards across the five subjects was D+. That's the bad news. The good news is that in every subject at least a few states developed exemplary standards—proof that this can be done well. I am also encouraged by the fact that many states took our criticism in a constructive vein and have indicated that improving their academic standards is a high priority. Let's hope they follow through.

Pierre van Hiele and Dina van Hiele-Geldof[33] described developmental standards by identifying five levels for understanding spatial concepts that children need to develop to arrive at geometric thinking. The levels are sequential, not age dependent, and they are influenced by experience and instruction. Students should move from levels 1 to 3 by the end of eight grades. Levels 4 and 5 should be achieved by high school or college. The van Hieles stress that all teachers should be aware of these levels. Box 2.12 contains the developmental standards used by Texas for geometric reasoning based on van Hiele's work.

Grade-level standards are grade-specific standards that identify outcomes expected at a particular grade level or as the result of a particular unit of study. The *backwards design process* developed by Wiggins[34] is a perfect example of how to plan to attain grade-level standards when you know what you wish to

---

Box 2.12   Samples of Developmental Standards in Mathematics from Texas

Van Hiele Levels of Geometric Reasoning

Levels:

1. Can name and recognize shapes by appearance, but cannot specifically identify properties.

2. Begins to identify properties of shapes and learns vocabulary related to properties, but cannot make connections between different properties and shapes.

3. Student can recognize relationships between properties and shapes, as well as follow logical arguments using such properties.

4. Can go beyond just identifying characteristics of shapes and able to construct proofs using postulates or axioms and definitions.

5. Student can work in different geometric or axiomatic systems.

Source: Cognitive and Development Issues, *Van Hiele Levels of Geometric Reasoning,* http://wwwdallassd.com/geometry/vanheile1.html

---

achieve. Take the end result (the standard) and work backwards. The process involves teachers planning in three steps: identifying results, determining valid evidence, and planning instruction that achieves results. These three steps can be viewed as a guide to backward design.

1. *Identifying results.* In this stage we ask, "What do we really need to understand?" Focus on what students need to understand—big ideas, concepts, theories, and principles. The goal is to obtain enduring understandings of concepts such as life, liberty, equality, honesty, and truthfulness. Lasting understandings go beyond disconnected facts or skills; they relate to future life experiences beyond subject matter.

2. *Determine valid evidence.* Students demonstrate understanding by providing convincing proof. Student understanding develops as a result of continual inquiry and rethinking. Total comprehension occurs over time; it should not be thought of as a single event. The backward design process determines acceptable evidence by having students explain, interpret, apply, and discuss their research data.

3. *Plan instruction.* Implement learning experiences that lead to understanding. This phase can only happen after you clearly identify results and suitable demonstrations of understanding. In designing backwards planning for instruction, it is the last step rather than the first that clinches the process.

Content-specific standards identify the expected outcomes for specific subjects with regard to content and conceptual knowledge. These types of standards can act as guideposts for teachers in determining effective lesson strategies. For example, check out a web page from Eduscapes, a site that depicts content-specific standards by matching various content areas to specific standards (http://eduscapes.com/sessions/cyberprairie/standards.htm).

Performance standards make content standards operational by describing how good is good enough. They essentially define what children should know and how they can demonstrate that knowledge. Performance standards describe expected outcomes for what students should be able to do. They depict expectations such as No Child Left Behind's Adequate Yearly Progress (AYP), the performance standard that "All students will experience a year of academic growth for each year of instruction."[35] The AYP is used to track the success of Title I schools and districts in improving student achievement. Schools and districts that exceed their AYP goals for two or more consecutive years are eligible for recognition and are encouraged to share their successful programs.

The Current Status of Standards

As of 2010, a veneer of performance standards existed in most states and school districts throughout our nation. However, they aren't all consistent and they don't all mesh with each other. Teachers will be given standards regardless of where they teach, and they will be asked to have students achieve at the mandated levels. The war over developing standards appears to be over, and now the battle to implement them has been engaged. Our cities and states have decided that fixed academic-content standards and performance standards are here to stay. No longer will norm-referenced tests be the sole indicator of student performance. The achievement of students will no longer be measured against their peers but rather by specific mandated content. It is likely that standards will also be used to increase the quality of our nation's teachers.

Common Core State Standards are presently being developed. As of this writing, forty-eight states, two territories, and the District of Columbia have agreed to participate in their development. The final version of the standards was released in June 2010; thirty-two states immediately agreed to adopt the standards.[36] The purpose of the standards is to establish a uniform rigorous set of expectations for what American students should know by the time they graduate high school, enter college, or prepare for careers. The immediate objective is to make it less difficult for students to change schools across district or state borders. The standards consist of two subject areas—Mathematics and English Language Arts—including Literacy in History/Social Studies, Science and Technical Subjects, all of which focus on literacy. These standards are not meant to *be* a curriculum; rather, they are intended to *achieve* through individual, content-rich curriculum.

The Common Core State Standards website describes the standards as a framework designed to "define the knowledge and skills students should have within their K–12 education careers so that they will graduate from high schools able to succeed in entry-level, credit-bearing academic college courses and in workforce training programs."[37] The Standards appear to be the result of President Obama's plan for a "Race to the Top" in 2009. The speech he gave emphasized the following reform areas:

- *Designing and implementing rigorous standards and high-quality assessments,* by encouraging states to work jointly toward a system of common academic standards that builds toward college and career readiness, and that includes improved assessments designed to measure critical knowledge and higher-order thinking skills.

- *Attracting and keeping great teachers and leaders in America's classrooms,* by expanding effective support to teachers and principals; reforming and improving teacher preparation; revising teacher evaluation, compensation, and retention policies to encourage and reward effectiveness; and working to ensure that our most talented teachers are placed in the schools and subjects where they are needed the most.

- *Supporting data systems that inform decisions and improve instruction,* by fully implementing a statewide longitudinal data system, assessing and using data to drive instruction, and making data more accessible to key stakeholders.

- *Using innovation and effective approaches to turn around struggling schools,* by asking states to prioritize and transform persistently low-performing schools.

- *Demonstrating and sustaining education reform,* by promoting collaborations between business leaders, educators, and other stakeholders to raise student achievement and close achievement gaps, and by expanding support for high-performing public charter schools, reinvigorating math and science education, and promoting other conditions favorable to innovation and reform.

The speech given by President Barack Obama, July 24, 2009, focused on promoting innovation, reform, and excellence in America's public schools.

> America will not succeed in the 21st century unless we do a far better job of educating our sons and daughters. . . . And the race starts today. I am issuing a challenge to our nation's governors and school boards, principals and teachers, businesses and non-profits, parents and students: if you set and enforce rigorous and challenging standards and assessments; if you put outstanding teachers at the front of the classroom; if you turn around failing schools—your state can win a Race to the Top grant that will not only help students outcompete workers around the world, but let them fulfill their God-given potential.[38]

National Standards for Teachers

The *National Board of Professional Teaching Standards (NBPTS)* was established in 1987 with the assistance of the Carnegie Corporation. The premise was that great schools begin with great teachers, and quality teaching is the key to improved student achievement. Today NBPTS is recognized for developing professional standards that define what accomplished teachers should know and be able to do. NBPTS also administers National Board Certification, which is a voluntary assessment program that certifies educators who meet those standards. The number of teachers achieving National Board Certification has increased by more than 90 percent in the past five years (from more than 47,000 in 2005 to more than 91,000 in 2010).[39] There are five core propositions that form the foundation for the NBPT standards. These standards create a vision for what the accomplished teacher should know. The standards can be retrieved at the National Board for Professional Teaching Standards website (http://www.nbpts.org).

The Interstate New Teacher Assessment and Support Consortium (INTASC) standards are an integral component of the new performance-based process for evaluating teachers that is still in use today. These standards reflect the requisite knowledge, skills, and attitudes necessary for teachers starting their career. To retrieve these standards, see http://www.wresa.org/Pbl/The%20INTASC% 20Standards%20overheads.htm.

Student Performance Standards

It's crucial that we recognize the relationship between teacher standards and student performance. We succeed when our students attain academic success. Performance standards are the haphazard products of content standards found in texts, states, city guides, and elsewhere. Performance standards are linked to content standards that were determined by various national councils of teachers. This process contains benchmarks for comparing our national standards with world standards. Performance standards specify what students should know and be able to do at each grade level in all academic areas. The performance standards make content standards operational. They provide a description of performance needed to meet a content objective. This can be clearly understood if one visualizes judges rating Olympic high dives. Each judge knows what the standard is and what surpasses it. This is what standards are attempting to do for education (more specifically, for reading and math). See examples of student performance standards in middle school mathematics at http://schools.nyc.gov/offices/teachlearn/documents/standards/math/ms/ 76overview.html.

How can standards be made a reality in the classroom? Standards are easy to accept, but implementation is a much more difficult proposition. Teachers should follow the suggestions outlined in their state education department guides. Most states have provided assessments aligned to test their performance standards. Teachers must implement standards-based instruction for students to thrive. This requires a process of staff development and self-training on the part of teachers. To have instruction put standards into practice and become an integral part of the fabric of a school and each classroom, District Comprehensive Plans and School Comprehensive Plans should be linked to the Classroom Teacher's Comprehensive Plan. For performance standards to be realized, they must be reflected in demonstrations of student learning. The goal is to bring standards-based planning into the classroom—planning that is directly related to state and national standards. See Case Study 2.1 for suitable strategies to use when appraising student and teacher performance.

The following case discusses the use of appropriate strategies when dealing with assessing student and teacher performance. The strategies and methods proposed focus on meeting the needs of the child and teacher. Read the case and compare the ideas it presents with the reality of everyday classroom life.

Case Study 2.1
Standards versus Learning

At Ridgemont School a schoolwide administrative memo had been distributed, stating that effective immediately all student grades would conform to national and state standards. If grades did not conform, students were to receive a failing grade. An addendum to this memo stated that teacher salaries would be based on the success of their students in achieving the standards. This memo prompted a discussion among three Ridgemont teachers on the topic of learning and standards.

One of these teachers, Philip Hill, loved to quote Einstein. He felt that using an authority gave credence to whatever he was discussing. "Imagination is more important than knowledge," Phil said, "and should be the standard for all learning." And since he was citing Einstein, he figured it had to be correct.

Beverly Macaw said, "I like what you're saying, but I think you need some knowledge to apply your imagination to. Both are important." Beverly further remarked that imagination might be characterized as a skill, so she felt that no problem existed.

"Good point," Philip retorted, "but I am still not sure how this is going to help our nation in its efforts to revise learning standards. That would be great if the problem was termed 'Learning standards: Imagination versus Knowledge.' Unfortunately, it isn't. Those like E. D. Hirsch and his Core Knowledge Foundation are the leading advocates for content knowledge at the expense of the skills-emphasis spotlighted in the 21st Century Skills Project. This project placed emphasis on the importance of skills that crossed disciplinary lines, such as skills for life. Diane Ravitch of the *Boston Globe* refuted it as a fad, saying that skill-centered, knowledge-free education has never worked.

Margaret Collins, a friend of Philip, said, "Please—give me a break! How can anyone consider standards without a content basis? Without standards and benchmarks, we would have no way of determining what our students have learned."

"Couldn't you just ask them?" inquired Beverly. "Or better yet have the children create authentic assessments for evaluation?"

"Beverly, what you are saying is unrealistic," Margaret responded. "Do you realize how much time that would take? We might as well return to the Middle Ages when all testing was oral."

The discussion was concluded when Philip said, "You know, actually we are all upset about that memo for no reason." "What do you mean no reason?" asked Beverly, and Margaret nodded her head. "Well," Philip responded, "To the best of my knowledge there are no national standards yet—only a core outline that hasn't been fully adopted or implemented."

"Oh! That means nothing: We *do* have state standards in place that are not going to go away. Just because the US Department of Education said that all states and schools will have challenging and clear standards of achievement and accountability for all children and effective strategies for reaching those standards doesn't mean it's going to be done," Beverly said archly, pleased that she could recall and recite the USDE mandate.

"Look, all you have to do is go to a good website like Education World* where you can retrieve your state's standards and get the new national standards when they are completed," said Philip. It wasn't an Einstein quotation, but he felt it was the most important statement in the whole conversation.

Discussion Topics and Questions to Ponder

1. List the arguments made by Philip to support his position that learning is part skill and a lot of imagination.

2. Contrast Philip's argument with Margaret's argument. Who had the stronger argument, and why? Whose side was Beverly on? Justify your response.

3. How has the standards movement affected the lives of teachers and students alike?

4. Describe your feelings with regard to standards versus learning.

5. Is there a need for teacher and student standards? How would you use them to better educate students and attract qualified and competent teachers?

What would you do if . . . ?

1. You were asked to lead a conference that was to place an emphasis on standards based on content knowledge.

2. Pedagogy, skills, and methods were to be emphasized rather than content.

3. You were asked to contribute ideas for the standards. Make specific suggestions and discuss your answer in class.

*The Education World URL is http://www.educationworld.com/standards/state/toc/index.shtml

Standards-Based Lesson Planning

No specific guides exist for developing standards-based lesson planning. The *Standards-Based Classroom Operator's Manual*[40] attempts to develop directions and provides a set of tools designed to answer such questions as what standards look like in lesson planning and in the classroom, and how to design learning experiences to achieve them. The activities move from the conjectural to actual implementation of standards. The approach consists of eight sequenced steps in a standards-based design process that includes planning, delivery, and evaluation of instruction:

1. Understanding content standards

2. Designing assessment tasks

3. Determining performance levels

4. Designing the curriculum

5. Planning instruction strategies

6. Implementing instruction

7. Assessing students

8. Evaluating and refining the whole process

Another approach is the *Standards Achievement Planning Cycle (SAPC)* that offers a first step in developing strategies for effective standards-based planning. SAPC is a synthesis of ideas associated with outcomes-based education, Japanese lesson-study technique, functional standards, and the use of state standards as instructional targets. In SAPC, learning outcomes are written from standards and frameworks that form instructional targets of standards-based lesson plans. The lesson objectives consist of observable skills or products that are demonstrable and can be evaluated by teachers.[41] See box 2.13 for assistance in achieving standards through lesson planning. See http://www.tc.edu/lessonstudy/lessonstudy.html for functional standards (the specific actions

Box 2.13   SAPC's Five-Step Process for Writing Lessons to Achieve Standards

1. **Identify standards.** This can be accomplished by perusing your state standards and state resources guides. Textbooks and authentic resource materials should be used to motivate lessons, not to identify appropriate standards. Once identified, standards provide focus for lesson objectives.

2. **Analyze standards.** Once you have identified the standards deemed essential, they must be analyzed as to the content knowledge students are expected to master. Student outcomes must be transformed into student performances that can be measured.

3. **Describe student performances.** Paint a picture of what students must accomplish in order to master the content standards you have selected. The guide for this step is to imagine the activities necessary to acquire the knowledge and skills appropriate to achieve mastery.

4. **Select learning activities.** After identifying the standards and analyzing the content to be learned, as well as the necessary student performances, you must then select specific learning activities. Activities must translate into coherent developmental experiences that result in achievement of lesson objectives.

5. **Evaluate student work.** Student achievement is determined by the quality of work produced. This is the purpose of the standards-based lesson. Student work must demonstrate comprehension of the standard as described in your vision of mastery in student performances. It should be noted that performance descriptions are the key to providing a rubric and should serve as the prime assessment tool in evaluation of student success.

Note: The author cautions that SAPC is really not a formula for translating state standards; it is essentially a guide for preparation. It only works well, he claims, when teachers share curriculum expertise to plan standards-based lessons.
Source: Adapted from M. R. O'Shea, *From Standards to Success* (Alexandria, VA: ASCD, 2005). Learn more about ASCD at www.ASCD.org.

taken to achieve the written standards). It is obvious that these strategies are essentially commonsense approaches to instructional planning. To be successful, teachers must plan effective lessons that link to specific, state-mandated curriculum objectives.

Best Practices

The effect of standards on classroom performance is enormous. (Read Case Study 2.2 to help you determine if standards are truly worthwhile.) Critics believe that teachers feel coerced into teaching for high-stakes tests. They also claim that students are driven by fear and the shame of being labeled a failure. To expect all students of a given age to achieve at the same level, they claim, is unrealistic and unfair. Arts and creative activities are forsaken in order to prepare students to pass standardized tests. Proponents claim that standards drive instruction and create an environment where quality learning is experienced.

Both sides would agree that teachers need to follow effective teaching practices regardless of pedagogical philosophy. These practices can be considered best practices, whether the focus is on teaching to meet standards or to augment students' knowledge bases.

The following case discusses the standards used to attain membership on a school honor roll, and whether the standards truly reflect academic success. Can learning be measured by quantifiable grades or percentages? Should the standard bar always be raised when success is near? When can we consider standards high enough?

Case Study 2.2
Honor Roll Standards: Good or Bad?

Two problems faced Mary Lewis, the school academic achievement coordinator: the numbers of students being placed on the honor roll, and school standards. The standard to obtain honor roll was an 85 percent academic and 75 percent non-academic average. Students also had to evidence good school citizenship with a passing grade in social behavior (in early times called a conduct grade). Because of this policy, 50 percent of all the students at Warwick Elementary School made the honor roll list every year. This created a problem for some parents and faculty, who claimed that the standards were too low and reflected poor teaching. The solution presented by this group was to raise the criteria, which they assumed would lower the number of eligible students. This, they said, would make selection truly an honor.

Mary agreed with the idea about raising the criteria. By agreeing she felt she would also appease those who thought that instruction was watered down and grades inflated. Before taking any action Mary decided to get some faculty opinions.

Lucille Salerno, Mary's best friend, told her that raising the standards would be heading for disaster. To raise the requirements every time someone complained was unfair to those previously selected. Standards would never be high enough using that approach. Lucille told Mary, "Why raise the standards when students were achieving? Rather than raising standards, just add other criteria to be assessed." Lucille suggested using authentic forms of evaluation, such as portfolios or learning logs.

Fran Judge, an inquisitive bystander, volunteered her opinion in a tentative voice: "I'm not sure, but it seems to me that by raising the requirements you just create more work for teachers." Fran also commented on Lucille's idea about using portfolios as being too time consuming. It would require teachers to construct assessment rubrics, which meant even more work. Fran asked Mary to consider using interviews for all potential candidates. As the coordinator, Mary could assess each student's oral communication skills, as well as grades and written work samples.

Mary agreed to consider all suggestions. She told Lucille and Fran that she had thought about raising the requirement from 85 to 95 percent but had decided that would not solve the problem and would only cause another one. She would have to deal with those who thought the standard too high.

Mary said she was seriously considering using a percentage of the total student population as the cutoff rather than a fixed, inflated grade. The only question was whether to allow the top 5 percent or 15 percent or 25 percent to be selected. Doing it this way wouldn't influence the quality of instruction and would still allow a goodly number in. Mary decided that she favored the top 25 percent: It would eliminate student disappointment and still have 25 percent less students make the list than under the current policy. The new policy would create a perception of fairness while still restricting admittance. She doubted that this new policy would be a strong predictor of a quality education, but it did address the need to have higher standards for student honor-roll selection.

Fran said, "Wait a minute! Why not create two lists—one for academics with a 95 percent standard, and a principal's list for social behavior and citizenship based on percentage? Wouldn't that satisfy everyone?"

Discussion Topics and Questions to Ponder

1. Compare and contrast the arguments for raising the standards for honor roll.
2. Contrast Mary's, Lucille's, and Fran's arguments. Whose was the strongest? Justify your answer.
3. How do you feel about raising standards because too many students achieve them?
4. If given the opportunity, how would you resolve this issue?
5. Read the following passage and react to the author's statement. Share your opinions in class.

The danger with standards is not in the standard but in the preparation. To prepare students for the necessary assessment that goes hand in hand with standards requires teachers to exchange a rigorous curriculum for repetition and drill on timed practice tests. Given up are exercises in which students write analytic essays, thoughtful research papers, original science experiments and advanced math applications. As these tests become part of our schools, students will only be asked to focus on skills necessary to pass. The rigorous instruction and high standards of the original reform movement will be replaced by test-driven lower standards. Of course a contrary argument could be made that claims this argument is based on assumption and faith that if standards were eliminated every classroom would offer expectations that were clear, rigorous, and objective. It also assumes that testing conducted by teachers would be inherently fair because it would be based upon the achievement of an objective result rather than comparison of one student to the other.

What would you do if . . . ?

1. A suggestion was made to eliminate the honor roll because it's an elitist tradition.
2. It was decided that only the top one percent was allowed to make the honor roll.
3. The school board suggested that pay raises be tied to the number of students who made the honor roll.

The way to incorporate the standards into lessons is simply to teach good lessons. Teachers who embody quality practices produce students who attain content mastery. The use of best practices allows standards achievement to become a reality. Eight items come to mind when reflecting on the instructional quality found in the first-rate lessons of first-rate practitioners:

1. *Achieving instructional clarity.* This occurs when students are engaged during a lesson.
2. *Linking familiarity with substance.* Structure and integrate concepts into the curriculum.

3. *Establishing expectations.* Present your lesson objectives before you teach the lesson.

4. *Varying your teaching style.* Plan for a variety of strategies that include interactive learning.

5. *Using an array of materials.* Use many different instructional aids and resources.

6. *Implementing learning and development principles.* Meet student needs through use of appropriate strategies.

7. *Diversifying communication with students on multiple levels.* Communicate clearly and focus on higher-order thinking skills.

8. *Being enthusiastic.* Enthusiasm is infectious, and a teacher's positive energy is usually reciprocated.

Theory into Practice

Most teachers will be required to use objectives in the planning and implementation of their instruction. Depending on the philosophy and beliefs of your school (and supervisor), your formulation of objectives may be general or precise. The set of questions below covers both possibilities.

General Objectives

1. Have you determined the major objectives you wish to stress?

2. Are your objectives related to the goals of the school (or grade level or department)?

3. Are your objectives related to sound principles of teaching and learning?

4. Are your objectives realistic in terms of students' abilities and the time and facilities available? Do your students use different cognitive processes?

5. Are your objectives related to important learning outcomes?

6. Have you arranged the objectives according to some order of importance, domains of learning, or high-order/low-order cognitive, social, or psychological categories?

7. Have you arranged the content and activities of the subject so they correspond with the objectives?

8. Are you satisfied that your objectives coincide with the views (or values) of the parents and community? Of established academic standards?

Precise Objectives

1. Have you clearly determined what you want the learner to accomplish? (Have you identified appropriate knowledge types and cognitive processes?)

2. Have you decided on who is to perform the desired behavior (e.g., the entire class, the more advanced group)?

3. Have you used an action word to describe the actual behavior required to demonstrate mastery of the objective (e.g., to write, to describe)?

4. Did you establish limiting and/or facilitating conditions under which the learner is to do what is asked (e.g., in one hour, with the textbook closed)?

5. Have you described the product or performance to be evaluated to determine whether the objective has been achieved (e.g., a report, a speech)?

6. Have you decided on a standard or achievement level that will be used to evaluate the success of the product or performance (e.g., 80 percent correct)?

CONCLUSIONS

- Aims are broad statements about the intent of education as a whole. Goals or standards are statements about what students are expected to learn. Objectives specify content and behavior and sometimes a proficiency level to be achieved at some level of instruction.

- Objectives are written at several levels, including program, grade, subject, course, classroom, unit plan, and lesson plan, and at several degrees of specificity, from broad to precise.

- The most popular approaches to formulating objectives are based on the work of Tyler, Bloom, Gronlund, and Mager. Tyler identifies purposes and then, to derive instructional objectives, interprets them in the light of philosophical and psychological concerns.

- Bloom's work (a taxonomy of educational objectives) entails three domains of learning: cognitive, affective, and psychomotor. The taxonomy was revised in 2001 to emphasize types of knowledge and cognitive processes.

- Gronlund distinguishes between general objectives and specific learning outcomes.

- Mager relies on three major characteristics for writing objectives: behavior, condition, and proficiency level.

- A number of recommendations for writing objectives exist to facilitate teacher planning.

- Standards greatly impact instructional practices, yet they need not be detrimental.

KEY TERMS

affective domain	course objectives	program objectives
aims/purposes	general instructional	psychomotor domain
classroom objectives	objectives	standards
cognitive domain	goals	taxonomy of
Common Core	lesson plan objectives	educational objectives
State Standards	objectives	unit plan objectives

DISCUSSION QUESTIONS

1. In terms of aims and goals, why is the answer to the question "What is the purpose of school?" so complex?

2. Why is it important for aims and goals to change as society changes?

3. What sources of information does Tyler recommend in formulating his objectives? Which source is most important? Explain your answer.

4. How does Gronlund distinguish between general objectives and specific learning outcomes?

5. What are the three components of Mager's objectives? Do teachers need to write objectives that include all three components?

MINI-CASES FROM THE FIELD

Case One: Aim of Education

Phil Simms was totally confused by the statement that there are really only two specific aims to education: to facilitate learning and to develop independent learning. He had read that statement somewhere, and it had stuck with him. The problem was that he wasn't sure whether this was accurate, and whether there were more and/or different primary aims for education. Phil was not sure of the difference between aims, goals, standards, and objectives, let alone the two most important aims for any teacher. And what of the two primary aims? Was this situation similar to the old unanswerable question, "Which came first—the chicken or the egg?"

1. Help Phil by providing a possible solution to his problem.

2. Discuss two aims that are inherent in all teaching situations. Justify your choices.

3. Write an example of a goal, an aim, and an objective.

4. Explain how Bloom's Taxonomy of General Objectives might be of assistance to Phil.

5. How do you feel about the two aims to education that put Phil into a quandary?

Case Two: Are Objectives and Standards Necessary?

Mrs. Founts was aware that objectives and standards had traditionally gone hand in hand. She knew that the state examinations were based on their standards. She had been told that what she taught in the classroom had to be directly related to the standards. This was exactly what she was opposed to. She and her colleagues at the Donning Middle School believed that they were doing a disservice to their students if they just taught to the test. She felt that it deprived students of the opportunity for an enriched education, one that included the arts, music, and theater. Her colleagues had decided to enrich their curriculums and not specifically teach to the test. Unfortunately, this strategy was met by an uncompromising administration that said it would move to dismiss any teacher who refused to follow legitimate state policy.

1. Are standards and objectives necessary for a formal assessment program to be effective? Explain your answer.
2. Should teachers teach to the test to maintain the standards? Explain your reasoning.
3. How can one have an enriched curriculum and still achieve standards?
4. If you were Mrs. Founts, what would you have said to your colleagues after they told you what they were going to do?
5. Despite the fact that the administration said there would be no compromise, how could one have been proposed?

Case Three: Do Standards Really Help?

Bob Pennell never realized how difficult it would be to teach his fourth-grade class and have them all meet the state-mandated standards. His children were all reading two to three years below grade and were similarly delayed in mathematics. When the principal, Mrs. Queen, had offered him the position, she had intimated that no child was to be left behind. She expected all lessons to be related to the curriculum standards and labeled accordingly. In answering the following questions, use the curriculum standards for the state in which you teach or intend to teach.

1. Were Mrs. Queen's expectations unrealizable? Explain your answer.
2. What is the relationship between standards and performance?
3. How can standards be used for instructional improvement?
4. How could teachers measure student achievement without standards?
5. Describe the differences between content standards and performance (functional) standards.

Case Four: Is There Really Such a Thing as Best Practices?

John Luau was a new teacher at Public School 102. He felt fortunate in being assigned to an innovative school where professionalism was appreciated. The school had a positive reputation. The principal, Mr. Bornocore, was a much admired administrator who was very proud of his school's academic successes. Parents and teachers were happy to be associated with such a fine school. The principal constantly stressed that teachers in his school used only the best practices in their approach to instruction. He favored standardized testing because it removed any subjectivity in assessment and helped maintain academic standards.

John couldn't help but wonder: If things were so wonderful at PS 102, why was he having such a difficult time adjusting?

1. John's job satisfaction appears to depend on professional growth, not financial considerations. Can a policy advocating standardized tests be perceived as limiting to academic freedom and professionalism? Discuss both sides of the issue in your response.

2. Is pay an important factor to be considered in the selection of your first teaching position? Could other things besides money influence you?

3. Is it possible to utilize best practices and maintain standards? Explain your answer.

4. Why do you think John had a difficult time adjusting?

5. What do you feel John was really looking for?

Case Five: What Is Standards-Based Lesson Design?

Sal Bacon had always used a developmental format when he wrote his lesson plans. Now his new department chairman had insisted that all lessons in the Language Arts Department were to follow a standards-based lesson format. The approach consisted of sequenced steps in a standards-based design process that included planning, delivery, and evaluation of instruction. Specifically, each lesson was to have a relationship to content standards, a method to assess the lesson, clearly stated performance levels, a description of instructional strategies, a log to indicate how the lesson was conducted, assessment of student understanding, and finally an evaluation of the whole process. This seemed like a cumbersome process to follow for each lesson he taught.

1. Is there a right way to design every lesson taught? Justify your answer.

2. Demonstrate how different lessons can require different approaches (for example, a lesson preparing a class for a guest speaker and a lesson where children are brainstorming a concept such as freedom of speech).

3. What facets are common to any lesson?

4. Are there standards that every lesson should contain?

5. Define and explain how the following practices could be used to design a standards-based lesson: instructional clearness, establishing expectations, different teaching styles, using dissimilar materials, implementation of learning and development principles, and enthusiasm.

FIELD EXPERIENCE ACTIVITIES

1. Find a list of program or course goals in a curriculum guide and revise them to conform to the guidelines for writing objectives at a particular subject and grade level that you plan to teach.

2. Arrange the six categories of the cognitive domain into a hierarchy from simple to complex. Give an example of an instructional objective for each category for the content that you plan to teach.

3. Arrange the five categories of the affective domain into a hierarchy from simple to complex. Give an example of an instructional objective for each category.

4. Write six objectives for the subject you wish to teach at the lesson-plan level. Use the methods of Bloom or Mager to write these objectives.

5. Identify the standards for your teaching area and examine them in relationship to a textbook that is being used by a local school district. Talk to a

teacher in that district to determine how he or she uses standards to shape classroom lessons.

6. Analyze the standards that are being used in the course for which this book is required. Comment on the following areas:

   • the performance standards expected

   • the content-specific standards expected

   • the practices employed to achieve the standards

   Use the same approach and analyze the standards evidenced in your local elementary school.

RECOMMENDED READING

Anderson, L., and David Krathwohl (eds). *Taxonomy for Learning, Teaching, and Assessing: A Revision of Bloom's Taxonomy of Educational Objectives.* New York: Longman, 2001.
    A revision of the taxonomical structure first put forth by Benjamin Bloom, this text illustrates the ways in which good instruction requires teachers to think broadly about the learning outcomes expected of students.

Bloom, Benjamin S. *Taxonomy of Educational Objectives, Handbook I. Cognitive Domain.* New York: Longman, 1984.
    Describes six categories of the cognitive domain and identifies objectives and test items related to knowledge and problem-solving skills.

Gronlund, Norman E., and Susan M. Brookhart. *Gronlund's Writing Instructional Objectives*, 8th ed. Upper Saddle River, NJ: Prentice-Hall, 2008.
    A complete guide for helping future teachers master the task of creating and using instructional objectives in teaching that describes—and illustrates with examples—step-by-step procedures for writing objectives that clearly define desired learning outcomes and expected student performance.

Krathwohl, David R., Benjamin S. Bloom, and Bertram Maisa. *Taxonomy of Educational Objectives, Handbook II: Affective Domain.* New York: Longman, 1984.
    Describes five categories of the affective domain and identifies objectives and test items related to feelings, attitudes, and values.

Marzano, Robert. *What Works in Schools.* Alexandria, VA: ASCD, 2003.
    An effective synthesis of the curriculum and instruction implementation process that documents the various types of research supporting current practices.

Oliva, Peter E. *Developing the Curriculum*, 7th ed. New York: Harper Collins, 2008.
    Provides a solid foundation of key models, concepts, and issues pertaining to curriculum today.

Ornstein, Allan C., Edward F. Pajak, and Stacey B. Ornstein. *Contemporary Issues in Curriculum*, 5th ed. Upper Saddle River, NJ: Pearson, 2011.
    Addresses issues in implementation, planning, and evaluation of curriculum at all levels of learning from the viewpoints of philosophy, teaching, learning, instruction, supervision, and policy.

Wiggins, G., and Jay McTighe. *Understanding by Design.* Upper Saddle River, NJ: Prentice-Hall, 2001.
    An excellent text that helps teachers discern the difference between understanding and knowing. Many teachers think of covering content; the authors argue for striving to facilitate understanding.

3

Planning Instruction for Learning

FOCUS POINTS

1. Learning how teachers plan for instruction, and the levels of planning.
2. Mapping a course of study and the main components of a unit plan.
3. Learning the main components of a lesson plan: a beginning, middle, and conclusion.
4. Identifying the components stressed in a mastery lesson plan.
5. Knowing how unit and lesson plans facilitate teaching and instruction.
6. Realizing that good planning relates to research on how students learn and to cognitive development.
7. Deciding whether to use methods of direct transmission or student construction of knowledge.
8. Recognizing that curriculum is the interaction between teacher and learner.
9. Learning that performance objectives are specific, measurable, attainable, results-oriented, and achievable within a precise time frame.
10. Realizing that supervisors look for learning: Fail to plan and you plan to fail.

OVERVIEW

Efficient planning is based on understanding six key ingredients for success: (1) state educational standards; (2) the general goals of the school; (3) the objectives of the course or subject and the concomitant disciplinary standards; (4) students' abilities, aptitudes, needs, and interests; (5) content to be included, and appropriate units into which the subject can be divided; and (6) techniques of short-range instruction or lesson planning.

Although planning is the shared responsibility of administrators, supervisors, and teachers, when you enter a school as a teacher, you must modify any existing plans and design your own plans for instruction in the classroom. Those plans are represented in the curriculum (both taught and hidden) that you emphasize in your classroom. There are many different definitions of the curriculum as a plan. Each definition represents a different view of the learner and the learning process. A curriculum viewed as a plan represents a behaviorist interpretation, which includes a teacher-defined strategy for achieving desired goals or ends (and is rooted in the ideas of such educators as Ralph Tyler and Hilda Taba). Such an interpretation is quite different from viewing a curriculum as a set of experiences or activities (a progressive view, wherein student interests drive instruction) or in terms of subject matter or academic content.

Along with the five keys for effective teaching (discussed in chapter 1), understanding how children learn provides a platform from which to explore, plan, and create effective lessons. Guidelines are needed for incorporating topics and objectives into plans whose effectiveness can be assessed. Effective yearly, term, unit, weekly and daily planning depend on a curriculum that provides topics for individual lessons. Topic selection determines the lesson objectives. A plan for instruction, either direct or indirect, and a summary assessment of learning completes the planning process. Planning and lesson design has been researched and discussed for many years. How do we write and plan effective lessons that facilitate learning? How do we get children to master the type of self-discipline that leads to success? This chapter focuses on how to plan lessons that help students to acquire knowledge and self-control. You will learn now to develop your presentation skills and survive the inevitable supervisory observation of your performance.

Defining Curriculum

Lesson planning does not exist in a vacuum. Before writing lesson plans, you must understand the curriculum and the standards by which it is measured. One problem with curriculum is deciding on the amount of content to include without losing quality. Addressing all content at a suitable level of depth and quality is nearly impossible. There are not enough hours in the day to concentrate on teaching all content, or even to attempt to achieve such a goal. A solution may be found in the concept of intensive and extensive curriculum. The *intensive curriculum* comprises what students should know in depth, and the *extensive curriculum* comprises knowledge of which all students should have some understanding.[1]

Before beginning to plan lessons the teacher should understand curriculum. Providentially, curriculum is a given—decided upon by state education departments and school boards—while lesson plans are teacher creations. Goals and objectives for courses of study are usually neatly laid out by respective boards of education. For most, there is no need to worry about goals and objectives: Teachers need only concern themselves with the preparation and delivery of lessons.

Since children learn by doing, begin the lesson-planning process by deciding on appropriate activities. Look at program standards and see the performance benchmarks that students are expected to achieve, and then write a plan based on achieving those benchmarks by using appropriate strategies that facilitate learning. Regardless of approach (expository, discovery teaching, scientific method, or plain discussion), student learning must be the focus of all instruction. This is so, regardless of whether one is a traditionalist, progressive, constructivist, essentialist, or just plain eclectic. An instructor's philosophy becomes evident upon presentation of a lesson. One lesson plan does not make for a course of study, however; it necessitates the development of unit plans and related daily lesson plans. These plans should reflect the details, methods, materials, and resources needed to understand the specific content area and related skills.

The last step in the lesson-planning process is for the teacher to assess her work and decide whether to enrich it or reteach it. The curriculum model for classroom instruction (figure 3.1) helps to clarify the process by highlighting four essential components, beginning with (1) curriculum vision activities, (2) program standards, (3) classroom practices, and (4) assessment.[2]

In order to bolster the curriculum model for instruction, students should be included in making planning decisions whenever possible. Show students how you use the curriculum model for classroom instruction and in developing lessons. Promote student participation by allowing them an active part in your planning. An outstanding way to develop student comprehension is to let stu-

Figure 3.1   Curriculum Model for Classroom Instruction

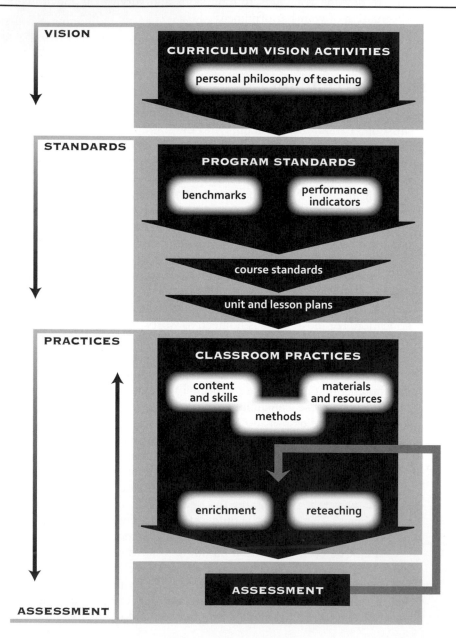

dents assist in making choices regarding types of activities; instructional approaches; and the amount of independent work, discussions, and assignments. Students who are comfortable with these procedures are students who will learn. Of course, no one can guarantee success in all cases, but using this approach is certainly a step in a positive direction.

Teacher Planning

Decision making is a form of teacher planning. Planning a course, unit, or lesson involves making decisions in two areas: (1) *subject-matter* (content) *knowledge*—concerning organization and presentation of content, knowledge of student understanding of content, and knowledge of how to teach the content; and (2) *action system* (pedagogical) *knowledge*—concerning teaching activities such as diagnosing, grouping, managing, and evaluating students and implementing instructional activities and learning experiences.[3] Both kinds of knowledge are needed for effective planning for instruction.

Some teachers have knowledge of subject matter but lack expertise in various aspects of action system knowledge. Research on out-of-field teachers (teachers who are teaching in areas in which they do not have an academic major) would suggest that they lack the content knowledge but may understand the process of grouping and managing students.[4]

John Zahorik, who sampled some 200 teachers, argues that most teachers do not engage in rational planning or make use of objectives. They tend to emphasize content, materials, resources, and learning activities.[5] Several years after Zahorik conducted his research, Clark and Peterson also found that teachers emphasize subject-matter knowledge or content and instructional activities when planning a daily lesson. They spend the least time on planning objectives.[6]

Many teachers simply do not value the use of objectives or of detailed or elaborate lesson plans. Although researchers and professional educators tend to see logic in planned lessons, Elliot Eisner points out that most of what happens in the classroom cannot be observed, measured, or preplanned, and much of teaching is based on impulse and imagination and cannot be designed in advance.[7] There is, therefore, a tension between those who advocate detailed planning and those who suggest that teaching is too artful for such detailed planning. This textbook is oriented toward the former, though we acknowledge that good teachers do on occasion "teach to the moment" and rely on hunches and intuitive judgment.

The emergence of assessment measures that make public how much students actually learn is impacting student learning. Assessments are based on standards that have been prescribed at the local, state, or national levels. Because teachers and schools are being held accountable for student performance on prescribed assessments, more teachers (and administrators) are ensuring a match between the taught curriculum and assessment. That makes sense! For teachers this means that they need to understand how to plan lessons around standards and the prescribed district curriculum, and how to assess the growth of students using a variety of low-stakes testing measures (assessments that do not have retention or promotion consequences).

Standards are organized around the facts, concepts, principles, and skills that disciplinary experts believe students at every grade level should know. Examples of such facts, concepts, principles, and skills categorized by various levels of learning are provided in table 3.1. Standards do not prescribe the limits of what students learn but rather establish a coherent structure for what is taught. Tomlinson observes,

> Standards should be a vehicle to ensure that students learn more coherently, more deeply, more broadly, and more durably. Sadly, when teachers feel pressure to cover standards in isolation, and when the standards are presented in the form of fragmented and sterile lists, genuine learning is hobbled, not enriched.[8]

Table 3.1   Examples of the Levels of Learning

Levels of Learning	Science	Literature	History
Facts	Water boils at 212° C. Humans are mammals.	Katherine Paterson wrote *Bridge to Terabithia*. Definition of *plot* and definition of *character.*	The Boston Tea Party helped to provoke the American Revolution. The first 10 amendments to the US Constitution are called the *Bill of Rights.*
Concepts	Interdependence. Classification	Voice. Heroes and antiheroes	Revolution. Power, authority, and governance
Principles	All life forms are part of a food chain. Scientists classify animals according to patterns.	Authors use voices of characters as a way of sharing their own voices. Heroes are born of danger or uncertainty.	Revolutions are first evolutions. Liberty is constrained in all societies.
Attitudes	Conservation benefits our ecosystem. I am part of an important natural network.	Reading poetry is boring. Stories help me understand myself.	It's important to study history so we write the next chapters more wisely. Sometimes I am willing to give up some freedom to protect the welfare of others.
Skills	Creating a plan for an energy efficient school. Interpreting data about costs and benefits of recycling.	Using metaphorical language to establish personal voice. Linking heroes and antiheroes in literature with those of history and current life.	Constructing and supporting a position on an issue. Drawing conclusions based on analyses of sound resources.

Source: Carol Ann Tomlinson, *The Differentiated Classroom: Responding to the Needs of All Learners* (Alexandria, VA: ASCD, 1999), 41. Learn more about ASCD at www.ascd.org.

Planning by Level of Instruction

Teachers should engage in four levels of planning: yearly (and in some cases semesters), unit, weekly, and daily. Planning at each level involves a set of goals, sources of information, forms or outlines, and criteria for judging the effectiveness of planning. Yearly planning usually is framed around state and school district standards or curriculum guides; whereas unit, weekly, and daily lesson planning permit wider latitude for teachers to develop their own plans, though teachers are still required to anchor what they teach to established goals and standards that exist in every disciplinary area. At the elementary school level, the principal is usually considered the instructional leader who is responsible for checking and evaluating the

Music	Math	Art	Reading
Strauss was The Waltz King. Definition of *clef.*	Definition of *numerator* and *denominator.* Definition of *prime numbers.*	Monet was an Impressionist. Definition of *primary colors.*	Definition of *vowel* and *consonant.*
Tempo. Jazz	Part and whole. Number systems	Perspective. Negative space	Main idea. Context
The tempo of a piece of music helps to set the mood. Jazz is both structured and improvisational.	Wholes are made up of parts. The parts of a number system are interdependent.	Objects can be viewed and represented from a variety of perspectives. Negative space helps spotlight essential elements in a composition.	Effective paragraphs generally present and support a main idea. Pictures and sentences often help us figure out words we don't know.
Music helps me to express emotion. I don't care for jazz.	Math is too hard. Math is a way of talking about lots of things in my world.	I prefer Realism to Impressionism. Art helps me to see the world better.	I am a good reader. It's hard to "read between the lines."
Selecting a piece of music that conveys a particular emotion. Writing an original jazz composition.	Expressing parts and wholes in music and the stock market, with fractions and decimals. Showing relationships among elements.	Responding to a painting with both affective and cognitive awareness. Presenting realistic and impressionistic views of an object.	Locating main idea and supporting details in new articles. Interpreting themes in stories.

teachers' plans, with the aid of any assistants she might have. At the secondary school level, the chair of the various subject or academic areas usually performs this professional role and works with teachers to improve instructional planning.

There are different sources of knowledge that influence teacher planning. Although each of those is addressed to some degree in this chapter, the primary emphasis relates to how the goals of learning are identified and defined. Those goals emerge out of a context, as illustrated by the following hierarchy that can also be loosely related to the curriculum model in figure 3.1:

- national standards,
- state curricular frameworks,
- district-level curriculum guides,
- teacher unit plans,
- teacher lesson plans, and
- teacher assessments.

Notice that while the top three are essentially controlled at the national, state, or district level, the bottom three are under the direct decision-making authority of the teacher. The teacher makes general decisions with an awareness of national standards, state mandates, and district requirements. So how do teachers make more specific decisions on what to include?

One researcher points out that at the yearly level a middle-school teacher relies most heavily on (1) previous successes and failures, (2) district curriculum guides, (3) textbook content, (4) student interest, (5) classroom management factors, and (6) the school calendar when they plan their lessons. At the unit, weekly, and daily levels, a teacher is mostly influenced by (1) availability of materials, (2) student interest, (3) schedule interruptions, (4) the school calendar, (5) district curriculum guides, (6) textbook content, (7) classroom management, (8) classroom activity flow, and (9) prior experience.[9] According to Robert Yinger, planning is perceived as rational, logical, and structured, and as being reinforced by a number of instructional and managerial routines. By the middle of the school year, about 85 percent of the instructional activities become habitual. In planning, teachers use instructional routines for questioning, monitoring, and managing students, as well as for coordinating classroom activities.[10]

However, in addition to structure and routine, the teacher needs to include variety and flexibility in planning to take into account the students' differing developmental needs and interests. Some students—especially high achievers, divergent thinkers, and independent learners—learn more in nonstructured and independent situations, whereas many low achievers, convergent thinkers, and dependent learners prefer highly structured and directed environments.

The capacity of the teacher to differentiate instruction appears to be closely linked to student achievement across ability levels. Studies by William Sanders, who has established himself in education because of his value-added concept (how much value or learning is added by a teacher), suggest that the teachers most able to close the achievement gap between groups of students yet foster learning in all students are those who know how to differentiate instruction.[11]

Mental versus Formal Planning

Gail McCutcheon maintains that the most valuable form of teacher planning at the classroom level is "the reflective thinking that many teachers engage in before writing a unit or lesson plan or while teaching a lesson (or even more important, *after* teaching a lesson)."[12] Often the weekly or daily lesson plan is sketchily outlined. Much of what happens is a reflection of what happened in other years when the teacher taught a similar lesson. The structure develops as the teaching–learning process unfolds and as teachers and students interact in the classroom. Many actions related to planning cannot be predetermined in a classroom of thirty or more students who are rapidly interacting with their teacher.

Mental planning is the teacher's spontaneous response to events in the classroom; the teacher considers situations and responds intuitively. (Of course, that intuition must be well-grounded in subject-matter and action system knowledge.) **Mental planning** is a part of teaching that is crucial for effectiveness, but it cannot easily be observed, recorded, or detailed. Therefore, it often goes unnoticed and unmentioned as part of the planning process.

Formal planning is what most educators and researchers recognize as a legitimate and necessary instructional activity. Perhaps it is examined so often simply because it can be prescribed, categorized, and classified. **Formal planning** is structured and task oriented; it suggests that teaching and instruction can be taught as part of teacher education and staff development. Further, if done correctly it can create a culturally responsive classroom and in a way that accommodates defined academic standards.

Specifically, the various academic standards created by organizations such as the National Council of Teachers of Mathematics (NCTM) and National Science Teachers Association (NSTA) can be used to create and organize lessons around certain culturally responsive principles. Beverly Armento takes three principles—one related to instruction, one to student engagement, and one to assessment—and then examines how those principles can be embedded in lessons in ways that benefit diverse student groups.[13] A teacher identifies specific lesson objectives (related directly to established academic standards) and then identifies specific instructional strategies with an orientation to the principles outlined in box 3.1. The teacher strives, for example, to allow different student voices to be heard (IE 4) and to help students see the purpose for a lesson (SE 1). These specific principles create inclusiveness for the lesson, but they do not compromise the rigor of what occurs. Lessons have clear objectives, are focused on standards, involve certain principles of culturally responsive instruction, and assess what students have learned—through a range of materials and techniques and in ways that address the unique learning needs of special learners.

The Culturally Responsive Classroom

A **culturally responsive classroom** is one in which the teacher plans in a way that is inclusive, offers alternative perspectives, suggests commonalities as well as areas of diversity, and relies on some student-constructed (and hence personally relevant) learning tasks. Further, students are engaged in learning as a result of understanding the purpose of learning, having a full range of learning modes avail-

---

Box 3.1 Culturally Responsive Curriculum Principles

Instructional Examples (IE)
IE 1 = Cultural examples used in the curriculum, inclusion
IE 2 = Alternative perspectives
IE 3 = Diversity and commonalities
IE 4 = Culturally relevant and student-generated images/metaphors/examples

Student Engagement (SE)
SE 1 = Purpose/curiosity/anticipation
SE 2 = Multiple learning preferences
SE 3 = Individual/unison/team communications
SE 4 = Cooperative/competitive/individual goals
SE 5 = Student choices/decision making

Assessment (A)
A 1 = Ongoing assessment using a range of materials
A 2 = Assessment information to provide feedback and inform instruction
A 3 = Special accommodations for special learners

Source: Jacqueline Jordan Irvine and Beverly Jeanne Armento, *Culturally Responsive Teaching* (Boston: McGraw-Hill, 2001), 26. Reproduced by permission of the McGraw-Hill Companies.

---

able, using a full range of communication and interaction patterns, and appreciating the various choices that can and must be made while learning to learn. Finally, the teacher assesses what students learn in a way that is ongoing and formative in nature (i.e., provides feedback that shows students how they are progressing) and that accommodates special learners.[14] Notice that a culturally responsive curriculum does not mean you "take it easy" on the students. It means that you base instruction on defined academic standards and then try to make it relevant!

Regarding cultural responsiveness, Ken Henson notes, "A truly democratic society values diversity. . . . Multicultural education is more than just curriculum reform that involves changing or restructuring the curriculum to include content about ethnic groups. . . . Future curricula must promote an appreciation for diversity."[15]

J. A. Banks outlines five dimensions of multicultural education that can help teachers create a culturally responsive classroom:[16]

1. *Content integration.* Teachers can promote diversity across the disciplines, integrating ethnic and cultural concepts in their lesson planning.

2. *The knowledge construction process.* Teachers can help students to understand that knowledge creation is impacted by racial, ethnic, and socioeconomic status of individuals and groups.

3. *Prejudice reduction.* Teachers can discourage stereotypes and negative student attitudes by promoting democratic values. (This may involve what is called a *teachable moment*—the time at which learning a particular concept or idea becomes possible or easiest).

4. *An equity pedagogy.* Teachers can modify their teaching in ways that enhance the learning of students from diverse racial/ethnic/gender/cultural backgrounds.

5. *An empowering school culture and social structure.* The hidden curriculum (discussed in chapter 1) can hugely impact schools' social structures. Effective teachers are aware of this influence and will plan their lessons to incorporate the first four dimensions discussed above, each of which addresses a specific aspect of cultural and/or social systems.

Questions for Reflection

The whole concept of culturally responsive teaching is controversial. Some conservative critics would argue that students learn best in highly teacher-centered classrooms, that content should be dictated by teachers, and that culturally responsive teaching (teaching that builds on student interests and backgrounds) is simply inappropriate. However, many educators—*especially* many teacher trainers—subscribe to the use of more student-centered strategies. They want to create classrooms where students' interests are considered part of the instructional sequence. The conflicting ideologies are increasingly evident in the debate about how to educate urban students.

What approach do you subscribe to? Can you find research that supports your view? A great source of information is Jeanne Chall's *The Academic Achievement Challenge* (see the recommended readings at the end of the chapter). Chall's book describes the problems inherent in poor student performance and recommends approaches similar to those promoted in culturally responsive teaching. She argues for a highly teacher-centered approach. Find research that supports the culturally responsive, student-centered approach and compare what you discover with what Chall concludes. How do the types of students you teach potentially influence how you teach?

One way to begin to address this question is to examine the literature of two groups of educational writers. The first includes those who argue for culturally responsive teaching. For example, Gloria Ladson-Billings, in her book *The Dreamkeepers* (see the recommended readings at the end of the chapter), identifies specific characteristics of teachers who know how to deal with diverse student populations in classrooms. They see their role as one of "pulling knowledge out" of students rather than "pouring it in." In the second group, many conservative educational critics see culturally responsive teaching as a new form of student-centered instruction. Read articles from journals or newspapers such as *Education Next* to familiarize yourself with these critics' arguments. They assert that the limited skills of poor, urban students demand a more teacher-centered approach, and they claim that the evidence on student achievement backs them up.

Courses of Study

A long-range teacher guide is usually called a **course of study** or curriculum guide. In large school districts it is often prepared by a committee of experts. In small school districts the teachers, working as a group or as individuals, may develop their own, within limits defined by state guidelines or academic content standards. As a teacher plans, he or she must consider (1) needs-assessment data, if available, for the school or district; (2) the goals of the school (or school district); (3) pre-assessment or placement evaluation data of the students, such as reading tests, aptitude tests, self-report inventories, and observational reports; and (4) instructional objectives of the course of study according to district or state guidelines and grade-level or departmental publications.[17]

The course of study details the content, concepts, skills, and sometimes values to be taught for the entire course. Ideally, a prescriptive course of study places the teacher in a better position to do unit and lesson planning. The document helps guide and connect the goals and objectives of the course. It helps teachers view the course as a whole and to see existing relationships. The teacher must know, before the term or school year begins, what the important content areas, concepts, and skills of the course are. Some states require school districts to have courses of study, so you will need to see if one is available for the area you teach. In general, the course of study provides a total view of the entire term's or year's work without specifying sequences or relationships of tasks.

Unit Plans

A **unit plan** is a blueprint to clarify what content will be taught, by what learning experiences, during a specific period of time. It incorporates goals and objectives from the course of study. One reason for developing unit plans is the theory that learning by wholes is more effective than piece-by-piece learning; units help learners see and make conceptual connections. Another is the need for teachers to plan experiences in advance to meet different kinds of objectives. Advance planning at the unit-plan level enables teachers to be more effective in designing and structuring the instructional process. The overall view such planning provides can help teachers anticipate problems that may arise, especially in terms of prerequisite content, concepts, and skills.

Components of the Unit Plan.   The number of components in a unit plan may vary, depending on the lesson. The six basic components in the most typical lesson plans are objectives, content, skills, learning activities, resources and materials, and assessment and evaluation (see box 3.2). All should be considered when planning a unit, although in many cases all six components do not have to be specified.

Objectives.   As was discussed in the previous chapter, objectives can be behavioral (e.g., given five fractions or decimal problems the student will be able to complete each pattern to 70 percent accuracy) or nonbehavioral (topics, problems, questions). Most teachers today rely on behavioral objectives partly because of recent emphasis on them in the professional literature. The method one uses as the core of a plan will depend on one's approach and the school's approach to planning units.

Content.   The scope of the content should be outlined. The content often includes two major categories: knowledge and cognitive processes. The development of factual and procedural knowledge is usually more important at the elementary school level and with teachers who emphasize mastery learning, although types of knowledge are being emphasized by more educators at all levels because of high-stakes testing. Abstract knowledge is more important at the secondary school level

Box 3.2   Unit Plan Components

1. Objectives
General objectives and specific objectives
Behavioral objectives or nonbehavioral objectives (topics, problems, questions)

2. Content
Knowledge (factual, conceptual, procedural)
Cognitive processes (remember, understand . . .)

3. Skills
Work habits
Discussion and specific communication skills
Reading skills
Writing skills
Note-taking skills
Dictionary skills
Reference skills (table of contents, glossary, index, card catalog)
Library skills
Reporting and research skills
Computer skills
Interpreting skills (maps, charts, tables, graphs, legends)
Inquiry skills (problem solving, experimenting, hypothesizing)
Social skills (respecting rules, accepting criticism, poise and maturity, peer acceptance)
Cooperative and competitive skills (leadership, self-concept, participation in group)

4. Learning activities
Lectures and explanations
Practice and drill
Grouping activities (buzz sessions, panels, debates, forums)
Role-playing, simulations, dramatizations
Research, writing projects (stories, biographies, logs)
Experiments, inquiry, and discovery
Field trips
Reviews

5. Resources and materials
Written materials (books, pamphlets, magazines, newspapers)
Audiovisual materials (films, records, slides, television, videotapes)
Programmed or computer materials
Models, replicas, charts, graphs, specimens

6. Assessment and evaluation
Demonstrations, exhibits, debates
Reviews, summaries
Quizzes, examinations
Reteaching
Remediation
Exhibitions

and with teachers who emphasize conceptual understandings. Teachers use the district's course of study and national or state standards to determine what knowledge and which cognitive processes to teach, including the sequence of the lessons.

Skills.   Some teachers create what is often an optional list of cognitive and social skills. The skills should be based on the content to be taught but are sometimes listed separately from the content. Important skills to develop include critical thinking, critical reading, skimming and scanning, problem solving, reading graphic materials (maps, diagrams, charts, tables), library skills, composition and reporting skills, note-taking skills, homework skills, study skills, social and interpersonal skills, discussion and speaking skills, cooperative and competitive skills, and leadership skills.

Learning activities.   Sometimes called student activities, learning activities should be based on students' needs and interests. Only special activities, such as guest speakers, field trips, debates and buzz sessions, research reports, projects, experiments, and summative examinations, need be listed. The recurring or common activities can be shown as part of the daily lesson plan.

Resources and materials.   The purpose of including resources and materials in the plan is to guide the teacher in assembling the reading material, library and research materials, and audiovisual equipment needed to carry out instruction. At the unit plan level this list should include only essential resources and materials. (Resources are often included in a list of learning activities and so are sometimes considered an optional element in a unit plan.) A wealth of online lesson plans, units, and other resources exist that can be utilized as well. For example, the Educators Reference Desk website provides a variety of ways to use the Internet as part of lesson planning (http://ericir.syr.edu/Virtual/Lessons/).

Assessment and evaluation procedures.   The major evaluation procedures and culminating activities, both formative and summative, should be included. Plans might list student exhibits and demonstrations, debates and discussions, quizzes and examinations, reteaching, remedial work, and special tutoring or training. Evaluation can be conducted by students or the teacher or both. The intent is to appraise whether the objectives have been achieved and to obtain information for improving the unit plan. See Tips for Teachers 3.1 for some suggestions for organizing and implementing unit plans.

Approaches to Unit Planning.   Teachers should check with supervisors before planning a unit. Some school districts have a preferred approach for developing units, and others permit more latitude for their teachers. For example, some supervisors require teachers to submit units for final approval, while other supervisors give more professional autonomy to teachers. What follows are basic approaches to unit planning that you may wish to consider. Regardless of the approach you use, it is imperative to consider depth over breadth when developing unit plans. Good teachers cover material but provide more opportunities for students to learn specific content material. Reform advocates in education such as E. D. Hirsch, Jr., reinforce this focus on specificity and depth:

There is another inherent shortcoming in the overreliance on large-scale abstract objectives (as opposed to "mere" content) as a means of determining a curriculum. These general objectives do not compel either a definite or a coherent sequence of instruction. That is because the large conceptual scheme and its concrete expressions (through particular contents) have a very tenuous and uncertain relationship to each other. A big scheme is just too general to guide the teacher in the selection of particulars. For instance, one multi-

---

TIPS

F O R

T E A C H E R S

3.1

Organizing and Implementing Unit Plans

As you prepare your unit and lesson plans, you should be aware of some common mistakes and how to minimize them by utilizing the following practical guidelines. This list of suggestions applies to all levels of unit planning and can be adapted to accommodate your school's requirements as well as your teaching style and instructional approach.

1. Ask your principal or supervisor for the standards and curriculum guides (or the course of study) pertaining to your subject and grade level.

2. Check the instructor's manual of the textbook or workbook if you are using one; many have excellent examples of unit plans, and many relate content to broader sets of disciplinary standards.

3. Consider vertical (different grades, same subject) and horizontal (same grade, different subjects) relationships of subject matter in formulating your unit plans. Be sure you understand the relationship between new information and prior knowledge.

4. Consider students' abilities, needs, and interests.

5. Decide on objectives and related content for the various units of the subject.

6. After objectives and content have been established, sequence the units.

7. Determine the order of the content by considering the cognitive processes (remembering, applying) and affective processes (attitudes, feelings, values) involved. You can use developmental theories, mastery learning, or task analysis to determine the order of the units.

8. Consider appropriate time allocation for each unit. Most units will take one to three weeks to complete.

9. Investigate resource materials and media available in your district and school; incorporate appropriate materials and media.

10. Provide opportunities for student practice and review.

11. Provide opportunities for evaluation (not necessarily testing or marks in early grades). Consider also what types of exhibitions might be appropriate.

12. Ask your colleagues or supervisor for feedback after you implement your unit plan. Discuss questions, problems, and proposed modifications.

13. Rewrite or at least modify your unit plan whenever you teach the same subject and grade level. The world changes, classes change, and students differ.

14. Be patient. Do not expect immediate results. Practice won't make you perfect, but it will make you a better teacher.

grade science objective in our superior local districts states, "Understand interactions of matter and energy." This is operationally equivalent to saying, "Understand physics, chemistry, and biology." The teachers who must decide what to include under such "objectives" are given little practical help.[18]

Taxonomic approach.   Table 3.2 illustrates a unit plan based on the taxonomy of educational objectives. The objectives are divided into three domains of learning: cognitive processes, attitudes and values, and psychomotor skills. The

Table 3.2   Unit Plan: Taxonomic Approach for Environmental Science

Problems	Cognitive Processes	Attitudes and Values
1. Identifying an environment	To identify environments based on physical and biological characteristics	To explore social and scientific issues; to ask questions
2. Comparing environments	To understand different environments	To discuss alternative viewpoints; to debate responsibility for health and welfare of others
3. Taking a field trip to compare environments	To analyze environments based on physical and biological characteristics	To formulate new ideas about natural resources
4. Experiencing other ways to compare environments	To evaluate environments based on physical and biological characteristics	To ask questions; to compare alternative viewpoints
5. Summarizing differences between environments	To evaluate different environments	To discuss balance and theorize ideas
6. Exploring the limits of environmental change	To deduce that environments change and still conserve their identity and that they lose identity when their capacity to change is exceeded	To ask questions; to define limits of biological and environmental systems
7. Understanding the consequences of changing environment	To appraise the results of changing environments	To seek alternative viewpoints; to revise ideas
8. Implementing a plan to improve the school environment	To recognize how to create environments that change and improve	To demonstrate responsibility for health and welfare of others
9. Surveying world environments that have changed	To detect how world environments have changed and assumed new identities	To demonstrate the need to use natural resources wisely; to organize a plan that contributes to the conservation of natural resources
10. Summarizing and evaluating	To remember facts, concepts, and principles	To argue, appraise, and judge in terms of scientific standards

Source: Adapted from Rita Peterson et al., *Science and Society: A Source Book for Elementary and Junior-High Science Teachers* (Columbus, OH: Merrill, 1984), 166–167.

unit plan provides a daily problem that leads to the objectives and shows corresponding activities, materials, and resources. Evaluation is not listed separately but is blended as part of the activities suggested for the ninth and tenth daily problem lessons. The approach requires that students use different cognitive processes to learn fully requisite content.

Topic or theme approach.   Box 3.3 illustrates this approach. The unit plan is organized by topics. Objectives introduce the lesson, but the topics serve as the

Psychomotor Skills	Learning Activities	Resources and Materials
	Class discussion	Video, Internet
To use tools that call for fine adjustment and discrimination	Debates	Pictures, replicas, models
To visualize different environments; to listen to tour guides present relevant information	Field trip to museum	Tape recorder
To manipulate laboratory equipment	Experiment (see text)	Plants, rocks, soil
	Class discussion	Visiting expert
To handle plants, rocks, soil	Class discussion	Graphs and maps showing weather, volcanoes, mountains
To use equipment that requires fine adjustments	Student interviews	"Old-timers" in community, old newspapers
To use and care for tools and equipment	Brainstorming sessions	Visiting administrator
	Oral reports judged by students	Technical journals, library materials
	Unit examination	

Box 3.3   Unit Plan: Topic Approach for American History

Objectives

I. Knowledge

   A. To recognize that the US Constitution is rooted in English law
   B. To identify the causes and events leading to the forming of the US Constitution
   C. To argue the advantages and limitations of the US Constitution
   D. To illustrate how amendments are enacted

II. Skills

   A. To expand vocabulary proficiency
   B. To improve research skills
   C. To improve oral reporting skills
   D. To expand reading habits to include historical events and people
   E. To develop debating techniques

III. Values

   A. To develop an understanding that freedom is based on laws
   B. To recognize the obligations of freedom (among free people)
   C. To appreciate how rights are protected
   D. To develop a more positive attitude toward minorities
   E. To develop a more positive attitude toward classmates

IV. Topics

   A. Historical background of the Constitution
      1. English common law
      2. Magna Carta
      3. Mayflower Compact
      4. Colonial freedom
      5. Taxation without representation
      6. Boston Tea Party
      7. First and second Constitutional Congress
      8. Declaration of Independence
      9. Age of Enlightenment and America
   B. Bill of Rights and the Constitution
      1. Constitutional Convention
      2. Framing of the Constitution
      3. Bill of Rights
         a. Reasons
         b. Specific freedoms
      4. Powers reserved to the states

5. Important amendments
   a. Thirteenth, Fourteenth, Fifteenth (slavery, due process, voting rights)
   b. Nineteenth (women's suffrage)
   c. Twentieth (progressive tax)
   d. Twenty-second (two-term limit to presidency)
   e. Others

V. Evaluation

A. Short quiz for IV.A. 1–9
B. Graded reports with specific feedback for each student
C. Discussion of students' roles as citizens in a free society; comparison of rights and responsibilities of American citizens with rights and responsibilities of students
D. Unit test; review IV.A. 1–9; IV.B. 1–5

VI. Activities

A. (Selected video) introducing part I
B. List of major points to be discussed in part I
C. Homework—reading list for each topic or lesson (IV.A. 1–9; IV.B. 1–5)
D. Television program on "American Freedom" and discussion after IV.A. 9
E. Field trip to historical museum as culminating activity for I and introduction to II
F. Topics and reports for outside reading, with two-day discussion of reports after II.C
G. Two-day debate (with four teams): "What's wrong with our Constitution?" "What's right with our Constitution?" after II.E
H. Internet search of selected websites on teacher approved historical topic.

major basis for outlining the unit and especially the lessons. The objectives coincide with the recommendation that content focus on concepts, skills, and values. Note that the objectives (related to knowledge, skills, and values) do not build upon one another (they are somewhat independent), nor are they divided into the general and the specific. The topics are arranged in the order in which they will be treated, suggesting that they correspond to the table of contents of a textbook. Indeed, it is appropriate to follow a text, as long as it is well planned and the teacher knows when to modify or supplement the text with related activities and materials.

The topics also represent daily lesson plans. The activities listed are nonrecurring, special activities; repeated activities can be listed at the lesson plan level. The activities are listed in the order in which they will occur, but there is not one particular activity listed for each topic (as in table 3.2). The evaluation component is separate and includes formative and summative tests, discussion, and feedback. Most secondary school teachers rely on the topic approach to unit planning, since they are subject or content oriented.

There is no right way to plan, although one method may better foster the types of learner outcomes that you desire. If you plan on using a taxonomic approach, you will likely be more oriented toward the explicit standards for your teaching area. What is prescribed? What is the sequence for the prescribed content? In contrast, the topic approach identifies areas to be covered, along with specific knowledge skills and attitudes for students to learn. If you use a topic approach, you might find it useful to review work by Howard Gardner on multiple intelligences and on a theme approach that he describes as "entry points" to learning. Gardner describes five such entry points:

1. *Narrational.* Presenting a strong narrative about the topic or concept in question

2. *Logical—quantitative.* Using numbers or deductive/scientific approaches to the topic or question

3. *Foundational.* Examining the philosophy and vocabulary that undergird the topic or concept

4. *Aesthetic.* Focusing on the sensory features of the topic or concept

5. *Experiential.* Using a hands-on approach where the student deals directly with materials that represent the topic or concept[19]

One advantage of Gardner's theme approach to unit planning is that it allows students to relate to content material in a more direct sense. The entry points foster curriculum relevance and also may coincide with what we know about how the brain works and processes ideas. Brain researchers argue for using knowledge meaningfully, and that's precisely what Gardner's entry points approach accomplishes.

Guidelines for developing unit plans. The number of units as well as the time allotted and emphasis for each unit are matters of judgment, although school practitioners tend to recommend about fifteen to thirty units for a year's course and about five to ten lessons per unit. Consideration is usually given to the organization of the textbook; the emphasis suggested by state and school district curriculum guides; and the special abilities, needs, and interests of the students. Increasingly, teachers tend to plan units around national, state, and school district testing programs.[20]

We've already examined the basic components of the unit plan. Now let's consider suggestions for addressing some of the details. These suggestions are applicable for all subjects and grade levels.

1. Develop the unit plan with a particular class and group of students in mind.

2. Indicate the subject, grade level, and length of time to teach the unit.

3. Outline the unit around a general theme or idea (the unit title).

4. Identify the relevant standards on which your unit will be based.

5. Identify the general objectives, problems, or topics of the unit. Each objective, problem, or topic should correspond to a specific lesson plan (discussed in the next section), and each should be tied directly or indirectly to an academic content standard.

6. Include one or more of the following: (a) content and activities, (b) cognitive processes and skills, (c) psychomotor skills, and (d) attitudes and values.

7. Identify methods for assessing and evaluating the outcomes of the unit. Possibly include a pretest and posttest to determine learning outcomes or improvement in learning.

8. Include the resources (materials and media) needed to supplement the text.

9. Plan an effective way of introducing the unit, possibly through an overview exercise, problem, or recent event.

10. Design parts of the unit for different types of learners (some hands-on activities, some inquiry strategies).

11. Develop the unit to include the life experiences of the students, or out-of-school activities such as field trips or work in the library or community.

Lesson Plans

A **lesson plan**, sometimes referred to as a *daily plan*, sets forth the instructional activities for each day. In general, the lesson plan should be planned around the fixed periods (usually thirty-five to fifty minutes) of the typical school schedule, allowing adequate time for teachers or students to arrive (if they are changing classrooms) and to leave at the end of the period. Shorter blocks of time may be planned for younger students or for those whose attention spans are limited. Longer time periods may be evidenced in high schools that have *block scheduling* (schools that schedule students into class, for example, every other day for longer time periods on each day they do meet). Good timing or scheduling is an aid to good instruction and good classroom management.

Although special school activities may require shortened or lengthened periods, most lessons should be planned for full periods. Sometimes students need more or less time than planned to finish an activity or assignment, and teachers need to learn how to be flexible in adjusting timing. As teachers develop their planning and pacing skills, they learn to plan better schedules in advance and to plan supplementary activities and materials for use as the need arises. Supplementary activities might include performing a committee function, completing a research assignment, finishing a workbook assignment, illustrating a composition or report, working on a study activity, performing an honor or extra credit assignment, or tutoring another student. Supplementary materials might include pictures, charts, and models to further demonstrate a major point in the lesson; review exercises for practice and drill; or a list of summary questions to review major points of the lesson.

To avoid omissions or an over- or underemphasis on a particular topic, the teacher needs to consider his or her style of teaching and the students' abilities and interests. The teacher should review the progress of each day's lesson and periodically take notes on important student responses to different methods, media, and activities—to apply with another class or at another time. Inexperienced teachers need to plan the lessons in detail, follow the plan, and refer to it frequently. As they grow in experience and confidence, they become able to plan with less detail and increasingly rely on their spontaneous responses to what happens in the classroom as the teaching–learning process unfolds (see Classic Professional Viewpoint 3.1).

| classic professional viewpoint **3.1** | **Lesson Plans and the Professional** |

Albert Shanker

Should teachers be required to prepare lockstep lesson plans? Of course, teachers need to plan, and most of them do. But does each teacher have to do the same amount of planning and use the same format? Do all the plans have to be inspected on the same morning? Do some teachers plan better in their heads than on paper? More important, what are the plans for? They are supposed to help teachers focus and improve their instruction. But now, in many schools, teachers are not given a satisfactory rating, no matter how good they are as teachers, unless they have complied with the ritualistic planbook requirements. This is clearly a case of management incompetence. Would anybody rate Pavarotti a poor opera singer because he fails to fill out bureaucratic forms telling management how he intends to approach each aria?

This reminds me of the morning many years ago when I appeared for the examination to become a New York City public school teacher. After we had assembled in the school cafeteria, someone appeared, blew a whistle, and ordered us to form a double line. We were then marched down a hall and told to form a single line to move to various classrooms in which we would take the test. Throughout this march, we continued to receive instructions. "Keep in single file." "Hurry up." "No talking." It was clear from the start that we were back in school. Even though we had gone to college and received our degrees, we were being treated very much like children again!

Rigid requirements for lesson plans are like that. They treat educated adults, veteran teachers among them, like children, requiring them to jump to a whistle and "keep in single file." Even after we have solved the problem of providing adequate financial rewards, we are not going to get good teachers or keep them so long as school management values blind obedience to authority above creativity and excellence.

Professionalism for teachers will come only through hard work. This means not only questioning outmoded practices but also offering better alternatives that serve the interest of student success rather than bureaucratic convenience.

Lesson Plans by Authorities.   Many current authorities who write about what a lesson plan should contain do so from the point of view of *direct instructional methods*—that is, a view of the classroom in which teaching is teacher directed, methods and materials are sequenced, content is extensive and focused, students are provided with practice as the teacher checks or monitors the work, and the teacher provides evaluation of performance. The objectives are clearly stated in the beginning of the lesson, and a review either precedes or follows the statement of objectives. Learning takes place in an academic, teacher-centered environment. There is little mention of or concern about student needs or interests; emphasis is on student achievement.

All three authors whose methods are synopsized in table 3.3 exhibit this direct, step-by-step approach to learning. The categories or components are lined up within the table to show similarities among approaches. All lesson plan components and classroom events are controlled by the teacher, little provision

Table 3.3   Lesson Plan Components by Authorities

Mastery Learning (Hunter)	Instructional Design (Gagne)	Instruction Behaviors (Good and Grouws, Good and Brophy)
1. *Review:* Focus on previous lesson; ask students to review questions orally or in writing; ask students to summarize main points.	1. *Gain attention:* Alert students to what to expect; get students started on a routine or warm-up drill.	1. *Review:* Review concepts and skills related to homework; provide review exercises.
2. *Anticipatory set:* Focus students' attention on lesson to be presented; stimulate interest in new material.	2. *Inform learners of objective:* Activate the learners' motivation by informing them of the objective to be achieved.	2. *Development:* Promote student understanding of new material; provide examples, explanations, demonstrations.
3. *Objective:* State explicitly what will be learned; state rationale or how it will be useful.	3. *Recall prior knowledge:* Remind students of previously learned knowledge or concepts germane to new material; recall relevant prerequisites.	3. *Assess student comprehension:* Ask questions; provide controlled practice.
4. *Input:* Identify needed knowledge and skills for learning new lesson; present material in logical and sequenced steps.	4. *Present the stimulus material:* Present new knowledge or skills; indicate distinctive properties of the concepts to be learned.	4. *Seat work:* Provide uninterrupted seat work; get everyone involved; sustain momentum.
5. *Modeling:* Provide several demonstrations throughout the lesson.	5. *Provide learning guidance:* Elaborate on directions, provide assistance; integrate new information with previous (long-term memory) information.	5. *Accountability:* Check the students' work.
6. *Check for understanding:* Monitor students' work before they become involved in lesson activities; check to see they understand the directions or tasks.	6. *Elicit performance:* Suggest, do not specify, methods for performing tasks or problems; provide cues or directions, not answers (students are to provide answers).	6. *Homework:* Assign homework regularly; provide review problems.
7. *Guided practice:* Periodically ask students questions or pose problems and check answers. The same type of monitoring and response formats are involved in checking for understanding as in guided practice.	7. *Provide feedback:* Reinforce learning by checking students' work and providing frequent feedback, especially during the acquisition stage of the new material. Use feedback to adapt instruction to individual students.	7. *Special reviews:* Provide weekly reviews (exercises, quizzes) each Monday to enhance and maintain learning; provide monthly reviews every fourth Monday to further enhance and maintain learning.
8. *Independent practice:* Assign independent practice or work when it is reasonably certain that students can work on their own with minimal effort.	8. *Assess performance:* Inform students of their performance in terms of outcomes; establish an "expectancy" level.	
	9. *Ensure retention and transfer:* Utilize various instructional techniques to ensure retention (outline; classify information; use tables, charts, and diagrams). Enhance transfer of learning by providing a variety of cues, practice situations, and interlinking concepts.	

Source: Allan C. Ornstein, *Secondary and Middle School Teaching Methods,* 3rd ed. (Boston: Allyn & Bacon), 141. Copyright © 1992 by Pearson Education. Reprinted by permission of the publisher.

is made for student choice or planning, and the classroom is highly structured and businesslike. Most important, the emphasis is on knowledge, skills, and tasks as well as practice, review, and testing. Very few, if any, of the prescriptions seem directed to problem solving, critical thinking, or creativity, much less personal, social, or moral development.

Although the authorities listed in the table might not admit it or agree, their approaches apply mainly to teaching basic skills and discrete processes (i.e., how to do something in a step-by-step fashion) in basic subjects such as reading, mathematics, and foreign language, where practice and drill are often recommended. They are not as effective, if they can be used at all, in teaching inquiry or discovery learning or creative thinking. Nevertheless, since the explicit approaches do receive much attention in the professional literature and since they are applicable in more than one teaching area, they should be considered. Later we present a less direct, constructivist approach that provides teachers with greater flexibility in teaching.

There are other types of lesson plan "authorities" as well—authorities that include other practicing teachers. Their efforts and ideas can be accessed online, for example, at the Marco Polo website (marcopolo.worldcom.com). Such sites provide free lessons and list the resources you will need to teach the lesson. Many of the practicing teachers we know rely heavily on the Marco Polo site as a resource for ideas. Websites of this type enable teachers to share with other teachers how to identify resources and materials that they can use to help build student understanding and to relate them to national and state standards.

Writing a Traditional Lesson Plan.   In the planning process, teachers think in terms of daily lesson plans that are usually confined to set periods of time depending upon the grade level. The most basic approach to writing a traditional lesson plan we have found is contained in the mnemonic AMMCASH. It recapitulates the areas that lesson plans usually address in one form or another: aim, motivation (including materials), content, application (practice or procedure), summary, and homework. These elements might be easier to understand if viewed from the perspective of a theatrical play. The play's purpose and mood are represented by a lesson's aims and motivations. The message of the play becomes its content, while the staging and props take the form of a lesson's material. The script is essentially the applications, procedures, and pivotal questions, while the critique or critics' review is the evaluation and summary. It is common knowledge that performers rarely write their own scripts and plays, but teachers always do.

Regardless of the terms used for traditional planning, the procedure in essence is the same. The mnemonic AMMCASH (box 3.4) provides an effortless and straightforward way to remember how to write traditional lesson plans. Each of the components in AMMCASH adds to the substance of a lesson plan. In most cases, a lesson would not be considered complete if one step in the process was discarded. This is not to say that AMMCASH is the only model for lesson planning. There is no one right way to write a lesson plan; this is just one of the most concise.

Box 3.4   AMMCASH

Aims are the spotlight for a lesson. They should be the focus of attention and aligned with specific standards. They act as a guide to focus learning in clear and unambiguous language. Aims must be achievable within the parameters and available resources at hand.

Motivations establish a purpose for learning that tells the student "what's in it for me." Reasons for learning must go beyond a simple reward, punishment, or grade. Motivation is either extrinsic (outside) or intrinsic (directly related to the topic).

Materials are the ingredients, resources, or substances that make up the lesson. A geography lesson would need a map as an art lesson needs paints. List the technology, handouts, chart paper, text resources (and so on) needed to complete the lesson.

Content is the body of the lesson; it describes the major ideas and concepts you expect to communicate. It is what you are teaching and what students are expected to learn. Align the content area with the standard number or key components applicable for the lesson.

Application or Procedures can best be described as how to teach what you expect students to learn. The steps can be seen as a set of directions or instructions that guide in the presentation of the lesson. Enumerate the procedure you expect to follow to teach the lesson to students.

Summary is where content presented is summarized to assess comprehension. Simply ask students what they have learned so far or ask them to write a statement on what was learned to be shared with classmates. Or just lead a question-and-answer session on what was presented during the lesson.

Homework is the cement that "seals in" learning if prepared and presented properly. The purposes of homework are to reinforce, concretize, and extend the concepts and ideas presented in class lessons. It can also be used to prepare for sequential lessons.

Source: Adapted from Richard T. Scarpaci, *Resource Methods for Managing K–12 Instruction: A Case Study Approach* (New York: Pearson Education, 2009).

In addition, online lesson-building sites are now available to teachers, such as TaskStream or the Educators Reference desk (http://www.eduref.org/Virtual/Lessons/Guide.shtml). Through such websites the components of the lesson plan can be customized based on user needs. National and state standards are built into these sites, and the user simply scrolls through the appropriate standards list in order to "pick and clip" selected objectives that are to be taught in lessons for a particular group of students and that meet the goals of a particular school. (See Case Study 3.1 to understand the reasons for writing lesson plans.)

The following case study emphasizes the importance of understanding proper lesson design as a necessity to effective teaching skills. Read the case and decide if formal lesson planning is truly necessary.

Case Study 3.1
Are Standards-Based Lesson Plans Necessary?

Joe Quinlan entered the teacher's lounge in a huff. Joe was a tall man who weighed in excess of 250 pounds. He usually prided himself on his appearance and fancied himself a model of middle-class fashion;—a man for all seasons, as he put it. Maureen Major, Joe's friend and professional confidante, offered a cheery hello, but Joe just shrugged and looked agitated and distracted. He seemed fatigued, washed out, and worn down. Joe finally said, "I feel terrible! Dr. Scase embarrassed me in front of my class by asking to see my lesson plans. I tried to explain that I didn't need to write formal plans because I always knew what I was going to teach. He asked if I were some kind of sage—or, as he put it, a fount of wisdom—that I didn't need plans. For all practical purposes he reprimanded me in front of my class for not having formal lesson plans." Maureen reminded Ed that the school policy was for every teacher to keep a set of plans for the week in the middle drawer of his or her desk. "No wonder the principal was mad," said Maureen. "Aside from that, the plans are also supposed to be standards based."

"Maureen," said Joe exasperatedly, "The problem with standards-based lesson planning is that there are no precise directions on how they should be written. I don't even know what a standard looks like, let alone how to achieve one."

Maureen looked reprovingly at Joe. "So you lied to Dr. Scase! It's not that you keep your plans in your head—you just don't know how to plan." Joe looked sheepishly at Maureen and said, "I guess you could say that."

"OK, Joe, let me make a suggestion," said Maureen, opening a book and showing it to Joe. "Why don't you just follow this guide I got from the *Standards-Based Classroom Operators Manual*? Look, it says right here in the preface that it consists of eight sequenced steps in a design process that includes planning, delivery, and evaluation of instruction. It begins with understanding content standards, followed by preparing an activity for a specific performance level while designing the curriculum and how to present it. Then you teach the lesson, assess the students, evaluate, and refine the whole process. That's what standards-based planning should look like. You know, Joe, there's a whole school of thought claiming that if you don't properly plan you'll be an ineffective teacher," she said, smiling to soften the criticism.

Bill Judge, a friend of both Joe and Maureen, said, "Since we all have to do this, why don't we just use the five Standard Achievement Planning Cycle steps; identify standards, analyze standards, describe the student performance, select learning activities, and evaluate student work. I think this process is easier."

Maureen said, "Most lessons have a beginning, middle, and an ending. What you've got to do is have a vision of what you want your students to know, and how to get them to understand. The key to good lesson design is in writing clear objectives so you know what you're looking to achieve. I use an acronym called SMART to guide me in writing performance objectives." (See box 2.7.)

Joe told Bill and Maureen "Thanks, but no thanks," saying he still didn't believe formal standards-based lesson plans were necessary. "I still like my own simple formula: I ask the students what they need to learn. Of course they have to complete the readings I assign from their text. This way I cover everything and don't have to write a plan. The authors of the text I use wrote everything for me. You could say I use a constructivist design by allowing my students to construct their own knowledge. My role as a teacher is not to write plans and instruct, it's to foster student learning."

Discussion Topics and Questions to Ponder

1. Describe the argument supporting the writing of lesson plans. Should they be written only because of school policy? Explain your reasoning.

2. Was Dr. Scase justified in reprimanding Joe in front of his class? How should the situation have been handled?

3. Compare Maureen's ideas on lesson design with Bill's. Explain how they are compatible.

4. Compare and contrast the various lesson designs discussed in the case study. Which would you choose? Justify your answer.

5. How would you respond to Joe's final statements?

What would you do if . . . ?

1. Dr. Scase said Joe's ideas regarding constructivism were confused. Can you explain why?

2. Dr. Scase asked you to write a policy all could agree to.

3. You put yourself in Maureen's place. Can you convince Joe that his method is faulty?

Aims or objectives.   The first questions a teacher considers when sorting out the content he or she plans to teach are, "What do I plan to teach?" and "What do I want the students to learn from the lesson that will be worthwhile?" The answers to these questions are the aims, also called objectives; they form the backbone of the lesson. Motivation, methods, and materials are organized to achieve the objectives. Establishing objectives eliminates aimlessness and focuses teaching and learning.

Objectives may be phrased as statements or questions. (Most people think they can only be written as statements.) The question form encourages students to think. Regardless of how they are phrased, they should be written on the chalkboard or distributed as a printed handout for students to see, or they should be stated at some point during the lesson. Here are some examples of general objectives for a lesson plan, written first as statements and then as questions:

Statement: To compare the prices of agricultural goods and industrial goods during the Depression

Question: Why did the prices of agricultural goods decline more than the prices of industrial goods during the Depression?

Statement: To explain how the production of oil in the Middle East affects economic conditions in the United States

Question: How does the production of oil in the Middle East affect economic conditions in the United States?

Statement: To identify how the skin protects people from diseases
Question: How does our skin protect us from diseases?

The major objective of a lesson may have ancillary (secondary) objectives. Ancillary objectives divide the lesson into segments and highlight or supplement important ideas. Here is an example of a lesson objective with two ancillary objectives (expressed as statements and then questions):

1-a. *Lesson objective:* To explain the causes of World War I.

Ancillary objectives: To compare nationalism, colonialism, and militarism; to distinguish between propaganda and facts.

1-b. *Lesson objective:* What were the causes of World War I?

Ancillary objectives: How are nationalism, colonialism, and militarism related? How can we distinguish between propaganda and facts?

Motivation.   Motivational devices or activities arouse and maintain interest in the content to be taught. Fewer motivational devices are needed for students who are intrinsically motivated (that is, are motivated to learn to satisfy some inner need or interest) than for students who are extrinsically motivated (that is, require incentives or reinforcers for learning). Lesson planning and instruction typically rely on both forms of motivation, and motivation is often a major issue with some groups of students.

Intrinsic motivation involves sustaining or increasing the interest students already have in a topic or task. This is the best type of motivation because it starts with what the student wants to know. The teacher selects and organizes the lesson so that it will (a) whet students' appetites at the beginning of the lesson; (b) maintain student curiosity and involvement in the work by using surprise, doubt, or perplexity; novel as well as familiar materials; and interesting and varied methods; (c) provide active and manipulative opportunities; (d) permit student autonomy in organizing time and effort; and (e) provide choices or alternatives to meet requirements of the lesson. Some activities and materials that can be used to enhance intrinsic motivation are:

- *Challenging statements.* "Nuclear power plants are unnecessary and potentially dangerous."

- *Pictures and cartoons.* "How does this picture illustrate the American public's feelings about American-made automobiles?"

- *Personal experiences.* "What type of clothing is best to wear during freezing weather?" or "How does this content relate to you and your life?"

- *Problems.* "What metals conduct heat well? Why is this so?"

- *Exploratory and creative activities.* "I need three volunteers to come to the chalkboard to fill in the blanks of the puzzle while the rest of you do it in your seats."

- *Charts, tables, graphs, maps.* "From a study of the chart, what characteristics do all these animals have in common?"

- *Anecdotes and stories.* "How does the paragraph I have just read convey the author's feelings about the South?"

Extrinsic motivation, in contrast, focuses on behavioristic strategies. Activities that enhance success and reduce failure increase motivation. High-achieving students will persist longer than low-achieving students, even when experiencing failure, so incentives for learning are more important for average- and low-achieving students. They are important for all students when the subject matter or content is uninteresting or difficult,[21] but they must be used cautiously. The following principles can guide teachers in enhancing motivation through the use of both intrinsic and extrinsic approaches.

- *Provide clear directions.* Students must know exactly what they are expected to do and how they will be evaluated.

- *Ensure a cognitive match.* Student motivation is highest when students work on tasks or problems appropriate to their achievement levels. When they are confused or when the work is above their abilities, they resist or give up. When it is below their abilities, they seek other interests or move through the lesson as fast as possible.

- *Provide prompt feedback.* Feedback on student performance should be constructive and prompt. A long delay between behavior (or performance) and results diminishes the relationship between them.

- *Relate past learning with present learning.* Use reinforcers to strengthen previously learned content.

- *Provide frequent rewards.* No matter how powerful a reward, it may have little impact if it is provided infrequently. Small, frequent rewards are more effective than large, infrequent ones. Praise is a particularly powerful reward, especially if delivered to students in a natural voice, and for specific achievements.[22]

- *Hold high expectations.* Students who are expected to learn will learn more and be motivated to learn more than students who are not expected to learn.

- *Show instrumental value of what students learn.* Help students see how to use and apply what they are learning in the classroom.

One cautionary note: Limit the use of explicit extrinsic motivators such as rewards. Although they seem like an easy way to motivate, they are not always the best way. Indeed, there are some critics who suggest that extrinsics should never be used. Paul Chance takes a more moderate stance:

> Rewards reduce motivation when they are given without regard to performance or when the performance standard is so high that students frequently fail. When students have a high rate of success and when those successes are rewarded, the rewards *do not have negative effects.* Indeed, success-contingent rewards tend to increase interest in the activity. . . .
>
> The evidence, then, shows that extrinsic rewards can either enhance or reduce interest in an activity, depending on how they are used. Still, it might be argued that, because extrinsic rewards *sometimes* cause problems, we might be wise to avoid their use altogether. The decision not to use extrinsic rewards amounts to a decision to rely on alternatives. What are those alternatives? And are they better than extrinsic rewards?[23]

Content or development.   The **development**, sometimes called the *outline,* can be expressed as topics and subtopics, a series of broad or pivotal questions, or a list of activities (methods and materials). Most secondary teachers use topics or questions, and most elementary teachers use activities to try to foster student engagement with content.

Emphasis on topics, concepts, or skills indicates a content orientation in teaching approach. Emphasis on activities has a more sociopsychological orientation; there is more stress on student needs and interests. For example, outlining the problems of the ozone layer on the chalkboard is content oriented, while interviewing someone about the ozone layer is an activity that encompasses a wide range of social stimuli.

Several criteria have been proposed for selecting and organizing appropriate content and experiences in the development section. The following criteria for content were developed by Ornstein and Hunkins:[24]

1. *Validity.* The content selected should be verifiable and standards based.

2. *Significance.* The content must be constantly reviewed so that worthwhile content—basic ideas, information, principles of the subject—is taught, and lessons do not become cluttered by the masses of more trivial content now available through the "information explosion."

3. *Balance.* The content should promote macro- and micro-knowledge; students should experience the broad sweep of content, and they should have the opportunity to dig deep.

4. *Self-sufficiency.* The content should help students learn how to learn; it should help them gain maximum sufficiency in the most economic manner.

5. *Interest.* Content is best learned when it is interesting to the student. Some progressive educators urge that the student should be the focus of the teaching and learning process. What are the students' interests?

6. *Utility.* The content should be useful or practical in some situation outside the lesson, either to further other learning or in everyday experiences. How *usefulness* is defined depends on whether a teacher is subject centered or student centered, but most teachers would agree that useful content enhances the human potential of the learner.

7. *Learnability.* It should be within the capacity of the students to learn the content. There should be a cognitive match between the students' aptitudes and the subject (and between their abilities and academic tasks).

8. *Feasibility.* There are limitations on what can be planned and taught. The teacher needs to consider the time needed, resources and materials available, curriculum guides, state and national tests, existing legislation, and the political climate of the community.

When considering how to develop a lesson, you should include the use of activities and approaches that ensure congruence with what you teach. If you want students to learn problem-solving techniques, you need to quite literally give them problems. Indeed, one of the first premises of what Murrell calls "African-centered pedagogy" is "that human cognition and intellectual development are socially and culturally situated in human activity."[25] Murrell then goes on to observe, "You cannot teach children cooperative behavior without situating them in the activity of cooperative behavior; you cannot teach systematic inquiry without doing systematic inquiry."[26]

Teaching Procedures: A Transmission View

Relying on the same methods day after day would be very boring. Different procedures sustain and enhance student motivation throughout the lesson. Many different procedures can be employed in a lesson. Four basic strategies for teaching specific concepts and discrete skills or processes are (1) lectures and explanations, (2) demonstrations and experiments, (3) questioning to check for understanding, and (4) practice and drill. The extent to which each of these strategies is used depends on the type of lesson as well as the students, subject, and grade level. At this juncture we'll consider the order in which they are used. Note that we begin with lectures/explanations (or teacher-centered content delivery), which Madeline Hunter might describe as *input* (see table 3.3), and we end with practice/drill, which is both guided by the teacher and performed independently once students exhibit mastery.

Lectures/Explanations.   Teachers are often required to give short lectures and explanations to emphasize an important point, to fill in content gaps in the workbook or textbook, or to elaborate on a specific content area. Lecture can be used in combination with a number of other teaching methods—for example, buzz groups, controlled discussion, brainstorming, debates, audiotapes—to enhance lessons and student learning. According to Donald Bligh, "The task facing new lecturers is to decide [on] and invent combinations suitable for their purposes."[27] The classroom teacher must keep this in mind as well. Short explanations may be embedded in the lesson without being noted in the plan. Keep in mind the 10–2 rule when lecturing: For every ten minutes of lecture, provide two minutes for students to process the content through the use of some type of summary.

In planning an explanation or short lecture, the following characteristics are important to consider.

- *Sequence of discourse.* The lesson should follow a planned sequence, with few diversions or tangential discussions. Explanations should be included at proper places to maintain the sequence of the lesson.

- *Fluency.* The teacher should speak in clear, concise, complete, grammatical sentences.

- *Visual aids.* Pictures, tables, charts, models, and computer graphics or videos can be used to enhance verbal explanations.

- *Vocabulary.* The teacher should use the students' normal vocabulary for effective explanations. Technical or new terms pertaining to the content should be introduced and clearly defined during the explanation.

- *Inclusion of elements.* The major ideas of the lesson should be elaborated with specific descriptions or examples.

- *Explicit explanations.* Causal and logical relationships should be made explicit.[28]

Ken Henson points out that a weakness of lecture as an instructional method is that it fails to consider the unique needs and interest of students. He criticizes

> . . . the effect it has on learners. . . . Interestingly, the lecture is favored by poorer students because it places less classroom responsibility on learners. Too often, the goal is to be able to recall information rather than to attempt to understand it. . . . It is a poor motivator for students.[29]

When teachers utilize the lecture method, they need to pay particular attention to extrinsic motivation, as discussed earlier in the chapter. Henson also cautions that difficult material should be introduced through each student's strongest "perceptual modality" (preferred learning style) and then reinforced through other modalities to ensure understanding.[30]

Demonstrations/Experiments.　These two characteristics play an important role in inductive inquiry. They are ideal for creative and discovery methods of learning, wherein the teacher and students approach the subject matter by collecting data, observing, measuring, identifying, and examining causal relationships. Young students and low-achieving students will need more instruction and feedback from the teacher. Older and high-achieving students will work more independently and participate more in demonstrations and experiments because they are better able to handle quantities of information, reorganize information into new forms, and transfer it to new learning situations.[31] The following recommendations ensure the effectiveness of the demonstration and experiment:

a. Plan and prepare for the demonstration (or experiment). Make certain that all materials needed are available when you begin. Practice the demonstration (if you are conducting it for the first time) before the lesson to see what problems may arise.

b. Present the demonstration in context with what students have already learned or as a stimulus for searching for new knowledge.

c. Make provisions for full participation of the students.

d. Maintain control over the materials or equipment to the extent that the students are unable to work on their own.

e. Pose both close-ended and open-ended questions according to students' capacity for deductive and inductive responses. ("What is happening to the object?" is a close-ended question; "What can you generalize from . . . ?" is open ended.)

f. Encourage students to ask questions as they arise.

g. Encourage students to make observations first and then to make inferences and generalizations. Encourage them to look for and express new information and insights.

h. Allocate sufficient time so that the demonstration can be completed, students can discuss what they have observed, students can reach conclusions and apply principles they have learned, students can take notes or write about the demonstration, and materials can be collected and stored.

When students are involved in experimentation and problem solving, it is important that they are not afraid to err in the process. Teachers should accept mistakes as part of the learning process. Risk taking should be supported and rewarded. Ken Henson further remarks,

> [I]f students are to become creators of knowledge, they must be empowered to take risks. [Teachers must] create classroom environments where students can hypothesize without fear of being ridiculed. In such classrooms students learn to view mistakes as doorsteps to success.[32]

Questioning.   Teachers should include questions to check for student understanding of the content being presented. Such questions should

- be simple and direct;
- be asked in an order that corresponds to the content of the lesson;
- build on each other (that is, be sequential);
- challenge students, yet not be above the level of the class;
- be framed, when possible, to meet the needs and interests of the students; and
- vary in difficulty and abstractness to encourage participation by different students.

Good questioning, according to Jerome Bruner, leads to higher modes of learning. We discuss this more fully in the section on constructivism. In asking questions that check for understanding of specific content, the teacher limits what content students explore. In answering a thought-provoking (higher-level) question, on the other hand, a high-achieving student explores content, analyzes parts of it, reformulates it, and decides on the best method to use for answering.[33] Thought-provoking questions usually ask how and why—not when, where, who, or what—unless introduced by a provocative comment. Questions that call for a yes-or-no answer or for a specific right answer do not promote discussion, nor do they stimulate critical thinking or problem-solving strategies.

Much research now exists on questioning and on the efficacy of different approaches. Box 3.5 lists James H. Stronge's synthesis of what we know about good questioning strategies used by teachers.

Practice/Drill.   It is generally agreed that students need practice exercises to help them transfer new information into long-term memory and integrate new with old learning. Practice problems may come from workbooks, textbooks, and teacher-made materials. Practice in the form of seat work can be helpful for students if it is given for limited time periods (no more than ten minutes per class session), the instructions for it are clear, and it is integrated into the lesson (not assigned to fill time or to maintain order). Drill can be helpful for basic skills, such as reading, mathematics, and language, and in lower grades and with low-achieving students who need more practice to learn new skills or integrate information; but even with these types of students some balance of teaching approaches is needed.[34]

A short practice/drill session provides a quick and efficient way for teachers to check on the effectiveness of instruction before moving to the next stage or level in the lesson. It is well suited for mastery and direct methods of lesson

> **Box 3.5   Good Questioning Strategies**
>
> • When questions receive responses—correct or incorrect—they are the most valuable, because responses encourage student engagement, demonstrate understanding or misconception, and encourage discussion.
>
> • Ideally, the level of difficulty and cognitive level of questions should reflect the context; the level of each question should reflect the type of content, the lesson's goals, and which students are involved, with sufficient variance of the type of question both within and across lessons to maintain interest and momentum.
>
> • Questions should be considered carefully and prepared in advance of a lesson to ensure that they reflect the goals, emphasize the key points, and are geared toward the achievement levels of the students.
>
> • Questions within a lesson are most effective when they are considered as a sequence, not as isolated units.
>
> • Longer wait times have been correlated to higher student achievement in several studies. Ideally, the amount of wait time should also be considered in terms of maintaining student engagement and lesson momentum.
>
> *Source:* Adapted from James H. Stronge, *Qualities of Effective Teachers*, 2nd ed. (Alexandria, VA: ASCD, 2007).

planning, and especially for low-achieving students.[35] Following are some drill techniques that can be used in lesson planning:

- Ask pupils to repeat answers.
- List facts or concepts to be remembered.
- Identify characteristics or attributes of the content.
- Review answers to questions.
- State answers in different ways.
- Have volunteers answer a number of questions and discuss answers.
- Give a short quiz and have students grade each other's papers.
- Assign exercises from the workbook or text.
- Monitor seat work and provide immediate feedback.
- Discuss or review common problems, as revealed by a short quiz or monitoring seat work.

Teaching Methods: A Constructivist View

In the previous section, we discussed procedures for teaching discrete skills and processes. Much of teaching involves such skills and processes (e.g., long division or how to solve a radical equation). The **transmission view** of teaching sees it as imparting to students what you know so they can use it just as you use it. In contrast, the **constructivist view** of teaching sees it as facilitating student co-construction of concepts. Table 3.4 clearly describes the differences between the two views. Your teaching set must also include methods for helping students explore content. What would this entail? The constructivist approach is not as easily outlined as the transmission view, but here are some principles that should be evidenced:

- Students should be encouraged to express and develop their personal points of view.

Table 3.4   Teaching and Learning as Transmission of Information versus as Social Construction of Knowledge

Transmission View	Constructivist View
Knowledge is a fixed body of information transmitted from teacher or text to students.	Knowledge is developing interpretations co-constructed through discussion.
Texts and teacher are authoritative sources of expert knowledge to which students defer.	Authority for constructed knowledge resides in the arguments and evidence cited in its support by students as well as by texts or teacher; everyone has expertise to contribute.
Teacher is responsible for managing students' learning by providing information and leading students through activities and assignments.	Teacher and students share responsibility for initiating and guiding learning efforts.
Teacher explains, checks for understanding, and judges correctness of students' responses.	Teacher acts as discussion leader who poses questions, seeks clarifications, promotes dialogue, and helps group recognize areas of consensus and of continuing disagreement.
Students memorize or replicate what has been explained or modeled.	Students strive to make sense of new input by relating it to their prior knowledge and by collaborating in dialogue with others to co-construct shared understandings.
Discourse emphasizes drill and recitation in response to convergent questions; focus is on eliciting correct answers.	Discourse emphasizes reflective discussion of networks of connected knowledge; questions are more divergent but designed to develop understanding of the powerful ideas that anchor these networks; focus is on eliciting students' thinking.
Activities emphasize replication of models or applications that require following step-by-step algorithms.	Activities emphasize applications to authentic issues and problems that require higher-order thinking.
Students work mostly alone, practicing what has been transmitted to them in order to prepare themselves to compete for rewards by reproducing it on demand.	Students collaborate by acting as a learning community that constructs shared understandings through sustained dialogue.

Source: Thomas L. Good and Jere E. Brophy, *Looking in Classrooms,* 8th ed., Table 10.1, 421. Copyright © 2003 by Pearson Education. Reprinted by permission of the publisher.

- Students should be questioned by the teacher, but in a way that helps them critically reflect on ideas and engage in sustained discourse.
- Students should be exposed to ideas that might contradict their own beliefs.
- Students should be expected to communicate their ideas to others and to do so in a way that enables them to more clearly articulate and understand their personal views.[36]

As you can see, with the constructivist view the control moves from the teacher to the student. We contend that good (effective) teachers know when to teach from a transmission view and when to teach from a constructivist view.

Materials and Media

Media and materials, sometimes referred to as *resources* or *instructional aids,* facilitate understanding and foster learning by clarifying verbal abstractions and arousing interest in the lesson. Many materials and media are available. The teacher's selection should depend on the objectives and content of the lesson plan; the age, abilities, and interests of the students; the teacher's ability to use the resources; the availability of the materials and equipment; and the classroom time available. Materials and media can be in the form of:

- visuals, such as posters, slides, graphs, films, computer simulations, and videos;
- reading materials, such as pamphlets, magazines, newspapers, reports, online information organized in a webquest, and books;
- listening media, such as radio, CDs, DVDs, and television;
- verbal activities, such as speeches, debates, buzz sessions, forums, role-playing, and interviews;
- motor activities, such as games, simulations, experiments, exercises, and manipulative materials; and
- construction activities such as collages, paintings, logs, maps, graphs, drawings, and models.

The materials and media you choose should be accurate and up-to-date, large enough to be seen by all the students, ready for use (check in advance of the lesson), interesting and varied, suited for developing the objective(s) of the lesson, and properly displayed and/or used throughout the lesson.

Many lessons fail because the required materials or media were inadequate, unavailable, or inappropriate for the level of the students. If students need to bring special materials for a task or project, they should be told far in advance so that they may obtain them. The teacher should be sure that necessary equipment is available, scheduled in advance, set up on the appropriate day, and in working order.

Summaries

Teachers cannot assume that learning is taking place in the class as a whole (or even with the majority) just because they have presented well-organized explanations and demonstrations or because some students give correct answers to questions. Some students might have been daydreaming or sitting there confused while other students answered questions and while the demonstrations/ explanations took place. To ensure understanding of the lesson and to determine whether the objectives of the lesson have been achieved, teachers should include one or more of the following types of summaries.

1. *Immediate summary*. There should be a short review of each lesson in which the lesson as a whole and important or confusing parts are summarized. A short review can take the following forms:

   - Posing several thought-provoking questions that summarize previous learning (or previous day's homework)
   - Asking for a comparison of what has already been learned with what is being learned
   - Asking a student to summarize the main ideas of the lesson; having other students make modifications and additions
   - Assigning review questions (on the chalkboard or in the workbook or textbook)
   - Administering a short quiz

2. *Medial summary*. During the lesson, at some point when a major concept or idea has been examined, it is advisable to present a **medial summary**—a series of pivotal questions or a problem that will bring together the information that has been discussed. Medial summaries slow down the lesson; however, they are important for low-achieving and young students who need more time to comprehend new information and more links with prior knowledge.

3. *Final summary*. A **final summary** is needed to synthesize the basic ideas or concepts of the lesson. If it is impossible to teach everything planned, you can end the lesson at some logical point and provide a summary of the content covered. Each lesson should be concluded or brought to closure by a summary activity, not by the bell. The summary activity enables students to ensure that they understand what the teacher just taught.

As your status changes from education student to beginning teacher, you must acquire appropriate subject and pedagogical knowledge and develop your own beliefs about teaching. Although teacher education programs can transmit some generalized principles of teaching and lesson planning, you need to learn to rely on your own experiences, capabilities, and reflections, incorporating them into your own classroom practices. You can also improve your instruction by observing experienced teachers, conversing with them, and getting feedback. Unfortunately, supervisors or principals rarely visit classrooms to observe teachers and provide feedback, unless a teacher is experiencing difficulties with the students or is new. Teachers must interpret their own instruction to grow professionally; they need mentors but they also need to know how to engage in self-reflection. The best barometers are the students. A teacher needs to learn to understand his or her instruction from the perspective of students, since they are the ones being taught and the ones who observe the teacher on a daily basis. Ask yourself: Which students are engaged? Which are disengaged? Why?

With experience, good teachers grow less egocentric (concerned about themselves) and more sensitive to student concerns. They learn to address the "Why?" question more thoughtfully. This shift in interest and focus helps them analyze what is happening in the classroom on an ongoing basis. By learning to read your students' verbal and nonverbal behaviors you will improve your instructional planning. As you put yourself in the place of your students, you should become more attuned to them as individuals—with particular needs and abilities—as opposed to viewing them as some amorphous group with generic problems or concerns[37] (see Case Study 3.2).

The following case study stresses the importance of understanding how to develop good lesson plans. It suggests various approaches that can be interesting and effective in your own lesson planning. Read the case and decide whether formal lesson planning is truly necessary or whether intuitive planning could actually be effective.

Case Study 3.2
Lesson Planning

Burt Carr didn't know what was wrong. He cared about his students and worked hard at his job as ninth-grade mathematics coordinator. He felt he was innovative because he sat down on the floor with students to read and complete the activities he assigned. He felt he engaged his small classes of no more than 20 students in curriculum-focused class activities. The school supported rigorous academic standards and state-of-the-art curricula and used a software program to analyze test results for each student, pinpointing which skills needed to be improved.

After getting over the shock when 55 percent of his students failed the midterms, Burt concluded that something was seriously wrong. He decided that possibly his traditional instructional approach was not all he had thought it to be. He used the textbook to sequence instruction and as the plan for his lessons. His methodology consisted of lecturing on a concept and then having students do exercises at the chalkboard or complete homework assignments on the material he covered in class. After thinking about it, he realized that of the twenty students in his class, probably no more than a few paid attention during his lectures. But homework assignments often were not turned in, or they were incomplete or done incorrectly. And only 5 or 10 percent of his students were able to pass his weekly quizzes.

Burt asked his colleague Roy Bunning if he was having similar problems with his classes. Roy said, "Absolutely not! I know how to teach and plan my lessons." He told Burt that *he* (Burt) was the one who was failing because when it actually came to teaching, the daily task of getting students to learn, Burt hadn't planned properly.

Burt looked bewildered and said, "What does planning have to do with students not following instructions, and class discussions that veer away from my lessons?" Burt said that in one class he had spent half a period debating a student about why he didn't have a pencil. He also explained to Roy that he had thought about ways to improve his work. He had tried to improve his lesson planning by using video presentations and more interactive exercises.

Roy asked Burt if he had ever considered a detailed plan rather than just depending on a video or the textbook to provide instructional materials. "You should try to make your lessons more relevant to your students, Burt. Why not use a simple guide called AMMCASH?" At this point, Roy handed Burt a card containing the information provided in box 3.4.

The card presented a simple way to quickly write a traditional lesson plan and allowed a systematic way to develop class work. Burt looked at the card and said, "This is the same thing in another form that I was given when I came to teach here." From his desk drawer Burt pulled out the following preprinted material:

Sample Lesson Plan

Your Name_____

Grade Level____ (College)_____   Date_____

Aim: (inform learner of object of the lesson)
To teach . . .
To understand . . .
Student aim . . .

Behavioral Objective: (At the conclusion of the session the student will understand . . .)

Motivation: (gaining attention)

Materials: (presenting the stimulus materials)

Procedure: (steps for eliciting desired behavior)

Summary: (stimulating recall of prerequisite learning)

Evaluation: (assessing instruction and behavior)

Follow-up: (providing feedback exercises and correctives)

Comments: (your feelings reflecting on the success or failure of the lesson)

Discussion Topics and Questions to Ponder

1. Do you agree with Roy's view that Burt had a problem? Why or why not?
2. Was Roy correct in identifying Burt's problem? Explain your answer.
3. Compare and contrast Roy's AMMCASH card and the sample lesson-plan form Burt already had in his possession.
4. Would effective planning resolve Burt's problems? Explain your answer.
5. What suggestions would you give both Burt and Roy regarding effective planning and class management?

What would you do if . . . ?

1. You were asked to recreate a lesson you observed or have previously taught to use as a model for Burt.
2. You reflected upon the lesson and the decisions you made to facilitate instruction and found they were wanting.
3. You were asked to create a discovery lesson rather than a traditional one.

Sample Lesson Plans

Three sample lesson plans are shown in boxes 3.6, 3.7, and 3.8 to illustrate how the various components of the lesson can be used. The lesson plans are written for different grade levels and subjects and are used to show the relation-

---

Box 3.6   Flexible Grouping Lesson Plan

Lesson topic: Vocabulary

Objectives: To define 10 new words

- To define the meaning of the words using a dictionary
- To write the meaning of the new words in a sentence

Review (both groups, 10 minutes):

- Correct homework, workbook, pp. 36–39.
- Focus on questions, p. 39.

Materials: Dictionaries, logs, supplementary books

Development:

Group I Activities	*Group II Activities*
Seat work (15 minutes)	**Seat work (15 minutes)**
1. Alphabetize the following 10 words: explicit, implicit, appropriate, inappropriate, potential, encounter, diminish, enhance, master, alligator.	1. Find each of the following 10 words in the dictionary: explicit, implicit, appropriate, inappropriate, potential, encounter, diminish, enhance, master, alligator (same words for both groups).
2. Find each new word in the dictionary.	2. Write a definition for each new word.
3. Write a definition for each new word.	3. Divide each new word into syllables.
Medial summary (15 minutes)	**Independent work (15 minutes)**
Teach new words; students give examples and discuss meaning of new words.	1. Continue reading supplementary books.
	2. Underline at least five new words in the pages you read.
	3. Find their meaning in the dictionary.
Independent work (10 minutes)	**Final summary (10 minutes)**
1. Update logs.	Discuss the 10 assigned words plus the 5 words students have chosen in their independent reading.
2. Include the 10 new words in logs.	

Homework (both groups):

1. Develop a picture for the meaning of each word. (artistic intelligence)
2. Create a song that has all 10 words. (musical intelligence)

ship of your overall instructional goals and the structure of a lesson. The explanations in this section give some sense of what the teacher is trying to achieve. The words in italics coincide with the previously discussed components of a lesson plan; they serve as anchors or highlight the major ideas of the lessons. Notice, in particular, how the homework requires students to use other forms of intelligence in order to assimilate the meaning of the words.

Lesson Plan for Flexible Grouping.   In box 3.6, the lesson topic is derived from the unit plan on vocabulary development.

1. The *primary objective* is to teach the meaning of ten new words. The two secondary objectives accomplish the primary objective and enhance dictionary and writing skills.

2. The teacher immediately starts the lesson with a *review* of the previous homework. The class as a whole discusses the homework.

3. Only *materials* specific to the lesson are noted in the lesson plan.

4. The teacher uses the term *activities* to describe the development or outline, since the focus of attention is on classroom activities.

5. The class is divided into *two groups* for the activities. Group I is lower achieving than group II.

6. Both groups do similar *seat work*. Group I is given the extra step of alphabetizing for extra practice in the process. Group II understands the need for alphabetical order in searching through the dictionary, so this step is omitted. Group II is given another, more difficult task of dividing words into syllables to make up for the one task that was omitted. The teacher monitors the seat work of the students and helps anyone with individual problems.

7. After seat work, the two groups engage in different activities. The teacher works with one group while the other is involved in independent work. For group I the teacher provides a *medial summary* for feedback, review, and assessment. (Prompt and varied feedback and review are needed for the less advanced group.) Group II engages in *independent* work, having selected their own books to read for enjoyment. The teacher then works with group II in a *summary* activity, connecting the original objective with the students' independent work, while group I does its independent assignment. Group I has fifteen fewer minutes for independent work and fifteen more minutes of teacher-directed summary work because these students need more teacher time, are less able to work independently, and are likely to have more problems that need to be directly remediated.

8. The whole class receives the same *homework* assignment. Group I is permitted to start the homework in class, so the assignment at home does not overwhelm them and so the teacher can check for understanding. The students use two forms of intelligence that they did not use during the formal lesson taught by the teacher, which fosters a type of *intrinsic motivation*.

Box 3.7   Thinking Skills Lesson Plan

Lesson topic: Classifying information

Objective: To classify information on the basis of similar or common attributes

Motivation:

- Into what groups would you classify the following information: Kennedy, table, elephant, Lincoln, Roosevelt, Chicago, Nixon, Boston, Bush, donkey, and San Francisco?
- Why should *we* learn to classify information into categories or groups?

Procedures	Pivotal questions
1. *Development:* Discuss at least three reasons for classifying information.	a. When do you classify information? Why? b. What happens to information that is not organized? Why?
2. Skim text (pp. 48–55) to get an idea of important items or ideas that might be classified.	
3. Agree on categories (groups or labels) to be used in classifying information in text.	a. What advantages are there to the categories? b. What are their unifying attributes? c. What other categories could we have used? Explain.
4. Focus on three practice items in the text and agree on related categories for the purpose of ensuring understanding.	
5. Carefully read the same pages and place selected items into appropriate categories.	Why did you identify these items with those categories?
6. Discuss similar or common attributes.	a. Why did you choose these common attributes as a category to classify the items? b. What other common attributes might you have chosen?
7. Modify (change, subtract, or add) categories, if necessary.	a. Why did you change these categories? b. What can we do with the items that fit into more than one category? Which items fit into more than one category?
8. Repeat procedures using other important items; read pp. 56–63.	What categories did you select? Why?
9. Combine categories or subdivide into smaller categories.	a. Why did you reclassify (add or subdivide) these categories? b. What should we do with the leftover items? Which ones are left over?

Summary:

1. What important things have you learned about classifying information?
2. What are different ways of classifying information?
3. When is it appropriate to subdivide categories?
4. Look at the chalkboard (text). Who wishes to categorize these five new items into one of the categories we have already established?

Homework:

1. Read Chapter 7 (intrapersonal intelligence).
2. Classify important information into pro/con categories listed on p. 68 (verbal intelligence).

Lesson Plan for Thinking Skills.   With the type of lesson plan shown in box 3.7, the lesson topic can be part of a separate unit on critical thinking skills, or it can serve as an introductory lesson for a unit in almost any subject.

1. There is only one *objective.* It pertains to classifying—a critical thinking skill.

2. The *motivation* assumes a certain amount of abstract thinking on the part of the students. It is verbal as opposed to visual or auditory. The first question is divergent and open-ended. The second question is more convergent and focused. The short exercise provides students with a challenge, introduces them to the main part of the lesson, and shows how they handle certain information before the lesson. Some words (*elephant, donkey, Lincoln,* etc.) can be categorized into various groups, and *table* does not belong in any category. (It serves as irrelevant information in order to observe how students handle it.)

3. The *development* is a set of *procedures* or operations to teach students how to classify information. The *pivotal questions* are to be introduced at different stages of the lesson. They stimulate discussion, clarify points, and check understanding. They are divergent in nature and provide students with latitude in the way they can answer; the teacher must listen carefully to the responses, since the answers are not necessarily right or wrong but involve, in part, viewpoints and subjectivity.

4. The *summary* is a series of important or key questions that lead to a discussion and elaboration of what has been taught. The length of the summary discussion is based on the time permitted. Question 1 is vague, and students may not respond or may respond in a way that the teacher does not expect. Questions 2 and 3 are more focused. Question 4 leads to a good overview and reinforcement exercise. (The teacher may or may not have time to use it.)

5. The *homework* is based on the lesson, leads to a slightly more advanced type of thinking, and relies on areas of verbal and intrapersonal intelligence.

Box 3.8   Mastery Learning Lesson Plan (Primary Grades)

Lesson topic: Subtraction

Objective: Students will complete the worksheet items on subtraction, with at least 80 percent accuracy after the lesson.

Review: Review yesterday's homework on subtraction.

Motivation (Sample items):

1. There are 25 students in the class, as you know. We are planning to go to a movie next Friday afternoon. Three of you—Joel, Jason, and Stacey—have soccer practice and will not attend the movie. How many tickets should we buy?

2. We are going to plan a Halloween party in class. Each of you may have one dessert choice with your milk. Most of us enjoy chocolate-chip cookies, but some might prefer vanilla-cream cookies. Let's see how many prefer vanilla-cream cookies. (Show of hands.) Good. Ten of you prefer the vanilla-cream cookies. Who can tell the class how many chocolate-chip cookies we will need for the party?

Materials: Overhead projector or computer with PowerPoint slides, checkers (distribute to students)

Development:

Problems	Activities
1. With an overhead projector or Power-Point presentation, explain how to solve 11–5, 11–7.	a. At their desks students use the checkers and perform 12–2, 12–5, 12–8. b. Students record work (and answers) in their notebooks. c. Discuss all items missed by more than 10 percent of the students.
2. With an overhead projector or Power-Point presentation, explain 20–5, 20–10.	a. At their desks students use the checkers and perform 21–3, 21–5, 21–7. b. Repeat b. in item 1. c. Repeat c. in item 1.
3. With an overhead projector or Power-Point presentation, explain 22–6, 22–10, 22–15.	a. At their desks students use the checkers and perform 23–5, 23–8, 23–12, 23–20. b. Repeat b. in item 1. c. Repeat c. in item 1.

Practice:

1. Distribute worksheet with subtraction problems.

2. Call on volunteer to do first sample item on worksheet.

3. Call on second and third volunteers to do next two sample items, then call on nonvolunteers.

4. Have students complete remaining worksheet on their own at their own pace.

Summary (evaluation):

1. With overhead projector or PowerPoint, show correct answers for all the items.

2. Ask students how many got each item right.

3. Discuss all the items, but reteach items that 20 percent or more missed.

4. Have students score their own papers and turn them in.

Homework:

1. Distribute homework or explain new worksheet that is to be answered.

2. Review assignment for next day.

3. Reteach problem items (items that 20 percent or more missed during previous lesson).

Lesson Plan for Mastery.   Box 3.8 features subtraction as a *lesson topic*, introduced in the second grade in most school districts and continued in the third grade.

1. The *objective* is written in terms of a performance level.

2. Mastery learning lessons entail a good deal of practice and *review*.

3. The *motivation* is in the form of two separate problems that involve real-life experiences and interests.

4. Only unusual *materials* are listed. Popsicle sticks, baseball cards, or any other items easy to count can be used in lieu of checkers.

5. The *development* is in the form of problems and related activities. The problems, involving one- and two-digit numbers, coincide with the work-sheet level the students have reached. The teacher explains each problem and then introduces the related activity. While students work on the activity, the teacher moves around the room and monitors their work. The problems get progressively more difficult. Each item that is missed by even a small percentage of students must be further explained, since the work builds on previous learning.

6. The teacher provides additional *practice* before asking students to complete the worksheet on their own. Only volunteers are called on because the work is new. Three items are explained. The teacher moves around the room, monitoring the students' work and providing additional help when necessary.

7. As a *summary*, all items are discussed. All items missed by students, especially those that are missed by 20 percent or more, are discussed in greater detail. Individuals' scores on the worksheet determine how much practice is needed the next day in the form of review.

8. The *homework* is related to the lesson; it is assigned and explained. The next day it will be reviewed.

9. Peer teaching can be useful in lessons like this one. The process is quite simple. Students work in pairs. If possible, pair one student who clearly understands the lesson with another who is having some difficulty. The student who understands the lesson teaches his or her partner. The teacher should walk around the room to ensure that students are explaining the material correctly.

Integrating Real-Life Experiences

Ralph W. Tyler

I have been teaching for more than sixty years, and in every one of my classes I have found some students who have difficulty in learning what I had hoped the class would help them learn. At first, I thought these students were unable to learn and that they would never be successful in their schoolwork. But then, I noticed that many of them were learning to play games, to deliver newspapers, to plan for field trips, and to carry out many other activities.

I asked several students, "Why are you so good at learning things outside of school and seem to have difficulty with schoolwork and with your homework?" Some said, "The things we learn outside of school are real, while schoolwork is dull and not real." Others said, "The things we do outside of school are *our* jobs. In school we are doing *your* job."

From these experiences, I began to realize that I must give my students responsibility for jobs in school, on the playground, and in the neighborhood. Then, when they accepted these responsibilities, I helped students learn to meet them successfully. Now, I try to find out from my students what they are trying to do outside of school, and then help them to learn how to use reading, mathematics, literature, science, art, and music by doing well in activities they believe to be important. As students understand that they need to learn what schools are expected to teach, I become their helper, not their slave driver. Then teaching becomes fun for me.

Guidelines for Implementing Lesson Plans

Several factors must be considered as you begin to move from planning to performance. Even after you have had some experience, it is wise to review the following factors to ensure your success in the execution of the lesson plan:

Student Differences.   You must consider individual and group differences as you plan your lesson and then teach it. Make provisions for student differences in ability, age, background, and reading level. The differences in how students learn are being accentuated because of the increasing diversity of the student population. Teachers can capitalize on the unique learning dispositions of students from different backgrounds by understanding that different students learn in different ways. Be careful not to stereotype how students learn in classrooms. African American students are not necessarily verbal learners, any more than European American students are analytical in their approach to learning, for example. The key is to understand that you have different types of learners, and this fact requires that you organize the classroom in different ways and then examine critically how those different structures impact student learning and achievement. Ask yourself: Which students learn best in cooperative structures? Which ones benefit from independent structures? All students from all different types of ethnic/racial backgrounds and ability levels can and do learn through some common strategies. But from the 1970s through the 1990s many researchers began to see that some approaches "played" more to certain students' cultural strengths. For example, Native Americans tend to stress interpersonal cooperation, and teachers who understand that fact can better help these students achieve their full potential. Teachers should not interpret these cultural dispositions as keys to *how* a group learns, but rather should use them to understand *why* some students may adjust more quickly to one particular learning situation than to another.

Length of Period.   One of the major problems for beginning teachers is planning a lesson that will coincide with time allotted (the thirty, forty, or fifty minutes of each period; with block scheduling the time frame may be as much as 100 minutes). New teachers must learn to pace themselves and not plan too much (and have to end abruptly) or too little (and have nothing planned for the last five or ten minutes of the period). Remember to select fewer concepts but find more ways to teach the concepts.

Flexibility.   The teacher must be flexible—that is, prepared to develop a lesson along a path different from the one set down in the plan. Student reactions may make it necessary or desirable to elaborate on something included in the plan or to pursue something unexpected that arises as the lesson proceeds (the *teachable moment*). Although effective teachers tend to encourage on-task behavior and discourage off-task behavior, they are willing to make corrections and take advantage of unforeseen developments. The basis for the change is more intuitive than objective, more unplanned than preplanned.

Student Participation.   Teachers must encourage the participation of the greatest number of students in each lesson. They should not permit a few students to dominate the lesson, and they should draw nonvolunteers into the lesson. They should not talk too much or dominate the lesson with teacher-directed activities. The need is to encourage student participation, student-to-student interaction, and increased performance among shy students, low-achieving students, and students on the sides and in the rear rows (as opposed to students in the middle or front of the room who tend to get the most attention).

Student Understanding.   There is often a gap between what students understand and what teachers think they understand. Part of the reason for this gap is the rapidity of the teaching process—so much happens at once that the teacher is unaware of everything that goes on in the classroom. Following are suggestions to increase student understanding as you teach the lesson:

- Insist that students respond to the questions put to them. Students who do not know answers or have trouble understanding the lesson tend to mumble or speak too quietly to be heard clearly, try to change the subject, or ask another question instead of responding to the original question. These are some of the strategies students adopt to outwit teachers.[38]

- If a student answer lacks detail, does not cover the major aspects of the problem, or is partially or totally incorrect, probe the student by rephrasing or simplifying the question, by using another question to lead the student toward the desired answer, or by providing additional information. As a last option, call on another student to help the first student.

- If, after calling on a few students you are unable to obtain the desired response, you may have to reteach parts of the lesson. Although this is not planned, you cannot ignore that several students are having problems understanding the lesson.
- Prepare students for demonstrations and experiments, ask questions during these activities, and follow up with written exercises in which students analyze or synthesize what they observed or performed.
- Include practice, review, or applications in every lesson. The amount of time you spend on these activities will depend on the students' abilities. Low-achieving and younger students need more practice, review, and concrete application.
- Be sure to include medial and final summaries. Low-achieving and younger students need more medial summaries than high-achieving students do.

Assessment and Evaluation. At the end of a lesson, the teacher should have a clear idea about how the students reacted and whether they understood and were engaged in the lesson. To appraise your lesson plan, ask yourself the following questions:

- Did my objectives align with state or local content standards?
- Was the instruction congruent with the objectives?
- Are certain questions targeted to the learning objectives?
- Do I need to spend more time reviewing parts of the lesson?
- Do I give feedback in a manner that is supportive and encouraging?
- Were the questions appropriate? Which ones came up that were not planned and that can be used in the future? Did I incorporate higher-order questions?
- What problems arose? How can I correct them?
- Was there sufficient time to complete the lesson?
- Did my students learn the skills, concepts, and generalizations I set out to teach in my learning objectives?
- What did I fail to accomplish in the lesson?
- What other forms of intelligence (musical, artistic, kinesthetic) might help students better understand the concepts?

Homework. Homework assignments are a critical part of the process for fostering student understanding. (See box 9.1 on pp. 444–445 for some "dos and don'ts" of homework.) Unfortunately, perspectives vary on the value of homework. Some claim that students are receiving higher grades with less outside preparation. According to Alfie Kohn, "There was no consistent linear or curvilinear relation between the amount of time spent on homework and the child's level of academic achievement."[39] Other researchers maintain that homework helps students develop responsibility and life skills as well as the ability to manage tasks. It also provides time for experiential learning, increased motivation, opportunities for learning to cope with difficulties and distractions, and academic benefits.[40]

While many researchers take either a positive or a negative stance on homework, Cooper takes a more balanced approach, stating, "Research on the effects of homework suggests that it is beneficial as long as teachers use their knowledge of developmental levels to guide policies and expectations."[41]

A good teacher, no matter how experienced, is a critic of his or her lesson and seeks new ways to improve the teaching–learning situation. The teacher takes time for self-reflection and self-analysis. The teacher is aware of what is happening during the lesson and intuitively judges what is worthwhile and what needs to be modified for the next time the lesson plan is used. See Tips for Teachers 3.2 for more ideas on lesson plan improvement.

TIPS FOR TEACHERS 3.2

Organizing and Implementing Lesson Plans

The teacher should always look for ways to improve the lesson plan. What follows are twenty-five research-based tips that correlate with student achievement. As many as possible (not necessarily all in one lesson) should be incorporated into portions of the lesson plan. Although most of the statements seem to be based on a mastery approach, the checklist can be used for most types of teaching.

1. Plan the lesson toward stated objectives or topics of the unit plan.
2. Make certain that lesson objectives are clear.
3. Develop objectives and activities that use a variety of higher-level and lower-level cognitive skills.
4. Provide a review of the previous lesson or integrate the previous lesson with the new lesson.
5. Indicate to students the objectives of the lesson; explain what is to be accomplished.
6. Present the lesson with enthusiasm; motivate students.
7. Present the lesson at an appropriate pace, not too slow or too fast.
8. Explain things clearly. Be sure students understand what to do and how to do it.
9. Give students a chance to think about what is being taught.
10. Try to find out when students don't understand.
11. Provide sufficient time for practice.
12. Ask frequent questions; be sure they are challenging and relevant.
13. Provide explanations, demonstrations, or experiments.
14. Elaborate on difficult points of the lesson; give details, provide examples.
15. Choose activities that are interesting and promote success.
16. Incorporate supplementary materials and media.
17. Summarize the lesson.
18. Schedule seat work: Monitor and assess student work.
19. Give homework, provide examples of how to do homework, and collect and check homework.
20. Evaluate (or reflect on) the lesson plan after teaching.

Theory into Practice

All school districts expect teachers to cover the appropriate goals/standards from the adopted course of study. Online lesson/unit builders are available that are designed to report on (and document) this kind of data, if teachers create their lesson using one of these databases. LiveText and TaskStream are two such online approaches. School districts will have their own approaches that may be either electronic or paper-and-pencil oriented. In essence, unit planning and lesson planning will vary according to the school district and school in which you teach. Some school settings and supervisors will be quite prescriptive and expect you to follow a specific method. Your plans may be collected and checked on a regular basis. In other schools and with other supervisors, there will be no prescribed method and very little feedback or concern about your unit and lesson plans, in which case you will be largely on your own when it comes to instructional planning. For this reason, you can use the following questions to avoid common mistakes and to guide you when you plan your own units and lessons.

Unit Planning

1. Did you consider state (or school district) requirements and standards as well as the course of study?
2. If your textbook features an instructor's manual, did you read it for suggestions? Does it contain samples that you can modify to your students' abilities and needs?
3. Are you clear about your instructional objectives? Are they appropriate?
4. Does the content tie together with the objectives? Is the content interesting and relevant?
5. Do the skills tie together with the content? Do they allow for differences in student abilities and needs?
6. Did you include interesting and relevant learning activities? Do some of the activities extend beyond the classroom?
7. Did you include varied resources and materials? Did you supplement the text with other resources and materials?
8. Are your evaluation procedures appropriate? Do they help assess your objectives?
9. Is your plan flexible enough to accommodate various students—in terms of abilities, interests, and learning styles?
10. Is your plan detailed enough so that another person would understand it and know what you intend to do?

Lesson Planning

1. Are your objectives clear in terms of the knowledge, skills, and values you wish to teach? Do they stem from the unit plan?
2. Is the content arranged in a logical order and in the way you wish to teach it?

3. Are your instructional methods clear? Do you vary the methods to prevent student boredom?

4. Are your materials and equipment ready to use? Did you order them far enough in advance?

5. Have you checked the previous work? Did you ask review questions or pose problems? Did you administer a short quiz on the previous lesson or homework? Did you reteach or provide additional practice when needed?

6. Have you checked the current work? Did you provide adequate summaries? Did you call on new volunteers? Did you reteach when necessary?

7. Are crucial or pivotal questions included?

8. Did you include an appropriate homework assignment? Were your directions clear? How did you check to see if the students understood yesterday's homework?

9. Have you budgeted sufficient time to complete the lesson? Did you finish too soon? Did you run out of time before finishing?

10. How do you intend to evaluate the lesson? Would you enjoy the lesson if you were a student? Would you learn from the lesson if you were a student?

CONCLUSIONS

- Teachers plan at five different levels: yearly, term, unit, weekly, and daily.
- Mapping takes place at different subject and grade levels; it helps clarify what content, skills, and values you wish to teach.
- Teachers use national and state standards to shape the lesson goals and objectives.
- The basic components of a unit plan are objectives, content, skills, activities, resources, and evaluation.
- Two types of unit plans are the taxonomic and topic.
- The basic components of a lesson plan are objectives, motivation, development, methods, materials and media, summaries, and homework.
- Three lesson plans were discussed: flexible grouping, thinking skills, and mastery learning.

KEY TERMS

constructivist view
course of study
culturally responsive
  classroom
development

extrinsic motivation
final summary
formal planning
intrinsic motivation
lesson plan

medial summary
mental planning
transmission view
unit plan

DISCUSSION QUESTIONS

1. Why do educators advise planning in cooperation with students? Why do many teachers ignore student input when planning?

2. What are the criteria for a good unit plan?

3. With what approach do you think a unit for your subject or grade could best be planned? Explain your answer.

4. Which are the most essential components to consider when planning a lesson? Explain your answer.

5. What are the problems of relying too heavily on either a transmission or social constructivist view of learning? Is it preferable or possible to adopt just one view?

MINI-CASES FROM THE FIELD

Case One: Just What Is Curriculum?

Paul Young was a student teacher who was concerned with teaching the prescribed curriculum. He had prepared for his fourth-grade class a unit on the legislative process titled *How a Bill Becomes a Law.* Political science had always been his best subject. He was confident that he could prepare and teach an effective unit of instruction. Mr. Kantor, Paul's cooperating teacher, was not pleased with Paul's request. He said that the legislative process should not take an entire unit; it really needed only one lesson. Paul discussed his proposed unit at length with Mr. Kantor. Paul said the unit would take five to six lessons, each for thirty-minutes. A final session would be devoted to a unit test. Mr. Kantor said that while he realized the work that Paul had put into developing the unit, it still did not meet his curriculum requirements. Paul asked, "Just what is curriculum if not the prescribed content?" Mr. Kantor replied that curriculum was simply the interaction between the teacher and his class.

1. Based on this vignette, write a sentence that would encapsulate Paul's definition of curriculum.

2. How would you describe Mr. Kantor's reasoning for not approving Paul's unit?

3. Was Paul's unit really a unit, or was it a lesson, as Mr. Kantor insisted? Justify your position.

4. Describe your feelings regarding Mr. Kantor's definition of curriculum.

5. What is your definition of what curriculum is?

Case Two: Are Unit Plans Necessary?

Joan Finkelman was a natural—she was born to teach. Her tenth-grade foreign-language arts class was filled with children who loved her. That was before she was instructed by Mrs. Green, her supervisor, to teach full-period lessons. In her attempt to meet Mrs. Green's demands Joan consistently planned more than what was necessary for forty-minute lessons. She was afraid that she would run out of material before the lessons were over. To compensate for this fear she always planned to teach more than was reasonable. As a result, Joan rushed through materials by using a lecture format and students were overwhelmed by her lessons. Mrs. Green had told Joan that a lesson should have a beginning, a middle, and an end (summary) that would leave students with a sense of accomplishment. Students were to be engaged in active listening while taking organized notes and developing the skills necessary for future learning. Students should be taught to evaluate, interpret, compare, analyze, and defend solutions. To achieve this Joan was to prepare a yearly plan made up of units, weekly plans, and daily plans directed toward meeting the objectives that were aligned to her curriculum standards.

1. How did Mrs. Green attempt to assist Joan?
2. Can a lecture format be effectively utilized with tenth-grade students? Justify your response.
3. What type of activities could have been useful to Joan in her planning?
4. How could this problem be solved and be turned into a benefit for both teacher and student?
5. Are unit plans really necessary? Explain your position.

Case Three: Is There a Correct Way to Plan a Lesson?

Peter DiLeo could not decide on the best way to go about writing a lesson plan. He believed that his plans had to reflect his teaching style—constructivist rather than traditionalist. He knew that in a constructivist teaching style the individual traditional lesson plan is often inappropriate. Specific objectives and timelines might be fine in a unit plan, but lesson plans were more fluid because they had to address student needs that were rarely the same. He wanted his lessons to engage students in problem solving or inquiry learning; rigid lesson planning with title, behavioral objectives, and specific outcomes were not his cup of tea. Unfortunately for Peter, his immediate supervisor, Mrs. Brown, insisted that her department use a traditional lesson design format. She wouldn't even listen to a suggestion that a constructivist lesson format could be used. She insisted that the basic problem with students' lack of academic achievement is that learning is hard work and should not be trivialized. She wanted a teacher-centered approach that included prepared lessons, discussions, and frequent interchanges of ideas in class. Mrs. Brown said that appropriate group work was fine as long as there was a clear sense of direction for every lesson.

1. What advice would you give Peter in dealing with Mrs. Brown?
2. Compare and contrast Peter's ideas with Mrs. Brown's.
3. How could Peter put a positive slant on his position?
4. Describe your own feelings regarding the proper way to develop a lesson plan.
5. Is there a best way to write a lesson? Explain your answer.

Case Four: Implementing a Lesson Plan

Eileen Kelly was very proud of her lesson plans. She believed that the AMMCASH approach (see box 3.4) she had read about was perfect for her style of teaching. Her supervisor, Mr. Battle, was disturbed by such a simplistic approach to preparing and implementing a lesson plan. He suggested the following format:

1. *Unit topic* is essentially the title for a unit. A unit is made up of lessons that are taught in a sequential order. The title reminds us of the relationship between the individual lesson and the unit as a whole.

2. *Objectives* form the heart of a lesson. They give the lesson a purpose and provide a means of assessment.

3. *Rationale* provides your reason for teaching a particular topic.

4. *Content* is the component that describes the major ideas you plan to teach.

5. *Procedures* are the ways in which you will teach the content.

6. *Materials* should be listed to remind the teacher of materials needed for the lesson.

7. *Assessment* is the component wherein a teacher considers how to evaluate what students have learned.

Eileen looked at what she had been given and exclaimed that this format was basically the same as she had been using with AMMCASH. She told Mr. Battle that she would use his format in conjunction with her own. She had decided to learn for herself what a good plan was and what a bad plan was by using trial and error. She told Mr. Battle that she felt this approach would be better for her students. He smiled and said, "I'm sure the children will let you know if your lessons are effective."

1. Why would Mr. Battle have thought Eileen's approach simplistic?
2. Compare and contrast Eileen's AMMCASH with Mr. Battle's suggestions.
3. Is there any justification for Eileen's position that we learn by trial and error?
4. How could a compromise have been made?
5. Are these plans constructivist or traditionalist? Explain your answer.

Case Five: A Constructivist Lesson Plan

Is there really such a thing as a constructivist lesson plan? Mrs. Wellington, the principal of Wingate High School, said yes. In a staff meeting with her teachers, she claimed that the constructivist approach is not as easily outlined as a traditional developmental lesson, but that it was doable nevertheless. She compiled a list of four basic principles that should be evidenced in every lesson taught:

• Students should be encouraged to express and develop their personal points of view.

• Students should be questioned by the teacher, but in a way that helps them critically reflect on ideas and engage in sustained discourse.

• Students should be exposed to ideas that might contradict their own beliefs.

• Students should be expected to communicate their ideas to others, and to do so in a way that enables them to more clearly articulate and understand their personal views.

Mr. Harriman raised his hand and asked, "What about content? All these principles are about points of views, beliefs, and ideas." He further went on to say that these so-called principles had nothing to do with the curriculum or standardized forms of assessment. "If we did what you want us to do, our students would fail the state graduation examinations." Mrs. Wellington responded by saying that students were already failing under the traditional approaches. "We need to be progressive and meet student needs. Remember, no one said you are not to include content and meet curriculum standards. Look at a constructivist lesson as just another path to student understanding."

1. What are the ingredients of a traditional lesson plan?

2. How does a constructivist approach differ from a traditional approach?

3. Describe how a traditional and constructivist approach can be interwoven into a successful lesson design.

4. Outline a brief lesson on a simple topic (e.g., how a bill becomes a law, how to balance a checkbook). Demonstrate how constructivist principles can be incorporated into the lesson.

5. Choose the approach you favor (traditional, constructivist, or eclectic) and explain your reasons.

FIELD EXPERIENCE ACTIVITIES

1. Prepare a unit for your subject or grade level grounded on existing content standards.

2. Speak to an experienced teacher. Ask the teacher to provide you with a series of unit plans for the subject or grade level you plan to teach. Examine the major components in class.

3. Select one of the units and list the activities and resources that could be incorporated into it.

4. Plan a lesson in your subject and grade level; then teach it using the lesson components listed in this chapter. What were the good parts of the lesson? What were the unsatisfactory parts?

5. List some common mistakes in lesson planning. Ask experienced teachers, "What are ways for preventing some of these mistakes?"

RECOMMENDED READING

Beyer, Barry K. *Teaching Thinking Skills: A Handbook for Elementary School Teachers.* Needham Heights, MA: Allyn & Bacon, 1991.
Explores how teaching skills can be planned and taught in most elementary classrooms. It includes sample exercises and lesson plans.

Brun, Peter. *The Lesson Planning Handbook*. New York: Scholastic, 2010.
Helps teachers craft lessons full of high-level student thought and engagement.

Chall, Jeanne S. *The Academic Achievement Challenge*. New York: Guilford Press, 2002.
Examines the research on teacher-centered versus student-centered instructional approaches.

Glass, Katherine Tuchman. *Lesson Design for Differentiated Instruction, Grades 4–9*. Thousand Oaks, CA: Corwin, 2009.
Step-by-step guidance and a detailed template for creating meaningful lessons that are differentiated according to students' learning characteristics.

Good, Thomas L., and Jere E. Brophy. *Looking in Classrooms*, 10th ed. Boston: Allyn & Bacon, 2007.
Research-oriented coverage of several aspects of teaching, including lesson planning.

Irvine, Jacqueline Jordan, and Beverly Jeanne Armento. *Culturally Responsive Teaching*. Boston: McGraw-Hill, 2001.
A thoughtful exploration of how culturally responsive lessons can be planned around established disciplinary standards.

Ladson-Billings, Gloria. *Dreamkeepers*. San Francisco: Jossey-Bass, 1994.
Describes the practices and characteristics of successful teachers working with students of color.

Ladson-Billings, Gloria. *Beyond the Big House: African-American Educators on Teacher Education*. New York: Teachers College Press, 2005.
Offers powerful, insightful portraits of seven well-known African American teacher educators.

McNeil, John D. *Curriculum: The Teacher's Initiative*, 3rd ed. Columbus, OH: Merrill, 2003.
Describes a constructivist view on curriculum and teaching.

Ornstein, Allan C., Thomas J. Lasley, and Gayle Mindes. *Secondary and Middle School Methods*. Boston: Allyn & Bacon, 2005.
Helps experienced teachers improve their teaching and instruction by combining a broad approach of methodology, from research to theory to practice.

Serdyukov, Peter, and Mark Ryan. *Writing Effective Lesson Plans: The 5-Step Approach*. Boston: Allyn & Bacon, 2008.
A five-step process that helps to streamline the process of lesson planning.

4

Instructional Methods

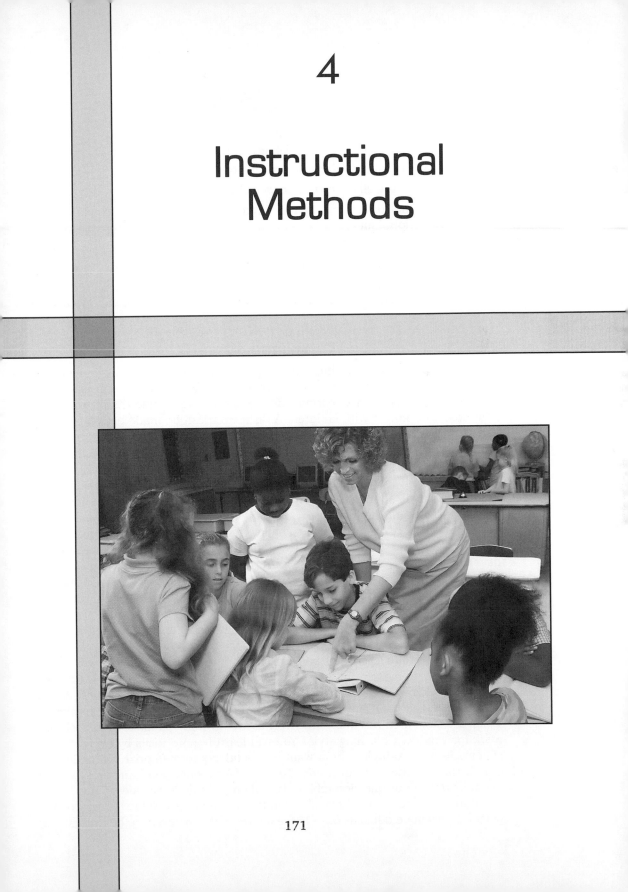

FOCUS POINTS

1. Understanding the usefulness of practice and drill.
2. Mastering more effective practice and drill.
3. Realizing that questioning is crucial to good instruction.
4. Recognizing the characteristics of well-formulated questions.
5. Realizing that direct and indirect approaches to instruction are basic for all instructional methods.
6. Learning to limit lecture times.
7. Discovering strategies for student problem solving and inquiry.
8. Recognizing that differentiating methods enhances achievement.

OVERVIEW

The difference between teaching and instruction is that teaching is what is done by the teacher during the instructional process, while instruction consists of the methods used to influence learning. Teachers must determine the instructional methods that connect with children. A distinction can be made between tactics and strategies: Tactics are short term and used during lessons, while strategies are long-term plans focused on learning. The methods employed are the basis for the tactics and strategies used. Learning has nothing to do with what a teacher covers; it has to do with what a student learns. Learning is the goal of any instructional approach. The specific approach may vary but the focus on learning is constant in every case.

This chapter reviews a basic arsenal of effective methods and approaches in order to facilitate student learning. Learning does not occur in a vacuum; it develops over time within a caring, nurturing environment. It can be passive or interactive. Today traditional passivity has been co-opted for interactive student participation. We also explore the pedagogical methods that are most often employed by teachers: (1) practice and drill; (2) questioning, discovery, and inquiry; (3) direct and indirect instructional methods; and (4) student-centered learning and problem solving.

Pedagogy is the science or art of teaching, knowing what and how to teach it. Fortunately, to master the "how" of teaching is a comparatively simple process. It consists of recognizing strategy and various lesson-delivery techniques. Which methods will you use? Why? What are the consequences of using these methods? When are these methods most effectively used? How do you make these methods work for your own teaching style? You will learn how to focus by using if–then statements. For example, if you want your students to memorize multiplication tables, then practice and drill are effective. If you want your students to think about how the multiplication tables work, then you might use questioning.

Bransford and his colleagues[1] argue that the appropriateness of a particular teaching technique depends on "(1) the nature of the materials to be learned; (2)

the nature of the skills, knowledge, and attitudes that learners bring to the situations; and (3) the goals of the learning situation and the assessments used to measure learning relative to these goals."[2] They show how to select teaching techniques using an if–then relationship. If students are to learn the characteristics of arteries, then use a mnemonic (or memory device) technique: "ART(ery) was *thick* around the middle so he wore pants with an *elastic* waistband."[3] This technique helps students learn that arteries are thick and elastic. However, if the question was *why* this is true (that is, Why are arteries thick and elastic?), then a more inquiry-oriented strategy would be more appropriate. The conditional (if–then) statement you make about your objectives determines your teaching strategy. You must also think about the goals for learning and the skill set that students bring with them to each learning task. "If students already know the properties of arteries, then they may be ready to consider the reasons for those properties."

The following instructional approaches suggest that teachers can (and must) use a range of teaching strategies and must know how to use both direct and indirect instructional models to foster student growth and development. Direct approaches such as practice and drill are transmission oriented, with the teacher explicitly teaching students the academic content they need to know. In contrast, indirect strategies are more constructivist oriented and require that students explore ideas to create more personally constructed understandings of salient concepts.

Instructional Approach I: Practice and Drill

When teaching a specific skill or process, use practice and drill.

The mention of practice and drill summons up images of the old-fashioned schoolmaster, the drillmaster, who made learning a repetitive process whereby students either memorized their lessons or experienced the teacher's wrath. Despite its less-than-flattering image, practice and drill is an instructional method that does serve certain purposes well and can be used to advantage in classrooms today. Practice and drill has a clear purpose: to help students learn discrete skills or processes well. As we begin the twenty-first century, we now know both the strengths and limits of this approach.

Applications of Practice and Drill

Practice and drill is a common method used by elementary teachers to teach the fundamentals, especially to young children. The method is also employed by secondary teachers with students who still lack basic skills or knowledge of academic subject matter before asking them to move on to other tasks or transfer their learning to a new situation. Some teachers believe lots of practice is essential in order to learn a basic skill or task. As a result, they repeatedly drill their students. Today, most teachers are less drill oriented and more open to other instructional approaches, but those different approaches rely heavily on Thorndike's **law of exercise,** which states that the more often a stimulus–response connection is made, the stronger it becomes. This law and Skinner's finding that reinforcement of a response increases the likelihood of its occurrence provide some basis for the old maxim that practice makes perfect.[4]

Practice and drill can be provided by instructional techniques such as computer-assisted instruction (CAI), which relies on a schedule of reinforcement. In this approach, instructional materials are arranged in logical order and broken down into units (called *frames*) that lead students through a program in small steps from the simplest to the most complex material. A program may have hundreds or thousands of frames. Repetition is used to maximize correct responses and to prevent misconceptions. Continuous reinforcement is supplied by getting answers right, and the program presents material in a way that enables students to have a high rate of success. From time to time, frames review previous material or present the same material in different contexts. After making a mistake, the student must practice more before he or she can advance to another level of difficulty.[5]

classic professional viewpoint 4.1

The Persistence of Practice and Drill

Herbert M. Klieband

The decade of the 1890s was one in which a spirit of reform in education permeated the atmosphere. A young pediatrician, Joseph Mayer Rice, was caught up in this desire to remake American education and embarked on a tour of thirty-six American cities to observe what was going on in American schools. In one New York City school, Rice observed how children learned tiny bits of information by memorizing facts and reciting loudly and rapidly. Rice was properly outraged and dedicated himself to eradicating as far as possible such puerile forms of teaching.

Now, about a century later, such extreme forms of drill are virtually unknown, but all contemporary evidence indicates that recitation remains the predominant form of classroom discourse. This is despite the fact that many astute and sensitive educational reformers have called for a much greater measure of teaching procedures that involve, say, critical thinking or discovery activities. But even if teachers are not quite as rigid as in Rice's day, they continue to rely on handout sheets and workbooks to an unconscionable extent.

Why, we may ask, have classroom practices changed so little from Rice's day to the present? To my way of thinking, the most plausible answer lies in a conflict between two seemingly compatible tasks that teachers are asked to perform: control and teaching. Hardly anyone will argue against the need for a measure of control in classroom situations in order to carry forward the task of teaching. In practice, however, the emphasis on control has so predominated that we can be counted as good teachers so long as our classrooms are orderly. It almost does not matter whether we really teach or not. Practice and drill of the sort that Rice observed persist, not because they have specific pedagogical sanction but because they are proven instruments of control. It is only when teachers are able to see their primary role as teaching, not as enforcing a precarious order, that routine practice and drill will be relegated to their appropriately subordinate role in the classroom.

The main goal of practice and drill is to make sure that students understand the prerequisite skills for the day's lesson. A high success rate on practice items is important for student learning. Similarly, short practice sessions at one sitting minimize the risk of student boredom or burnout. The amount of time for practice varies with the age of the students.

In elementary and secondary grades, the technique of beginning a lesson by checking or reviewing the previous day's assignment is common in many direct instructional approaches. In a forty-five-minute period in mathematics, for example, educators recommend that daily practice and drill be used to start the lesson for approximately five to ten minutes, and that it be related to homework assignments and computation exercises. Educators also recommend practice as part of seat-work activity, when students are engaged in learning new concepts and skills.[6] Practice and drill usage varies by subject and grade level. Teachers need to decide what concepts and skills require this type of focus to ensure that students learn content material sufficiently for mastery.

At the secondary level, unscripted direct instruction takes a slightly different form, but it still consists of a set of explicit steps. Marzano and colleagues provide an example of what it might look like when teaching new terms or phrases:

Step 1: Present students with a brief explanation or description of the new term or phrase.

Step 2: Present students with a nonlinguistic representation of the new term or phrase.

Step 3: Ask students to generate their own explanations or descriptions of the term or phrase.

Step 4: Ask students to create their own nonlinguistic representation of the term or phrase.

Step 5: Periodically ask students to review the accuracy of their explanations and representations.[7]

Notice the common elements of direct instruction, whether elementary or secondary focused: clear explanation of what is to be learned, teacher modeling, student practice, and repetition or drill.

Two methods of instruction are often associated with practice and drill (the transmission view of education): mastery learning and direct instruction. They are discussed in the following two sections.

Mastery Learning Methods. Instruction that is arranged in a logical, progressive order and that matches materials and activities to individual needs and abilities is most effective in fostering achievement. The basis of mastery learning is making certain that adequate learning and mastery of certain concepts and skills have taken place, usually through practice and drill, "before progressing to more complex concepts and skills."[8] To understand mastery learning one must be able to justify the statement, "The more time on task a student spends, the more he will comprehend." Instruction is based on the notion that learning depends largely on the amount of time one spends attempting to understand. The idea is that all students, regardless of ability, can master a subject when given sufficient time.

A student who has difficulty attaining a specific level of performance or mastery can improve by working on the necessary prerequisites with practice and drill. The most important techniques for teaching simple tasks or reinforcing prior learning tasks involve practice and drill.

Direct Instruction Methods.   One of the most popular forms of group-based drill and practice is direct instruction (DI). This model was first popularized by Siegfried Engelmann several decades ago as a means of teaching basic academic skills to students. It has recently grown in popularity as a result of the systemic reform efforts within many urban school contexts. Teachers ask questions in a rapid sequence by following a script, and students respond with either a choral or individual response. Some teachers use the method for teaching vocabulary or specific skills. The DI method can also be unscripted, consisting of a sequenced set of explicit teaching steps.[9] In such instances the teacher would follow the guidelines in box 4.1 to conduct the lesson.

Box 4.1   Unscripted (Explicit) Direct Instruction

1. **Conduct daily reviews.**
   Check the previous day's work.
   Check homework.
   Reteach if necessary.

2. **Present new content/skills.**
   Introduce with concrete examples.
   Proceed in small steps.
   Give detailed instructions and explanations if necessary.
   Gradually phase in the material or task.

3. **Provide guided practice.**
   Provide teacher-led practice.
   Provide varying contexts and exercises for student practice.
   Use prompts, cues, visuals, and so on, when appropriate.
   Monitor students' work.
   Continue practice until student responses are firm.
   Aim for an 80 percent or higher success rate.

4. **Provide feedback.**
   Offer teacher-led feedback.
   Provide checklists.
   Correct by simplifying the material or task, giving clues, and explaining or reviewing steps.
   Reteach if necessary.

5. **Increase student responsibility.**
   Diminish prompts, clues, explanations, and so on.
   Increase the complexity of the material or task.
   Ensure student engagement during seat work.
   Monitor student work.
   Aim for a 95 percent minimum success rate.

6. Provide independent practice.
Encourage students to work on their own.
Provide extensive practice.
Facilitate application of new examples.

7. Conduct weekly and monthly reviews.
Check for understanding on an irregular basis.
Reteach if necessary.

Source: Adapted from Barak V. Rosenshine, "Teaching Functions in Instructional Programs," *Elementary School Journal* (March 1983): 338.

Traditionally, direct instruction stems from the expository approach. It is a teacher-centered strategy that uses a lecture–recitation design. When done effectively, it can promote teacher–student interactions. The teacher's role is to pass on facts and rules, while modeling how to solve problems. This transmission or direct instructional model contains basic practices for preparing and presenting lessons: (1) daily review, (2) presentation of new content, (3) guided practice, (4) feedback and corrections, (5) independent practice, and (6) periodic review.

The lesson objectives most suited to direct instruction relate to three domains: the cognitive, affective, and psychomotor. Your mind, feelings, and physical actions are what determine learning. Combining these three domains with an understanding of the learning paradigm produces the learning process. Box 4.2 illustrates lesson objectives in the three domains that work well with direct instruction.

Implementing Practice and Drill

In order to acquire many basic skills—especially in arithmetic, grammar, and foreign languages—you need to learn certain things to the point of automatic response, such as simple rules of grammar and speech, word recognition,

---

Box 4.2   Lesson Objectives Most Suited to Direct Instruction

Cognitive	Affective	Psychomotor Objectives
to recall	to listen	to repeat
to describe	to attend	to follow
to list	to comply	to place
to summarize	to value	to perform accurately
to paraphrase	to follow	to perform independently
to distinguish	to obey	to perform proficiently
to use	to display	to perform with speed
to organize	to express	to perform with coordination
to demonstrate	to prefer	to perform with timing

and mathematical calculations (adding, subtracting, multiplying). These skills, which are needed for more advanced learning, are best learned through practice and drill.

Although practice and drill are accepted in theory, realistic guidelines need to be applied to the classroom setting in order to make it work. Below is a list of guidelines based on practice and research.

1. *Practice must follow understanding and can enhance understanding.* Students will learn more easily and remember for a longer period of time if they practice what they understand. At the same time, understanding can be further increased through practice and drill of what is to be learned.

2. *Practice is more effective if students have a desire to learn what is being practiced.* Students will practice if they are motivated, and if what they are practicing is believed by them to have value or relevance. For these reasons, it is important for the teacher to provide situational variety (because repetition can become boring), interesting aspects of a particular skill as well as interesting drill items, situations in which students can use their skill or knowledge in other phases of learning, drill items related to students' experiences and interests, and explanations of the relationship between the skill or knowledge being learned and more advanced learning.

3. *Practice should be individualized.* Exercises should be organized so that each student can work independently at his or her own level of ability and rate of learning. In this way low-achieving students can devote more time to items that are difficult for them, and high-achieving students can advance without waiting for the others.

4. *Practice should be specific and systematic.* A drill exercise should be related to a particular objective or skill, and students should know in advance what is being practiced. Drill on specific skills in which students need practice will produce better results than will indiscriminate drill. Digressions should be avoided. A systematic, step-by-step procedure fits well with all learners, especially low-achieving students.

5. *Practice should be intermixed with different materials and parts of the lesson.* Drill items can constitute part of chalkboard exercises, photocopied materials, workbook and textbook exercises, homework, and reviews for tests.[10] Drill may also be used in conjunction with independent seat work, small-group learning, or student team learning.

6. *Practice should focus on a few skills rather than on many skills.* It is best to focus practice on one or two skills at a time and master those few skills before moving on to others.

7. *Practice should be organized so that students experience high rates of achievement.* Effective drill is characterized by high rates of correct response. Correct responses serve as reinforcement. When students discover that their answers are correct, they are encouraged to move on to the next question or item. This is especially important for students who

learn slowly. Research suggests that most students need at least a 90 percent rate of correct response while doing practice and drill activities (also for completing homework) in material that has supposedly been learned.[11] Success rate can be lower for students who become overly confused or frustrated, but this situation is avoidable as long as the teacher is available to correct their work immediately. Students who are confident in their learning skills view themselves as competent.[12] They are often willing to persist, even when they occasionally experience failure. Students who view themselves as incompetent will not persist in the same way.

8. *Practice should be organized so that students have immediate feedback.* Drills should be either student or teacher scored, with correct answers provided as soon as possible. The teacher needs to know scores or results in order to know whether students are ready to proceed to the next point or skill. Students—especially low-achieving students—need to know the correct responses immediately, not next week or when the teacher has had time to mark the papers.[13] Classroom practice also should be graded each day, with the teacher giving suggestions on how to proceed with wrong answers.

9. *Practice material should be used for diagnostic purposes.* Drill items should be constructed to reveal individual problem areas. Much of the practice material can be used for diagnostic purposes as long as the teacher knows what skills each student is working on and has mastered. Studying and keeping a record of students' performance can help the teacher recognize and treat problems before they become habits, seriously affect later work, or cause students to be branded as "remedial" or having a "learning disability."

10. *Practice material should provide progressive continuity between learning tasks.* Too often, teachers teach a skill and then move on to a new skill without testing. To foster continuous mastery and systematic recall, teachers should implement a whole sequence of practice for a specific unit or course, with intermittent drill at desirable intervals. Practice should occur frequently; it should cover tasks in order of difficulty, and the range of items should be wide enough to connect prerequisite learning tasks with new learning tasks.[14] See Tips for Teachers 4.1 for more insight into how to use practice and drill effectively.

As you can see, drill and practice are not an uncomplicated strategy. They must be used purposefully to direct and then reinforce student learning.

Instructional Approach II: Questioning

When checking for student understanding, use various forms of questioning.

Good teaching involves good questioning, especially when large groups of students are being taught. **Discovery teaching** based on questioning is an approach to instruction in which students interact with their environment—by

TIPS FOR TEACHERS 4.1

Improving Practice and Drill

Research has identified several recommendations for improving practice and drill and other seat-work activities to enhance academic learning:

1. *Have a clear system of rules and procedures for general behavior.* This allows students to deal with personal needs (e.g., seeking permission to use the bathroom pass) and procedural routines (sharpening a pencil) without disturbing classmates.

2. *Move around the room to monitor students' seat work.* Students should feel that the teacher is aware of their behavior and alert to difficulties they may encounter. The extent of monitoring correlates with the level of students' academic abilities and need for teacher attention.

3. *Provide comments, explanations, and feedback.* The more recognition or attention students receive, the more they are willing to pursue seat-work activities. Watch for signs of student confusion and deal with it quickly; this increases students' willingness to persist, helps you know how your students are doing, and helps you plan the next instructional task. Explain common problems immediately by interrupting the practice exercise if the problems are serious, or after the practice if students can wait.

4. *Spend more time teaching and reteaching the basic skills.* Elementary and low-achieving students should be exposed to more skill-focused learning, which requires practice and drill. When students have difficulty, it is important to instruct in small steps.

5. *Use practice during and after learning.* Practice and drill should be used after teaching a specific skill or process. It is most effective when mixed with other activities as learning progresses (e.g., demonstrations, explanations, and questions), depending on the students' age and abilities. However, for purposes of review or reteaching, in terms of efficient use of time, activities such as games and simulations for young children and field trips and buzz sessions for older students are not as effective as practice and drill and other paper-and-pencil activities.

6. *Provide variety and challenge in practice and drill.* Practice can easily drift into busy-work and frustrate or bore students if it is too easy, too difficult, or too monotonous.

7. *Keep students alert and focused on the task.* Teachers need to keep students on task—occasionally questioning them, calling on both volunteers and nonvolunteers, and elaborating on incorrect answers.

8. *Maintain a brisk pace.* There should be little confusion about what to do during practice and drill, and activities should not be interrupted by minor disturbances. A snap of the finger, eye contact, or other "signal" procedures should help deal with inattentive or disruptive students without stopping the lesson.

exploring and manipulating objects, wrestling with questions and controversies, or performing experiments—the idea being that students retain concepts they discover on their own. Skillful questioning arouses curiosity and stimulates imagination, both of which motivate students to search out new knowledge. Discovery teaching may or may not be totally teacher centered depending upon how it is used. If the teacher decides which problems students work on, it is teacher centered and called guided discovery. **Guided discovery** falls in the middle between direct and indirect instruction. Teachers using this approach must prepare by identifying the concepts and skills children need to learn, to lead them in understanding those concepts. A progression of questions that lead to concept discovery using the guided discovery approach consists of

1. Explaining the purpose of the lesson by stating the objective as a "to discover" or "to understand" question,

2. Presenting the first question to guide students,

3. Getting student responses,

4. Framing the rest of your questions to lead student discovery of the concept, and

5. Summarizing the lesson by asking students what they have discovered.

This type of questioning can challenge them, make them think, and help clarify concepts and problems related to the lesson. The type and sequence of the questions and the way students respond to them will influence the quality of classroom discussion and the effectiveness of instruction. Good teachers usually are skilled in striking a balance between factual, thought-provoking questions and questions that emphasize major points and stimulate lively discussion.

Types of Questions

Questions can be categorized in many ways, for example: according to the thinking process involved, from low level to high level (or, according to the cognitive taxonomy, from knowledge to evaluation); according to the type of answer required, whether convergent or divergent; and according to the degree of personal exploration or valuing.

Low-level questions emphasize memory and recall of information (e.g., Where is the Statue of Liberty?). This type of question focuses on facts and does not test understanding or problem-solving skills. Most typically, low-level questions begin with *what, when, where,* or *who.* Low-level questions are used to assess readiness for abstract thinking and to determine whether students can deal with higher-level questions that involve analysis, synthesis, and problem solving.

Low-level questions can foster learning for students who lack prerequisite knowledge. Low-level questioning is effective when used for instructional activities involving basic reading and math, or to build a foundation for future learning. The new low-level information must be related in a meaningful way to the knowledge and information the learner already possesses and in a manner that enables learners to personally discuss and describe their thoughts and ideas.[15]

High-level questions go beyond the level of memory and factual information and call for complex and abstract thinking. They usually begin with *how* or *why.* They typically are used after the teacher establishes that students possess certain fundamental understandings of the content. The ideal is to reach a balance between the two types of questions, with low-level questions typically preceding high-level questions. Regrettably, it is not uncommon to find that 70 to 90 percent of the questions teachers ask are low level.[16]

Criticism of the use of low-level questions is complicated by recent research indicating that low-level and narrowly defined questions (often evident in direct instructional approaches) characterize effective instructional programs for inner-city and low-achieving learners.[17] Some argue that teachers who ask high-level questions and encourage student-initiated comments and inquiry (or discovery of knowledge) are less effective with these types of students.[18] Those who advocate this point of view argue that these students lack a knowledge base and need more explicit instruction, low-level questions, and feedback from teachers before they can move to problem-solving skills and high-level questions. Teachers who subscribe to this practice unfortunately may become set in their use of low-level questions (and concomitant low expectations) and thus keep these students permanently in a cognitively second-rate instructional program. This may be part of the reason for the achievement gap between diverse student groups that is evidenced in so many urban school environments. Asking high-level questions demands patience and clear thinking on the part of the teacher. Creating appropriate timing, sequencing, and phrasing is no easy task for even the experienced teacher, but such factors are critical in motivating pupils.[19]

Benjamin Bloom's cognitive taxonomy can be related to the categories of low-level and high-level questions just described. Low-level questioning and knowledge correspond to the knowledge category of the taxonomy—what Bloom calls the "simplest" form of learning and the "most common educational objective."[20] High-level questioning and problem-solving skills correspond to the next five categories of the taxonomy—comprehension, application, analysis, synthesis, and evaluation (see table 4.1). The six categories of the cognitive taxonomy form a hierarchy of complexity levels from simplest to most advanced, with each level dependent upon the acquisition of skills at the lower levels. The sample questions in the table correspond to the cognitive categories of the taxonomy.

Questioning for Learning.   The relationship between thinking and questioning is unmistakable. "Thinking itself is questioning" is a classic quote from Dewey. Thinking is one of the basic objectives for teaching. To understand approaches to learning one must consider strategies that promote thinking. The first step in understanding is thinking, and to do that one must understand questioning and the procedures for promoting thinking. According to Andrade,

1. *We teach for thinking* when establishing safe environments by modeling risk taking and acceptance behaviors. By conducting classes that invite interaction and openness, we create a positive climate for thinking. Our use of verbal and nonverbal messages communicates to students that we also are learners and listeners.

2. *We teach of thinking* when we teach directly and define terms, post aims and objectives, and vary our classroom presentations.

3. *We teach with thinking* when we structure groups that invite participation and allow students to process information, while interacting with material in experimental activities.

4. *We teach about thinking* when we get children to think about their thinking.[21]

The ancient Greeks believed that good questioning was equivalent to good teaching. It made good teaching possible by developing interest, focusing attention, and correlating new content with prior student knowledge. Questions

Table 4.1   Questions Related to the Cognitive Taxonomy

Category	Sample Question
Knowledge	
Knowledge of specifics	Who discovered the Mississippi River?
Knowledge of ways and means of dealing with specifics	What type of word does an adjective modify?
Knowledge of universals and abstractions in a field	What is the best method for calculating the circumference of a circle?
Comprehension	
Translation	What do the words *hasta la vista* mean?
Interpretation	How do Democrats and Republicans differ in their view of spending?
Extrapolation	Given the present birth rate, what will be the world population by the year 2015?
Application	How has the Miranda decision affected civil liberties?
	Given a pie-shaped lot 120 ft. × 110 ft. × 100 ft. and village setback conditions of 15 ft. in all directions, what is the largest one-story home you can build on this lot?
Analysis	
Analysis of elements	How would you distinguish between fact and opinion in the article we just read?
Analysis of relationships	How does Picasso organize colors, shapes, and sizes to produce images?
Analysis of organizational principles	How does John Steinbeck use his characters to discuss the notion of friendship in *Of Mice and Men*?
Synthesis	
Production of a unique communication	Who can write a simple melodic line?
Production of a plan or proposed set of operations	How would you go about determining the chemical weight of an unknown substance?
Derivation of a set of abstract relations	What are the common causes for cell breakdown in the cases of mutations, cancer, and aging?
Evaluation	
Judgment in terms of internal evidence	Who can show the fallacies of Hitler's *Mein Kampf?*
Judgment in terms of external evidence	Who can judge what is wrong with the architect's design for the plumbing and electricity?

Source: Allan C. Ornstein, "Questioning: The Essence of Good Teaching." *NASSP Bulletin* (May 1987): 73–74. Copyright © 1987. Reprinted by permission of Sage Publications.

organize and fix our knowledge by forcing us to review what we know. Good questioning is truly a search for meaning, which centers on objective facts rather than personal interpretations. Meanings are understood within the framework of our own experiences, which allows us to learn and teach. We cannot assume that a body of information is in itself meaningful since much of what we teach is in itself meaningless. This is so because we assume that knowledge has value for the one who acquires it, apart from its meaning.[22]

When related to questioning, Bloom's Taxonomy can be interpreted as suggesting ways of sequencing questions inductively and deductively. This is important, since you must decide on the approach you are going to use when you design a lesson. Will you be like Sherlock Holmes and find one solution from many clues, or will you find many solutions, all stemming from one starting place? The lessons you design will utilize either inductive reasoning (specific to general) or deductive reasoning (general to specific).

The number of questions you ask depends on your purpose. If you are testing for knowledge or attempting to facilitate in the solution of a problem, you should ask as many as needed. Questions are essentially classified into two categories: drill and thought.

1. *Drill* (fact) questions are lower-level questions that ask for knowledge, comprehension, and application. They begin with words such as *where, when, who, what,* and *which*.

2. *Thought* questions are higher-level questions related to analysis, synthesis, and evaluation. They begin with words and phrases such as *why, if, suppose, compare, how, compose, can you contrast,* or *would you*.

Question Design.   A good question is direct, concise, simple, clear, and to the point. It is logical and stated in language that everyone can understand. It should be sufficiently difficult to promote critical thinking. A good question appeals to students' interests and needs. The best questions are directed toward solving a problem. They consist of pivotal questions that focus students and encourage interactive discussion. To develop positive social interaction, discourage responses directed to the teacher, and ask students to direct their responses to their classmates instead. There are specific steps one should take while questioning students. Box 4.3 provides general steps that will make questioning more effective.

Convergent questions tend to have one correct or best answer. For this reason they are often mistakenly identified as low-level (knowledge-level) questions. They can, however, involve logic and complex data, abstract ideas, analogies, and multiple relationships. Use convergent questions when students are attempting to solve difficult problems in math and science, especially those involving analysis of equations and word problems.[23]

Divergent questions are open ended and can have many different answers. Stating a "right" answer is not always the most important goal; what's more important is to select a method for arriving at an answer. Students should be encouraged to state their reasoning and to provide supporting examples and evidence. Divergent questions are associated with high-level thinking processes and can encourage creative thinking and discovery learning.

Box 4.3   Steps to Effective Questioning

Follow these steps when asking questions:

1. Organize your questions before asking.
2. First pose your question, then call on a student.
3. Allow an appropriate amount of time before you elicit a student response.
4. Respond to any student queries that arise from the original question and move to next item.

The following poor questioning techniques should be avoided:

- "Yes or no" questions should be avoided. (Was it tasty?)
- Stay away from echo questions. (Washington was the first president. Who was the first president?)
- Avoid double questions. (Where did Cortez go and why did he go?)
- Pass up "guess" questions. (Was Hamlet a good or bad character?)
- Avoid leading questions that tell the answer and insult the recipient's intelligence. (Eight is the sum of 4 and 4, right?)
- Tugging questions are mind-numbing. (What has replaced the Soviet Union's communistic government? Isn't it nationalistic capitalism?)
- Questions should not be repeated. If necessary, have a student repeat.
- Inaudible questions are never good. You can't get an answer to a question that is not heard.
- Unclear or poorly phrased questions can be impossible to answer. (What about the stimulus package?)
- Never call on a pupil *before* you ask the question. First, ask the question, then call on the student by name. This gives students time to think and allows for response time.

Source: Richard T. Scarpaci, *Resource Methods for Managing K–12 Instruction: A Case Study Approach* (Boston: Allyn & Bacon, 2009).

Convergent questions usually start with *what, who, when,* or *where;* divergent questions usually start with *how* or *why. What* or *who* questions, followed by *why,* are actually divergent questions. For example, *"Who* won the Civil War?" leads to the ultimate question *"Why?"* The differences are highlighted by the sample questions in table 4.2. Most teachers ask far more *what, who, when,* and *where* questions than *how* or *why* questions.[24] This is so because convergent questions are simple to phrase and grade, and they make good questions for practice and review. In contrast, divergent questions require more teacher flexibility, and they necessitate skill on the part of students to handle uncertainty and possible lack of teacher approval. In general, the pace of divergent questioning is slower. Students have more opportunity to exchange ideas and differing opinions, and disagreement among students and between students and teacher is more likely.

Table 4.2 Sample Convergent and Divergent Questions

Subject and Grade Level	Convergent Questions	Divergent Questions
Social studies, 5th–7th	Where did the Boston Tea Party take place? When did it take place?	Why did the Boston Tea Party take place? Why did it take place in Boston, not New York or Philadelphia?
Social studies, 7th–8th	What are the three export products from Argentina?	How does wheat production in Argentina affect wheat export in our country?
English, 5th–7th	What is the verb in the sentence "The girl told the boy what to do"?	How do we write the present and future tense of the verb in the sentence "I told the boy what to do"?
English, 10th–11th	Who wrote *A Farewell to Arms*?	How might Hemingway's experience as a news reporter have affected his writing of the novel *A Farewell to Arms*?
Science, 2nd–5th	Which planet is closest to the sun?	How would you compare living conditions on Mercury with those on Earth?
	Who was the first American astronaut to travel in space?	What planet, other than Earth, would you prefer to visit if you were an astronaut? Why?
Science, 9th–11th	What are two elements of water?	Why is water purified?
Math, 4th–5th	What is the definition of a triangle?	How have triangles influenced architecture?
Math, 6th–9th	What is the shortest distance between two points?	What is the best air route to take from New York City to Moscow? Why?

Right Answers Count

In the majority of American classrooms, teachers ask convergent questions that entail a "right" answer, and students are expected to give that answer—often resulting in teacher approval. These questions and answers, when coupled with the students' need for approval (especially at the elementary grade level), permit teachers to dominate classroom interaction. According to Jules Henry, students "learn the signal response system called docility and thus obtain approval from the teacher."[25] Indeed, what usually counts in school are right answers, not necessarily how students arrived at the answer.

For low-achieving students and for students who need teacher approval, the magic word from the teacher is often yes or *right*. The teacher determines what is right in the classroom, and the easiest way to test students is to ask convergent questions. Divergent questions, on the other hand, lead to novel responses—responses that the teacher does not always expect and responses that take up class time.

John Holt points out that, as students become right-answer oriented, they become producers who produce what teachers want—not thinkers who construct personal understandings of what the content suggests. It is the rare student who is willing to play with ideas, not caring whether the teacher confirms an answer is right. The average child has a need to be right because that is what teachers in American schools expect: "She [the student] cannot bear to be wrong. When she is wrong . . . the only thing to do is to forget it as quickly as possible."[26] Few teachers understand that wrong answers are just as important as right answers. When students provide wrong answers they are showing the teacher *how* they are thinking about a particular question or idea and constructing the content, which in turn suggests what reteaching the teacher needs to do. Instead of dismissing wrong answers, instead ask students how they derived them and then make a decision on how to reteach. Interestingly, the Japanese, who consistently perform well in international comparisons, place more focus on *how* a student derives an answer than on whether a student has the right answer.

Asking questions to which there is only one right answer fosters a view of learning that is self-limiting—one that looks for simple solutions to complex problems, one that relies on authority rather than on rational judgment. It also breeds a rigid and narrow mind that fails to recognize or is unwilling to admit that facts and figures are screened through a filtering process of personal and social experience and interpretation.[27] The current emphasis on academic standards in American education has enhanced America's right-answer orientation. That need not be the case in your classroom. Remember, you want to teach content and to help students explore that content. To do that successfully requires variability.

Asking Questions Correctly

Good questioning is both a methodology and an art; there are certain rules to follow that have been found to apply in most cases, but good judgment is also needed. See Tips for Teachers 4.2 and 4.3 for some pointers on formulating questions and recommendations for procedures when asking questions.

In preparation for asking questions in class, a number of instructional strategies have been shown to be effective for a large number of different teachers and students. Most of these instructional strategies come from educational psychology and researchers who study teacher effectiveness, not from the curriculum, instruction, or teaching methods that one might think would contribute to this field of knowledge.

Wait-Time.   The interval between asking a question and the student response is referred to as **wait-time.** One study by Mary Budd Rowe indicated that the average amount of time teachers wait is one second. Increasing the

TIPS FOR TEACHERS 4.2

"Don'ts" in Asking Questions

Good questioning techniques have to be developed slowly and over time. They must become second nature—a habit. Just as you can form good or bad habits in driving a car or swinging a golf club, you can develop good and bad habits in questioning. Try to eliminate any bad tendencies you've acquired in asking questions before they become ingrained as habits. What follows is a list of types of questions a teacher should *not* ask:

1. *"Yes or no" questions or questions that give a guesser a fifty-fifty chance of getting the right answer.* "Did Orwell write *Animal Farm*?" and "Who won the battle at Gettysburg?" are the kinds of questions that encourage guessing, impulsive thinking, and right-answer orientation, not conceptual thinking or problem solving. If the teacher accidentally asks this kind of question, he or she should follow up immediately with a why or how question.

2. *Indefinite or vague questions.* "What are the important cities of the United States?" and "How would you describe the following sentence?" are confusing questions and must be repeated or refined. Questions should be clearly worded and coincide with the intent of the teacher.

3. *Guessing questions.* Guessing questions can also be "yes or no" questions, indefinite or vague questions. Ask students to explain ideas and show relationships rather than requesting detailed or trivial information.

4. *Double or multiple questions.* Asking, "What is the chemical formula for salt? What is its chemical weight?" confuses students. Which question does the teacher want answered?

5. *Suggestive or leading questions.* "Why was Andrew Jackson a great president?" appears to be asking for an opinion, but the opinion has already been given or implied.

6. *Fill-in questions.* In "The New Frontier occurred during whose presidency?" the question is embedded. It is better to express the question clearly: "Which president implemented the New Frontier?"

7. *Overload questions.* "In connection with pollution factors and the sun's rays, what conclusions can we make about the future water level?" and "How did Manifest Destiny lead to imperialism and colonialism while enhancing the industrialization of the country?" are indefinite, multiple, and wordy. Trim excess verbiage; use simple rather than overly formal or obscure vocabulary; and ask clear, simple questions to avoid confusing the student.

8. *Tugging questions.* "What else?" and "Who else?" tug at the student and do not really encourage thought.

9. *Cross-examination questions.* You may be able to assist a student by asking a series of questions to draw out information. However, this should be distinguished from asking many or rapid questions of the same student, which not only can overwhelm the targeted student but also can make the rest of the class feel neglected.

Several more important "don'ts" are important to mention:

10. *Never call the name of a student before asking a question.* As soon as the other students know that someone else is responsible for the answer, their attention lessens. First ask a question, then pause to allow time for comprehension, and then call on someone to answer.

11. *Never answer a question asked by a student if the student should know the answer.* Turn the question back to the class and ask, "Who can answer that question?"

12. *Never repeat questions or repeat answers given by students.* Reiteration fosters poor work habits and inattentiveness. A good practice is to say, "Who can repeat that question (or that answer)?"

13. *Never exploit bright students or volunteers.* The rest of the class becomes inattentive and loses the thread of the discussion.

14. *Never allow choral responses or hand waving.* Both are conducive to undesirable behavior.

15. *Never allow improper speech or incomplete answers to go unnoticed.* Young people are quick to cultivate bad habits. Supply the correction without stopping the recitation.

Source: Adapted from Allan C. Ornstein, "Questioning The Essence of Good Teaching: Part II." *NASSP Bulletin* (February 1988): 77.

TIPS FOR TEACHERS 4.3

"Do's" in Asking Questions

Now that you know what *not* to do after reading Tips for Teachers 4.2, here is a list of things you *should* do in questioning. Practice them so they become second nature in your instructional process.

1. *Ask questions that are stimulating and not merely memory testing or dull.* A good teacher arouses students and makes them reflect with thought-provoking questions. Questions that ask for information recall will not sustain the attention of a class, and that's when discipline and management problems begin.

2. *Ask questions that are commensurate with students' abilities.* Questions that are dramatically below or above the abilities of students will bore or confuse them. Target questions, even on difficult subjects, within the ability level of the majority of the class.

3. *Ask questions that are relevant to students.* Questions that draw on students' life experiences will be relevant.

4. Ask *questions that are sequential.* Questions and answers should be used as stepping stones to the next question, which contributes to continuous learning.

5. *Vary the length and difficulty of questions.* Questions should be diversified so that both high- and low-achieving students will be motivated to participate. Observe individual differences and phrase questions to ensure that all students take part in the discussion.

(continued)

6. *Ask questions that are clear and simple.* Questions should be easily understood and trimmed of excess verbiage.

7. *Encourage students to ask questions of each other and to make comments.* This results in students becoming active learners and cooperating on a cognitive and social level, essential for reflective thinking and social development. Good questions stimulate further questions by both teacher and students. Encouraging student comments and interaction and referring student questions and comments to other students (even when they are directed at the teacher) promotes discussion.

8. *Allots sufficient time for deliberation.* Pausing for a few seconds until several hands go up gives everyone, particularly the learners who need more time, a chance to consider the question. As a result, everyone profits from the discussion, and learning takes place for all.

9. *Follow up incorrect answers.* Take advantage of incorrect or marginal answers. Probe the student's mind. Encourage the student to think about the question. Perhaps the student's thinking is partially correct, even novel!

10. *Follow up correct answers.* Use a correct answer as a lead to another question. A correct answer sometimes needs elaboration or can be used to stimulate student discussion.

11. *Call on nonvolunteers as well as volunteers.* Some students are shy and need coaxing from the teacher. Other students tend to daydream and need assistance from the teacher to keep attentive. Distribute questions among the entire class so that everyone can participate.

12. *Call on disruptive students.* This practice involves troublesome students without interrupting the lesson. It is important, however, not to call on them as a disciplinary technique. Call on "problem" students when they are already involved. Reinforce the behavior that you desire.

13. *Prepare five or six pivotal questions.* Such questions test students' understanding of the lesson as well as enhance the lesson's unity and coherence.

14. *Write the objective and summary of the lesson as a question, preferably as a problem.* Questions encourage the class to think. Students are made to consider the new work when asked about it.

15. *Change your physical position and move around the room.* Teacher energy and vitality induce class activity, rapport, and socialization. Circulating around the classroom also fosters an active audience and prevents daydreaming and disciplinary problems.

wait-time to three to four seconds has several beneficial effects on student responses: (1) length of response increases, (2) unsolicited but appropriate responses increase, (3) failure to respond decreases, (4) confidence (as reflected in an affirmative rather than a questioning tone of voice) increases, (5) speculative responses increase, (6) student-to-student responses increase, (7) evidence-inference statements increase, (8) student questions increase, and (9) responses from students rated by teachers as relatively slow increase.[28]

No negative side effects of increasing wait-time have been observed and the positive effects are numerous, yet many teachers do not employ this wait-time instructional strategy. Other data suggest that asking one to four questions per minute is reasonable and that beginning teachers ask too many questions, averaging only one second of wait-time.[29] It's important to note that although all students need time to process information, low-achieving students need more time—but the data indicate that teachers tend to wait less time for an answer from the students they perceive as academically slow. In such cases the teacher must be willing to slow down the lesson, cover fewer topics, focus on the most important ideas, ask more questions, and develop explanations.

Directing.   The recommended strategy in directing questions to students is to ask the question first and then call a student's name, because that way more students will think about it. Research on classroom management also confirms that it is better to be unpredictable in calling on students to answer questions but to do so in a way that maximizes participation. Indeed, Evertson and her colleagues suggest that "This can be done by using a checklist or shuffled stack of name cards. Some teachers [even] place a strip of construction paper on each student's desk as a marker. As a student contributes . . . the marker is removed."[30] On the other hand, when calling on students to read, using a predictable order seems to be more effective with the lower grades and with low-achieving students.[31] The reason is perhaps that predictability reduces anxiety, which is important for young children who are reading in front of the class.

The research also indicates that calling on nonvolunteers can be effective as long as students who are called on can answer the question most of the time. It is a good idea to call on nonvolunteers when you believe that students can respond correctly, but it is not appropriate to embarrass them with their inability to answer the questions or to catch them off-task so that you can discipline them. This is probably true at all grade levels and subjects. If you call on a nonvolunteer and get an incorrect response, you can do two things: (1) match the correct statement to the wrong answer (e.g., if you ask, "Should public employee unions be allowed to retain collective bargaining rights?" and a student responds "Teachers shouldn't strike," say, "Collective bargaining rights do not mean the right to strike: I'm looking for an understanding of the term *collective bargaining*"; or (2) ask the student to explain his response. Quite frankly, some student explanations of wrong answers will make sense, which provides the teacher with more opportunities to probe and question. The key is that, to the extent possible, a teacher should stick with the student who was originally asked the question.

Although some research indicates that teachers should call on nonvolunteers no more than 15 percent of the time, practice indicates this figure may be too low.[32] Asking questions primarily of volunteers increases the tendency to call on high-achieving students more often than low-achieving students. Calling on more nonvolunteers increases the likelihood that low-achieving students will be included in the discussion. It is generally a good idea to call on low achievers who usually do not volunteer, and they should periodically be called on as nonvolunteers as long as they are likely to be able to answer the question correctly.

If they do give a wrong answer, you have several choices. You can, as suggested earlier, (a) provide the right "lead" for the answer the student gave, (b) reword the question and probe, or (c) ask another student (through a question redirect) for a correction. We'll examine the redirect and probing options next.

Redirecting and Probing.   If a student response to a question is incorrect or inadequate, rather than providing the answer an effective strategy is to redirect the question to another student or to probe for a better answer from the same student. In general, teachers overuse redirecting. Redirecting the question is better for high-achieving students, but probing is better for low-achieving students. High-achieving students seem more able to cope with minor academic failure in front of their peers and thus are better able to accept redirection. This is especially true if a teacher knows how to "honor" a wrong answer (i.e., treat the answer as logical but incorrect). Teacher persistence in seeking improved responses from low-achieving or at-risk students is a reflection of positive teacher expectations, which is important in trying to reach and teach such students.

In **probing** the teacher stays with the same student, asking for clarification, rephrasing the question or asking related questions, and restating the student's ideas. It is important not to overdo it, lest the probing become a cross-examination.[33] On the other hand, if the teacher feels that the student was not paying attention, it is best not to probe and give the student a second chance; otherwise the teacher would unwittingly be condoning (even rewarding) the student's lack of attention. During the probing process the teacher may ask a series of easier questions that lead toward the answer to the original question. If the student answers correctly (either initially or in response to a rephrased question), the teacher may want to follow up with a related question to pursue the implications of the answer and to ensure student understanding.

Probing is acceptable for all students. With high-achieving students it tends to foster high-level responses and discussion. With low-achieving students it tends to reduce the frequency of no responses or incorrect responses. In both cases probing is positively correlated with increased student achievement, especially if it fosters students' ability to engage in personal problem solving by pushing them to solve intellectual problems themselves rather than to have problems solved for them.[34]

Commenting and Praising.   While the results of research on the use of praise vary, it is generally agreed that honest, thoughtful praise increases achievement and motivation. Positive reactions can simply mean a smile, a nod of approval, or a brief comment ("Good," "Correct," "That's true") indicating approval or acceptance.

Most teachers do not use sufficient or genuine praise while questioning or with other methods of instruction. Yet it is clear that praise and other positive reinforcement strategies can have positive effects on student behavior.[35] Experts have noted that praise of good answers to questions or good work in general needs to be spontaneous and genuine, not for the purpose of controlling student behavior or tacitly expressing teacher expectations.[36] Phony praise or public praise can have detrimental effects.

The research results about negative comments are also mixed. It is suggested that teachers use criticism and disapproval sparingly, even less than praise, which is a good thing since criticism can have a detrimental effect on student achievement. Similarly, if used by a teacher in response to a student question or comment, criticism can curtail further student questions or responses.[37] Low achievers receive more criticism than high achievers—and it is possible that low achievement causes teachers to use more criticism. Boys receive more criticism (and also more attention) from teachers than do girls. We know that boys often achieve less than girls because teachers tend to emphasize physical activities with boys and intellectual exercises with girls.[38] In other words, a correlation seems to exist between criticism (or negative attention) and lowered achievement levels, but a cause-and-effect relationship is uncertain.

We have explored a series of ideas and observations about questioning. Questions can be used for different reasons and to achieve different goals. Ideally, though, they are always used to assess what students know and how they are making sense of what the teacher is teaching. (See Case Study 4.1 to review your own understandings regarding questioning.)

The following case discusses the importance of understanding specific approaches to learning by utilizing effective questioning techniques. Compare and analyze the various approaches, and decide if a teacher should be held responsible for student learning.

Case Study 4.1
Questioning for Learning

Silvia Levin just knew that there was an unmistakable relationship between thinking, questioning, and learning. She remembered that Dewey said, "Thinking itself is questioning." Silvia wanted to *question for learning* so that her students would develop critical thinking skills. The problem was to identify which methods and approaches to learning promoted the critical thinking skills that lead to learning. The first step in understanding thinking was to understand questioning, and that process would lead to promoting the thinking and learning processes.

Unfortunately, Silvia's principal, Mrs. Howard, was more concerned with student achievement than with questioning strategies. Mrs. Howard was not someone who could be described as easy going, even though she did listen and at times was known to change her mind. She could be aptly described as strong-willed, opinionated, extremely self-confident, and very set in her ways. She had observed Silvia teaching a social studies lesson to her fifth-grade class. When the lesson ended, she had asked Silvia what she thought of her own performance. Silvia said she had asked thought-provoking questions that required her children to develop higher-order thinking skills. Mrs. Howard actually smiled and said, "So you judge your effectiveness on your questioning technique?"

Silvia responded that good questioning leads to student learning, so she felt the answer to Mrs. Howard's question was yes. "Wouldn't it be better to judge your lesson on how much the students had learned rather than on the form of questions you used?" Mrs. Howard inquired. Silvia responded, "I evaluated my effectiveness by the way the children answered my questions. Besides, giving a test—or even a short quiz—would have taken too much time." Mrs.

Howard then asked Silvia why she had not asked the students what they had learned, or just asked them to turn and tell their neighbor what the lesson was about while she, Silvia, moved about the room. Silvia responded that she did use a final summary question.

Mrs. Howard began discussing the history of questioning in education. She spoke about the ancient Greeks, who believed as Silvia did that to question well was to teach well. "What they forgot," said Mrs. Howard, "is that teaching is really about learning, not questioning. Good questioning is in reality a search for meaning; it is a distinctly personal search. You should remember that learning centers on objective facts rather than personal meanings. Just because a student thinks critically and constructs personal meanings does not mean that learning has occurred. You can't assume that a body of information is in itself meaningful. Much of what we teach is in itself meaningless because we assume that knowledge in itself is valuable no matter what meaning is constructed by the student."

Mrs. Howard continued by saying that questioning is essentially a tool. "The number of questions you ask depends on your purpose. If you're assessing knowledge or guiding students to a solution of a problem, you should ask as many as needed. Questions come basically in two categories: drill and thought. The drill or fact questions are lower-level questions that ask for knowledge, comprehension and application. They usually begin with words such as where, when, who, what, and which. Thought questions, on the other hand, are higher-level questions related to analysis, synthesis, and evaluation. They usually begin with why, if, suppose, compare, how, compose, can you contrast, or would you."

Mrs. Howard continued, "Various factors should be considered when designing a question. A good question is direct, concise, simple, clear, and to the point. It is logical, and stated in language that all can understand while still being sufficiently difficult to promote critical thinking. The question should also appeal to a majority of the class's interests. The best questions are usually directed toward solving a problem." Finally, Mrs. Howard told Silvia that she should try to integrate her belief that *questioning leads to learning* with *teaching is really about learning.*

Discussion Topics and Questions to Ponder

1. List the questions asked by Mrs. Howard and the responses given by Silvia. How would you have responded?

2. What was Principal Howard attempting to achieve by her line of questioning?

3. Compare and contrast the two statements, "questioning leads to learning" and "teaching is really about learning."

4. Analyze the following statement: "Much of what we teach is in itself meaningless because we assume that knowledge in itself is valuable, no matter what meaning is constructed by the student." Do you agree or disagree? Explain your answer.

5. Was Silvia correct in believing that when you question for learning your students develop critical thinking skills?

What would you do if . . . ?

1. You were given the list below as the be-all and end-all guide to questioning.

   Steps to follow when asking questions

   • Prepare questions before asking.

   • Ask your question first, then call on students to answer.

   • Give children time to think before they answer.

   • Elicit questions from the students, making sure they understand the content before moving on.

2. You were told that effective questioning is "similar to a lawyer's never asking questions that elicit unwanted responses. You should always know what response you should get. If your question fails to get the desired response, rephrase it until it does." What's wrong (or right) with this statement?

3. You were asked to prepare a list of poor questioning techniques that should be avoided. Where possible, rewrite the examples in parentheses to make an effective question.

   Example: Never ask yes or no questions. (Was it good?)
   Answer: How do you feel about it?

   - Do not ask echo questions. (New York is noted for diversity. What is noted for diversity?)
   - Avoid double questions. (Where did Columbus go, and why did he go?)
   - Do not be cute and ask "guess the answer" questions. (Is the prize behind the door big or small?)
   - Leading questions that tell you the answer insult the recipient's intelligence. (4 is the sum of 2 and 2, right?)
   - Tugging questions are boring for both you and the student. (4 is ¼ of 16, isn't it?)
   - Vague or poorly phrased questions do not deserve an answer. (What about the products of Japan?)

Instructional Approach III: Selecting Direct or Indirect Instructional Practices

There are two basic approaches to selecting the instructional methods you will employ in your teaching: direct and indirect.

Although this seems simple enough, instruction and teaching are more complicated than that. Each approach has benefits and drawbacks, and both require some preliminary preparation. There may be occasions when more than one method is appropriate for a lesson. Good teachers know this and work at developing skills to make the process seamless. In general, the appropriateness of a lesson depends upon the age and developmental level of the students. You would not teach the philosophical implications of indentured servitude to a first-grade class, for example. Nor would you teach what is already known, except as a review. The instructional method chosen should fit your teaching personality and be suited to the lesson's objectives inclusive of time, space and materials, and physical setting. No one has come up with a "right way" for teaching all lessons, but there are guides to assist a teacher in making the best possible decision.

Direct Instructional Practices

Below is a list of instructional methods showing the advantages, drawbacks, and the type of teacher preparation needed to put them into practice. The methods are divided into direct and indirect teaching strategies.

Direct Teaching.   *Advantages*: Direct teaching focuses students on unambiguous learning objectives. The teacher explains the purpose for content and discusses its significance. The practice of explanation assists in clarifying lesson objectives and in maintaining task orientation. This method of teaching is a quick and efficient way to teach facts and skills. Assessment is relatively straightforward.

Drawbacks: Direct teaching can become boring, since in most cases the process depends on repetitive scripted lessons leading to rote learning, which stifles creativity. It requires a great deal of preparation and excellent communication skills. Direct instruction is not thought to be effective for teaching higher-order thinking skills.

Preparation: All materials must be organized in advance, and the teacher should know the level of student readiness for the content to be taught. To be successful, teachers must be aware of the necessary prerequisites for every lesson.

Lecture/Explanation.   *Advantages*: **Lectures** must be presented in a logical, clear manner using a direct instructional methodology. An effective lecturer is eloquent and able to paint verbal pictures that can engage listeners by providing inspirational experiences. It is most valuable when endeavoring to put across a great deal of content to large groups in a limited period.

Drawbacks: The lecturer must be an excellent speaker. Passive listeners rarely become engaged in lessons. A test must be used to assess lesson effectiveness. Young children below grade 4 have limited attention spans that make this approach inappropriate.

Preparation: Lecture requires content expertise. Ideas and concepts must be clearly presented in a timely fashion and developed with anecdotes and examples so that the class is motivated by the introduction and convinced by the final lesson summary.

TIPS FOR TEACHERS 4.4

Enhancing Your Explanations

There are numerous methods for improving your lectures and explanations in class. Evaluate your lesson with regard to the following guidelines:

1. Maintain eye contact with the class.
2. Use handouts and overheads to help students follow the presentation and focus on important ideas.
3. Avoid high levels of detail unless supplemented by graphs, tables, or illustrations.
4. Write important information on the chalkboard
5. Define new terms and concepts.
6. Provide an outline for note taking.
7. Present relevant examples to explain major ideas.
8. Relate new information to prior information.
9. Summarize important ideas.

Explanation Combined with Discussion.   *Advantages:* Students become involved by being allowed to ask questions during or after a presentation. This approach provides a more engaging atmosphere.

Drawbacks: Time spent answering questions takes away from the amount of material that can be covered. Questions that are irrelevant can change the direction of the lesson, sacrificing clarity and focus. Untoward questions can become unmanageable.

Preparation: Attempt to anticipate difficult questions and prepare fitting responses in advance. Don't just allow for student questions; use the opportunity to question the class to evaluate the effectiveness of the lesson.

Discussion.   *Advantages:* Discussion provides a necessary process to learning by allowing information to be questioned, interpreted, and assimilated. Discussion affords opportunity for the collection of ideas and experiences while developing a sharing environment. It works very well with small groups of 15 or less because it allows everyone to participate. In small groups it is usually easy to reach a consensus on any particular issue. Students can attain a greater depth of understanding.

Drawbacks: Effective discussion is difficult with more than 20 students, and careful planning and thought are needed on how the group should be composed. Be aware that often a few students will tend to dominate all discussion, and some will not participate at all. The process can also be time consuming, especially if the teacher is thrown off track by irrelevant questions.

Preparation: Skillful planning is required to guide lessons to the desired conclusion. Organize a large class into small effective groups that can work independently on specific topics, while using a question outline to guide the discussion.

Guest Speakers.   *Advantages*: Guest experts provide different opinions and points of view. A guest speaker can provoke an exchange of ideas and generate better discussion opportunities. Different speakers with controversial views create an exciting setting for learning. Guest speakers personalize and add character to topics and issues.

Drawbacks: A speaker's magnetic personality may eclipse important positions taken by less engaging speakers. Not all guest speakers will be articulate; some may even do their cause damage! All experts are not effective speakers and may present accurate material unclearly and unscientifically.

Preparation: Students must be prepped to know what to listen for. They must be taught how to make unprejudiced critical judgments. Getting everyone in the same place at the same time can be a tiring experience, and the logistics for a good panel presentation can be quite troublesome. The teacher must coordinate panelists and focus, introduce, and summarize positions. Teachers must contact speakers and coordinate programs so that they are relevant to the issues the class is researching.

Indirect Instructional Practices

Indirect Teaching.   *Advantages:* Indirect teaching develops critical thinking skills that are necessary for life. It encourages creativity and thinking outside the box. It adds to construction of meaning and knowledge, and it encourages students to assume responsibility for their own learning.

Drawbacks: It is difficult to manage and can seem vague, which will cause students to lose focus and direction. It is not an efficient way to teach facts and skills. Evaluation is tricky since creativity can be relative. It goes against a teacher's natural instinct to direct and instruct students.

Preparation: The role of the teacher must change from instructor to guide. Teachers must assist students in developing higher-order thinking skills, and they must create supportive settings that will inspire students to learn independently. Students must be highly motivated by the teacher's actions and suggestions.

Cooperative Learning.
Advantages: This practice cultivates mutual responsibility, and it helps students develop social skills and learn to be understanding, patient, and team players. Students learn how to analyze data in a scientific fashion and arrive at solutions to predetermined problems. It replicates many life skills and gives students the opportunity to communicate findings with others. It is a practice that most students like, since they are social beings and prefer working in cooperative settings.

Drawbacks: Some students do not work well in groups; they prefer to be individualists and find it difficult to share work and credit. Aggressive, bright students tend to take charge, do all the work, and may act superior. Some may have difficulty in analyzing data and need teacher guidance. This method is not useful for learning facts and skills since it is difficult to focus students on curriculum objectives. The products may be subjective and difficult to evaluate.

Preparation: Worksheets must be prepared to guide and instruct students with regard to objectives, skills, and content to be covered. Students must be taught how to work in groups; organizing and analyzing data obtained from surveys can require large blocks of instructional time. Teachers must devise a strategy that is fitting for evaluation (usually accomplished through the creation of a rubric fitted to the specific project).

Group Brainstorming.
Advantages: Students learn to listen while developing the creative-thinking skills required for new ideas. This process encourages full participation because all ideas are shared and recorded. *Accountable talk*, a practice that goes well with brainstorming, develops children's ability to speak to the topic, based on information they are required to cite and reference.

Drawbacks: Brainstorming is unwieldy, and direction can be lost if not focused. Students have individual experiences and may find it difficult to think outside of the box. Unconstructive criticism and personal remarks may be made if students have not been taught to use "accountable talk."

Preparation: Planning is difficult because it is hard to select suitable issues that will motivate students. Brainstormed topics must be related to the curriculum yet relevant to students' own interests and experiences.

Multimedia and Technology.
Advantages: Videos, slides, and PowerPoint presentations enhance instruction and keep attention focused. Today's students live in a multimedia world and expect to be entertained on occasion. The use of technology makes any presentation look professional while inspiring questions and discussion.

Drawbacks: It can overstimulate and allow too many issues to be raised. Uninterested students may not participate in discussion because of a loss of clarity and focus in a lesson. Malfunctions can occur, which distract from any presentation.

Preparation: Students must be prepped for follow-up questions before the actual presentation. A major problem for the teacher is learning how to obtain, assemble, and run the equipment.

Case Studies. *Advantages:* Case studies encourage higher-order thinking skills to assist in analytic problem solving. They can be used to explore complex issues and topics. This is an engaging approach, which stimulates student participation in a real and meaningful way. Students see studies as stories that they can relate to their own experiences to create understandings.

Drawbacks: If relevance is not apparent, students tend not to participate. If a study provides insufficient information, it can lead to unsuitable results. Students may not possess the abilities necessary to diagnose individual studies.

Preparation: Case studies require a great deal of preparation. They must be clearly written and defined. Teachers need to spend a great deal of time preparing studies or finding case studies that correlate to the content being taught.

Role Playing. *Advantages:* Role playing introduces problems in a dramatic fashion and allows children to assume the roles of others. The process helps develop an appreciation for other points of view. It provides for a problem-solving methodology through an exploration of solutions from different viewpoints, at the same time developing human-relations skills in real-life simulation activities.

Drawbacks: Some students are too shy and self-conscious to participate. Role playing is not suitable for large groups, because it allows for limited involvement and participation. Students may not grasp the relevance of the role they are expected to portray.

Preparation: Each situation, and the roles children are playing, must be explained. Students need a great deal of time to learn how to role-play in an academic structure. Belief that children learn by doing and not solely by instruction is an article of faith for this practice. (See box 4.4 for a list of teacher-centered and student-centered instructional practices.) Case Study 4.2 will enhance your understanding of these basic strategies.

Box 4.4   Instructional Practices

Teacher-Centered Instruction	**Student-Centered Instruction**
Direct Teaching/ Instructional Practices	*Indirect Teaching/ Instructional Practices*
lecture/explanation	cooperative learning
explanation combined with discussion	group brainstorming
discussion	multimedia technology
guest speakers	case studies
	role playing

The following case study presents the basic methods of instruction that must be mastered if one is to become a successful pedagogue. Read the case and compare and contrast the ideas presented to determine what exactly makes up effective instructional strategies.

Case Study 4.2
Direct versus Indirect Instructional Strategies

The debate was titled *The Key to Effective Teaching: Direct or Indirect Instruction?* Professor Hughes' students had been asked to prepare position papers and brief statements in support of their position regarding direct or indirect instruction. The class was fairly evenly divided between those who favored one or the other. After having read his students' position papers he selected one student to summarize the argument for each point of view.

The first to speak was Irwin Kantor, who felt that there was only one method for a teacher to master in order to become an effective teacher. All one had to do was use a direct instructional approach. He stressed the point that children needed to be motivated in order to learn, and that could only be accomplished by using punishments and rewards. Children needed a basic method of instruction which they could all relate to and understand. Irwin claimed that his approach to teaching had always been expository; children didn't discover meaning indirectly, it had to be transmitted through the teacher's efforts. All one had to do to be an effective teacher was to establish clear goals while using the lecture and discussion methods of instruction as tools. A direct instructional teacher-centered approach, said Irwin, was the key to effective teaching.

Marylou Valletta stood up next to respond to Irwin's remarks. She felt he was totally off course in arguing for direct instruction. Indirect instructional methods were the key to effective teaching. Indirect strategies such as inquiry teaching (incorporating open-ended discussions with student research) were the key to effectiveness. Children should be allowed to select projects and participate in activities aimed at developing creative thinking. When used properly, this approach results in self-motivated children seeking to create and understand new knowledge. The idea of discovery learning is that students participate in problem-solving activities of their own choosing. An indirect instructional approach, said Marylou, guarantees effective teaching.

Professor Hughes asked the class if anyone had questions for Irwin or Marylou. Sal Evans stood up and asked if discussion could only be used with direct instruction. Marylou said she would like to respond to that question. She explained that discussion can take many different forms, from student centered to teacher centered. Activities such as brainstorming, debates, role-playing, simulations, and small-group discussions could be described as either direct or indirect, depending upon your approach.

Professor Hughes looked at his class and said that they had covered a great deal during this session. He suggested that the class take some time before the next class meeting to digest and reflect on the positions taken during the debate on direct and indirect instruction. "Try to determine if you favor teacher- or student-centered instructional methods. I would also suggest that you look at the term *eclectic* to decide if your viewpoint is somewhere in the middle. I caution you not to forget that personality and enthusiasm are effective motivators and attention getters. Also remember that enthusiasm is infectious, and few will learn from a teacher who is not liked or respected."

Discussion Topics and Questions to Ponder

1. List and contrast the teacher-centered and student-centered methods discussed during the debate. Note the instructional methods that go well with either approach. Be sure to justify your choices.

2. Was either Irwin or Marylou (or both) inconsistent or eclectic in their thinking? Defend your reasoning.

3. Why did Professor Hughes remind the class to consider teaching personality when they were to reflect on indirect and direct instructional approaches as the key to effective teaching?

4. Describe the basic methods for instruction used by effective teachers you have known.

5. How would you determine if the instructional practice you used was appropriate and effective?

What would you do if . . . ?

1. You were asked to select a teacher-centered and a student-centered practice you could employ for each of the following topics. Justify your choices.
   - Space travel
   - Alternative energy sources
   - Midyear elections
   - Holiday class play
   - Note taking

2. You were handed the following chart and asked to explain it.

   Instructional Strategies

Teacher-Centered Strategies	**Student-Centered Strategies**
Direct instruction	Indirect instruction
Expository teaching	Discovery teaching
Guided discovery	Problem-solving inquiry approach
The scientific method	Seminars
Direct Teaching	**Indirect Teaching**
Lecture	Cooperative learning
Lecture and discussion	Group brainstorming
Discussion	Multimedia technology
Small-group discussion	Case studies
Guest speakers	Role playing
	Research surveys

Character education

3. You were asked to take a position for or against one of these positions. What would you say?

Instructional Practices Require Explanations of Content

Whether using indirect or direct strategies, all instructional practices require varying degrees of content explanation at times. This is crucial for student comprehension. The question is how to explain clearly and succinctly while maintaining an environment of sharing and caring. The following steps and suggestions may be of assistance:

- *Establish rapport with students.* At the beginning of a talk, take measures to make a connection with students. (Periodically telling a story or using humor helps maintain student interest in the subject and rapport with you.) Always keep in mind the need to maintain the interest of students and the fact that students will react to you first on a personal basis and then on a cognitive basis.

- *Prepare addresses.* Outline the major concepts or ideas in advance, especially for hierarchic talks. Indicate the corresponding activities and materials—say, in the lesson plan—to introduce at a certain point. Except for short passages or quotations to make a point, you should not read from notes. You must know the material well enough to speak clearly and with animation, and to speak extemporaneously as you sense the need of the moment and the interests of the students.

- *Control the length of explanations.* Brief explanations are suitable for elementary school students. Short explanations of five to ten minutes are acceptable at the middle grade and junior high school levels. High school students can tolerate longer periods of interesting teacher talk. Always try to limit your explanations by using questions, discussions, various student activities, and media as supplementary tools of instruction. Overall, though, remember the 10–2 rule—for every ten minutes of talk a couple of minutes of interaction are necessary to assess learning.

- *Motivate students to pay attention.* Relevance motivates students. To achieve relevance consider the students' age, ability, educational experiences, environment, interests, needs, perceived goals, and career aspirations. You can make the lesson more understandable and interesting by combining other methods, materials, and media with your talk. When students perceive the relevance of, understand, and are interested in the topic, they become success oriented and are more intrinsically motivated—that is, they pursue "the goal of achievement for the sake of achievement."[39]

- *Establish structure and sequence.* A disorganized talk confuses and bores its audience. Present major concepts and difficult ideas in a linear and logical fashion, with examples and questions to test students' understanding. Develop facts and concepts systematically and sequentially from statement to statement. Relate the overall topic to the topic of the previous lesson. Make your sentence structure and vocabulary appropriate for the students' level of development. Although this seems an obvious point, many beginning teachers overestimate the vocabulary level and content understanding of students.

The criteria for a structured explanation are (1) *continuity*, or a sequenced arrangement of ideas expressed in intelligible and grammatically correct sentences; (2) *simplicity*, or the absence of complex sentences and the use of language within the students' vocabulary range; and (3) *explicitness*, or the identification and explanation of major concepts and relationships.[40]

Effective explanatory talk tends to correspond with what we often mean by coaching. More effective teachers engage in highly structured explanations and are more responsive to student questions, more adequate in presenting content, more complete in providing specific information, and better at giving students feedback to help them learn.[41]

- *Provide appropriate graphic organizers.* Research suggests that teachers who use graphic organizers enhance student achievement.[42] Graphic organizers help students assimilate content. They allow students to organize the ideas to be presented by telling them in advance what they will focus on and how it will be structured. Another technique is to outline the major topics or parts of the lesson, either orally or in writing (on the chalkboard), as they unfold (not in advance) during the discussions. This is especially helpful when students are listening to the teacher and must select, process, and assimilate the information with which they are working.

- *Avoid vagueness.* Lectures and explanations that are free of vague language are easier to follow and to understand.

Another factor that leads to vagueness is discontinuous and irrelevant content. The content may be important at another time, but when introduced at an inappropriate time it distracts from the main ideas. In an effective talk, the sequence of ideas from sentence to sentence is clear, and the language is free of ill-defined and redundant terminology. You need to be clear and concise—using short and precise sentences; providing examples; using simple, jargon-free language; and including the minimum number of concepts to make a point. As a presenter you need to be decisive, avoid fillers and long pauses, and generally display confidence in order to maintain your credibility.[43]

- *Combine instructional materials and strategies.* The use of audiovisual aids and special materials and activities can enliven a talk and reinforce its content. The use of informal cooperative learning strategies can also enhance talks. Varied stimuli are important for all learners, but younger students especially benefit from less verbalization and more illustrations and activities. Display such aids only when you talk about them; explain visuals to your audience; use a marker or highlighter when using an overhead to focus students on key points; and use the *k-i-s-s* (keep it short and simple) principle—minimize detail. Make sure visuals (whether overhead or PowerPoint) are readable from the back of the room.

- *Encourage students to take notes.* The activity of recording notes serves as an encoding (comprehension) function, helping to integrate content into long-term memory. Note takers outperform listeners (those who don't take notes) about four to one at the high school and college level. Effective note taking serves as both a storage function and a review function prior to tests.[44] You can also provide an outline for students to use in helping them take their notes.

- *Summarize content.* Classroom discussions should always end with **final summaries** or conclusions—what some educators call *post-organizers*.

The lesson may also have **internal summaries,** sometimes called *medial summaries, conceptual frameworks,* or *chunking strategies.*[45] *Medial summaries,* with accompanying summary activities and transitions, subdivide a lesson into clear parts. It is more important to incorporate medial summaries for low-achieving and young students than for high-achieving or older students.

The best type of summary (medial or final) briefly reviews the presentation and gives students a chance to see whether they understand the material by asking them to explain ideas, provide examples, evaluate data, and do some exercises. It makes them aware of what they have learned and helps identify the major ideas of the lesson.

After the final summary, the teacher should explain related homework and prepare students for any problems they may encounter in their assignments. The teacher also might establish a connection between the just-completed lesson and the next lesson.

Questions for Reflection

There is a wonderful scene in the movie *Ferris Bueller's Day Off* when the teacher (played by Ben Stein) is lecturing to students. He talks and then asks questions, but he gives the students little time to respond. Yet, even if they did have time, they could not respond because they really are not listening. Watch that section of the movie and identify a way in which the same content could be delivered effectively. Stein is doing everything wrong for comedy effect, but it is funny because we have all experienced it. Identify specific things that he is doing wrong. How could he have done the lecture right? It would not, then, be funny, but it would be educational. How can a lecture be both funny and educational? Explain and discuss your answer.

Instructional Approach IV: Student-Centered Learning

When fostering critical or creative thinking, use strategies that emphasize student-centered learning.

Since the beginning of the twentieth century, a great deal of literature has focused on students' problem solving and related thinking skills. Ever since Charles Judd (at the University of Chicago) and Edward Thorndike (at Columbia University) showed that learning could be explained in terms of general principles of thinking and that methods of attacking problems could be applied to different situations, educators and psychologists have worked to identify ways to teach students how to solve problems.

Problem Solving

From 1910 until the 1950s, John Dewey's **reflective thinking** was considered the classic model for problem solving. In the 1950s Piaget and others introduced new models of various cognitive and information-processing strategies.

Although Dewey's model is viewed as an oversimplification by cognition theorists, it is still considered practical. He wanted to improve students' reasoning process, so he recommended adopting the reflective thinking method for all subjects and grade levels. Reflective thinking involves five steps: (1) become aware of difficulty, (2) identify the problem, (3) assemble and classify data and formulate hypotheses, (4) accept or reject tentative hypotheses, and (5) formulate and evaluate conclusions.[46] This reflective model is based on a mixture of theory and practice. Bransford and Stein outline a similar model for problem-solving: (1) identify the problem, (2) define it, (3) explore possible strategies, (4) act on the strategies, and (5) look at the effects of your efforts.[47]

Heuristic thinking is engaging in exploratory processes that only have value in that they may lead to the solution of a problem. This is similar to physicians who diagnose problems by doing tests to eliminate what is *not* the problem in order to narrow the possibilities. Good teachers know their content, know how to assess students relative to that content, and know how to make appropriate interventions.[48] According to Newell's and Simon's method for dealing with a problem, the person first constructs a representation of the problem, called the *problem space,* and then works out a solution that involves a search through the problem space. The problem solver may break the problem into components, activate old information from memory, or seek new information. If an exploratory solution proves to be successful, the task ends.[49] If it fails, the person backtracks, sidetracks, or redefines the problem or method used to solve it.

In terms of actual teaching, the problem-solving process might look something like the three approaches presented in table 4.3. In concept formation the students are taught how to create their own concepts; in generalizing the students are taught to critically look at ideas; and in application of principles the students are taught how to predict. Look carefully at the questions in the table to see the unique perspective of each approach.

Does it make a difference whether the teacher hierarchically presents content or the students construct it? The answer is yes. When students *induce* their own concepts, they tend to recall the information longer and better.[50] In Linda Darling-Hammond's words,

> In effective classrooms, teachers use diverse strategies ranging from whole class lecture and recitation to guided inquiry, small group work, discussions, independent work, projects, experiments . . . and teacher interaction with individuals and small groups.[51]

Teachers use these different approaches to ensure that all students have multiple ways to assimilate content.

Students as Problem Solvers

Individuals are confronted with problems when they encounter situations to which they must respond but do not know immediately what the response should be. Regardless of the problem-solving method, students need relevant information to assess a situation and arrive at a response—that is, to solve the problem. The strategies used relate to a student's age and the specific problem

Table 4.3   Cognitive Operations and Levels of Questions

Overt Activity	Eliciting Questions
Cognitive task 1: Concept formation	
1. Enumeration and listing	What did you see? Hear? Note?
2. Grouping together	What belongs together? On what criterion?
3. Labeling, categorizing	What would you call these groups? What belongs under what?
Cognitive task 2: Generalizing and inferring	
1. Identifying points	What did you note? See? Find?
2. Explaining identified items of information	Why did such and such happen? Why is such and such true?
3. Making inferences or generalizations	What does this mean? What would you conclude? What generalizations can you make?
Cognitive task 3: Application of principles	
1. Predicting consequences, explaining unfamiliar phenomena, hypotheses	What would happen if . . . ?
2. Explaining and supporting predictions and hypotheses	Why do you think this would happen?
3. Verifying predictions and hypotheses	What would it take for such and such to be true? Would it be true in all cases? At what times?

Source: Hilda Taba, *Teaching Strategies and Cognitive Functions in Elementary School Children*, Cooperative Research Project No. 2404 (San Francisco: San Francisco State College, 1966), 39–40, 42.

at hand. Not all successful students will use the same strategy to solve the same problem, and often more than one strategy can be used.

Even in simple math, students use different strategies to solve problems and therefore have different frameworks about the relative difficulty of the problems. For example, if John has 6 marbles and Sally has 8, how many marbles do they have together? Most students simply add 6 and 8, in what we might term a *common strategy*. In a *joint strategy*, students add elements (6 + 6 = 12; 2 more is 14). With a *separate strategy;* students remove elements (8 + 8 = 16, 2 less is 14). A *part-part-whole strategy* involves undertaking two or more elements ("I tabulated both numbers by adding 1 and 6 and subtracting 1 from 8; that makes 7 + 7, which is 14"). All student approaches are potentially correct strategies.[52]

As problems become more abstract, so do students' problem-solving strategies. The teacher who insists on one strategy and penalizes students who use another appropriate strategy is discouraging their problem-solving potential. Teachers need to become aware of how students process information and what strategies they use to solve problems in order to teach problem solving according to the way students think. They can accomplish this by asking questions, listening to responses, and inspecting student work. They can also do so by using different types of deductive and inductive strategies that help different students understand content.

Some basic problem-solving strategies emerge when the behavior of successful and unsuccessful problem solvers is explored. Successful students do the following:

1. *Comprehend the problem.* Successful problem solvers react to selected cues and immediately begin to work out a solution. Unsuccessful students miss cues and often misinterpret the problem.

2. *Employ previous knowledge.* Successful students utilize previous knowledge to solve a new problem. Unsuccessful students possess the accessory information but do not utilize it. They often do not know where or how to start.

3. *Use active problem-solving behavior.* Successful students are more active than unsuccessful students, and they verbalize what they are doing. They simplify the problem, whenever possible, or break it down into parts. The unsuccessful students are unable to clarify or state concisely what they are doing. They often do not attempt to analyze the various parts.

4. *Display confidence toward problem solving.* Successful students have confidence and view the problem as a challenge. Unsuccessful students lack confidence, become frustrated, and give up.[53]

Metacognitive skills (or processes) are transferable competencies that play a significant role in students' high-order thinking. These skills represent knowledge of how to do something (usually involving a plan, a set of steps, or procedures) as well as the ability to evaluate and modify performance. Based on a review of the research, some metacognitive skills have been found to distinguish successful problem solvers from others and to translate into instructional methods. Ten of these skills are listed below.

1. *Comprehension monitoring:* knowing when one understands or does not understand something; evaluating one's performance

2. *Understanding decisions:* comprehending what one is doing and the reasons why

3. *Planning:* taking time to develop a strategy; considering options; proceeding without impulse

4. *Estimating task difficulty:* gauging difficulty and allocating sufficient time for difficult problems

5. *Task presentation:* staying with the task; being able to ignore internal and external distractions; maintaining direction in one's thinking

6. *Coping strategies:* staying calm; being able to cope when things are not going easily; not giving up or becoming anxious or frustrated

7. *Internal cues:* searching for context clues when confronted with difficult or novel problems

8. *Retracking:* looking up definitions; rereading previous information; knowing when to backtrack

9. *Noting and correcting:* using logical approaches; double-checking; recognizing inconsistencies, contradictions, or gaps in performance

10. *Flexible approaches:* willingness to use alternative approaches; knowing when to search for another strategy; trying random approaches that are sensible and plausible when the original approach has been unsuccessful.[54]

It should be noted that low-achieving and younger students have fewer metacognitive skills than high-achieving and older students.[55] The implication for teaching is that an increase in knowledge of subject matter does not necessarily produce changes in metacognitive skills. These generally reflect high-order thinking processes that cannot be learned or developed overnight or in one subject. Developmental age is crucial in limiting potential metacognitive skills among students. An 8-year-old student is capable of just so much and cannot be pushed beyond his or her cognitive stage. According to Piaget, not until about age 11 is a child capable of employing many of these metacognitive skills (corresponding to formal mental operations), and not until approximately age 15 is the child capable of fully employing all metacognitive skills in an efficient manner.[56] One of the advantages of using multiple instructional approaches is that the teacher is explicitly helping students understand different ways to explore content.

Sternberg points out that students don't learn how to solve problems by osmosis. Encourage students to use their "practical intelligence"—inferred knowledge that is not taught but used explicitly by problem solvers. Student problem-solving techniques can be improved by taking notes; getting organized; understanding questions; asking questions, especially when they don't understand something; following directions; underlining main ideas in texts; outlining text information and classroom discussions; seeing likenesses and differences in subject matter; keeping track of time; and getting things done on time.[57]

Most of these techniques are basic learning strategies that are based on common sense and correlate with school achievement. By providing knowledge of and practice in applying learning strategies we enhance student self-concept and coping abilities, which provides the means for problem solving. (See Case Study 4.3 to explore how a teacher can aid students in problem solving.)

The following case study presents a situation in which a teacher poses a conceptual problem about prejudice to students. The teacher wants students to create their own concept and then explore the meaning of that concept in relationship to a broader concept: prejudice. Read carefully how this strategy is used, with an eye for identifying areas where you could use this approach.

Case Study 4.3
Concept Formation

Lucille Salerno had decided to teach a lesson that she felt her sixth-grade social studies class needed to learn. It was a lesson on prejudice. Negative remarks had been made regarding the number of diverse peoples who had recently moved into the community. This, combined with the fact that the Afghanistan war was in danger of being lost and withdrawal of troops from Iraq had hardly begun, created a tense situation. Students had expressed strong views about Afghanistan and Iraq that occasionally erupted into heated words. Lucille wanted her students to understand how their remarks and views had the potential for fostering prejudice. She decided to teach her lesson in an indirect fashion *without* beginning by formally defining prejudice. Rather, she wanted her students to construct their own understanding of the term and its meaning and implications.

She began by asking students to consider Gordon W. Allport's ladder of prejudice that outlines how people progress in their levels of enmity toward others. She wrote the following list on the chalkboard:

1. *Speech,* or the process of talking negatively about a group.

2. *Avoidance,* or the disregard for a group that manifests the trait or characteristic perceived as "wrong."

3. *Discrimination,* or the treatment of the "defined" group in a different, diminished way.

4. *Physical attack,* or the victimization of those who are within a threatened group.

5. *Extermination,* or the excessive use of physical attack to the point that it becomes deadly.

The children were then asked to list the times they had observed in their own lives, or in their study of history, when speech and avoidance relative to the treatment of a group of people have become commonplace and accepted as the "right" way to respond to others. Lucille guided her students in a brainstorming session in which a wide variety of personal examples of groups being treated differently was discussed. Finally a list of historic instances emanating from the brainstorming was placed on the board that included:

- Jim Crow laws
- Segregation policies
- Nuremberg laws
- Ku Klux Klan

The personal examples included:

- Name calling
- Creating groups with special membership rules to exclude "undesirables."
- Bullying weaker children
- Making fun of others' national origin, religion, and culture

After a great deal of discussion Lucille divided the children into small groups and asked them to select examples of inappropriate actions. They were then asked to come up with a title for their selections. She then asked the students to draw a large circle on some chart paper that she provided, to place terms within the circle that fit together, and then to create a generic label for those terms. One group created the following list but could only think of four terms.

1. Ku Klux Klan

2. Street Gangs

3. Nazis

4. Terrorists

The title they gave the grouping was: *Groups that See Themselves as Superior to Others.*

Lucille then asked the rest of the class two questions: (1) Can you think of other groups that you think fit into this category? and (2) Why might a feeling of superiority lead to "climbing" Allport's ladder of prejudice?

The class identified some other examples and spent the rest of the period discussing a definition of prejudice provided by the teacher. They also discussed the "concepts" that each group developed. Lucille then collected all the concepts and wrote three homework questions for everyone to explore. The questions were:

Why did the Ku Klux Klan and the Nazis form? What events led to their creation?

Who have been the primary spokespersons for the views of the respective groups?

How have they attempted to get their message out?

Discussion Topics and Questions to Ponder

1. What are the advantages of having students create their own concepts?
2. What are the problems?
3. What other approaches could have been used to teach this same set of ideas about prejudice and its consequences?
4. Would the teacher have been better off to just give them the concept, its definition, and then examples? Why or why not?
5. How would you teach a lesson in your content area that had students form concepts indirectly?

What would you do if . . . ?

1. The children felt that there was nothing wrong with exclusion.
2. The children said that everyone has the right to free speech.
3. A parent complained, stating that prejudice was not a topic on the state examinations and that you were just wasting time.

Students as Inquirers

While most teachers acknowledge that experiential approaches are important, many need help incorporating them into their lessons. Good and Grouws have identified five processes for mathematics, but they can be applied to the teaching–learning process in all subjects.

1. *Attending to prerequisites.* Solving new problems is based largely on understanding previously learned skills and concepts of the subject. The teacher should use skills and concepts previously mastered by the students as a basis for solving (new) problems.

2. *Attending to relationships.* Students need to understand how ideas are related; the teacher should emphasize meaning and interpretation of ideas to help them understand.

3. *Attending to representation.* The more students are able to represent a problem in context with concrete or real-world phenomena, the better able students are to solve the problem.

4. *Generalizability of concepts.* Teachers need to explain the general applicability of the idea; students should practice skills and processes that apply to many settings.

5. *Attending to language.* Teachers should use the precise terminology of their subject; students must learn basic terms and concepts of the subject.[58]

The test for problem solving is the ability to apply or use the learned strategies in new situations, or at least in a variety of situations. Many times teachers erroneously think students have "mastered" relevant facts and procedures when in reality, according to Alan Schoenfeld, they often have blindly learned a strategy and can use it only in circumstances similar to those in which they were taught. When given a slightly different version of a problem, or when they must make inferences or leaps in thinking, such students are stymied.[59] Similarly, most of the problems found in textbooks and those assigned for homework are not problems in the true sense. They are, instead, exercises or tasks that reinforce specific, usually rote, procedures for solving a problem. In math, for example, most word problems are solved by students who rely on a key word without fully understanding the procedures involved. A real problem presents a student with a difficulty; the answer cannot be obtained by relying on rote procedures. It calls for relating or rearranging learned concepts or procedures with new ideas generated by the problem. This is not straightforward process. A student's understanding of the procedures and of the transfer of that understanding to new situations is crucial. Most students cannot function in this arena because traditional instructional methods tend to emphasize rote procedures.

Teachers can help students become better problem solvers and inquirers by using a variety of student- and teacher-centered instructional approaches. Class time must incorporate experimental, discovery, and/or reflective processes and activities. An expectation or norm is created in the classroom that *acquiring* knowledge is only the first step to understanding and is not as important as actually *using* knowledge.

---

classic professional viewpoint 4.2

Methods for Teaching

Benjamin S. Bloom

There is much rote learning in schools throughout the world. However, in a small number of countries—for example, Japan, South Korea, Israel, and Thailand—I find great emphasis on such higher mental processes as problem solving, application of principles, analytical skills, and creativity. These countries have very active central curriculum centers charged with responsibility to constantly improve textbooks and other learning materials, and to provide in-service training for teachers, especially as it relates to the curriculum and teaching methods.

In these countries, subjects are taught as methods of inquiry into the nature of science, mathematics, the arts, and the social studies. Subjects are taught as much for the ways of thinking they represent as for their traditional content. Much of this learning makes use of observations, reflections on observations, experimentation with phenomena, and the use of firsthand data and daily experiences, as well as primary printed sources.

In sharp contrast to these teaching methods, teachers in the United States use textbooks that rarely pose real problems. The textbooks I observe emphasize specific content to be remembered and give students little opportunity to discover underlying concepts and principles—and even less opportunity to attack real problems in their environments. I estimate that over 90 percent of the test questions that American students are expected to answer deal with little more than remembered information. Our instructional materials, classroom teaching methods, and testing methods rarely rise above knowledge.

Theory into Practice

Teachers and students across grade levels spend a majority of their classroom instructional time on practice and drill, questioning, explaining, problem solving, inquiry, and discovery. The remaining time is spent on other instructional methods and activities such as role-playing, simulations or games, small-group discussions, independent projects, class reporting, and monitoring.[60]

Some basic recommendations in the form of questions can help you implement these various methods in classrooms:

1. Is your lesson planned in advance? Is it based on clear academic standards? Do students know what to expect and when to change activities? Is the pace of the lesson brisk? Do you slow down when further detail or explanation is warranted?

2. Are your materials and methods prepared in advance and incorporated without hindering the momentum of the lesson?

3. Do you combine explanations, illustrations, and demonstrations with your methods and with what is to be learned?

4. Does the lesson proceed in sequenced steps? Do academic tasks or skills build on the preceding ones? Are students able to see relationships between previous and present learning?

5. Do you use practice and drill activities before and after other new learning to ensure that students have mastered required academic tasks? Have you incorporated practice exercises into several parts of the lesson, including preliminary reviews and end summaries?

6. Do you give younger students and low-achieving students more practice and drill activities than older and high-achieving students? Are practice exercises checked and corrected promptly?

7. When asking questions, do you make sure all students have the opportunity to respond by using a variety of types of questions (low-level, high-level, convergent, divergent, valuing, etc.)? Do you allow sufficient wait-time? Do you call on nonvolunteers as frequently as or more than volunteers? Do you call on low achievers as frequently as or more than high achievers?

8. Are you aiming at a high rate of success in student responses to your questions? Do you ask easier or more concrete questions of low achievers to ensure high success rates?

9. Are your questions sequenced to ensure understanding and to build a knowledge base before proceeding to more difficult questions? Do you ask clear and concise questions? Or do you find you have to rephrase and repeat questions?

10. While lecturing or explaining, do you readily ask questions to maintain student attention and to gauge student understanding and progress? Do you test and assess students frequently?

11. Do you provide supportive groups in the classroom (i.e., sharing dyads, cooperative learning groups, tutors, or homework helpers) to overcome anxiety in problem solving? Do you identify the strengths and resources of the students to enhance their confidence level?

12. Do you take time to model or show, or let students discover, *different* ways to solve problems, including how to compare, analyze, modify, guess, hypothesize, and predict? (Weak teachers explain problem concepts a second time, LOUDER. Strong teachers use different explanations, metaphors, or analogs.)

13. Do you modify your instructional approaches to ensure that classroom structures (such as tracking) do not limit instructional opportunities for some students?

14. Do you use different instructional approaches during the duration of a unit?

CONCLUSIONS

- Most teaching activities can be categorized as one of these instructional methods: practice and drill, questioning, or problem solving. No one approach, whether teacher-centered or student-centered, is inherently good or bad. How you teach is dictated by who and what you teach.

- The method of practice and drill has applications for teaching skills and processes.

- Questioning is used as part of many different types of lessons, including low level and high level, convergent and divergent, and valuing. Questioning is crucial to good instruction.

- Differentiating methods enhance achievement and add to an eclectic approach to instruction.

- Direct and indirect approaches to instruction are basic for all instructional methods.

- Explaining/lecturing is one of the oldest instructional methods. Different types of teacher talk can be effective with different students, but in general the length, complexity, and frequency of teacher talk should be kept brief for younger and slower students.

- Problem-solving approaches help students actively take responsibility for their own learning. Such approaches, which are inductive in nature, help students discover knowledge, not just assimilate teacher-identified content, and help them retain information better and longer.

KEY TERMS

convergent questions	heuristic thinking	low-level questions
discovery teaching	high-level questions	probing
divergent questions	internal summaries	reflective thinking
final summaries	law of exercise	wait-time
guided discovery	lectures	

DISCUSSION QUESTIONS

1. Why is practice and drill used more often in elementary grades than in secondary grades? Should it be? Explain your answers.

2. What is the difference between convergent and divergent questions? Why do most teachers rely on convergent questions?

3. What are the advantages and disadvantages of student-centered approaches as an instructional method?

4. Does the national emphasis on academic standards suggest that teachers should favor one type of instruction over another?

5. How would you teach a lesson using direct instruction, problem solving, or indirect instruction? Outline the structure of the lesson.

MINI-CASES FROM THE FIELD

Case One: Practice and Drill

Bill Judge could not believe he was going to teach his eleventh-grade chemistry class using a practice-and-drill approach. This strategy went against everything he had been taught in graduate school. As a science teacher he was supposed to be imbued with the scientific method. His lessons were supposed to encourage critical thinking and develop problem-solving skills. Bill had been directed to prepare his class for the state examination by reviewing past tests and then drilling the students on those portions of the test that were repeated every year.

1. Was Bill given bad advice? Justify your answer.

2. There are strengths and limitations to any approach. What are the strengths of practice and drill? What are the limitations?

3. How could Bill's task have been accomplished using a different approach?

4. How could a computer program be used to teach a review lesson?

Case Two: Questioning

Tina had been asked to redo her lesson on the differences between adjectives and adverbs because of a lack of clear and concise questions. Tina thought that was really unfair. She had spent over an hour preparing her lesson for her third-grade class. When she taught the lesson she had simply explained the difference and had her class do an exercise in which they had to circle every adjective and adverb that appeared in the selection they were reading. Yet Tina's mentor had said that was not enough.

1. Identify any weaknesses in the approach Tina had taken to teach the lesson.

2. Why did Tina's mentor feel that it was not the explaining that was weak but the lack of questioning?

3. How could Tina have employed questioning in this lesson?

4. Give an example of a question that might bring closure to this lesson. Explain your reasoning.

5. How could questions have been used to motivate the lesson? To develop the content?

Case Three: Direct Instructional Practices

Lisa was asked to prepare a lesson to be presented for demonstration at a staff departmental conference. Her department consisted of five colleagues who had a total of less than ten years experience among them. Their chairperson, Mrs. Weston, had explained that she wanted her staff to teach demonstration lessons for each other. In that way they could help develop and improve different instructional strategies. She began by assigning each teacher a direct instruction practice from the following list: direct teaching, lecture/explanation, explanation combined with discussion, discussion, and guest speakers.

1. Had Mrs. Weston chosen a good strategy to help develop her staff's skills? Explain.
2. Give an example of another way that these teachers could have been assisted.
3. How could brainstorming have been used?
4. How could technology or multimedia be used to accomplish this task?
5. If Mrs. Weston's procedures had been followed, would the teachers have been able to improve their skills? Explain your reasoning.

Case Four: Indirect Instructional Practices and Child-Centered Learning

Doris asked her friend Betty to explain the difference between student-centered instruction and indirect instructional practices. Betty responded by saying that no difference existed: They were both the same thing described in different ways. Doris disagreed and said that she felt strategies such as indirect teaching, cooperative learning, group brainstorming, multimedia and technology, case studies, and role playing were indirect instructional practices. Student-centered instruction, said Doris, was instruction in which young students' learning, not the instructional approach, was the focus of the lesson.

1. What was Doris confused about?
2. How did Betty attempt to resolve the problem?
3. What is the difference between student-centered learning, child-centered learning, and indirect instructional practices?
4. Why couldn't a lecture be considered a student-centered approach?
5. Why is cooperative learning an example of both student-centered instruction and an indirect instructional approach?

Case Five: Student-Centered Learning

Doris said, "Now I am really confused! I don't know the difference between student-centered learning and child-centered learning!" Betty responded by saying, "I told you before, no differences exist!" Doris said, "I understand that any practice is as good as its success rate. If a student learns, then that strategy worked. What I don't understand is how a practice can be child centered, student centered, and an indirect instructional practice at the same time."

1. Give examples of strategies that could be classified as all three practices mentioned by Doris.
2. Which practices would you favor, and why would you favor them?
3. How would you describe each of the following with regard to child or student centered:
   - Cooperative learning
   - Group brainstorming
   - Multimedia and technology
   - Case studies
   - Role playing
4. When would you use a strategy other than a child-centered one?
5. Are student-centered strategies interchangeable from grade to grade? Explain your answer.

FIELD EXPERIENCE ACTIVITIES

1. List five recommendations for conducting practice and drill. Indicate any that you feel particularly comfortable or uncomfortable with as a teacher. Based on these preferences, what conclusions can you make about how you will use practice and drill?
2. Outline ten "do's and don'ts" in asking questions. Which of the "don'ts" have you most often experienced in your own education? Observe a classroom teacher during a field experience and identify "do's and don'ts" that you observe in real practice.
3. Teach a short lesson to your class by asking questions. Have an observer use Tips for Teachers 4.2 and 4.3 as guides to assess how well you performed.

RECOMMENDED READING

Bligh, Donald A. *What's the Use of Lectures?* San Francisco: Jossey Bass, 2000.
　　Offers a thorough discussion of how and when to lecture.
Block, Cathy Collins, and Michael Pressley. *Comprehension Instruction.* New York: Guilford, 2001.
　　Research-based cognitive practices and schema theory for teachers K–12.
Brookhart, Susan M. *How to Assess Higher-Order Thinking Skills in Your Classroom.* Alexandria, VA: ASCD, 2010.
　　Provides essential background, sound advice, and thoughtful insight into an area of increasing importance for the success of students in the classroom.
Gage, Nathaniel L., and David C. Berliner. *Educational Psychology,* 6th ed. Boston: Houghton Mifflin, 1998.
　　An examination of the research pertaining to practice and drill, lecturing, and problem solving—among other topics.
Hargreaves, Andy, Lorna Earl, Shawn Moore, and Susan Manning. *Learning to Change.* San Francisco: Jossey-Bass, 2000.
　　Focuses on how reform proposals have brought new complexities to teaching practices.

Hollingsworth, John R., and Silvia E. Ybarra. *Explicit Direct Instruction (EDI): The Power of the Well-Crafted, Well-Taught Lesson.* Thousand Oaks, CA: Corwin, 2009.
Research-based explanation of how EDI can improve instruction and raise achievement levels in diverse classrooms.

Johnson, Stephen, Harvey Siegel, and Christopher Winch. *Teaching Thinking Skills (Key Debates in Educational Policy),* 2nd ed. London: Continuum, 2010.
Considers the philosophical debates surrounding the existence, teaching, and transferability of thinking skills.

Kaplan, Phyllis, Virginia Rogers, and Rande Webster. *Differentiated Instruction Made Easy: Hundreds of Multi-Level Activities for All Learners.* Hoboken, NJ: Wiley, 2008.
A hands-on resource designed for teachers to support the individual learning needs of their students as they participate in similar tasks.

Kohn, Alfie. *What to Look for in a Classroom.* San Francisco: Jossey-Bass, 2000.
Raises several provocative issues that challenge traditional views on teaching and instruction.

Lasley, Thomas J., Thomas Matczynski, and James Rowley. *Instructional Models: Teaching Strategies for a Diverse Society.* Belmont CA: Wadsworth, 2002.
Focuses on eight different specific teaching models that can be used to teach students content and skills.

Marchand-Martella, Nancy E., Timothy A. Slocum, and Ronald C. Martella. *Introduction to Direct Instruction.* Boston: Allyn & Bacon, 2004.
A comprehensive introduction to the highly effective system of direct instruction.

Parks, Sandra, and Howard Black. *Building Thinking Skills: Critical Thinking Skills for Reading, Writing, Math, Science,* 4th ed. Seaside, CA: The Critical Thinking Company, 2006.
Helps students develop the broad range of analytical skills they need to improve academic performance and score higher on standardized tests and college entrance exams.

Scarpaci, Richard T. *Resource Methods for Managing K–12 Instruction: A Case Study Approach.* Boston: Allyn & Bacon, 2009.
Offers an excellent comprehensive analysis of various strategies and methods for K–12 instruction.

Tomlinson, Carol Ann, and Jay McTighe. *Integrating Differentiated Instruction & Understanding by Design: Connecting Content and Kids.* Alexandria, VA: ASCD, 2006.
Describes how teachers can differentiate teaching to meet the diverse learning needs for students.

Tomlinson, Carole. *The Differentiated Classroom.* Alexandria, VA: ASCD, 1999.
Provides fresh perspectives on two of the greatest contemporary challenges for educators: crafting powerful curriculum in a standards-dominated era and ensuring academic success for the full spectrum of learners.

Walsh, Jackie A., and Elizabeth Dankert Sattes. *Quality Questioning: Research-Based Practice to Engage Every Learner.* Thousand Oaks, CA: Corwin, 2005.
Provides tools teachers can use to support students in becoming active, responsible learners through a reciprocal process of questioning, discussion, and response.

5

Instructional
Resources

FOCUS POINTS

1. Knowing what factors to consider when selecting instructional resources.
2. Linking instructional resources to your state's academic standards.
3. Understanding the advantages and disadvantages of using textbooks.
4. Estimating the reading difficulty of textbooks.
5. Knowing some common textbook aids to enhance student learning.
6. Understanding workbook pros and cons.
7. Using magazines or newspapers in class.
8. Using simulations, games, and other electronic devices to enhance student learning.
9. Making literacy the main objective in using any instructional resource.

OVERVIEW

Real-life experiences provide the most direct type of learning, but they are difficult to supply in the traditional classroom. Most experiences in the classroom occur through verbal symbolism—written and spoken words. These classroom experiences may be easier for teachers to supply, but they may be more difficult for many students to understand. Verbal symbolism depends on the ability to conceptualize and think in the abstract, whereas the impact of firsthand experience is immediate and concrete. Various multisensory instructional aids—texts, computers, pictures, games, simulations—can substitute for firsthand experiences and enhance understanding, so they are an integral part of the learning activity. Children often struggle to learn from content-area textbooks that don't match their reading levels. This problem of mismatched teaching resources is aptly summarized by Richard Allington, who claims, "You can't learn too much from books you can't read," especially if the same textbook is used as the main instructional resource for all students.[1]

The essence of this chapter is devoted to providing various options for instructional practices that can facilitate teaching for literacy. Its focus is on written instructional materials and on the technological tools and media equipment that can assist in delivery of instruction.

Selecting Instructional Resources

Selecting appropriate commercial materials, especially textbooks, is the responsibility of teachers and administrators, sometimes acting in small professional groups (at the district, school, department, or grade level), in professional lay groups that include parents and community members, or as individuals. The professional lay group, according to Elliot Eisner, is subject to controversy when lay members have particular views about what students should be exposed to or when they start objecting to what teachers are teaching.[2] This has been especially noticeable most recently in several states where divisive views on evolution and intelligent design have surfaced.

Although curriculum committees make decisions about the purchase or adaptation of materials on a schoolwide or districtwide basis, the teacher still needs to make professional judgments about the appropriateness and worth of the materials, since he or she is closest to the students and knows their needs, interests, and abilities. The evaluator (committee or individual) should examine as many available materials as possible. The following general questions should be considered:

1. *Do the materials fit the course objectives?* Materials should fit the objectives of the course as well as the unit plan and lesson plan. Given the general nature of published materials, some may fit only partially; or it may not be possible to find materials to cover all the objectives. In such cases teachers need to create all (or at least some) of their own materials. There may also be times when the teacher expands the objectives or activities to include an outstanding set of instructional materials.

2. *Are the materials well organized?* Good instructional materials will relate facts to a few basic ideas or concepts in a logical manner.

3. *Do the materials prepare the students for the presentation?* The materials should include instructional objectives or advance organizers.

4. *Do the materials provide sufficient repetition through examples, illustrations, questions, and summaries to enhance understanding of content?* Young students and low-achieving students need more repetition, overviews, and internal summaries, but the material should be paced properly for all students, and they should have sufficient time to digest and reflect on it.

5. *Is the material suitable to the reading level of the students?* Many teachers can make this type of judgment intuitively by reading through the material, and others can make the judgment after students experience the materials; that is, in listening to students read material the teacher can assess the miscues the students are making and determine whether the material is producing learning or frustration. In general, less than 90 percent accuracy in reading will produce frustration and diminish the motivation to learn.[3]

6. *Does the difficulty of the material match the abilities of the students?* Research indicates that highly motivated students require a minimum success rate when working with reading materials (or on related tasks) to maintain motivation and interest. Materials for low-achieving students, especially seat work and drill materials, require minimum success rates of 70 to 80 percent when the teacher is nearby to provide corrective feedback, and over 90 percent (depending on individual confidence level) when students work independently.[4]

7. *Are the materials compatible with state standards?* The materials a teacher uses should reflect national or state academic expectations. Make certain that you know the academic standards for your state and match them with the materials that are available for you to use in your classroom. Most state standards are accessible through websites (or see www.achieve.org).

Box 5.1 lists some questions more specifically related to content than are these general considerations. Committees and teachers should vary the questions they ask to suit their own goals. The teacher may want to observe students using the materials for several weeks and use their reactions to the materials in making final judgments. It is also worthwhile to consult with students about the worth of textbooks and other web-based resources, since they are the ultimate consumers of these materials. They represent a fresh and different perspective. With the proper guidance from the teacher, students can offer questions and comments that provide valuable insight into the texts they prefer (and why), those they understand, and those they consider most interesting. See Tips for Teachers 5.1 for more insight into selecting materials.

Duplicating Materials

The types of educational materials used most by teachers are written texts (textbooks, workbooks, pamphlets, magazines, and newspapers), pictures and models, and supplies for classroom activities. They may be printed materials (prepared and published commercially) or duplicated materials (prepared by the teacher or school). Duplicated materials include those that teachers produce on their own and already printed material not easily available for students. Instructional aids that involve special materials and equipment, such as films, slides, computers, video recordings and, of course, web-based resources, can also be considered duplicated materials.

Box 5.1   Questions to Consider in Selecting Instructional Materials

1. Does the material further the objectives of the lesson?
2. Does the material contribute meaningful content to the unit or lesson plan?
3. Does the material build on previous learning?
4. Is the material suitable to the reading level of the students?
5. Is the material free from bias, stereotyping, sexism?
6. Is the physical presentation of the material acceptable? Are there appropriate margins, headings, summaries, review exercises, and questions?
7. Will the materials last over a period of time so the initial cost will be worth the investment?

Source: Adapted from Allan C. Ornstein, "The Development and Evaluation of Curriculum Materials." *NASSP Bulletin* (November 1995): 28.

TIPS F O R T E A C H E R S 5.1

Selecting and Using Instructional Materials

How do instructional materials best serve students? Following are some guides for selecting, using, and even developing instructional materials, with emphasis on reading and subject-related tasks:

1. Materials should be relevant to the instruction that is part of the unit or lesson.

2. Materials should provide for a systematic and cumulative review of what has already been taught.

3. Materials should reflect the most important aspects of what is being taught in the course or subject.

4. Materials should contain extra tasks for students who need extra practice.

5. The vocabulary and concept level of materials should relate to that of the rest of the subject.

6. The language used in the materials must be consistent with that used in the rest of the lesson and in the textbook or workbook.

7. Instructions to students should be clear, unambiguous, and easy to follow.

8. The layout of pages should combine attractiveness with utility.

9. Materials should contain enough content so that students will *learn* something and not simply be *exposed* to something.

10. Tasks that require students to make discriminations must be preceded by a sufficient number of tasks that provide practice on individual components.

11. The content of materials must be accurate and precise; the materials should not present wrong information or use language that contains grammatical errors or incorrectly used words.

12. The instructional design of individual tasks and of task sequences should be carefully planned.

13. The number of different materials should be limited so as not to overload or confuse students.

14. Cute, nonfunctional, and space- and time-consuming materials should be avoided.

15. When appropriate, materials should be accompanied by brief explanations of purpose for both teachers and students.

Adapted from Jean Osborn, "The Purposes, Uses, and Contents of Workbooks and Some Guidelines for Publishers," in R. C. Anderson, J. Osborn, and R. J. Tierney, eds., *Learning to Read in American Schools* (Hillsdale, NJ: Erlbaum, 1984), 110–111.

Developing Materials

Sometimes slight modifications or supplements to published materials will make them suitable to use. Other times totally different materials are needed. If none of the printed materials seem usable, you must consider developing your own.

Before developing new materials, you should examine the district-pre-scribed materials carefully. There must be a sufficient number of "no" responses to the evaluating questions in box 5.1 to warrant producing your own resources and to justify the time, effort, and cost of their development. If you decide to produce your own materials, take factors of time and cost into consideration. Take no more than one to two hours to develop materials for each forty to forty-five minute lesson; any more is not worth the time and effort. Too often teachers make their own instructional materials at a high personal cost to themselves and their schools. There may be better uses for the teacher's time and the school's money.[5] It is important that you identify materials already available that relate to the district's curriculum and interface with textbooks or other instructional materials.

One example of developing innovative materials comes from Ogden, Utah, where two junior high school art teachers created a technological bridge between their school's art programs by use of video conferencing. They also created a website (www.theartmachineonline.org) that allows students to display their art work and poetry.[6]

Copying Materials

Many teachers supplement the required text or workbook with instructional materials obtained from various sources—library texts, magazines and journals, government reports, and newspapers. They duplicate these materials without being aware that there is a copyright law that controls their use. The **copyright law,** enacted in 1976, permits an educator to make a *single* duplication for scholarly or instructional purpose of the following: (1) a chapter from a book; (2) an article from a magazine, journal, or newspaper; (3) a short story, essay, or poem; and (4) a chart, graph, drawing, or table from a book, periodical, or newspaper.[7]

Multiple copies for students, not to exceed one copy per student for a course, may be made without permission providing the following requirements are met:

1. *Brevity.* The material may be no more than 250 words from a poem; no more than 1,000 words or 10 percent, whichever is less, from a prose work; no more than 2,500 words from a complete story, article, or essay; and no more than one chart, graph, drawing, or table per book or periodical issue.

2. *Spontaneity.* The materials are considered necessary for scholarly or teaching effectiveness, and the time required to obtain permission would interfere with the scholarship or teaching.

3. *Cumulative use.* No more than one entire source (story, article, essay, poem) or two excerpts may be copied from the same author. No more than three sources may be copied from the same collective work, magazine, or journal during one class term.

4. *Prohibition.* The duplicated material should not create a substitute for a text or compilation of works, nor should it restrict the consumption or purchase of a published work. No charge shall be made to the student beyond the actual cost of duplication.[8]

5. *Computers and web pages.* When it comes to the law we should understand that computers never make copies, only human beings make copies. Computers are given commands, not permission. Only people can be given permission. Absence of a copyright notice does not mean it is permissible to copy something from the web. Under US copyright law, any original work fixed in a tangible medium is automatically protected by copyright, regardless of whether any copyright formalities are done.[9]

Teachers should be aware of the potential consequences of violating copyright laws; ignorance is no defense. When in doubt, it is best to follow the school district's policy (if it has one) or request written permission from the publisher or copyright holder to use the work.

Presenting Instructional Materials

The teacher must incorporate instructional materials into the unit plan and lesson plan and modify them in a way that considers the students' developmental stages or age, needs and interests, aptitudes, reading levels, prior knowledge, work habits, learning styles, and motivation. The following factors should be considered when presenting materials (both published and teacher-made).

- *Understanding.* Teachers must match materials to the learner's abilities and prior knowledge. If students don't understand the material, frustration sets in, making learning even more difficult. The teacher must know whether the materials are appropriate for the students to begin with and whether the students are able to understand the material as it is being presented.

  Teachers must check for student understanding—especially important when working with younger and slower-learning students and when teaching new information. Teachers can ask students questions to check for understanding or try to observe if students understand; if they know what they have learned; if they know what they need to know; and if they know how to detect errors and improve.[10]

- *Structuring.* Teachers must organize the material so it is clear to students. This means clearly stating directions, objectives, and main ideas. Internal and final summaries cover the content. Transitions between main ideas are smooth and well integrated. Writing is not vague, sufficient examples are provided, and new terms and concepts are defined. Adequate practice and review assignments reinforce new learning.[11] Clarity is especially important when new subject matter is introduced and when it is being integrated into previous learning.

- *Sequencing.* Teachers should arrange the material to provide continuous and cumulative learning and to give attention to prerequisite skills and concepts. There are four basic ways to sequence materials: (1) simple to complex—materials gradually increase in complexity and become broader and deeper in meaning; (2) parts to whole—parts of information are presented first to enable the student to grasp the whole; (3) whole to parts—whole concepts or generalizations are presented first to facilitate organizing and integrating new and isolated items, and (4) chronological sequence (a favorite organizer for many teachers)—topics, ideas, or events are studied in the order in which they take place.[12]

- *Balancing.* The materials must be vertically and horizontally related or balanced. *Vertical relationships* refers to building content and experiences at the lesson, unit, and course levels: Ninth-grade math concepts build on eighth-grade concepts, the second unit plan builds on the first, and so on. *Horizontal relationships* establish a multidisciplinary and unified view of different subjects: The content of a social studies course is related to English and science.

- *Explaining.* This refers to the way headings, terms, illustrations, and summary exercises are integrated and elucidate the content. Do the examples illustrate major concepts? Are the major ideas identified in chapter objectives and overviews? Do the headings outline a logical development of the content? Do the materials show relationships among topics, events, or facts to present an in-depth view of major concepts? The students should be able to discover important concepts and information and relate new knowledge to prior knowledge on their own through the materials. In short, the content of the materials should be explicit, related, and cumulative in nature.

- *Pacing.* This refers to how much and how quickly material is presented. The volume or length of material should not overwhelm students, but there must be enough to keep students challenged. As students get older, the amount of material can increase, the presentation can be longer and more complex, and the breadth and depth can be expanded.

- *Elaborating.* Students can learn better when they are learning in different ways. The idea is to teach students to transform information from one form to another and to apply new information to prior knowledge—by using various techniques such as comparing and contrasting, drawing analogies, drawing inferences, paraphrasing, summarizing, and predicting. Students can be taught a broad list of "generating" questions (e.g., previewing, self-questioning, visualizing) to use while reading materials. With *previewing*, for example, a good generating question for a narrative (story-like) text might be "Based on the title, what might be the focus of this story?" A student who is about to read expository material on the American Civil War might ask, "What do I already know about the events occurring during the war?" The teacher can also raise *generating* questions in class when discussing the materials: "What is the main idea of the story?" "If I lived during that period, how would I feel?" "What does this remind me of?" "How can I use the information in the project I am working on?" "How do I feel about the author's opinions?" "How can I put this material in my own words?"[13]

- *Motivating.* Instructional materials, according to Posner and Strike, may be classified as (1) concept related, drawing heavily on structure of knowledge or the concepts, principles, or theories of the subject; (2)

inquiry related, derived from critical thinking skills and procedures employed by learning theorists or scholars in the field; (3) learner related, or related to the needs, interests, or experiences of the students; and (4) utilization related, showing how people can use or proceed with them in real-life situations.[14] The first two "organizers" seem to work best with intrinsically motivated (self-motivated) students, but all four draw on the intrinsic interests of students.

---

classic professional viewpoint 5.1   **On Using Many Materials**

Barak Rosenshine

Judith was a student teacher I supervised in an MA intern program. She was a thin, quiet, almost mousy person who received only average ratings in the summer microteaching program because she didn't have the necessary verbal pizzazz to lead a discussion. I worried about her during that hot, dry summer.

The school year started, and as part of her intern year Judith was assigned to teach three social studies classes in a local high school. Then, something new happened. Judith started writing extremely good worksheets that contained well-developed integrative questions and thought questions. The students prepared these before class, and much of the class time focused on having students compare their answers, with Judith elaborating upon those answers. Judith also took charts and tables from the various sources and developed extremely good factual, analytic, and skill-based questions based on those materials. The students were excited because they were learning new skills and developing an integrated map of the material, but they weren't doing it through the usual teacher–student discussion. Judith's means were different, but they were effective.

Judith taught me that effective teachers come in many varieties; even quiet people can be effective. We should remember that the goal of teaching is the learning, processing, and skill development that goes on in the students' heads, and there is a variety of instructional methods for achieving this: It can be done by leading discussions, by developing special materials, by finding suitable materials developed by others, by developing thoughtful assignments, by explaining with guided note taking, and/or by having students explain concepts and material to each other. Judith taught me to focus on what goes on in the students' heads, and less on whether a currently prescribed method was used.

Recognizing Field Dependent/Field Independent Learners

Embedded within all of these considerations is the teacher's awareness of the different types of learners in American classrooms. American classrooms evidence a great deal of diversity in students. Good teachers see the possibilities in all students, regardless of ethnic background or racial-group affiliation. They also know how to use the backgrounds of the students to enhance the ways in which young people can learn content and experience success. There are many different ways to classify or think about students as learners, as opposed to students of a particular racial or ethnic group. Teachers need to consider two primary ways of classification: field dependent and field independent. Simply speaking, different students possess different cognitive styles and exhibit different levels of psychological differentiation. **Field-dependent learners** are those who tend to do best on verbal tasks that have a significant relational component. **Field-independent learners** are those who think more analytically and can process impersonal and often abstract ideas more effectively.[15]

Students possess several different cognitive styles. We use psychological differentiation (field dependence and field independence) for illustrative purposes to show how important it is to recognize and teach with attention to student differences. If you treat all students the same and assume that they are all field-independent learners, those who are field dependent will begin to experience frustration. Similarly, if you assume that the students are all field dependent, those who learn more analytically will become frustrated. Good and Brophy highlight research that illustrates the importance of teachers' accommodating different types of learners:

> . . . Field-independent and field-dependent students . . . [learned] content from taped lectures under four conditions: (1) no notes, (2) student's notes only; (3) outline framework plus student's notes, and (4) complete outline plus student's notes. [The researcher] . . . found that field-independent students performed well under the student's-notes-only condition, because they tended to take efficient notes and to organize them within an outline format. The field-dependent students, however, seemed to need the teacher-provided outline. [The researcher] . . . contended that the typical classroom procedure in which the teacher lectures and students take notes may favor the performance of field-independent students. To reduce this effect, he suggested that teachers provide students with external aids [or materials] (e.g., an outline on the board or a handout that organizes the presentation) that may help the field-dependent students without harming the field-independent students.[16]

As you can see, you would not use varied instructional materials to be "cute" or to arbitrarily satisfy a supervisor. There are learners with different backgrounds and learning styles in any classroom, and you must remember that your goal is not content coverage but rather student learning. Teachers who practice adaptive pedagogy vary the way they teach and the materials that they use. They know that students who come to them from poor, rural, urban, or highly ethnic communities need varied experiences that connect the standards to be achieved with the materials that are provided.

Questions for Reflection

Research clearly demonstrates that a large gap exists between the reading achievement of disadvantaged students and their advantaged peer counterparts. A relationship also exists between socioeconomic status (SES) and reading achievement. That said, what does it suggest about the types of skills you may need to possess if you teach in an urban (low-SES) middle school as opposed to a suburban (high-SES) middle school? Consider the reading problems of students in both situations. If you want students to comprehend an expository text (a typical textbook), what must you do differently with students who come from a literary-poor environment as opposed to those from a literary-rich one? Notice that these questions do not suggest an inherent difference in students' abilities. If student abilities are often a reflection of their experiences, how do you adjust for those differences? As you consider possible solutions, consider what a wide variety of researchers have found relative to the most significant ways to close the academic achievement gap between diverse student groups:

- High-quality teaching
- Reduced class size
- Clear standards of performance for students to achieve
- Assessments that are clearly aligned to standards
- Enhanced parental involvement in a child's education

Which of these can you most directly impact? How?

Special note to readers: A wide variety of resources are now available on the achievement gap issue. See, for example, *Bridging the Great Divide: Broadening Perspectives on Closing the Achievement Gaps* (Naperville, IL: North Central Regional Educational Laboratory, 2002, www.ncrel.org).

Instruction with Textbooks

Traditionally, the textbook has been the most frequently used instructional material at all levels beyond the primary grades, and in some cases it is the only one used by the teacher. "The textbook and its partner, the workbook," asserts Eisner, "provide the curricular hub around which much of what is taught revolves."[17] In terms of purchasing decisions, textbooks receive the highest priority, with the exception of costly hardware such as computers and copying machines. Textbooks strongly influence or even dominate the nature and sequence of a course and thus profoundly affect the learning experiences of most students. Reliance on the textbook is consistent with the stress on written words as the main medium of education, and it is the way that many teachers were educated. Educators have estimated that 70 to 95 percent of instructional time centers around some sort of textbook material (or workbook material for younger students).[18] This figure is supported by other research, especially in reading and math classrooms, where there is excessive dependence on textbooks.[19]

Disadvantages. In order to have wide application and to increase potential sales, textbooks tend to be general, noncontroversial, and bland. Because they are usually written for a national audience, they do not consider local issues or community problems. Because they are geared for the greatest number of "average" students, they may not meet the needs and interests of any particular group of students. Moreover, issues, topics, and data that might upset potential audiences or interest groups are omitted. A type of censorship is currently occurring that is creating heated ideological debate.[20] This is evident when school boards remove texts from school lists based on political or ideological precepts.

Because textbooks summarize large quantities of data, they may become general and superficial and may discourage conceptual thinking, critical analysis, and evaluation. With the exception of mathematics textbooks, most quickly become outdated because of the rapid change of events. Because they are costly, however, they are often used long after they should be replaced. There is also a concern that textbooks unnecessarily dumb down topics. Because some states require certain reading levels in the textbooks that they adopt, there is a tendency for publishers to modify sentences in ways that compromise the integrity of the ideas. Also problematic is the emphasis in the United States on breadth versus depth. Sadker and Sadker describe this as the **mentioning phenomenon,** in which textbooks endeavor to mention everything so as not to forget anything. The by-product of this phenomenon is diminished student learning. Students who need richer descriptions of concepts with more examples are limited in their ability to acquire the content.[21]

Advantages.   Considering these criticisms, you might ask why teachers rely so heavily on textbooks when they have access to other instructional materials. The answer is, of course, that textbooks offer many advantages. A textbook (1) provides an outline that the teacher can use in planning courses, units, and lessons; (2) summarizes a great deal of pertinent information; (3) enables the students to take home in convenient form most of the material they need to learn for the course; (4) provides a common resource for all students to follow; (5) provides the teacher with ideas regarding the organization of information and activities; (6) includes pictures, graphs, maps, and other illustrative material that facilitates understanding; (7) includes other teaching aids, such as summaries and review questions; and (8) relieves the teacher of preparing material for the course, thus allowing more time to prepare the lesson.[22]

Good textbooks have many desirable characteristics. They are well organized, coherent, unified, relatively up-to-date, accurate, and relatively unbiased. They have been scrutinized by scholars, educators, and minority groups. Their reading level and knowledge base match the developmental level of their intended audience. They are accompanied by teachers' manuals, test items, study guides, and activity guides. The textbook is an acceptable tool for instruction as long as it is selected with care, is kept in proper perspective so that it is not viewed as the only source of knowledge, and does not turn into the curriculum. In most cases you will have no choice about the textbook you use, but you can decide how to supplement the content covered in the textbook and what topics warrant extended coverage. Remember, most textbooks suffer from the mentioning phenomenon. To help you make a choice about where your *depth* decisions should be made, focus on the following:

1. *The school district's curriculum guide.* What does the district require you to teach?

2. *The academic standards for the state in which you teach.* What are the academic standards for your state, and what topics *may not* be adequately covered in textbooks relative to defined standards?

Stereotyping in Textbooks

Basic readers and textbooks began to be criticized in the 1960s and 1970s as irrelevant to the social realities of the inner-city and minority child. Many years ago, Fantini and Weinstein suggested that school books depicted "happy, neat, wealthy, white people whose intact and loving families live only in clean, grassy suburbs. . . . Ethnic [and racial] groups comprising so much of our population are often omitted" or included only "as children from other lands."[23] Such stereotypic representations are far less explicit than they used to be, but they are still evident.

According to one educator, for many years all American Indians in textbooks and readers were called "Big Horn" or "Shining Star"; people with Italian, Greek, or Polish names were likely to appear as peddlers or organ grinders, wearing red scarves and ragged clothes. Either there were no blacks, or one black boy might be inserted in the background. Yellow, brown, or black people were depicted in stories about China, India, and Africa, but they were always strangers and foreigners. Women were almost always portrayed as mothers, nurses, or teachers. Religion was rarely mentioned—except in relation to church attendance on Sunday morning. In short, the readers of these books were presented with a monocultural view of society. Nonwhite children were learning to read from books that either scarcely mentioned them, omitted them entirely, or represented them stereotypically.[24]

Today, many readers, workbooks, and textbooks exclude racial, ethnic, religious, and sexual stereotyping. (Obscenity, violence, and sexual topics are still generally avoided, as are such unpleasant issues as disease and death.) Major racial, ethnic, and minority groups, including the handicapped and elderly, are represented more often in story characters and pictures. Women are depicted as airplane pilots, police officers, construction workers, lawyers, and doctors. Blacks, Hispanics, and other minorities are featured with professional and managerial jobs and are no longer all represented as basketball players and musicians. Thankfully, overt stereotyping is largely avoided in current textbooks.

Still, balanced textbook development remains an ongoing topic of debate. On one end of the political continuum are the charges that the content and pictures in textbooks still transmit racial and gender stereotypes, albeit more covertly than they did in the past. Glazer feels that textbooks appear to overemphasize science, capitalism, and formal rationality, values traditionally associated with the once-dominant (white, male) power group.[25] Critics maintain that subtle, tacit stereotyping still exists (e.g., women are portrayed as passive, or mainly in service industries or family roles.) Ethnic groups are still given stereotypical treatment, even in the twenty-first century. (As late as 2010, a best-selling nursing textbook with the ironic title *Guide to Culturally Competent Health Care* came under fire for racially stereotyping African Americans.)[26]

On the other end of the continuum are the critics who say that too much pressure is being placed on publishers (and now on textbook authors) to be "politically correct"—not just to reflect the cultures of all students but to disparage any hint of "common culture." Nearly everything that is European, white, or male is, according to these critics, perceived as a vehicle for racism, sexism, and oppression.

Oakes and Lipton eloquently describe how a 1991 revision of a California text still compromises the real story of how pioneers expanded Westward and how American Indians responded. They first provide a quote from the text:

Although some Indians were content on the missions, many others were unhappy with this new way of life. By living at the missions the Indians gave up their own culture, the way of life they had known in their tribal villages. They could only leave the mission grounds with permission from the padres. They were not free to hunt or to pick berries.

Mission Indians were not allowed to return to their tribes once they agreed to take part in mission life. Some ran away. But soldiers usually brought them back and sometimes whipped them. Others wanted to revolt. They wanted to rise up against their leaders, the Spanish padres and the soldiers at the mission communities. . . .

Oakes and Lipton comment:

. . . [T]his version waffles as it portrays the stunning violations of decency and human rights that California Indians endured. That "some Indians were content" must be seen as the moral equivalent of references to happy Negro slaves on the plantation. That the Indians "gave up" their culture seems close to a free and neutral choice. The text explains offenses against the Indians in the familiar language of what grownups do to naughty children—whippings, not being able to leave without permission, not free to hunt or pick berries. Indian deaths seem sanitized, kept a safe distance from the killers; disease, crop failure, and a change in diet reduced the Indian population by half, not theft of land and enslavement. On the other hand, Indians, with *their* offenses, are downright uncivilized; they violently revolt, attack and burn missions, and kill padres.[27]

We are forced to struggle with two opposing, highly emotional views about the politics of information and what textbook content is acceptable. Finding good literature or good texts that reconcile all these concerns is difficult. To accommodate some of the new criteria, many classic works of literature have been eliminated from the curriculum, and many bland texts and instructional materials have been included. Writes Connie Muther, "The idea is to please all and offend none [and thus] many textbooks [and related materials] have no clear point of view."[28] An example of "blanding down" texts so as not to offend is the 2011 single-volume version of Mark Twain's *The Adventures of Tom Sawyer* and *Huckleberry Finn* in which every instance of the word *nigger* has been replaced by the word *slave,* and *Injun Joe* replaced with *Indian Joe*. Some argue that this will make Twain's work much more acceptable for classroom use, replacing "'two hurtful epithets' that have caused the book to often fall off of school curriculum nationwide."[29] The other side argues that readers need to be made aware that culture (whether good or bad) consists of value judgments that define the time in which they were made:

What's the point of reading a censored version of the book? By the time that we Americans dilute our literary heritage, taking away both impact and historical significance from what we read, we will have thoroughly become a nation of imbeciles and may not even notice the loss. As the famous Mark Twain said, "The difference between the almost right word and the right word is really a large matter—it's the difference between the lightning bug and the lightning."[30]

Although many new books portray the populace more accurately, they remain safe, boring, and watered down.

One of the authors of this textbook made it clear, in a book about 9/11, that most texts are watered down for purposes of being neutral, entertaining, positive, and politically correct. He wrote the following opinionated introduction about textbooks:

> You may feel life is too difficult and there is no need to read a book that requires a literate mind. If you cannot be entertained by glossy pictures and smiling faces, or with sidebars of cartoons or case studies, then you might rationalize that you should not be bothered or expected to read or think about serious issues.

Later, the author puts the issue more directly in the reader's face, claiming his textbook is opinionated and deals with tough issues that most education textbooks avoid.

> . . . this is not intended to be light reading, or a "Dick and Jane" reader. For those with an urge to be politically correct on all topics, you will find plenty to be upset with—not [being] willing to admit your own form of racial, ethnic, religious, or gender prejudice. Finally, there will be some who find fault that the content lacks restraint, sobriety, and optimism, and that my expressions are somewhat disruptive and upsetting.

Finally, the author pokes fun at the publishing industry.

> Life has become pretty flat and dull when reading typical education texts. That the content has become so oblique and middle-of-the-road is a tribute to mainstream society that publishers wish to convey a neutral or positive picture of the human condition.[31]

Readability of Textbooks

Concern about student reading problems has prompted educators to identify textbooks and other reading materials that are suitable for specific student populations, especially below-average readers. One strategy used in this endeavor is **leveling**, a fairly subjective assessment method that enables teachers to determine the level of a specific text through the use of reading formulas. **Reading formulas**, first devised in the 1920s to estimate the reading difficulty of a text, is another strategy that has lately increased in popularity. Some reading formulas count the number of syllables or the number of letters in a word; some count the number of words that are not on a specific word list; others measure sentence length; and still others remove words from a passage to test whether students can fill in the exact word that was removed.[32] Some formulas use graphs, regression statistics, and percentiles and range scores to calculate reading difficulty. Computer programs are now available for doing the counting and calculation chores involved in reading-level determinations. There are a variety of formulas in existence, and all attempt to provide educational professionals with a means of assessing text difficulty and suitability for potential readers.

The best known reading formula was developed by Edward Fry. It is an estimate of grade level based on average number of sentences and syllables in three passages taken at random.[33] The Raygor Reading Estimate, developed by Alton

Raygor, is easier to use than the Fry method (counting letters instead of syllables) and is of equal accuracy.[34] Examples of other formulas are provided in box 5.2.

Box 5.2   A Closer Look at Readability Formulas

Because there are over 100 readability formulas, what follows is only a small sample.

Betts Levels

This formula is based on errors made in oral reading. The independent level is less than 5 percent errors; the instruction level is about 5 percent errors (one in twenty words); the frustration level is more than 5 percent errors.

Chinese

Because Chinese is written in characters, not words, you count the number of brush strokes per character.

Cloze

To use the cloze method to rank books, simply take a text passage and delete every fifth word, and then ask a group to fill in the blanks. This method is objective and accurate but time-consuming. To translate cloze scores to grade level, see the Dale-Chall manuals.

The New Dale-Chall Readability Formula

You can obtain a grade level, and a cloze score if you wish, by taking a 100-word sample (every fiftieth page) and counting the number of sentences in the sample. Next, determine the number of unfamiliar words (those not on the Dale list of 3,000 words). Use the table to get a grade level or cloze score. (The manual is required for the tables and the 3,000 word list.)

The Flesch-Kincaid Grade Level Formula

This formula is widely used in industry. Here's an example of how to find grade level:

$$0.39 \left(\frac{\text{total words}}{\text{total sentences}} \right) + 11.8 \left(\frac{\text{total syllables}}{\text{total words}} \right) - 15.59 = \text{grade level}$$

The Fry Readability Graph

Randomly select a minimum of three 100-word samples and count the number of sentences in each sample. Then count the number of syllables in each sample. Average the sentence count and syllable count and use the graph to obtain grade level. (The graph is not copyrighted and is readily available on the Internet.)

Lix and Rix

These formulas are used in Europe for many languages. Lix is average sentence length plus average word length. Rix is the number of long words divided by sentence length.

Leveling

Each of several authors suggests a different mix of factors. [Leveling is a much more modern term and is used primarily at the beginning reading levels.]

Lexiles, DRP Units, ATOS Grade Level

These formulas are applied by large companies to a large number of books. It is perhaps best to buy their book lists.

Source: Edward Fry, "Readability Versus Leveling," *The Reading Teacher* (November 2002): 290. Copyright © 2002. Reprinted with permission of the International Reading Association.

Critics of the various reading formulas say that they fail to consider students' prior knowledge, experience, and interests, all of which influence reading comprehension; they assume that words with fewer syllables and shorter, simpler sentences are easier to comprehend than words with more syllables and longer sentences with subordinate clauses, which is not always true; publishers have reacted to these formulas by adjusting sentence and word length to give the appearance of certain levels of readability without necessarily providing them;[35] and strict adherence to formulas robs prose of the connective words, vocabulary, and sentence structure that make it interesting, comprehensible, and stylistically worth reading. In short, rigid adherence to reading formulas may result in the adoption of a boring and bland text. It is imperative for you, the teacher, to determine the match between textbooks used by a school and the learning needs of students and then to supplement the textbook when additional resources are needed to ensure student learning.[36]

Another criticism of the readability formulas is that they are not useful with texts for young children in the very early grades. Because text passages frequently have fewer than 100 words, the formulas do not work with the texts appropriate for early grades. When formulas cannot be applied, teachers need to develop skill in making their own assessments by taking into account such factors as text length, the size and layout of the print, the vocabulary and concepts introduced, the pattern of language, and the illustrations that support the narrative (i.e., do they help clarify material?). In essence, teachers need to be attentive to the vocabulary of the books they use and to develop skill in matching books with children.

Whatever their faults, reading formulas do help teachers to assess reading difficulty and select printed material that is appropriate for the students' abilities. Since most teachers work with groups of students in which there is a range of abilities, it is advisable that the difficulty of the material not be more than one year below or above the average reading grade level of the group. If there is more than a one- to two-year spread in reading ability in a group, the teacher should use more than one set of instructional materials.

Some educators now urge that comprehensibility, not readability, is the major quality to consider when adopting a text. Comprehensibility is usually defined as the criterion one uses for judging textbooks based on aids that enhance understanding. Teachers and textbook committees are identifying various textbook aids such as structural overviews, introductory objectives, summaries, and review exercises as devices that contribute to comprehensibility. One reading expert lists more than forty aids that might be considered when selecting a text.[37]

Electronic Reading Devices

More and more educators believe that the classroom of the future may contain portable readers or e-books for every student, class program, and activity. A number of teachers are now supplementing textbook material with information easily accessible through the Internet. The use of electronic reading devices such as Amazon's Kindle, Sony's Reader, Apple's iPad, and Barnes & Noble's Nook have burst onto the scene with the potential for revolutionizing educational practices in the future. The learning world of the twentieth century was driven by textbooks; the learning world of the twenty-first century is driven by information accessed through the Internet.

In today's high-tech marketplace, electronic reading devices have created a movement that can potentially deliver textbooks in fast, inexpensive ways. Many different types of electronic reading devices are available today. They offer an alternative to traditional paper texts in that they are small and portable, offer an unlimited potential to learning resources, and are relatively inexpensive. They are softly readable, with little of the glare often associated with computer screens. The question presently being asked is what type of e-reader is easiest on the eyes: the grayscale screens that simulate ink on the printed page, or the back-lit color screens used by computers, including the iPad and iPhone (which have a Kindle app). All e-readers can download e-materials in seconds, from potential listings of millions of books, for very little cost. They also offer instant access to academic tools such as dictionaries and thesauruses. It seems that traditional paper and hardcover books—at least textbooks—might someday go the way of the abacus, chalkboards, and ink pens, to be replaced by a small, plastic gadget that offers immediate access to unlimited potential learning resources. Portability, accessibility, and enhanced reading clarity, plus adaptability for updating features, make these technologies an enticing new avenue for schools. Portable electronic readers deserve serious consideration by boards of education and school leaders. Teachers need to become familiar with them, too, to keep pace with their high-tech students—a real, continuing, but worthwhile challenge.[38]

Disadvantages.   Before school leaders are tempted to put one of these devices into the hands of every student in their districts, they should spend some time contemplating a few important issues. Some potential risks and disadvantages do exist concerning e-books:

- *Domination of free trade.* There is the potential for too much control by a few technologically dominant publishing companies over curriculum and instruction, especially if electronic textbooks listings are limited by copyright laws. At this stage no one knows which companies will succeed and which will fail. Schools investing in the wrong companies' merchandise stand to lose a great deal of taxpayer monies.

- *Unforeseeable expenditures.* Portable reading devices are relatively new and untested on a large scale. Not even taking into consideration the initial cost of purchasing such devices, many school districts would not be willing to gamble with funds in the selection of materials (opting to be safe rather than sorry). Some might prefer to avoid risk and wait to see what happens in the market for portable reading devices, letting others take the risks of early adoption.

- *Technical apprehensions.* What would the initial costs of e-books mean to a school's budget (e.g., more electrical outlets, buildings to be reconfigured for wireless providers)? Would the schools purchase the devices, or would students be required to purchase them? Amazon's Kindle, as an example, has a $139 price tag! For poorer districts, access to such technology might be prohibitive (and, some would say, discriminatory).

Advantages. The advantages and potential benefits of electronic reading devices can be summed up in four phases:

- *Transportability.* Students would not be burdened with carrying a multitude of heavy textbooks.
- *Expense.* The cost of one electronic reading device compared to the price of numerous textbooks could be quite substantial.
- *Freedom of choice.* Instructors would no longer need to limit their choices of reading matter. Reading and content selections could be differentiated for individual students.
- *Environmental friendliness.* Electronic devices have the potential to lower carbon emissions and reducing the demand for paper.

See Case Study 5.1 to clarify your feelings regarding the printed page.

The importance of understanding the various forms texts can take is a topical issue across the country. The following case discusses views regarding learning with textbooks, trade books, and e-books. Compare and analyze the various views expressed and decide what position you would take.

Case Study 5.1
Learning with Textbooks, Trade Books, and Electronic Texts

Mona Childress realized that textbooks by themselves are not enough; in order to extend the curriculum, trade books had to be employed. Mona understood the difference between trade books and textbooks. Trade books were produced and published for distribution to the public in general while textbooks are not.

Teachers used trade books to integrate a variety of print and multimedia environments into the curriculum. Mona believed her primary role was to instruct students in how to think and learn with textbooks. In her mind textbooks contained the blueprint for classroom learning.

Unfortunately there are problems with textbooks: Due to their comprehensive and encyclopedic natures they tend not to treat subject matter in great depth.

Robin Mumford, an associate of Mona's, had gone into a tirade on the problems of black-and-white texts, which was unusual for Robin. He was really quite mild mannered. In his diatribe he pointed out four specific problems:

1. They may contain inaccuracies.

2. They could be written at high levels of difficulty.

3. They often lacked appeal to students.

4. They frequently were organized in confusing ways, making them "inconsiderate text."

Robin wanted Mona to use trade books; they were cheaper and more attractive than textbooks. He insisted that a basic rationale for using trade books was they complemented textbooks and could be chosen to meet a broad range of reading levels. He maintained that in many cases you didn't need a textbook to teach, only a trade book. He described a method for choosing quality trade books which he casually called *Five A's For Evaluating Trade Books.*

1. *Authority:* Does the author identify and cite experts to support his view?
2. *Accuracy:* Is text content accurate?
3. *Appropriateness:* Is information geared to level of readers and effectively organized?
4. *Literary artistry:* Is the author's style engaging and lively?
5. *Attractiveness:* Is the layout enticing to readers?

Susan Jennings overheard their discussion and couldn't stop herself from blurting out, "Are you two for real? The age of paper print is almost dead. We live in a digital age where more is better. Our students are already immersed in a world of digital technology. The question is not textbooks or trade books, but when should we move our classes toward digital readers."

Susan continued, "Don't shun your responsibilities and become victims who fear bureaucratic reprimand. The advantages for adopting e-readers are simply overwhelming; daily they're becoming more refined and less costly. On average it costs 50 percent less to obtain material digitally than it does to regularly purchase textbooks." "I'm not even considering the obvious health benefits from not having children overloaded with heavy texts. Digital textbooks have everything a paper textbook or trade book can offer, and they allow us to customize materials to specific class needs."

Robin inquired as to where Susan had gotten all her information. Susan replied that it was from an AFT Journal called *The American Teacher,* the February 2010 issue. Robin pointed out that he also had read the article and had found it wanting. He further indicated that Susan hadn't revealed everything contained in the article. A major portion of the piece was devoted to a teacher survey on the question, "Should classrooms go completely digital?" The results showed that 28 percent of teachers said yes and 72 percent said no. Robin looked at Susan and triumphantly exclaimed, "So much for your point of view!"

Discussion Topics and Questions to Ponder

1. Discuss your feeling regarding whether or not textbooks are a necessary resource for instructional purposes.
2. Do the faults with textbooks mean they should be replaced by trade books or electronic texts? Explain your answer. How can textbooks be used to encourage learning?
3. Should trade books be used to enhance learning or to eliminate textbooks?
4. Was Robin correct in proclaiming that the teacher survey on e-books confirmed his view that they should not be used solely?
5. Compare and discuss the strengths and weaknesses of textbooks, trade books and electronic texts.

What would you do if . . . ?

1. You were asked to prepare criteria for the selection of electronic texts.
2. Mona said, "Why can't we use all three forms?"
3. You were given the choice to select only one form of text.

classic professional viewpoint **5.2**

Beyond the Textbook

Diane Ravitch

Don't be afraid to be a critic of textbooks. Sometimes they contain inaccuracies or are poorly written. Sometimes they don't provide enough background information for students to understand their meaning.

The biggest drawback of textbooks is that they may bore students. Today's students are accustomed to getting information about the world from television and movies; increasingly they know how to get information electronically. A textbook alone may not hold the students' interest. When your students are turned off by the dull writing in their textbooks, blame the textbooks, not the kids.

Put yourself in the students' place and then ask yourself: Would you read this if you didn't *have* to? Does it hold your attention? Would you be tempted to read more than the assigned number of pages? If the answer is "no" to all of these questions, then think about de-emphasizing the textbook in your classes.

The best way to use a textbook is to treat it like a reference work. Use it as background. The main source of learning should come from the other materials, experiences, and technology that you supply, either through hands-on activities (in or out of the classroom) or through the use of supplementary materials that are livelier, more vivid, and more motivating for students than the textbook.

Cognitive Task Demands

Critics have found that textbooks in nearly every subject and grade level cover too many topics; the writing is superficial, choppy, and lacking in depth and breadth (you'll recall that this phenomenon is called *mentioning*); and content wanders between the important and the trivial.[39] Many texts also fail to capture the imagination and interest of the students or make students think, and they spurn current knowledge about cognitive information and linguistic processing.[40] The so-called "best" textbooks are often designed to entertain and to be decorative, but they provide only surface information on topics, lack adequate integration of subject matter, and do not stretch the student's mind. They are unintentionally geared to oversimplify and to limit thinking.

Textbook adoption committees have contributed to the superficiality problem with their demands for topic coverage and easy-to-read prose. Special interest groups, with their political passions and legal challenges, have added to the problem, causing publishers to become politically sensitive to the content at the expense of linguistic and cognitive processes. Teachers have done their part, too, since far too many teachers emphasize "right" answers rather than a focus on exploring ideas critically.

Several years ago, Bennett and colleagues analyzed 417 language and math tasks assigned in texts by teachers and found that 60 percent were practice tasks, or content already known to the students. New tasks accounted for 25 percent, and tasks requiring students to discover, invent, or develop a new concept or problem made up only 7 percent of the tasks. Another study found that approximately 84 percent of teachers rely on *textually explicit instruction*, a method of selecting verbatim information from the textbook or workbook to provide a correct answer to a question. Rarely do teachers employ *textually implicit instruction*, in which a correct answer requires students to make an inference from the textual information supplied. Even more rarely do they use *scripturally implicit instruction*, in which a correct answer requires students to go beyond the information given and call on prior knowledge and reasoning skills.[41]

Many teachers are unwilling or unable to change from textbooks that are characterized by low-level cognitive demands and divorced from how students think or reason. One might expect mathematics teachers, at least, to stress problem solving, but many teachers of mathematics—especially at the upper elementary and junior high school grades—are not much different from their colleagues in this regard. Indeed, some data strongly suggest that many of these "teachers don't know mathematics. [As a result] they assign the basic problems but skip word problems because word problems are harder to teach."[42]

Word problems can also require a level of content understanding that some teachers, even "reasonably well-trained" teachers, do not have. For example, one researcher asked teacher candidates to create a story problem for $1\frac{3}{4}$ divided by $\frac{1}{2}$. According to Harriet Tyson,

> A whopping 69 percent of the elementary education students were unable to do so. But a surprising 55 percent of the mathematics majors and minors who were planning to teach in secondary schools were also unable to devise a life situation that would call for that division problem. All could "work" the problem, of course, through the mechanical approach they had learned. But in trying to imagine a real-life situation using $1\frac{3}{4}$ divided by $\frac{1}{2}$, many created a problem that involved dividing by 2 rather than by $\frac{1}{2}$. This study makes it clear that those math majors and minors didn't understand the *concept* of dividing by $\frac{1}{2}$. If they had, they would have known that dividing by 2 produces a smaller number, whereas dividing by $\frac{1}{2}$ produces a larger number. Engineers may not need to understand that concept, but teachers do.[43]

The point here is straightforward: Good teaching is intellectually demanding. It requires complex and sophisticated decision making, and textbooks cannot do that for a teacher. However, it's important to remember that textbooks are a resource, not a content mandate. Some teachers are actually experimenting with creating a textbook-free curriculum. Geoff Ruth claims that the less he uses the book, the more his students learn. "You don't learn stuff from textbooks," one student wrote. "You just memorize for a test, then forget it." Ruth says, "I won't settle for that in my classroom; without a textbook, I don't have to." Monya Baker suggests that although textbooks may be the right way to go for some educators and subjects, teachers can "slowly ease away from them—unit by unit or lesson by lesson—to develop a series of activities and lessons crafted specifically for your students."[44]

Textbook and Pedagogical Aids

Textbook aids, sometimes called *text-based aids, instructional aids, textbook elements,* or *reader aids,* are designed to enhance understanding of the content and to facilitate learning. Aids used before students start to read a chapter acquaint them with the general approach and the information and concepts to be learned, while fostering enhanced comprehension. Aids used while students are reading a chapter focus on the organization of content, provide examples, supply supplementary information, and repeat objectives. Those used after the chapter reinforce learning through summaries and exercises and encourage critical thinking through problems and activities. See Tips for Teachers 5.2 for insight into the use of textbook aids.

TIPS FOR TEACHERS 5.2

Student Use of Textbook Aids

Textbook aids (textbook elements) have continued to grow, as publishers and authors respond to growing needs of teachers and textbook selection committee criteria for selecting texts. Following is a list of features now commonly found in textbooks, with questions to ask students to help them understand how to use these tools.

Features of Text:

Sample Questions for Students

Contents
How do you use the table of contents?
What is the difference between major and minor headings?
In what chapters would you find information about _____?

Index
What information do you find in an index?
On what pages would you find the following information _____?
Why is the subject on _____ cross-referenced?

Opening Material (overview, objective, focusing questions, outline)
What are the main points or topics of the chapter? How do we know?
Do the objectives correspond with the outline of the chapter?
In what section can we expect to find a discussion of _____?

Graphic Material (charts, graphs, diagrams) and tabular material
How does the legend at the bottom of the chart explain the meaning of data?
Based on the lines plotted on the graph, what will happen in the year 2015? What do the dotted lines represent?
Where in the narrative does the author explain the table?

Summaries
If you could read only one page to find out what the chapter is about, what page would you read? Why?
Where can we find a summary of the main ideas of the chapter?
Does the summary correspond to the major headings?

(continued)

Pictures
Are the pictures relevant? Up-to-date?
What is the author trying to convey in this picture?
How do the pictures reveal the author's biases?

Headings
What main ideas can you derive from the headings? Subheadings?
How are the subheadings related to the headings?
On what pages would you find a discussion of _____?

Information sources (footnotes, references)
Where did the author get the information for the chapter?
Are the footnotes important? Up-to-date?
What references might you use to supplement those at the end of the chapter?

Key Terms in text
Which are the important terms on this page?
Why are some terms in bold print? Why are others in italics?
Where can you find the meaning of these terms in the text?

Marginal notes (or trigger items)
Do the marginal notes catch your eye?
Why are these terms or phrases noted in the margin?
Quickly find a discussion of the following topics: (Provide a list of appropriate topics.)

Supplementary discussion (point/counterpoint tables, list of suggestions, case studies)
Why are the point/counterpoint discussions interesting? Which side do you take?
What are the important issues on this topic?
Which tips make sense to you? Why?

End-of-chapter material (review exercises, questions, activities, sample test items)
Are the exercises meaningful? Do they tie into the text?
Which discussion questions seem controversial? Why?
Why should we do the activities?
Take a practice test. Answer the sample test questions to see what we need to study.

Pedagogical aids, sometimes called *instructional aids* or *teaching aids,* are materials designed for teacher use and provided as supplements to a textbook. See table 5.1 for a list of commonly used pedagogical aids.

The teacher may combine approaches and guide students with questions to facilitate comprehension: "Where can you find the information you need to know?" "Which words are unknown to you?" "Where in the text can you find a clue for understanding them?" "How do the tables and graphs help you understand?" "Why should we pay close attention to the bold print (or print in italics)?" "What do the marginal notes tell you?" "Does the order of discussion (homework) questions correspond with the order of the narrative?" Then teacher and class can practice finding the answers to selected questions in the discussion (homework) section.

Textbook aids, in particular, can facilitate the development of cognitive processes. Table 5.2 (on p. 244) lists four developmental stages of cognitive pro-

Table 5.1   Pedagogical Aids

Teacher's manuals	Lesson plans
Test questions	Bulletin board displays
Skills books or exercise books	Supplementary tables, graphs, charts, and maps
Transparencies or cutouts to duplicate	Parental involvement materials
Reinforcement activities	Teacher resource binders
Enrichment activities	Computer software
Behavioral objectives	Audio- and video recordings

cesses and corresponding cognitive operations, reader activities, and their relationship to various textbook aids. In theory, the cognitive processes, operations, and reader activities each form an untested hierarchy in which one level is prerequisite to the next. The aids are not hierarchical but overlap—any one aid may facilitate learning at more than one level of the hierarchy.

Without good textbook aids, poor readers will learn little and capable readers will develop default strategies or partially ineffective strategies for processing text information. A default strategy is likely to involve focusing on topic sentences or unusual and/or isolated information, instead of main concepts and principles.[45] A default strategy also leads to copying and memorizing long lists of information, rather than organizing, inferring, and transferring ideas of the text. A textbook may have excellent aids; however, the teacher may not know how to make good use of them. (See Tips for Teachers 5.2.)

One other type of textbook aid (or supplement) has emerged recently as a consequence of the heavy emphasis on academic standards: supplements that align textbooks with state standards. Although publishers put out national textbooks, in states like Virginia (and Texas and California) special editions of texts are being published to align with state standards.[46] For example, in Virginia, Harcourt Brace and Scott Foresman have brought K–3 textbooks in line with the Virginia Standards of Learning for history and social science. Prior to this development, teachers who focused heavily on state academic standards created their own supplements.[47]

Reading across the Content Areas

All teachers are reading teachers, whatever the subject or grade level. One role of teachers is to help their students read and understand textbook material. The purpose of content area reading instruction is to improve students' learning through the integration of instructional strategies in the subject-matter curriculum, rather than to present strategies in isolation. Success on all types of assignments and tests—even math tests—requires reading ability. "Every teacher should be, to a certain extent, a teacher of reading."[48] Box 5.3 (on p. 245) contains Guiding Principles of Content Area Reading Instruction.

The apparent lack of interest by many secondary teachers in combining reading instruction with disciplinary content instruction is problematic. Content

Table 5.2   Levels of Cognition and Reading, with Implications for Using Textbook Aids

Cognitive Process	Cognitive Operations	Reader Activities	Textbook Aids
Identifying	Focusing on selective information Sequencing selective information	Copying Underlining Simple note taking or discussion	Overviews Instructional objectives Prequestions Key words or terms Marginal notes Summaries Review exercises
Conceptualizing	Classifying main ideas of text Comparing main ideas of text	Logical or structured note taking or discussion Distinguishing relevant information Relating points to each other	Headings, subheadings Marginal notes Point-counterpoint discussion Summaries Postquestions Problems Review exercises
Integrating	Analyzing main ideas of text Modifying ideas of text into variations or new ideas Deducing main ideas of text Expanding main ideas of text Applying main ideas of text to problems	Elaborate note taking or discussion Making generalizations Hierarchical ordering of items Making inferences from text information	Headings, subheadings Graphs, tables Models, paradigms Postquestions Case studies Problems Activities
Transferring	Evaluating text information Verifying text information Going beyond text information Predicting from text information	Elaborate note taking or discussion Evaluating, problem solving, and inferring based on text information Using text information to create new information	Graphs, tables Models, paradigms Simulations Case studies Problems Activities

Source: Allan C. Ornstein, "Textbook Instruction: Processes and Strategies." *NASSP Bulletin* (December 1989): 109. Copyright © 1989 by National Association of Secondary School Principals (www.principals.org). Reprinted with permission of Sage Publications.

Box 5.3   Guiding Principles of Content Area Reading Instruction

1. Content area reading instruction is based on the supposition that students obtain meaning through the application of strategies, skills, and previous information to text material.

2. The classroom is an active social, cultural, and intellectual environment where students gain information and create meaning.

3. Students gain information in content area reading because of the diversity of sources.

4. Content reading instruction aims to facilitate active learning.

5. Instructional strategies and activities in the content areas are malleable to the constraints presented in most classrooms.

Source: Adapted from R. J. Ryder and M. F. Graves, *Reading and Learning in Content Areas*, 3rd ed. (New York: Wiley, 2002).

---

teachers have historically been resistant to accepting responsibility for reading instruction, "perceiving reading to be additional content for which they have neither the training nor the time."[49] Nationwide, for example, 44 percent of 466 surveyed teachers maintained that reading instruction is not the responsibility of content area teachers. Moreover, 30 percent admit they lack the skills needed to participate in reading instruction or to combine it with content instruction.[50] The great majority of secondary teachers (over 90 percent) report that they assign pages to read without providing a purpose for or comprehension guides for the reading.[51] The level of support a teacher needs to provide will vary with the information a teacher knows about each student. Box 5.4 outlines a set of considerations essential for using and selecting texts to enhance learning.[52]

Researchers suggest that students' comprehension of what they read in the content areas is enhanced by previewing (by helping students with background knowledge); relating their knowledge and experience (or making connections) to the information in the text, relating one part of the text to another, discussing and summarizing the meaning of important new words; and self-questioning that entails having students create questions about the content as they are reading.[53] Students need practice in inferential reasoning and other comprehension processes, but this cannot occur if they are occupied with word recognition and vocabulary demands or if they simply do not comprehend the material.[54]

According to Sara Bernard, "Students need a personal connection to the material, whether that's through engaging them emotionally or connecting the new information with previously acquired knowledge (often one and the same). Without that, students may not only disengage and quickly forget, but they may also lose the motivation to try."[55] Teachers can relate the text to students' experience by asking their opinions, having them imagine themselves part of the events described in the text, or having them think of examples from their own experience. Relating parts of the text to one another can be achieved by asking students to summarize and analyze main points, to explain relationships and

Box 5.4   Text Information for Classrooms

Once you have gathered information about each student, you must consider what texts you will use. The following steps facilitate this process:

1. *Identify the texts already available in the classroom.* These may include basals, anthologies, trade books, textbooks, magazines, poetry books, and picture books.

2. *Organize the texts to facilitate guided comprehension.* Use the following questions to accomplish this:

   • Does this text add to existing content area study or knowledge?
   • Can this text be used in a genre study?
   • Does this text exemplify a particular style, structure, language pattern, or literary device? Can this text be used to teach a comprehension strategy?
   • Are there multiple copies of the text available?
   • Does this text match a particular student's interests?
   • Is this a good example of a text structure?
   • Is this text part of a series?
   • Is this text written by a favorite author?

These questions can be used with both narrative and expository texts, which include individual stories in literature anthologies as well as individual articles within magazines.

3. *Acquire additional materials to assure ample accessible texts for all readers.* It is important to have some small sets of books to use during teacher-guided comprehension groups, but it is also necessary that the classroom contain a variety of texts, varying in type, genre, length, and content. These books must represent a wide range of readability and genre. It is important to include novels of varying length, nonfiction trade books, picture books, poetry books, and magazines.

Keep in mind the following ideas when adding to classroom collections:

   • *Content areas*—nonfiction and narrative text to supplement studies in math, science, and social studies
   • *Student interests*—a variety of texts (fiction, nonfiction, poetry) to match students' interests
   • *Read aloud*—texts that offer examples of a variety of text structures and engaging story lines to be used to demonstrate comprehension processes and fluency
   • *Anchor books*—texts used in whole-group and small-group instruction to demonstrate a specific strategy or routine
   • *Sets of books*—small sets (four to six copies) of books to be used in guided comprehension groups; these should be based on students' learning levels as well as the strategies that can be taught and used
   • *Text sets*—series books, books by a favorite author, books in a particular genre or topic; several books that have a common characteristic

Authors' note: The purpose of all these questions is to focus the teacher's decision-making process about the texts.

Source: Maureen McLaughlin and Mary Beth Allen, *Guided Comprehension: A Teaching Model for Grades 3–8* (Newark, DE: International Reading Association, 2002), 68–69. Reprinted with permission of the International Reading Association.

elaborate with examples, and to note main and minor headings, marginal notes, key terms, and summary statements. Defining new terms can be accomplished by in-class discussion of selected terms that have conceptual meaning and by encouraging students to use the dictionary and glossaries on their own. Providing repetitive sentence patterns and familiar words and concepts eases word recognition and comprehension tasks for students who have trouble reading. Paying close attention to instructional objectives or focusing questions and answering review questions can help students determine whether they understand the text material and what sections they need to reread or skim.

Advance organizers, developed by David Ausubel to enhance concept thinking, can be used in teaching students how to read.[56] Advance organizers characterize the general nature of the text, the major categories into which it can be divided, the similarities and differences among categories, and the examples within different categories. The organizers state the abstraction or generality under which data can be subsumed. Armstrong and colleagues[57] say that advance organizers help students sort out fragmented pieces of information and help clarify the purpose of the lessons. According to Ken Henson, students who read and paraphrase an advance organizer prior to study are better able to answer both lower-order and higher-order study questions than students who do not encounter an organizer.[58] To be useful, the organizers should be stated in terms that are already familiar to the students prior to their reading the text material.[59] They are especially useful when the text is poorly organized or students lack prerequisite knowledge of the subject. Although Ausubel and most other educators believe organizers should be presented before the text is read, others maintain that presenting them in the middle or after the text can also facilitate learning.[60]

Other types of textbook aids or cues—such as instructional objectives, overviews, prequestions, and specific instructions—presented prior to chapter reading can also facilitate learning of reading materials.[61] These aids are similar to advance organizers because they provide advance information about the nature of the material to be learned. In addition, postquestions and summary activities that apply textbook material to concepts, problems, or creative projects also enhance learning.

The idea is to get students to think out loud and to elaborate on the strategies they use to process information they read. Students use different strategies. If they become aware of what they are doing, they can improve their approaches to reading texts. Teachers should discuss these strategies with their students on a regular basis. (See Case Study 5.2 to clarify some strategies in use for adolescent readers.)

The following case discusses approaches to teaching reading in the content areas. Teachers in adolescent education at times find it difficult to teach reading. The views presented in this case study emphasize the importance of the saying, "We are all essentially teachers of reading." Compare and analyze the various views expressed on what reading is to learning. Evaluate the directed reading lesson (DRL) method and determine its effectiveness in a secondary content classroom.

Case Study 5.2
Reading in Content Areas

Alan Hanson made an excellent point at a faculty conference on teaching reading across the content areas. Alan had stood up and in a clear, resonating voice had said, "Reading is easy if you already know how to do it." He went on to say that he did not understand how any high school teacher could claim that it was not their job to teach students how to read.

Clark Spellings got up and said, "I for one don't think it's my responsibility. Our students should have learned to read before they got into high school. And if they didn't, they should be placed in remedial classes where they can be taught to read properly. Besides, I have too much content to cover already without teaching reading."

Alan responded by saying, "I certainly empathize with your having a heavy workload, but it's still our job. I read a recent article in an educational journal that said a survey of secondary teachers who included reading strategies in their lessons significantly increased their students' chances of mastering the subject content they taught. It went on to say that students learn better by reading than by listening and viewing."

Clark said, "I understand all that. I not only assign text materials to read, I also use trade books and a multi-text approach."

"Good for you, Clark," said Alan, "but I think you need to stop *assigning* content reading and begin *teaching* content reading. It's really not that difficult if you use a direct reading lesson approach. All you have to do is model by reading passages aloud, and then analyze them for your students by showing them how to apply what they read to problem solve. Model, analyze and apply—that's the secret. The DRL (directed reading lesson) plan is an outline for a teacher-guided, learner-centered lesson that uses reading as the primary source of content knowledge."

Velvet Dileo spoke up and exclaimed, "As a certified reading instructor I'd have to say that Alan is on the right track. Don't worry, I'm not afraid of talking myself out of a job. Reading in the content area is not just sounding out words: It means comprehension." Velvet briefly consulted her notes. "To comprehend in reading your brain must activate five different cueing systems:

1. Graphic cueing, which is the printed representation of sound.

2. Semantic cueing, or making meaning out of printed material.

3. Syntax cueing, which is when patterns of language are used to assist you in developing meanings.

4. Experiential background cueing, or relating to your past experiences and history.

5. Text structure cueing, which is the major thought pattern you must use to comprehend the text."

After consulting her notes again, Velvet continued, "Text structure revolves around various patterns such as *narrative text structure,* the "story grammar," setting, characters, plot, conflict, significant events, and outcome or solution. Another example is *expository text structure,* when a text is written to inform based on thought patterns of cause and effect, classification or categorization, chronological order or sequence, comparison and or contrast, description, definition, enumeration or simple listing, pro and con, and finally problem solutions."

Velvet wound up her remarks by saying that teachers must teach the cueing systems necessary for reading comprehension in the secondary classroom! Clark looked at Velvet and said, "Boy that was a mouthful. But it still doesn't change my point of view, it just confirms it. I understand that reading can be defined as using graphic, semantic, syntactic, background and text structure clues in a recursive manner to construct meaning with the text. I think I said it much more succinctly than you did, Velvet."

Velvet replied, "Don't be so difficult, Clark. As Alan said, it's really not difficult at all. There are a number of ways to plan directed reading lessons, and all contain five basic procedures: readiness preparation, motivation and background; guided reading/silent reading; discussion and oral reading; rereading, and follow-up. That's the way to teach reading in the content area."

Discussion Topics and Questions to Ponder

1. Is reading in the content area really essential to learning? Explain your answer.
2. What was wrong with Clark's argument? What was right with his argument?
3. Was Velvet correct not to be worried about losing her job? Justify your answer.
4. In your opinion would DRL lessons be effective at the secondary level?
5. What would your position be regarding reading in the content area?

What would you do if . . . ?

1. Clark continued to be recalcitrant regarding content area reading.
2. Clark handed you the following list and then said, "I don't get paid enough to teach all this *and* my subject!"

   Guiding Principles of Content Area Reading Instruction

   - Content area reading instruction is based on the assumption that students acquire meaning through the application of strategies, skills, and prior knowledge to text material.
   - The classroom is a dynamic social, cultural, and intellectual environment where students acquire information and construct knowledge.
   - Content area reading allows students to learn from numerous sources of information.
   - Content reading instruction aims to facilitate active learning.

3. Clark said he wouldn't use the DRL method but he would use the traditional SQ4R approach for teaching comprehension, where the letters in the acronym stand for the following six steps:

   - Survey the chapter by reading it quickly.
   - Question what you have read.
   - Read to answer the questions you asked.
   - Recite your answers to your questions.
   - Record the important items from the chapter and add to your notes.
   - Review it all for retention.

In addition, he asks you to compare and contrast DRL and SQ4R.

Text Structure

In general, **narrative structure**, which deals with a broad theme and conveys information in story form, is easier for readers to understand than is **expository structure**, which the reader encounters in textbooks. Children who learn to read in elementary school first learn through narratives. By the fourth or fifth grade, students begin to move into the more complex organizational patterns of the content areas that are conveyed through texts and expository writing. The emphasis on textbooks and thus expository structure increases with the grade level. Students who are unable to cope with this type of reading are bound to be low achievers since most learning in school depends on the ability to read and understand expository text.

Students, in general, have more difficulty with expository text than with narrative text, because of insufficient prior knowledge, poor reading ability, lack of interest and motivation, and lack of sensitivity to how texts are organized.[62] In addition, a good many texts are poorly written, boring, and even confusing to students.[63] Narrative writing possesses a structure that likely will engage many readers who are unable to deal with the inherent abstractness of expository texts.

Researchers argue that the reason some students have more difficulty comprehending expository texts relates to their prior experiences. Specifically, the backgrounds of students will dictate the ease with which they can comprehend a text. Students from literary-rich home environments may be better able to comprehend expository texts that emphasize comparison–contrast, description, and cause and effect.[64] Students from poor socioeconomic areas or from homes that lack substantial reading materials may be limited by the background reading experiences they bring to expository text.

The teacher cannot take for granted that students understand text structure—that is, how information is organized, as well as the verbal and contextual cues (such as the headings and subheadings or the bold or italic print) that bring unity to the text. Good texts are written with certain expository structures that can be taught to students. Some of the common textbook structures are defined next.

Response.   Sometimes referred to as "question/answer" or "problem/solution," these structures are most common and crucial for meeting classroom or homework assignments. Often a problem is introduced, a plan discussed, an action presented, or an outcome described. The teacher needs to help students become aware of what is being asked and where the solution can be found or how the problem can be worked out. In the middle grades and with low achievers, students as a group should discuss the difficulties encountered and what they did about them.

Cause–Effect.   Students need to be taught to search for main ideas: What is happening? To whom? Why? The teacher needs to clarify the task or problem, present guided practice to the group, and then introduce independent practice. Whereas most texts, especially in science, usually deal in cause–effect relationships, the process is often reversed in social studies texts to effect–cause (i.e., an event is described and then the causes are explained).

Comparison–Contrast.   This structure is common in most science and social studies texts. The author explains likenesses and differences—sometimes with tables, charts, or graphs. When tables or charts are used, categories and columns usually help cluster the information. Students must be taught to slow down, deduce, and extrapolate data from the tables, charts, or graphs.

Collection.   Texts often classify, enumerate, or list information. Although this text structure is easy for students to understand, the information is more difficult to recall because of overload (the list is too long), and the information is rarely integrated into larger concepts. Students must be taught to summarize or synthesize from long lists. Most low achievers will attempt to memorize or write down long lists as opposed to conceptualizing the major points.

Generalizations.   This structure is sometimes referred to as argument–persuasion in science texts, and as main ideas in social studies and English texts. The author presents concepts, summary data, or conclusions with supporting information. Students need to identify the generalizations and their supporting information for each chapter. One method is to view major topics in relation to subtopics.

Topics and Subtopics.   Good textbooks sequence topics (sometimes called headings) in logical form and then integrate subtopics (or subheadings) within topics. Most middle school and junior high school texts contain between seven and fifteen pages per chapter; they should have three to four topics per chapter and two to four subtopics per topic. High school texts may have as many as twenty pages per chapter, although fifteen is the average. These texts should have four to five topics per chapter and the same number of subtopics per topic. More than four or five subtopics per topic will confuse or overload most readers.

Guidelines for Using Textbooks

The following general guidelines should help increase the value of the text for students.

1. *Do not become so hypnotized by the textbook that you follow it rigidly.* Supplement the textbook with other instructional aids and printed materials (such as paperback books for all students; web searches; and journals, magazines, and reports for junior high and high school students). And be certain to determine if your state offers supplements that align state academic standards with textbook content.

2. *Adapt the textbook to the needs of the students and the objectives of the lesson.* Do not allow the textbook to determine either the teaching level or course content exclusively.

3. *Appraise the worth of the textbook by critically examining its content and structure.* See Tips for Teachers 5.3 for more information on this topic.

Textbooks of the Future

Textbooks in the future will be flexible, adaptive, and interactive. They will garner student attention because they will provide different types of visualizations, self-motivating simulations, and interactivity. Technology in the form of electronic reading devices will make e-books interactive learning tools that stand

TIPS FOR TEACHERS 5.3

Appraising the Worth of a Textbook

Here are some questions to keep in mind when assessing the worth of a textbook for teacher and student. The first group of questions deals with text content, the second with mechanics, and the third with overall appraisal.

Content

1. Does the text coincide with the content and objectives of the course?
2. Is it up-to-date and accurate?
3. Is it comprehensive?
4. Is it adaptable to the students' needs, interests, and abilities?
5. Does it adequately and properly portray minorities and women?
6. Does it foster methodological approaches consistent with procedures used by the teacher and school?
7. Does it reinforce the type of learning (such as critical thinking and problem solving) sought by the teacher and school?
8. Does it provide the student with a sense of accomplishment because it can be mastered and yet is still challenging?

Mechanics

1. Is the size appropriate?
2. Is the binding adequate?
3. Is the paper of adequate quality?
4. Are the objectives, headings, and summaries clear?
5. Are the contents and index well organized?
6. Is there a sufficient/appropriate number of pictures, charts, maps, and so on for the students' level?
7. Does it come with instructional manuals and study guides?
8. Is it durable enough to last several years?
9. Is it reasonably priced relative to its quality? To its competitors?

Overall Appraisal

1. What are the outstanding features of the text?
2. What are the shortcomings of the text?
3. Do the outstanding features strongly override the shortcomings?

Source: Adapted from Allan C. Ornstein, "The Textbook-Driven Curriculum," *Peabody Journal of Education* (Spring 1994), 71–72.

alone. The Internet has made information so easily and quickly available that the role of the textbook as a comprehensive reference has been diminished. The next evolutionary milestone of the textbook will be as an authoritative means to sanction the credibility of information, by signifying what information is reputable.[65] Today's vast amount of online information makes it increasingly difficult for young students to assess the origin and veracity of what they find there. Teachers should address the topic of Internet source credibility with their students.[66]

Workbook Materials

At the lower grade levels, workbooks are often used separately or independently to provide practice-and-drill exercises in language arts, reading, and math. Along with the textbook, the workbook tends to dominate elementary school classrooms as a major instructional tool.

Teachers exhibit wide variations in the use of workbooks—variations based primarily on content area. Workbooks and other "guide" materials tend to be used chiefly in reading and language arts (as much as 19 percent of the instructional time), but they are used to a much more limited extent in social studies and in math.[67]

At the secondary grade levels, workbooks are often used in different content areas keyed to or as a supplement (rarely independently) to the textbook for the purpose of practice. For example, student manuals with drill exercises (sometimes problems) may be available that cover most of the course content. Students first engage in new learning derived from the textbook or another source; then the workbook is used to reinforce the new learning. Ideally, the exercises or problems are concrete examples of abstract learning. For this reason, many teachers view the workbook as a pedagogical aid and always check with publishers to see whether a workbook accompanies the textbook.

Disadvantages

The value of the workbook depends on how the teacher uses it. Unfortunately, the workbook is sometimes used as busywork to keep students occupied, or even worse, as a substitute for teaching. Workbooks tend to overemphasize factual and low-level information. Students can spend hours, especially at the elementary grade level, filling in blanks, completing sentences, recognizing correct words, and working on simple mathematical computations. According to critics, workbook exercises have little to do with—and often discourage—critical thinking; creativity; developing a whole, abstract thought; or relevant hands-on activities and materials.[68] One way that some teachers deal with the fact-based orientation of workbooks is to supplement workbook assignments with questions or activities that require higher-level thinking.[69]

The teacher may assign workbook exercises in order to keep students busy while he or she grades papers, performs clerical functions, or confers with an individual student or group of students. Such approaches are used, sometimes overused, in conjunction with seat-work activities. When workbooks are assigned either as busywork or merely to facilitate seat-work activities and fail to link the exercises in a meaningful way to new information or to content coverage, the routine produces what critics call *management mentality* in both students and teachers. Such dependence "de-skills" teachers (they become ineffective) and curtails creative instruction.[70]

Advantages

The merit of the workbook is that it performs the practice-and-drill function well. It helps young students who need to learn a knowledge base and low-achieving students who need extra concrete activities to understand abstract learning and repeated exercises to integrate new learning. To the extent that the workbook is used in one of these instructional contexts and that its exercises make learning more meaningful to students, it has value. In essence, workbooks can be very useful for skill reinforcement.

To judge a workbook's merit, ask the following questions:

- Are the exercises (or problems) related to abstract or new learning?
- Are the exercises interesting, and do they maintain students' interest?
- Do exercises exist in proper quantity (not too many or too few)?
- Can students understand the directions? (Young students and low-achieving students often don't understand written directions.)
- Can students perform or answer the majority of the exercises? (If they cannot, frustration will mount and most students will no longer persist.)
- Can teachers provide needed direction and guided practice to help students learn the necessary skills and strategies for workbook comprehension or performance? (The sheer ability to do something does not guarantee performance.)
- Do teachers use the exercises discriminately (i.e., Do they supplement with other instructional methods and materials)?[71]

Workbooks are desirable for many students, but they are especially important for those students having difficulty in learning to read. It is for these children that workbooks should be geared. Many students are also deficient in note-taking skills, and Uma Iyer found that using workbooks as an educational tool helped train these students in organized note taking, enhancing their classroom experience.[72] For workbooks to be effective, Jean Osborn insists that they focus on a sequenced review of what has been taught, on the most important content, and on content that needs to be reinforced. Workbooks can provide a means of practicing details of what has been taught; extra practice for students who need it; intermittent reviews of what has been taught; ways for students to apply new learning with examples; practice in following directions; practice in a variety of formats that students will experience when they take tests; and an opportunity for students to work independently and at their own pace.[73]

Guidelines for Using Workbooks

In choosing, working with, or evaluating workbook materials, keep the following questions in mind. They should act as guidelines to help you decide if the workbook materials are appropriate for your specific teaching and learning situation.

1. *Objectives.* Do the workbook materials meet the goals of the school? Which ones? Do the workbook materials meet the program objectives? Course objectives? Unit or lesson plan objectives?

2. *Readability.* What evidence is there that the workbook exercises coincide with the reading level of the students? Do the students understand the written directions? The wording of the exercises or problems?

3. *Utility.* What evidence is there that the workbook materials are helpful for the students? What evidence is there that students are interested in the exercises?

4. *Cognition.* Do the workbook exercises supplement or reinforce abstract thinking? Are the exercises intellectually stimulating? Are sample exercises or problems worked out step by step?

5. *Content coverage.* Do the exercises cover the content in depth? Do they have balance in terms of the scope and sequence of the content?

6. *Audiovisuals.* Is the workbook material user friendly? Are there a variety of appropriate illustrations—charts, tables, pictures, drawings, and so on—to facilitate learning?

7. *Learning theory.* Do the workbook exercises coincide (or conflict) with current learning theory? Which theory? In what ways do the exercises stimulate learning? In what ways are individual differences provided for?

8. *Pedagogical aids.* Is the workbook used as a separate text or used in conjunction with another text? Does the workbook have a teacher edition or instructor's manual to provide assistance? Is the assistance valuable?

Key Characteristics for Educational Software and Materials

Electronic workbooks have permitted interactive and customized learning. Such workbooks may be used on computers and PDAs. High-quality educational software and materials have six key characteristics that suggest areas to use for measuring and judging the relative worth of different materials. These characteristics are:

- *Evenhandedness and exactness.* Is the material intellectually accurate, as well as unbiased?

- *Depth.* Does the product explore the subject relative to the needs of your students?

- *Skill building.* Does the software focus on the skills that need to be developed?

- *Action orientation.* Does the material offer opportunities for interactive use by your students?

- *Teaching reliability.* Would you expect the software to achieve what the marketers claim?

- *Usability.* Will the product fit into your classes' curriculum?

When it comes to reaching young people, your biggest challenge is keeping their attention long enough to help them build and gain necessary skills. Teachers need to provide compelling alternatives to the barrage of media messages and peer influences to which today's students are exposed. Educators must develop their capacity to use technology effectively in education. Although the information potentially available to anyone with Internet access is rapidly expanding, in many cases its proper use has become obscure. We need to provide tools that actually increase learning. Among other things this means—as always in education—addressing the diversity of students' intelligences, backgrounds, and interests. A focus must be placed on best practices while simultaneously avoiding unevaluated materials that make unrealistic claims. In the area of educational technology, therefore, even more so than in others areas of education, teachers need to work together to develop learning communities, and explore the potential social changes surrounding the use of educational technology.[74]

Journals, Magazines, and Newspapers

Journals, magazines, and newspapers offer an alternative to textbook material that can also be accessed online. All three resources can be used to update materials found in standard textbooks. Since they are all primary sources, they are excellent for enhancing thinking skills and research skills. Journals are the publications of professional and academic associations and as such are more technical than magazines and newspapers. Their uses with young students are quite limited. The most popular magazines used by teachers are *Time, Newsweek,* and *U.S. News and World Report,* although there are many others that can supplement or be the focal point of learning. The magazines are topical and usually readily available to a large number of students either at home or through a school or local library. It is appropriate to start students with the local newspaper at the middle grade and junior high school level, but the teacher should also consider *The New York Times, Washington Post,* or *The Wall Street Journal* at the high school level. These papers are written at the tenth- to twelfth-grade reading level; carefully assess the reading abilities of your students before using these papers. Many local newspapers will even deliver copies (for a limited time) to the whole class if you need them for some type of systematic study.

To enrich content, teachers in most subjects can encourage students to read journals, magazines, and newspapers. Many of these publications are interesting and more informative and up-to-date than the textbook. Gathering suitable magazine and newspaper materials can be delegated to the class, or it can be conducted primarily by the teacher.

Journal and magazine articles have not been sanitized or toned down to the same extent as textbooks. The content expresses a point of view, and it can be used to enhance critical thinking and hone research skills. Newspapers, in theory (although not always in practice), deal in reporting, not analyzing or interpreting data. It is up to the student to evaluate and draw conclusions about what is being reported. Editorials, story columns, op-ed (opinion) columns, and letters to the editor are quite different, and students need to understand that such material is subjective.

Although a student may understand that a particular point of view may be expressed in a journal, magazine, or newspaper article, he or she may be unable to identify distortions or biases and therefore accept the view as fact. In general, biases can be conveyed in eight ways: (1) through length, selection, and omission; (2) through placement; (3) by title, headline, or headings; (4) through pictures and captions; (5) through names and titles; (6) through statistics; (7) by reference source; and (8) by word selection and connotation.[75] Although the teacher must use professional judgment in interpreting or assigning these instructional materials, students can learn to evaluate the information contained in them by being trained to answer the following questions:

- Is the account slanted?
- Is important information treated accurately?
- Are controversial topics discussed rationally?
- Is there a clear distinction between fact and opinion?
- Do the headlines, captions, and opening statements present the news accurately?
- Are editorials and commentaries clearly designated?[76]

The five most popular uses of journals and magazines in classrooms are for extension activities, recreational reading, motivation to read, change of pace, and current information.[77] Use varies by grade and subject area. One study reports that in junior high school, 76 percent of the language arts teachers, 43 percent of the social studies teachers, and 23 percent of the science teachers used journals or magazines in their classrooms. In high school, 57 percent of the science teachers, 31 percent of the English teachers, and 24 percent of the social studies teachers use them. Actual frequency of use and type of student (student's ability or achievement) were not reported.[78]

Considering that textbooks are adopted for a period of five years or longer in some states, it is not surprising that teachers across the curriculum look to current magazines for updated information in their respective subject areas. These magazines are excellent up-to-date instructional tools for promoting student research skills and for independent projects. They offer multiple viewpoints and thus encourage critical reading and controversial discussions, as well as in-depth understanding and learning of current and relevant content. Box 5.5 contains some helpful guidelines for using these instructional materials, incorporating available classroom technology.

Simulations, Games, and Technology

During the past two decades, simulations have been extensively used to understand complex systems and situations. They have become a mainstream use of computational technology. **Simulations** in education are basically imitations of real-life situations, a method of managing life's problems with the added advantage that any possible consequences of risk taking are virtually absent. According to Ken Henson, virtual problem solving is a good way to encourage students to take risks, which they must learn to do if they are to become creators of knowledge.[79]

Box 5.5   Guidelines for Using Journals, Magazines, and Newspapers

1. Check all websites before assigning students articles to read. Offer students the choice of a hard copy or an e-copy. Provide appropriate website listings.

2. Be sure that journal, magazine, and newspaper articles are within the students' reading and comprehension range.

3. Select those materials that are readily available and affordable and can be found online without cost.

4. Make sure the journal, magazine, or newspaper articles are compatible with your teaching goals, given the fact that these materials often express a particular view.

5. A guided reading exercise can be used to train students in reading and evaluating materials. Children and adolescents tend to believe that whatever is printed is true. A useful project is a comparative analysis of articles that take different views on a controversial subject.

6. Train students in the use of card catalogs, periodical catalogs, and the classification and retrieval systems of journals and magazines so they can use these materials in independent study and research. Also demonstrate the need to use reputable online materials.

7. Many students, especially at the secondary school and college level, clip excerpts from journals, magazines, books, or even entire articles found in the library or online. As a teacher you must alert your students to the possibility of online plagiarism, discuss copyright laws with them, and provide instruction in the proper use of the author-date reference system.

8. Journal, magazine, and newspaper articles are excellent sources for student reports. Encourage students to take notes, summarize main ideas, and interpret ideas in these instructional materials.

9. Assist students in doing research reports by providing a list of journals and magazines that are relevant to the topic at a level that can be understood by the student. Show students how to cut, paste and edit online materials.

10. Keep a file of pertinent journal, magazine, and newspaper articles and websites to supplement the text and incorporate into the unit or lesson plan. Update the file on a frequent basis. Be sure to stress copyright laws so students understand.

The act of simulating something generally entails representing its key characteristics or behaviors. Play offers a natural format for children and adolescents to express themselves. They provide a wide range of social and cognitive experiences. Simulations can be further thought of as abstractions of the real world, involving objects, processes, or situations. *Games* are activities that may include a variety of goals, rules, and rewards. Simulated games mimic real-life situations with appropriately associated goals, rules, and rewards.

Simulations have become increasingly popular among educators, after much success in military, business, medical, and public administrative arenas. Many simulations are now produced commercially for teachers, especially for use in conjunction with computers and DVDs. Teachers sometimes have trouble distinguishing so-called "virtual field trips" from WebQuests that engage students in higher-level thinking processes. According to Tom March,

> A real WebQuest is a scaffolded learning structure that uses links to essential resources on the World Wide Web and an authentic task to motivate students' investigation of a central, open-ended question, development of individual expertise and participation in a final group process that attempts to transform newly acquired information into a more sophisticated understanding. The best WebQuests do this in a way that inspires students to see richer thematic relationship, facilitate a contribution to the real world of learning, and reflect on their own metacognitive processes.[80]

Teacher-made simulations (not for computer and DVD use) are increasingly used in the classroom since they can be geared to specific students, subjects, or grade levels. Several "how-to-do-it" publications have been produced by teacher associations for would-be developers of simulations and games.

There is no doubt that educational games and simulations have been found to be effective in motivating students to learn, and games that encourage exploration may be particularly engaging to students, especially girls.[81] An example of a game that fosters exploration is *Discover Babylon*,[82] in which students travel through Mesopotamian time using math, reading, and writing skills.

Simulations offer many advantages in the classroom:

1. [They are] an excellent motivating device.

2. A successful simulation demands the use of many study skills and techniques. . . . A practical relationship is forged between study and fun.

3. A full-dress simulation is a powerful way to make many . . . topics . . . come alive.

4. A successful simulation is very rewarding to the teacher. [He or she] takes a back seat to let things develop [and watches] students live, talk, and enter into [active learning].[83]

In short, simulations permit students to experience the nearest thing to reality. They come in a variety of forms. One excellent resource for identifying appropriate simulations for content material that you are teaching is the Thinkfinity website (http://www.thinkfinity.org). Another good source of top issue-oriented computer simulations can be found at the Edutopia website.[84] More information on simulations, lesson plans, interactive games, and video/podcasts are readily available on one of the links found at http://www.nationalgeographic.com/resources/ngo/education/xpeditions/activities/.

If you visit the site you can select one of the many standards-based activities listed there. For example, if you selected an activity described as "Lewis and Clark Expedition: Create Your Own Adventure," you would be asked to accomplish a mission by completing a series of engaging hands-on-activities. Two examples of simulated missions (or "Xpeditions") from the National Geographic website appear in box 5.6. One is for younger children, and the other is for older students. The questions are oriented toward the K–12 students being taught.

Box 5.6   Examples of Online Simulations

Younger Xpeditioners

Print the world map from the Xpeditions atlas. On the map, mark the location of your home and of your destination. Make a list of what you know about that area, and what you would like to know.

What would you need to bring on your trip? To answer this question, you will need to answer other questions first. What will you need to know about your destination before you decide what to bring? Make a list of questions you will have to answer and then answer as many as possible by using an atlas, encyclopedia, or other sources of information.

Now make a list of things you would need to do to prepare for your trip. How would you get there? Whom would you go with? What else could you do to help you prepare for the "unknown"?

Make a travel brochure about the place you would visit. Draw pictures and write about things you might see on your trip. You could describe the people you might meet, the climate you expect or the animals, landscapes, and plants you might find. You could also make a map of the place and include features that you might see.

Try to find an actual travel brochure of the area and compare your brochure to the real one. What is different? What is the same? Why do you think there are differences?

Older Xpeditioners

The journey that Lewis and Clark made in the early 1800s would be similar to an "extreme adventure" by today's standards. It was challenging, dangerous, and most importantly, it had never been done before. This same spirit of adventure is alive and well today in people who take on "extreme" challenges for a variety of reasons.

What kind of "extreme adventure" would you like to do? For an idea of the kinds of things adventurous people do these days; check out the *National Geographic Adventure magazine* website. After exploring this site, try to think of an "extreme adventure" that is challenging, dangerous, and something that no one has ever done before in a place where no one has ever done it.

Find a map of your destination from the Xpeditions atlas and print out the map that shows the area where you want to go. Make a list of what you know about that area, and what you would need to know to prepare for your adventure. How will you get there? What will you take? Whom will you go with? What arrangements will you make to ensure your safety? Write a proposal to explain your proposed adventure, pretending you were going to submit it to *National Geographic Adventure*.

Source: Xpeditions@nationalgeographics.com. Family-X Files. Reprinted by permission of the National Geographic Society.

Although simulations and games are similar in many ways, **games** differ from simulations by including a goal or challenge.[85] Games have been an important instructional tool in kindergarten and elementary school since the early nineteenth century and were utilized by educational pioneers such as Froebel, Pestolozzi, and, later, those in the Progressive Movement who advocated children's learning through game playing. Games are more informal and cover a wide range of situations, whereas simulations reflect real-life situations and are more structured. Before designing a game the teacher must understand the cognitive side of instruction, which is essential for all learning. To design an instructional game well, you must be systematic and intuitive, analytic and artistic. You must clearly understand your instructional objectives. At this juncture you can then address the affective side of instruction and answer questions such as: Why are some games fun and others not? How can you create and design games for classroom instruction that maximize enjoyment without giving up instructional quality?

Almost any teacher guide, for almost all grade levels and subjects, will list several games for enriching learning. Educational games have social and cognitive purposes; they are not designed solely to amuse. Any game, however, may contribute to learning. For example, even Monopoly, a game normally played for amusement, has some value for young children in learning to count and deal with money. Checkers and chess, besides being enjoyable, challenge the mind; they involve math, logic, and sequencing of moves.

For younger students the value of the game may lie in the game itself, in the experience it gives them in learning to discriminate sounds or objects, to manipulate and gain facility in motor skills, or to play together and socialize.[86] For older students, the value may lie more in the postgame discussion, or what some educators call the *debriefing sessions*. (Simulations can also incorporate postactivity discussions or debriefing sessions.) Through proper questioning, the teacher brings out instances of questionable behavior, when the rules were ignored, and the reasons for such behavior. Life situations can be perceived as a series of games, in which there are winners and losers, in which there is cooperation and competition, and in which rules are broken and enforced. In this connection, games are an excellent means for teaching morality and ethics, value clarification, and affective education.

One potential disadvantage of games is that by their very nature they tend to emphasize competition. Depending on the students and the situation, teachers need to assess whether the positives of the game outweigh whatever negatives emerge as students compete against one another.

Guidelines for Using Simulations, Games, and Technology

Electronic games are powerful motivators that can create a social context, connecting learners to others who share their interests; they also lower the threat of failure for students and motivate them to do additional research.[87] Numerous simulations and games are commercially produced, but teachers must judge whether these are suitable for their students, whether they need modification or can be modified, or whether the teachers need to develop their own materials. Here are some guidelines to follow when incorporating simulations and games:

1. Computer-based games and simulations are more effective when some form of guidance is provided to students.
2. Every simulation and game must have an educational objective. Distinguish between amusement games and educational games, between game objectives and instructional objectives.

3. The purpose of using simulations is to enable students to understand the nature of a problem and how to solve the problem.

4. Games should be used for teaching thinking and socialization to children in the lower grades.

5. Simulations and games should be viewed as an experience for learning content. Students learn by organizing and familiarizing themselves with the content—by experiencing as much as possible the object, process, or situation.

6. Simulations and games must be related to the content (skills, concepts, values) you wish to teach; this content should correspond with reality, and the relationship between the real world and the simulation or game should be clarified to the participants.

7. The postgame (or post-simulation) discussion is crucial for older students to clarify skills, concepts, and values to be learned.

8. The postgame (or post-simulation) discussion should incorporate case studies, draw on student experiences, apply what was observed to real-life situations, and lead to suggestions for further study.

9. Employ a series of questions that require students to discuss their thoughts during the activity: What thoughts governed their behavior? What experiences resulted in certain behaviors? What strategies did they use to make decisions to achieve their goals? Which strategies were most effective? Could they predict the behavior of others?

10. In most simulations and games, students will interact. Participants and observers should discuss the interaction, if they are old enough, in terms of cooperation and competition and rational and emotional behavior.

11. To determine whether your objectives have been achieved by the simulations or games, use some form of evaluation, feedback, or discussion. Remember that electronic games and simulations can provide a safe environment for exploration and experimentation.[88]

Theory into Practice

For each subject and grade level, you need basic instructional materials to implement successful teaching and learning. Teachers, both beginning and experienced, should become familiar with the curriculum bulletins and guides for their subjects and grade levels. Such bulletins list necessary, recommended, and supplementary materials. Teachers should be familiar with the materials available in their school by discussing them with experienced colleagues or supervisors. Teachers must also find out how to construct supplementary materials in order to address areas of weakness in prescribed textbooks and materials used by a school district.

The following questions provide a guide for effective use of instructional materials.

- What instructional materials do you plan to use?
- What do you hope to achieve by using these materials? Do they correspond with your objectives? Do they help students meet defined academic standards?
- How will you prepare students to use the instructional materials?
- How will you incorporate the instructional materials into the lesson?
- Is the content of the materials suitable for your students? Consider sequence, scope, vocabulary, and so on.
- Are there a variety of materials to coincide with various topics of the lesson?
- How will you follow up the presentation of the materials? Are your follow-up activities appropriate?
- How do students react to the materials? Are they engaged by the materials? Are the students learning the required content?

Conclusions

- Good teachers become better teachers when they use appropriate materials in their lessons. They relate the materials they use to the curriculum and academic standards for the subject they teach. Learning what materials to use and how to use them comes with experience.
- Instructional materials may be printed (available from professional, governmental, and commercial sources) or duplicated (if teacher-made or copied from printed material) or may be electronically based on the Internet.
- Materials should be selected in terms of well-defined and agreed-upon criteria— for example, do they coincide with the teacher's objectives, are they well organized and designed, and are they suited to the reading level of the students?
- In presenting materials, teachers need to consider student understanding as well as structure, sequence, balance, explanation, pace, and elaboration strategies.
- Types of instructional materials include textbooks and workbooks; journals, magazines, and newspapers; and simulations and games as well as electronic reading devices. Textbooks and workbooks tend to dominate as the major instructional materials in most classrooms.
- Important aspects of selecting textbooks are stereotyping, readability, textbook and pedagogical aids, and aids to student comprehension.
- Textbook aids are designed to facilitate student comprehension, and pedagogical aids are designed to facilitate the teacher's instruction.
- Several strategies can be used for incorporating simulations and games into the daily lesson.
- It is important to remember that the purpose of all materials is to foster literacy.

KEY TERMS

copyright law	games	narrative structure
expository structure	leveling	pedagogical aids
field-dependent learners	mentioning	reading formulas
field-independent learners	phenomenon	simulations

DISCUSSION QUESTIONS

1. What is the main purpose of using instructional materials?

2. How would you determine if a textbook presents a stereotypical picture of an ethnic or religious group, gender, labor group, or any other minority?

3. Which textbook aids are most important? Why?

4. Is there a danger in using too many supplementary materials in a class? What factors should you consider when supplementing? Explain your answer.

5. How would you compare and contrast paper textbooks with those contained on electronic reading devices?

MINI-CASES FROM THE FIELD

Case One: Selecting Instructional Materials

John Grove had been chosen by his colleagues teaching the fourth grade to select all instructional materials for the coming school year. John wondered if the choice of a single person (himself) was an appropriate grade strategy. He did feel confident in his ability to make the choices involved, since he had been teaching the fourth grade for the past two years. He wanted to be sure that any choice he made would further the literacy objectives for the grade. All materials would be on a fourth-grade reading level and free from any stereotyping.

1. Were the fourth-grade teachers using a justifiable approach in selecting one of their members to choose materials for the entire grade? Explain your reasoning.

2. How would you describe the criteria that John intended to use?

3. Prepare a brief list of criteria that John could have used.

4. How would you select materials that met the literacy requirement of all the children in the fourth grade?

5. How can cost be factored in as one of your criteria?

Case Two: Paper Textbooks or Electronic Reading Devices?

As the teacher representative, Susan Steinberg was faced with the challenge of preparing remarks to explain to the parents of her elementary school's students why her school favored the use of electronic reading devices rather than the traditional paper textbooks. Her remarks were focused on convincing parents that electronic reading devices were the educational wave of the future.

Susan spotlighted four key points: cost, choices, environment, and ease of move-ment. The cost was less for one reading device than for many texts. The choices of materials were practically unlimited. Less use of paper was environmentally friendly, and because of the devices' small size students would not be burdened carrying heavy book bags. Susan was sure she had covered every possible point that could be brought up at the meeting.

1. Discuss your reasons for agreeing or disagreeing with Susan's position.

2. Was Susan correct regarding her claim that choices were unlimited?

3. How could copyright law be used to oppose her argument?

4. Describe your feelings with regard to whether or not the environment plays a role in the selection of instruction materials.

5. Look at Susan's argument regarding cost. Is she really being honest? Explain your response.

6. Describe how you would decide the issue of using electronic reading devices, textbooks, or both.

Case Three: Selecting Texts to Enhance Learning

George Mussen was about to begin his first year as an eighth grade lan-guage arts teacher at the Donaldson Middle School. He felt that he had gotten the position because of his enthusiastic responses during his job interview. When he had been asked how he would advance student learning, he had responded that the trick was in the selection of texts that would enhance learn-ing. He would identify all the instructional materials presently available, and then organize based on grade objectives; this would improve student compre-hension. He would balance materials between expository and narrative texts to help motivate student interest. The texts he chose would represent a wide range of readability and genre. George was sure he had the right formula to enhance students' learning.

1. Describe your feeling regarding George's formula.

2. Would George's formula guarantee that the materials he selected would reflect the most important aspects of his course? How could his formula be improved?

3. Why did George insist that narrative materials be used to balance exposi-tory materials? Is this a good strategy?

4. Would you agree or disagree with the following statement: *The number of different materials for any one course should be limited so as not to over-load or confuse students.*

5. Can any text really enhance student learning? Justify your answer.

Case Four: Are Workbooks Necessary?

Merrill Hall wasn't sure how to handle the use of workbooks for her third grade class. After using them for a month she was convinced that workbooks were an important addition to any instructional materials she chose to use with her class. She felt that their essential purpose was to reinforce the skills that she knew her children had to master. She had been brought up to utilize the maxim, "Practice makes perfect." She knew that most of her students needed materials that were appropriate to their reading levels and she made sure to use leveled reading materials. At times she wondered if she really needed textbooks.

1. Describe your reactions to Merrill's feelings about workbooks.

2. How can workbooks be used for other purposes beside practice?

3. What do you feel is the proper role of workbooks in primary classrooms and secondary classrooms?

4. How would you respond to someone who claimed that the use of workbooks focused too much on facts and limited critical thinking?

5. List five uses for textbooks and five for workbooks.

Case Five: Simulations, Games, and Technology

Jerrie Johnson had always prided herself on being an innovative person. She believed that children learned best through games and storytelling. As a seventh grade social studies teacher she had devised a "Constitutional Convention" game as the highlight of her unit on the branches of government and the United States Constitution. The game required her class be divided into three groups (legislative, executive, and judicial). The purpose of the simulation was to create a classroom constitution based on the United States Constitution. Each group was to draft rules regarding homework, class work, and appropriate behavior from the perspective of their branch of government. A convention would be held for the entire class to debate and vote on a constitution for Ms. Johnson's social studies class.

1. Describe your reaction to Ms. Johnson's idea of a classroom constitution drafted by her students.

2. What should Ms. Johnson's role be in the implementation of the simulation?

3. Should this activity be termed a game or a simulation? Explain your answer.

4. How could technology have been used to assist students in performing their roles?

5. What additional instructional materials could have been used to bolster instruction for the unit presented in this case study?

FIELD EXPERIENCE ACTIVITIES

1. Discuss with other prospective teachers ten questions to consider when evaluating instructional materials. Which questions or concepts are the most important? Why?

2. List five steps in developing your own instructional materials.

3. Prepare a checklist for evaluating textbooks. Select a textbook for your disciplinary area that is used in a proximate school district and evaluate it using *your* criteria and using the criteria we provide in this chapter.

4. Give specific guidelines for using the following materials: (a) workbooks, (b) journals and magazines, (c) simulations and games, and (d) DVDs.

5. Visit the state department of education website for the state in which you teach. For example, if you live in Virginia, you would go to www.pen.k12.va.us. See if there is a link there to textbooks and instructional materials. What resources are listed for teachers to use in your disciplinary area? Does your state provide clear linkages to the mandated academic standards?

RECOMMENDED READING

Aldrich, Clark. *Learning Online with Games, Simulations, and Virtual Worlds: Strategies for Online Instruction*. San Francisco: Jossey-Bass, 2010.
   A practical guide that shows faculty members how to identify opportunities for building games, simulations, and virtual environments into the curriculum; how to successfully incorporate these interactive environments to enhance student learning; and how to measure the learning outcomes.

Allington, Richard L., and Peter H. Johnston. *Reading to Learn*. New York: Guilford, 2002.
   Lessons from exemplary classrooms along with reading strategies and methods that work for teachers.

Carnine, Douglas W., Jerry Silbert, Edward J. Kame'enui, and Sara G. Tarver. *Direct Instruction Reading*, 5th ed. Upper Saddle River, NJ: Merrill/Prentice-Hall, 2009.
   A specific repertoire of carefully sequenced, highly prescriptive procedures for teaching decoding, comprehension, content reading, and study skills.

Cunningham, Patricia M., and Richard L. Allington. *Classrooms That Work: They Can All Read and Write*. New York: Allyn & Bacon, 2007.
   Provides a comprehensive, balanced treatment of instructional reading methods for struggling and culturally diverse students.

Ellington, Henry, Joannie Fowlie, and Monica Gordon. *Using Games and Simulations in the Classroom: A Practical Guide for Teachers*. New York: Kogan Page Ltd., 1998.
   Explains how to develop and implement games and simulations at the primary and secondary levels—case studies are included.

Goeke, Jennifer L. *Explicit Instruction: Strategies for Meaningful Direct Teaching*. Boston: Allyn & Bacon, 2009.
   A challenge to the view of explicit instruction as an outdated, mechanistic instructional strategy that presents it as timely, proven, and accessible.

Kellough, Richard D. A *Resource Guide for Teachers K–12,* 5th ed. New York: Allyn & Bacon, 2007.
   Examines various methods, materials, and resources for teaching middle school students and how to incorporate these resources into lesson plans.

Ludewig, Alexis, and Amy Swan. *101 Great Classroom Games: Easy Ways to Get Your Students Playing, Laughing, and Learning*. New York: McGraw-Hill, 2007.
   Easy-to-learn games in reading, logic, science, measuring, listening, social studies and math, designed to be both fun and educational.

Pressley, Michael. *Reading Instruction That Works: The Case for Balanced Teaching (Solving Problems in the Teaching of Literacy)*, 3rd ed. New York: Guilford Press, 2006.
   A focus on comprehension problems, decoding, vocabulary instruction, development of word knowledge and both skills and whole language instruction.

Morlan, John E., and Leonard J. Espinoza. *Preparation of Inexpensive Teaching Materials,* 6th ed. Belmont, CA: Fearon, 1998.
> Use this book to learn about several ways to plan, prepare, use, and evaluate materials.

Scarpaci, Richard T. *Resource Methods for Managing K–12 Instruction.* New York: Pearson, 2009.
> A practical, case-based text organized around the five keys to effective teaching: management, mastery, method, expectation and personality.

Strong, Richard, Harvey F. Silver, and Matthew J. Perini. *Teaching What Matters Most.* Alexandria, VA: ASCD, 2001.
> A thoughtful analysis of how to use standards in ways that enhance instruction and foster student learning.

Tyner, Beverly. *Small-Group Reading Instruction: A Differentiated Teaching Model for Beginning and Struggling Readers.* Newark, DE: International Reading Association, 2009.
> Easy-to-use lesson plans and activities support the five stages of reading—emergent, beginning, fledgling, transitional, and independent—and the accompanying CD features materials to help you implement the model.

Vacca, Richard T., and JoAnne L. Vacca. *Content Area Reading.* New York: Allyn & Bacon, 2004.
> These reading practices across content areas help students improve their reading skills.

Wisniewski, E. Robin. *Evidence-Based Instruction in Reading: A Professional Development Guide to Culturally Responsive Instruction.* Boston: Allyn & Bacon, 2012.
> An effective literacy program that supports all students, providing teachers with friendly tips and research-based strategies along with guidance on how to make instructional decisions for students who have fallen behind in reading.

6

Grouping for
Instruction

FOCUS POINTS

1. Understanding the use of whole-group, small-group, and individual instruction.
2. Learning the advantages and disadvantages of the different types of instruction.
3. Effectively organizing students for different types of instruction.
4. Identifying the methods to use when individualizing instruction.
5. Understanding how to differentiate instruction to personalize it for students.

OVERVIEW

In this chapter we discuss grouping and how important it is to effective instruction. Grouping your students for instruction should be based on your beliefs with regard to how children learn. Grouping is encumbered with uncertainty and ambiguity. Despite the insecurity it is essential for successful instruction. The reason for this uncertainty is the confusing variety of terms used in discussing the theoretical and practical issues surrounding grouping practices. The most common grouping pattern is by age. Students are organized for instruction in groups of twenty to thirty students according to age, grade level, and sometimes ability. When instruction occurs in this type of setting, it is called a **self-contained classroom**. The terms ungraded, nongraded, continuous progress, and mixed or multiage grouping are usually used interchangeably, causing confusion among many. Box 6.1 contains a list of definitions that should bring clarity to the issue of grouping by age.

At the elementary school level a teacher is assigned to the class for the whole day. Students may travel as a class to another classroom for one or two periods a day to receive special instruction (e.g., in corrective reading, music, or physical education), or other teachers may visit the class to provide special instruction.

At the secondary level the self-contained classroom is modified by what is commonly called **departmentalization**. Students are assigned to a different teacher for each subject and may have six or seven different teachers each day. Departmentalization usually begins at the sixth, seventh, or eighth-grade level—depending on the school district and on the state. Ohio has licensure standards for teachers that make departmentalization prevalent as early as the fourth and fifth grades.

There are three basic ways of grouping for instruction: (1) *large-group instruction,* sometimes called whole-group instruction, in which the entire class is taught as a group; (2) *small-group instruction,* in which the large group is broken up into subgroups according to ability, interest, project, or other criteria; and (3) *individualized instruction,* in which the individual student works alone or with another person on a specific task or assignment. Different groupings require different physical settings, so in this chapter we take a look at some

---

Box 6.1   Grouping by Age

Nongraded or ungraded grouping refers to placing children of differing ages in classes without grade-level designations. The purpose of this type of grouping was to increase heterogeneity, and avoid achievement expectations linked to age. The result, however, has been different; children are actually grouped homogeneously based on ability, regardless of age. This approach results in an increase of homogeneity rather than the heterogeneity it intended. The ungraded or nongraded approach acknowledges age as a crude indicator of what children are ready to learn.

- *Combined grades in bridge classes.* Includes more than one grade level in a classroom. This is usually done for budgetary or programming reasons, such as when classes do not have enough children to make a full register. It normally is not done to facilitate learning or complement an instructional approach.

- *Social promotion (continuous progress).* Children remain with their classroom peers in an age-based class, regardless of achievement level. The term is associated with a strong emphasis on individualizing the curriculum. The goal is to let children progress according to their individual rates of learning and development, without being compelled to meet age-related achievement expectations. Social promotion is a developmentally appropriate alternative to a rigid, lock-step curriculum that denies grade advancement based on test achievement. It also provides a way to sensitize teachers to the variability of child and adolescent development.

- *Mixed-age or multi-age grouping.* Refers to grouping children so the age span of the class is greater than one year. The goal is to focus on curriculum practices that maximize the benefits of interaction and cooperation among children of various ages. Mixed-age grouping generates social benefits, especially for at-risk children.

Source: Adapted from Richard T. Scarpaci, *Resource Methods for Managing K–12 Instruction: A Case Study Approach* (New York: Allyn & Bacon, 2009).

---

designs for seating arrangement and then look at the characteristics of instruction for each grouping.

American teachers spend more time in front of students (actually teaching) than do teachers from many other countries, such as those in Japan and China. And yet, US students perform no better than their international counterparts.[1] Time makes a difference in student learning, but for it to make a value-added difference, it's important for you to understand that what occurs must be *vital*—must be linked to standards and entail high expectations on your part for what the students will do. Let's take a look at how you arrange the classroom environment for learning—but never forget that it is the substance of a lesson, not the arrangement of the desks, that really dictates whether the learning will be significant for students.

Classroom Seating Arrangements

Room arrangements are a reflection of your teaching philosophy. They also necessarily influence the types of interactions that occur in the classroom. In a classic study on teaching, Adams and Biddle found that, for the most part, what takes place in the classroom requires the attention of all the students. Teachers tend to stay in front of the classroom more than 85 percent of the time when teaching the whole class, but they change their location on the average once every thirty seconds. Elementary teachers tend to move around through the aisles more than secondary teachers do.[2]

Adams and Biddle further found that student participation is restricted by the environment or physical setting itself in ways in which neither the teacher nor students seem to be aware. It appeared to them that students who sit in the center of the room are the most active learners, or what they called "responders." The verbal interaction is so concentrated in this area of the classroom and in a line directly up the center of the room (where the teacher is in front most of the time) that they coined the term "action zone" to refer to this area (figure 6.1).

Teachers who are student centered, indirect, and warm or friendly as opposed to teacher centered, direct, and businesslike tend to reject the tradi-

Figure 6.1 "Action Zone" Seating Arrangement

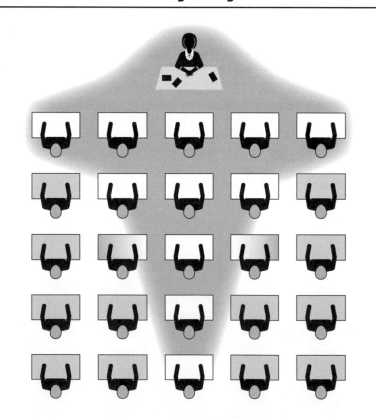

tional formal seating pattern of rows of students directly facing the teacher at the front of the classroom. Formal seating patterns tend to reduce student-to-student eye contact and student interaction as well as increase teacher control and student passivity. Student-centered teachers tend to favor informal seating patterns, such as rectangular (seminar), circular, and horseshoe (U-shaped) patterns, in which students face each other as well as the teacher (figure 6.2 on the following page).

Some conservative reform critics would argue against using student-centered instruction and seating patterns. Others who are more progressivist in their approach (and student centered in orientation) would argue for more open (and less traditional) classroom arrangements. Neither argument is absolutely right. Your goals for instruction dictate how you arrange the classroom. A direct instruction lesson might require a traditional student-in-rows format. A jigsaw, cooperative learning lesson focused on the causes and consequences of the Civil War might require a very different classroom arrangement. Your learning goals and beliefs, in essence, determine your classroom arrangement.

Special Classroom Designs

The rectangular, circular, and horseshoe arrangements in figure 6.2 assume that there are no more than 20 to 25 students. Double rectangular, double circular, and double horseshoe (w-shaped) arrangements are needed to accommodate more than 25 students (figure 6.3 on p. 275).

An open classroom seating arrangement is appropriate for elementary, middle grade, and junior high school students (figure 6.4 on p. 276). The many shelves, tables, and work areas allow for small-group and individualized instruction. The formal rows of fixed desks of the traditional classroom are gone. The desks are arranged in groups or clusters that can be moved. The open classroom increases student interaction and gives students the opportunity to move around and engage in different learning activities in various settings.

Figure 6.5 shows two additional seating designs—both of which correspond to special activities. The design on the left is well suited for whole-class debates and forums. The design on the right is conducive to cooperative learning or "buzz sessions." Whereas the seating patterns in figures 6.2, 6.3, and 6.4 are home-based or permanent arrangements, the ones in figure 6.5 (on p. 277) are temporary designs.

Because of the resulting increased student interaction, discipline problems may arise with these special seating arrangements, unless the teacher has good managerial skills (see chapter 7). However, all these designs allow the teacher flexibility in activities. They create feelings of group cohesion and cooperation, they allow students to work in small groups, and they also allow the teacher to present a demonstration, lead the class in a brainstorm or debate, or use audiovisual materials, among other methods.

Figure 6.2   Seating Patterns

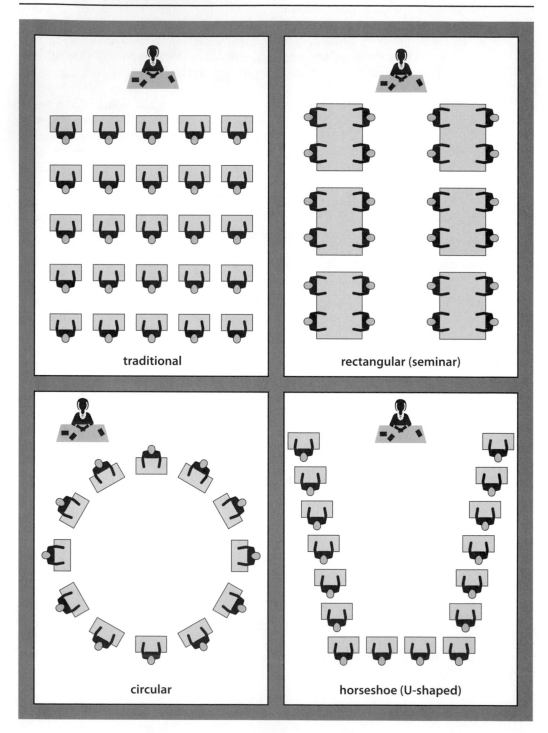

traditional

rectangular (seminar)

circular

horseshoe (U-shaped)

Figure 6.3   Modified Seating Patterns

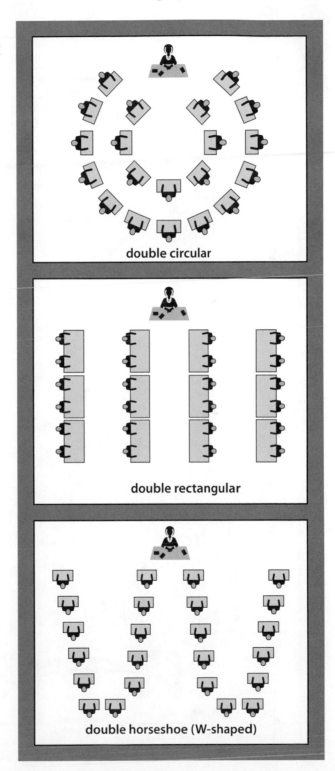

double circular

double rectangular

double horseshoe (W-shaped)

Figure 6.4   Open Classroom Seating Pattern

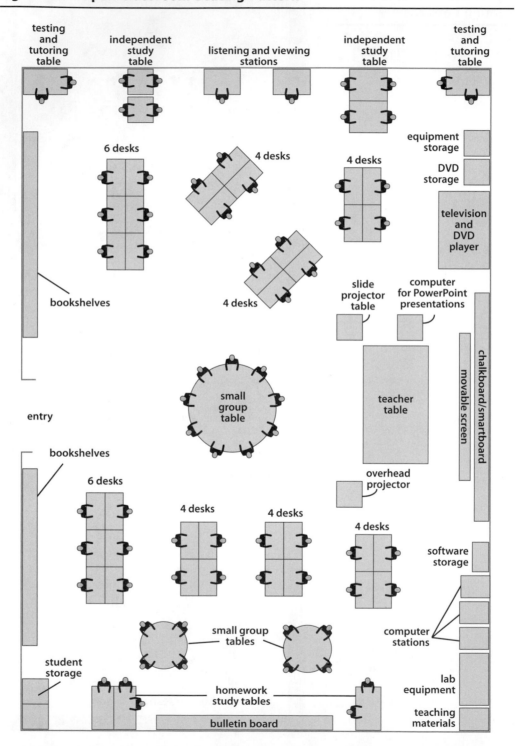

Figure 6.5 Group Formations

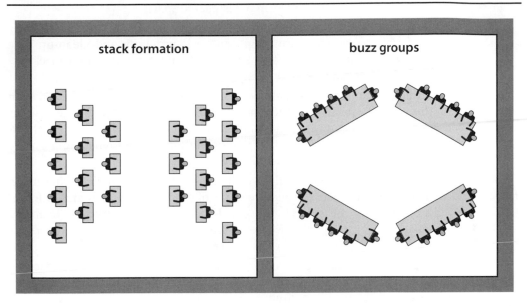

stack formation buzz groups

Factors to Consider in Classroom Designs

Classroom design will be determined by the size of the room; the number of students in the class; the size and shape of tables and chairs; the amount of movable furniture; the location of fixed features such as doors, windows, closets, and chalkboard; the audiovisual equipment to be used; the school's philosophy; and the teacher's approach and experience. Several factors should be considered in arranging the classroom:

1. *Fixed features.* The teacher cannot change the "givens" of a room and must take into account the locations of doors, windows, closets, electric outlets, and so forth. For example, seats should not be too close to doors or closets. Electrical equipment needs to be near an outlet, and wires should not run across the center of the room. (If they must, they should be taped to the floor.)

2. *Traffic areas.* High-traffic areas such as supply areas, the area around closets, and space near the pencil sharpener and wastebasket need to be open and easily accessible. The teacher's desk should be located in a low-traffic area.

3. *Work areas.* Work areas and study areas should be private and quiet, preferably in the corners or rear of the room, away from traffic lanes and noisy areas.

4. *Furniture and equipment.* The room, furniture, and equipment should be kept clean and in repair so that they can be used. Desks and chairs may be old, but they should be clean and smooth (make the appropriate requisition to the janitorial department or supervisor), and graphics and doo-

dling on furniture should be discouraged immediately. Classroom equipment should be stored in a designated space.

5. *Instructional materials.* All materials and equipment should be easily accessible so activities can begin and end promptly and clean-up time can be minimized. Props and equipment that are not stored in closets should be kept in dead spaces away from traffic.

6. *Visibility.* The teacher should be able to see all students from any part of the room in order to reduce managerial problems and enhance instructional supervision. Students should be able to see the teacher, chalkboard, projected images, and demonstrations without having to move their desks and without straining their necks.

7. *Flexibility.* The classroom design should be flexible enough so that it can be modified to meet the requirements of different activities and different groupings for instruction. As you look at your classroom's flexibility, make certain that you are able to see all students and that all students can see you during whole-class presentations.[3]

Elementary teachers often need to be more flexible, since they are teaching several subjects; they *can* be more flexible, since they rarely share the room with other teachers. The room is entirely theirs for setting up learning areas, interest areas, and work and study areas for reading, mathematics, science, and arts and crafts. At the secondary level, where teachers teach one subject and several teachers may share a room, the possibilities are reduced, but the room can still be divided into areas for small groups, audiovisual activities, projects, and independent study. Cooperation among the teachers who share the room is essential for a positive school climate.

Unfortunately, too few high school teachers are flexible in their classroom arrangements. Students usually sit in rows, facing the chalkboard and teacher, just as they did 100 years ago. One possible explanation is that most high school teachers stress content and ignore socialization and personal relations as classroom goals.

Only through experience and time will teachers learn whether a given arrangement suits their teaching style and the needs of their students. It may take several tries and continual revision to come up with a classroom design that helps students work efficiently, in which materials and equipment can be used to their best advantage, from which unnecessary equipment is removed, and where the teacher finds it easy to instruct and to supervise the students.

Whole-Group Instruction

Whole-group instruction is the most traditional and common form of classroom organization. Teachers generally gear their teaching to the "mythical" average student on the assumption that this level of presentation will meet the needs of the greatest number of students. A common block of content (in any subject) is taught through whole-group instruction because it is most often perceived as the most effective and convenient format for teaching it.[4]

In the large group, the teacher lectures, explains, and demonstrates material related to a topic; asks and answers questions in front of the entire class, provides the same practice-and-drill exercises to the entire class, works on the same problems with the entire class, and employs the same materials with all students. Instruction is directed toward the whole group, but the teacher may ask specific students to answer questions, monitor specific students as they carry out the assigned activities, and work with students on an individual basis.

Whole-group instruction can be an economical and efficient method. It is especially convenient for teaching the same skills or subject content to the entire class, administering tests, or setting group expectations. Bringing members of a class together for certain activities strengthens the feeling of belonging and can help establish a sense of community and class spirit. The whole group learns to cooperate by sharing available resources, setting up rules and regulations for the learning environment, and exchanging ideas. This method of grouping students is most effective for large numbers of students, especially when the focus is on learning distinct skills or processes (see Tips for Teachers 6.1). It is also one of

TIPS FOR TEACHERS 6.1

Components of Direct Instruction

Evidence suggests that for teaching low-achieving and at-risk students in the whole-group setting, a highly structured approach is the most effective method. This approach is often called *direct instruction* or *explicit instruction.* We discussed it in chapter 5. The major aspects of direct instruction listed here are especially appropriate for teaching a specific skill, concept, or process:

1. Begin a lesson with a short statement of goals (and anchor those goals to defined academic standards).

2. Review previous, prerequisite learning.

3. Present new material in small steps, with student practice after each step.

4. Provide clear and detailed instructions and explanations.

5. Provide a high level of active practice for all students, and call on a variety of volunteers and nonvolunteers.

6. Guide students during initial practice, and monitor and assess the ongoing practice of the students.

7. Check for student understanding by asking many questions of all students.

8. Provide systematic feedback and corrections.

9. Monitor and help students during seat work and independent practice.

10. Provide for review, testing, and assessment.

Note: Since Rosenshine published his work on explicit instruction in the 1970s and 1980s, a variety of subtle variations have been introduced by all who have an interest in this form of instruction. The steps outlined are fundamental to the explicit approach and should be evidenced in any lesson that uses this approach.

Source: Adapted from Barak Rosenshine, "Explicit Teaching and Teacher Training," *Journal of Teacher Education* (May–June 1987), 34.

the most common forms of instruction, despite the fact that a wide variety of educators have encouraged teachers to incorporate instructional alternatives that are more student centered. Whole-group instruction is often used in conjunction with small-group instruction: When working with whole groups, teachers usually present new information to the total group and then have students split off into smaller groups for review and practice or enrichment activities.

The critics of whole-group instruction contend that it fails to meet the needs and interests of individual students. Teachers who use this method tend to look upon students as a homogeneous group with common abilities, interests, styles of learning, and motivation. Instruction is geared to a hypothetical "average" student—a concept that fits only a few students in the class—and all students are expected to learn and perform within narrow limits. Students are evaluated, instructional methods and materials are selected, and learning is paced on the basis of the group average, with a tendency for high-achieving students to eventually become bored and low-achieving students to eventually become frustrated.[5] The uniqueness of each student is often lost in the large-group context. Extroverted students tend to monopolize the teacher's time, and passive students are usually not heard from or do not receive necessary attention. Finally, students sometimes act out their behavioral problems in teacher-centered, whole-group instructional formats.

Different group patterns are essential for variety, motivation, and flexibility in teaching and learning. They are also essential for meeting the needs of diverse learners who are now a part of American classrooms.[6] Eugene Garcia describes teachers who are effective with language minority students:

> These [successful] teachers [of language minority students] organized a good portion of class time around a series of learning activities that children pursue either independently or with others. During science and math, children work in small groups doing a variety of hands-on activities designed to support their understanding of a particular concept . . . or subject. . . .[7]

To work effectively with the wide variety of students in whole-group learning classrooms, many educators are actively arguing for smaller classes, especially in the early grades. In the next section we discuss the research on class size. It seems logical to believe that the number of students in your class makes a difference. However, the real issue is how much of a difference there is in student achievement if teachers have smaller classes.

Class Size and Achievement

Does class size affect whole-group learning? Some state legislatures think it does. In the late 1990s, California embraced smaller class size as a way of dealing with the learning needs of young children. Has it made a difference? Many researchers question whether a slightly smaller class size makes a difference in achievement. (California looked at classes of twenty children, and Tennessee's Project STAR focused on classes of fifteen children). The key seems to be the interaction between class size and the effectiveness of the teacher's instructional practices—that is, a large class with an effective teacher may be better than a smaller class with an ineffective teacher. Indeed, many who are interested in the effects of class size are now calling for research that investigates the relationship between class size and the factors that help students learn.[8]

When it comes to improving student performance, common sense would indicate that there is a clear relationship between class size and student achievement. Conservative critics suggest that class size does not automatically lead to better student performance. Several studies have found that class size does not have an impact on student achievement overall.[9] In one review of 152 studies that analyzed smaller classes and student achievement, 82 percent found no significant impact, 9 percent saw positive results, and about 9 percent found negative results.[10] That research has now been influenced by additional research that illustrates some of the complications (financial and practical) of smaller class size; in particular, teacher quality.[11] For example, the California class size "experiment" resulted in many poorly qualified teachers being placed in classrooms. Nearly all schools needed more teachers, but schools in poor urban environments added the fewest number of highly qualified teachers.

In still another review of eight studies of low-achieving students, Robert Slavin found that differences in achievement levels of students in larger classes (twenty-two to thirty-seven students) compared to small classes (fifteen to twenty students) were insignificant. Across the eight studies the effect was only +.13—a low figure, given that the average class size in the large groups was 27 students compared to 16 in the small groups (a 40 percent difference).[12] In another review, Slavin found that only when class size is reduced to a one-to-one teacher/student ratio, as in tutoring, does size make a truly dramatic difference.[13]

A more recent Northwestern study in 2008 questioned commonly held assumptions about class size and the academic achievement gap. Northwestern researchers worked with data from Project STAR to determine whether small classes positively impacted the academic achievement of students. That data showed that on average, small classes had a positive impact on student academic performance. The Northwestern study, however, found an exception in the STAR data in that the children who already were high achievers were the primary beneficiaries of the extra attention smaller classes afforded. Northwestern researchers claim that the STAR data provided weak or no evidence that class reduction benefited lower-achieving students more than others.

These findings suggest that small classes produce significantly higher unpredictability in achievement than regular-sized classes in kindergarten mathematics and in first-grade reading. Overall the results indicate that class-size reduction increases achievement for all students on average, while simultaneously demonstrating an inconsistency in student achievement as well.[14]

It appears that small classes in early grades improve test scores in later grades for students of all achievement levels, but low achievers get an extra boost. That's the finding of a study on the long-term effects of class size that appeared in the November 2009 issue of the *American Journal of Education*. The study suggests that reducing class size in early grades provides a dual benefit: It raises achievement for all students through middle school, while also closing the persistently large gap between high and low achievers.[15]

The National Assessment of Educational Progress (NAEP) reading examination to analyze the effect of class size on academic achievement provides the most comprehensive database on educational outcomes available to researchers. Among the major findings of this analysis of NAEP data are that:

- On average, being in a small class does not increase the likelihood that a student will attain a higher score on the NAEP reading test, and

- Children in the smallest classes (those with 20 or fewer students per teacher) do not score higher than students in the largest classes (those with 31 or more students per teacher).[16]

Class-size data at times receive conflicting interpretations, depending on who is doing the reporting. According to Biddle,

> Class size reduction in the early grades helps kids who are at risk primarily. In other words, it's not an across the board thing. That doesn't mean that middle class kids aren't helped, they are helped by class size reduction, but the evidence suggests that the amount of help is greater for kids from minority backgrounds and from impoverished homes.[17]

At the secondary level, however, the impact of class size seems to have no significant influence on student achievement.[18] One possible reason is that class size may have different effects with different tracks (honors, academic, vocational, etc.); different subjects (English, social studies, etc.); different students (depending on prior ability level, motivation level, study habits, and high versus low achievement level); and/or different presentation of content (consistent review and practice, problem solving, questioning or discussion)—variables that may blur research results.

If reduced class size seems to have modest effects overall on school achievement and since reduction in class size is expensive (the cost in California is by some estimates close to $1 billion), that cost should be weighed against the cost of other innovations to determine the best policy or programs for fostering academic achievement. For example, research suggests that increasing school attendance among students, increasing academic time in reading (or any other subject area), improving the quality of instruction (hiring better teachers for low-achieving students), and providing more review or practice for learning the material on tests have more positive effects than just reducing class size.[19]

Dividing the whole group (say, 25 students) into smaller, homogeneous groups (of four or five), with the teacher spending more time with the low-achieving groups, is perhaps more beneficial than small whole-group instruction (say, 15 students), as long as the teacher knows how to take advantage of the extra time for the low-achieving groups without shortchanging the other groups. Such different grouping patterns within whole groups also are essential for variety, motivation, and flexibility in teaching and learning.

What can we conclude? First, American schools have been trying to reduce the size of classes for years. In the 1970s, classes averaged 22.3 students, and in the 1990s, the average class size was 17; some research from the *Digest of Education Statistics* suggests that in the early 2000s the class sizes began to be even smaller.[20] Second, whether smaller class size makes a difference is difficult to ascertain. Through an analysis of National Assessment of Educational Progress (NAEP) data, Johnson examined variables related to race and ethnicity, parents' education, reading materials in a child's home, free and reduced lunch participation, gender and, of course, class size. Johnson concluded the following:

> After controlling for all these factors, researchers found that the difference in reading achievement on the 1998 NAEP reading assessment between students in small classes and students in large classes was statistically insignificant. That is, across the United States students in small classes did no better on average than those in large classes, assuming otherwise identified circumstances.[21]

Does that mean schools should not strive for smaller classes? Not if resources are available! What the class-size research suggests, however, is that the key to a good learning environment is the teacher. That news is good for you. You are the key factor that will make a difference in a student's learning. Whether you have 25 or 15 students, their learning depends primarily on what you do to structure the classroom into a meaningful environment. The tasks you assign and the learning experiences you arrange mean more than the number of students you have in the class.

Classroom Tasks

Instructional tasks are at the core of decisions about the classroom setting. Most teachers maintain control over instructional tasks by choosing what is to be taught, what materials and methods are to be used, and how much students are to be allowed to interact.

With the current emphasis on academic standards in most states, this circumstance is even truer than it was several years ago. Secondary school classrooms tend to be more controlled settings than elementary school classrooms. The key variable, of course, is the teacher and not the grade level. When the teacher has complete control over instruction, it is likely that most students, if not all, will be engaged in a single classroom task at one time and work toward the same goal with the same content. There are teachers, however, who do permit student input in planning content and activities. When students have input, it is likely that they will work on different classroom tasks.[22]

Teacher control over tasks affects the social setting and nature of evaluation. Under single-task conditions with high teacher control, students usually work alone, and evaluation of academic abilities and achievement is based on comparison to others in the class or to standardized achievement levels. Under multiple-task conditions with low teacher control, there is more social interaction and cooperative learning. Evaluation is conducted more on the basis of individual progress than on comparison to others.[23]

Classroom learning falls into one of three basic categories: (1) knowledge or facts (e.g., what is the capital of Chile?); (2) skills (i.e., reading, writing, spelling, computer literacy); or (3) high-order thinking processes (e.g., analysis, problem solving, concepts).[24] A majority of classroom tasks initiated by teachers in traditional classrooms are what might be called low-level cognitive processes, involving facts or skills. Only small portions are high-order cognitive tasks. The reason is that in a whole-group classroom setting the range of ability is usually wide, and it is easier to keep things simple and focused so students can perform the tasks without frustration. Focusing on low-level tasks, facts or skills, and right answers emphasizes short-term goals at the expense of critical thinking and integration of prior and past knowledge for long-term benefits. Students learn the answer, not the process, and they work toward completing the assignment on time and getting it out of the way (as if it were taking medicine). Interestingly, one way that you can foster more process-oriented (higher-order) answers on the part of students is to engage yourself in more reflection about the lessons you teach. Your in-depth reflection will lead to higher-level student thinking.

Most classroom tasks are initiated and structured by the teacher and focus on the acquisition and comprehension of knowledge. Students usually act in response to the teacher's expectations. Basically, classroom tasks that are initiated by the teacher fall into four categories:

1. incremental tasks, which focus on new skills or ideas and require recognition;
2. restructuring tasks, which involve the discovery of an idea or pattern and require some reorganization of data;
3. enrichment tasks, which involve application of familiar skills and ideas to new problems; and
4. practice tasks, which are aimed at making new skills and ideas automatic so they can be used in other task situations and for other cognitive processes.

In order to facilitate learning, the teacher must learn to match appropriate tasks with the students' abilities and background knowledge. Matching becomes more difficult as students get older and have the potential to learn more. It is also more difficult in heterogeneously grouped classrooms because of the range in students' abilities and interests. The teacher must consider which tasks contribute most to students' learning and when it is appropriate to introduce these tasks so students gain new insights and skills.

Success in matching can be judged by student performance. The more errors that students make in working on the tasks, the greater the mismatch. Fewer errors mean that students are capable of working on the tasks but not necessarily that a good match has been made, because the tasks may be too easy to contribute to learning. *Matched* tasks are at an appropriate level of difficulty and foster learning. *Mismatched* tasks are either too easy or too difficult. Matching tasks to student learning needs is one of the biggest challenges that new teachers and experienced teachers face. For example, the pattern of over- and underestimation of tasks was found in a study of 21 third- to sixth-grade classes in math, language arts, and social studies.[25] In this study 500 academic tasks were analyzed, and the extent of mismatching was significant for both high- and low-achieving students.

Teachers more often tend to overestimate than underestimate tasks. In fact, in the study cited, no teacher saw any task as too easy. Both types of mismatching lead to failure to meet the needs of the students. When tasks are underestimated, too many students are not learning up to potential, and they also may become bored. When tasks are overestimated, too many students fail to learn because they don't understand what they are being asked to do, and they are likely to become discouraged. If the assumption that matching becomes more difficult in the upper grades is correct, then mismatching may help explain why so many students drop out of school during adolescence. Far too many tasks are either too difficult or too easy for them to accomplish. As a result, they fail to understand the relevance of the tasks they are assigned.

Actually, understanding classroom tasks is not an "all-or-nothing" experience. Students seldom experience flashes of insight while in a classroom. Rather, they gain gradual understanding with further practice or explanation as well as through exposure to a variety of tasks. High achievers, more often than low achievers, have a larger knowledge base (i.e., more prior learning that helps them acquire the new information faster) so they quickly integrate relevant information pertaining to the tasks; moreover, they have more confidence in their ability to learn so they remain on task and work on various tasks for longer periods without giving up. In fact, some are even challenged by difficult tasks. Not so for low achievers, who are often frustrated by difficult tasks—and easily give up. That is why varied instructional approaches are needed. Teachers who group students in only one way (e.g., teacher-centered classrooms) give greater advantage to high achievers (who need no advantage) and disadvantage the low achievers. Cooperative (student-centered) learning approaches, coupled with teacher-centered instruction, potentially maximize the learning for all students, especially if

1. students know why they are being asked to work together,
2. students are shown how to interact with one another, and
3. student groups systematically analyze and reflect on their own effectiveness.[26]

A good deal of concept learning (high-order tasks) involves multidimensional understanding, not singular or specific representations.[27] That means that, in presenting new concepts such as symmetry, you need to help students learn the material in a number of different ways (e.g., drawing lines of symmetry on figures and having students look at different visual representations). A single task or approach, repeated several times, may not effectively represent all features of a concept but rather may capture only particular concept attributes. Thus, the low-level tasks accompanied by concrete materials often designed for low achievers may have their limitations, since this instructional approach fails to capture all the representations needed for full understanding. Thus, the cycle of low achievement may be repeated by the way classroom tasks (involving facts and skills) are introduced by teachers. Simonsen and colleagues identified features that can be associated with effective classroom task management: maximizing structure; posting, teaching, reviewing, monitoring, and reinforcing expectations; and actively engaging students in observable ways. Think of this dilemma when you introduce tasks in your own classroom.[28]

Instructional Variables

Researchers are focusing on elements of the classroom that teachers and schools can change, or what some call *alterable environments,* for purposes of measuring the effect they have on student achievement. According to Robert Slavin, there are four components of instruction: (1) quality of instruction, (2) appropriate level of instruction, (3) incentives to work on instructional tasks, and (4) time needed to learn tasks. He concludes that all four components must be adequate for instruction to be effective. For example, if the quality of instruction is low, it matters little how much students are motivated or how much time they have to learn.[29] Notice also that all four of these components are matters that you, the teacher, can control. Although there are limits to the total amount of time you have with students, you can dictate what you do with students when they are in your classroom.

Several years ago, Benjamin Bloom listed 19 teaching and instructional variables based on a summary of several hundred studies conducted during the past half century. His research synthesized the impact these variables have on student achievement. The five most effective ones in rank order are (1) tutorial instruction (1:1 ratio), (2) instructional reinforcement, (3) feedback and correction, (4) cues and explanations, and (5) student class participation. The next most effective variables for student achievement are improved reading and study skills, cooperative learning, graded homework, classroom morale, and initial cognitive prerequisites.[30]

Bloom concluded that the quality and quantity of instruction (teacher performance and time devoted to instruction) are the most important factors related to teaching and learning. Most of the instructional variables that are effective tend to be emphasized in individualized and small-group instruction. Bloom assumed that two or three variables "used together contribute to more learning than any one of them alone, especially those in the first five rankings."[31] In essence, it is not any one thing that you do but rather the array of practices that you have in place that begin to influence student achievement.

Good and Brophy have highlighted the notion that how teachers behave and arrange the learning environment and who they are teaching make a difference. Good teaching is not about doing one thing right but rather doing a combination of things correctly, purposefully, and in a timely manner. Good teachers alter how they arrange the class environment (whole-class versus small-group) and the focus of their teaching (thinking-skill oriented versus learning-time oriented).[32]

Marzano writes that teacher-level variables associated with raising the academic achievement of all students are commonly grouped into three categories: instruction, classroom management, and curriculum design.[33] Marzano also conducted a theory-based meta-analysis of meta-analyses of studies on instruction, which he defines as "those direct and indirect activities orchestrated by the teacher to expose students to new knowledge, to reinforce knowledge, or to apply knowledge."[34] Based on his meta-analyses, he identified nine categories of instructional variables. His list analyzed 395 experimental studies and calculated effect sizes for nine instructional practices shown to contribute to higher levels of student achievement. He reports these findings along with their effect sizes, which range from .59 to 1.61 as follows:

1. Identifying similarities and differences (1.61)
2. Summarizing and note taking (1.0)
3. Reinforcing effort and providing recognition (.80)
4. Homework and practice (.77)
5. Nonlinguistic representations such as mental images, graphs, acting out content (.75)
6. Cooperative learning (.73)
7. Setting objectives and providing feedback (.61)
8. Generating and testing hypotheses (.61)
9. Activating prior knowledge via questions, cues, advance organizers (.59)[35]

The general conclusion is that both the quality and quantity of instruction can and must be modified for the students' benefit. The instructional variables (what you teach and how you teach it) provide excellent guidelines for improving instruction. The variables seem to be effective across school districts, ethnicity and gender, grade level, classroom size, and subject area. They deal mainly with the process, not with inputs or educational spending. They call attention to classroom variables that can be altered, rather than to such practices as IQ testing or to various cognitive deficits of students. You, the teacher, determine what can be altered. You decide how to adjust learning time for the whole group and *when* to develop thinking skills within small groups.

Guidelines for Teaching Whole Groups

When teaching whole groups or regular classes of 20 or more students, it is important to be organized and to start on time. You need to make good use of allocated time. Here are some practical suggestions to get the instructional ball rolling on the right path:

1. Be in the room before the class arrives. Your appearance helps the class start on time.
2. Ready your materials: attendance book, lesson plans, and other instructional materials (charts, pictures, maps) that you may need.
3. Obtain the full attention of the students. Start the students on a review exercise, warm-up drill, or set of problems. Explain instructions clearly and be sure students begin the assignment.
4. Attend to special student needs. While the students are completing the assignment, respond to special student requests or problems. Attend to one student at a time; otherwise, you may lose control.
5. Circulate among students. This bolsters classroom management and ensures that students are prepared with books, pens, assignments, and the like.
6. Check notebooks, homework, or other written work. If time permits, check to see that students have their notebooks, homework, or texts with them.

7. Review assignments. Take extra time to discuss or reteach specific aspects of the assignment.

8. Summarize the lesson. Learn to pace your lesson. Remind students that class work continues until you give the word that the class has ended.

Small-Group Instruction

Dividing students into small groups provides an opportunity for students to become more actively engaged in learning and for teachers to better monitor student progress. Evidence suggests that an optimal number to ensure successful small-group activity is between five and eight students. When there are fewer than five, especially in a group discussion, students tend to pair off rather than interact as a group.[36]

Small groupings can enhance student cooperation and social skills. Appropriate group experiences foster the development of democratic values, cultural pluralism, and appreciation for differences among people. Small-group instruction can provide interesting challenges, permits students to progress at their own pace, provides a psychologically safe situation in which to master the material, and encourages students to contribute to class activities.

Dividing the class into small groups helps the teacher monitor work and assesses progress through questioning, discussions, and checking workbook exercises and quizzes geared for the particular group. Small groups also give the teacher a chance to introduce new skills at a level suited to particular students. Because the number of students assigned to each group is often determined by their level of progress, group size will vary. Students may move from group to group if their progress level exceeds or falls below that of their assigned group. In effect, the teacher uses grouping to restructure a heterogeneously grouped class into several homogeneous subgroups.

Small groups are typically used in elementary school reading and mathematics. The teacher divides the class into two or three groups, depending on the number of students, their range of ability, and the number of groups the teacher is able to handle. The teacher usually works with one group at a time, while the other students do seat work or independent work.

The use of small groups can be extended beyond the typical grouping in elementary reading and mathematics to all grade levels and subjects. There are several other reasons to form small groups: (1) special interests or skills in a particular topic or activity; (2) ability grouping or regrouping within a class for specific subjects (reading or mathematics) or specific content (different assignments or exercises), thus reducing the problems of heterogeneity in the classroom; and (3) integration to enhance racial, ethnic, religious, or gender relations.

Regardless of the basis of the grouping, assignments given to small groups should be specific enough and within the range of the students' abilities and interests so that each group can work on its own without teacher support. This permits the teacher to single out one group for attention or to help individuals by explaining, questioning, redirecting, and encouraging.

Ability Grouping

The most common means of dealing with heterogeneity is to assign students to classes and programs according to ability. In high schools, students may be tracked into college preparatory, vocational or technical, and general programs. In many middle and junior high schools, students are sometimes assigned to a class based on ability—**ability grouping**—and stay with that class as it moves from teacher to teacher. In a few cases, and more often in elementary schools, students are assigned to a class on the basis of a special characteristic, such as being gifted, handicapped, or bilingual. Elementary schools may use several types of ability grouping. In addition to the types used in the secondary schools, they may assign students to a heterogeneous class and then regroup them homogeneously by ability in selected areas, such as reading and mathematics.

Between-Class Ability Grouping

Despite widespread criticism of **between-class ability grouping** (separate classes for students of different abilities), many teachers support the idea because of the ease of teaching a homogeneous group. In addition, many parents of high-achieving students perceive tracking to be in their children's best interests. Reality is also a consideration. By the time students are in middle school, the achievement and motivation gaps between the top third and lowest third achievers have grown extremely wide, and teachers cannot accommodate this range of student abilities. Hence, the norms of the school culture resist detracking.[37] In addition, a number of neoconservative education reform critics debunk detracking because they believe it results in "teaching to the average."

One primary criticism of separating students by ability is that it results in low expectations for low-ability students, lowered self-esteem, less instruction time, less homework, less learning, and worst of all, a compounding and stigmatizing effect on low achievers.[38] The negative consequences of these practices disproportionately affect minorities and female students in math classrooms.[39]

Given our democratic norms and the need to deal with diversity in schools (and society), and given the notion that abilities are multifaceted and developmental (not genetic), differences in abilities can become assets in classrooms rather than liabilities.[40] Earlier studies seemed to indicate that high-ability students benefit from separate ability groups because the curriculum and instruction are tailored to the students' abilities, and the classroom work and homework driving the group require extra effort. There are fewer competing values that curtail the academic ethos, and less time is devoted to management problems.[41]

But such arguments tend to run up against democratic thinking—that is, the drive to reduce inequality and differences (including outcomes) that may exist between high- and low-achieving students. Ability-grouping critics contend that the gains made by high achievers do not compensate for the loss of self-esteem and achievement among low achievers, who often find themselves slotted into groups where the instruction is less engaging. Performance of low-achieving groups may suffer because the students themselves are less responsive, because of management problems, or because the instruction is really inferior, as critics suggest.

More recent studies have found that ability grouping with curriculum differentiation may be implicated in increasing the achievement gap. This research indicates that students' academic self-concept is related to the extent of ability grouping, with students in high-ability groups having significantly higher self-concepts than students in low-ability groups, and that students' intentions to learn in the future were more strongly affected by self-concept than by achievement.[42]

After reviewing sixty years of research on the issue, Slavin claimed that the achievement gains of all students (high and low achieving) in ability-grouped classes canceled each other out or "clustered closely around zero."[43] In other words, ability grouping rarely adds to overall achievement in a school (although it may for a particular class), but it often contributes to inequality (highs do better, lows do worse). In addition, studies show that instruction in mixed-ability, untracked classes more closely resembles instruction in high-achieving and middle-track classes than it does instruction in low-track classes—that is, the mixed-ability grouping tends to benefit low-ability students.[44] Similarly, average-ability students who are grouped in high-ability math classes achieve significantly higher math grades and higher scores on achievement tests than do their cohorts who are placed in average classes, perhaps since their teachers have higher expectations for them and the content is more advanced (see Tips for Teachers 6.2).[45]

Ability grouping is a controversial issue. Most academics are against between-class ability grouping, as evidenced by recent studies.[46] Although no consensus from the research is evident to suggest exactly what teachers and administrators *should* do with regard to between-class ability grouping, some policy implications do emerge. Good and Brophy suggest, for example, that between-class ability grouping (or tracking) "should be minimized, should be delayed as long as possible, and when used, should be confined to grouping by curriculum rather than by ability or achievement."[47] A recent study suggests that inequalities are magnified by national-level tracking institutions and that standardization decreases inequality.[48]

Within-Class Ability Grouping

Within-class ability grouping, on the other hand, has been assessed as effective for almost all students.[49] This is especially true if the groups are fluid and evolving. Students in heterogeneous classes who are regrouped homogeneously learn more than students in classes that do not use such grouping, particularly in reading and mathematics (for which within-class grouping is common) as well as for low-achieving students.[50]

The research data suggest that a small number of within-class groups (two or three) is better than a large number, permitting more monitoring by and feedback from the teacher and less seat work time and transition time.[51] For example, in a class of three ability groups, students spend approximately two-thirds of the time doing seat work without direct supervision; but with four groups they spend three-quarters of the class time doing seat work without the teacher monitoring their work.

When within-class ability groups are formed, students proceed at different paces on different materials. The tasks and assignments tend to be more flexible than those in between-class groups. Teachers also tend to try to increase the tempo of instruction and the amount of time for instruction in low-achieving within-class groups to bring students closer to the class mean.[52] There is less stigma for low-ability groups in within-class grouping than in between-class grouping, since grouping is only for part of the day and the class is integrated the rest of the time. Regrouping plans tend to be more flexible than with between-class groups, because moving students from group to group is less disruptive within a class than it is between classes. Finally, regrouping is most beneficial when it is based on achievement levels that can be assessed frequently

---

TIPS

F O R T E A C H E R S

6.2

Grouping Practices in Classrooms

Teachers and schools can provide alternatives to grouping without ignoring the needs of high-achieving and exceptional students. Here are some recommendations to consider:

1. *Postpone tracking.* Defer tracking as late as possible and implement it only in selected subjects at the middle school level. Organize elementary grades around within-class ability groups in reading and mathematics.

2. *Limit tracking.* At the high school level, limit ability grouping to a few academic subjects in which student differences in skill areas are critical for whole-group instruction or prerequisite requirements influence each step of learning.

3. *Modify placement procedures.* The use of a single criterion—such as the student's rank, report card average, or score on a standardized test—to determine track placement is misleading. Replace it with the use of recent grades and tests in each subject area.

4. *Make group assignments flexible.* Disband groups once they have achieved their goals, and regroup students for a new task.

5. *Provide tutoring assistance.* Encourage students having academic difficulties to participate in special tutoring or coaching sessions (before or after school) before assigning them to a lower track. Find ways to provide lower-achieving students with extra help.

6. *Limit the degree to which group membership determines other school experiences.* Group members of a group (reading or math) only for the learning time they have on one topic or activity.

7. *Use instructional alternatives.* Consider other useful methods such as mastery learning, continuous progress, independent study, and ungraded plans—all which permit students to complete subject units at different rates—for heterogeneous classes.

Source: Adapted from Thomas L. Good and Jere E. Brophy, *Looking in Classrooms* (New York: Addison Wesley Longman, 2000), 281–282; Jomills H. Braddock and James P. McPartland, "Alternatives to Tracking," *Educational Leadership* (April 1990): 76–79; Jeannie Oakes and Martin Lipton, "Detracking Schools: Early Lessons from the Field," *Phi Delta Kappan* (February 1992): 448–454.

(but not daily or weekly), so students can be regrouped during the school terms and when teachers adapt their instruction to the level and pace of the students' abilities and needs. Tips for Teachers 6.2 provides a synthesis of practices that teachers should consider in dealing with ability grouping practices.

Two researchers describe two approaches to within-class ability grouping. Structural grouping occurs when teachers form groups and then proceed to instruction. The groups may be formed in a variety of ways, but the grouping occurs before instruction and is appropriate when grouping by curriculum area. Situational grouping, which is the preferred approach, occurs when teachers form groups after instruction. The teacher sees who needs review or reinforcement and then moves students into groups based on their immediate needs.[53] Above all, researchers tend to agree that homogeneous grouping should be practiced partially and not completely—that the segregation of students into permanent groups is not appropriate. On the other hand, grouping heterogeneously, defined as the placement of students randomly without regard for academic ability or achievement, is not always appropriate. It is important to remember that homogeneous groups in one area will prove to be heterogeneous in other areas: Children with strengths in language arts, for example, may not have strengths in the sciences. (See table 6.1 for a comparison of ability grouping and heterogeneous grouping.)

Table 6.1   Ability Grouping versus Heterogeneous Grouping

Ability Grouping	Heterogeneous Grouping
1. Instruction is aimed to ability level.	1. Instruction is aimed at the class's average learner.
2. Homogeneous groups are easier to work with.	2. Mixed groups are more difficult to work with.
3. Students are more comfortable and learn better with peers of similar abilities.	3. Children work in a democratic environment with children of differing abilities.
4. Works well for gifted students.	4. Higher-achieving students positively influence lower-achieving students.
5. Works well for special children.	5. Students show more desirable democratic behaviors.

Source: Richard T. Scarpaci, *Resource Methods for Managing K–12 Instruction: A Case Study Approach* (Boston: Allyn & Bacon, 2009), 79. Copyright © 2009. Reproduced by permission of Pearson Education, Inc.

Peer Tutoring

Peer tutoring is the assignment of students to help one another, on a one-to-one basis or in small groups, in a variety of situations. There are three types of pairing: (1) students may tutor others within the same class; (2) older students may tutor students in lower grades outside of class; or (3) two students may work together on learning activities and help each other as equals. The purpose of the first two types is to pair a student who needs assistance with a tutor on a one-to-one basis, although small groups of two or three tutees and one tutor may also be effective. The purpose of the third type, called *peer pairing* or **cooperative learning,** is more than tutoring.

Of the three pairing arrangements, peer tutoring within the same class is the most common in elementary and middle schools. A student who has mastered specific material or who has completed a lesson and has shown understanding of the material is paired with a student who needs help. The research suggests that, because students are less threatened by peers, they are more willing to ask fellow students questions that they fear the teacher might consider "silly." Jeanne Ormrod reports that in one study students in peer teaching situations asked 240 times more questions than they did during whole-class teaching.[54] In addition, students are less afraid in peer tutoring that fellow students might criticize them for being unable to understand an idea or problem after a second or third explanation.[55] It has also been found that a fellow student is sometimes better able to explain a concept in language that another student can grasp. Unfamiliar vocabulary is cut to a minimum, and sometimes a few choice slang terms can make a difficult concept comprehensible. Also, because the faster student has just learned the concept, he or she may be more aware than the teacher of what is giving the slower student difficulty. Peer tutors also benefit from the relationship; their own understanding is reinforced by explaining the idea or problem, and their social skills are enhanced.[56] The teacher benefits by having additional time to work with students who have more severe learning problems.

David and Roger Johnson find these advantages of peer tutoring:

1. Peer tutors are often effective in teaching students who do not respond well to adults.

2. Peer tutoring can develop a bond of friendship between the tutor and tutee, which is important for integrating slow learners into the group.

3. Peer tutoring allows the teacher to teach a large group of students but still gives slow learners the individual attention they need.

4. Tutors benefit by learning to teach a general skill that can be useful in an adult society.[57]

Student help can be explanatory or terminal. Explanatory help consists of step-by-step accounts of how to do something. Terminal help consists of correcting an error or giving the correct answer without explaining how to obtain the answer or solve the problem. Most studies of explanatory and terminal help conclude that giving explanations aids the tutor in learning the material, whereas giving terminal help does not.[58] In giving explanations the tutor clarifies the material in her own mind and builds a better grasp of the material. Giving terminal help involves little restructuring of concepts.

Not surprisingly, receiving explanatory help is correlated with achievement. Students who receive terminal help or receive no help tend to learn less than do students who receive explanatory help.[59] The benefit of receiving explanations seems to be that it fills in incomplete understandings of the material and corrects misunderstandings; it also increases effort and motivation to learn. Receiving terminal help or receiving no help is frustrating and causes students to lose interest in learning.

Studies have shown increased oral reading fluency and reading comprehension when classwide peer tutoring is implemented.[60] In two separate studies (involving eight and fifteen classrooms respectively), the most effective tutoring situations occurred when the tutor (1) elaborated information, (2) directed attention to task features, (3) offered procedural assistance, and/or (4) showed how to use information. The problem is, however, that most student tutors do not provide adequate explanations unless explicitly trained.[61] With proper tutor training and experience, student questions during tutoring sessions—one indicator of learning activity—increase dramatically compared to the normal classroom setting.

Student questions in whole-classroom settings are infrequent and unsophisticated. The estimated frequency of student questions per hour ranges from 1.3 to 4.0, with an average of 3.0. Given an average class of 26.7 for the studies conducted on the frequency of questioning, the number of questions per student for one hour is 0.11 (3 questions ÷ 26.7). On the other hand, teachers ask 30 to 120 questions per hour, or an average of 69—with math teachers tending to ask the most questions. Therefore, about 96 percent of the questions in a regular classroom are formulated by teachers.[62] The low frequency and low sophistication of student questions may be attributed to student difficulty in identifying their own knowledge deficits (their inability to understand when they don't know or to discriminate superficial from necessary information) and their loss of self-esteem, or the social barriers involved in asking questions in front of their peers. A one-to-one tutoring situation removes many of the barriers. Tutors, if experienced or trained properly, can tailor questions or explanations to a particular deficit. Peer embarrassment is minimized by the privacy of the sessions.

Benjamin Bloom argues that tutoring (with preferably a 1:1 student-student ratio and no more than 3:1) is the most effective method of grouping for instruction compared to conventional methods (30:1 student-teacher ratio) and even mastery learning methods (which he helped develop), when the mastery methods are used in a class of about thirty students. Bloom found that as many as 90 percent of the tutored students and 70 percent of the mastery learning students attained a level of increased achievement reached by only 20 percent of the students who received conventional instruction over a three-week period.[63] Figure 6.6 compares achievement with conventional, mastery, and tutor instruction.

The most effective tutoring programs, both for tutors and tutees, have the following characteristics: procedural rules established by the teacher, instruction focused on basic skills and content, no more than three tutees per tutor and ideally one tutee per tutor, and tutorial sessions of short duration (about four to eight weeks).[64] When a tutorial program with these features is combined with regular classroom instruction, "the students being tutored not only learned more than they did without tutoring, they also developed a more positive attitude about what they were studying." In addition, the "tutors learned more than students who did not tutor."[65]

Figure 6.6   Achievement Distribution

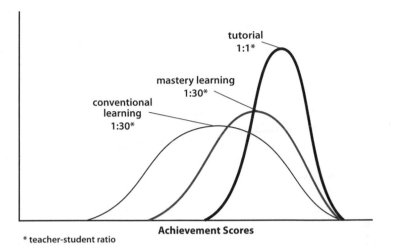

*teacher-student ratio

Source: Benjamin S. Bloom, *Educational Researcher* (June–July 1984). Copyright © 1984 by Sage Publications. Reprinted by permission of the publisher.

There are, of course, some drawbacks as well. Peer tutoring is problematic if tutors do not believe they can really help other students because they fear losing face (What happens if I can't help?) or if they perceive that they are too smart to help another student (Why should I have to waste my time helping another student?). Teachers can limit these problems through the use of cross-age tutoring (e.g., fourth graders tutoring second graders) or through carefully constructed cooperative learning arrangements.

Guidelines for Peer Tutoring

Peer tutoring, like ability grouping, can be effective if implemented properly, but it takes substantial time and effort to get off to a good start. Following are some suggestions for effective peer tutoring:

1. Provide directions (or structure) for each tutor about time schedules and exactly what to do (e.g., "Read the sentence to the group and get at least two students to identify the adjectives and nouns").

2. Prevent the tutor from assuming the role of substitute teacher. Whenever possible, use cross-age tutoring.

3. Be sure that students understand their respective roles. The teacher should model appropriate tutor behavior, providing examples of what is to be achieved and how.

4. Plan tutoring arrangements so that tutors understand and use a mix of materials, media, and activities (e.g., one week doing review and drill in the workbooks, the next week doing library research, the following week writing and discussing stories).

5. Inform parents of the organization, purpose, and procedures of the tutoring program.

Cooperative Learning

Cooperative learning is an instructional approach that received a lot of attention in the 1990s. It involves students working together in small groups instead of competing in a whole-group situation for recognition or grades. Rarely used in American classrooms before the 1970s, the idea is rooted in John Dewey's notion of group activities and group projects, as well as in his theories in *Democracy and Education* (recommending that students work together to learn civic and social responsibility). Participating and sharing in mutual school experiences, Dewey maintained, prepares students for democratic living. Although reintroduced in the 1960s by Japanese educators to promote the ideal of teamwork and group effort, cooperative learning was popularized in the United States by Robert Slavin and the Johnsons (David and Roger) in the 1970s and 1980s.

In the traditional classroom structure, students compete for teacher recognition and grades, and the same students tend to be "winners" and "losers" over the years. High-achieving students continually receive rewards and are motivated to learn, and low-achieving students continually experience failure (or near-failure) and frustration, and subsequently many psychologically and then physically drop out of school. Reducing competition and increasing cooperation among students may diminish hostility, prejudice, and patterns of failure among many students.

This does not mean that competition has no place in the classroom or school. Even the advocates of cooperation feel that competition, under the right conditions and with evenly matched individuals or groups, can be a source of motivation, excitement, fun, and improved performance—for example, in simple drill activities, speed tasks, low-anxiety games, psychomotor activities, and athletics. Competition among groups is also accepted as a means for enhancing academic achievement for all grade levels and subjects, as long as two elements are present: group goals and individual accountability.[66] However, there are some data (a minority view) suggesting that group grading decreases individual motivation and lowers individual levels of performance, since the rewards are extrinsic. High-achieving students also feel that group activity is a waste of their time and express resentment in having to explain academic material to low achievers or uninterested students.[67]

Teachers have reported that their lessons were more interesting, their students learned more and felt more confident, and they often learned to work more closely with their peers through cooperative learning.[68] According to a review of the research, cooperation among participants helps build positive and coherent personal identity, self-esteem, knowledge and trust of others, communication skills, acceptance and support of others, wholesome intergroup relationships, and reduction of conflicts. These data also suggest that cooperation and group learning are considerably more effective in fostering these social and interpersonal skills than are competitive or individualistic efforts.[69] When cooperative learning methods are used, achievement effects are consistently positive compared to those of traditional methods. These conclusions applied in thirty-seven of forty-four controlled experiments at all grade levels (2–12); in all major subjects (although most of the research deals with grades 3–9 in reading and mathematics); and in a wide diversity of geographic settings[70] (see Tips for Teachers 6.3).

In cooperative learning, students divide their own workload, help one another, praise and criticize group members' efforts and contributions, and receive a group performance score. It is not enough for a teacher simply to tell students to work together. They must have a reason and relate as a team. The idea is to create some form of interdependence "in such a way that each individual's actions benefit the group, and the group's actions benefit the individual."[71] The teacher needs to clarify learning goals, student roles, and expectations; divide resources within and among groups; provide tasks and rewards that promote team spirit; and most important, provide some kind of incentive and recognition for individual achievement.

The difference between cooperative groups and small groups can be stated in one word: accountability. In a cooperative group all members are assessed

---

TIPS
FOR TEACHERS 6.3

Meaningful Methods for Cooperative Learning

Research on specific applications of cooperative learning that began in the 1970s has now expanded in different parts of the world and includes various methods and techniques. Here are some practical questions for teachers to consider when organizing appropriate cooperative learning lessons:

1. Which cooperative learning model are you using? Why?

2. How did you form your groups? Did you consider ability, ethnicity, gender?

3. What objectives, directions, and timelines did the groups receive?

4. How did you motivate the students to perform as a group, to respect differences, and to interact with and accept peers from different ethnic, religious, or socioeconomic groups?

5. What have you observed about how the groups function? Do student groups use a variety of skills—reasoning, hypothesizing, predicting—or do they rely on rote procedures? Do students help one another understand concepts and skills?

6. What tasks will the groups be expected to perform during the cooperative lesson? Are the roles of students clear?

7. How will individual and group evaluation (academic and social) take place? Are students held accountable for individual learning through testing, individual work, or specific activities? Is the group accountable for its work and for the achievement of each member of the group?

8. Do you monitor group progress and intervene when necessary (when problems arise)? Do you merely provide answers, or do you assist groups in working out their problems?

9. Do you provide feedback about how progress is being made and about how problems can be resolved? Do you clarify, elaborate, and reteach when necessary?

and monitored as team members and as individuals. Competition and rivalry in the pursuit of team goals and objectives are encouraged. The employment of *group goals* and *individual accountability* are the key elements accounting for cooperative learning success as an instructional approach. In contrast, traditional small-group instruction has limited accountability (see box 6.2). Cooperative groups can be set up by following five easy steps:

1. *Set the goals* for all groups while focusing student attention on outcomes.
2. *Structure tasks* for students while introducing the problem to solve.
3. *Model and demonstrate* how to go about solving the problem. Explain that students are expected to communicate respectfully, negotiate, and share with team members. Collaboration is the key word for students to understand.
4. *Monitor each group*, especially those that are faltering. Your role as the teacher is to encourage and promote individual and group success.
5. *Debrief and summarize* the way each group operated. Discuss both the positive and negative aspects of their performance, and encourage students to offer their opinion while discussing how they will function in the future.[72]

Box 6.2   Benefits of Cooperative Learning

The cooperative learning method develops social, problem-solving, and interpersonal skills.
- It maximizes student involvement in learning.
- When more minds work on a problem, superior results can be expected.
- It teaches the value of cooperation and prosocial behavior.
- It builds a learning community in the classroom.
- It promotes critical thinking and the development of problem-solving skills.
- It improves academic achievement, self-esteem, and attitude toward school.
- It offers an alternative to tracking and can temper the negative aspects of competition.

Source: Richard T. Scarpaci, *Resource Methods for Managing K–12 Instruction: A Case Study Approach*, 80. Copyright © 2009. Reproduced by permission of Pearson Education, Inc.

Other formal cooperative learning approaches are structured around a particular team learning model. Three examples of team learning approaches—Student Teams-Achievement Divisions (STAD), Teams-Games-Tournaments (TGT), and Jigsaw—are discussed below:

Student Teams-Achievement Divisions (STAD).   Team membership consists of four students, based on heterogeneous abilities. The teacher presents the lesson to the whole group in one or two sessions, and then the class divides into teams for mastery. Students who have mastered the material help slower teammates. Drill and practice is stressed in groups, although students can engage in discussion and questioning. Class quizzes are frequent, and student scores are averaged into a team score to ensure cooperation and assistance within groups. Quizzes are scored in terms of progress so that low-performing groups have the opportunity to gain recognition and improve. Team rewards are given based on the performance of the team as a "good," "great," or "super" team. Teams are changed every five or six weeks to give students an opportunity to work with other students and to give members of low-scoring teams a new chance.[73]

Teams-Games-Tournaments (TGT). Like STAD, TGT was developed by Robert Slavin. Instead of quizzes there are weekly "tournament tables" composed of three-member teams, with each member contributing points to the particular team score. Low achievers compete with other low achievers, and high achievers compete with other high achievers for equal points. Thus, the impact of low achievers is equal to that of high achievers. As with STAD, high-performing teams earn certificates or other team rewards. Student teams are changed weekly on the basis of individual performance to equalize them.[74]

Jigsaw. Originally designed for secondary schools (grades 7–12), Jigsaw has students working in small groups (four to five members) on specific academic tasks, assignments, or projects. They depend on each other for resources, information, and study assignments. Each team member becomes an "expert" in one area, meets with similar experts from other teams, and then returns to the original group to teach other team members.[75] After the time for team study, the students are tested and, once again based on each student's individual performance and the team performance, awards for "good," "great," and "super" teams are given.

Informal cooperative learning occurs when a teacher asks questions and then has students discuss possible answers among themselves or with the teacher. It can happen when teachers read stories or lecture and then ask students questions or encourage students to summarize or synthesize ideas. Several forms of informal cooperative learning can be used. In general, informal approaches are clearly linked to other instructional strategies such as direct instruction. The following formats for informal groupings, coupled with another teaching strategy such as direct instruction, were developed by one educator:

1. The teacher asks a question that serves as an anticipatory set or advance organizer for the story, video, demonstration, or lecture that is to follow. Student discussion is encouraged.

2. The teacher reads a story, shows a video, or delivers a lecture—stopping every few minutes and asking students to discuss a teacher-prepared question or problem. Questions and problems might be factual or conceptual; they might focus on the material that has just been presented or might help students make the transition to a new segment of the presentation. Again, student discussion is encouraged.

3. The teacher asks a question that helps students summarize and synthesize the material that has been presented and provides closure for the lesson. Students are again encouraged to discuss what they have learned.[76]

Following are two specific examples of informal cooperative learning strategies.

1. *Numbered Heads Together*

- The teacher has students number themselves off within their groups, so that each student has a number: 1, 2, 3, 4, or 5. (Groups can consist of three to five students.)
- The teacher asks a question.
- The teacher tells the students to "put their heads together" to make sure that everyone on the team knows the answer. (All students need to discuss the material relevant to the question and be able to respond.)
- The teacher calls a number (1, 2, 3, 4, or 5) and the students with that number can raise their hands to respond.[77]

2. *Think-Pair-Share*

- The teacher provides the students with a topic or idea.
- The students then reflect independently on the meaning of the topic. (The teacher should give students three to five seconds for independent thinking.)
- The students pair up with other students to discuss the topic and to share their respective thoughts. (This can be a random pairing.)
- The students then share their thoughts with the entire class. The teacher needs to wait for approximately three to five seconds after each student shares to allow time for all students to think about what has been shared.[78]

Marzano and his colleagues provide a description of what informal learning might look like in a classroom. Notice how the teacher is making no effort to create "arranged" teams or to assess how the pairs function together.

Mr. Anderson likes to read aloud original source documents about slavery to his fifth graders. After reading for ten minutes, he gives the students a discussion task to complete in pairs for three to four minutes. The task requires students to answer a specific question that he provides. After each member of a pair formulates a response and discusses it with his or her partner, Mr. Anderson begins to read aloud again. After ten minutes, Mr. Anderson stops and asks students to complete a second paired discussion task. Occasionally, he asks two or three pairs to share a brief summary of their discussions. At the end of the class, Mr. Anderson asks the paired students to summarize in written form what they have learned from the readings and discussions and turn their summaries in to him.[79]

Activities for Cooperative Learning Lessons

Many projects can be made to fit when designing cooperative lessons. These activities are essentially action oriented, in that students are required to build, describe, or assess something.

- *Project building* requires student teams to construct something based on the content being studied, for example, writing a diary, a journal, or a commercial or brochure to convince people to go to Alaska—in 1849!

- A *describing activity* requires students to analyze, compare, and contrast subject materials, as in a unit on deceptive advertising or propaganda. It could also be used to have students solve a problem related to the material being studied. An exercise on women's rights or the Civil War that asked students to predict outcomes would come under this category (e.g., What if the South had won the Civil War?).

- An *assessment activity* might call for students to debate points of view, judge the effectiveness of proposed solutions to problems, or rank and rate (as with a list of "The Three Best Decades in the Past 100 Years"). Students could be asked to predict the outcome of a story being read or a current events situation.[80]

To design cooperative learning activities you should hold fast to some basic rules, regardless of grade level. First, teach students the *procedures* they are to follow, and then *name teams* and determine the *group size.* Next, discuss the *purpose* of the activity, the *materials,* and *steps* needed to achieve objectives. *Teach cooperation* by establishing rules for teamwork that hold all accountable. Explain collaboration as an important skill and a necessary goal to build a classroom learning community. Encourage student reflection and evaluation for group success. A wonderful ending to any cooperative learning activity is a debriefing session where both positive and negative outcomes are explored. Box 6.3 provides some guidelines for cooperative learning. The organization of cooperative learning groups can be either heterogeneous or homogeneous:

- Students can be paired with a learning partner to share workloads.

- Students can be seated in cluster groups consisting of four to six students. Smaller groups make it difficult to monitor the teams' work.

- Tests can be administered for individuals or teams. Team competition can be encouraged as long as a cooperative ethic has been established.[81]

In a review of cooperative learning, the Johnsons point out that each lesson in cooperative learning should include five basic elements:

1. *Positive interdependence*—students must feel they are responsible for their own learning and that of other members of the group;

2. *Face-to-face interaction*—students must have the opportunity to explain to each other what they are learning;

3. *Individual accountability*—each student must be held accountable for mastery of the assigned work;

4. *Social skills*—each student must communicate effectively, maintain respect for group members, and work together to resolve conflicts; and

5. *Group processing*—groups must be assessed to see how well they are working together and how they can improve.[82]

Those assessments can take different forms. The teacher might keep some anecdotal notes on how groups function or make more structured observations using a matrix such as the one shown in figure 6.7. The teacher might also ask students how they thought their groups functioned (see box 6.4 on p. 303).

Box 6.3   Guidelines for Cooperative Learning

1. Determine goals and then decide on the appropriate formal or informal cooperative learning approach.

2. Arrange the classroom to promote cooperative goals.

3. Communicate intentions and expectations. Students need to understand what is being attempted.

4. Encourage a division of labor when appropriate. Students should understand their roles and responsibilities.

5. Encourage students to share ideas, materials, and resources. Students should look at each other and not the teacher.

6. Encourage supportive behavior and point out rejecting or hostile behavior. Behaviors such as silence, ridicule, personal criticism, one-upmanship, and superficial acceptance of an idea should be discussed.

7. Monitor the group. Check progress of individuals in a group and of the group as a whole. Explain and discuss problems, assist, and give praise as appropriate.

8. Evaluate the individual and group. In evaluation, focus on the group and its progress. Evaluate the individual in the context of the group's effort and achievement. Provide prompt feedback.

9. Reward the group for successful completion of its task.

Source: Adapted from H. Brown and D. C. Ciuffetelli (Eds.), *Foundational Methods: Understanding Teaching and Learning* (Toronto: Pearson Education, 2009); David Johnson and Roger Johnson, *Reaching Out: Interpersonal Effectiveness and Self-Actualization,* 10th ed. (Needham Heights, MA: Allyn & Bacon, 2008).

Figure 6.7   Observation Form

Assess the types of interactions using this matrix.

	John	Tom	Amanda	Lucette
Asks other group members questions	XX	X	X	
Takes notes on what others say		XX	X	
Helps others clarify their thoughts		XX	XXX	X
Rephrases the statement of others		XXXX		
Offers encouragement to other students	X	XX	X	XXX

Box 6.4   Personal Assessment of Work in Groups

Name: _____

   Place checkmarks in the three boxes that best describe you in your work today. Circle one behavior that you want to make sure you use tomorrow.

☐ I stayed with my group.

☐ I made sure my voice did not get TOO LOUD!

☐ I reminded others to stay on task in an agreeable way.

☐ I helped manage the materials and made sure they got put back in "good shape."

☐ I participated.

☐ I asked others to participate.

☐ I helped my group make a plan.

☐ I helped my group stick with the plan.

☐ I helped summarize our work.

Source: Adapted from Lynda Baloche, *The Cooperative Classroom* (Upper Saddle River, NJ: Prentice-Hall, 1998).

Group Activities

Although there is no clear research showing that group activities, also known as *group projects,* correlate with student achievement, it is assumed that under appropriate circumstances instruction in small groups can be as effective as or more effective than relying on the teacher as the major source of learning. It is also assumed that many kinds of group activities help teachers deal with differences among learners, provide opportunities for students to plan and develop special projects on which groups can work together, and increase student interaction and socialization. In short, they achieve social and emotional as well as cognitive purposes.

If planned and implemented properly, group activities tend to promote five group-oriented characteristics in the classroom: (1) task structures that lend themselves to cooperation among group members, (2) a chance for students to work at their own pace but think in terms of group goals, (3) the development of social and interpersonal skills among participants—students learn to communicate with and trust one another, (4) a reward structure based on the performance of the group (which encourages helping behaviors), and (5) a variety of team-building strategies—students learn to work together, appreciate individual characteristics, and capitalize on individual strengths.

By participating in group activities, students engage in helping and sharing experiences. Ideally, they experience positive expectations of peers and learn to be considerate, cooperative, and responsible in mutual endeavors. If groups are organized properly, with clearly defined roles and/or rules, then positive discipline (actually self-discipline) should evolve as part of the classroom culture. Finally, students should come to appreciate and better understand people: their needs, intentions, and feelings. All of these new group learning experiences are important, since education and work environments increasingly involve people working together in programs, units, and departments.

According to researchers, when students (as well as adults) work on group projects, they need to focus on specific problems, not personalities; provide feedback that the receiver can understand; and provide feedback on actions that the receiver can change.[83] Honest communication demands that individuals learn to appreciate the strengths and uniqueness of others, to listen to others, and to give and receive supporting feedback—all of which require maturity, understanding, and respect. Effective student group activities can nurture and reinforce such qualities.

Group Techniques

During group activities, the teacher's role changes from that of engineer or director to that of facilitator or resource person, and many leadership functions transfer from the teacher to the students. Certain small-group techniques can assist students in their group projects and shift learning from originating with you to originating with them.

- *Brainstorming* is a technique for eliciting large numbers of imaginative ideas or solutions to open-ended problems. Group members are encouraged to expand their thinking beyond the routine. All suggestions are accepted without judgment, and only after all the ideas are put before the group do the members begin to focus on a possible solution.

- A *buzz session* provides an open environment in which group members can discuss their opinions without fear of being "wrong" or being ridiculed for holding an unpopular position. Buzz sessions can also serve to clarify a position or bring new information before the group to correct misconceptions.

- The *debate* and *panel* are more structured in format than some of the other small-group techniques. In a debate, two positions on a controversial issue are presented formally; each debater is given a certain amount of time to state a position, to respond to questions from others in the group, and to pose questions to the other side. The panel is used to present information on an issue and, if possible, to arrive at group consensus. Several students (three to eight) may sit on a panel. Each panel member may make an opening statement, but there are no debates among panel members.

- *Role-playing* and *improvisation* are techniques that allow students to place themselves in another's situation. Role-playing also serves as a technique for exploring intergroup attitudes and values.

- *Fish bowl* is a technique in which group members give their full attention to what one individual wants to express. The whole group sits in a circle. Two chairs are placed in the center of the circle. A member who wants to express a point of view does so while sitting in one of the chairs. Any other member who wants to discuss the view takes the other chair, and the two converse while the others listen. To get into the discussion, students must wait for one chair to be vacated.

- *Round table* is a quiet, informal group technique. Usually four or five students sit around a table conversing among themselves (similar to a buzz session) or before an audience (similar to a forum).

Using group techniques in flexible and imaginative ways can have important instructional advantages. They give students some control over their own behavior as well as over their own cognitive learning. Teachers can inject them into different lessons to meet the needs and interests of different groups. Teachers can use them to make activities more interesting and active. They can supplement lecture, questioning, and practice and drill methods.

Questions for Reflection

Although the relationship between class size and student achievement is unclear, class size can influence the quality of a teacher's life and students' educational experiences. For example, it is logical (and documented) that fewer students in a class result in fewer management and discipline problems for the teacher. With smaller classes the teacher has a better set of options for dealing with the problems that do emerge. The teacher can use more one-on-one or personalized disciplinary techniques with fewer students. Factors other than discipline and management may be influenced by class size: assessment of student learning, the use of effective teaching practices, the creation of a positive classroom learning community, and the time available to work with individual students. Consider each of these "other factors" and compare results from having 15 students as opposed to 25. Also, are there times when larger classes are more advantageous? Why?

Another issue to consider is why, even with smaller classes, the instructor tends not to change how instruction is delivered. Holloway* documents that, even with smaller classes, teachers make "no substantial changes in their content coverage, grouping practices, or pedagogical strategies." If that is true, what would be the argument for smaller classes?

*John H. Holloway, "Do Smaller Classes Change Instruction?" *Educational Leadership* (February 2002), 91.

Guidelines for Group Activities

Students can be assigned to group projects by interest, ability, friendship, or personality. The teacher must know the students and the objectives for using small groups before establishing the groups. If the objective is to get the job done expeditiously, the teacher should assign a strong leader to each group, rely on high-achieving students to lead the activities, avoid known personality conflicts, and limit the group size to five. If the objective is more interpersonal than cognitive, the students may be grouped according to their differences rather than similarities, and the groups might be larger.

In order to organize such group activities, consider the following recommendations. They are basically sequential, although each recommendation should be used only if it coincides with your circumstances and teaching style.

1. Decide on a group project that enhances specific objectives and outcomes.
2. Solicit volunteers for membership in group projects, reserving the right to decide final membership.
3. Go over directions for each phase of the group activity (in writing or orally) to the point of redundancy.
4. Explain the roles of participants, the way they are to interact, and potential problems. Give examples and model interactions.
5. Allot class time for groups to organize, plan, and develop some of their projects or assignments, with supervision as needed.
6. Allow group members to decide on the nature of the class presentation, within general rules that have been established.
7. Do not allow any individual to dominate the activities or responsibilities of the group.
8. Evaluate the completed group project with the students. Discuss the problems and decisions that participants faced and the strategies chosen. (See Case Study 6.1 to review the various methods for grouping.)

The following case study deals with strategies used to effectively group children for instruction. Teachers in the study wonder whether class size and academic grouping are related to student achievement. Explore the arguments expressed and develop your own strategy for grouping students for learning. Carefully compare and analyze the issues and reflect on what class grouping means for learning.

Case Study 6.1
Grouping for Learning

Jiana De Marco told her colleagues that the way you group students for instruction should support your approach to learning. She knew that grouping children for instruction is always difficult and burdened with doubt. She realized that despite the uncertainty, organizing for instruction was essential for any effective educational gains to be made by students. The reason for the imprecision involved in grouping students is the confusing variety of terms used to describe grouping practices. Terms such as ungraded, nongraded, continuous progress, and mixed or multiage grouping are used interchangeably. (See box 6.1).

Nicoletta, Jiana's older sister and professional colleague, told Jiana that when it came to grouping for instruction there really was only one effective way: by ability. "It's a type of grouping that has many nuances, such as grouping by reading and mathematics scores," she said." The idea is to assign students' classes based on some measure of achievement or ability. Another name for it is homogeneous grouping."

Deidra Petronas, Jiana's friend, attempted to stick up for her by saying that students could be regrouped according to math/reading ability while being kept in heterogeneous classes: "I read somewhere in an educational journal that heterogeneous grouping reduces the risk of student labeling and recognizes that some students may be weak in reading and strong in math or vice versa. The article said that this strategy was effective if two conditions were met: (a) instructional level and pace are adapted to student performance level, and (b) students are regrouped for only one or two subjects."

"Then what you are really saying," said Jiana to Nicoletta, "is that there are just two ways to effectively group students: homogeneously or heterogeneously." Nicoletta chimed in and said, "I didn't say that. What I said was that ability grouping—or, as you call it, homogeneous grouping—in whatever form is effective. Mixed ability or heterogeneous grouping is ineffective." Deidra said, "That's not necessarily true. Ability grouping produces conflicting evidence by promoting achievement in superior groups while uniformly producing lower achievement rates in average and slower-functioning groups."

Jiana looked at both Deidra and her sister and said, "I think I've got the best answer for grouping my classes. Why not have within-class ability grouping by sending students to homogeneous subgroups for specific subjects? That way the class benefits from the social positives of heterogeneous grouping and the academic benefits of homogeneous grouping." Deidra said, "Not so fast Jiana, socioeconomic and social class differences are increased by grouping and reduced by not grouping. You have your benefits all mixed up."

"No I don't," said Jiana. "Within-class ability grouping allows the children to remain in a fairly homogeneous setting for most of the day and avoids management problems."

Another colleague, Shirley Mumford, said, "I overheard your discussion, and I have the solution. You do know that there are other approaches to learning that center around cooperative learning strategies such as peer tutoring, team teaching, individually programmed instruction, multiple intelligence teaching, and constructivist teaching strategies. These strategies offer alternatives to the traditional ability grouping approach that Nicoletta is advocating. It provides Deidra and Jiana the means to assign students by ability into heterogeneous rather than homogeneous subgroups within a class, usually to perform a specific project or assignment. It offers group rewards based on the individual learning of all group members. You get the best of both worlds with cooperative learning by combining ability grouping within heterogeneously formed classes."

Discussion Topics and Questions to Ponder

1. Describe Nicoletta's position regarding grouping for instruction.
2. Contrast and compare Nicoletta's views with Deidra's.
3. Was Jiana's compromise position really a compromise? Justify your response.
4. How did Shirley try to resolve the issues at hand? Would her positions have satisfied everyone? Explain.
5. Briefly describe the conflicts that exist between Jiana's, Nicoletta's, Deidra's, and Shirley's views with regard to grouping.

What would you do if . . . ?

1. You were asked to explain the best way to group for learning: ability-oriented or heterogeneous. Take another look at table 6.1 and decide.
2. You were asked to explain which type of class you would prefer to teach: one that was grouped by ability (homogeneous), or one grouped with children of random abilities (heterogeneous).
3. You were asked to identify the grade and subject you (intend to) teach and then react to the following statement: "Cooperative learning is the wave of the future."

Individualizing Instruction for Enhanced Student Learning

Thus far we have examined different forms of whole-group and small-group instruction. These are by far the most common forms of instruction used in American classrooms. Another type of instruction is individualized instruction. We conclude this chapter with examples of such approaches. They are important to understand, even though they are not evidenced in any "pure" form in many of today's schools. The individualized and mastery learning techniques that were popular in the 1960s to 1980s represented important precursors to the instructional modeling that is being used today.

Individualized Instruction

Individualized instruction is a method of instruction in which content, instructional materials, instructional media, and pace of learning are based on the abilities and interests of each individual learner. Individualized instruction is a prime component of special education programs, even though it is not limited to special-needs children. Instruction is simply designed to meet the needs of the individual student.

Several systematic programs for individualized instruction were advanced in the 1970s and 1980s. Although the individualized instruction approaches varied somewhat, all the programs attempted to maximize individual learning by diagnosing the student's entry achievement levels or learning deficiencies; providing a one-to-one teacher-to-student or machine-to-student relationship; introducing sequenced and structured instructional materials, frequently accompanied by practice and drill; and permitting students to proceed at their own rate. Although the approaches combined behavioral and cognitive psychology, the behaviorist component seems more in evidence because of the stress on instructional objectives and drill exercises, as well as small instructional units and sequenced materials that maximize student success. In essence, it was believed that learners would learn and be motivated if they experienced instruction "staged" to ensure success.

One of the early programs for individualized instruction was the Project on Individually Prescribed Instruction (IPI), developed at the University of Pittsburgh in the late 1950s and early 1960s. For every student an individual plan was prepared for each skill or subject based on a diagnosis of the student's proficiency levels. Learning tasks were individualized, and the student's progress was continually evaluated. Most important, the lessons for students were sequenced so that students could master skills within a single class period.[84]

Individually Guided Education (IGE) was a total educational system developed at the University of Wisconsin and introduced in several thousand schools. Planned variations were made in what and how each student would learn. The program included individual objectives, one-to-one relationships with teachers or tutors, diagnostic testing, independent study, small-group instruction, and large-group instruction.[85]

A more behaviorist and teacher-directed approach was the Personalized System of Instruction (PSI), sometimes called the *Keller plan* after its originator. It was developed initially for high school and college students. PSI made use of study guides, which would break a course down into small units with specific objectives. Individuals progressed through the units as quickly or slowly as they wished, mastered units (80 percent or better) before proceeding to the next unit, and acted as proctors (high-achieving students assisting others).[86]

Some reports on IPI, IGE, and PSI showed significant gains in student achievement, especially with low-achieving students, who seemed to prefer a structured approach to learning.[87] Of the three programs, IPI and IGE were the most widely used and seemed to report the most consistent rise in student test scores. Because individualized plans were (and are) expensive to implement, most schools today continue to employ the "group" methods of instruction.[88]

Though once popular, the IPI, IGE, and PSI approaches are used today only in a very limited number of schools, and the research on them is even more limited. Indeed, in the *Handbook of Research on Teaching,* which was published in 2001 and is the most comprehensive synthesis of research on educational practices, only the IPI model is referenced.

---

classic professional viewpoint 6.1   **Psychology of Instruction**

Ernest R. Hilgard

The shift in emphasis in the last few years from a psychology of learning (which might hopefully be applied in the classroom) to a psychology of instruction has had promising consequences, encouraged both by the development of cognitive psychology and by a greater awareness of the contexts in which instruction is effective. The mastery model, in which instruction is engineered to reach goals set by the teacher, is being contrasted with the acquisition of self-regulatory skills in which knowledge is structured for problem solving in various contexts.

If the teacher understands the difference between such strategies, steps can be taken to improve the interaction with the student as learner.

Although these individualized approaches are out of vogue as "formal" strategies, they continue in instructionally mutated forms in many school districts today. Indeed, if you look at some school districts that are endeavoring to close the achievement gap between African American and mainstream white students, you will see that they are using forms of individualized instruction to maximize the learning potential of typically disenfranchised and poorly performing students. That is, by identifying specific academic standards and diagnosing students' prior knowledge of the requisite content, teachers are arranging learning experiences to ensure more student success (see figure 6.8). After analyzing data on what students know or don't know, teachers provide appropriate instruction, check to see if students understand, and determine how students should continue their learning.

Figure 6.8   Plan-Do-Check-Act Instructional Cycle

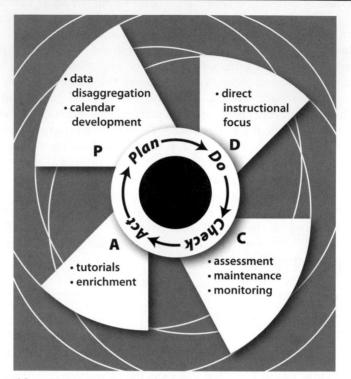

Source: Adapted from Patricia Davenport and Gerald Anderson, *Closing the Achievement Gap* (Houston, TX: American Productivity and Quality Center, 2002), 60.

The PDCA (Plan-Do-Check-Act) instructional cycle in figure 6.8 (based on the classic model by Davenport and Anderson) is predicated on securing and disaggregating data so that teachers can act (teach) in ways that make instructional sense for student learning. The first key is for a teacher to determine whether students are mastering the content prescribed by the school district. That occurs through careful assessment. The second key is to determine if all groups are mastering the content to the same degree, which can occur by disaggregating data by the different student groups. How are female students performing? Male students? African American students? Are there apparent differences between and among the groups?

Once they have identified learning deficiencies, teachers make instructional decisions about how to cover the content, which can be done through whole-group, small-group, or even individualized models. As we will further discuss, assessment is a critical key to good individualized instruction. You must know where your students are in their learning progress if you are going to teach them the particular academic skills they need for their future success. Individualized instruction is essentially a method of managing instruction by decreasing teacher time spent talking and lecturing. The time that is freed can then be allocated to working with individual students.

Mastery Instruction

Mastery learning was originally associated with John Carroll and later with James Block and Benjamin Bloom and focused on specifically orienting instruction to ensure student acquisition of content. Their mastery learning ideas earned supporters, particularly in urban school districts, where there was an obvious need to improve academic performance. It may seem unusual to those who really understand mastery learning to include it in the individualized instruction section, since mastery learning is usually more focused on whole-group or large-group instruction. It is included here because it constitutes a type of whole-group individualized model. The teacher teaches to a large group but seeks to identify those individual students who do not understand.

---

classic professional viewpoint 6.2

On Being "Dumb"

Anonymous

I am writing as a parent and not in my usual role as professor.

It was two years ago when the standardized reading test, administered at the beginning of the term, sealed my son John's fate. The results revealed that his reading grade declined from 1 year above level in the previous school year to 1.2 years below level. He was shunted into the "slow" reading group by Mrs. Smith, his fourth-grade teacher, and was assigned three times a week to a special reading teacher, Mrs. Jones, who thrived on Prussian rules of order and drill activities.

The boy who only a few months ago during the summer had read for enjoyment, including the abridged versions (100–150 pages) of *Treasure Island, Robinson Crusoe, The Swiss Family Robinson*, and *Dr. Jekyll and Mr. Hyde*, was now unable to answer questions about "Tony's Visit to the Zoo" and unable to do his homework. The reading teacher's phone call at home confirmed his "lack of comprehension and inability to keep up with the class."

A new nail-biting habit, repeated outbursts at the dinner table, fights with his brother and sister, and frequent remarks about his new reading group and "dumbness"—all in six weeks—prompted me to make an appointment with the school principal, the popular Mr. Murphy, who knew every child in school by name and whose office magazine rack contained the latest issues of *Educational Leadership, Elementary Principal, Phi Delta Kappan*, and *Reading Teacher.*

When I mentioned John's behavior at home, the principal suggested further testing. "No," I responded. "If you test a child long enough, the school will find more things wrong with him and slap more labels on him." When I elaborated on my child's summer reading habits, Mr. Murphy pointed to recent research that concluded that poor readers don't understand what they read.

Somewhat frustrated, I asserted, "Only a fool or nitwit would misread a book for one hour before bedtime each evening and then, after finishing the book, want to read another book."

The principal was flexible but did not give ground easily. He alluded to John's age—that he was the youngest person in his class—and then reviewed Piaget's development stages of growth. I responded with the principles of test reliability and boring methods of instruction. A compromise was eventually reached. My wife and I would make an appointment with the school social worker so she could assess family conditions, and John would be retested.

(continued)

After three additional weeks of school bureaucracy, the principal called with good news: John's retest score was .75 above grade level! In order to preserve the reading teacher's ego, however, he suggested that the program transfer take place in January, when the semester ended.

Today John is in the sixth grade, still bored with his school reading assignments but is reading Dick Gregory, John Steinbeck, Jack London, and Pearl Buck for his own pleasure. It's sad to think what might have happened to my son had I not intervened. But what about all the children who don't have fathers sitting at the dinner table or checking homework, much less a parent with the knowledge to challenge the system? Armed with test data and reading labels, Mrs. Smith and Mrs. Jones had boxed a nine-year-old child into a no-win, no-escape situation in which he could not cope or fend for himself. The school, with its professional jargon, had labeled and grouped a bright child so that he no longer wanted to learn and no longer felt he could learn. His means of expression was rebellion—reacting with feigned stupidity in class and anger at home. In only a few weeks the classroom's ability group, coupled with the teacher's self-fulfilling prophecy, had overshadowed John's past performance and behavior.

My son had all the advantages: high SES, two educated parents, a bright peer group, and a top-rated school—yet he could not cope with these new labels. Think of all the millions of students who don't have these advantages, who by chance are classified into the other side of the socioeconomic and school continuum. Then think of their test scores, their "stupidity" in school, and their anger inside and outside of school. Ask yourself, as an educator, who is responsible; then ask yourself what you intend to do that is different from what these educators did.

Carroll maintained that if students are normally distributed by ability or aptitude for some academic subject and are provided appropriate instruction tailored to their individual characteristics, the majority should achieve mastery of the subject and learning should be dramatically improved. He also held that if a student does not spend sufficient time to learn a task, he or she will not master it. However, students vary in the amount of time they need to complete a task. Nearly all students (assuming no major learning disability) can achieve average outcomes if given sufficient time.[89] Mastery learning attempts to ensure that individual students have the time they need to learn the content taught in a whole-group setting.

Carroll, and later Robert Slavin, distinguished between time needed to learn (based on student characteristics such as aptitude) and time available for learning (a factor that is under the teacher's control). High-achieving students need less time than low-achieving students to learn the same material. Group instruction, large or small, rarely accommodates varying learner characteristics or considers the time needed to learn. The teacher has the ability to vary instructional time for different individuals or groups of students with mastery instruction, especially for low-achieving students who usually need additional time.[90]

Block and Bloom argued that 90 percent of the public school students can learn much of the curriculum at the same level of mastery, with the slower 20 percent of students in this 90 percent needing 10 to 20 percent more time than the fastest 20 percent.[91] Although slower students require a longer period of time to learn the same materials, they can succeed if their initial level of knowledge is correctly diagnosed, and if they are taught with appropriate methods and materials in a sequential manner beginning at their initial competency level.

To accomplish this goal, criterion-referenced tests must be used to determine whether a student possesses the skills required for success at each step of the learning sequence. Also, small units of instruction must be used. An entire course such as third-grade mathematics or seventh-grade social studies is too complex to be studied in large units. Instead it should be broken down into smaller pieces, following some of the principles of programmed instruction.

In a review of more than 25 studies, Block and Burns found that 61 percent of the mastery-taught students scored significantly higher on achievement tests than nonmastery-taught students.[92] The results of studies of entire school districts show that mastery approaches are successful in teaching basic skills (e.g., reading and mathematics) that form the basis for later learning; moreover, inner-city students and disadvantaged students profit more from this approach than from traditional groupings for instruction.[93]

The favorable findings associated with the mastery approach do not mean that all the important questions about this technique have been answered. Mastery strategies have their critics. For example, some claim that, when basic skills—reading, writing, and mathematics—are broken down into discrete tasks that students can master, the students still do not acquire the more comprehensive skill (i.e., they cannot read, write, or compute any better than before the skill mastery). Students may show gains in small skill items, but this does not necessarily prove learning.[94] Critics ask a powerful, rhetorical question: What happened to the notions of wholeness and the importance of concepts and problem-solving skills? There are students who know the difference between a noun and a verb but who cannot write a whole sentence, much less a paragraph. Students may be capable of memorizing vocabulary words but are still unable to read with comprehension (or understanding) at their grade level.

Traditionally, teachers have held time constant so that individual differences were reflected in achievement differences. A mastery learning situation, which varies time for learning among students, narrows achievement differences among students in favor of those who need extra time at the expense of other students.[95] In a situation in which high-achieving students must wait for slow students to catch up, and high achievers must wait for the teacher's attention (because the teacher spends an inordinate amount of time with low achievers so they can gain mastery), the high achievers may be discriminated against. As a result, they will become bored, and their learning outcomes will probably suffer.

These criticisms do not nullify the importance of mastery learning or other direct instructional approaches.[96] However, questions arise about whether any instructional approach that breaks learning into tiny, sequenced items has desirable end results for all students, especially high-achieving, talented, or creative students; whether all students need so much practice to master fundamental skills and tasks; and whether it is acceptable to vary instructional time to the disadvantage of higher achievers.

During the past two decades, mastery approaches have been adopted in more than 5,000 schools. The research suggests they require extensive diagnostic criterion-reference testing, and it is necessary to determine different standards of mastery for each class depending on the students' abilities. Teachers have to devise alternative assignments (remedial, corrective, or enrichment) for different students at different stages and at least two forms of tests to measure changes in learning. Teachers must cope with individual rates of learning and vary content coverage and time. It takes a master teacher who is willing to work hard to implement mastery instruction successfully. Actually, it takes a master teacher to implement any instructional method effectively. But if you look carefully at the mastery model, it consists of nothing more than solid instruction. In simplified form, mastery teaching consists of the steps in box 6.5.

To understand mastery learning one must be able to justify the statement that, "The more time on task a student spends, the more he will comprehend." This method is based on the idea that learning depends largely on the amount of time one spends attempting to understand. The method maintains that all students in a classroom regardless of ability can master a subject when given sufficient time. If you feel this is true, mastery learning will appeal to you. The method is a systematic way of learning and teaching. The objective of this strategy is to master at least 85 percent of any topic being taught. All course work is organized into one- or two-week units, and comprehension is assessed by testing and retesting materials not mastered. This approach to learning begins with assessing student prior knowledge, followed by teacher-led instruction, which is evaluated by nongraded tests. The process affords the teacher an opportunity to correct errors and guide students to mastery. (Box 6.5 illustrates the steps to be taken when using the mastery learning method.) (See Case Study 6.2 to further explore the concepts involved in this learning strategy.)

Box 6.5   The Mastery Learning Process

All course work is organized into one- or two-week units. Each student's unit work is first assessed by a diagnostic test and then a retest to correct any errors related to non-mastery of the unit of study.

Basic Components of Mastery Learning

- Orientation: Goals are clearly stated so that all are aware of the expected outcomes. The objectives of the curriculum are discussed.
- A letter explaining the program is sent to parents.
- Pre-assessment of student's prior knowledge is completed before the unit begins.
- Subject unit taught: Primary instruction is teacher directed.
- The first test, called a formative assessment, is not graded.
- A corrective process takes place: Additional instruction is provided to clarify any errors.
- If a student demonstrates mastery on formative assessment test A or B, s/he can move on to new materials.
- Summative Assessment: Final mastery is reached when 85 percent of material is understood.

Source: Benjamin S. Bloom, "Mastery Learning and Its Implications for Curriculum Development," in E. W. Eisner (ed.), *Confronting Curriculum Reform* (Boston: Little Brown, 1971).

The following case study suggests we look at mastery learning as an alternative when discussing direct and indirect instructional approaches. Read the case and compare and contrast the ideas presented regarding what exactly can be done to advance student understanding through the use of effective instructional strategies.

Case Study 6.2
Mastery Learning

Jerry Grieco had been present at the debate held last week in Professor Hughes' class. He remembered the heated words and arguments between Irwin Kantor, who was for direct instruction, and Kendra Jackson, who was for indirect instruction. He recalled Professor Hughes telling the class to digest and reflect on the positions taken during the debate. He also thought about the reminder to consider the term *eclectic* in his decision making.

The problem as Jerry saw it was the lack of a consistent philosophy regarding how children learned best. Irwin had just rehashed the traditional transmission approach to learning as opposed to Kendra's idea of students discovering and creating meaning on their own. Irwin felt it was the teachers' role to guide students to learning and not allow them to create their own knowledge. Jerry realized that the instructional strategies mentioned, such as whole- and small-group discussions, brainstorming, debates, role-playing, and simulations, could be used in either a direct or indirect way.

When Jerry researched the problem he came across a strategy called *mastery learning* that was easy to understand and offered an alternative approach to learning. All one had to do to understand it was to be able to justify the statement, "The more time on task a student spends, the more he will comprehend." The method, he discovered, was based on the concept that learning depends largely on the amount of time one spends attempting to understand, and not on a student's intellectual abilities. The idea that all students in a classroom, regardless of ability, can master a subject when given sufficient time was revolutionary to Jerry. Mastery learning claimed that all children could learn when provided with appropriate learning conditions in the classroom.

Jerry decided to do further research and present his findings in Professor Hughes' class. He found out that students essentially had to follow five steps if they wanted to master this systematic way for learning and teaching. The first was to master at least 85 percent of any topic being taught. Second, all work was organized in small weekly units and evaluated by testing and retesting materials not mastered. The third step required teachers to have prior knowledge of students' learning levels before beginning instruction, which were evaluated by nongraded tests. The fourth step required that students be given an orientation regarding the process. The final step was a letter sent to parents explaining the program. Students and parents had to understand that the objective is mastery and not finding fault.

Jerry presented his material in class and summed up by saying that the idea of mastery learning amounted to a radical shift in responsibility for teachers; the blame for a student's failure rests with the instruction, not a lack of ability on the part of the student. In a mastery learning environment the challenge becomes providing enough time and employing effective instructional strategies so that all students can achieve the same level of learning.

Upon hearing Jerry's presentation, Irwin stood up and said that Jerry had just confirmed his position about direct instruction. Mastery learning works best with the traditional content-focused curriculum, one based on well-defined learning objectives organized into smaller and sequentially organized units. Kendra said, "You're wrong again, Irwin. Mastery learning works best when it doesn't focus on content, but on the process of mastering it. It captures the elements of independent functionality. The teacher directs a variety of activities, but students still construct their own meanings."

Discussion Topics and Questions to Ponder

1. Was Jerry correct in his analysis of the problem of inconsistency in learning methodology? Explain your answer.

2. How do you feel about Jerry's alternative? Was it really an alternative? Explain your answer.

3. Compare and contrast Kendra's and Irwin's positions.

4. On a continuum between Kendra's and Irwin's arguments, where did Jerry's argument belong?

5. If you were asked to use a mastery learning approach, how would you go about it?

What would you do if . . . ?

1. You were asked to look at box 6.5 (The Mastery Learning Process) and compare it to box 6.2 (Benefits of Cooperative Learning).

2. You were asked by Jerry to help him prove that mastery learning could be both direct and indirect in its approach.

3. Professor Hughes asked you to decide whether students could all learn, given enough time on task, or whether they could only learn as a result of intellectual ability.

Theory into Practice

Just as it is important to use different instructional methods and materials, it is important to mix instructional groupings to meet varied classroom conditions and student needs and to provide variety. No one grouping approach is appropriate for every circumstance. A mixture of whole-group, small-group, and individualized instruction should be used. Here are a few commonsense methods written as questions.

For Whole-Group Instruction

1. Is your classroom attractive and safe? Are the spacing and furnishings flexible?

2. Have you involved all students in the instructional activities? Do you avoid emphasizing teacher-student interaction on one side or in the middle of the room?

3. Have you arranged instructional materials and media equipment so that all students can readily see and participate in the activities?

4. Do you direct and monitor classroom activities?

5. Do you combine whole-group (direct-instruction) approaches with small-group (informal cooperative learning) approaches?

6. Are you able to make smooth transitions for large-group activities to either small-group or individualized instruction? Do you maintain a brisk pace when making transitions?

For Small-Group Instruction

1. Have you made sure students know what to do and how to proceed? Do they understand the objectives or tasks and when they have achieved them?

2. Have you made sure students are aware of their responsibilities while working in small groups?

3. Do you enhance communication and minimize conflicts by discussing appropriate behavior for individuals within groups?

4. When organizing groups, do you consider the abilities and interests of students? Do you mix groups by ethnicity, social class, and gender for purposes of integration and by ability so they are relatively equal on a cognitive basis?

5. Have you taken into account special learning and behavior problems? Do you separate students who do not work well together?

6. Do you permit students to work at their own pace within their respective groups? Do you permit each group to work at its own pace?

7. Do you monitor the work of each group? Do you make comments, ask questions, and assist the group as necessary?

8. Are you providing knowledge of group results by emphasizing the positive? Do you provide immediate feedback and group rewards for achievement?

CONCLUSIONS

- Instruction may take place in whole-group, small-group, and individualized settings. The teacher is responsible for varying these three groupings according to the needs of the students and the objectives of the lesson.

- Classroom seating arrangements include traditional, rectangular, circular, horseshoe, and various special formations designed for special activities.

- Large-group or whole-group instruction is the most common form of classroom organization, suitable for the teacher when lecturing and explaining, questioning, and providing practice and drill.

- Whole-group instruction tends to be geared to the average learner, and the students are expected to perform within a narrow range. Most classroom tasks performed by students are either too easy or too difficult.

- Small groups give the teacher flexibility in instruction and an opportunity to introduce skills and tasks at the level suited to a particular group of students.

- There are several methods for organizing students in small groups. Small-group activities are best conducted when group size is limited to five to eight students per group.

- Individualized instruction permits the student to work alone at his or her own pace and level over short or long periods of time. Individualized instruction permits the teacher to adapt instruction to the abilities, needs, and interests of the learner.

KEY TERMS

ability grouping	individualized instruction	self-contained
between-class	informal cooperative	classroom
ability grouping	learning	within-class
cooperative learning	mastery learning	ability grouping
departmentalization	peer tutoring	

DISCUSSION QUESTIONS

1. What types of seating arrangements do you prefer during whole-group instruction? Does this suggest anything about your teaching approach?

2. Which small-group instructional methods do you prefer? Why?

3. How might class size influence how you teach in either a whole- or small-group situation?

4. In general, which methods do you expect to emphasize (or presently emphasize) in your own class—whole-group, small-group, or individualized? Why?

5. Why do most consider cooperative working activities effective?

MINI-CASES FROM THE FIELD

Case One: Grouping for Instruction

Kyle Wilson was a newly appointed teacher to Wallington High School. He had been interviewed by his department chairperson, Erica Reed, who said she would be his immediate supervisor. Two months into the term Mrs. Reed told him that he was not meeting the needs of all the students in this tenth-grade heterogeneously organized social studies class. She further said that the direct instructional lecture approach he was using might work for some but not all students. She asked Kyle to consider using cooperative learning activities as a basis for planning cooperative lessons. This approach, she claimed, would work exceptionally well with his present unit on social justice and civil rights.

1. Why does Mrs. Reed consider cooperative learning activities a viable idea for a tenth-grade social studies class?

2. How should Kyle group his class to best meet Mrs. Reed's expectations?

3. Does Mrs. Reed have a right to request instructional approaches that she believes in? Explain your answer.

4. In planning how the unit should be taught, should Kyle involve his students? (Should he use a lecture approach or a cooperative approach?)

5. What suggestions would you offer Kyle to aid in his preparation?

Case Two: Teaching Whole Groups

Jeanne Emmons had read her notes on how to be successful in teaching whole groups. Most of the notes were commonsense, especially those regarding appearance, prior preparation, and being on time. What she was most interested in was how to obtain her students' attention and keep them focused on the lesson. She had found that her second-grade class became too excited with highly motivated warm-up exercises and bored with simple reviews. Her friend Alice told her, "That's just the way it is! It doesn't matter: Just keep circulating about the room and monitor student work. Keep them busy—don't give your class a chance to be unruly!"

1. How do you feel about Alice's suggestions?
2. How does the quality of instruction affect student focus?
3. What types of incentives could Jeanne use to keep her second-grade class on task?
4. Does time on task affect focus? If so, how?
5. How would Jeanne's class function if she used the appropriate level of instruction for each child? How can that be done?

Case Three: Small-Group Instruction

Mr. Chan was Gloria's third-grade teacher leader. He had been assigned the role of mentor teacher for all new teachers at Cambridge Academy Elementary School. After having observed Gloria, he noted that all she did was teach whole-group lessons. After five weeks he felt it was about time that Gloria organized her class for some small-group instruction. He was tired of seeing all her lessons revolve around a direct instructional approach in which she taught and spoke for the entire lesson and her children acted as passive learners—and he suspected her students were tired of it too! He asked her to use a small-group approach as an alternative to constant whole-group instruction.

1. How would you describe Mr. Chan's understanding of his role as a mentor teacher?
2. Did Mr. Chan have the right to request that Gloria use a small-group instructional approach?
3. How could Mr. Chan have explained the potential benefits of small-group instruction?
4. Describe how Gloria could organize a class of 21 into small learning groups.
5. Compare small-group instruction to cooperative learning.

Case Four: Ability Grouping versus Heterogeneous Grouping

Silvia Ortiz had been asked by her principal to speak at the school's Parent Association on the topic of ability grouping. She was asked to stress the positive aspects of both types of student classroom grouping: homogeneous and heterogeneous. She began her address by stating that ability grouping was preferred by most of the teachers at the school. They felt that homogeneous instruction focused on students' ability level and allowed students to work more effectively. It worked well for both gifted and at-risk children. Finally, homogeneous grouping allowed students to interact with their peers, which was comfortable for them. On the other hand, heterogeneous grouping was much more difficult for the teacher. It was most effective when instruction was aimed to the "center" of the class (i.e., toward the "average" student). Silvia concluded, "It's certainly more democratic and some research has shown that higher-achieving students positively influence lower-achieving children."

1. How would you describe Silvia's approach to her assignment?
2. Compare her positions for homogeneity and heterogeneity.
3. If you were a member of the parent association, what type of organization would you request for your child?
4. How could a stronger argument have been made for heterogeneous grouping?
5. What question would you have asked Silvia to address?

Case Five: Individualized Instruction

Professor Kornbluth distributed his lecture notes to his undergraduate methods class. He expected that his students would follow his lecture and take notes atop the pre-prepared remarks he had distributed to the class. His notes first defined individualized instruction as "a method of instruction where content, materials, and pace of learning are based on the individual learner's ability." Kornbluth followed up by stating that as a result, a teacher's instruction should highlight each student's unique learning style, as is done in the field of special education. He further stated that individualization was not the same as one-to-one tutoring, which economically is too costly. He also noted that lectures, unfortunately, are used about 80 percent of the time by most teachers, even though it is an inherently inefficient form of instruction. Students, he claimed, on average retain only 10 percent of what is presented, and without reinforcement only 2 percent, after 24 hours. The answer to this dilemma is to place greater reliance on well-designed instructional materials, audio, video, multimedia, computer-assisted instruction (CAI), or simply a good textbook. They can hardly be less inefficient than the lecture method, and they free teachers to focus on the needs and problems of individual students. Computer- and Internet-based education holds the promise of an enormous increase in the use of individualized instruction methodology.

1. Do you agree with the professor's definition of individualized instruction? Justify your response.
2. How can individualized instruction become cost effective?
3. Individualized instruction has been compared by some to direct instruction, which also places great reliance on carefully prepared instructional materials and explicitly prepared instructional sequences. Do you agree with this analysis? Explain your answer.
4. Is the use of technology the key to individualized instruction? Explain your answer.
5. Was the professor correct in using an explanatory method (lecture) to teach his lesson? How could he have used an individualized approach?

FIELD EXPERIENCE ACTIVITIES

1. Discuss the advantages and disadvantages of three different seating arrangements for the subject level and grade level you wish to teach.

2. Observe two or three teachers at work in the classroom and describe in writing the classroom tasks taking place. Do the students appear to view the tasks as relevant to their lives?

3. Defend or criticize the nature of competitive and cooperative classrooms. Be sure to describe the advantages of each, whatever your overall preference. How would you change the reward structures in school?

4. Observe a tutoring program for students in a local school. How does the program operate in terms of student responsibilities?

5. In what content areas do students tutor other students?

RECOMMENDED READING

Baloche, Lynda. *The Cooperative Classroom.* Upper Saddle River, NJ: Prentice-Hall, 1998.
Describes different types of formal and informal cooperative learning approaches.

Benjamin, Amy. *Differentiated Instruction: A Guide for Elementary School Teachers.* New York: Eye on Education, 2006.
Demonstrates how to make your classroom more responsive to the needs of individual students with a wide variety of learning styles, interests, goals, cultural backgrounds, and prior knowledge.

Bloom, Benjamin S. *Human Characteristics and School Learning.* New York: McGraw-Hill, 1976.
Emphasizes individual instruction and school learning and offers mastery approaches to changing the level and rate of learning.

Chubb, John E., and Tom Loveless. *Bridging the Achievement Gap.* Washington, DC: Brookings Institution Press, 2002.
An exploration of the cause of the achievement gap between different student groups, with particular attention to ways of "bridging" the gap through different school and classroom practices.

Hacsi, Timothy. *Children as Pawns: The Politics of Educational Reform.* Cambridge, MA: Harvard University Press, 2003.
A thoughtful discussion of a wide range of issues with particular focus on class size research.

Marzano, Robert J., Debra J. Pickering, and Jane E. Pollock. *Classroom Instruction That Works.* Alexandria, VA: ASCD, 2001.
Describes the different ways of teaching content and documents the research base to support each approach.

Slavin, Robert E. *Cooperative Learning: Theory, Research, and Practice,* 2nd ed. Upper Saddle River, NJ: Prentice-Hall, 1995.
Discusses how to set up and use cooperative learning in classrooms.

Tomlinson, Carol Ann. *How to Differentiate Instruction in Mixed Ability Classrooms,* 2nd ed. Alexandria, VA: ASCD, 2001.
Provides guidance, principles, and strategies for teachers who are interested in creating learning environments that address the diversity typical of mixed-ability classrooms.

Vermette, Paul J. *Making Cooperative Learning Work.* Upper Saddle River, NJ: Prentice-Hall, 1998.
Describes how cooperative learning structures can be used to enhance student learning.

7

Classroom Management and Discipline

FOCUS POINTS

1. Realizing that classroom management is an integral part of teaching.
2. Understanding the approaches to classroom management that best fit your personality and philosophy, and realizing that similar management problems can be handled in different ways.
3. Choosing the approach that best fits your classroom management goals.
4. Knowing the characteristics of successful classroom managers, and understanding those characteristics that coincide with your management behaviors.
5. Recognizing that preventive disciplinary measures improve classroom management.
6. Analyzing your strengths and weaknesses as a classroom manager, with the goal of developing techniques that will help you evaluate your management abilities.
7. Recognizing that technology can influence classroom management.

OVERVIEW

In order to teach, you must be able to manage your students. No matter how much potential you have as a teacher, if you are unable to control the climate in your classroom, little learning will take place. Classroom management is an integral part of teaching. How do you develop a personal approach for classroom management that fosters learning and augments order and discipline? Disciplinary problems are a prime concern for most teachers, and always will be. Teachers have agonized over some students' lack of discipline, cooperation, and respect. Many teachers and parents believe that because of a few disobedient students, the majority suffers. The solution is to teach good classroom procedures. The lack of appropriate procedures is the prime cause for unruly classes. The teacher is the most important person responsible for classroom management and student achievement. The correlations between good classroom management and academic success are self-evident.[1]

As you prepare to teach you need to understand two fundamentals. First, schools are largely governed by middle-class social rules. Second, student behavior is bound by the rules with which students are raised. Teachers have one set of expectations about how students should behave, but students come to school having learned a set of behaviors that may be incompatible with those teacher expectations. The vast majority of problems in classrooms are caused by conflicts between what the teacher expects and what the students have learned. Negotiating this conflict requires that teachers help students learn new sets of behaviors and procedures, but it also demands that teachers try to understand what it is that students bring with them to school. Because most teachers fail to understand the interplay between the school and home cultures, many problems can occur that limit teacher control and student learning.

The public widely considers inadequate classroom management and discipline to be the major educational problem, even though the media have centered on school busing, school financing, declining test scores, and student drug abuse. Annual Gallup polls in education taken among parents since the late 1960s have shown student discipline, or the lack of it, listed as the number one, two, or three school problem each year.[2]

According to an NEA teacher opinion poll, 90 percent of the teachers maintain that student misbehavior interferes with their teaching, and nearly 25 percent claim that it greatly interferes. The same poll revealed that approximately 100,000 teachers suffer personal verbal or physical attacks from students annually, most often in front of other students in the classroom.[3] Moreover, nearly 8 in 10 teachers (78 percent) say that there are persistent troublemakers in their school who should have been removed from regular classrooms. The vast majority of both teachers (85 percent) and parents (73 percent) say the school experience of most students suffers at the expense of a few chronic offenders.[4]

The problem of discipline is persistent, especially in inner-city schools, because many students lack self-control and are unwilling to defer to teacher authority, and many teachers lack systematic methods for dealing with discipline problems.[5] Compounding the problem, many school administrators do not provide adequate support for teachers, and many parents are not adequately involved in their children's education.

Approaches to Classroom Management

Your personality, philosophy, and teaching style will directly affect your managerial and disciplinary approach. There are many approaches, but the one you adopt must be comfortable for you and coincide with your personal characteristics.

---

classic professional viewpoint 7.1

Effective Classroom Management

Carolyn M. Evertson

The foremost concern of new teachers is managing the classroom effectively, but managing effectively is too often seen as simply dealing with misbehavior. To view good classroom management as a set of strategies for disciplining students is to misunderstand the basis on which good management rests. Effective classroom managers are distinguished by their success in preventing problems from arising in the first place, rather than by special skills in dealing with problems once they occur. Good management practice begins on the first day of school with carefully organized, systematic plans for accomplishing classroom tasks and activities. Good managers also make clear their expectations for students' work and behavior, rules and procedures, routines for checking and monitoring student academic work, procedures for grading and giving feedback to students, incentives and deterrents, methods for grouping students, and a whole variety of seemingly minor but essential procedures. Proactive planning helps avert behavior problems by providing students with ways to be successful.

We'll consider six approaches or models. Each is grounded in research, and each is applicable to classrooms. Although they are presented as distinct approaches, they do share common features, and most teachers use them in some combination, depending on their personalities and the maturity level of their students. All are based on a mixture of psychology, classroom experience, and common sense, and all blend elements of prevention with techniques for intervention. They differ in the degree of control and supervision exercised by the teacher and the relative emphasis on tasks and personalities. They form a continuum from firm, direct, and highly structured (a high level of teacher control) to flexible, indirect, and democratic (a moderate teacher control level). Teachers, in general, should move from high teacher control to moderate control systems as the year progresses and as the maturity of students increases. Specifically, if the goal of the teacher is to foster student self-discipline (and this is in fact what *should* occur), then the teacher needs to find ways to help students learn how to control their own behavior. This cannot occur if teachers are always directing and controlling students. Teachers may need to start the school year—or their careers—with a high control level, but as they create engaging lessons and as students come to understand teacher expectations, the students should become more engaged in self-monitoring their own behavior.

A basic theoretical rationale underpinning classroom management is that management style is directly related to a person's personality and beliefs. If this assumption is correct, then it should be possible for teachers to understand their own style through a process of self-reflection and analysis. Box 1.12 in chapter 1 contains twelve scenarios related to classroom managerial situations. Your response to the choices offered should give you an opportunity to assess your relative management style. Your beliefs will be somewhere on a continuum from lowest, to moderate, to highest level of classroom control.

Assertive Approach: High Intervention Level

Teachers need control within their classrooms to facilitate learning. The problem for most is in selecting the best method to achieve control. Traditionalists evidence the common belief that students need and want to be controlled and managed by teachers. Practicing teachers tend to favor proven management models despite the negative or authoritarian connotations associated with some.

The **assertive approach** to classroom management requires that teachers specify rules of behavior and identify consequences for disobeying them; they also must communicate these rules and consequences clearly. The classroom is managed in such a way that students are not allowed to forget who is in charge of the classroom. According to Duke and Meckel, "Students come to realize that teachers expect them to behave in a certain way in class." Teachers hold students accountable for their actions. For example, students who disobey rules might receive one warning and then be subject to a series of one or more sanctions; the idea is for the teacher to respond to a student's misbehavior quickly and appropriately.[6] Mild misbehavior is followed by mild sanctions, but if the misbehavior continues, the sanctions toughen. The approach assumes that misbehavior is contagious and will snowball (or ripple) unless checked early. If misbehavior is ignored or not stopped at an early stage, it will eventually become uncontrollable; more and more students will become disruptive. Paul Chance likens behavior problems to cancer: "It's easier to treat in its earliest stages."[7] The assertive approach is based on Lee and Marlene Canter's model of discipline in which teachers insist on responsible behavior by their students. The teacher takes charge of the classroom immediately, sets the ground rules, and interacts with students in a calm yet forceful way.[8] The teacher is expected to combine clear expectations, an active response to misbehavior, and consistent follow-through with warmth and support for all students.

The technique assumes that good teachers can handle discipline problems on their own and that teaching failure is directly related to inability to maintain adequate classroom discipline. Success is, if not predicated on, at least correlated with good discipline. The approach is probably most effective with students who are emotionally immature and who are having difficulty controlling their own behavior.[9]

The Canters make the following suggestions for teachers applying assertive discipline:

1. Clearly identify positive expectations for students.
2. Take positions. (Say, "I like that" or "I don't like that.")
3. Use a firm tone of voice.
4. Use eye contact, gestures, and touches to supplement verbal messages.
5. Give and receive compliments genuinely.
6. Place demands on students and enforce them.
7. Set limits on students and enforce them.
8. Indicate consequences of behavior and why specific action is necessary.
9. Be calm and consistent; avoid emotion or threats.
10. Persist; enforce minimum rules; don't give up.[10]

The assertive model holds that teachers must establish firm management at the beginning of the year by (1) clarifying appropriate expectations of responsible behavior, (2) identifying existing or potential discipline problems, (3) deciding on negative and positive consequences of behavior that fit the students and situation, and (4) learning how to follow through and implement defined consequences. The plan is best achieved through mental rehearsal (having a good idea of what to do before something occurs) and practice (learning from mistakes).

When to Use. Assertive discipline can be used at any time a teacher decides to gain control of a classroom. This method appeals to most teachers who wish to facilitate learning in a structured, teacher-dominated environment. It supports the inherent belief that teachers must exert strong control over children to create an atmosphere in which learning can thrive. It essentially favors those who feel that classroom management is the job of the teacher. This strategy is also useful as an interventionist or preventative approach to classroom management.

Strengths. The strength of this model is in its simplicity and reinforcement of teachers' management belief systems. The method encourages teachers to take charge and develop clear and defined relationships with their students. Teachers build confidence in their ability to avoid the powerlessness of the non-assertive teacher and shun the hostility and anger formerly directed at students. The method advocates a discipline process involving parents and administrators as team members. The goal is to maneuver the child to conform to the norms of traditional, appropriate behavior.

Weaknesses. The weaknesses of this method are in its confrontational approach, which may anger students to the point of rebellion against sanctions. This approach does not support students in developing personal efficacy or in becoming self-directed. It fails to deal with the underlying causes of discipline problems, such as emotional illness, divorce and other family problems, poverty, and racism. It promotes harsh consequences such as suspensions for extreme mis-behavior, at a time when far too many children are suspended already. Detractors of the approach say that basing classroom management on punishment kindles rebellion and promotes the very behavior it was designed to eliminate.[11]

Applied Science Approach (Instructional Practice): High Intervention Level

Well-run classrooms that are free from disruptions, in which students behave in an orderly manner and are highly involved in learning, are not accidental. They exist if teachers have a clear idea of the type of classroom conditions (arrangement, materials), student behaviors (rules, procedures), and instructional activities (assignments, tasks) they wish to produce. The **instructional practice** or **applied science approach**, developed by Evertson and Emmer, emphasizes the organization and management of students as they engage in academic work.[12] Their method is based on real-world observations of effective and ineffective classroom managers. Their work suggests that task orientation—that is, focusing on the businesslike and orderly accomplishment of academic work—leads to a clear set of procedures for students and teachers to follow.

Instructional practice is based on the basic concept that good lessons prevent management problems. Effective momentum management theory provides the theoretical rationale for this approach. It concludes that interesting, relevant, appropriate curriculum and instruction move lessons along smoothly while avoiding management problems. By establishing effective classroom routines and giving clear directions you create a positive class environment. Showing interest in students and being sensitive to student needs makes for a positive learning environment, which should be misbehavior-free according to this approach. This practice is evidenced by the fact that we have all been in classes where misbehavior was inconceivable, since the teacher—through his/her enthusiasm, pedagogical skills, content mastery, winning personality, and empathy for student needs—was a poster child for the instructional approach.

Evertson and Emmer divide the organization and management of student work into three major categories: establishing and communicating work assignments, standards, and procedures; monitoring student work; and providing feedback to students.

1. *Clear communication of assignments and work requirements.* The teacher must establish work assignments, features of the work, standards to be met, and procedures to be followed and must clearly explain them to students.

   a. *Provide clear instruction for assignments.* Teachers should provide explanations in both oral and written forms. In addition to telling the students about assignments, teachers should post assignments on the chalkboard or distribute duplicated copies. Students should be required to copy assignments posted on the chalkboard into their notebooks.

   b. *Develop standards for the form, degree of neatness, and due dates of papers.* Before students start any written assignment, they should be given general rules to follow: type of paper and writing material to use (pencil, pen, word processor), page numbering system, form for headings, due dates, and so forth. Students will then know what is expected of them without having to be told each time.

   c. *Develop procedures for absent students.* Routines should be established for makeup work for students who missed class. Teachers must meet briefly with such students at a set time before or after school, assign class helpers to be available at particular times of the day (usually during seat-work activities) to assist the students, and designate a place where students can pick up and turn in makeup work.

2. *Monitoring student work.* Monitoring student work helps teachers detect students who are having difficulty and encourages students to keep working.

   a. *Monitor group work.* Before helping any individual student with work, the teacher must be sure that all students start work and are able to do the assignment; otherwise, some students will not even start the assignment and others may start incorrectly.

   b. *Monitor individual work.* Monitor work in several ways, by circulating around the room and giving specific feedback where needed, reviewing each student's work at some designated point during an activity, and establishing due dates that correspond with stages in an assignment.

   c. *Monitor completion of work.* Establish and enforce procedures for turning in work. When all students are turning in work at the same time, the best procedure is to have the work passed to the teacher in a given direction, with no talking until all the work is collected.

   d. *Maintain records of student work.* It is important for teachers to keep a record of the students' work and to incorporate it into the grade. The record should be divided into several headings, such as workbook assignments, major assignments or projects, daily homework, and quizzes and tests.

3. *Feedback to students.* Frequent, immediate, and specific feedback is important for enhancing academic monitoring and managerial procedures. Work in progress, homework, completed assignments, tests, and other work should be checked promptly.

    a. *Focus attention on problems.* It is important for teachers to pay careful attention, particularly at the beginning of the year, to completion of classroom and homework assignments. The first time a student fails to turn in an assignment without a good reason is the time to talk to the student. If the student needs help, provide it but insist at the same time that the student do the work. If the student has persistent problems completing work, then parental communication may be needed. Do not wait until the grading period is over to note the problems that exist.

    b. *Focus attention on good work.* Part of giving feedback is acknowledging good work. This may be done by displaying the work, giving oral recognition, or providing written comments.[13]

According to Evertson and Emmer, an effective manager incorporates eleven managerial methods, all of which have been shown to correlate with improved student achievement and behavior. These methods are listed in box 7.1.

The general approach and methods used by Emmer and Evertson are appropriate for both elementary and secondary teachers. The approach coincides with various instructional techniques; especially as a complement to teacher-centered approaches such as direct instruction.

The applied science approach involves a high degree of time on task and academic engaged time for students. *Time on task* refers to the time allocated to learning, and *engaged time* (or time-on-task) refers to the portion of instructional time that students spend directly involved in learning activities.[14] Successful students are typically engaged students. The applied science approach maintains that when students are working on their tasks successfully, and when those tasks have meaning and relevance, there is little opportunity for discipline problems to arise. The teacher organizes students' work, keeps students on task, monitors their work, gives them feedback, and holds them accountable by providing rewards and penalties.[15] It is a no-play, no-frills approach, corresponding to the old-fashioned "three Rs" and now packaged as part of the *academic productivity movement* in education.

Ornstein compares the instructional practice approach to the business-academic approach developed by Evertson and Emmer in 1981.[16] The strategy stresses procedures that allow for a well-functioning classroom, in which an effective instructional pace is maintained. Procedures in the classroom are similar to those that run a profitable business and should be clear and well defined. Ornstein cites eleven managerial methods taken from Evertson and Emmer that they claim have shown improvement in student achievement and behavior (see box 7.1). Even though these eleven methods are dated, they still demonstrate a practical guide for a traditional approach to classroom management that attempts to facilitate learning. The essential premise is that by teaching effective lessons, which by definition include effective pedagogical practices, you lessen the risk for classroom disruption.

When to Use.   The applied science approach/instructional practice method is a natural for effective teachers who use momentum to pace their lessons. Paul Chance says that "when students are actively engaged in learning tasks and making progress, they are inclined to remain engaged"—a process he refers to as *instructional momentum.*[17] Good instruction limits opportunity for misbehavior and allows teachers to concentrate on teaching. The applied science approach needs to be combined with an interventionist management strategy such as assertive discipline to be effective. This gives the approach a method for dealing with infractions of classroom rules.

Box 7.1   Traditional Methods of Classroom Managers

1. *Readying the classroom.* Classroom space, materials, and equipment are ready at the beginning of the year. Effective managers arrange their rooms in the best possible configurations, and they cope more effectively with existing constraints than less effective teachers.

2. *Planning rules and procedures.* Teachers make sure students understand and follow rules and procedures; they spend time at the beginning of the year explaining and reminding students of rules. They also provide feedback to students on rule compliance.

3. *Teaching rules and procedures.* Rules and procedures (e.g., lining up, turning in work) are systematically taught and reinforced. Most of these teachers teach their students to respond to certain cues or signals, such as a bell or the teacher's call for attention. They also discuss with students how their behavior conforms to expectations.

4. *Consequences.* Consequences for not following rules and procedures are clearly established by teachers; there is consistent follow-through.

5. *Beginning-of-school activities.* The first few days are spent getting students ready to function as a coherent and cooperative group. Once the group is established, efficient teachers sustain a whole-group focus.

6. *Strategies for potential problems.* Strategies for dealing with potential problems are planned in advance. Armed with these strategies, teachers can deal with misbehavior more quickly than less effective managers can.

7. *Monitoring.* Student behavior is closely monitored; student academic work is also monitored.

8. *Stopping inappropriate behavior.* Inappropriate or disruptive behavior is handled promptly and consistently—before it worsens or spreads. The teacher has a variety of techniques to handle misbehavior.

9. *Organizing instruction.* Teachers organize instructional activities at levels suitable for all students in the class. There is a high degree of student success and content related to student interests.

10. *Student accountability.* Procedures have been developed for keeping students accountable for their work and behavior.

11. *Instructional clarity.* Teachers provide clear instructions that help keep students on task, allow them to learn faster, and reduce discipline problems. Directions are clear, and thus confusion is minimized.

Sources: Adapted from Edmund T. Emmer, *Classroom Management for Middle and High School Teachers* (Boston: Allyn & Bacon 2006); Carolyn M. Evertson, *Classroom Management for Elementary Teachers* (Boston: Allyn & Bacon, 2003); Edmund T. Emmer and Carolyn M. Evertson, "Synthesis of Research on Classroom Management," *Educational Leadership* (January 1981), 342–347.

Strengths. The model is based on empirical research showing that both positive and negative actions by teachers influence student behavior. Teacher actions may even affect students for whom the action was not intended. The basic arguments for the instructional practice/applied science approach can be summed up in the following three statements:

1. Carefully designed and implemented instruction will prevent most managerial problems and solve those it does not prevent.

2. The role of the teacher is to plan and implement "good lessons" while developing learning tasks that are tailored to meet the needs of each student.

3. Good managerial strategies consist of well-planned and conducted activities centered on abilities and interests with clear, explicit directions that have smoothness and momentum.[18]

Weaknesses. The model basically can be used only during classroom recitation sessions, and it is limited in that it is not readily adaptable to many classroom situations or teaching approaches. No matter how it is stated, the model is essentially preventative and shows how to avoid discipline problems. It does not provide corrective measures to solve serious discipline problems, nor does it assist students in becoming responsible for their behavior, since behavior is not really addressed.

Behavior Modification Approach: High Intervention Level

Behavioral modification is rooted in the classic work of James Watson and the more recent work of B. F. Skinner. The **behavior modification approach** involves a variety of techniques and methods, ranging from simple rewards to elaborate reinforcement training. Behaviorists argue that behavior is shaped by environment, so they pay limited attention to the causes of problems.

Teachers using the behavior modification approach strive to increase the occurrence of appropriate behavior through a system of rewards and reduce the likelihood of inappropriate behavior through punishments. According to Albert Bandura, such teachers would ask the following questions: What is the specific behavior that requires modification, and is the intention to increase, reduce, or eliminate it? When does the behavior occur? What are the consequences of the behavior (or what happens in the classroom when the behavior is exhibited)? How do these consequences reinforce inappropriate behavior? How can the consequences be altered? How can appropriate behavior be reinforced?[19]

The basic principles of the behavioral modification approach are as follows:

1. Behavior is shaped by its consequences, not by the causes of problems in the history of the individual or by group conditions.

2. Behavior is strengthened by immediate reinforcers. **Positive reinforcers** consist of praise or rewards. **Negative reinforcers** take away something or stop some process that the student enjoys; by removing a particular unpleasant stimulus, an increase in desired behavior occurs.[20] For example, the student is reprimanded by the teacher; the student agrees to behave according to classroom rules and the teacher

First-Day Procedures

Sara Eisenhardt

Classroom management is something that an accomplished teacher does almost intuitively. From my perspective, classroom management involves knowing my students and developing and consistently implementing comprehensive strategies for "doing the work." In 25 years of teaching I have developed a system for all the routines I needed to enable me to teach and my students to learn, which I modify according to each class's respective needs and dynamics. Developing these strategies is a very complex and challenging activity. It involves knowing your students and being able to predict how they might respond to particular situations. It involves identifying what you want them to know and be able to do by the end of the first day, week, month, and so on, to enable them to shift their focus from the "routine" to the academic work you prepared. You must be clear about what you want them to know and be able to do, planning the most effective way to enable them to reach your goals.

The old saying "You don't know what you don't know until you learn it" certainly applied to one developing teacher I know and for whom I acted as an informal mentor. I drew a T-chart and asked him to identify what he wanted the students to know and be able to do by the end of the first day of school. He said he wanted the students to do a getting-acquainted activity. I reminded him that that was an activity and asked him to identify what he wanted them to know and be able to do. After exhausting his list of first-day activities he was still unable to identify what he wanted the students to "know and be able to do," and half-believing that this was trick question, he said he did not know the answer. One major difference between a highly effective teacher and a less effective teacher is that the effective teacher clearly knows and understands the *why* of each and every activity.

I shared with him my strategy for communicating to the students how I want them to respond to my questions. I clarified the difference between when it is important for one student at a time to respond (communication of a conceptual understanding) and when I want the whole class to respond (recitation of facts). I showed him that when I want one student to respond, I raise my own hand as I ask the question and lower my hand when I call the student's name. This is what I want my students to do. I also explained that I want my students cognitively engaged the entire time they are in my class, and so I teach them how to actively listen with their eyes, ears, and hearts when a student is responding. I explained that I always repeat this process, as I encourage multiple perspectives and dialogue between students. I demonstrated how I preface a recitation or recall of information question with "Class, . . ." and a short pause to command their attention.

Once I explained this to the teacher, he created a list of "know and do" that included things such as how to greet him and enter the classroom, how to store and collect materials, how to independently work on the Daily Calendar Math Problems, and how to participate in discussions and respond chorally. We worked collaboratively and developed connected and integrated lessons that taught the students the routines within the authentic context in which those routines would occur. He seemed to understand the importance of creating highly structured learning opportunities to teach the students classroom behaviors and routines and recognized that many of the challenges he faced stemmed from a lack of effective management strategies.

If someone were to ask me what classroom management was, I would say, "knowledge of student organization—clear communication—consistency—empathy."

stops reprimanding. In a negative reinforcing situation, the student behaves in such a way as to remove aversive stimuli (such as nagging, scolding, and threats) from the environment.

3. Behavior is strengthened by systematic reinforcement (positive or negative). Behavior is weakened if not followed by reinforcement. Reinforcers can take several different forms: social (praise), material (tangible rewards), or token (stars, points).[21]

4. Students respond better to positive reinforcers than they do to punishment (aversive stimuli). Punishment can be used to reduce inappropriate behavior if used sparingly.

5. When a student is not rewarded for appropriate or adaptive behavior, inappropriate or maladaptive behavior may become increasingly dominant and will be utilized to obtain reinforcement.

6. Constant reinforcement—the reinforcement of a behavior every time it occurs—produces the best results, especially in new learning or conditioning situations.

7. Once the behavior has been learned, it is best maintained through intermittent reinforcement—the reinforcement of a behavior only occasionally.

8. Intermittent reinforcement schedules include (a) variable ratio, supplying reinforcement at unpredictable intervals; (b) fixed ratio, supplying reinforcement after a preselected number of responses; and (c) fixed interval, supplying reinforcement at preselected intervals.[22]

9. There are several types of reinforcers, each of which may be positive or aversive. Examples of positive reinforcers are (a) social reinforcers, such as verbal comments ("Right," "Correct," "That's good"), facial expressions, and gestures; (b) graphic reinforcers, such as written words of encouragement, gold stars, and checks; (c) tangible reinforcers, such as cookies and badges for young students and certificates and notes to parents for older students; and (d) activity reinforcers, such as being a monitor or sitting near the teacher for young students and working with a friend or on a special project for older students.[23]

10. Rules are established and enforced. Students who follow rules are praised and rewarded in various ways. Students who break rules are either ignored, reminded about appropriate behavior, or punished immediately. The response to rule-breaking differs somewhat in different variations of the behavioral modification approach.

Each teacher has an undetermined value as a potential reinforcing agent for each student. This value is initially assigned by students on the basis of past experiences, and it changes as a result of the teacher's actions. The teacher must realize that this evaluation process is ongoing in the student, and that a positive relationship with the student will enhance the teacher's potential for influencing behavior in class. Moreover, the teacher is just one of many adults who serve as reinforcing agents in the student's life. In order to facilitate the classroom management process, the teacher may have to enlist the support of others.

There are a number of systems or variations on behavioral modification that are applicable to classroom management. They basically build limits and consequences into behavior and employ various rules, rewards, and punishments. A well-known system utilized in various social learning situations is termed **modeling**. Models are effective in modifying behavior to the degree that they capture attention, hold attention, and are imitated. Effective models may be parents, relatives, teachers, other adults (community residents), public figures (sports people, movie stars), and peers. The best models are those with whom individuals can identify on the basis of one or more of the following traits: sex, age, ethnicity, physical attractiveness, personality attractiveness, competence, power, and ability to reward imitators. The sources for these models are classic researchers in the field of behavioral psychology. Teachers who want to use modeling in classroom management should recognize that the first five traits are personal characteristics that are hard to change, but the last three are institutional and role characteristics that are easier to manipulate to increase the models' effectiveness.

Building good discipline through modeling includes:

1. *Demonstration.* Students must know exactly what is expected. In addition to having expected behavior explained to them, they see and hear it.

2. *Attention.* Students must focus their attention on what is being depicted or explained. The degree of attention correlates with the characteristics of the model (teacher) and the characteristics of the students.

3. *Practice.* Students have an opportunity to practice the appropriate behavior.

4. *Corrective feedback.* Students receive frequent, specific, and immediate feedback. Appropriate behavior is reinforced; inappropriate behavior is suppressed and corrected.

5. *Application.* Students are able to apply their learning in classroom activities (role-playing, modeling activities) and other real-life situations.[24]

Teachers who do not know much about how students learn from "modeling" produce less learning in their students and have more disciplinary problems than teachers who are successful at using modeling.

Miltenberger describes several different ways in addition to modeling of using behavior modification in the classroom.

1. *"Catch them being good" approach.* The teacher observes students doing what he or she desires and then makes a positive statement: "I like how row one is sitting" or "I like how Bobby is working on his assignment."

2. *Rules-ignore-praise approach.* The teacher develops clear rules, ignores mild inappropriate behavior, and praises compliant actions.

3. *Rules-reward-punishment approach.* The teacher establishes clear rules and rewards appropriate behavior while punishing infractions.

4. *Contingency management approach.* The teacher rewards appropriate behavior by creating tangible reinforcers that can be cashed in at some point for a variety of different rewards. One high school Algebra I teacher gave "lucky bucks" to students when they exhibited appropriate rule-compliant (and positive mathematical) behavior in the classroom. The

students then exchanged the lucky bucks for several different types of Girl Scout cookies.

5. *Contracting approach.* The teacher creates a contract that specifies the behaviors expected of a student and the rewards for appropriate behavior.[25]

When to Use.   To use modeling effectively, teachers should understand and accept its underlying principles and philosophy. Since behaviors are understood to be learned, it behooves teachers to create learning experiences combined with reinforcers to modify misbehavior and improve classroom management.

Strengths.   Modeling's strength is its essential simplicity and ease of implementation. Results are evident almost immediately. It combines feelings of success with obtaining rewards by utilizing rules and standards that are clear and consistent for all students. The strategy is appropriate for students of all ages, as well as being efficient since time is never lost discussing rules. Finally, it is well researched and consistently works with most students.

Weaknesses.   The prime weakness of modeling is its manipulative use of stimuli in lieu of faith in free will. Results may not last because responsibility for individual actions is not stressed, just rewards. When reinforcers are removed, poor behavior can return. Using rewards undermines a child's intrinsic motivation to behave properly. Behavior modification ignores causes stemming from the home situation and the society in which the child resides. It affords no opportunity to clarify emotions, weigh alternatives, decide on solutions, or develop the intellect.

Group Managerial Approach/Effective Momentum: Moderate Intervention

The group managerial approach to discipline is based on Jacob Kounin's research. Almost all the major applied science theorists of classroom management—Brophy, Doyle, Emmer, Evertson, and Good—have been influenced by Kounin. Much of what they have to say now was said by Kounin in some form forty years ago.

Kounin was one of the first researchers to systematically study classroom management procedures, especially as they related teacher behaviors to student behaviors. The **group managerial approach** emphasizes the importance of responding immediately to group student behavior that might be inappropriate or undesirable in order to prevent problems rather than having to deal with problems after they emerge. He describes what he calls the "ripple effect."[26] If a student misbehaves but the teacher stops the misbehavior immediately, it remains an isolated incident and does not develop into a problem. If the misbehavior is not noticed, is inappropriately ignored, or is allowed to continue for too long, it often spreads throughout the group and becomes more serious and chronic.

Kounin analyzes classroom activities for purposes of management by dividing them into categories of pupil behavior and teacher management behavior (see table 7.1). Major categories of pupil behavior are work involvement and deviancy. Major categories of teacher behavior are desist techniques, movement management, and group focus.

Table 7.1   Kounin's Behaviors and Categories for Observing Classroom Management

Categories of Pupil Behavior

I. Work Involvement	*II. Deviancy*
A. Involved	A. No misbehavior
B. Mildly involved	B. Mild misbehavior
C. Not involved	C. Serious Misbehavior

Categories of Teacher Management Behavior

I. Desist Techniques	*III. Group Focus*

A. "With-it-ness:"
 Dealing with students in a timely fashion
	A. Alerting
	   1. Encourage suspense
	   2. Pick reciter randomly

B. Overlapping: Dealing with multiple behaviors	3. Call on nonvolunteers 4. Present new materials
C. High Profile: Publicly reprimanding a student	5. Ignore group in favor of recite 6. Select reciter before asking question
D. Low Profile: Moving closer to a misbehaving student	7. Ask question, then call recite
II. Movement Management	B. Accountability 1. Ask students to hold up props

A. Smoothness-Jerkiness
   1. Flip-flopping topics
   2. Abbreviating lessons
	2. Actively attend to mass unison response
	   3. Call on others
	   4. Ask for volunteers and nonvolunteers

B. Momentum
   1. Overdwelling
   2. Fragmenting lessons
	5. Require student to demonstrate performance
	   6. Review frequently

Source: Adapted from Jacob Kounin, *Discipline and Group Management in Classrooms* (New York: Holt, Rinehart & Winston, 1970), chaps. 3 and 7.

Work Involvement. *Work involvement* is the amount of time students spend engaged in assigned academic work. (It closely resembles what other researchers call "time on task" or "academic engaged time.") Students who are involved in work (e.g., writing in a workbook, reciting, reading, watching a demonstration) exhibit fewer disciplinary problems than do students who are not involved in any assigned task. If the teacher keeps students involved in work, there is less chance that boredom and discipline problems will arise.

Deviancy. *Deviancy* ranges from no misbehavior to serious misbehavior. *No misbehavior* means the student unwittingly is off task, is upsetting another student or teacher, or is temporarily (deliberately but nondisruptively) off task. *Mild misbehavior* includes such actions as whispering, making faces, teasing, reading a comic, and passing notes. *Serious misbehavior* is aggressive or harmful behavior that interferes with others or violates school or social codes. The point is to prevent mild misbehavior from degenerating into serious misbehavior. Mild misbehavior needs to be dealt with promptly.

Desist Techniques.   Actions that teachers take to stop misbehavior are called **desist techniques.** Kounin feels that they depend on two abilities. **With-it-ness** is the ability to react on target (react to the proper student) and in a timely fashion. It also involves communicating to students that the teacher knows what is happening or, as Kounin puts it, that the teacher "has eyes in the back of [his or her] head." **Overlapping** refers to the teacher's ability to handle more than one matter at a time. He or she can attend to more than one student at the same time—say, one student who is reciting and another student who is interrupting with a question or comment.

Movement Management.   The organization of behavior in transitions from task to task within and between lessons is called *movement management.* Movement may be characterized as smooth or jerky. The terms are not especially sophisticated, but they are quite apt. *Smoothness* is an even and calm flow of activities. It involves uninterrupted work periods and short, fluid transitions that are made automatically and without disruption. In particular, the teacher (1) avoids unnecessary announcements and interruptions when students are busy doing work, (2) finishes one activity before starting on the next, and (3) doesn't abruptly end or start an activity. In contrast, *jerkiness* is a disorderly flow of activities that may result if the teacher tries to do too many things at once or does not make clear to students the procedures for ending one task and changing to a new one. The teacher may have to raise his or her voice during transitions, disorder may arise as students have to ask questions about what to do, and unengaged students may create disruptions. In order to prevent jerkiness, the teacher should avoid five subcategories of behavior:

1. The teacher is so immersed with a small group of students or an activity that he or she ignores other students or misses an event that is potentially disruptive.

2. The teacher bursts into activities without assessing student readiness and gives orders, makes statements, or asks questions that only confuse the students.

3. The teacher ends an activity or drops a topic before it is completed.

4. The teacher ends an activity abruptly.

5. The teacher terminates one activity, goes to another, and then returns to the previously terminated activity. The teacher lacks clear direction and sequence of activities.

Movement management also involves *momentum*—that is, keeping activities at an appropriate pace. Effective momentum is slowed or impeded if the teacher engages in over-dwelling or fragmentation. *Overdwelling* may take the form of giving explanations beyond what is necessary for most students' understanding or lecturing, preaching, nagging, overemphasizing, or giving too many directions. *Fragmentation* is giving too much detail, breaking things down into too many steps, or duplicating or repeating activities. For example, a teacher who calls students to his or her desk to read on a one-by-one basis, rather than having one student read aloud to the class while the others listen, is engaging in fragmentation.

Group Focus.   *Group focus* refers to the students' concentration on the group activity or task. It can be achieved through what Kounin calls *alerting*. Alerting activities include creating suspense, presenting new material, choosing reciters randomly, and selecting reciters (see table 7.1 for other methods Kounin lists). Group focus can also be achieved by using *accountability*. This involves such methods as asking students to hold up props or circulating to check the products of nonreciters, and requiring students to perform and then checking their performance.

In summary, Kounin believes that student engagement in lessons and activities is the key to successful classroom management. Students are expected to work and behave. The successful teacher monitors student work in a systematic fashion, clearly defines acceptable and unacceptable behavior, and exhibits with-it-ness and overlapping abilities. The successful teacher has a clear sense of direction and sequence for tasks. Smooth transitions are made from one activity to another, so that student attention is turned easily from one activity to another. Similarly, lessons are well paced.

In essence, Kounin argued that as a classroom manager, the teacher should do the following:

1. *Maintain a group focus.* The teacher knows what students need to do (to be organized) and then expects students to do what is outlined.

2. *Have a degree of group accountability.* The teacher makes all students feel a sense of responsibility for what happens in the classroom. All students feel included.

3. *Obtain the attention of the group.* The teacher finds ways to get students' attention easily and begins class on time.[27]

Kounin's greatest contribution may be his emphasis on prevention. Good teachers structure classroom environments so that misbehaviors are minimized if not prevented. Student misbehavior will never be eliminated totally, but a teacher who understands concepts such as *momentum* and *smoothness* will see far less misbehavior than one who has too few activities or jumps from one lesson to another without proper transitions. See Tips for Teachers 7.1 for an overview of some practical suggestions for effectively managing your classroom.

When to Use.   The group managerial approach, based on maintaining effective momentum in the classroom, is key to successful teaching. By maintaining group focus and providing good instruction, the opportunity for misbehavior is limited and teacher time spent on instruction is increased.

Strengths.   The approach is based on Kounin's empirical research, which documented the behaviors of teachers that aided or interfered with learning. This strategy offers several procedures for making desists effective, such as targeting the proper students, timing of desists, overlapping, and with-it-ness. Through the use of with-it-ness teachers create the impression that they are aware of anything happening in the classroom.

Enhancing Your Classroom Management Approach

TIPS FOR TEACHERS 7.1

How do you develop and maintain a positive approach to classroom management or whatever discipline approach you wish to adapt? Here are some practical suggestions that will work in most situations.

Affective Dimensions

1. *Be positive:* Stress what should be done, not what should not be done.

2. *Use encouragement:* Show that you appreciate hard work and good behavior.

3. *Trust:* Trust students, but don't be an easy mark. Make students feel you believe in them as long as they are honest with you and don't take advantage of you.

4. *Express interest:* Talk to individual students about what interests them, what they did over the weekend, and how schoolwork is progressing in other areas or subjects. Be sensitive and respectful of social trends, styles, and school events that affect the behavior of the group. Be aware that peer group pressure affects individual behavior.

5. *Be fair and consistent:* Don't have "pets" or "goats." Don't condemn an infraction one time and ignore it another time.

6. *Show respect, avoid sarcasm:* Be respectful and considerate toward students. Understand their needs and interests. Don't be arrogant or condescending or rely on one-upmanship to make a point.

Procedural Dimensions

7. *Establish classroom rules:* Make rules clear and concise and enforce them. *Your* rules should eventually be construed as *their* rules.

8. *Discuss consequences:* Students should understand the consequences of acceptable and unacceptable behavior. Invoke logical consequences—that is, use appropriate rewards and punishment. Don't punish too often; it loses its effect after a while.

9. *Establish routines:* Students should know what to do and under what conditions. Routine procedures provide an orderly and secure classroom environment.

10. *Confront misbehavior:* Don't ignore violations of rules or disruptions of routines. Deal with misbehavior in a way that does not interfere with your teaching. Don't accept or excuse serious or contagious misbehavior, even if you have to stop your teaching. If you ignore it, it will worsen.

11. *Reduce failure, promote success:* Academic failure should be kept to a minimum since it is a cause of frustration, withdrawal, and hostility. When students see themselves as winners and receive recognition for success, they become more civil, calm, and confident; they are easier to work with and teach.

12. *Set a good example:* Model what you preach and expect. For example, speak the way you want students to speak; keep an orderly room if you expect students to be orderly; check homework if you expect students to do the homework.

Weaknesses.   Kounin's approach is limited in that it is not readily adaptable to many classroom situations or teaching methods. The strategy is primarily preventative and affords no interactive intervention procedures. No corrective measures for solving serious discipline problems are offered. The emphasis on the group tends to delay the development of individuals' responsibility for their own behavior.

Acceptance Approach/Logical Consequences: Moderate Intervention Level

The **acceptance approach** to discipline is rooted in humanistic psychology. It maintains that every person has a prime need for acceptance. Students, like everyone else, strive for acceptance. They want to belong and to be liked by others. Their need for acceptance is more important to them than learning. Similarly, they would rather behave than misbehave. The acceptance approach is also based on the democratic model of teaching, in which the teacher provides leadership by establishing rules and consequences but at the same time allows students to participate in decisions and to make choices.

The acceptance approach, also known as *logical consequences,* is a management theory developed in Vienna, Austria, by a psychiatrist named Rudolf Dreikurs (1897–1972). His model highlighted a basic premise that children should be given a choice rather than being forced to behave as directed. Behavior is driven by an individual's own purposes and is founded on one's own biased interpretations of the world; each of us acts according to our own subjective appraisal of the reality that surrounds us. When we are able to assess the consequences associated with our behaviors, our course of actions becomes more knowledgeable. Applied to the classroom, we can say that students misbehave because their needs are not met. When these needs (such as attention and acceptance) are met, misbehavior tends to disappear. Dreikurs felt that misbehavior in general was due to the students' need for recognition, which led to four mistaken goals: (1) attention getting, (2) power seeking, (3) revenge seeking, and (4) withdrawal.[28]

Rudolph Dreikurs' disciplinary approach is based on the need for acceptance.[29] He maintains that acceptance by peer and teacher is the prerequisite for appropriate behavior and achievement in school. People try all kinds of behavior to get status and recognition. If they are not successful in receiving recognition through socially acceptable methods, then they will turn to mistaken goals that result in antisocial behavior. Dreikurs identifies four mistaken goals:

1. *Attention getting.* When students are not getting the recognition they desire, they often resort to attention-getting misbehavior. They want other students or the teacher to pay attention to them. They may act as "class clowns," ask special favors, continually seek help with assignments, or refuse to work unless the teacher hovers over them. They function as long as they obtain their peers' or teacher's attention. Teachers can determine if misbehavior has this goal by asking, "Am I annoyed?"

2. *Power seeking.* Students may also express their desire for recognition by defying adults in what they perceive as a struggle for power. Their defi-

ance is expressed in arguing, contradicting, teasing, temper tantrums, and low-level hostile behavior. If the students get the teacher to argue or fight with them, they win, because they succeed in feeling powerful. Teachers can determine if a misbehavior has this goal by asking, "Am I threatened?"

3. *Revenge seeking.* Students who fail to gain recognition through power may seek revenge. Their mistaken goal is to hurt others to make up for being hurt or feeling rejected and unloved. Students who seek revenge don't care about being punished. They are cruel, hostile, or violent toward others. Simple logic doesn't always work with them. Being punished gives them renewed cause for action. The more trouble they cause for themselves, the more justified they feel. Teachers can determine if misbehavior has this goal by asking, "Am I hurt?"

4. *Withdrawal.* If students feel helpless and rejected, the goal of their behavior may become withdrawal from the social situation rather than confrontation. They guard whatever little self-esteem they have by removing themselves from situations that test their abilities. Such withdrawal displays their feelings of inadequacy. If not helped, they eventually become isolated.[30]

The first thing teachers need to do is identify students' "mistaken goals." The type of misbehavior indicates the type of expectations or goals students have.

1. If students stop the behavior and then repeat it, their goal tends to be getting attention.

2. If students refuse to stop or increase their misbehavior, their goal tends to be power seeking.

3. If students become hostile or violent, their goal tends to be revenge.

4. If students refuse to cooperate or participate, their goal tends to be withdrawal.

After teachers identify the student goals, they need to confront the students with an explanation of what they are doing. Dreikurs maintains that by doing this in a friendly, nonthreatening way, teachers can get students to examine—even change—their behavior. The teachers should then encourage students in their efforts to recognize their mistaken goals and to change their behavior. Dreikurs sees an important distinction between encouraging and praising. Encouragement consists of words or actions that convey respect and belief in students' abilities. It tells students they are accepted; it recognizes efforts, not necessarily achievements. Praise, on the other hand, is given when a task is achieved.

The teacher needs to be sure the students are aware of and understand the consequences of inappropriate behavior. The consequences must be as closely related to the misbehavior as possible, and the teacher must apply them consistently, immediately and in a calm manner, displaying no anger or triumph. For example, the consequence for failing to complete a homework assignment means staying after school and finishing it. The consequence for disturbing others in class is isolation from the group for a short period. Students gradually learn that poor choices result in unpleasant consequences that are nobody's fault but their own.

Eventually, students learn to control their actions and to make better decisions, and thus they reach a point at which they control their behavior through self-discipline.

Dreikurs suggests several strategies for working with students who exhibit mistaken goals to encourage them and to enforce consequences. Some examples of what he suggests are listed in table 7.2.

Dreikurs rejected the use of punishment and any type of positive or negative reinforcement. He considered them unsuitable because eventually they would produce dependency. He advocated the encouragement of children to experience success by charging them with responsibility for their behavior. Responsibility, he felt, was fundamental to a democratic society, as was the idea that children must experience the consequences of their misbehavior. He applied standards such as relatedness, respectfulness, and reasonableness to potential consequences so that they are logical and not punishments. Examples might include:

1. A child (or his or her parents) will pay the custodian for cleaning up the child's graffiti or refuse.
2. A child will be responsible for refinishing (or pay for the refinishing of) marked school furniture.

Table 7.2   Sample Strategies for Carrying Out the Acceptance Approach

To Encourage Students	To Enforce Consequences
1. Be positive; avoid negative statements.	1. Give clear directions.
2. Encourage students to improve, not to be perfect.	2. Establish a relationship with each student based on mutual trust and respect.
3. Encourage effort; results are secondary if students try.	3. Use consequences that are logical; a direct relationship between misbehavior and consequences must be understood by students.
4. Teach students to learn from mistakes.	4. Perceive behavior in its proper perspective; avoid making issues out of trivial incidents.
5. Encourage student independence.	5. Permit students to assume responsibility for their own behavior.
6. Exhibit faith in students' abilities.	6. Combine friendliness with firmness; students must see the teacher as a friend, but limitations must be established.
7. Encourage a cooperative or team effort among students.	7. Set limits at the beginning, but work toward a sense of responsibility on the part of the student.
8. Send positive notes home; note students' improvement.	8. Keep demands or rules simple.
9. Show pride in students' work; display it.	9. Mean what you say; carry out your rules.
10. Be optimistic, enthusiastic, supporting.	10. Close an incident quickly; mistakes are corrected, then forgotten.

Source: Adapted from Rudolph Dreikurs, *Maintaining Sanity in the Classroom,* 2nd ed. (New York: Harper & Row, 1982).

3. A child who starts a fight is not allowed to partake in any group activities until a plan is developed to avoid fighting.

4. Poor or sloppy work is considered incomplete and will be graded as a failure until the work is redone.

5. A child who is unruly at dismissal will be dismissed after the rest of the class.[31]

When to Use.   Although listed as a moderate teacher intervention model, the logical consequences/acceptance approach can be utilized in practically any situation. It works well in combination with most other classroom management strategies. The model provides the teacher with a method to facilitate students' understanding for responsibility with regard to their actions. When children understand that there is a consequence for negative behavior, their desire to seek some benefit from that misbehavior diminishes.

Strengths.   The approach promotes student autonomy by encouraging students to understand and correct their behavior. It is a preventative approach to discipline that relies on logical consequences instead of arbitrary punishment. This strategy also endorses the concept of mutual respect among students. Teachers who use this strategy tend to reflect on causes before they take action.

Weaknesses.   Children may not admit their real motives simply because they are unable to understand what motivated their negative behavior. Consequently, teachers may have trouble determining the actual motives for student behavior as well. Some teachers may have problems in dialoguing with students as well as finding it difficult to respond to students in a non-controlling way.

Success Approach/Choice Theory/Reality Therapy: Moderate Intervention

Influenced by this approach, William Glasser created a method of counseling that he called **reality therapy**. Applied to education, it is a method of counseling and dialoguing—basically a technique for managing classroom behavior that meets students' basic psychological needs. Reality therapy falls into the category of management styles known as the guidance approach or **success approach** (rooted in humanistic psychology), which many teachers find difficult to implement because they feel they are not qualified to act as guidance counselors or psychologists.

Glasser insists that although teachers should not excuse bad behavior on the part of the student, they need to change the negative classroom climate and improve conditions so they lead to student success.[32] One of those conditions is creating and maintaining successful social relationships, a key tenet of reality therapy. To foster social interaction, a teacher may jointly establish rules with student assistance and then enforce those rules fairly. Reality therapy works toward that end by establishing a caring relationship with a student, keeping the focus on current (versus past) behavior, helping a student take personal responsibility for his or her own behavior, and then together developing a plan for behavior change and obtaining the student's commitment to that plan.

The reality therapy process involves asking students four questions that will help them understand the responsibility for their actions.

1. What do you want?

2. What are you doing?

3. Is it helping you get what you want? (If students explain why they think their behavior is helping them [or are unable to say that this is so], they are a step closer to understanding why they are misbehaving.)

4. What is your plan now?

Questions do not need to be asked in any specific order. A prime rule is to never ask why a student misbehaves; that only gets excuses. A unique aspect of this strategy is that there is no punishment for poor behavior, given that students take responsibility for their actions. Teachers have to realize that they do not lose authority by giving up control; they gain respect.[33]

In the 1970s, William T. Powers created what he called control theory systems. Glasser applied Powers' knowledge of how systems work to the field of human behavior and called it choice theory. **Choice theory** explains how the brain functions as a control system that selects behaviors. It is an internally motivated psychology that sees all behavior as coming from within and not from any outside stimulus. All behavior is chosen, except for reflex reactions such as sneezes, itches, or twitches. Glasser believes that individuals are knowingly responsible for their own actions as a result of having free choice. To make the theory practical, reality therapy or responsibility training must be used.

Choice theory is a natural extension of Glasser's reality therapy. The aspect of reality therapy that encourages students to take responsibility for their own behavior doesn't infringe on students' rights and allows for implementation of choice theory. Recall the four questions that teachers should ask a misbehaving student. If a student's choice of behavior is not helping the student or is harming the student, he or she needs to choose new and better behaviors.

The basic premise underlining choice theory revolves around satisfying four basic psychological needs, which Glasser views as genetic: love and belonging, power and achievement, fun and enjoyment of work, and freedom and the ability to make choices. This theory posits that the reduction of misbehavior is achieved by creating an environment and developing a curriculum that meets students' generic needs. Glasser defines disruptive classrooms as environments that interfere with the educational process and infringe on the rights of others. Disruptive behavior is caused when the inner needs of students are not met, and they then choose to misbehave. According to Glasser, teachers who can avoid a disruptive classroom by applying choice theory and utilizing reality therapy/responsibility training will have taken a positive step to create quality schools and quality classrooms.

Applying Glasser's Theories to Classroom Management

Choice theory and reality therapy go hand in hand. In essence, Glasser argues that misbehavior does not occur in isolation; rather, discipline problems occur because of a myriad of human needs, and teachers must be cognizant of those needs if behaviors are to be managed effectively.[34] Glasser stresses the importance of the teacher attending to certain student needs, such as belonging, love, control, and freedom—a central tenet of reality therapy.[35]

Glasser's noncoercive view of discipline is simple but powerful. Behavior is a matter of choice. Good behavior results from good choices; bad behavior results from bad choices. A teacher's job is to help students make good choices. Students make choices according to how they perceive the results of those choices. If bad behavior gets them what they want, they will make bad choices.

Students who have feelings of positive self-worth and who experience success will make good choices most of the time. The road to positive self-worth and to success begins with a good relationship with people who care—a central tenet of choice theory. For some students school may be the only place where they meet people who genuinely care for them, yet some students resist entering into positive relationships with adults, especially teachers. Teachers, therefore, must have positive attitudes, show that they care, and be persistent about conveying both. The emphasis is on helping—exactly what the teaching profession is about—and therefore the approach is attractive to many educators.

Glasser makes the following suggestions:

1. *Stress students' responsibility for their own behavior continually.* Since good behavior comes from good choices, clarify students' responsibility for their choices and behavior on a regular basis.

2. *Establish rules.* Rules are essential, and they should be established and agreed upon early in the term by the teacher and students. Rules should facilitate group achievement and group morale. Rules can be evaluated and changed, but as long as they are retained they must be enforced.

3. *Accept no excuses.* The teacher should not accept excuses for inappropriate behavior as long as the student is able to distinguish right from wrong. This is especially true if the student has made a commitment to a rule.

4. *Utilize value judgments.* When students exhibit inappropriate behavior, the teacher should call on them to make value judgments about the behavior. This enhances the students' responsibility to make better choices.

5. *Suggest suitable alternatives to inappropriate behavior.* The students should make the choice, which reinforces their responsibility.

6. *Enforce reasonable consequences.* Reasonable consequences must follow whatever behavior the students choose. The consequences of inappropriate behavior should not be erratic, emotional, sarcastic, or physically punishing. The consequences of good behavior should be satisfying to students. The teacher should never manipulate events or make excuses so that reasonable consequences do not occur after a behavior is exhibited.

7. *Be persistent.* The teacher must make sure, repeatedly and constantly, that students are committed to desirable behavior. The teacher must always help students make good choices and make value judgments about bad choices.

8. *Continually review.* During a classroom meeting separate from academic activities, discuss and develop these procedures. This is the time for stu-

dents and teacher to seek plausible solutions to problems together. Students should never be allowed to find fault with or place blame on others, to shout, or to threaten. If attention is directed to real matters of concern, a bonding or caring attitude between teacher and students may have a chance to take form.[36]

Student misbehavior is often inextricably linked with academic problems. The failing student, frustrated by an inability to function in the classroom, frequently expresses uneasiness by acting out. Too often the student is unaware of how to deal with the problem, the teacher is too burdened with other problems, and the school lacks the resources for helping the student and teacher. To correct an academic problem, the student, teacher, and school must make a specific commitment.[37] Glasser makes the point that teachers must be supportive of and meet with students who are beginning to exhibit difficulties, and they must get students involved in making rules, committing to the rules, and enforcing them. School must be a friendly, warm place, especially for students who have previously experienced failure in school. For Glasser, school reform is not about stimulating teachers and students to work harder. People, including students, will not be more productive unless what is being asked of them is psychologically satisfying. We must change schools—not by changing the length of the school day or school year or the amount of homework, but by making school more satisfying to students and more consistent with their interests so that they gain a sense of power, fulfillment, and importance in the classroom. Solutions to the problems of discipline and achievement are related to and based primarily on making students feel that someone listens to them, thinks about them, cares for them, and feels they are important.

Many of Glasser's ideas involve setting aside time for classroom meetings and group discussion. Glasser generally argues for three different types of meetings: social conduct meetings, at which teachers and students discuss the students' behavior; open-ended meetings, at which teachers and students discuss topics of intellectual significance; and curriculum meetings, at which teachers and students discuss how well students are doing relative to curricular objectives.

Reality therapy and choice theory coincide with the democratic model of teaching. Glasser sees teachers not as lecturers or leaders but rather as a facilitators and modern managers. A manager is a person who creates conditions under which children can control themselves and develop self-control. This idea is opposed to the traditional role of the teacher as someone who metes out punishments or consequences. Students are taught to accept responsibility for their actions and to visualize their own "quality world" (Glasser's term for self-discipline which, in effect, is a self-imposed ideal). The teacher can help students to accomplish this objective through the use of questioning, guiding, and brainstorming.

Teachers using this strategy change the structure of teaching by using learning teams, ignoring past failures, and focusing on present achievements. Glasser's Learning Team Model (table 7.3) is an attempt to express relevance by empowering students through involvement. It does away with competition and memorization, using a team model concept similar to a sports team model. The team model moves away from a short-term focus on rote learning to long-term

Table 7.3   Comparison of Learning-Team Approach and Traditional Approaches

Learning Team Model	Traditional Approach
1. Students gain a sense of belonging by working in heterogeneous teams.	1. Students work as individuals.
2. Students achieve success from motivation, see that knowledge is power, and want to work harder.	2. No motivation from belonging, no motivation if a student doesn't succeed. Knowledge is not seen as power.
3. Strong students feel fulfilled by helping weak students and feel the power and friendship associated with being part of a high-performing team.	3. Strong and weak students hardly get to interact with and know one another.
4. When a weak student contributes, it is helpful and need fulfilling.	4. Weak students contribute less and are not valued.
5. Students depend on themselves and the team, not just the teacher.	5. Students depend solely on the teacher. No incentive to help each other.
6. Learning teams build a structure for getting past superficial facts to vital knowledge.	6. Students are bored and don't want to work.
7. Teams choose how to prove they have learned the material, with encouragement from the teacher.	7. Teacher-designed evaluation encourages little more than studying for a test.
8. Teachers can change the responsibility levels associated with team membership. Sometimes all members get the team score, other times individual scores, to create incentive.	8. Students compete as individuals; winners and losers are evident.

Source: Richard T. Scarpaci, *A Case Study Approach to Classroom Management,* Figure 7.3, 113. Copyright © 2007. Reproduced by permission of Pearson Education, Inc.

assignments based on depth and involvement. Classes are viewed as teams, not as individuals, and assignments are structured to demand student cooperation in achieving established objectives. Students are given as much responsibility as they can handle. Glasser claims that any management strategy can be used to support choice theory.

Glasser's work continues to evolve. His concepts of reality therapy and choice theory have been refined with his publication of *The Quality School.* In this text he examines how the management of a school influences the behavior of the students, and in *Every Student Can Succeed* he offers specific strategies for teachers to use in creating quality schools.[38] The Glasser approach continues to be very popular with a wide variety of teachers and administrators. The straightforward approach requires teachers to:

1. Be involved with students on an ongoing basis; be connected to the students in terms of knowing their interests and abilities.

2. Focus on behavior and deal with "what happened," not "who is to blame."

3. Help students learn to accept responsibility for behavior. As suggested previously, *accept no excuses.*

4. Help the student evaluate the behavior.

5. Develop a plan for preventing the behavior from recurring.

6. Help the student make a commitment to change his or her behavior. This requires dialogue and a clear indication of the positive and negative consequences.

7. Monitor behavior on an ongoing basis.[39]

When to Use.   Choice theory and reality therapy are quite valuable when used as an intervention technique immediately after the occurrence of misbehavior. The first time the four questions are used, students may have difficulty responding. Students fear punishment and may be mystified by an approach that instead attempts to meet their needs through questioning. This approach can be used at any time, whether looking for immediate intervention or long-term prevention.

Strengths.   The strategy works with most because it is simple to master, requiring only the use of the four questions to intervene in any incident of misbehavior. The approach is effective with at-risk students because of its individual guidance approach. The process exposes students to an intervention strategy that also acts in a preventative capacity by causing students to reflect upon their inappropriate actions.

Weaknesses.   Many teachers feel uncomfortable in the role of a guidance counselor and lack the ability to achieve the intimacy needed to interact with students. Since there is no direct punishment involved in this approach, some teachers feel that it enables students to get away with misbehavior. The process takes an inordinate amount of time away from standardized class work. (See Case Study 7.1 to explore the underlying beliefs related to developing your own classroom management strategy.)

The following case discusses principles that can be relied on to assist in formulating your own management strategy. The beliefs presented may not be appropriate for everyone. Compare and analyze the various beliefs expressed on what goes into classroom management. Evaluate their effectiveness in relation to your own beliefs.

Case Study 7.1
Twelve Beliefs that Lead to Effective Management Strategies

Professor Patane, a calm, cultured, erudite man, began his lecture by saying that standard teaching practice can be viewed through a prism consisting of twelve beliefs that lead to effective classroom management. He claimed that these ideas were a compilation of various strategies and could be described as an assorted tote-bag approach to management. The beliefs could be categorized into three generalized areas: behaviors, understandings, and strategies. The *behaviors* are a composite of psychological beliefs, skills, and practices that effective teachers exhibit in common, that satisfy student needs. The *understandings* support the realization that self-discipline is the prime objective for behavioral management. Teachers who accept responsibility for both student success and student shortcomings encourage development of student internal controls and academic success. The third component, *strategies*, leads to specific management approaches such as the IOSIE method (see box 1.10). The beauty of these constructs is that they offer everyone an opportunity to create their own management strategy.

Jeanne Barca asked Professor Patane to explain what these twelve beliefs were. He said they were qualities that allow a teacher to use specific tactics and methods to manage classrooms effectively. He further explained that tactics differ from strategies in that they are short term and used during classroom episodes, while strategies are long-term plans focused on how to deliver instruction. Methods in this scenario become the fundamental structures behind how to manage instruction and behavior. They also form the theoretical beliefs used in developing the IOSIE method of behavioral analysis (Scarpaci, 2007). Putting these behaviors, understandings, and strategies into practice establishes teachers as effective classroom managers.

Professor Patane looked Jeanne squarely in the eyes and said, "Remember, no discipline program can be effective unless its theories can be put into practice. Your goal, Jeanne, is to develop a plan whose theories and practices can be translated into a useful diagnostic, corrective, and prescriptive tool. By building a management 'tote bag' you will develop your own method for instructional and behavioral classroom management. Just be sure that the method you choose is related to your own personality and beliefs." (Review box 1.12 Style, Personality, Beliefs, and Discipline Inventory.) Professor Patane then distributed the following list.

Twelve Beliefs of Effective Teachers

Behaviors
Effective teachers:
1. Have a teaching personality that allows them to discourage misbehavior and enhance learning.
2. Have mastered content and understand management approaches and pedagogical methods, while having high student expectations and an engaging teaching personality.
3. Apply positive, rather than negative, discipline.
4. Meet students' psychological needs.

Understandings
Effective teachers:
1. Recognize that authority can be constructive or unconstructive.
2. Are aware that the goal of discipline is self-discipline (internal control) and that teachers should teach ways to acquire self-discipline.
3. Know that the biggest problem in classrooms is not discipline, but rather a lack of procedures and a teacher's unwillingness to take responsibility for their students' learning.
4. Recognize that students choose their behavior and teachers choose their management style.

Strategies
Effective teachers:
1. Are aware that there are three approaches to resolving behavioral issues: a consequence approach, a group-guidance approach, and an individual-guidance approach.
2. Understand that to determine causality we must understand the different categories, types, and causes of misbehavior.

3. Know that individuals are an accumulation of choices and experiences.

4. Recognize that an effective management plan consists of generic strategies that may be called authoritarian, permissive, eclectic, group-guidance, or individual guidance. They can run the gamut from management models, such as assertive discipline, to judicial discipline and choice theory.

Discussion Topics and Questions to Ponder

1. Is there anything else that could go into a management strategy aside from behaviors, understandings and strategies? Explain your answer.

2. What did Professor Patane mean when he said that by putting these behaviors, understandings, and strategies into practice a teacher would become an effective classroom manager? How do you feel about this position?

3. Which one of the four behaviors in the list would you consider the most essential to effective teaching? Why?

4. Analyze the four understandings in the list, and describe the most relevant to instructional practice.

5. Explain what is meant in the twelfth belief, "An effective management plan consists of generic strategies that may be called authoritarian, permissive, eclectic, group-guidance, or individual guidance."

What would you do if . . . ?

1. You were asked to explain the relationship between box 1.12 and your development of an individual management plan.

2. You were asked to describe what you would put into your management plan.

3. You were asked to research and then describe the three management plans: assertive discipline, judicial discipline, and choice theory (mentioned in the twelfth belief)?

Implementing Alternative Approaches to Classroom Management

All six approaches that are discussed in this chapter have elements of prevention and intervention, and all, regardless of how firm or flexible they appear to be, require a set of rules, limitations, and consequences of behavior. In all the approaches students must complete academic work and they are held accountable for their behavior and work. A brief overview of the six approaches is shown in box 7.2.

All the approaches advocate having clear and well-communicated rules. The moderate teacher intervention (MTI) approaches rely on mutual trust and respect between teacher and students. They emphasize positive expectations of students; they have more faith in the students' ability to exhibit self-control and to work out the rules with their peers and the teacher. In contrast, the high teacher intervention (HTI) approaches (teacher-centered approaches) look to the teacher to take control of the classroom, quickly establish rules, and assert more power and authority with students.

Although all the approaches establish limitations, the MTI approaches permit greater latitude in enforcing rules and allow the students to share power with the teacher. All the approaches rely on consequences, but the HTI approaches advocate stricter imposition of generally more severe sanctions as a consequence of disobedience. Punishment for inappropriate behavior is permis-

---

Box 7.2   Overview of Classroom Management Models

High-Intervention Approaches

1. *Assertive Approach*
   - Firm, assertive approach
   - Insistence on appropriate behavior
   - Clear limits and consequences
   - Taking action promptly
   - Follow-through, checking, and reinforcing rules

2. *Applied Science/Instructional Practice Approach*
   - Identifying and enforcing school and classroom rules
   - Procedures for seat work, teacher-led activities, transition between activities
   - Purposeful academic instruction, student accountability
   - Procedures for assignments and monitoring student work

3. *Behavior Modification Approach*
   - Reinforcement through rewards
   - Constant and then intermittent reinforcement to produce the best results
   - Shaping desired behavior quickly and strongly
   - Modeling appropriate behavior
   - Use of verbal comments, observations, practice, prizes, etc.

Moderate-Intervention Approaches

4. *Group Management Approach/Effective Momentum*
   - Group focus and group management
   - On task, work involvement
   - With-it-ness, overlapping, smoothness, and momentum
   - Variety and challenging instruction
   - Teacher alertness, student accountability

5. *Acceptance Approach/Logical Consequences*
   - Acceptance of and belonging to a group
   - Student recognition and praise
   - Routines and limitations
   - Firmness and friendliness
   - Teacher leadership, corrective action by teacher

6. *Success Approach /Choice Theory/Reality Therapy*
   - Student success and achievement
   - Reasonable rules with reasonable consequences (some student input)
   - Student responsibility and self-direction
   - Good choices resulting in good behavior
   - Teacher support, fairness, and warmth

sible as long as it is logical and related to the severity of the disturbance. The MTI approaches impose sanctions but emphasize making students aware that their behavior influences others, helping them to examine their behavior and to identify the consequences of their misbehavior.

All the approaches hold students accountable for academic work. The HTI approaches limit students' socializing and group activities, determine academic tasks, and demand that they complete assignments. Students are told what is expected of them, and little time is spent on any activities other than academic work. The classroom is organized so that students' engagement in academic work is continuous. In the MTI approaches students are still held accountable for academic work, but they participate in planning the curriculum, and socializing is tolerated. Engagement in academic tasks is less intense, and work is often performed on a cooperative or group basis.

In choosing an approach, you must be objective about your personality and philosophy and what you are trying to accomplish. It is important that you be honest about yourself—acknowledging your strengths and weaknesses. To help determine the approach that is best, you must also consider your students—their developmental needs, abilities, and interests—and how they behave as a group. Adjustments in your approach may be required for certain classroom situations; reality, not theory, will dictate whether adjustments are necessary. Generally, HTI approaches are better for younger, more emotionally immature students; MTI approaches are better for older, more emotionally mature students.

Questions for Reflection

Some reform-minded educators argue that high academic standards and high expectations result in enhanced student achievement. Other educators who are more progressivist in orientation feel that schools need to connect academic content with the real-world problems of students. In a *Miami Herald* story (October 27, 2002), a reporter noted that teachers should change how they teach students to make classroom practices more culturally congruent in response to the diversity of American classrooms. Then the reporter quotes a University of South Florida professor discussing one strategy for working in a diverse classroom:

> Instead of classroom rules, the children . . . were presented with traditional African values associated with the Kwanzaa celebration, among them unity, self-determination, and faith. They also are encouraged to follow the "I got your back" concept of policing each other's behavior in the classroom.

Do you think this is an appropriate way to teach students who come from diverse environments? What might make it right for you? Wrong for you? Right for your students? Wrong for your students?

Some teachers turn to package programs that are discussed in the professional literature or advertised as "reforms" or quick fixes. Don't be fooled by the allure of such programs. It is wrong to assume that a process as complicated and multidimensional as managing students can be fully understood by reading a list of "do's and don'ts" or by attending a two-day workshop.

Certain rules are central to all the models, but they are conceptual and must be modified according to the classroom situation and personalities involved. The models should not be construed as set in stone, just as rules should not be viewed as inviolate. There are many gray areas involved in managing students that require common sense and maturity on the part of the teacher. The models, if taken literally, actually limit teacher discretion and judgment.

The point is that teachers need to be flexible and examine the models in relationship to their own classroom situations and personalities. Each of the models is supported by some research, and all provide a way for teachers to respond to real discipline problems. You will likely use some combination of the strategies in your approach to discipline. We seldom see teachers who are purists in terms of how to manage student behavior.

In considering what is best for you, you must consider your teaching style, your students' needs and abilities, and your school's policies. As you narrow your choices, remember that approaches overlap and are not mutually exclusive. Also remember that more than one approach may work for you. You may borrow ideas from various approaches and construct your own hybrid approach. The approach you choose should make sense to you on an intuitive basis. Don't let someone impose his or her teaching style or disciplinary approach on you. Remember, what works for one person (in the same school, even with the same students) may not work for another person because of the unique nature of personal chemistry.

As a new teacher, it is imperative that you begin by learning a relatively narrow set of skills, and perhaps one HTI approach and one MTI approach. Expand the number of approaches as you develop your professional repertoire of skills and your understanding of classroom dynamics.

Box 7.3 contains the *essential* survival management skills and the specific behaviors you *must* know how to exhibit. These are beginning points for the novice—a skill-based strategy. As you become more experienced, you will begin to shape and redefine your approach, and you will find that you focus more on instruction techniques to prevent problems than on the disciplinary skills to deal with misbehaviors.

Paul Burden identifies a large number of different low and moderate desist behaviors (skill 3 in table 7.4). They include a process whereby the teacher first attempts to provide situational assistance, then moves to a low-profile (mild) desist/response, and then to a moderate response for behaviors that persist.[40] Table 7.4 (on p. 356) provides an illustration of the behavior progression on the part of the teacher.

The recommended approach (and that of Burden) parallels the disciplinary sequence that the Joneses recommend in their comprehensive classroom management approach. Specifically, they argue that the teacher should follow the sequence below.

- *When misbehavior occurs:* Nonverbally try to stop a misbehavior when it first occurs (e.g., make eye contact or move closer to a student). In essence, start by using a low profile desist.

Box 7.3   Essential Teaching Skills and Behaviors

Skill 1: Teachers should organize instruction to maximize student time on task.
 Behavior 1: Start class on time.
 Behavior 2: Move around the room to monitor student behavior.
 Behavior 3: Establish clear procedures for turning in work.
 Behavior 4: Establish clear routines for transition times.

Skill 2: Teachers should identify and implement specific classroom rules.
 Behavior 1: Rules should be reasonable, enforceable, and understandable.
 Behavior 2: Rules must be taught to students. They must be rehearsed. The students
 must receive feedback on their rule comprehension.

Skill 3: Teachers should know how to use both low- and high-profile desists in dealing
with mild misbehavior. (Note: Low-profile desists stop misbehavior without drawing atten-
tion to it; high-profile desists stop misbehavior by drawing attention to it.)
 Behavior 1: Use misbehaving students' names as part of the classroom lesson (low
 profile).
 Behavior 2: Move close to the disruptive student (low profile).
 Behavior 3: Use nonverbal cues such as eye contact (low profile).
 When behaviors 1–3 do not work, attempt the following:
 Behavior 4: Say the student's name and direct the student toward appropriate and
 assigned tasks (high profile).
 Behavior 5: Give punishment (detention) for misbehavior (high profile).

Skill 4: Teachers should identify specific consequences for severe, chronic misbehavior.
Know how and when to use different types of punishment.

- *If misbehavior does not stop:* Ask the misbehaving student to state the rule
  he or she has broken.

- *If misbehavior does not stop then:* Provide the misbehaving student with an
  option to stop the misbehavior or develop a plan for improving behavior.

- *If misbehavior does not stop then:* Ask the student to move to a designated
  area and develop a plan that addresses the following questions:

  1. What rule did I violate?

  2. What specific behaviors violated the rule?

  3. What problems did my behavior cause for others in the classroom?

  4. What can I do to be more responsible?

  5. How can the teacher help me obey the rule?[41]

As you can see, there is a progression in the degree to which the student
must clearly articulate the nature of the rule infraction. Remember, your goal is
to enhance student responsibility and self-control. The way that becomes possible is by getting students to think about their misbehavior.

Table 7.4   A Three-Step Response Plan to Misbehavior Using the Principle of Least Intervention

Teacher response	Step 1 *Provide Situational Assistance*	Step 2 *Use Mild Responses*	Step 3 *Use Moderate Responses*
Purpose	To help the student cope with the instructional situation and keep the student on task	To take nonpunitive actions to get the student back on task	To remove desired stimuli to decrease unwanted behavior
Sample Actions	• Remove distracting objects. • Provide support with routines. • Reinforce appropriate behaviors. • Boost student interest. • Provide cues. • Help the student over hurdles. • Redirect the behavior. • Alter the lesson. • Provide a nonpunitive time-out. • Modify the classroom environment.	**Nonverbal Responses** • Ignore the behavior. • Use nonverbal signals. • Stand near the student. • Touch the student. **Verbal Responses** • Call on the student during the lesson. • Use humor. • Send an I-message. • Use positive phrasing. • Remind students of the rules. • Give students choices. • Ask "What should you be doing?" • Give a verbal reprimand.	**Logical Consequences** • Withdraw privileges. • Change the seat assignment. • Have the student reflect on the behavior and write down his or her thoughts. • Place student in time-out. • Hold the student for detention. • Contact the parents. • Have the student visit the principal.

Source: Paul R. Burden, *Classroom Management*, 4th ed., 219. Copyright © 2009 John Wiley & Sons. Reproduced with permission of John Wiley and Sons, Inc.

Guidelines for Using Punishment

According to Good and Brophy, a number of general principles apply to meting out punishment:

1. The threat of punishment is usually more effective than punishment itself, especially when phrased in such a way that there are unknown consequences.

2. Punishment should be threatened or warned before being implemented (but teachers should threaten only once!)

3. The punishment should be accompanied with positive statements of expectations or rules, focusing on what the students should be doing.

4. Punishment should be combined with negative reinforcement, so that the student must improve to avoid the punishment.

5. Punishment should be systematic and deliberate.[42]

Educators also point out that teachers should avoid punishing while angry or emotional; punish when inappropriate behavior begins (don't wait until things build up); and make their motivation clear (without preaching or overexplaining) while the student is being punished.[43] Two other suggestions are worth noting: First, do not punish an entire class or group because of the misbehavior of one student, and avoid excessive punishment. These practices are signs of weakness, and eventually the class or group will unite against you.) See Tips for Teachers 7.2 for more punishment strategies.

It would be nice to say that teacher decisions are usually rational and reflective. Unfortunately, this is not so. Many managerial problems are caused by teachers themselves: by overreaction to minor incidents, by ignoring small problems and letting them build until they are out of control, or by meting out inappropriate punishment (mismatching the incident and response to the incident).

Educators would have you believe that teachers' decisions in classrooms and reactions to student behavior are reflective in nature and can be understood within a psychological context of prior beliefs, personal perspectives, and embedded theories of behavior.[44] The fact is, the complexity and immediacy of many classroom situations require teachers to make intuitive rather than reflective or clinical decisions. Thus, disciplinary decisions, which are often complex and require immediate decisions, are likely to be more reactive than prescriptive and more influenced by prior social experiences and personality than by well-thought-out techniques.

The guidelines listed here can be used for all disciplinary approaches. Underlying the guidelines is the idea that punishment should be flexible and tailored to the specific student and situation.

1. *Don't threaten the impossible.* Make sure the punishment can be carried out. Telling a student to stay after class at 3:00 PM when you have a 3:30 appointment with the dentist illustrates that you reacted hastily and cannot follow through.

2. *Don't assign extra homework as punishment.* This creates dislike for homework as well as for the subject.

3. *Be sure the punishment follows the offense as soon as possible.* Don't impose punishment two days after the student misbehaves.

4. *When possible, be sure the punishment fits the misbehavior.* Don't overreact to mild misbehavior or underplay or ignore serious misbehavior.

TIPS FOR TEACHERS 7.2

Strategies for Managing Problem Students

Following are general strategies for dealing with problem students, sometimes called "difficult" students, based on the experience of teachers. Although originally developed for junior high school inner-city students, the strategies apply to most school settings and grade levels.

1. Accept the students as they are, but build on and accentuate their positive qualities.

2. Be yourself, since these students can recognize phoniness and take offense at such deceit.

3. Be confident; take charge of the situation, and don't give up in front of the students.

4. Provide structure, since many of these students lack inner control and are restless and impulsive.

5. Explain your rules and routines so students understand them. Be sure your explanations are brief; otherwise you lose your effectiveness and you appear to be defensive or preaching. Also, explain why punished behavior is unacceptable.

6. Communicate the positive expectations that you expect the students to learn and that you require for academic work.

7. Rely on motivation and not on your prowess to maintain order; an interesting lesson can keep the students on task.

8. Be a firm friend, but maintain a psychological and physical distance so your students know you are still the teacher.

9. Keep calm and keep your students calm, especially when conditions become tense or upsetting. It may be necessary to delay action until after class, when emotions have been calmed.

10. Administer punishment, whenever possible, privately.

11. Anticipate behavior: Being able to judge what will happen if you or a student decide on a course of action may allow you to curtail many problems.

12. Expect, but don't accept, misbehavior. Learn to cope with misbehavior, but don't get upset or feel inadequate about it.

13. Follow through on consequences for misbehavior. It is acceptable to threaten once, but NOT *repeatedly.*

14. Inform students ahead of time that certain types of behavior will be punished.

Source: Adapted from Jeanne Ellis Ormrod, *Educational Psychology: Developing Learners*, 4th ed. (Upper Saddle River, NJ: Merrill Prentice-Hall, 2003); Allan C. Ornstein, "Teaching the Disadvantaged," *Educational Forum* (January 1967), 215–223; Allan C. Ornstein, "The Education of the Disadvantaged," *Educational Research* (June 1982), 197–221.

5. *Be consistent with punishment.* If you punish one student for something, don't ignore it when another student does the same thing. However, students and circumstances differ, and there should be room for modification.

6. *Don't use double standards when punishing.* You should treat both genders, as well as low-achieving and high-achieving students, the same way. (Perhaps the only allowance or difference can be made with emotionally disturbed children.) Avoid having teacher's "pets."

7. *Don't personalize the situation.* React to misbehavior, not to the student. Do not react to the student's anger or personal remarks. He or she usually doesn't mean them and is emotionally reacting. Stay focused on the deed. Remind the student he doesn't mean what he is saying and that things will worsen unless he calms down. When the student is out of control, the main thing is to get him to control himself. Punishment comes later, if it is required, after the student is calm.

8. *Document all serious incidents.* This is especially important if the misbehavior involves sending the student out of the room or possible suspension.[45]

Preventing Misbehaviors through Feedback, Trust, and Communication

David Johnson has written several books on interpersonal relations, cooperation, and self-actualization. His methods of enhancing self-awareness, mutual trust, and communication among people serve as excellent preventive strategies. Johnson's methods correspond with flexible and democratic approaches to discipline such as the acceptance and success approaches. They might be used by anyone who wishes to build a humanistic classroom based on student rapport and understanding. The specific methods can be applied on a one-to-one basis or on a group basis in which teachers emphasize interpersonal relations and cooperative processes.[46]

Building Self-Awareness through Feedback

Feedback tells students what impact their actions have on others. It is important for the teacher to provide feedback in a way that does not threaten the student. The more threatened and defensive the student becomes, the more likely it is that he or she will not understand the feedback correctly. Increasing a student's self-awareness through feedback gives the students a basis for making informed choices in future behavior. Follow these guidelines:

1. *Focus feedback on behavior, not on personality:* Refer to what the student does, not to what you believe her traits to be. The former is a response to what you see or hear, but the latter is an inference or interpretation about character.

2. *Focus feedback on objective descriptions, not on subjective judgments.* Refer to what occurs, not to your judgments of right or wrong, good or bad. Say, "You are not spelling the word correctly" or "We cannot hear you,"

rather than "You are a terrible speller" or "You don't know how to speak up in public."

3. *Focus feedback on a specific situation, not on abstract behavior.* Say, "Your homework has not been turned in for three days" instead of "You are so irresponsible." Feedback tied to a specific situation leads to self-awareness. Feedback that is abstract is open to interpretation and is often misunderstood.

4. *Focus feedback on the present, not on the past.* The more immediate the feedback, the more effective it is. Say, "You are becoming angry now as I talk to you," rather than "Sometimes you become angry."

5. *Focus feedback on actions that the person can change.* It does little good to tell a person that you don't like the color of his or her eyes, for example. This is something that cannot be changed.

Paul Chance provides the following caveat:

> [Although] positive feedback usually results in faster learning and tends to uplift and motivate, . . . negative feedback tends to depress and demoralize. This is not to say that all feedback needs to be positive. Pointing out where a student has gone astray is not only helpful but sometimes essential. But if most feedback is negative, the prevailing mood is negative.[47]

Developing and Maintaining Trust

To build a healthy relationship among students and between students and teacher, a climate of mutual trust must grow and develop. Fears of rejection or betrayal must be reduced, and acceptance, support, and respect must be promoted. A study by Gregory and Ripski found that students' perceptions of their teachers as trustworthy authority figures mediated defiant behavior and reduced the need for discipline.[48] Trust, like order, is not something that can be built once and forgotten about; it constantly changes and constantly needs nourishment. Consider these ideas about trust:

1. *Building trust.* Trust begins as people take the risk of disclosing more and more of their thoughts and feelings to each other. If they do not receive acceptance or support, they back off from the relationship. If they receive acceptance or support, they will continue to risk self-disclosure, and the relationship continues to grow.

2. *Being trusting.* The level of trust that develops between two people is related to both individuals' willingness and ability to be trusting. Each must be willing to risk the consequences of revealing oneself to and depending on the other person. Each must be openly accepting and supporting of the other to ensure that he or she experiences beneficial consequences from the risk taken.

3. *Trusting appropriately.* A person must be able to size up a situation and make a wise judgment about when, whom, and how much to trust. Trust is appropriate when a person is reasonably confident that the other person will not react in a way that will be harmful.

4. *Trusting as a self-fulfilling prophecy.* Assumptions affect an individual's behavior. That behavior often elicits the expected reactions from the other person, and the assumptions become a self-fulfilling prophecy. If you make other people feel they can trust you, they probably will.

Communicating Effectively

All behavior conveys messages. A person sends messages to evoke a response from the receiver. The messages and responses are verbal and nonverbal. Effective communication takes place when the receiver interprets the sender's messages in the way that was intended; effective communication enhances understanding and cooperation among individuals. Ineffective communication arises when there is a discrepancy between what the sender meant and what the receiver thought the sender meant. This reduces understanding and cooperation. Mutual trust enhances the possibility of effective communication; distrust is a primary cause of miscommunication. Understanding communicative tools and strategies helps teachers to develop individual learning methods such as discovery learning and social interaction to develop peer collaboration.[49] Skill in sending messages can increase communication between teachers and students. Follow these guidelines for effective communication:

1. *Use the first person singular.* Take responsibility for your own ideas or feelings. People doubt messages that use terms like "most people" and "some of your classmates." Say, "I think . . ." or "I feel . . ."

2. *Make messages complete and specific.* People often make incorrect assumptions about what their listeners know, leave out steps in describing their thinking, and do not mention specifics or ideas that would clarify their intent.

3. *Make verbal and nonverbal messages congruent.* Communication problems arise when a person's verbal and nonverbal messages are contradictory.

4. *Be varied in delivering key ideas.* Use more than one means of communication, such as verbal and nonverbal cues, to reinforce your message.

5. *Ask for feedback.* The only way to learn how a person is actually receiving and interpreting your message is to seek feedback from the receiver.

6. *Consider the listener's frame of reference.* The same information might be interpreted differently by a child than by an adult. It may be necessary to use different words or different nonverbal cues depending on the listener's age, maturity level, educational level, and cultural background.

7. *Make messages concrete.* It is important to be descriptive, to use verbs ("You *worked* hard on this project"), adverbs ("Your homework is due *tomorrow*"), and adjectives ("Marco is an *excellent* student") to communicate your feelings clearly.

8. *Describe behavior without evaluating it.* Describe the student's behavior ("You are interrupting Alisha") rather than evaluating it ("You are self-centered and won't listen to anyone else's ideas").[50]

During the past several years an alarming number of troubling incidents have occurred at schools involving violent actions by students. Great debate rages about who is at fault: teachers, parents, the students themselves, or society. Affixing blame seldom solves problems.

To just describe actions or interventions that teachers and school personnel can take to prevent Columbine-like episodes does not provide solutions. Many actions may be well intentioned but "off the mark." The key is to better match solutions with problems—a process that requires thought, dialogue, an understanding of young people, and research on what works.

Basically, there are two classes of intervention: root cause interventions and peripheral interventions. In my judgment, some of the so-called "cures" outlined in box 7.4 have merit; others are useless; still others are foolish and almost certain to cause more harm than good. But they are all peripheral interventions in that none of them (not even the useful ones) succeed in getting to the root of the problem. If a peripheral intervention (like gun control or metal detectors, for example) proves to be effective, there is no reason why it cannot be utilized. However, we must realize that the deeper underlying problem will remain, and before we implement any kind of intervention we must make sure that there is evidence supporting its use. What is immediately apparent is that most of these "cures" are not based on solid evidence; rather, they rest on emotion, wishful thinking, bias, and political expediency.[51] (See Case Study 7.2 to help you determine how you might behave when faced with common management problems.)

Box 7.4   Politically Expedient Interventions

Problems

- There is not enough moral training in our educational institutions.
- There is too much violent imagery in the media.
- There are too many guns that are too easily available.
- Youngsters are not respectful enough.
- Some students act differently from what is considered the norm.

Quick-Fix Solutions

- Allow prayer in schools, or post the Ten Commandments in every classroom.
- Clamp down on violent movies, TV, and video games.
- Institute more stringent gun control.
- Make rules that require students to call teachers "sir" and "ma'am."
- Identify students who behave abnormally and either keep them under surveillance, remove them from the school, or subject them to intensive therapy until they are able to be like everybody else.

Source: Adapted from Eliot Aronson, *Nobody Left to Hate: Teaching Compassion after Columbine* (New York: Henry Holt, 2000).

This chapter concludes with a discussion about prevention. Many teachers think that the key to classroom management is in knowing how to deal with students who are disruptive. But as we've said numerous times, the real key is to know how to prevent problems from occurring, or at least how to lessen the likelihood that they will occur. Prevention comes from creating an environment in which students are welcomed and learning is encouraged. (See Tips for Teachers 7.3 on p. 365 for suggestions for analyzing preventive measures.) To drive home the point about prevention, here is a vignette about a (former) first-year teacher who has drawn national attention as a result of her work with urban students. ABC News, on a *Prime Time Live* segment, captured the story of Susan Gruell, a first-year teacher in Long Beach, California.[52]

> Ms. Gruell was struggling. Her students, at least some of them, wanted her to fail, and some even wanted to make her cry or break down in front of the class. One day, Ms. Gruell confiscated a student note that depicted in caricature a black boy with big lips. The caricature was derisive and degrading. Many teachers would have responded with high teacher control (and punishment) procedures. Ms. Gruell did not. She reacted, instead, out of a learning paradigm. She wanted students to see what the note meant in personal and interpersonal terms. She introduced the concept of prejudice, drawing connections to the Holocaust and the Nazi dehumanization of Jews. Her passion to help her students learn about why people act as they do rather than punish them for acting as they do started a journey for her class that was truly extraordinary. Over the next weeks and months they studied prejudice and injustice, in their lives and in the lives of others. The students were pulled outside of themselves to connect with lives of others such as Anne Frank and Zloto Vilapovich, people whose lives were changed or ended by prejudice. In the process, the students acquired an incentive to behave responsibly and maturely. They became so invested in their work that they no longer had any reason to misbehave.

See Case Study 7.2 to explore how to deal with prejudice in a classroom setting.

The following case discusses the process that should be taken when faced with classroom management problems. It suggests that the "twelve beliefs of effective teachers" can be relied on to assist in formulating one's own management strategy. It also advocates the use of the IOSIE method (see chapters 1 and 10). Mini problems are presented that require appropriate solutions. Compare and analyze the solutions offered and see if one's beliefs, understandings and strategies underlie the process used.

Case Study 7.2
Preparing for Management Problems

Jeanne Barca was really excited when she left Professor Patane's class. For the first time she felt she had a grip on how to manage a class. She had previously learned about the IOSIE analysis model (see box 1.10), which she saw as a road map to resolving whatever problem she might encounter. The IOSIE model, when combined with the twelve beliefs (see Case

Study 7.1), would give her the confidence she needed to face any situation; especially now that she had been offered an interview for a position at the Cambridge Comprehensive K–12 School. She had been briefed by her university supervisor that the school had various classroom management problems that the principal was sure to highlight during her interview.

Upon her arrival Jeanne was greeted by the principal, Dr. Rodriguez. He offered Jeanne a seat and began by describing the school, focusing on his belief that to be a successful teacher you had to be able to manage behavior as well as instruction. The interview followed the basic stages that Jeanne had been taught. It began with an introductory phase, followed by a question about her background in order to establish her qualifications. Finally, Dr. Rodriguez came to the focus of the interview. He handed Jeanne a list containing typical problems that occurred at school and in class. He told Jeanne he would give her ten minutes to review the list and then he would call upon her to offer her solutions.

The first problem concerned students (both primary and secondary) who constantly asked to leave the room to go to the restroom. Using IOSIE, Jeanne first had to identify the problem. It could be either a physical problem or just mischievousness. She decided to respond that in either case she would speak with the student privately and explain that he or she was missing too much instructional time and could not leave the room again without a doctor's note.

The second problem concerned a fourth grader who was inciting violence due to his use of racial slurs directed at his classmates. Again Jeanne identified the problem as ignorance on the part of the child, who apparently did not understand that name calling can hurt. She would solve the problem by using a group guidance approach that would allow all the children to see how bad racial slights could be. She would read *The Diary of Anne Frank* aloud in class and have the children discuss it.

The third problem dealt with the theft of outer jackets taken from student lockers in the high school building. Jeanne thought and said that the problem was one of plant security and, short of giving lessons on honesty, she could see very little that she could accomplish.

The fourth problem dealt with secondary students who were absent on Mondays and Fridays. Jeanne felt that once she could identify a pattern, she would have to ask for assistance to address the problem. The solution she proposed involved working with the attendance officer and guidance counselor to let the students know that school was a five-day proposition (despite the fact that some school board members had been calling for a four-day week as a money-saving strategy).

The final problem dealt with complaints by other teachers that her classes left the room filthy and that desks had been written on. Jeanne would try to identify the students responsible, have them clean the room, and notify their parents of the vandalism.

Dr. Rodriguez ended the interview by asking Jeanne if she could define what the real goal of discipline was.

Discussion Topics and Questions to Ponder

1. Was Jeanne really prepared for this interview? Explain your answer.

2. Was Jeanne justified in following the IOSIE model as a guide for her responses? What other approaches could she have taken?

3. Look at problem number two in the list Dr. Rodriguez gave to Jeanne. Is group guidance the best approach to take when combating violence caused by derogatory remarks about a person's race? Justify your answer.

4. Was Jeanne too harsh in resolving problem number four? What else could she have done?

5. Analyze Jeanne's solutions and determine which beliefs, understandings, and strategies she used in her decision-making process.

What would you do if . . . ?

1. Dr. Rodriguez asked you to define what the real goal of discipline was.

2. You saw students smoking on school grounds in direct violation to school guidelines.

3. You were asked to write a brief description of the process you would use to resolve classroom management problems.

TIPS

F O R   T E A C H E R S

7.3

Suggestions for Analyzing Preventive Measures

Some of the causes of misbehavior are beyond your control. Knowing what measures to take to avoid common discipline problems and to handle problematic student behaviors will increase your time for teaching and your general effectiveness as a teacher. Here are suggestions for analyzing your measures for preventing student misbehavior:

1. Meet privately with other teachers to discuss problems and successful strategies for dealing with difficult students.

2. Identify and analyze the strengths of colleagues in dealing with discipline problems. Watch other teachers teach. What works for them with some students you find difficult to teach?

3. Determine which supervisors and administrators will provide support when necessary. What approach to dealing with misbehavior do they subscribe to?

4. Ask another teacher, supervisor, or administrator to visit your classroom on a regular basis to analyze your classroom management approach.

5. Communicate with parents on a regular basis to learn about their management philosophies for purposes of support and follow-up in the class.

6. Keep informed on current legal issues concerning discipline. Read education journals and state law digests; talk to union representatives.

7. Document carefully all serious student behavior problems.

8. Evaluate your expectations about your disciplinary measures and review what you ought to accomplish.

Source: Adapted from Daniel L. Duke and Adrienne M. Meckel, *Teacher's Guide to Classroom Management* (New York: Random House, 1984).

This chapter introduced a great deal of information about how to manage students. Use that knowledge selectively. You need to have control of a classroom in order for students to learn. But you also really need to use good instructional strategies (and good planning), and you need to use prevention strategies and deal with problems when even the best plans fail.

The relationship between good classroom management and student learning is something that even students understand. Almost all the students you teach want and expect you to have control of the class so that they can learn. A *Christian Science Monitor* article noted that 43 percent of teenagers believe that misbehavior of peers is hurting their learning. Equally important, 83 percent of all teachers and administrators assert that the major barrier to success of new teachers is classroom management.[53] Far too many new teachers are oversensitive to what misbehavior means (usually it is a ploy to get attention; it is not personally directed at the teacher) and are apprehensive about taking action. If you watch good classroom managers, you will notice that they do not take personally what students do (though they may reflect on what it means!), and they act to deal with misbehavior before it spreads. They also try to have a meaningful relationship with their students. Students who know you and know that you believe in them are much easier to manage. Students who are engaged by what you plan as learning activities will be more on-task and successful.

Theory into Practice

To move from theory to the practice of good management and discipline, you must consider the overview or wrap-up questions in box 7.5. Ideally you should be able to say *yes* to all thirty of the questions. This will probably not be the case if you have a problem managing students. More than five negative responses suggests that you are probably contributing to your own problem and/or that you are heading for bigger problems unless you take corrective action. Ask yourself these questions about each of your students.

Box 7.5   Classroom Management Checklist

	Yes	No
1. Background Information		
a. Do I know the student's personal needs as a learner?	☐	☐
b. Have I examined the student's records?	☐	☐
c. Have I spoken to colleagues (other teachers) about the student?	☐	☐
d. Is the student's home life psychologically safe and secure? (Does he or she eat a good breakfast, get enough sleep, have a quiet place to work, and so on?)	☐	☐
e. Do I know which peers influence the student and which students he or she influences?	☐	☐
2. Attitude		
a. Do I interact positively with the student?	☐	☐
b. Do I listen to the student?	☐	☐
c. Do I show respect toward the student?	☐	☐
d. Do I provide helpful feedback?	☐	☐
e. Do I communicate high expectations to the student?	☐	☐
f. Do I compliment or praise the student when it is appropriate?	☐	☐
g. Do I recognize (call on) the student in class?	☐	☐
h. Do I emphasize the strengths of the student in front of the class?	☐	☐

3. Routines and Procedures	**Yes**	**No**
a. Have the routines or rules been clearly stated to the student?	☐	☐
b. Are the classroom routines appropriate and succinct?	☐	☐
c. Is there consistent routine in the classroom that the student can understand and model?	☐	☐
d. Are the routines enforced equally with all students, including the student exhibiting inappropriate behavior?	☐	☐
e. Have I been clear about the consequences of inappropriate behavior?	☐	☐
f. Are the consequences fair and consistent with the misbehavior?	☐	☐
g. Do I remain calm when the student exhibits inappropriate behavior?	☐	☐

4. Instruction

a. Are the instructional demands appropriate to the ability and needs of the student?	☐	☐
b. Are the students interested in the classroom tasks?	☐	☐
c. Does each student understand how to do the homework?	☐	☐
d. Are special academic provisions (enrichment, tutorial) made for the students?	☐	☐

5. Preventive Measures

a. Have I followed through with my warnings to the students?	☐	☐
b. Have I changed a student's seat when problems warrant such a change?	☐	☐
c. Have I spoken to a student privately when misbehavior needs to be discussed?	☐	☐
d. Am I willing to spend extra time talking to and getting to know each student outside of class?	☐	☐
e. Have I communicated with each student's parent(s) or guardian(s)? Is there consistent follow-up with them?	☐ ☐	☐ ☐
f. Have I spoken to the guidance counselor or dean of discipline for advice about students who misbehave?	☐	☐

CONCLUSIONS

- Six approaches to establishing and maintaining good discipline are presented in this chapter. All of them establish clear rules and expectations, all include recommendations for preventive measures, and all are positive and practical. They differ in the degree of control exercised by the teacher and in the emphasis on tasks.

- Which approach or combination of approaches a teacher adopts largely depends on the teacher's philosophy, personality, teaching style, and teaching situation. Teachers should begin their teaching by learning one high-level and one moderate-level intervention strategy extremely well. Do not try to use all of them until these first two approaches are fully mastered.

- Punishment is sometimes necessary to enforce rules and regulations. The punishment you choose should fit the situation and take into consideration the developmental stage of the student. It should also be in line with school policy.
- Preventive measures for maintaining and enhancing discipline are based on the need to curtail classroom problems before they become disruptive and affect teaching.

KEY TERMS

acceptance approach	desist techniques	negative reinforcers
applied science approach	group managerial approach	overlapping positive reinforcers
assertive approach	instructional practice approach	reality therapy
behavior modification approach	modeling	success approach
choice theory		with-it-ness

DISCUSSION QUESTIONS

1. What goals do you expect classroom management to achieve?
2. What approaches to classroom management do you prefer? Why?
3. How do a teacher's personality characteristics affect his or her disciplinary strategies?
4. Under what conditions, if any, might you touch a student? Under what conditions, if any, would you use corporal punishment?
5. Which preventive measures discussed in the chapter appear to coincide best with your personality and philosophy?
6. Discuss in class how you would respond as a teacher to the following classroom situations: (a) a student constantly calls out; (b) a student refuses to do work; (c) a student uses improper language as an affront to a classmate; (d) a student begins to argue with another student.
7. Prepare a list of preventive disciplinary techniques and common errors of discipline. Discuss them in class. Which common errors could have been prevented, with which preventive techniques?

MINI-CASES FROM THE FIELD

Case One:
Assertive Approach (High Level of Teacher Control)

After visiting and observing your seventh grade math class, your supervisor informs you that she is not satisfied with your approach to class management. She suggests that you should move away from the assertive discipline model you have been using. She feels you are restricting the students' intellectual growth by using such a high teacher-control approach to classroom management. She suggest you choose a moderate teacher intervention approach utilizing a group management model.

1. Prepare a response to your supervisor in which you refute her claim that a high level of teacher control restricts intellectual growth.

2. Write a rebuttal as if you were the supervisor, explaining the weaknesses of assertive discipline.

3. Explain the differences between a moderate teacher intervention model and a model of high-level teacher control.

4. Which of these two models would you select? Justify your reasons.

5. As a compromise, could these two approaches be commingled? Explain your answer.

Case Two:
Behavioral Modification Approach (High Level of Teacher Intervention)

Your class is not doing well academically. You have reflected on your students' behavior and have come to the conclusion that they appear to share a value system that advocates that "might is right" and "do unto others before they do unto you." You have seen evidence throughout the school year that demonstrates the correctness of your judgment. José, a known bully in your high school social studies class, is constantly singing and disturbing the class. You have spoken to him politely and have been rebuffed by his response that he is not disturbing anyone. José has even gone as far as to tell you to ask the class if anyone is upset with his singing.

1. How could you use behavior modification to curb José's actions without taking away his democratic right of free speech?

2. Describe some positive and negative reinforcers you might use.

3. Explain how you would implement a contracting approach with José.

4. Identify the specific misbehavior and propose a plan to eliminate it. Explain your reasoning.

5. How could you model appropriate behavior for this class?

Case Three:
Acceptance Approach/Logical Consequences (Moderate Level of Teacher Intervention)

Bobby is a fourth-grade youngster who has done everything he could to undermine your class management. He has tested your patience on numerous occasions. He constantly calls out and requests that you call on him. When you do, he says he really doesn't know the answer to the question you had posed. When you speak to him about his behavior he refuses to talk and looks out the window. You have decided to use an acceptance approach based on the use of logical consequences to alleviate this situation.

1. Discuss four steps you would use that would be approved in this model.

2. Dreikurs identified four mistaken goals to which students may aspire in order to obtain status and recognition. Discuss those mistaken goals as they apply to Bobby's behavior.

3. Describe some logical consequences that might alter Bobby's behavior.

4. What rule might you establish for this class?

5. How might Bobby react to a rule that called for isolation when he disturbs the class?

Case Four:
Success Approach/Choice Theory/Reality Therapy (Moderate Level of Teacher Intervention)

Betty, a third-grade youngster and class leader, had refused to allow her classmate June an opportunity to play "jump rope" with the rest of her class. June, who is much smaller and less articulate than Betty, began to cry. Upon seeing June crying, Betty began encouraging everyone to laugh and make fun of June. As the lunch-duty teacher you took both Betty and June aside and spoke to them in a corner of the school play area. You then proceeded to question Betty, utilizing the four questions central to reality therapy.

1. A colleague who had seen you using the reality therapy questions with the children during lunch recess asked you to explain it to him. Outline your response.

2. Your colleague also asked you to justify your questioning technique as opposed to the punishment he would have inflicted for the child's misbehavior. How would you justify your actions?

3. How would you handle Betty if she tried to explain why she didn't want to play with June?

4. When you asked Betty what she was doing, she just looked at you. What would you do then?

5. How would you respond if your colleague said that your approach took too much time and that he would have simply not allowed Betty to continue playing? What do you think of your colleague's approach?

Case Five:
Guidelines for Using Punishment

Children in your tenth-grade social studies class have very poor social skills. They make statements to each other that lack any empathy or concern for the feelings of their classmates. They are constantly pushing each other and allowing their aggressive tendencies to direct their actions. Clark, a learning-disabled child, has been mainstreamed into your class. He appears to be frustrated in his attempts to keep up with the class work. His classmates show no empathy and basically ignore him. This frustrates him, causing him to act out and lie about his class work. You have attempted to control his misconduct by talking to him, but he has not responded positively.

You have also found that your class is becoming lethargic and lacking in positive enthusiasm. You are not sure which is worse: the lethargy or the acting out. No one volunteers for anything, and they are only excited when the dismissal bell sounds.

1. Identify the problems facing the teacher of this class.

2. How can the teacher improve learning and encourage self-discipline?

3. What types of punishments would fit the misbehavior evidenced in this class?

4. Describe the rule that should be used to turn this class around.

5. Which is worse: lethargy or acting out? Explain your answer.

FIELD EXPERIENCE ACTIVITIES

1. Arrange a conference with a teacher who is known as a "good" disciplinarian. Which of the approaches described in the chapter does the teacher's approach resemble? What are the constructive or positive factors in the teacher's methods and strategies?

2. Arrange to visit a nearby school to observe a teacher. Does that teacher have any special "tricks of the trade" for preventing disorder or confusion? What methods do you like? Dislike? Why? What low-profile desists are used? What moderate and high-profile approaches are used?

3. Create a set of classroom rules for your first teaching assignment. Are they clear? Reasonable? Understandable? Ask a peer to critique them. Describe how you would teach these rules to your students.

4. Visit a neighboring school and ask a teacher in your subject area to offer a solution for the following management episodes. Compare the answers to what you would have offered as a solution. Each of the cases can also be reviewed in class, using a role-play format to arrive at appropriate solutions.

   a. A child constantly asks to leave the room to go to the bathroom.

   b. A student makes fun of smaller classmates and calls them derogatory names.

   c. A sixth grader claims a classmate took her pen and refuses to return it.

   d. A fourth grader is crying in class and claims that no one likes her.

   e. A tenth grader is always late to class and never has assignments completed on time.

   f. You see students smoking on school grounds in direct violation to school guidelines.

   g. A student is absent from your class two or three times each week.

   h. A kindergarten child cries all the time, making it difficult for you to complete a lesson.

   i. Items are constantly missing from the area where students store their coats, boots, and umbrellas.

   j. A student in your third grade class is very fearful of strange adults.

RECOMMENDED READING

Burden, Paul. *Classroom Management: Creating a Successful K–12 Learning Community,* 4th ed. New York: Wiley, 2009.

A thoughtful research-based approach to classroom management that is appropriate for a wide range of teaching contexts.

Charles, Carol M. *Building Classroom Discipline,* 10th ed. Prentice-Hall, 2010.

Outlines various disciplinary models and practices.

Emmer, Edmond T., et al. *Classroom Management for Secondary Teachers*, 6th ed. Boston: Allyn & Bacon, 2003.

A business-academic approach to organizing and controlling students that includes several practical techniques for secondary teachers.

Evertson, Carol M., et al. *Classroom Management for Elementary Teachers*, 7th ed. Boston: Allyn & Bacon, 2006.

This companion book to the one above is mainly for elementary teachers.

Scarpaci, Richard T. *A Case Study Approach to Classroom Management*. Boston: Allyn & Bacon, 2007.

Surveys various management approaches and offers a simplified behavioral management strategy called IOSIE.

Weinstein, Carol. *Secondary Classroom Management: Lessons from Research and Practice*, 4th ed. New York: McGraw-Hill, 2010.

An applied science approach to the research on classroom management and discipline.

Weinstein, Carol. *Elementary Classroom Management: Lessons from Research and Practice*, 5th ed. New York: McGraw-Hill, 2010.

A companion book to the secondary text that focuses on the elementary grades.

Wolfgang, Charles. *Solving Discipline and Classroom Management Problems*, 7th ed. New York: John Wiley, 2008.

A wealth of information about methods and practical advice for solving classroom discipline problems with a wide range of management strategies that have been proven successful in the field.

8

Academic Standards and Student Assessment

FOCUS POINTS

1. Recognizing that academic standards influence assessment.
2. Grasp the importance of understanding the methods for testing reliability and validity.
3. Understanding the differences between norm-referenced measurements and criterion-referenced measurements.
4. Learning how classroom tests can be improved, which short-answer test questions generate the most controversy and why, and how the teacher can improve the writing and scoring of essay test questions.
5. Learning the test-taking skills that can be taught to students.
6. Recognizing how the standards movement has influenced the way that teachers teach, students learn, and curriculum is created.
7. Understanding how standards help us assess learning in relation to clear benchmarks.
8. Learning the positive aspects of standards with regard to curricula and in clarifying high expectations.

OVERVIEW

In this and the next chapter we discuss the issues of standards, student assessment, and student evaluation. During the past several years, especially since the passage of the No Child Left Behind legislation in 2002, educators have acquired a "new" understanding of what it means to teach in an American classroom. Not all would concur that the emphasis on standards, assessment, and accountability has led (or will lead) to better education, but almost all would agree that it has impacted and will continue to impact schools and the teachers who teach in them.

Of the several different ways being used to improve the quality of schools (e.g., competition through the use of vouchers, legislated class-size reductions), none has the potential for direct impact on teachers that the standards movement has. This chapter begins with a description of the standards movement, followed by a discussion of student assessment. In the next chapter we will address ways teachers evaluate the performance of students and how teachers, quite likely, will be evaluated and held accountable for what students learn.

Standards

Most states have some form of statewide standards in place. Under the Obama administration a movement is presently underway to supersede state standards with comprehensive national standards. Governors and state commissioners of education from 48 states, two territories, and the District of Columbia have developed a common core of state standards in English-language arts and mathematics for grades K–12. These career-readiness standards were released for public comment in September 2009.[1] These standards define the knowledge and skills students should have to succeed in entry-level, credit-bearing, academic college courses and in workforce training programs. The Common Core State Standards were completed June 2, 2010. The Council of Chief State School Officers and the National Governors Association Center for Best Practices completed them on behalf of 48 states, two territories, and the District of Columbia. These English language and mathematics standards represent a set of expectations for student knowledge and skills that high school graduates need to master to succeed in college and careers. When finally implemented these standards are to:

- Align with college and work expectations,
- Include rigorous content and application of knowledge through high-order skills,
- Build upon strengths and lessons of current state standards,
- Be internationally benchmarked so that all students are prepared to succeed in our global economy and society, and
- Be evidence and/or research based.[2]

E. D. Hirsch writes that standards should encourage good teaching and learning, and their creators have the obligation to develop standards that do just that. The word *standards* has become a vague term, leading people to believe that real curricular guides are being created when in effect they are not.[3] Historically, American authors put forward the same myths, facts, and values for all Americans to share. America has never really had an official national curriculum.[4] It is imperative for all teachers to know standards appropriate for their disciplines, whether state or (at some time in the future) national, because students will be assessed relative to those standards.

Standards evolve from three basic propositions:

1. Students, teachers, and parents need a clear idea of what students will be expected to learn.
2. Teachers need to know whether students are learning what they need to learn.
3. Results should be connected with appropriate incentives and supports.[5]

These propositions are not something that most people would contest, though clearly even the most innocuous of statements about standards will draw critics' comments. It is not our intention to explore the debate in all its complexity. Instead, the purpose of this chapter is for you to understand that although standards are being contested, they are already in place in most states and they will impact what and how you teach. Therefore, you should know about them and understand that most people who currently administer state and local education systems believe that standards are essential for improved education.

The Significance of Standards

Content standards now exist for almost all disciplinary areas—even for the early childhood areas. Teachers need to know the content standards for the subjects that they teach, even if they do not actively create lessons around those standards.

Good academic teaching standards have two essential qualities: clarity and parsimony.[6] *Clarity* means that sufficient detail is given to ensure that someone who reads the standard will know what students are expected to learn. Clear standards tend to be free of jargon and ambiguity. *Parsimony* refers to the narrow focus of the standards. (If they were written to ensure that students learn *everything,* students would likely be unsuccessful.)

As states set standards that are clear and focused, they also strive to ensure that the standards are reasonable yet rigorous. Some states also generate associated grade-level indicators for defined standards. (For an example of associated grade-level indicators for a standard, visit www.battelleforkids.org.)

Marzano recommends the national, broad-level implementation of standards. He argues that standards can improve student achievement, and many others who are concerned with educational reform would agree.[7] However, according to Marzano, for standards to make a difference, policy makers must take some specific steps:

1. *Reduce the number of overall content standards and ensure clear focus.* Marzano claims that a review of the different content standards (see www.mcrel.org) turns up 130 documents across fourteen different disciplinary areas! Any teacher who attempts to meet all these standards simply cannot cover all that needs to be taught within a K–12 context.

2. *Create monitoring systems to track student progress.* Students are extremely mobile—they don't stick around at one school for their entire educational careers. How are teachers supposed to monitor student progress when the data for even the nonmobile students are often unavailable? Teachers need this data, and they need to use it to clearly document the progress of students with a form of standards-based grading (i.e., plot the progress of students relative to specific standards).[8]

What are the implications for a specific teacher? Teachers must decide what to teach, have a clear focus, find out what students have learned, and then remediate. The prescription is simple; the actual implementation process is a bit more complex.

Can Standards Make a Difference?

When used appropriately, standards make a difference. Standards-based education can make a real value-added difference in the learning of students. Does that mean that you are locked into what you must teach? In most cases, the answer is *no.* Good teachers make decisions about what to teach and how to teach it. Standards form the basis for the curriculum, and a concomitant requirement is to assess what is taught. This assessment process is the focus of the remainder of this chapter. The goal of assessment is not an objective grade for a report card, but rather a clear understanding of what a student knows, does not know, and still needs to learn. "Standards without curriculum is like a bird without wings. It is not skills alone that prepare young people for college, work, and life, but knowledge as well."[9] It should be noted for the purpose of clarity that the authors of this text distinguish between the terms *assessment* (the process of collecting or discovering what students are learning in order to make instructional decisions—an ongoing daily process) and *evaluation* (making a judgment or assigning value to a program or student work—*after* the completion of instruction).

Questions for Reflection

As indicated at the beginning of this chapter, the focus on standards-based reform is not something that is universally embraced. Indeed, many argue that the narrow focus on standards results in an overemphasis on factual material and rote learning. Some also question whether the emphasis on standards works against creating educational opportunities that help students achieve their full potential. In essence, although most states have embraced standards reform, many educators continue to question the efficacy of the approach.

Articulate what you see as the arguments for and against standards-based education. You might begin by carefully examining the standards in your disciplinary area (or for the grade level that you want to teach). In what ways might standards make your job easier? More difficult?

Evaluating Student Learning

The process of evaluating student learning is central to teaching. Teachers must know how to diagnose learning and assess performance. Evaluation is a two-step process that utilizes assessment data. The first step is *measurement,* in which one or a series of tests generate data. The second step is to make judgments about the adequacy of the performance. Students who are required to perform beyond rote memorization and to analyze creatively while engaging with content learn better. Researchers assert that when teachers teach material in a variety of ways, students are more likely to understand the content.[10] Think about testing and evaluation as extensions of instruction, not as separate from the instructional process.

Criteria for Selecting Tests

Two major criteria for selecting tests, especially standardized tests, are reliability and validity. By **reliability** we mean that a test yields similar results when it is repeated over a short period of time or when a different format is used to test the same knowledge. A reliable test can be viewed as consistent, dependable, and stable. By **validity** we mean that the test measures what it is represented as measuring. An invalid test does not measure what it should. For example, a pen-and-pencil test is not suitable for measuring athletic abilities. A third criterion for selected tests, *usability,* refers to the characteristics (e.g., cost and simplicity of administration) that make it a reasonable choice.

Reliability.   Test reliability can be expressed numerically. A coefficient of .80 or higher indicates high reliability, .40 to .79 fair reliability, and less than .40 low reliability. Many standardized tests are comprised of several subtests or scales and thus have coefficients to correspond to each of the subtests, as well as the entire test. For example, reliability for a reading test might be reported as .86 for comprehension, .77 for vocabulary, .91 for analogies, and .85 for the test as a whole.

There are three basic methods for determining test reliability. In the method called *test-retest* a test is administered twice, usually with ten to thirty days between tests.[11] The rank ordering of individual test scores on the two tests is compared. If the rank ordering of scores is exactly the same, then the correlation coefficient is 1.00, or perfect reliability. A correlation of .86 indicates that the test is highly consistent over time.

A number of objections have been raised to the test-retest method. If the same items are used on both tests, the respondents' answers on the second test may be influenced by their memory of the first test and by discussions about the items with classmates or teachers between tests. If the interval between tests is too short, memorization is a factor. If the interval is too long, scores may change as a result of learning. The two test conditions might also differ. Lack of interest on the student's part during one of the test situations, a change in a student's health or diet, or a change in the mood of the student or the test administrator may affect the scores.

To overcome the problems introduced by repeated test items in the test-retest method, the *parallel forms* method may be used. In this method, two different but equivalent forms of the test are produced, and students are given both forms of the test. The correlation between scores on the two tests provides a good estimate of reliability.[12] One drawback to this method is that parallel forms are not always available, especially with teacher-made tests, but even with many standardized tests. And when two forms do exist they are not always equivalent and may differ in difficulty.[13] Also, the parallel forms method does not address the problem of differing test conditions.

The difficulties associated with the test-retest and parallel forms methods have led to the development of the *split-half reliability* method. In this method, a single test is split into reasonably equivalent halves, and these two subtests are used as if they were two separate tests to determine reliability coefficients. One common method of splitting a test is to score the even-numbered and odd-numbered items separately. It should be noted that by splitting a test in half the reliability is determined by half the number of items. Too few items in calculations can lead to greater distortions and more chance effects. In short, test reliability is higher when the number of items is increased, because the test involves a larger sample of the material covered.[14]

Each of the measures (or different methods of estimating reliability) has different strengths and weaknesses. In general, there are more sources of error with the first two than with the split-half reliability method.[15] The key is to look not just at the numerical value of a reliability estimate, but also at the reported method.

Another type of reliability is *scorer* reliability. This refers to the consistency of the scorer (typically the teacher) in scoring test items. Quite obviously, a true/false test can be more reliably graded than an essay test. High scorer reliability is not always possible, but it is important that you as a grader understand the fact that you can increase or decrease scorer reliability by simply changing the type of test you give.

In conclusion, keep in mind that reliability generally can be enhanced by giving longer tests.

Validity.   Depending on a person's knowledge of research and reason for administering the test, he or she can choose from many different types of validity. We will only examine those that a classroom teacher should know. You won't formally use these forms of validity in constructing teacher-made tests, but knowing them will help you shape your assessments. Professional testing services go to great expense to ensure that tests have validity. You should go to great effort to ensure that your tests have reasonable validity as well. Validity means that a test measures what it claims to measure. If a test is expected to measure geographic knowledge, it will not have questions focused on historical accuracy. The three basic areas measured for validity are content validity, curricular validity, and predictive validity, which are the same areas used by the nationally administered college admissions examinations, the Scholastic Aptitude Tests (SATs).[16]

Content Validity.   When constructing a test for a particular subject, teachers should ask whether the items adequately reflect the specific content of that subject. If test items can be answered on the basis of basic intelligence, general knowledge, or test-taking skills, understanding of the content and subject knowledge is not being tested adequately. The test lacks content validity.

Of all the forms of validity, content validity is perhaps the most important. An eighth-grade science test should measure scientific knowledge and skills taught in eighth grade—not reading comprehension, not mathematics, and not tenth-grade science.

Curricular Validity.   A standardized test that covers a good sample of a subject but not the subject or course as taught in a particular school has content validity but not curricular validity. A test that reflects the knowledge and skills presented in a particular school's curriculum has curricular validity. In such a test the items adequately sample the content of the curriculum the students have been studying.[17]

The problem of curricular validity arises more often with standardized tests than with teacher-made tests. Many standardized tests have excellent content validity on a nationwide or statewide basis, but the items are not targeted for local school use.

Predictive Validity.   Predictive validity is concerned with the relation of test scores to performance at some future time. For example, valid aptitude tests, administered in the twelfth grade or the first year of college, should predict success in college. This is what the SATs that students take in high school are supposed to do. Information on how a student is likely to perform in an area of study or work can be helpful in counseling students and in selecting students for different programs. (It is important to consider other factors as well, including previous grades and letters of recommendation.)

Usability.   A test may be valid in content, but the questions may be so ambiguous or the directions so difficult to follow that a student who understands the material may not do well on the test. The questions may be phrased in such a way that a student who does not understand the material may give the right answer. For example, students expect a true-false or multiple-choice item containing the word "always" or "never" to be false or an inappropriate choice. They sometimes answer such an item correctly when they are ignorant of the facts. By the same token, the vocabulary of the test should not be too difficult for students taking the test, or the test will no longer be measuring only content but also reading comprehension. Placing too many difficult items at the beginning of the test will cause students to spend too much time on them at the expense of reaching items at the end that they could have answered easily. Finally, if a test is too short, representative content will not be adequately tested—resulting in lower test validity.[18]

In general, for a test to be usable it should be easy for students to understand, easy to administer and score, within budget limitations if it has to be purchased, suitable to the test conditions (for example, time available), and appropriate in its degree of difficulty.[19]

Standardized and Nonstandardized Tests

A **standardized test** is an instrument that contains a set of items that are administered and measured according to uniform scoring standards. The test has been pilot tested and administered to representative populations of similar individuals to obtain normative data. Most standardized tests are published and distributed by testing companies (e.g., Educational Testing Service and Psychological Corporation); publishing companies (e.g. Houghton Mifflin and Macmillan), which usually publish reading and math tests to accompany their textbooks; and universities (e.g., Iowa State University and Stanford University) that have developed and validated specific achievement and IQ tests.

The scores from standardized tests will typically appear in the student record, sometimes called the *cumulative record.* Often these tests are scored externally.

Standardized tests are widely used in schools, and you most certainly have taken a number of them throughout your academic career. Standardized tests usually have high reliability coefficients and good validity, because they have been tested on representative sample populations. Most unreliable or invalid test items have been eliminated through pilot testing over the years. Normative data are useful in interpreting individual test scores and in ranking individual scores within a comparative population. However, normative data are less useful in special school or class situations in which the students have abilities, aptitudes, needs, or learning problems that are quite different from those of sample populations. A test manual should provide a comprehensive description of procedures used in establishing normative data. Although norms can be reported for almost any characteristic (gender, ethnicity, geographical setting, and so forth), such data are not usually shown or are incomplete for students who have special characteristics or backgrounds.

Sometimes an educator is concerned not with how well a student performs compared to other students, but with whether the student exhibits progress in learning. The educator establishes a set of objectives with corresponding proficiency or achievement levels and then determines whether the student can achieve at an acceptable level but does not compare the student to the normative population. The content of standardized tests does not always coincide with the content in a particular school or classroom—that is, the tests may lack curricular validity for that school or classroom.

Nonstandardized tests, usually referred to as **teacher-made tests** or classroom tests, have not been tested on several sample populations and therefore are not accompanied by normative data. These test scores cannot indicate an individual's position with reference to a larger sample. Standardized tests are usually administered on a limited yearly basis; teacher-made tests provide more frequent evaluations. Teacher-made tests are more closely related to the school's and/or teacher's objectives and content of the course. Who knows better than the teacher what content was covered and emphasized and hence should be tested? Who knows better than the teacher what the needs, interests, and strengths of the students are, when to test, and when, based on test outcomes, to proceed to the next instructional unit?

Norm-Referenced Tests

In **norm-referenced tests**, the performance of sample populations has been established and serves as a basis for interpreting a [student's] relative test performance. The test measures a student's level of achievement compared to students elsewhere. An example would be if the highest number of correct responses on a 100-item test were 70, the raw score of 70 would be reported as the 100th percentile. A norm-referenced measure allows comparisons between one individual and other individuals.[20] The purpose of norms (especially if the norms are based on a larger population, nationwide or statewide) is to compare the score of a student on a test with the scores of students from other schools. Suppose, for example, on a statewide achievement test that Jack's score places him in the 98th percentile in his school and the 58th percentile in the state. Although Jack's score is extremely high when compared with the scores of students in his school, it is barely above average compared to scores of a large pool of students. Students who attend inner-city schools may exhibit excellent performance when compared with classmates or peer groups but poor performance on a national or statewide basis. If their scores are compared only with those at other inner-city schools (or even with the city norms rather than statewide or national norms), their percentile scores are likely to be higher since the norm group has lower scores than the larger population.

Norm-referenced tests tend to have high estimates of reliability and validity because the norms are based on large populations. Scores can demonstrate progress (or minimal progress) in learning over time.

Criterion-Referenced Tests

Criterion-referenced tests measure individuals' abilities in regard to a criterion—that is, a specific body of knowledge or skill. The individual scores do not represent a relative level of achievement. Criterion-referenced tests are scored based on specific recall of course information. This means that a raw score of 70 would be worth 70 percent, for example. These tests are used to determine what students know or can do in a specific domain of learning rather than how their performance compares with other students'.

Criterion-referenced tests are usually locally or regionally developed. They allow the teacher to judge students' proficiency in specific content areas, and therefore they usually have better curricular validity than norm-referenced tests (i.e., the criterion-referenced tests are usually linked more directly to specific instructional objectives).

Criterion-referenced measurements may be practical in areas of achievement that focus on the acquisition of specific knowledge (for example, the Civil War in history or gas laws in physics) and in special programs such as individually prescribed instruction, mastery learning, and adaptive instruction. This type of test is important in that it considers the context of the classroom, what has actually been taught, and learning that may not be reflected on textbook or other pre-planned tests.[21] It is important to note, however, that it is difficult to develop reliable or valid criterion measurements that test for high-order or abstract thinking.

Your assessment should consider the kinds of learning (i.e., knowledge or problem solving) you expect from students, the content of the curriculum, and the context of the classroom. Your tests should be fair, provide incentives for students to learn, and give you information for purposes of instruction and curriculum decision making. See Tips for Teachers 8.1 for insight on improving your assessment procedures.

TIPS FOR TEACHERS 8.1

Improving Your Assessment Procedures

The following tips reflect the assessment policy of the Washington-based National Forum on Assessment (an advocacy organization intent on protecting the rights of students) and the National Council on Measurement in Education. The suggestions can be used with norm-referenced and criterion-referenced tests.

1. Educational standards—specifying what students should know and be able to do—should be clearly defined before assessment procedures and exercises are developed. Assessment should be based on a consensus definition—based on input from teachers, administrators, parents, and policymakers—of what students are expected to learn and the expected level of performance.

2. The primary purpose of assessment systems should be to assist educators in improving instruction and advancing student learning. All purposes and procedures of assessment should benefit students; for example, the results should be used to improve instruction or remediate learning problems.

3. Assessment standards and procedures should be fair to all students. Assessment tasks and procedures must be sensitive to class, cultural, racial, and gender differences.

4. The assessment exercises should be valid and appropriate representations of the standards students are expected to achieve. A sound assessment system provides information about the full range of knowledge and skills that students are to learn.

5. Assessment results should be reported in the context of other relevant information. Student performance should consist of a multiple system of indicators. Generally speaking, the more indicators there are, the more valid is the information about the student's performance.

6. Teachers should be involved in designing and using assessment systems. To correlate with instruction and to improve learning outcomes, teachers need to be involved in assessment practices and be committed to and use the test outcomes for decisions involving curriculum and instruction.

7. It is inappropriate to limit instruction to the objectives of a test or assessment program. Tests should not drive the curriculum. Focusing on the specific content or skills of a test limits the students' ability to learn the larger content and skills of the subject or course.

8. Assessment practices and results should be understood by students, teachers, parents, and policy makers. Test results reported in technical terms, such as grade equivalents and stanines, are often misunderstood or misleading to the public. Results should be reported in terms of educational standards or performance levels.

9. Assessment programs should provide appropriate information and interpretation when test scores are released to students, parents, employment agencies, or colleges and universities. The interpretation should describe in simple language (free of jargon) what the test covers, what the scores mean, the norms in which comparisons are being made, and how the scores will (or can) be used.

10. Assessment systems should be subject to continuous review and improvement. Even the so-called best testing (and grading) systems need to be modified to adapt to changing conditions (of community, class of students, etc.), resources (expenditures per student, staffing, etc.), and programs (class size, curriculum objectives. etc.).

Source: Adapted from Conn Thomas, et al., "Portfolio Assessment: A Guide for Teachers and Administrators," *National Forum of Educational Administration and Supervision Journal, 23*, 4E [electronic] (2004–2005). See also Douglas B. Reeves (2002), *Making Standards Work*, 3rd ed. (Denver, CO: Advanced Learning Press) for a more detailed discussion of these types of tips.

Comparing Norm-Referenced and Criterion-Referenced Tests

The difference between these two types of tests is that norm–referenced tests are based on the median scores of students, while criterion-referenced tests are focused on a predetermined level of performance to be given a grade. Simply stated, a *criterion-referenced test is based on content*, whereas a *norm-referenced test is based on judgments of how individual scores compare to others.*[22] Scores from a criterion-referenced test, however, do not indicate a relative level of achievement or produce standards because no comparisons are made. The criterion-referenced test indicates how proficient a student is in terms of a specific body of learning. It can measure changes in learning over time, but it cannot produce meaningful comparisons among students.

The norm-referenced test is valuable for heterogeneous groups in which the range of abilities is wide, and when the test is intended to measure a wide range of performance and then compare student performance. The criterion-referenced test is more useful in homogeneous classroom situations in which the range of abilities is narrower, and when the test is intended to measure a limited or predetermined range of objectives and outcomes. With norm-referenced tests, external standards can be used to make judgments about a student's performance relative to a geographically diverse student population; criterion-referenced tests lack broad standards, and the interpretation of the scores is only as good as the process used to set the performance levels.[23]

Gronlund and Linn point out five differences between the two types:

1. Whereas the norm-referenced test covers a large or general domain of learning tasks, with only a few items measuring each task, the criterion-referenced test covers a limited or specific domain, with a relatively large number of items measuring each task.

2. The norm-referenced test discriminates among students in terms of relative levels of learning or achievement, whereas the criterion-referenced test focuses on description of what learning tasks students can or cannot perform.

3. The norm-referenced test favors average difficulty and omits easy or difficult items; the criterion-referenced test matches item difficulty to the difficulty of learning tasks and does not omit easy or difficult items.

4. The norm-referenced test is used for survey or general testing, while the criterion-referenced test is used for mastery or specific test situations.

5. Interpretation of a norm-referenced score is based on a defined group, and the student is evaluated by his or her standing relative to that group. Interpretation of a criterion-referenced score is based on a defined learning domain, and the student is evaluated by the items answered correctly.[24]

Criterion-referenced tests are used by teachers to assess student performance relative to specific objectives, to develop more efficient and appropriate teaching strategies, and to fit the needs of the classroom population. Because norm-referenced tests are prepared for many different school districts with different curricular and instructional emphases, they are unable to do these individualized things. Criterion-referenced tests better coincide with the actual teaching–learning situation of a particular class or school, and they tend to provide answers to questions that are quite specific, for example: What is the capital of Missouri? What river flows through eastern New York? One problem with this type of test is that local school officials and teachers often lack the expertise in test construction needed to develop it. Norm-referenced tests are usually more carefully constructed than are criterion-referenced (teacher-made) tests, since the former are developed by test experts and test items are pilot tested and revised. Thus, it is recommended that teachers develop criterion-referenced tests in a group, so they can exchange information with colleagues and perhaps with a test consultant.

Table 8.1 provides an overview of the difference between norm-referenced and criterion-referenced tests.

Table 8.1   Comparison of Norm-Referenced and Criterion-Referenced Tests

Characteristic	Norm-Referenced Test	Criterion-Referenced Test
Major emphasis	Measures individual achievement (or performance) in relation to a similar group at a specific time. Survey test, achievement test	Measures individual change in achievement (or performance) over an extended period of time. Mastery test, performance test
Reliability	High reliability; usually test items and scales are .90 or better.	Usually unknown reliability; when test items are estimated, they are about .50 to .70.
Validity	Content, construct, and predictive validity are usually high.	Content and curricular validity are usually high if appropriate procedures are used.
Usability	For diagnosing student difficulties; estimating student performance in a broad area; classifying students; and making decisions on how much a student has learned compared to others. Administration procedures are standardized and consistent from class to class. Large group testing	For diagnosing student difficulties; estimating student performance in a specific area; certifying competency; and measuring what a student has learned over time. Administration procedures are usually varied among teachers or schools. Small group, individual testing
Content covered	Usually covers a broad area of content or skills. School (or teacher) has no control over the content being tested. Linked to expert opinion.	Typically emphasizes a limited area of content or skills. School (or teacher) has the opportunity to select content. Linked to local curriculum.
Quality of test items	Generally high. Test items written by experts, pilot tested, and revised prior to distribution; poor items are omitted before the test is used.	Varies, based on ability of test writer. Test items are written by teachers (or publishers); test items are rarely pilot tested; poor items are omitted after the test has been used.
Item selection	Test items discriminate among individuals to obtain variability of scores. Easy and confusing items are usually omitted.	Includes all items needed to assess performance; makes little or no attempt to deal with item difficulty. Easy or confusing items are rarely omitted.

(continued)

Characteristic	Norm-Referenced Test	Criterion-Referenced Test
Student preparation	Studying rarely helps students obtain a better score, although familiarity with the test seems to improve scores.	Studying will help students obtain a better score.
	Students are unable to obtain information from teachers about content covered.	Students are able to obtain information from teachers about content covered.
Standards	Norms are used to establish a standard or to classify students.	Performance levels are used to establish students' ability.
	Intended outcomes are general, relative to performance of others.	Intended outcomes are specific, relative to a specified level.
	Scores are determined by a ranking, average, or stanine.	Scores are determined by an absolute number (e.g., 83 percent correct).

Source: Adapted from Craig A. Mertler, *Interpreting Standardized Test Scores* (Los Angeles: Sage, 2007); R. K. Hambleton and M. Pitoniak, "Setting Performance Standards," in R. L. Brennan (ed.), *Educational Measurement,* 4th ed. (Lanham, MD: Rowman & Littlefield, 2006), 433–470; Allan C. Ornstein, "Norm-Referenced and Criterion-Referenced Tests," *NASSP Bulletin* (October 1993), 28–40.

Types of Standardized Tests

There are basically four types of standardized tests: intelligence, achievement, aptitude, and personality.

Intelligence tests have come under attack in recent years. Most school systems now use them only for special testing. The two most commonly used intelligence tests are the Stanford-Binet (SB) and the Wechsler Intelligence Scale for Children (WISC). The first is a group intelligence test; the second is administered on an individual basis. Intelligence tests sample a wide range of behaviors including, for example, general knowledge ("What is the square root of 25?"), vocabulary (with some intelligence tests scoring students pass-fail on definitions and giving points for different levels of definitions), comprehension, sequencing, analogical reasoning ("A is to B as D is to?") and pattern completion.[25]

Achievement tests have increased in recent years, replacing intelligence testing as the prime source of information for educators about students and how they perform in comparison to each other. Every elementary student is exposed to a series of standardized reading, language, and mathematics tests to evaluate performance at various grade levels. There are several types of achievement tests: The most common *survey* or *general achievement tests* are the Stanford Achievement Test, 9th edition (SAT9; grades 2 through 9) and the Iowa Test of Basic Skills (ITBS). These tests, used in a number of different states, give teachers a sense of what students have learned. The National Assessment of Educational Progress (NAEP) exams have been administered since 1969 and are designed to measure the knowledge and skills of American students in several different subject areas (mathematics, science, writing, US history, civics, geography, and the arts). The No Child Left Behind (NCLB) legislation of 2002 changed the stakes with regard to the use of NAEP tests. Whereas NAEP testing was at one time optional, the NCLB now requires that states receiving Title I funds participate in the state NAEP testing in reading and mathematics at grades 4 and 8 every two years. Participation in the areas of science and writing remains optional.[26]

Many elementary and junior high school students are required to take *diagnostic tests*, usually in the basic skills and in study skills, to reveal strengths and weaknesses for purposes of placement and formulation of appropriate instructional programs. One of the several different diagnostic tests commonly used by schools is the Stanford Diagnostic Reading Test 4 (SDRT4). This test, intended for lower-achieving students, includes items that focus on phonetic analysis, vocabulary, comprehension, and scanning. The SDRT4 mixes difficult and easy items. Most diagnostic tests rank the items by level of difficulty.[27]

An increasing number of students in many school systems must pass *proficiency tests* to prove they are competent in reading, language, and math. Students who fail are provided some type of remediation. In some cases the tests are used as "break points" or "gate guards" between elementary, junior high, and high school and as a requirement for graduation from high school. Students in some states are denied promotion or a diploma until they pass the examinations.[28] One of the real problems with the proficiency tests is the fact that they are not linked to clear national standards, which adds impetus to the move toward national standards. The reality is that in many states there is a poor alignment between standards and proficiency tests. *Subject exit tests* are increasingly being used at the high school level. Students must pass tests to graduate, to receive a particular diploma, or to enroll in certain programs. These tests act as a screen for eligibility to matriculate full time in a state college or university; the student must pass these examinations to receive an academic diploma. These exams also may be considered competency tests.

Aptitude tests differ from achievement mainly with regard to their purpose. Achievement tests provide information about present achievement or past learning on a cumulative basis. Aptitude tests predict achievement or what students have the capacity to learn. Whereas achievement tests deal with content that the schools teach (or should be teaching), aptitude tests may stress what is not taught in schools. There are two common types of aptitude tests:

1. *General aptitude tests.* Most students who wish to go on to college have to take a number of these tests to provide information to college admissions officers. You probably have taken the Scholastic Aptitude Test (SAT) or the American College Testing program (ACT) exam. Students applying to graduate school may take the Miller Analogies Test (MAT) or the Graduate Record Examination (GRE). The MAT is a general aptitude test in logic and language skills. The GRE is a general aptitude test, but the advanced parts are considered a professional aptitude test.

2. *Special* or *talent aptitude tests.* These tests are frequently administered as screening devices for students who wish to enroll in a special school (such

as for music, art, or science), for students who wish to enroll in a special course (such as an honors course or a college course with credit), or a special program (such as a creative writing or computer program). Specialized batteries of tests are available for assessing clerical ability (Hay Aptitude Battery Test), mechanical ability (SRA Mechanical Aptitude Test), psychomotor ability (Minnesota Manual Dexterity Test), artistic ability (the Meier Art Test), and musical ability (The Musical Aptitude Profile).[29]

Personality tests are generally used for special placement of students with learning problems or adjustment problems. Most students in school are not tested for personality. The most commonly used personality tests are the California Test of Personality and the Thematic Apperception Test. Both are intended for use in primary grades through college and designed to measure various social and personal adjustment areas. Several other types of tests measure a person's qualities:

1. A number of general *attitudinal scales* estimates attitudes in diverse economic, political, social, and religious areas; among the more common ones are the Allport Submission Reaction Study and the Allport-Vernon-Lindsey Study of Values.

2. *Occupational attitudinal tests* are available, such as the Occupational Interest Inventory, which is suitable for students with at least a sixth-grade reading level, and the Kuder Preference Record, which is designed for high school and college students.

Questions to Consider in Selecting Tests

Hundreds of standardized tests exist, and selecting an appropriate one is difficult. Individual classroom teachers usually do not have to make this choice, but you may be called upon to make selections if you serve as a member of a test or evaluation committee for your school district. Following are twelve questions to assist you in selecting an appropriate standardized test. They are based on criteria formulated by W. James Popham.

1. *Is the achievement test in harmony with course instructional objectives?* An achievement test should correspond with the objectives of the course, and it should assess the important knowledge, concepts, and skills of the course.

2. *Do the test items measure a representative sample of the learning tasks?* The test items cannot measure the entire course or subject matter, but they should cover the major objectives and content.

3. *Are the test items appropriate for measuring the desired outcomes of learning?* The test items should correspond to behaviors or performance levels consistent with the course level.

4. *Does the test fit the particular uses that will be made of the results?* For example, a diagnostic achievement test should be used for analyzing student difficulties, but an aptitude test should be used for predicting future performance in a given subject or program.

5. *Is the achievement test reliable?* The test should report reliability coefficients for different types of students, and they should be high for the student group you are testing.

6. *Does the test have retest potential?* Equivalent forms of the test should be available so that students can be retested if necessary. There also should be evidence that the alternative forms are equivalent.

7. *Is the test valid?* Standardized tests usually have poor curricular validity, but . . . should have good construct validity [e.g., show relationship to intelligence].

8. *Is the test free of obvious bias?* It is difficult to find a test that is totally free of bias toward all student groups, but teachers should look for tests that are considered culturally fair (or at least sensitive toward minority groups) and that provide normative data (reliability and validity data) for minority groups.

9. *Is the test appropriate for students?* The test must be suitable for the persons being tested in terms of reading level, clarity of instructions, visual layout, and so forth. It must be at the appropriate level of difficulty for students of a given age, grade level, and cultural background.

10. *Does the test improve learning?* Achievement tests should be seen as part of the teaching and learning process. This means a test should provide feedback to teachers and students and be used to guide and improve the teacher's instruction and the student's learning.

11. *Is the test easy to administer?* Tests that can be administered to large groups are more usable than tests that can only be given to small groups or individuals. Tests that require less time and are still reliable are more usable than lengthy tests.

12. *Is the cost of the test acceptable?* The total cost of the test, including the time involved in administering and scoring it, should be commensurate with the benefits to be derived. If similar information can be obtained by some other method that is just as reliable and valid and less costly, then that method should be considered.[30]

Teacher-Made Tests

Teachers are expected to write their own classroom tests. Most of these tests will be subject related, will focus on a specific domain of learning, and will assess whether a subject has been mastered and when it is time to move on to a new content area. One researcher estimated that a student may take between 400 and 1,000 teacher-constructed tests prior to high school graduation.[31] Teachers must create assessment mechanisms that match (or align with) the curriculum and do so with some sensitivity to the particular group of students that is being taught. Given the number of tests students take, such alignment is imperative.

It may be said that teachers and schools are in the business of testing and that they are highly influenced (sometimes hypnotized) by test scores. However,

---

classic professional viewpoint **8.1**

Testing What We Intend to Teach

Robert E. Yager

Too often, testing never goes beyond determining what a student can remember from reading, discussions, and/or class activities. And yet, the course goals and lesson objectives seldom begin with the verbs *remember* or *recall*. It is reasonable, then, to expect skills and competencies in quizzes and examinations that coincide with the verb forms in the statement of goals and objectives.

Some who are intimately involved with competency-based and/or behavioral learning strategies are guilty of defining the *competencies*, or behaviors for mastery, as lists that can be transferred to test items that require recognition of definitions in multiple-choice items, matching terms with definitions, or short-answer items requiring a straightforward definition or elaboration. Such recall does not assure learning and often negates the value of identifying goals and objectives for the classroom.

Effective teachers use their goals to select a curriculum that is a vehicle for meeting those goals, instructional strategies to drive the vehicle, and skills in testing that match the actions used in the goal statements. Too many of us espouse general goals, proceed to tell students whatever information we know, and evaluate student retention of this information. This is a common temptation for many beginning teachers. However, as we mature and have time to ponder what our testing actions do, we are humbled as we note the mismatch between what we purport to be our goals and the measures we select or create to assess student success.

---

according to researchers, the bulk of the testing is done with teacher-made tests that have unknown reliability; and most teachers do not know how to check for reliability or how to ensure appropriate weighing of content (which impacts on validity), even though most teachers have increased the time they devote to testing.[32] Analysis of teacher-made tests reveals that about 80 percent of test questions emphasize knowledge or specific content; tests frequently do not give adequate directions or explain scoring; and about 15 to 20 percent contain grammatical, spelling, and punctuation errors.[33]

Testing Practices.   In spite of their limitations, classroom tests still serve important and useful purposes. Teacher-made tests should have high content validity, largely because in most cases the material being tested by the teacher is the material that was just taught. In addition, this type of test provides timely information for teachers related to (1) understanding what students do and do not know, (2) determining how to group students for appropriate remediation, (3) monitoring student academic progress, and (4) evaluating pupils on their performance.

For all intents and purposes, four basic ways exist to assess student performance: essays, multiple-choice questions, portfolios, and authentic performances. Available testing choices range from subjective written responses to objective short answers, to evidence of student work, to actual live performance and demonstration. The most common test-construction tools used by teachers are short-answer questions and questions that require an essay for a response. These two basic test forms, combined with oral questioning, constitute the basic types of tests administered by teachers. Teachers, however, rarely consider oral questioning as part of objective testing, even though good oral questioning can be useful in generating precise and incisive responses. It is also valuable and far superior to written tests when it comes to providing evidence of student comprehension.[34] Table 8.2 outlines basic strategies used in developing classroom tests and their purposes.

Differences between Short-Answer and Essay Tests

Student evaluation can take many forms, from objective to subjective, from rational to whimsical. The practices you follow should allow you to be as accurate as possible in your appraisal of students. Your assessments are measurements of students' content knowledge, test-taking ability, comprehension, and the ability to read and understand questions. To be effective you should enhance written tests through the use of discussion and classroom observation.

Most classroom tests fall into two categories: short-answer tests (multiple choice, matching, completion, and true-false), sometimes called selected response/

Table 8.2   Basic Testing Practices

1. Use oral or written answers to a series of questions (e.g., essay questions, short-answer questions, and oral disputations).
2. Use a product-produced assessment (e.g., a portfolio, a research paper, piece of work).
3. Require a person to perform an act, to be evaluated against certain criteria and assessed using a rubric (e.g., excellent = 5, very good = 4, satisfactory = 3, less than satisfactory = 2, unsatisfactory = 1). Be sure to make clear to students by concise description the meaning of each item in the rubric.
4. Select an answer to a question from among several options (e.g., multiple-choice or true/false items).

Short-Answer Tests	Essay Tests
Provide good item pool	Call for higher levels of thinking
Sample objectives and broad content	Measure ability to select and organize
No writing ability needed	Test writing ability required
Specific answers required	Measure problem-solving/thinking skills
Objective, easy to score	Subjective scoring

Oral Tests

1. If phrased properly, call for higher-level thinking skills.
2. Measure students' grasp of both objective and subjective conceptual ideas.
3. Test the ability to speak and think on one's feet.
4. Require both specific and problem-solving skills.
5. Feature subjective scoring.

Source: Richard T. Scarpaci, *Resource Methods for Managing K–12 Instruction: A Case Study Approach* (Boston: Pearson, 2009), 218.

objective tests, and essay (or discussion) tests, sometimes called constructed response/*free-response tests.* **Short-answer tests** require the student to supply a specific and brief answer, usually consisting of only a few words; essay tests require the student to organize and express an answer in his or her own words, rather than being restricted to a list of responses.

An **essay test** usually consists of a few questions, each requiring a lengthy answer. A short-answer test consists of many questions, each taking little time to answer. Content sampling and reliability are likely to be superior in short-answer tests. Essay tests provide an opportunity for high-level thinking, including analysis, synthesis, and evaluation. Most short-answer items emphasize low-level thinking or memorization, not advanced cognitive operations.

The quality (i.e., reliability, validity, usability) of an objective test depends primarily on the skill of the test constructor, whereas the quality of the essay test depends mainly on the skill of the person grading the test. Short-answer tests take longer to prepare but are easier to grade. Essay tests may be easier to prepare but are more difficult to grade. Short-answer items tend to be explicit, with only one correct answer. Essays permit the student to express an individual style and opinion; the answer is open to interpretation, and there may be more than one acceptable answer. Short-answer tests are susceptible to guessing and cheating; essay tests are susceptible to bluffing (writing "around" the answer) unless the teacher has a clear rubric for grading them.[35] Table 8.3 provides an overview of some relative advantages of short-answer and essay tests.

Table 8.3   Reasons for Selecting Short-Answer or Essay Tests

Short Answer*

1. Allows for selection from many content items
2. Samples objectives and broad content
3. Is independent of writing ability (quality of handwriting, spelling) and verbal fluency
4. Discourages bluffing by writing or talking "around the topic"
5. Is easy and quick to score
6. Scoring and grading are reliable procedures
7. Scoring is more objective

Essay

1. Calls for higher levels of cognitive thinking
2. Measures students' ability to select and organize ideas
3. Tests writing ability
4. Eliminates guessing or answering by process of elimination
5. Measures problem-solving/thinking skills
6. Encourages originality and unconventional answers
7. Scoring is more subjective, though good rubrics limit subjectivity

*Multiple choice, matching, completion, and true-false questions

---

According to Mehrens and Lehmann, there are several factors to consider in choosing between short-answer and essay tests:

1. *Purpose of the test.* If you want to measure written expression or critical thinking, then use an essay. If you want to measure broad knowledge of the subject or results of learning, then use short-answer items.

2. *Time.* The time saved in preparing an essay test is often used up in grading the responses. If you are rushed before the test and have sufficient time after it, you might choose an essay examination. If you must process the results in one or two days, you should use short-answer items—provided you have sufficient time to write good questions.

3. *Numbers tested.* If there are only a few students, the essay test is practical. If the class is large or if you have several different classes, short-answer tests are recommended.

4. *Facilities.* If word processing facilities are limited, you may be forced to rely on essay tests. You can administer completion and true-false questions by reading the questions aloud, but it is best that all short-answer tests be typed, reproduced, and put in front of students to respond to at their own pace.

5. *Age of students.* Not until about the fifth or sixth grade should students be required to answer essay questions. Older students (sixth grade and above) can deal with a variety of types of short-answer items, but younger students are confused by changes in item formats and the directions that accompany them.

6. *Teacher's skill.* Some types of items (true-false) are easier to write than others, and teachers tend to prefer one type over another. However, different types should be included. Test writing is a skill that can be improved with practice.[36] See Tips for Teachers 8.2 for insight on test preparation.

Before we discuss the different types of assessments, let's focus on a critical question about which type of assessment is preferred: selected response or constructed response? The answer, quite simply, is that the goal is balanced assessment, so both are needed. Good teachers collect achievement data about students in different ways. Your goals dictate your approach. You need to know how to develop and use a myriad of different assessments ranging from short-answer (selected response) to essay (constructed response).

Short-Answer Tests

Short-answer or selected response tests include multiple choice, matching, completion, and true-false questions. Regardless of the type of objective test, composing the test questions or items generally involves finding the most appropriate manner in which to pose problems to students.[37] The test questions or items often involve the recall of information, exemplified by knowledge of facts, terms, names, or rules, but they can also involve higher-order cognitive abilities. (Multiple-choice items are easier to devise for testing advanced cognitive abilities; the other short-answer types are more difficult.) Consider these suggestions when preparing and writing short-answer tests:

1. The test items should measure all the important objectives and outcomes of instruction.

2. The test items should not focus on esoteric or unimportant content.

3. The test items should be phrased clearly so that a knowledgeable person will not be confused or respond with a wrong choice. The test items should not contain clues that might enable an uninformed person to answer correctly.

TIPS
FOR TEACHERS
8.2

Preparing Classroom Tests

Teacher-made tests are frequently the major basis for evaluating students' progress in school. Good tests do not just happen! They require appropriate planning so that instructional objectives, curriculum content, and instructional materials are related in some meaningful fashion. Here is a checklist to consider when preparing your classroom tests:

1. Have the expectations for what students should know been clearly communicated?
2. What is the purpose of the test? Why am I giving it?
3. What skills, knowledge, attitudes, and so on, do I want to measure?
4. Have I clearly defined my instructional objectives in terms of student behavior?
5. Do the test items match the objectives?
6. Are the objectives tied to standards, and are they both communicated to students in language they understand?
7. What kind of test (item format) do I want to use? Why?
8. How long should the test be?
9. How difficult should the test be?
10. What should be the discrimination level of my test items?
11. How will I arrange the various item formats?
12. How will I arrange the items within each item format?
13. What do I need to do to prepare students for taking the test?
14. How are the pupils to record their answers to objective items? On separate answer sheets? On the test booklet?
15. How is the objective portion to be scored'? By hand or machine?
16. How is the essay portion to be graded? Will a rubric be used?
17. For objective items, should guessing instructions be given? Should a correction for guessing be applied?
18. How are the test scores to be tabulated?
19. How are scores (grades, or level of competency) to be assigned?
20. How are the test results to be reported?

Source: Adapted from Jeanne Ellis Ormrod, *Educational Psychology: Developing Learners,* 7th ed. (Boston: Allyn & Bacon, 2011).

4. Trick or trivia test items should be avoided, since they penalize students who know the material and benefit students who rely on guessing or chance.

5. Test items should not be interrelated. Knowing the answer to one item should not furnish the answer to another.

6. Test items should be grammatically correct.

7. Test items should be appropriate to the students' age level, reading level, and cognitive and developmental levels.

8. Test items should not be racially, ethnically, or gender biased.

9. Test items should have a definite correct answer—that is, an answer that all experts (other teachers) can agree on.

10. Tests should not be the only basis for evaluating the students' classroom performance or for deriving a grade for a subject.[38]

In order to create an appropriate test the teacher must obviously know the course content (specific knowledge, skills, concepts, common misconceptions, difficult areas, etc.). But knowledge of content is not enough. The teacher must be able to translate the objectives of the course into test items that will differentiate between students who know the material and those who do not, items that will measure qualitative differences (preferably in higher-order thinking) related to the course as well as knowledge. When formulating your questions be clear, concise, and precise with the language you use. Each item (question) should test only one idea and contain only material that is relevant to its solution. Avoid using acronyms in the questions unless they are defined or you are asking for a definition of the acronym. After your own review and editing, ask someone else to review your tests for clarity and grammar.

---

classic professional viewpoint 8.2

Rules of Thumb for Taking a Short-Answer Test

Bruce W. Tuckman

Once upon a time, when I was a student, I was a good test taker. While all my friends were busy being overcome by test anxiety and forgetting everything they had crammed into their heads the night before, I was being focused and super "cool" and looking for any advantage I could get. I figured that all was fair in love, war, and test taking. I had studied hard, outlined all my notes and all the chapters that would be covered, and tried to figure out what the teacher thought was important enough to ask about on the test. But I also had some ideas about what kinds of clues to look for on the test itself. Back then I was working on intuition. But today, as a person who teaches teachers how to build tests, I have tried to identify all those clues I used back then so that the teachers I taught wouldn't inadvertently provide them for their students.

Since we don't want to reward test-taking skills as a substitute for acquiring knowledge through hard work (such as coming to class and studying), these are the clues that students should not be given in the tests that you build:

(continued)

1. Do not include any obviously wrong answer choices. If you do, students can just cross them out and thereby reduce their odds of guessing the incorrect answer.

2. Do not write one item that actually contains the answer to another item on the same test. If you do, clever students will skim over the whole test, find the items that overlap, and then use one to answer the other.

3. Do not make the right answer choice longer, more complex, or in any way visibly different from the wrong answer choices or else the wise test taker, when in doubt, will always choose the "meatier" choice and invariably be right.

4. Do not follow a pattern in choosing which choice (a, b, c, d, or e) will be the correct one. Pick letters out of a hat, or use some other truly random procedure. Otherwise, when in doubt, the "wily fox" will choose the letter choice that has not been right for the longest time.

5. Make all the answer choices grammatically consistent with the question. Any choices that are not will be automatically disregarded by the sharp-eyed student.

Beyond these five rules of thumb, in scoring the test include a penalty for guessing (for example, test score equals number right minus number wrong) if you do not want students to benefit unduly from guessing. In addition, while giving the test be wary of students who ask a lot of questions about the items that require you to give them explanations. You may be giving away the right answer without knowing it.

If you want to try to help your students, tell them to skip items they cannot answer and come back to them, to guess at answers they do not know (if there is no penalty for guessing), and to try to answer each question before they look at the answer choices. And tell them to put forth their best effort rather than wishing them luck.

Multiple-Choice Questions

These are the most popular objective test items, especially at the secondary level. Some students think they are fun to answer because they see the task almost as a puzzle—putting pieces together, doing easy pieces first and saving the hard pieces for last. The basic form of the **multiple-choice test** item is a stem or lead that defines the problem and is to be completed by one of a number of alternatives or choices. There should be only one correct response, and the other alternatives should be plausible but incorrect. For this reason the incorrect alternatives are sometimes referred to as *distractors*. In most cases three or four alternatives are given along with the correct answer.

The idea in writing the question is to have the knowledgeable student choose the correct answer and not be distracted by the other alternatives; the other alternatives serve to distract the less knowledgeable student. The effect of guessing is reduced but not totally eliminated by increasing the number of alternatives. In a twenty-five-item, four-alternative multiple-choice test, the probability of obtaining a score of at least 70 percent by chance alone is 1 in 1,000. Achieving a similar freedom from the effect of guessing in a true-false test requires 200 items.[39]

Like the other forms of tests, good multiple-choice test items are difficult to construct. The use of plausible distractors helps the teacher control the difficulty of the test. They should not be tricky or trivial. The major limitation of the multiple-choice format is that the distractors are often difficult to compose, particularly as the number of choices increases to five. Unless the teacher knows the content of the course well, he or she is usually limited in the number of good multiple-choice test items that can be constructed.

Box 8.1 features three examples of multiple-choice questions. The first tests simple knowledge, the second the application of a formula, and the third the application of a concept.

Box 8.1   Multiple-Choice Questions

1. Henry Kissinger is a well-known (a) corporate lawyer, (b) avant-garde playwright, (c) surrealist artist, (d) international statesman, (e) pop musician.
2. What temperature, in degrees Fahrenheit, is equivalent to 10° Centigrade? (a) 0°F (b) 32°F (c) 50°F (d) 72°F (e) 100°F
3. Based on the map provided, which product is most likely to be exported from Bango (a fictitious country for which longitude, latitude, and topography are shown)? (a) fish (b) oranges (c) pine lumber (d) corn

Although some teachers disdain multiple-choice (recognition) items because of their perceived simplicity, if well constructed they are very intellectually demanding. Multiple-choice items take time to develop and can come in several different forms: direct question, incomplete statement, and best answer. An example of each is provided below.

Direct question:
In what war was Thadeus Lowe's invention *The Intrepid* (an observational balloon) first used for making observations of troop movements?

a. War of 1812

b. Mexican-American War

c. Civil War

d. Spanish American War

Incomplete statement form:
The higher-education institution that trained the most military officers for the Civil War was

a. Harvard College.

b. West Point.

c. Annapolis.

d. Oberlin College.

Best answer:
Which of the following best explains why Black regiments were not more prominent in fighting for the North?

a. Most Blacks refused to fight for the North.

b. Northern Whites, like Southerners, held stereotypes that the Blacks were not brave enough to fight.

c. Too few Blacks were in the North, and those limited numbers made it difficult to form Black regiments.

d. Training Blacks was difficult because they were relatively unskilled.

Guidelines for Writing Multiple-Choice Questions

Here are some suggestions for writing multiple-choice questions:

1. Wherever possible, use a direct question rather than an incomplete statement in the stem. (A direct question will result in less vagueness and ambiguity, especially among inexperienced test writers.)
2. Avoid negative statements in the stem, since they lead to confusion.
3. Use numbers to label stems and letters to label alternatives.
4. Avoid absolute terms (*always, never, none*), especially in the alternatives; a testwise person usually avoids answers that include them.
5. Each distractor should be reasonable and plausible.
6. Arrange alternatives so that they are parallel in content, form, length, and grammar. Avoid making the correct alternative different from wrong alternatives: longer or shorter, more precisely stated, having a part of speech the others lack.
7. Make certain that correct responses are in random order. Do not use one particular letter more often than others or create a pattern for the placement of correct responses.
8. Use alternatives such as "All of the above" and "None of the above" sparingly.

Matching Questions

In a **matching test** there are usually two columns of items. For each item in one column, the student is required to select a correct (or matching) item in the other. The items may be names, terms, places, phrases, quotations, statements, or events. The basis for choosing must be carefully explained in the directions.

Matching questions have the advantages of covering a large amount and variety of content, being interesting to students (almost like a game), and being easy to score. Matching questions may be considered a modification of multiple-choice questions in which alternatives are listed in another column instead of in a series following a stem. The questions are easier to construct than multiple-choice questions, however, since only one response item has to be constructed for each stem.

One problem with matching tests, according to test experts, is finding homogeneous test and response items that are significant in terms of objectives and learning outcomes. A test writer may start with a few good items in both columns but may find it necessary to add insignificant or secondary information to maintain homogeneity.[40] Another problem is that matching questions often require recall rather than comprehension and more sophisticated levels of thinking. Higher levels of cognition may be called for in matching questions that involve analogies, cause and effect, complex relationships, and theories, but such items are harder to construct.[41]

Box 8.2 contains an example of a matching exercise.

Box 8.2   Matching Test Questions

Famous American presidents are listed in Column I, and descriptive phrases relating to their administration are listed in Column II. Place the letter of the phrase in Column II that describes each president in the space provided in Column I. Each match is worth one point.

Column I. Presidents
1. George Washington _____
2. Thomas Jefferson _____
3. Abraham Lincoln _____
4. Woodrow Wilson _____
5. Franklin Roosevelt _____

Column II. Descriptions or Events
A. Civil War president
B. "New Deal"
C. First American president
D. Purchased Louisiana Territory
E. "New Frontier"
F. World War I president

Guidelines for Writing Matching Questions

The following suggestions may improve the construction of matching questions:

1. Provide directions that briefly and clearly indicate the basis for matching items in column I with items in column II.

2. Ensure that column I contains no more than ten test items; five or six items is probably ideal.

3. Provide more responses in column II than there are premises in column I in order to prevent answering the last one or two items by simple elimination. Column II should contain six or seven items if column I contains five. A list of ten items in column I should be accompanied by about eleven or twelve items in column II.

4. Number the column I items, as they will be graded as individual questions, and assign the letters to the column II items.

5. Present either column I or column II items in a logical order (Column II is preferable), such as alphabetical or chronological (but not in an order that gives away the answers), so students can scan them quickly in search for correct responses.

6. Ensure that items in both columns are similar in terms of content, form, grammar, and length. Dissimilar alternatives in column II could give clues to the testwise student.

7. Avoid negative statements (in either column), since they confuse students.

Completion Questions

Completion tests present sentences from which certain words are omitted. Students are to fill in the blanks to complete the meaning. This type of short-answer question, sometimes called a *fill-in* or *fill-in-the-blank* question, is suitable for measuring a wide variety of content. Although it usually tests recall of information, it can also demand thought and ability to understand relationships and make inferences. Little opportunity for guessing and for obtaining clues is provided, as it is with other short-answer questions.

The major problem with this type of test question is that the answers are not always entirely objective, so the scoring is time-consuming for the teacher and the grading outcomes may vary with the grader. Combining multiple-choice and completion is an effective method for reducing ambiguity in test items and making scoring more objective. However, this combination does restore the opportunity for guessing.

The following examples illustrate how guessing is reduced. To answer the completion item (question 1), the student must know the capital of Illinois. To arrive at an answer to the multiple-choice question (question 2), the student may eliminate alternatives through knowledge about them or simply choose one of them as a guess.

1. The capital of Illinois is _____.

2. The capital of Illinois is (a) Utica, (b) Columbus, (c) Springfield, (d) Cedar Rapids.

Guidelines for Writing Completion Questions

Following are general suggestions for writing completion items.

1. Ensure that completion items have only one possible correct answer.

2. Ensure that the fill-in is plausible to the knowledgeable student; it should not be based on trivia or trick data.

3. In any item, use one blank (to fill in), or certainly no more than two, since using more than two blanks per item often leads to confusion and ambiguity.

4. Use completion items that are specific terms (e.g., person, place, object, concept), since an item requiring a more general phrase may elicit more subjective responses and be harder to score.

True-False Questions

True-false questions are another form of authentic assessment to use in short-answer tests. Here are some suggestions for writing true-false items.

1. Ensure that each true-false item tests an important concept or piece of information.

2. Ensure that true-false statements are completely true or false, without exception.

3. Avoid specific determiners and absolute statements (*never, only, none, always*), since they are unintentional clues. Be sure not to use them in statements you want to be considered true.

4. Avoid qualifying statements and words that involve judgment and interpretation (*few, most, usually*). Be sure not to use them in statements you want to be considered false.

5. Avoid negative statements and double negatives, since they confuse students and may cause even knowledgeable students to give the wrong answer.

6. Avoid verbatim textbook and workbook statements, since their use encourages memorization.

7. Use the same form and length for true and false statements. For example, do not make true statements consistently longer than false statements; testwise students will recognize a pattern.

8. Present a similar number of true and false items.

9. Use simple grammatical structures. Avoid dependent clauses and compound sentences, since they may distract students from the central idea. There is also a tendency for the knowledgeable student to see a more complex item as a trick question or to read more into the meaning than is intended.

True-False Questions: Pros and Cons

True/false questions are used primarily to measure students' ability to identify the veracity of statements, facts, principles, and generalizations. They can be used to poll an entire class to evaluate levels of understanding. Of all types of short-answer questions used in education, **true-false test questions** are the most controversial. Advocates contend that the basis of "logical reasoning is to test the truth or falsity of propositions" and that "a student's command of a particular area of knowledge is indicated by his [or her] success in judging the truth or falsity of propositions related to it."[42] The main advantages of true-false items are their ease of construction and ease of scoring. A true-false test can cover a large content area and can present a large number of items in a prescribed time period. This allows the teacher to obtain a good estimate of students' knowledge. If the items are carefully constructed, they can also be used to test understanding of principles.

Critics assert that true-false items have almost no value, since they encourage (and even reward) guessing and they measure memorization rather than understanding. Others note that true-false questions tend to elicit the "response set of acquiescence"—that is, the response of people who say "yes" (or "true") when in doubt.[43] The disadvantages of true-false questions outweigh their advantages unless the items are well written. Precise language that is appropriate for the students taking the test is essential so that ambiguity and reading ability do not distort test results. Here are two examples of ambiguous true-false questions.

1. Australia, the island continent, was discovered by Captain Cook.

2. Early in his career Will Rogers said, "I never met a man I didn't like."

In question 1 two statements are made, and it is unclear whether the student is to respond to both or only one; moreover, the meanings of *island* and *continent* are also being tested. In question 2, is the student being asked whether Rogers made the statement early or late in his career or whether this exact statement can be attributed to Rogers? A testwise person might say "False," because there are two ways of being wrong in this question, but the answer is "True."

Guessing is the biggest disadvantage to true-false tests. When students guess, they have a fifty-fifty chance of being right. Being able to sense clues in the items and being testwise improve these odds. The purpose of the test is to measure what students know, not how lucky or clever they are. To some extent, this disadvantage can be compensated for by increasing the number of test items and by penalizing (deducting a quarter point or one-third point) for an incorrect answer. True-false items should be used sparingly for older students, who are more test-wise and able to sense clues in questions. They are more appropriate for younger students, who respond more to the content than to the format of questions.

Overview of Short-Answer Questions.   Table 8.4 summarizes many of the points we have discussed about short-answer test questions. The different types of short-answer tests all have advantages and disadvantages. Different teachers

Table 8.4   Advantages and Limitations of Short-Answer Test Questions

Question Type	Advantages	Disadvantages
Multiple choice	1. They are flexible in measuring objectives or content. 2. Well-constructed items have the potential to measure high-level thinking. 3. Easy to score; little interpretation to count correct responses.	1. A correct answer can sometimes be determined without knowledge of content. 2. Susceptible to guessing and eliminating incorrect choices. 3. Time-consuming to write.
Matching	1. Relatively easy to write, easy to score. 2. Well suited to measure associations. 3. May be used to test a large body of content; many options available.	1. Often necessary to use single words or short phrases. 2. Cannot be used to assess all types of thinking; lists or individual pieces of information assess limited knowledge. 3. Harder to write than other short-answer items, because all items must fit together and be distinguishable from each other.
Completion	1. Easy to write test items 2. Minimal guessing; clues are not given in choices or alternatives. 3. Can test knowledge of what, who, where, and how many. 4. No distractors, options, or choices to worry about.	1. Difficult to score 2. Some answers are subjective or open to interpretation. 3. Usually measures simple recall or factual information. 4. Test items are sometimes confusing or ambiguous; constrained by grammar.
True-False	1. Easiest test items to write; easy to score. 2. Comprehensive sampling of objectives or content. 3. Guessing can be minimized by a built-in penalty. 4. No distractors to worry about; highly reliable and valid items.	1. Sometimes are ambiguous or too broad. 2. Simplicity in cognitive demands; measures low-level thinking. 3. Susceptible to guessing. 4. Dependence on absolute judgments, right or wrong.

Source: Adapted from M. David Miller, Robert L. Linn, and Norman E. Gronlund, *Measurement and Evaluation in Teaching,* 10th ed. (Boston: Allyn & Bacon, 2008).

will have different preferences. Although each type has features that make it useful for specific testing situations, the different types can be used together to add variety and to test different types and levels of knowledge.

Multiple-choice questions are the most difficult and time-consuming to construct. However, they can be used more readily to test higher levels of learning than can the other short-test items. Matching questions are also difficult and time-consuming to write, but they are interesting for students and can be used for variety. Completion questions are open to subjective interpretation and scoring, but they can be used also to test higher levels of learning. True-false questions force students to choose between alternatives, and they are a good way of assessing in a general sense what students know or do not know.

Essay Questions

Short-answer questions—especially for most teacher-developed tests—are not intended to measure divergent thinking or subjective or imaginative thought. To learn how a student thinks, attacks a problem, writes, and utilizes cognitive resources, something beyond the short-answer test is needed. Essay questions, especially when there is no specific right answer, produce evaluation data of considerable value. One test expert considers the essay to be the most authentic type of testing for middle-school students on up through college and perhaps the best one for measuring higher mental processes.[44]

Authorities disagree on how structured and specific essay questions should be. For example, some authorities advocate using words such as *why, how*, and *what consequences*. They claim that questions worded in this way (*type 1 essay questions*) call for a command of essential knowledge and concepts and require students to integrate the subject matter, analyze data, make inferences, and show cause-effect relations.[45] Other educators recommend words such as *discuss, examine*, and *explain*, claiming that this wording (*type 2 essay questions*) gives the student less latitude in responding but provides the teacher with an opportunity to learn how the student thinks.[46] Although more restricted than the first type, this type of question may still lead to tangential responses by some students. It is useful when the object is to see how well the student can select, reject, and organize data from several sources. Others advocate more precision, providing more structure and focus in a question by using words such as *compare* and *contrast*[47] (*type 3 essay questions*). In addition to giving more direction to the student, such wording demands that the student select and organize specific data. Box 8.3 lists thought processes elicited by different essay questions.

In effect, the descriptions of the different types of questions stress different degrees of freedom permitted the student in organizing a response to a question. The first two types of essay questions allow an *extended response*; they can lead to disjointed, irrelevant, superficial, or unexpected discussions by students who have difficulty organizing their thoughts on paper. The third type of essay question suggests a *focused response*; it can lead to simple recall of information and a mass of details.

Box 8.3   Sample Thought Questions and Cognitive Levels of Thinking

1. **Comparing**
   a. Compare the following two people for . . .
   b. Describe the similarities and differences between . . .

2. **Classifying**
   a. Group the following items according to . . .
   b. What common characteristics do the items below have?

3. **Outlining**
   a. Outline the procedures you would use to calculate . . .
   b. Discuss the advantages of . . .

4. **Summarizing**
   a. State the major points of . . .
   b. Describe the principles of . . .

5. **Organizing**
   a. Trace the history of . . .
   b. Examine the development of . . .

6. **Analyzing**
   a. Describe the errors in the following argument . . .
   b. What data are needed to . . .

7. **Applying**
   a. Clarify the methods of . . . for purposes of . . .
   b. Diagnose the causes of . . .

8. **Inferring**
   a. Why did the author say . . . ?
   b. How would (person X) more likely react to . . . ?

9. **Deducing**
   a. Formulate criteria for . . .
   b. Based on the premise of . . . , propose a valid conclusion.

10. **Synthesizing**
    a. How would you end the story of . . . ?
    b. Describe a plan for . . .

11. **Justifying**
    a. Provide a rationale for . . .
    b. Which alternatives below do you agree with? Why?

12. **Identifying**
    a. Identify three characteristics of . . .
    b. Based on the following . . . identify two qualities of . . .

13. **Predicting**
    a. Describe the likely outcomes of . . .
    b. What will most likely happen if . . . ? Why?

Source: Allan C. Ornstein, "Essay Tests: Use, Development and Grading," *Clearing House* (January–February 1992): 176. Used by permission of Taylor & Francis. See also M. David Miller, Robert L. Linn, and Norman E. Gronlund, *Measurements and Evaluation in Teaching,* 10th ed. (Boston: Allyn & Bacon, 2009).

Advantages and Disadvantages.   Essay questions can be used effectively for determining how well students can analyze, synthesize, evaluate, think logically, solve problems, and hypothesize. They can also show how well students can organize their thoughts; support a point of view; and create ideas, methods, and solutions. The complexity of the questions and the complexity of thinking expected of students can be adjusted to correspond to their ages, abilities, and experience. Another advantage is the ease and short time involved in constructing an essay question. The major disadvantages of essay questions are the considerable time needed to read and evaluate answers and the subjectivity of scoring. The length and complexity of the answers as well as the standards for responding can lead to reliability problems in scoring.

Some studies report that independent grading of the same essay by several teachers results in appraisals ranging from excellent to failing. This variation illustrates a wide range in criteria for evaluation among teachers. Even worse, one study showed that the same teacher grading the same essay at different times gave the essay significantly different grades.[48] It has also been demonstrated that teachers are influenced by such factors as penmanship, quality of composition, and spelling, even when they are supposed to grade on content alone.[49]

One way to increase the reliability of an essay test is to increase the number of questions and restrict the length of the answers. The more specific and restricted the question, the less ambiguous it is to the teacher and the less affected it will be by interpretation or subjectivity in scoring.[50] Another way is for teachers to develop an outline of what information a desirable answer might contain. The more clearly the teacher defines the expected outcomes, the more reliably the various student responses can be graded. Note that "more reliably" does not mean reliability. The reason for this is clear: Because essay tests are somewhat subjective, there will always be a level of unreliability in assessing student responses.

A test composed entirely of essay questions can cover only limited content because only a few questions can be answered in a given time period. However, this limitation is balanced by the fact that in studying for an essay test high-achieving students are likely to look at the subject or course as a whole and at the relationships of ideas, concepts, and principles.

The essay answer is affected by the student's ability to organize written responses. Many students can comprehend and deal with abstract data but have problems writing or showing that they understand the material in an essay examination. Students may freeze and write only short responses, write in a disjointed fashion, or express only low-level knowledge.[51] One way to alleviate this problem is to discuss in detail how to write the answer to an essay question. Sadly, few teachers take the time to teach students how to write essay answers. They often expect language arts teachers to perform this task, and language arts teachers are often so busy teaching grammar, spelling, and punctuation that they cannot approach the mechanics of essay writing.

On the other hand, there are students who write well but haven't learned the course content. Their writing ability may conceal their lack of specific knowledge. It is important for the teacher to be able to differentiate irrelevant facts and ideas from relevant information. Even though essay questions appear to be easy to write, careful construction is necessary to test students' cognitive abilities—that is, to write valid questions. Many essay questions can be turned around by students so that they merely list facts without applying information to specific situations, without integrating it with other information, and without showing an understanding of concepts. "What were the causes of World War II?" can be answered by listing specific causes without integrating them. A better question would be "Assume that Winston Churchill, Franklin Roosevelt, and Adolph Hitler were invited to speak to an audience on the causes of World War II. What might each of them say? What might each select as the most important causal factors? On what points would they agree? Disagree?"

Factors to be considered in deciding whether to use essay questions are the difficulty and time involved in grading essays, the low reliability of grading, the limited sampling of content, the validity of the essay itself, the ease in formulating questions, the testing of advanced levels of cognition, and the fostering of the integration of the subject as a whole. Many teachers take advantage of what both short-answer questions and essay questions have to offer by writing tests consisting of both, perhaps 40 to 60 percent short-answer and the remainder essay. This balance is determined to some extent by grade level. In the upper grades there is a tendency to require students to answer more essay questions, since it is believed they should have the ability to formulate acceptable answers. According to Piagetian developmental stages, students should be able to handle short essays at the formal operation stage, beginning at age 11.

Guidelines for Writing Essay Questions

Here are suggestions for preparing and scoring essay tests.

1. Make directions specific, indicating just what the student is to write about. Write up to three or four sentences of directions if necessary.

2. Word each question as simply and clearly as possible.

3. Allow sufficient time for students to answer the questions. A good rule of thumb is for the teacher to estimate how long he or she would take to answer the questions and then multiply this time by two or three, depending on the students' age and abilities. Suggest a time allotment for each question so students can pace themselves.

4. Ask questions that require considerable thought. Use essay questions to focus assessment on organizing data, analysis, interpretation, and formulating theories rather than on reporting facts.

5. Give students a choice of questions, such as two out of three, so as not to penalize students who may know the subject as a whole but may be limited in the area addressed by a particular question.[52]

6. Determine in advance how much weight will be given to each question or part of a question. Give this information on the test, and then score accordingly.

7. Explain your scoring technique to students before the test. It should be clear to them what weight will be given to knowledge, development,

and organization of ideas, grammar, punctuation, spelling, penmanship, and any other factor to be considered in evaluation.

8. Be consistent in your scoring technique for all students. Try to conceal the name of the student whose answer you are grading to reduce biases that have little to do with the quality of the student's response and more to do with the "halo effect" (the tendency to grade students according to impressions of their capabilities, attitudes, or behavior).[53]

9. Grade one question at a time, rather than one test paper at a time, to increase reliability in scoring. This technique makes it easier to compare and evaluate responses to each specific question.

10. Write comments on the test paper for the student, noting good points and explaining how answers could be improved. Do not compare a student to others when making comments.

11. As an alternative essay form, attempt to develop **one-minute essay questions** focused on specific goals that can be answered within a minute or two. One-minute essay questions can be used to check understanding, provide feedback, and promote reflection. They should be short, clear, concise questions that require students to demonstrate comprehension quickly, and they can be used to determine areas of a lesson that are not understood. An example might state: "In one to three minutes, describe what was most confusing in today's lesson about short answers. Why was this concept confusing?" The obvious advantage of the one-minute essay is that it promotes reflection and critical thinking skills. Teachers can assess their own effectiveness in the delivery of lessons, as well as reveal student misconceptions and background knowledge. These questions are easy to construct and do not require formal grading aside from traditional requirements associated with class participation. A disadvantage is that they do not measure in-depth understanding, and students may not take them seriously if they are not graded.[54]

Administering and Returning Tests

Teachers must decide when and how to give tests. Those teachers who consider testing important often give several tests at short intervals of time; those for whom testing is not so vital may give fewer tests. Teachers who prefer a mastery or competence approach to instruction generally give many criterion-referenced tests for the purposes of diagnosing, checking on learning progress, and individualizing instruction, as well as for grading student performance. Those who prefer a broad, cognitive approach may rely on fewer classroom tests that assess student knowledge of the subject matter. Whatever their approach to testing, it is recommended that teachers announce tests (or any type of assessment) well in advance. Discuss what will be covered, how it will be evaluated, and how much it will count toward a final grade.

Test-Taking Skills

Conditions other than students' knowledge can affect student performance on tests. One such factor is their general test-taking ability, which is completely apart from the subject matter of particular tests. Test-taking skills are important for all students. Almost any student who has taken a few tests and who has common sense can learn certain skills that will improve his or her scores. Developing good test-taking strategies should not be construed as amoral or dishonest. Rather, it is a way of reducing anxiety in test situations. A number of test authorities contend that all students should be given training in test-wiseness.[55]

Important test-taking skills can be taught to students. When students are given practice in diagnosing test questions and in strategies involved in taking tests, their test scores usually improve (although researchers differ as to the size of the effect).[56]

Tips for Teachers 8.3 will help you prepare students for test taking. You will note that some of the ideas are related to general test-taking skills and others to test-specific skills that might be useful if tests are not constructed properly by developers.

TIPS FOR TEACHERS 8.3

Testwise Strategies

Testing is an integral part of the education process, and it affects the lives of all students. As students become more testwise, they should perform better on classroom and standardized tests. The following suggestions are aimed at high school and college students:

1. Get a good night's sleep prior to major tests, and don't sit near a friend.
2. Read the test directions and each test item *carefully.*
3. Be aware that both human scorers and machine scorers place a premium on neatness and legibility.
4. Establish a pace that will permit you sufficient time to finish; check the time periodically to see if you are maintaining the pace.
5. Do easy items first; bypass difficult test questions or problems and return to them as time permits.
6. If credit is given only for the number of right answers or if correction for guessing is less severe than a wrong response (e.g., −1 for a wrong response and +1 for a correct response), it is appropriate to guess.
7. Eliminate items you know are incorrect on matching or multiple-choice questions before guessing.
8. Make use of relevant content information on other test items and options.
9. Don't get stuck on one item or question.
10. Recognize idiosyncrasies of the test constructor that differentiate correct and incorrect options; for example, notice whether correct (or incorrect) options (a) are longer or shorter, (b) are more general or specific, (c) are placed in certain logical positions within each set of options, (d) include or exclude one pair of diametrically opposed statements, and (e) are grammatically inconsistent or consistent with the stem.

11. Use of *an* instead of *a* may imply that the correct response begins with a vowel. Eliminate alternatives.

12. True items may be longer than false items because they require qualifying phrases.

13. Words such as *always, never,* and *none* are associated with false items.

14. Words such as *usually, often,* and *many* are associated with true items.

15. On multiple choice tests, if you cannot finish then fill in all the remaining answers with the same letter if there is no penalty for guessing.

16. Periodically check to be sure the item number and answer number match, especially when using an answer sheet.

17. Reflect on and outline an essay before starting to write; decide how much time you can afford for that question given the available time. In all cases, attempt an answer, no matter how poor, to gain some points.

18. Write short paragraphs for an essay; develop one idea or concept in each paragraph to make your points easier for the reader (teacher) to discern. Include several short paragraphs as opposed to a few long paragraphs that tend to blend or fuse distinct ideas.

19. If time permits, return to omitted items (if any): then check answers and correct careless mistakes.

Source: Adapted from Anita E. Woolfolk, *Educational Psychology,* 10th ed. (Boston: Allyn & Bacon, 1998).

For example, here are some general test-taking strategies:

1. Attend carefully to the test directions and then periodically check your work to make sure you are following them exactly.

2. Ask questions if you are unclear about what to do.[57]

3. Consistent studying or review over the duration of the course is more effective than cramming.

Here are examples of some test-specific strategies:

1. The answer option that is longest or most precisely stated is likely correct.

2. The use of vague words (e.g., *some, often*) in one of the answers usually signals the correct option.[58]

Reading is critical to students' academic growth in all academic areas and is a part of the standardized assessment process found in states as a result of the No Child Left Behind legislation. Following are some specific examples of test-taking strategies in reading.

1. Whisper-read the title/subtitles. Predict what the passage is about.

2. Carefully study any charts, graphs, or diagrams.

3. Number the paragraphs.

4. Whisper-read the questions carefully, circling the key words. Make sure you understand what the question is asking.

5. Beginning with the title, whisper-read the passage thoroughly at least two times. Make a mental picture of what you are reading.

6. Whisper-read the first question-and-answer choices, getting an idea of what the answer may be. Do not mark your answer choice.

7. Return to the passage and underline the clues that support the possible answer.

8. Return to the question and eliminate the wrong answers.

9. Mark the correct answer and record the paragraph's number where the answer/clues were located. Remember, you have to prove your answer is correct.

10. Repeat steps 6 through 9 for the remainder of the questions.

11. Check to make sure you answered all questions reasonably.[59]

Test Routines

Both short-answer and essay tests must be administered carefully to avoid confusion. You should establish a routine for handing out the test questions and accompanying materials. Answer sheets, papers, or booklets should be passed out first, for example, with the exact number for each row given to the first student in each row, who then passes them back along the row. Students should be instructed to fill out information required on the answer papers, such as their names and class. To avoid confusion the test itself should not be handed out until the answer papers or booklets have been distributed. To save time, insert the answer paper into the test and then hand out both.

Before the test begins, be sure that students understand the directions and questions; that the test papers are clear, complete, and in proper order; and that students have any necessary supplies, such as pencil or pen, ruler, calculator, or dictionary. You need to have on hand extra copies of the test and extra supplies.

Establish a procedure for clarifying directions and test items during test time. Once the test begins, a student with a question should raise his or her hand without talking out loud or disturbing classmates. With young students, go to the student's desk and whisper. Older students may be permitted to come to you. If several students have the same question or a problem with the same item, interrupt the students briefly to clarify it for all. This should be done sparingly to limit distractions.

To further reduce distractions or interruptions, close the door to the hallway and post a sign, "Testing—Do Not Disturb," on the door. No matter how quiet they are, late students will disturb the others in picking up the test papers and getting seated. Unless they have a proper pass or excuse for being late, do not give them extra time to complete the examination. If students enter the room late for a standardized examination, they should not be permitted to take the exam since the norms are based partially on time allotments.

Pressure on students for good grades (or for successful performance on high-stakes tests) causes some to cheat. Short-answer teacher-made tests are particularly susceptible to student cheating, because a student can easily see someone else's answer by glancing at his or her neighbors' papers.[60] To reduce cheating, have students sit in alternate seats if sufficient seating is available or have students sit at a distance from each other if seats can be moved. Using two versions of the same test or dividing the test into two parts and having students in alternate rows start on different parts also helps reduce cheating. One of the best deterrents to cheating is your presence. To what extent you need to police students during the test depends on how common cheating is among your students. Even if there is no cheating problem, stay alert and don't bury your head in a book while the test is being administered.

Defined routines should be established for collecting tests at the end of the period. Remind students who finish early to review their answers. When the test period ends, the papers should be collected in an orderly fashion. For example, you might ask that papers be passed forward to the first student in each row where you can collect them.

Box 8.4 lists some things a teacher can do to improve test conditions and help students perform to their full potential. Most of these strategies are geared to limiting confusion and interruptions before and during the test, ensuring that students know what to do, curtailing their anxieties and nervousness, and motivating them to do their best.

Box 8.4   Test Giver's List of Things to Do

1. Before giving a standardized test:
   a. Order and check test materials (in advance of the testing date).
   b. Be sure there are a sufficient number of tests and answer sheets.
   c. Securely store all test materials until the testing date.
   d. Read the testing instructions, including how to administer the test.

2. Before giving a teacher-made test:
   a. Check the questions for errors and clarity.
   b. Be sure there are a sufficient number of tests and answer sheets.
   c. Be sure the test pages are sequenced properly.
   d. Securely store all test materials until the testing date.
   e. Announce the testing date; avoid days that precede holidays or coincide with major events.

3. Be sure classroom conditions are adequate:
   a. Is there adequate work space, desks, chairs?
   b. Is there sufficient light, heat, and ventilation?
   c. Is it a quiet location?

4. Study the test materials before the test:
   a. Are the directions clear?
   b. Are the time limits clear?

5. Minimize distractions and interruptions during the testing period:
   a. Decide the order in which materials are to be distributed and collected.
   b. Be sure that students have pencils or pens and other needed supplies. Have extra pencils or pens handy for students who are unprepared.

(continued)

    c. Close the hallway door.

    d. Post a sign: "Testing in Progress: Do Not Disturb."

    e. Decide what students who finish early are to do.

6. Motivate students to do their best:

    a. Explain the purpose of the test.

    b. Ask students to make their best effort: "I will be pleased if you try your best."

    c. Reduce test anxiety: "Take it easy." "Take a deep breath." "Shake your fingers and wrists." "Relax, it's only a test."

7. Reassure students; provide positive expectations and strategies:

    a. "Some test questions are difficult. Don't worry if you can't answer all of them."

    b. "If you don't finish, don't worry about it. Just try your best."

    c. "Don't work too fast—you might start making careless mistakes."

    d. "Don't work too slowly—you could start falling behind. Work at a moderate pace."

    e. "Don't dwell on a difficult question; return to it when you finish, if there is time to do so."

    f. "Pay close attention to your work and to the time."

    g. "Good luck" (or better, "I know you'll do well").

8. Follow directions and monitor time:

    a. Distribute materials according to the predetermined time allotment.

    b. Read test directions, if permitted.

    c. Give the signal to start.

    d. Do not help students during the test, except for mechanics (e.g., providing an extra pencil or answer sheet).

    e. Stick to the time schedule, especially if you are administering a standardized test.

    f. Periodically post or announce time; provide five- to ten-minute time announcements during the last fifteen to twenty minutes of test.

9. Observe significant events:

    a. Pay attention to students; monitor the test situation.

    b. Make sure students are following directions and answering in the correct place.

    c. Note if any student is displaying behavior that might affect his or her test results; curtail cheating.

    d. Note any major distractions or interruptions that could affect the test results. If administering a standardized test, bring these problems to the attention of the administration.

10. Collect test materials:

    a. Attend to students who finish early; remind them to check their answers before handing in the test.

    b. Collect materials promptly and without confusion.

    c. If administering a teacher-made test, perhaps provide a few minutes extra for slow students or students who walked in late. Use good judgment.

    d. Count and check to see that all materials have been turned in.

11. Help students know when to guess:

    a. yes . . . when only right answers are scored.

    b. yes . . . when some alternatives can be eliminated.

    c. no . . . if a penalty is assessed for guessing.

Source: Adapted from Norman E. Gronlund, *Measurement and Evaluation of Teaching,* 10th ed. (Boston: Allyn & Bacon, 2009); Anita E. Woolfolk, *Educational Psychology,* 10th ed. (Boston: Allyn & Bacon, 2010).

Test Anxiety

Test anxiety (that is, potentially debilitating emotions and worry) among students is common and should not be ignored. Most of us who are studying to become teachers can recall our own anxieties about certain subjects (usually our weaker ones), about certain tests (midterms, finals, and standardized) when the stakes were high, and with certain teachers who used test scores and grades as a weapon and who rarely gave students the benefit of the doubt.

Several recent studies indicate that there is a relationship between anxiety and academic achievement.[61] A meta-analysis of 562 studies involving more than 20,000 students found that test anxiety correlates with feelings of academic inadequacy, helplessness, and anticipation of failure. A child's original view of self, before entering school, is likely to be positive. However, after grade 4, students who exhibit high test anxiety wish to leave the test situation and consistently score low on tests; this creates a cyclical pattern that reinforces a negative self-image.[62] Performance on tests also strongly varies with students' perceptions of the test's difficulty; average-achieving students are impacted more than other groups.[63]

Elementary teachers, particularly, have reported a host of anxiety-related symptoms experienced by their students. The six most common are (1) excessive concern over time limitations, 44 percent; (2) perceptions of freezing temperatures in the testing classroom, 41 percent; (3) headaches, 40 percent; (4) irritability, 38 percent; (5) increased aggression, 33 percent; and (6) stomachaches, 29 percent. Secondary teachers reported fewer signs of stress, probably because of greater student experience in taking tests. Nonetheless, older students' symptoms are (1) truancy, 29 percent; (2) increased aggression, 25 percent; (3) irritability, 21 percent; (4) excessive concern over time limitations, 17 percent; (5) complaints about freezing classroom temperatures, 14 percent; and (6) headaches, 12 percent.[64] Between 10 percent and 25–30 percent of school-aged children experience significant levels of test anxiety, and poorly performing students experience it the most—especially children with learning disabilities.[65] Students also said that they dreaded essay tests more than multiple-choice and short-answer tests, reporting "freezing" when faced with essay questions.[66] Anxiety is the highest during standardized tests.[67] More than 80 percent of high-school student respondents in one state felt that scores on standardized tests are not a true reflection of what they have learned, and more than 65 percent felt too much is at stake with the exam.[68] Though this research is now a decade old, there is little new research to suggest that such findings are now invalid. Teachers express similar anxiety over state-mandated and annual achievement tests, and teacher anxiety has been shown to have a direct impact on students, increasing their anxiety levels as well.[69] Nearly 40 percent report feeling pressure from administrators to raise test scores, and over two-thirds feel threatened by the results of the tests.[70]

The anxiety caused by tests is not likely to be mitigated anytime soon. Consider that in Texas starting in 2005 a student has to successfully pass TAAS (the Texas proficiency exam) to graduate from high school, and in Louisiana students are retained in either the fourth or eighth grade if they fail the mandated proficiency exam. Given such tests, student anxiety will be high and manifest itself in everything from physical symptoms (headaches and irritability) to social dysfunctions (cheating and aggressiveness).

The high test anxiety/low test performance cycle is difficult to reverse. Incentives, praise, rewards, and prompt feedback all have minimal benefits, as do frequent tests, detailed test instructions, and test reviews. Although earlier research recommended teaching students study skills (how to take good notes or how to use memory devices to remember information) and test-taking skills,[71] more recent studies indicate that cognitive behavioral therapy and relaxation techniques can reduce text anxiety.[72] Teachers can also help to reduce anxiety on teacher-made tests by (a) eliminating time requirements when what they are trying to measure is not how quickly students perform, (b) explaining very carefully to the students the assessment procedures that are to be used, and (c) simply affirming with students that the purpose of testing is to *assess* what students know and need to learn—tests are not "gotcha" situations.[73]

In essence, little things can make a difference in reducing student anxiety around tests. Imagine yourself as a student with a teacher who is preparing to administer a standardized test telling you, "You really need to do well on this because poor performance will have serious consequences for you." Now picture yourself with another teacher prior to taking the same test. This one says, "Class, you have worked hard. Now try to do your best work on this test."

Returning Tests and Providing Feedback

One major problem you might confront is the speed with which the results of standardized tests are provided for you. Unlike teacher-made tests that can be graded quickly, standardized tests are returned by outside sources often after a significant time lag.

Teacher-made tests should be returned to students as quickly as possible. As you return the papers, make some general comments to the class about your awareness of the group effort, the level of achievement, and general problems or specific areas of the test that gave students trouble.

Discuss in class each question on the test, giving particular emphasis to questions that many students missed. If the missed test items are fundamental for mastery, take extra time to explain the material and provide similar but different exercises for students to review. Some teachers call on volunteers to redo and explain parts of the test that were missed, although this method may not always be the most profitable use of time.

To students who have achieved a good grade, especially an unexpectedly good grade, provide approval. Give students who have performed poorly special help in the form of extra reading, selective homework, or tutoring. In some cases, you may retest them after they have restudied the material. After class, meet privately with students who have questions about their grades, possibly in a small group if several students have the same question. Regardless of the type of test, make some comments about the individual student's answers and progress, directing more personal comments toward younger children. Personal comments, as long as they are objective and positive, help motivate students and make them aware that they need to improve in specific areas.

Authentic Assessments

Authentic assessment is a form of assessment in which students are asked to perform tasks that demonstrate that they have an understanding of essential knowledge and are able to apply it in real-world situations. Authentic assessments such as research projects, group projects, scientific experiments, oral presentations, exhibits, and portfolios for various subject areas enable teachers to monitor and assess what students know. Authentic assessment techniques encourage learners to stretch their capacities, undertake independent assignments, and generate new ideas and projects. **Alternative assessment**, a form of authentic assessment, is the utilization of nontraditional approaches in judging student performance. Robert Rothman asserts that these forms of assessment cause students to demonstrate complex thinking, not just isolated skills; they challenge the view (implicit in multiple-choice tests) that there is only one right answer to every question and that the goal is to find it and to find it quickly.

According to critics, standardized tests do not tap the high-order skills and abilities that students need later in life. They encourage students to do little more than recall information instead of preparing them to solve problems, evaluate alternatives, and create ideas or products.[74] Authentic tests, however, assess essential skills or tasks. They are not needlessly intrusive or esoteric; they are contextualized and involve complex thought processes, not atomized tasks or isolated bits of information.

The students are graded in reference to a performance standard or expectation, not on a curve or absolute standard. Authentic tests often involve a panel, such as classmates or other teachers in the role of examiner. The performance provides room for various student learning styles, aptitudes, and interests—and comparisons among students are minimized.[75]

Authentic tests take the appearance of evidence tests such as portfolios, projects, and performance outcomes. These forms of authentic assessment are used as evidence of student learning and have come into vogue whenever discussing student evaluation.

Portfolios

Portfolios have become the prime alternative means of assessment for the majority of teachers, who increasingly recognize that there are advantages in involving students in their own ongoing evaluation.[76] They should be made up of original student work that can be used to monitor students' progress. Portfolio entries should be made by students and should include a wide variety of original products highlighting what a student has achieved. Box 8.5 describes items that should be included in most student portfolios.

Ideally, **portfolios** should be a compilation of a student's best work—a record of completed work. Long popular with artists and photographers, portfolios have emerged as a new means of documenting what students accomplish. Following are some guidelines for working with portfolios:

Box 8.5   Preparing Student Portfolios

1. Students should prepare a table of contents divided into the major aspects of the work they have completed, with an explanation of each item's worth.

2. The student should select samples that evidence the work accomplished. Students should also include a written description of each specific project completed.

3. A portfolio might also include any multimedia demonstrations that could be presented in the form of photographs, CDs, DVDs, and other forms of video and audio media.

   Note: This certainly is not an all-inclusive list and most certainly can be expanded. It should be noted that portfolios can provide a rich variety of information about students, which can be useful in making sound decisions regarding individual performance. The importance of portfolios should not be underestimated, but to be effective they must be more than just a collection of items. They must provide evidence that bears a direct relationship to the highlighted learning outcome.

---

1. Developing a portfolio offers the student an opportunity to learn about learning. Therefore, the end product must contain information that shows that a student has engaged in self-reflection.

2. The portfolio is something that is done *by* the student, not *to* the student. Portfolio assessment offers a concrete way for students to learn to value their own work and, by extension, to value themselves as learners. Therefore, the student must be involved in selecting the pieces to be included.

3. The portfolio is separate and different from the student's cumulative folder. Scores and other cumulative folder information that are held in central depositories should be included in a portfolio only if they take on new meaning within the context of the other exhibits found there.

4. The portfolio must convey the student's activities explicitly or implicitly; for example, the rationale (purpose for forming the portfolio), intent (its goals), contents (the actual displays), standards (what defines good and not-so-good performance), and judgments (what the contents tell us).

5. The portfolio may serve a different purpose during the year from the purpose it serves at year's end. Some material may be kept in a portfolio because it is instructional, such as partially finished work on problem areas. At the end of the year, however, the portfolio may contain only material that the student is willing to make public.

6. A portfolio may have multiple purposes, but these must not conflict. A student's personal goals and interests are reflected in his or her selection of materials, but information included may also reflect the interests of teachers, parents, or the district. One purpose that is almost universal in student portfolios is showing progress on the goals represented in the instructional program.

7. The portfolio should contain information that illustrates growth. There are many ways to demonstrate growth. The most obvious is by including a series of examples of actual records of school performance that show how the student's skills have improved. Changes observed on interest inventories, in records of outside activities such as reading, or on attitude measures are other ways to illustrate a student's growth.[77]

There are a number of different types of portfolios. Elementary teachers might consider having students develop a portfolio that deals with (a) writing (with a wide variety of writing samples), (b) literacy (including material students have read or have written about), (c) a unit to include all the different materials generated as part of a unit assigned by the teachers, or even (d) examples of the ways in which students are meeting or are fulfilling the standards dictated by the state or school district.[78]

Each of these types of portfolios represents a different way of showing what students are learning within the classroom. The type of portfolio will be dictated by the purpose you have in mind. Ask yourself: Are you trying to document student performance relative to local or state standards? Are you trying to document a student's developmental growth?

Students' portfolios are increasingly published online for viewing by parents, teachers, and other relatives and students. Sharing is as simple as sending your intended audience the link to the portfolio. A recent study found that use of electronic portfolios resulted in "positive impacts on students' literacy and self-regulated learning skills when regularly used and integrated into classroom instruction."[79]

Performance-Based Assessment

Another form of authentic assessment is **performance-based assessment**. This type of assessment requires that students demonstrate their knowledge or skill in some tangible way, relative to a specific task that is contrived rather than real. Some of the emerging state standardized tests have performance components to them.

Perhaps one of the most popular representations of performance assessment is Sizer's concept of *exhibitions*. Sizer, who is founder of the Coalition of Essential Schools, argues that a "student must exhibit the products of his learning. If he does that well, he can convince himself that he can use knowledge and he can so convince others. It is the academic equivalent of being able to sink free throws in basketball."[80] Box 8.6 provides several examples of exhibitions that students must perform to demonstrate their memory skills. Exhibitions can emerge in a variety of forms—some require memory, others require writing, and others entail some form of skill demonstration. Each exhibition, though, holds the common element of making students *do* what the teacher wants them to *know*. Exhibitions enable students to represent knowledge in more personal and, ideally, meaningful ways. Personal representations foster greater ownership of ideas and help students be more motivated in their learning.

Performance-based assessment has its drawbacks. Such assessments require teacher thought and significant student time. (However, when evaluating the

---

Box 8.6   An Exhibition: Performance from Memory

As part of your final exhibitions, you must show yourself and us that you can do the following, from memory:

1. Recite a poem or song or story that is special to your family or community.

2. Draw a map of the world, freehand (conventional Mercator projection), and be prepared to place properly on your map at least twelve of fifteen members of the United Nations that we shall randomly select for you.

3. Draw a map of the United States, freehand, and accurately position on your map at least twelve of fifteen states that we will select for you at random.

4. Identify and answer questions about the current United States president and vice president, this state's two United States senators, the representative from your district, your state representative and senator, and the mayor of this city.

5. Recite for us from memory a speech from history or literature that you find compelling and that we agree is appropriate for this exercise.

6. Present a time line since 1750 that you have assembled over the last several years and be prepared to answer questions about any event that appears on it.

7. Be prepared to identify five birds, insects, trees, mammals, flowers, and plants from our immediate local environment.

8. At a time mutually agreed on, we shall give you a text or an analogous "problem" (such as a machine to disassemble and reassemble) and three days in which to memorize or master it. We will then ask you to show us how well you have done this exercise.

9. Be prepared to reflect with us on how you completed this memory task; that is, how you best "learned" to memorize.

Source: "An Exhibition from Memory," from *Horace's School* by Theodore R. Sizer, Copyright © 1992 by Theodore R. Sizer. Reprinted by permission of Houghton Mifflin Harcourt Publishing Company. All rights reserved.

---

time taken for performance-based assessment it is important to remember that the time students take to generate products or performances for assessment is also learning time.) Another drawback is the difficulty of assessing student performance and projects unless teachers create and use clear scoring rubrics.

Project Work

Another form of authentic assessment is **project work**. "Project-based learning is a dynamic approach to teaching in which students explore real-world problems and challenges, simultaneously developing cross-curriculum skills while working in small collaborative groups."[81] Whereas performances tend to require short-term demonstration of a skill (e.g., reciting a poem), a project is a more long-term and usually collaborative endeavor.

Students work over an extended time period to show what they know and to earn some recognition, reward, or grade. Projects foster a certain measure of student self-discipline and motivation. Indeed, the daughter of one of the authors had a project-oriented German teacher who substantially enhanced her self-discipline and motivation. The projects were unique opportunities for the daughter to demonstrate what she knew in representational forms that played to her personal strengths.

> Because project-based learning is filled with active and engaged learning, it inspires students to obtain a deeper knowledge of the subjects they're studying. Research also indicates that students are more likely to retain the knowledge gained through this approach far more readily than through traditional textbook-centered learning. In addition, students develop confidence and self-direction as they move through both team-based and independent work. . . . Project-based work is often more meaningful to [students]. They quickly see how academic work can connect to real-life issues. . . . Students also thrive on the greater flexibility of project learning. . . . Adopting a project-learning approach in your classroom or school can invigorate your learning environment, energizing the curriculum with a real-world relevance and sparking students' desire to explore, investigate, and understand their world.[82]

Kay Burke effectively assesses the long-term benefits of authentic learning:

> The educated students of tomorrow must be able to "learn how to learn" by explaining, interpreting, applying, synthesizing, evaluating, and creating. They must also be able to develop their own perspective of the world, empathize with others, develop a sense of self-knowledge about their strengths and weaknesses, and recognize their prejudices that could impede their understanding.
>
> It is self-awareness that helps students become *independent learners*. Independent learners do not need a teacher with a red pen following them through life correcting their mistakes. . . . The ultimate goal of education is for students to be able to analyze their own actions: What did I do well? If I did this task over, what would I do differently? Do I need help? Where do I go if I don't know what to do? . . . Intelligent behavior is "knowing what to do when you don't know what to do."[83]

The following case discusses how teacher-made tests are the basic form of assessment used by teachers. The case reflects on four ways that students are evaluated. Look at the spectrum of options, from subjective written responses to objective short answers, and compare and analyze their relative strengths and weaknesses.

Case Study 8.1
Teacher-Made Tests and Authentic Assessment

Phil Minster was really upset after reading the principal's staff memo, which indicated a change in school policy. Of the various ways to assess student performance—essays, multiple-choice questions, portfolios, and authentic performances—the memo stated that this school would rely solely on authentic assessments. The memo went on to define *authentic assessment* as a form of evaluation based on judging whether the instruction had led to student behavior that evidenced learning. Students were expected to be able to produce and use the intended learning outcomes. The goal is to gather substantiation that students can use knowledge effectively and are able to analyze their own efforts.

Phil turned to his friend Lin Chang and exclaimed, "I haven't got the foggiest idea about what this memo means!"

"Don't get so upset, Phil. I don't think that this memo is going to go too far." Lin went on to explain that the memo was really a trial balloon intended to get faculty input as to the importance of teacher-made tests and how they are to be assessed. The real question is how classroom tests can be improved.

Marlene Anion, a part of the group that had come closer to hear the discussion, said that testing can be improved by limiting test anxiety and feedback time. "We could use innovative strategies, such as open-book or take-home examination. Of course, this presupposes that we are testing higher-order thinking skills such as analysis, evaluation, synthesis and the use of judgment."

Lin agreed and said that Marlene's interpretation sounded great. Phil, however, said that he thought Marlene's ideas were unrealistic. "If you only used authentic assessments, the time and effort needed to evaluate them would certainly take away from instructional time. What's wrong with our traditional short-answer questions and questions that require an essay for a response? When you combine these basic test forms with oral classroom questioning, they constitute sufficient evidence to evaluate student performance. It's really simple: If you want to measure written expression or critical thinking, use an essay. If you want to measure broad knowledge or learning outcomes, use short-answer items. This makes it easy to assess your effectiveness by measuring student comprehension. You could even use one-minute tests if you're so concerned about innovation."

Lin asked Phil to explain what one-minute tests were. He began by saying that one-minute tests contain essay questions with a specific goal that can be answered within a minute or two. "They can be used to check understanding, provide feedback, and promote reflection. They're short, clear, concise questions that require students to demonstrate comprehension by writing a sentence or one or more complete paragraphs. They can also be used to help you determine areas in a lesson that need to be rethought."

Lin said that Phil might have a valid point. Most teachers are more than satisfied to prepare their own tests because they expect children to understand and apply what they have taught them.

Marlene said that although she was glad to see that Phil and Lin agreed, that was not what was said in the memo. "How can short-answer tests, essays, and oral questioning ever be considered authentic forms of assessment? Authentic forms of performance testing range from student portfolios to teacher supervisory or peer evaluation!"

Discussion Topics and Questions to Ponder

1. Describe your interpretation of the principal's memo.

2. Express your reasons for agreeing or disagreeing with Phil's arguments.

3. Was there any validity to Lin's understanding of the principal's intentions? Explain your answer.

4. Do you agree with Marlene's categorization of open-book tests and take-home examinations as examples of authentic performances? Explain your answer.

5. In your opinion, can traditional tests be considered forms of authentic assessment? Why or why not?

What would you do if . . . ?

1. You were asked if assessment was really about categorizing students as "those who can" and "those who cannot."

2. You were asked if assessment was really about diagnosing the needs of each student so that the teacher and student can together set goals and identify learning experiences to lead to those goals.

3. You were asked to choose between traditional teacher-made tests or authentic performances.

The Purpose of Assessment

As we conclude this chapter, it is important to review the purpose of all the testing you might be responsible for as a teacher. You test (assess) in order to help students learn requisite content and to achieve learning goals effectively. A teacher who has clear standards of learning and who knows what the local district requires and what the state mandates is in a good position to make certain that each child learns to his or her full potential. Good assessment starts with knowing what you need to teach, and why and how you will teach it. The assessment process itself is most effective when you use a variety of strategies to measure what students have learned and to figure out whether you need to reteach any material they failed to learn.

If you are a teacher in a standards-based classroom, you will find yourself using all the tools we articulated in this chapter. More specifically, you will be able to address or consider the following:

1. The specific content standards in place for the areas of instructional responsibility that you have.

2. The benchmark standards in place for students in your school and state. (What must the students know at grades 4 or 8 or 10? What are you required to assess at the grade level you teach?)

3. The relative strengths and weaknesses of students you teach. You need to determine what students know or do not know relative to the standards. That will dictate what you teach and how you teach them.

4. Students need to be held accountable for achieving the standards and the learning goals you establish. Helping students to see that their success is important will lead to your success.[84]

It should be noted that assessments are both diagnostic and evaluative. They are diagnostic, for the purpose of ongoing instructional effectiveness (formative), and evaluative for the purpose of final grades (summative). The final evaluation is precisely the purpose for understanding basic assessment practices. As teachers, we are part of the standardized test movement. We are given the responsibility of administering diagnostic tests at the behest of state and local governments. These standardized tests have little to do with the everyday conduct of classrooms. They do, however, play a primary role in determining students' final scores and class placements. Managerial decisions are based on the diagnostic tests that are either norm-referenced or criterion-referenced tests.

The impact of standardized testing on instructional practices is apparent in that it determines how a course of instruction is developed, and how that instruction is managed. The content stressed reflects the content in the standardized test. Lessons are focused on meeting mandated standards and local curriculums. The problem of maintaining intellectual integrity with regard to the instructional process is ongoing. See Case Study 8.2 for a further look at the purpose for testing.

The following case centers on a debate regarding the purpose of testing. It describes the view that standardized testing forces teachers to focus on the curriculum and improves student's grades. It also suggests that a national curriculum may be the best thing that could happen to our nation's schools. The case also presents the view of those who say education means more than just passing a test. Reflect on both sides of the issue and see if you can arrive at a satisfactory solution.

Case Study 8.2
Testing for Learning

Phil Minster couldn't believe his eyes. The school board had issued a new memo that thanked the teachers for responding to the principal's memo on authentic assessment and performances. As a result of their suggestions the school board had overruled the principal and changed the policy. In the future, all teaching would be conducted with an eye to state standardized tests. This would help students attain high scores and better prepare them for the anticipated core national curriculum. The memo went on to state that "teaching to the test" is not a bad thing. It does not make children sick or render test scores meaningless or create a "dumbing-down" effect on all instruction. If teachers prepare children for exams in careful, sensible ways, they are more likely to enhance learning, not dumb it down.

The board memo said, "When we say *teaching to the test*, we want you to understand that we are not talking about just drilling students on test preparation skills. Teachers do this all the time when preparing children for teacher-made tests. It should be the same with annual state assessment examinations required under the No Child Left Behind Act. We share the teacher's view that what you are doing is helping students to learn the material, not to ace the test. No one is expected to adhere to someone else's views on teaching and present content in an inappropriate fashion."

Phil commented, "This is going out of the frying pan into the fire. No matter how tactful they try to be, the board really is implying that the only purpose for instruction is to pass a state assessment. "Teaching to the test also means teaching to the test *format*, and doing so at the expense of large portions of the curriculum."

Lin Chang asked, "What's wrong with teaching to the test?" "What's wrong," replied Phil, "is that it's turning teaching and learning into a mere exercise in prepping students to test well."

Marlene Anion said, "According to the board's logic, 'teaching to the test' is as unavoidable as a force of nature, as inevitable as gravity. And the choice between good instructional practice and good test scores is really no choice at all, since those who choose not to bow to the pressure will reap consequences under our tough accountability systems. I would like to know if high-stakes testing always forces educators to "dumb down" instruction to focus on rote skills and memorization. I would also like to know if schools that spend a lot of time on test preparation and 'drill and kill' instruction actually perform better on standardized tests than those that don't."

Lin said that she couldn't answer Marlene's questions but that she would like to find some middle ground. "Teaching to the test to me means aligning classroom instruction and curriculum to standards; that's called the *practice of teaching*. I think it's a good one that should be supported." Marlene replied, "There are two kinds of test preparation: teaching to the curriculum or to specific items. When teachers match their teaching to what they expect to appear on state tests, students are going to get more facts and routines rather than the opportunity to develop the conceptual understanding and problem-solving skills necessary to understand the curriculum. The test *becomes* the curriculum. In a way, I guess you are testing to learn—if what you want to learn is how to pass a specific test!"

Discussion Topics and Questions to Ponder

1. How would you describe the school board's memo: appropriate and reasonable, or inappropriate and unreasonable? Justify your response.

2. Explain your feeling towards the following statement from the board's memo. "No one is expected to adhere to someone else's views on teaching and present content in an inappropriate fashion."

3. Make two lists to compare and contrast what's good and what's bad about teaching to the test.

4. Discuss Lin's idea of middle ground by analyzing the following statement: Teaching to the test to me means aligning classroom instruction and curriculum to standards; that's called the *practice of teaching*.

5. How do you feel about teaching to the test?

What would you do if . . . ?

1. You were asked if "drill and kill" strategies for teaching to the test actually produce higher test scores than other forms of instruction.

2. You were told that research has shown that accountability and standardized tests need not be in conflict with good instruction.

3. You were asked your views as they relate to the following statement: Overreliance on "drill and kill" and test-preparation materials is not only unethical in the long term but ineffective in the short term, because there really is no trade-off between good instruction and good test scores.

In the next chapter we will discuss what happens after the assessments are made. The teacher holds students accountable for their learning by making an evaluation (or judgment) of their progress. It seems fitting that, especially in the case of standardized tests, teachers are then held accountable for what the students learned as a result of their instruction.

Theory into Practice

Although the specific purposes of tests and intended use of outcomes vary among teachers and schools, tests play an important part in the life of students and teachers. One of your goals as a teacher should be to improve your tests. Box 8.7 contains a checklist to use when constructing your classroom and/or criterion-referenced tests.

Box 8.7   Checklist for Constructing Tests

1. Is my test appropriate?
   - Does it match defined standards?
   - Does it fit my objectives?
   - Do the test items reflect a wide representation of subject content and skills?
   - Does the test have credible and worthwhile items to anchor the scoring system?
   - Does it consider reality (i.e., does it take into consideration the conditions of the classroom, school, and community)?

2. Is my test valid?
   - Does it discriminate between performance levels?
   - Does it fit external and agreed-upon standards?
   - Will my colleagues in the subject or at the grade level agree that all necessary items are included?
   - Does the test measure actual performance, not the students' reading levels or simple recall of information?

3. Is my test reliable?
   - Are all test items clear and understandable?
   - Are the items consistent with test performance?
   - Are there at least two items per objective, and do students who get one item of a pair correct get the other item correct?
   - Are there sufficient test items to measure important content and skills?

4. Is my test usable?
   - Is my test short enough to avoid being tedious?
   - Does it have sufficient breadth and depth to allow for generalizations about student performance?
   - Are there clear and standard procedures for administration of the test?
   - Is it authentic (i.e., does it measure worthwhile behaviors and tasks, not what is easy to score)?

CONCLUSIONS

- Good teachers know the standards for their local district and for their state.
- A good test is reliable and valid. Methods for establishing reliability are test-retest, parallel test forms, and split-half reliability. Forms of validity are content, curricular, construct, criterion, and predictive, with content validity being most important.

- There are two major types of tests: norm referenced and criterion referenced. Norm-referenced tests measure how a student performs relative to other students. Criterion-referenced tests measure a student's progress and appraise his or her ability relative to a specific criterion.

- For general appraisal of an individual's performance or behavior, the standardized (norm-referenced) test is an excellent instrument. There are four basic types of standardized tests: intelligence, achievement, aptitude, and personality.

- Teacher-made tests may be short-answer tests or essay tests. Short-answer questions include multiple choice, matching, completion, and true-false. Essay (or free-response) questions also include discussion questions.

- Proper test administration reduces confusion, curtails students' anxieties, motivates them, and helps them do as well as possible.

- Important test-taking skills can be taught to students.

KEY TERMS

achievement tests	matching test	portfolios
alternative assessment	multiple-choice test	project work
aptitude tests	nonstandardized tests	reliability
authentic assessment	norm-referenced tests	short-answer tests
completion tests	one-minute essay	standardized test
criterion-referenced	questions	teacher-made tests
tests	performance-based	test anxiety
essay test	assessment	true-false test questions
intelligence tests	personality tests	validity

DISCUSSION QUESTIONS

1. What are the academic standards for the subject you teach?

2. Compare the curriculum for a school district with the established state academic standards. How do they match up?

3. Identify the advantages and disadvantages of each of the following types of assessment.

   - essay questions

   - short-answer questions

   - multiple-choice questions

   - true-false questions

   - norm-referenced test

   - criterion-referenced test

4. When are they appropriate for use?

5. What are the advantages of teacher-made tests over standardized tests? What are the advantages of standardized tests over teacher-made tests?

MINI-CASES FROM THE FIELD

Analyze the following brief case studies, utilizing your common sense and the information contained in this chapter.

Case One: Using Standards

Richard Doyle was new to teaching and quite concerned about his assignment as a fourth-grade teacher at the Barton School. The school, located in an economically depressed area, was struggling with the impact of gentrification and an overly active parent association. The children in his class were delayed in reading by one to two years. His class had demonstrated little evidence of improvement since September. The state's standardized reading test for the fourth grade was scheduled to be given within two months. Mr. Doyle had worked hard in his attempt to implement the school's traditional reading program. In addition, he had selected books that he knew were appropriate for his students. He believed in a balanced approach to literacy; his only problem was that he couldn't tell whether it was working. He just felt deep down that his children were not learning.

1. Describe the types of tests that Mr. Doyle could have used to ascertain his students' reading progress.

2. Compare Mr. Doyle's intuitive approach to assessment with a properly prepared formative test.

3. What procedures should be followed when preparing for a standardized test?

4. How could Mr. Doyle have provided students and parents with a clear idea of what students would be expected to learn?

5. How could the standards have been used to assist Mr. Doyle in determining whether his students are learning what they need to learn?

Case Two: Test Selection

Carol Benbow loved to teach. She never felt better than when she was interacting with her sixth-grade language arts class. She was a serious person who had a great desire to see her students succeed. When she was preparing to become a teacher, her main thrust had been on learning theory and classroom management. What she had not done was actually teach a class and evaluate their success in understanding the required curriculum and content. She understood that she was responsible for determining the success of her students' learning and assessing their performance. Her problem was in selecting a test she could use that was reliable and valid. Carol's friend, Blanche, asked Carol why she was looking for a test, telling her to just make up her own test.

1. How would you describe Carol's approach to test selection?

2. Compare Blanche's approach to testing with Carol's.

3. How can reliability be obtained in a teacher-made test?

4. Explain the difficulty Carol would face in attempting to create a valid test for her class.

5. What suggestions would you have given Carol regarding her approach to test selection?

Case Three: Homework as an Assessment Tool

The principal asked Sally Callan to speak at the next Parent Association meeting. He wanted her to explain to the parents how homework could be used to evaluate student comprehension. He wanted her to stress that this could only be accomplished if children did their own homework. Sally was flattered that she had been asked to speak, but she was not sure whether she had a positive or negative view to express regarding the topic. She wondered if she should explain the two purposes for assessment. The first, known as formative assessment, was based on teacher observations and data collection during instruction to determine if students were learning what was being taught. Teachers used formative assessments as a guide for preparing future lessons. Summative assessments, on the other hand, were simply the evaluations done by teachers upon the conclusion of a unit of study.

1. What advice would you give Sally as to the correct position to take?

2. Explain the parents' role with regard to the amount of assistance they should give their children.

3. Discuss homework as a primary source for determining whether children are learning what is being taught.

4. How would you design a homework assignment to reflect what a child has learned?

5. How would you advise parents with regard to the proper amount of time for homework?

Case Four: Types of Tests

As a high school teacher, Phyllis Taylor understood that she had the responsibility to grade her students conscientiously. She realized that admission to college could be jeopardized by a poor grade, and that the assessment process consisted of evaluation and measurement. She understood tests but was unclear about how formal and informal approaches should be used in assessing her students. How much weight should each carry? She decided to make a list of the various assessment procedures she was aware of. Her list included teacher-made tests, standardized tests, portfolios, observation, performance assessment, interviews, and questionnaires. Even after constructing the list, Phyllis was still unsure of herself regarding the worth of the various approaches to evaluation. Her friend Gail told her to just be fair and treat all the data she collected on an equal basis.

1. Which of the assessment tools on Phyllis's list would you consider formal or informal?

2. Describe the difference between a formal and informal assessment.

3. How could you combine the idea of performance assessment with a teacher-made test?

4. Are your observations important in assessing student understandings? Justify your answer.

5. Which type of teacher-made test (true-false, completion, multiple choice, matching-items tests, or an essay) would you consider most effective for a final summative evaluation?

Case Five: Administering a Standardized Test

Janis Bowden was a new teacher who felt fortunate to have been appointed to the Harriman Elementary School. The school had a well deserved reputation for innovation and professionalism and was considered to be one of the best in the school district. The principal, Mrs. Berman, was a conscientious, fair-minded administrator. She always stressed to students, parents, and faculty the importance of doing well on the state comprehensive standards test. She viewed high-stakes standardized testing as the wave of the future. Mrs. Berman told her staff that before long, national standards would be a reality. She claimed this would remove the subjectivity of individual teachers' grading methods while maintaining academic standards. Mrs. Berman selected Janis for the position of teacher leader with regard to administering the test because she was new and would not have any preconceived ideas about administering a standardized test.

1. How would you respond to a colleague who claimed that talented teachers have abandoned the profession after having been turned into what they perceived as glorified test-prep technicians as a result of standardized tests?

2. How would you react to a parent who said that countless inventive learning activities have been eliminated in favor of prefabricated lessons pegged to state standards?

3. What would you say to those who claimed that standards alone should not drive teaching and learning?

4. Harold Howe II, a former US commissioner of education, said that we should make standards as vague as possible, to avoid becoming a nation that would create a de facto national curriculum. Do you agree or disagree with this statement? Explain your reasoning.

5. What are some suggestions to give Janis with regard to administering a standardized test?

FIELD EXPERIENCE ACTIVITIES

Visit a school and talk to a few teachers, the school counselor, or one of the administrators about the standardized tests the school uses. Try to find out which ones are used and why. What are the advantages and disadvantages of the tests? Report back to the class.

1. Invite a test specialist to class to discuss strategies that students can learn to increase their "test-wiseness."

2. Visit a class when the teacher is giving a test or quiz. Describe how the teacher deals with the following issues:

   • test reliability and validity

   • directions to students (oral or written)

   • proctoring the test

   • grading procedures

3. Observe two classroom teachers with regard to their task orientation. Compare their performance using the following rubric.

   • Is the lesson related to a specific standard?

   • Are clerical tasks handled efficiently?

   • Has the teacher developed an appropriate discipline plan?

   • Are children motivated because of the instructional strategy used by the teacher?

RECOMMENDED READING

Airasian, Peter W., and Michael Russell. *Classroom Assessment: Concepts and Applications*, 6th ed. Boston: McGraw-Hill, 2007.
  Focuses on assessment needs of preservice teachers, including special emphasis on standardized testing, performance tests, and authentic testing.

Burke, Kay. *How to Assess Authentic Learning*, 5th ed. Thousand Oaks, CA: Corwin, 2009.
  Documents the different ways teachers can assess student learning by using alternative assessment protocols.

Cizek, Gregory J., and Samantha S. Burg. *Addressing Test Anxiety in a High-Stakes Environment: Strategies for Classrooms and Schools*. Thousand Oaks, CA: Corwin, 2006.
  A research-based guide that offers recommendations for dealing with test anxiety.

Elliot, Stephen N., Jeffrey P. Braden, and Jennifer L. White. *Assessing One and All*. Arlington, VA: Council for Exceptional Children, 2001.
  An excellent resource that helps readers understand how to assess the wide variety of learners evidenced in most classrooms.

Gronlund, Norman E., and C. Keith Waugh. *Assessment of Student Achievement*, 9th ed. Boston: Allyn & Bacon, 2008.
  A thoughtful description of the development and use of practical assessment tools for teachers.

Koretz, Daniel. *Measuring Up: What Educational Testing Really Tells Us*. Boston: Harvard University Press, 2008.
  Everyday examples to show what tests do well, what their limits are, and how they can be used sensibly to help discover what students have learned.

Popham, W. James. *Classroom Assessment: What Teachers Need to Know*, 6th ed. Boston: Allyn & Bacon, 2010.
  Describes the differences between norm-referenced and criterion-referenced tests and their applications.

Reynolds, Cecil R., Ronald B. Livingston, and Victor Wilson. *Measurement and Assessment in Education*, 2nd ed. Boston: Allyn & Bacon, 2009.
    Includes a thorough discussion of performance and portfolio assessments and a practical discussion of professional best practices in educational measurement.
Salvia, John, James Ysseldyke, and Sara Bolt. *Assessment*, 11th ed. Belmont, CA: Wadsworth, 2009.
    A comprehensive resource for understanding all the different formal and informal assessment approaches that teachers might use.
Wiggins, G., and Jay McTighe. *Understanding by Design*, 2nd ed. Alexandria, VA: ASCD, 2006.
    Describes the subtle differences between understanding and knowing and how teachers explore and assess those differences.

9

Student Evaluation

FOCUS POINTS

1. Determining the meaning of the term *evaluation*.
2. Understanding that informal and formal methods are available for assessing students.
3. Contrasting the advantages and disadvantages of absolute grade standards and relative grade standards.
4. Comparing traditional grading to standards-based grading.
5. Comprehending the importance of teacher–parent communication.
6. Developing procedures to improve communication with parents.
7. Appreciating the relationship between student performance and school performance with regard to accountability.

OVERVIEW

In this chapter we address student evaluation and accountability. Testing students is more objective than evaluation, since it is based on quantifiable data. Evaluation is more subjective, since it involves human judgment. We make evaluations of people and their performance not only in school, but also on the job and at home. Similarly, we make evaluations of consumer goods (e.g., food, clothing, cameras, televisions) and services (e.g., auto repair, insurance, medical treatment, legal advice). We use various kinds of information, including test data and other objective measurements, to do these evaluations. As teachers we strive to reduce the chance for misjudgment in the evaluation of students by carefully designing evaluation procedures.

Students must feel that their academic efforts will lead to success. The evaluation process should motivate them; it should encourage them to set progressively higher goals for personal achievement. Students must feel that the evaluation of their performance is objective and the criteria are the same for all students. If students feel the evaluation process will lead to failure, or if they feel the process is unfair, they will be discouraged by it.

The evaluation process should also be realistic. Students should be able to assess their own performance in relation to that of classmates, and to normative standards. In a class in which most students cannot read well, a student who is an average reader may get an inflated impression of his or her real abilities. Evaluations are more effective when students are provided with valid norms of what constitutes success. Evaluation is also more effective when teachers think beyond the use of just criterion or normative tests. Good teachers provide students with a wide variety of ways to *show* what they know.[1]

Every student, during his or her school career, will experience the pain of failure and the joy of success as a result of the evaluation process. According to Philip Jackson, the student must learn "to adapt to the continued and pervasive spirit of evaluation that will dominate . . . [the] school year." Although school is not the only place "where the student is made aware of his strengths and weaknesses," school evaluation is the most common type and has the most lasting impact on how students view themselves.[2]

The impact of school evaluation is profound, because students form their identities during their school years, when they are going through their most critical stages of development, and because they lack the maturity to cope with the feelings they experience when confronted with the poor evaluations and their lack of knowledge about how to take steps toward remediation. Whether evaluation focuses on academic work, social behavior, or personal qualities, it affects the student's reputation among his or her peers, confidence in his or her abilities, and motivation to work. The student's popularity, confidence, personal adjustment, career goals, and even physical and mental health are related to the judgments that others communicate to him or her throughout school. We are what we see ourselves to be, and like it or not, we see ourselves as others perceive and evaluate us. The self is a social product that emerges as we grow and interact with others. Many students drop out of school (either psychologically or physically) because they simply do not believe they can learn—and they have learned to view themselves that way from teachers!

Types of Evaluation

Evaluation is normally defined as making a judgment or assigning a value to a program or student work, after the completion of instruction.[3] For our purposes, we discuss four basic evaluation techniques that are appropriate for and commonly used in the classroom: (1) placement evaluation, which helps to determine student placement or categorization before instruction begins; (2) diagnostic evaluation, which is a means of discovering and monitoring learning difficulties; (3) formative evaluation, which monitors student progress; and (4) summative evaluation, which measures the products of instruction at the end of instruction.

Placement Evaluation

Sometimes called *pre-assessment,* **placement evaluation** takes place before instruction. The teacher wants to find out what knowledge and skills the students have mastered in order to establish a starting point of instruction. Sufficient mastery might suggest that some instructional units may be skipped or treated briefly. Insufficient mastery suggests that certain basic knowledge or skills should be emphasized. Students who are required to begin at a level that is too difficult or beyond their understanding will encounter frustration and will most likely be unable to acquire new knowledge and skills. In contrast, students who are required to review old material they already know are wasting instructional time and may eventually become bored.

It is also important to find out how much a student knows and what his or her interests and work habits are in order to decide on the best *type* of instruction (group or independent, inductive or deductive) and instructional *materials*

Reasons for Evaluation

Daniel L. Stufflebeam

The most important reasons to evaluate are:

1. To assure that one is doing all one can to help each student to learn,
2. To find ways to conduct group instruction as efficiently and effectively as possible,
3. To provide students and their parents with progress reports they can use to guide the learning process,
4. To certify levels of achievement, and
5. To provide records and reports that will help other professionals work with individual students.

It is noteworthy that four of the five purposes denote the need for individualized evaluation and continuous assessment and feedback. While evaluation is also needed to assist the search for efficient teaching methods that work well with groups, it is crucial that the teacher become skilled in those kinds of evaluation that can lead to individual diagnoses, reinforcement, and direction for growth. Unfortunately, many of the evaluation devices for sale, especially standardized tests, and many of the evaluation designs in the literature, especially pre-test/post-test designs, have little utility to teachers for doing the types of evaluation that are most important to them and to the individual students and families they serve. Hence, teachers should not fall into a pattern of using whatever standardized measures are available but instead should become proficient in designing evaluations that produce useful information about their students, and in devising homespun instruments that will respond well to the pertinent data requirements.

---

for that student. We have previously referenced the idea of standards-based reform. That reform has implications for how you teach. Specifically, you must be able to assess student strengths and weaknesses in order to identify strategies for moving students forward in their own learning. The word *purpose* gives meaning to a teacher's evaluation. A teacher's evaluation is a judgment with regard to a student's ability. The purpose of evaluation is for the teacher to provide appropriate instruction. Unfortunately, testing has come to be associated with negative consequences that result from poor performance. Sadly, this difference in purpose between judgment for instruction and testing for consequences has been a major drawback to the standards movement.[4]

A third reason for placement evaluation is to assign students to specific learning groups. Although this procedure may lead to tracking, which is criticized by many researchers, teachers find that appropriately grouping students facilitates teaching and learning. Placement evaluation is based on readiness tests, aptitude tests, pretests on course objectives, teacher observational techniques, and teacher assessment of student progress toward achieving certain content standards.

Diagnostic Evaluation

Diagnostic evaluation attempts to discover the causes of students' learning or behavioral problems. If a student continues to fail a particular subject, or if she is unable to learn basic skills in elementary school or basic content in secondary school, diagnosing the cause of the failure may point to ways to remedy it. According to Bruce Tuckman, "Where proficiency has not been demonstrated, remedial instruction aimed directly at those [deficiencies] can be instituted," and evaluation can "provide the kind of information that will make it possible to overcome failure."[5]

In many cases diagnostic and formative evaluation overlap each other. Formative evaluation is mainly concerned with student progress, while diagnostic evaluation focuses on the lack of progress through identification and remediation. According to Gronlund and Linn, formative evaluation serves as a guide to general, everyday treatment, but diagnostic evaluation is necessary for detailed, remedial treatment.[6]

Some diagnostic information is developed as a result of the administration of standardized tests. Such tests are intended to examine specific social, academic, or emotional dispositions that the child evidences.[7] Other diagnostics are prepared by teachers in order to assess what students are doing wrong and why they are behaving the way they are. One problem with standardized tests is that they tend to be broad and may not yield the type of detailed information you need. Teacher-made diagnostics can be much more focused.

Formative Evaluation

Formative evaluation and *summative evaluation* are terms coined by Michael Scriven in his classic analysis of program and curriculum evaluation.[8] **Formative evaluation** monitors student progress during the learning process, while summative evaluation measures the final results at the end of an instructional unit or term. Benjamin Bloom and his associates described formative evaluation as a major tool of instruction: "Too often in the past evaluation has been entirely summative in nature, taking place only at the end of the unit, chapter, course, or semester, when it is too late, at least for that particular group of students, to modify either . . . the teaching [or] learning . . . process."[9]

If evaluation is to help the teacher and student, it should take place not only at the end point of instruction, but also at various points during the teaching–learning process when there is still time for modifications to be made. Instruction can be modified, based on the feedback that formative evaluation yields, to correct learning problems or to move ahead more rapidly.

Formative evaluation focuses on small, comparatively independent units of instruction and a narrow range of objectives. It is based on teacher-made and published tests administered throughout the term, on homework, on classroom performance of students, on informal teacher observations of students, on student-teacher conferences, and on parent-teacher conferences.

Formative assessment and evaluation are critical to student success. Several studies, including a systematic review of assessment studies by a group of researchers, revealed that enhanced formative assessments resulted in "significant and substantial learning gains" for students.[10] And those learning gains appear to be even more dramatic for lower achievers. If teachers use assessments in ways that show students can improve their performance, enhanced student learning appears to be a real and substantive result. Teachers can do this by determining specific ways in which students can use more practice on skills or by revising what and how to teach based on what students need to learn.

Summative Evaluation

Summative evaluation takes place at the end of an instructional unit or course. It is designed to determine the extent to which the instructional objectives have been achieved by the students, and it is used primarily to certify or grade students.[11] Summative evaluation also can be used to judge the effectiveness of a teacher or a particular curriculum or program. Whereas formative evaluation provides a *tentative* judgment of teaching and learning, summative evaluation is a *final* judgment.

Summative evaluation focuses on a wide range of objectives and relies on an accumulation of student work and performance. Although teacher-made tests can be used for this purpose, summative evaluation is often based on formal observation scales or ratings and standardized tests.

Table 9.1 provides a summary of the four types of evaluation a teacher can use during the instructional process. It's important to understand that the problem with this construct of evaluation is that it focuses almost exclusively on the child. It does not take context into consideration—that is, how do environmen-

Table 9.1　Types of Evaluation

Type	Function	Illustrative Instruments Used
Placement	Determines skills, degree of mastery before instruction to determine appropriate level and mode of teaching	Readiness tests, aptitude tests, pretests, observations, interviews, personality profiles, self-reports, video recordings, anecdotal reports from previous teachers
Diagnostic	Determines causes (cognitive, physical, emotional, social) of serious learning problems to indicate remedial techniques	Published diagnostic tests, teacher-made diagnostic tests, observations, interviews, anecdotal reports from current teachers
Formative	Determines learning progress; provides feedback to facilitate learning and to correct teaching errors	Teacher-made tests, tests from test publishers, observations, checklists
Summative	Determines end-of-course achievement or student performance on statewide proficiency tests	Teacher-made tests, rating scales, standardized tests administered locally or on a statewide basis

Source: Adapted from Peter Airasian and Michael Russell, *Classroom Assessment*, 6th ed. (New York: McGraw-Hill, 2008); M. David Miller, Robert L. Linn, and Norman E. Gronlund, *Measurement and Evaluation in Teaching*, 7th ed. (New York: Prentice-Hall, 2009).

tal factors influence the problems young people face? Environmental factors can have a tremendous impact on children's ability to learn. (See Classic Professional Viewpoint 9.2.)

---

classic professional viewpoint 9.2

Evaluating Students in Schools

Martin Haberman

I learned two lessons while teaching second grade (way back in the stone age). The first was from Arthur, who should have been in a special class; but we liked each other and I never sent him to the school psychologist to be tested. Arthur had trouble learning anything and when he did, he had trouble remembering it in the next hour. In order to "encourage" him (but also to be fair to the others) I gave him Cs on his first report card. The next day he came in with a black eye and some facial cuts. His sister explained that their parents had beaten him because he hadn't come home with all As. After meeting the parents I learned that they were religious zealots who believed that God told them to beat Arthur to shape him up; indeed, it was their duty. I saw to it that Arthur got all As on his subsequent report cards and included some specific information on the permanent record of just what Arthur's achievements were in the various subjects.

My second lesson also came from parents. Martha was a sweet little second grader who played with a doll all day, every day. When I met with her father, I was surprised to see a Danish sailor who was at least 6 foot 6 inches tall. He picked Martha up and perched her on his shoulder while I gave him a half hour of jargon about how he might interpret norm-referenced test scores related to Martha's achievement. I used every bit of jargon that I knew. But I noticed he was holding her just like she held her doll, and the only thing I thought to say was that it was a real pleasure to have Martha in class.

I never did learn how to communicate honestly with abusive parents, but with doting ones I learned to enjoy how much they loved their kids. I'll bet some people might not think this has anything to do with "evaluation."

Evaluation Methods and Approaches

To some degree, everyone is evaluated and makes evaluations on a daily and informal basis. Students and teachers continuously evaluate each other informally in class. When teachers observe students at work or answer students' questions, they are engaging in **informal evaluation**. When evaluation is impressionistic or based on thoughtful hunches, it is informal. **Formal evaluation** is more precise and defined and usually entails a lot more planning on the part of the teacher. As you will see as we examine different ways to collect data, some forms of assessment have both formal and informal elements.

Evaluation without tests (or informal evaluation) occurs on a daily basis and is considered to be more powerful and influential than tests by some. This is due to the impact of teacher judgment on student self-worth. Informal assessment can be made by noting class attendance, assessing the atmosphere in the class (e.g., attentiveness of students, noise level, student posture, and activity) and observing the performance of students in class work, projects and so on.

A second source of daily informal evaluation is the *judgment of peers.* Peer judgment is a two-sided sword: It can be both harmful and beneficial; harmful if children are ridiculed or receive destructive criticism, and positive when they work cooperatively to achieve objectives.

A third source of daily informal evaluation is student *self-judgment.* Students appraise their own performance without the intervention of the teacher. This type of evaluation is more difficult to discern and describe, but it occurs throughout instruction, such as when the student works on the chalkboard and knows that the work is correct or incorrect, even if the teacher does not bother to indicate one way or another.[12] "Correctly implemented, student self-assessment can promote intrinsic motivation, internally controlled effort, a mastery goal orientation, and more meaningful learning."[13] It should be noted that students' self-judgment of their performance without the intervention of a teacher is the most difficult to assess. The simplest approach would be to just ask the child, "How are you doing?"

There are many other types of evaluation that are both *private,* such as IQ and personality test scores (which may lead to labeling) or certain communications to parents or other teachers about students, and *public,* such as the display of work for others to see or a teacher review of a student's mistake for the benefit of the entire class. Evaluations in class and school never cease.

Some educators criticize the evaluation process, but evaluation is necessary. Although it can be argued that tests are not always necessary for grading, classifying, or judging students, evaluation is. Teachers need to evaluate students' performance and their progress toward defined school and state standards; otherwise, they are relinquishing an important role. On the other hand, the evaluation process should consider the student's feelings and self-concept; it should avoid labels that lead to traps, embarrassment, and despair in students whose performance is less than average. Various informal methods and approaches that can be used to supplement formal test data are summarized in Tips for Teachers 9.1.

Specific Evaluation Techniques and Tools

Teachers use a wide variety of assessment strategies to evaluate student academic growth. Some require the collection of explicit data about student learning and others gather more informal types of information. Each type of data, however, should give you a sense of *what* and *how much* students are learning so that you can evaluate performance. In most instances you will have considerable discretion in selecting how to assess student learning. But remember that a good assessment is based on clearly defined objectives. Alignment is critical to good teaching: objectives → instruction → assessment.

Quizzes. **Quizzes** are brief, informal assessments of student knowledge. They provide a basis for checking understanding and for evaluating students' daily progress. Some teachers give unannounced quizzes (or "pop" quizzes) at

TIPS
F
O
R
T
E
A
C
H
E
R
S
9.1

Alternative Assessment Criteria

The Aurora (Colorado) School District has implemented a nontraditional method of grading students based on judging their abilities to perform complex tasks that are not just cognitive but also psychological, social, and civic in nature. The five categories (which the district calls the "big outcomes") and their nineteen components or examples can be used for all grade levels and subjects. These criteria are listed below. This new method suggests a radical change in student assessment.

1. *Self-directed learner*
   - Sets priorities and achieves goals.
   - Monitors and evaluates progress.
   - Creates options for self.
   - Assumes responsibility for actions.
   - Creates a positive vision for sell and future.

2. *Collaborative worker*
   - Monitors own behavior.
   - Assesses and manages group functioning.
   - Demonstrates interactive communication.
   - Demonstrates consideration for individual differences.

3. *Complex thinker*
   - Uses a wide variety of strategies for managing complex issues.
   - Selects strategies appropriate to the resolution of complex issues and applies the strategies with accuracy and thoroughness.
   - Accesses and uses topic-relevant knowledge.

4. *Quality producer*
   - Creates products that achieve their purpose.
   - Creates products appropriate to the intended audience.
   - Creates products that reflect craftsmanship.
   - Uses appropriate resources/technology.

5. *Community contributor*
   - Demonstrates knowledge about his or her diverse communities.
   - Takes action.
   - Reflects on role as a community contributor.

Source: Nora Redding, "Assessing the Big Outcomes," *Educational Leadership* 49(8), 50. Copyright © 1992 by ASCD. Reprinted with permission. Learn more about ASCD at www.ascd.org.

irregular intervals, especially quizzes related to specific assignments. Others give regular, scheduled quizzes to assess learning over a short period of time, perhaps every week or two. Quizzes encourage students to keep up with the assignments, and they show them evidence of their strengths and weaknesses in learning.

Frequent and systematic monitoring of students' work and progress through short quizzes helps teachers improve instruction and student learning. Errors that students make serve as early warning signals of learning problems that then can be corrected before they worsen. According to researchers, student effort and achievement improve when teachers provide frequent evaluation and prompt feedback on quizzes.[14] Quizzes are relatively easy to develop, administer, and grade, thus providing an avenue for multiple and prompt evaluation.

In essence, student performance and progress can be measured through a variety of methods other than the pencil-and-paper tests described in the previous chapter, although testing is the most common source of data and should be included as part of the total evaluation.

Observation of Student Work.   The teacher has the opportunity to watch students perform various tasks on a daily basis, under various conditions, and either alone or with different students. The teacher observes students more or less continually, simply by virtue of being in the classroom, but he or she needs to know what to look for and to have some relatively objective system for collecting and assessing data.

Although the teacher should observe all students, individuals who exhibit atypical behavior or learning outcomes are often singled out for special study. The keys to good observation are objectivity and documentation. Teachers cannot depend on memory or vague statements, such as "Trent misbehaves in class." They must keep accurate, specific written records that contain objective statements of what students are doing: "Cheli is unable to use apostrophes correctly with possessive nouns" or "Han was out of his seat five times today without permission."

If observations are free from bias and tempered with common sense, this informal, nonstandardized evaluation method can provide more insightful information about a student than test scores alone. The key for a teacher is to make observations of students and then make specific learning prescriptions based on those observations.

There are many different types of observation instruments you can use to evaluate students. Some teachers create learning prescriptions that highlight strengths and weaknesses but also outline specific ideas for improving weaknesses (see Tips for Teachers 9.2). One of the simplest instruments is a *sign instrument*, on which you simply indicate the presence or absence of a behavior (see table 9.2 on p. 442). Another form of simple observation instrument is a rating instrument, on which you evaluate the degree to which some behavior is occurring in the classroom. Table 9.3 (on p. 442) is an example of a rating instrument. There are many other types of instruments that you can use, but these are two of the simplest and easiest. The sign instrument would be appropriate for collecting information simultaneously on a large number of students. The rating instrument is oriented toward individual assessments.

Observation data are valuable for understanding the daily performance of students in a more detailed way. Don't trust your memory to recall how a student is behaving. Purposefully collect observation data to better determine how students are behaving and what skills they do or do not possess.

Group and Peer Evaluation and Feedback.   Teachers can set aside a time to allow students to participate in establishing instructional objectives and to evaluate their strengths and limitations and their own progress in learning. Stu-

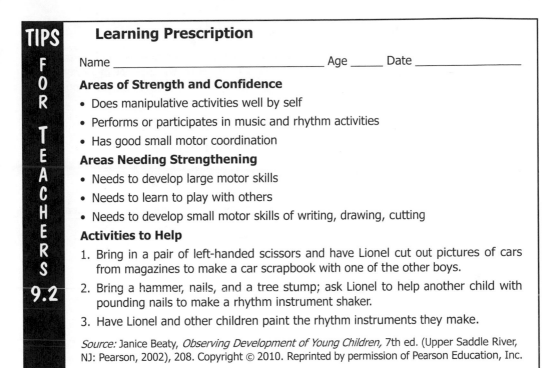

Source: Janice Beaty, *Observing Development of Young Children,* 7th ed. (Upper Saddle River, NJ: Pearson, 2002), 208. Copyright © 2010. Reprinted by permission of Pearson Education, Inc.

dents can evaluate themselves or their classmates on study habits and homework, class participation, quizzes, workbook or textbook activities, and other activities. They can keep anecdotal reports or logs about their own work in which they record successes and difficulties. They can check off assignments they complete and evaluate their work in group discussions. Evaluation techniques such as these make it possible for teachers to diagnose and measure student progress quickly and efficiently. Group evaluation strategies can be especially useful when teachers use cooperative learning strategies.

Group and peer evaluation enhances student interaction and enables students to learn from one another, enhances group spirit, and contributes to student empowerment. It also helps students develop higher-order thinking skills while learning discipline-specific course concepts.[15] Research suggests, too, that when students provide and receive feedback to and from peers about their academic work, social responsibility and student achievement are enhanced.[16] Students can serve as peer evaluators for quizzes or peer editors for written projects. Ideally, the answers or a preset criterion should be provided to enable students to evaluate others.

Students can also provide valuable ideas and information to each other regarding various cooperative activities and projects. Here the teacher's role in initiating and fostering trust and cooperation among students is important. Teachers can promote these aims by (1) encouraging students to contribute openly, (2) sharing materials and resources, (3) expressing acceptance and support during

Table 9.2   Student Behavior Observation Checklist

Identify behaviors that you would like to observe during a cooperative learning lesson. List those behaviors and then evaluate the degree to which students evidence the behavior during cooperative learning lessons. (Some common misbehaviors are identified for illustrative purposes.)

Teacher: _____ Class: _____ Date: _____

Target Skills: _____

Mark observed behaviors with a + and behaviors not observed with a −.

Name of student	Leaves seat without permission	Is late to class	Is disruptive to classroom activities	Keeps other students from doing work	Comments
1					
2					
3					
4					
5					
6					
7					
8					
9					
10					
11					
12					
13					

Table 9.3   Student Skill Checklist

Directions: Identify specific skills that you expect students to demonstrate in a particular learning context, and assess the degree to which you believe students possess that skill.

Student: _____

Date Observed: _____

Time Observed: _____

	Not Evident	Somewhat Evident	Very Evident
1. Students demonstrate an ability to think critically about an issue.			
2. Skill 2:			
3. Skill 3:			
4. Skill 4:			

their interactions, and (4) pointing out rejecting and nonsupportive behaviors that hinder peer evaluation and cooperation.[17]

Recitations.   Many teachers consider a student's participation in class to be an essential source of data for evaluation. Teachers are impressed by students who volunteer, develop their thoughts logically, and discuss relevant facts and relationships. Answering the teacher's questions frequently and carrying out assignments in class are considered evidence of progress. The inability to answer questions and the inability to perform assignments in class are indications of learning problems or lack of motivation. The key during recitation is to make certain that full student participation is evidenced. Some teachers call on a small group of volunteers who know the content well and ignore a larger group of nonvolunteer students who may either fail to understand the content or be unwilling to participate. All students need to learn, and it is the responsibility of the teacher to find ways to help all students engage in the learning process.

In fact, there may be a number of reasons students do not respond to teachers correctly. Observers outline some possibilities:

> A particular feature of the talk between teacher and pupils is the asking of questions by the teacher. . . . One common problem is that, following a question, teachers do not wait long enough to allow pupils to think out their answers. When a teacher answers his or her own question after only two or three seconds and when a minute of silence is not tolerable, there is no possibility that a pupil can think out what to say.
>
> There are then two consequences. One is that, because the only questions that can produce answers in such a short time are questions of fact, these predominate. The other is that pupils don't even try to think out a response. Because they know that the answer, followed by another question, will come along in a few seconds, there is no point in trying. . . .
>
> There are several ways to break this particular cycle. They involve giving pupils time to respond; asking them to discuss their thinking in pairs or in small groups, so that a respondent is speaking on behalf of others; giving pupils a choice between different possible answers and asking them to vote on the options; asking all of them to write down an answer and then reading out a selected few; and so on. What is essential is that any dialogue should evoke thoughtful reflection in which all pupils can be encouraged to take part, for only then can the formative process start to work.[18]

Homework.   The teacher can learn much about students' achievements and attitudes by checking homework carefully. A good rule is not to assign homework unless it is going to be checked in some way, preferably by you, and in some cases by another student or by the student him- or herself. The idea is to provide prompt feedback to the student, preferably emphasizing the positive aspects of work while making one or two major recommendations for improvement. As Walberg points out, student achievement increases significantly when teachers assign homework on a regular basis, students conscientiously do it, and teacher comments and feedback are provided when the work is completed.[19] But, for homework to be effective in accomplishing its purposes, it must be assigned properly. Box 9.1 outlines general teacher guidelines for assigning homework.

Box 9.1   Homework "Do's and Don'ts"

The following homework "do's and don'ts" are part of a selective list of the most important considerations.

For Principals

1. *Don't* believe everything you hear about a teacher's homework practices.
2. *Don't* expect all teachers to be equally enthusiastic about a schoolwide homework policy.
3. *Don't* expect a schoolwide homework policy to please all parents.
4. *Don't* expect teachers with the heaviest instructional loads to assign as much homework as those with the lightest loads.
5. *Do* check out all rumors that come your way about teachers' homework practices.
6. *Do* put the teachers you least expect to be pleased by a schoolwide homework policy on the committee that formulates it.
7. *Do* involve parents in the development of schoolwide homework policies.
8. *Do* everything possible to assist teachers with managing homework paper loads, including use of school aides and parent volunteers.

For Teachers

1. *Don't* ever give homework as punishment.
2. *Don't* make up spur-of-the-moment homework assignments.
3. *Don't* assume that because there are no questions asked about a homework assignment students have no questions about the assignment.
4. *Don't* expect students (even your best students) always to have their homework assignments completed.
5. *Do* understand that not all types of homework assignments are equally valuable for all types of students.
6. *Do* explain the specific purpose of every homework assignment.
7. *Do* listen to what students say about their experiences in completing your homework assignments.
8. *Do* acknowledge and be thankful for efforts students make to complete their homework.

For Parents

1. *Don't* try to help with homework if you are confused and really cannot figure out what is expected.
2. *Don't* hesitate to have your child explain legitimate reasons that homework simply cannot be completed.
3. *Don't* place yourself in an adversarial role between your child and the teachers over homework issues until all other alternatives are exhausted.
4. *Don't* feel your child always has to be doing "something productive." (There are few things sadder than a burned-out 14-year-old.)
5. *Do* make sure your child really needs help before offering to help with homework.
6. *Do* help your child see some value or purpose in homework assignments.
7. *Do* encourage your children to complete assignments after absences from school.
8. *Do* suggest an alternative to watching TV on nights when no homework is assigned, such as sharing a magazine article, enjoying a game together, or going to an exhibit or concert.

For Students

1. *Don't* expect that your parents will be able to help with all your homework. (Parents forget things they have learned, and some of what is taught in school today is foreign to adults.)

2. *Don't* ask teachers to help with any homework assignment you really can complete independently.

3. *Don't* confuse excuses for incomplete homework assignments with legitimate reasons.

4. *Don't* think doing your homework "most of the time" will be satisfactory for those classes in which homework counts the most. (In such classes, even a 75 percent completion rate may not be enough.)

5. *Do* ask your parents for help with your homework only when you really need help.

6. *Do* ask the teacher to help before or after class if you are confused about a homework assignment.

7. *Do* explain to teachers any legitimate reasons that sometimes make it impossible to complete some homework assignments.

8. *Do* make every effort to complete homework assignments when they are very important for a particular class.

Source: D. A. England and J. K. Flatley, *Homework—and Why* (Bloomington, IN: Phi Delta Kappan, 1985), 36–38. Reprinted with permission of Phi Delta Kappa International, www.pdkintl.org. All rights reserved.

Good and Brophy suggest that homework can be effective in fostering student learning and is advantageous for accomplishing teacher-defined goals if the teacher is seeking to achieve any of the following purposes: providing practice in a skill or procedures, preparing students for exams or summative learning experiences, enhancing personal student development in a particular area, or fostering parent-child relations (e.g., finding ways for parents and children to talk about ideas together).[20] Box 9.2 provides some homework guidelines based on current research.

Homework Controversy.   A controversy with regard to the value of homework has been ignited by the work of Harris Cooper, a noted education researcher at Duke University. A study he co-authored found that elementary school students gain little from most homework assignments, and that excessive amounts of homework might even be bad for middle and high school students. Cooper has claimed that elementary school students get no academic benefit from homework—except reading and some basic skills practice—and yet schools require more than ever.[21] His findings were compounded by Alfie Kohn in his book, *The Homework Myth.* Kohn called for the complete elimination of homework, which he blames for stress, family conflict, and slackened student motivation. Other education experts disagree with this view. They believe that the problem isn't homework per se, but the types of assignments teachers give— or are forced to give—and a general lack of clarity about the purpose of homework. They feel that solely relying on research is problematic. Rather than wait-

Box 9.2   Research-Based Homework Guidelines

Research provides strong evidence that, when used appropriately, homework benefits student achievement. To make sure that homework is appropriate, teachers should follow these guidelines:

Assign purposeful homework. Legitimate purposes for homework include introducing new content, practicing a skill or process that students can do independently but not fluently, elaborating on information that has been addressed in class to deepen students' knowledge, and providing opportunities for students to explore topics of their own interest.

Design homework to maximize the chances that students will complete it. For example, ensure that homework is at the appropriate level of difficulty. Students should be able to complete homework assignments independently with relatively high success rates, but they should still find the assignments challenging enough to be interesting.

Involve parents in appropriate ways (for example, as a sounding board to help students summarize what they learned from the homework) without requiring parents to act as teachers or to police students' homework completion.

Carefully monitor the amount of homework assigned so that it is appropriate to students' age levels and does not take too much time away from other home activities.

Adapted from R. J. Marzano and D. Pickering, "The Case For and Against Homework," *Educational Leadership* 64 (2007, March), 74–79.

ing until research proves that a practice is effective, practitioners should use their own professional judgment to develop specific homework practices. They can do so by combining research-based generalizations with research from related areas that enhance their practice. Like medical practitioners, education practitioners must develop their own "local knowledge base" on homework and all other aspects of teaching.[22]

Notebooks and Note Taking.   Notebooks should be used as an assessment tool for evaluating students' writing and understanding of subject matter in elementary school and, to a lesser extent, in the middle grades and junior high school.

Note taking is more important for secondary school students, especially at the high school level. At this level students should begin to be able to take notes on some of the unwritten ideas that emerge from the classroom discussions. Good note taking consists of arranging information in a systematic form, focusing on major points of discussion, condensing material, and integrating new with old information.[23] Verbatim note taking or simple paraphrasing or listing of information is not as effective.[24]

Note taking can take different forms. One especially useful form is summarizing. Students synthesize the material that they have been learning by analyzing the notes they have taken and by writing a brief summary. Such strategies are well established in areas such as reading for their effectiveness in enhancing student achievement.[25] Once the summaries are written, you can collect and read them to see what understandings and misunderstandings the students have, or you can pair students and have them share and evaluate the material.

Reports, Themes, and Research Papers.   Written work serves as an excellent way to assess students' ability to organize thoughts, to research topics, and to develop new ideas. In evaluating projects, the teacher should look to see how well students have developed their thoughts in terms of explanations, logic, and relationship of ideas; whether ideas are expressed clearly; whether facts are documented or distinguished from opinion; and what conclusions or recommendations are evidenced. Spelling and grammar should not be the focus of evaluating students' work, but neither should they be dismissed; rather, the emphasis should be on the thinking process of the students, their use of reference materials, and their ability to keep to the topic and develop it logically.

Quite obviously, how you grade and assess student work is largely dictated by your purpose in making the assignment. Your instructional goals and the rubrics you will use in assessing student work should be transparent to students. Some teachers hand out performance standards with assignments, communicating to the student what he or she is expected to do and how it will be graded.[26] Zmuda and Tomaino observe that, with such evaluation explicitness, "the grading process . . . [becomes] concrete, up front, and honest."[27]

Discussions and Debates.   Evaluating oral work is more difficult than evaluating written samples, but oral work may reveal creative and critical thinking that cannot be measured with other methods. David and Roger Johnson and others point out that, when students freely discuss topics that are of interest to them, their thinking is based on many skills, insights, and experiences not evidenced in a one-hour written test.[28] In discussion and debate students discover, in front of their peers, that they can succeed. Because they are in front of their peers, it is essential that no humiliation, no sarcasm, and no negativism be introduced into the discussion or evaluation process.

During discussions students can be rated not only on their mastery of and ability to analyze material, but also on several social and cognitive characteristics. Such characteristics include the way in which the student (1) accepts ideas of others, (2) initiates ideas, (3) gives opinions, (4) helps others, (5) seeks information, (6) tries to make the best decision as opposed to trying to "win," (7) encourages others to contribute, (8) works well with all group members, (9) raises provocative questions, (10) listens to others, (11) disagrees in a constructive fashion, (12) shows willingness to reverse an opinion, and (13) makes an overall positive contribution to the group.[29]

Before discussing the assignment of grades, let's summarize. There are multiple layers of assessment. School districts will administer large-scale assessments (common assessments required in all teachers' classrooms), and teachers have the option to decide on a variety of classroom assessments. The former have efficacy in determining the overall performance of a school or school district or group of teachers, while the latter are most useful in helping students (and parents) understand specific strengths and weaknesses associated with the particular content that has been taught. Your classroom assessments are important because they provide detailed information and feedback regarding a particular student's academic growth. With such information you are now ready to consider the assignment of a grade.

Traditional and Standards-Based Grading

The purpose of grading is somewhat different for teachers at different grade levels. Some studies indicate that elementary school teachers tend to say they give grades because the school district requires it, not because grades as a yardstick for achievement are important to them. In contrast, secondary school teachers feel grades are necessary for informing students, other teachers, and colleges about performance.[30] The same studies show that elementary school teachers rely heavily on their observations of student participation in class, motivation, and attitudes. Secondary school teachers assign grades mainly on the basis of test results and specific assignments.

Teachers need to recognize that young students (grade 2 or lower) have a limited understanding of the meaning of grades and that understanding of grading concepts increases with age. Grades at the elementary level are usually for the benefit of parents. Parents expect to see where a student stands, and, regrettably, that usually means in relationship to other students in class. It is not until the upper grades that most students understand complex schemes such as a grading curve, grade point average, and weighted grading. Older students are more likely than younger students to be critical of grading practices and less accepting of low grades received.[31] Such findings indicate that teachers might consider postponing formal grading until grades 5 or 6, if school policy permits, and that teachers should expect concern and even criticism among older students regarding "issued" grades, especially since they increasingly see grades as important for their future.

There are a number of general purposes for testing and grading: *certification,* or assurance that a student has mastered specific content or achieved a certain level of accomplishment; *selection,* or identifying or grouping students for certain educational paths or programs; and *motivation,* or emphasizing specific material or skills to be learned and helping students to understand and improve their performance.[32]

Interestingly, traditional grading is often taking a back seat in terms of importance to the standardized testing occurring in many schools and school districts. The high-stakes testing is all too often becoming more significant than the traditional grades that emerge from a series of low-stakes-assessment teacher measures. As a new teacher, pressures will be on you to address and deal with the demands and requirements of standardized testing. That reality, however, should not mitigate your daily instructional decision making regarding the learning needs of each student. You will know the students best, and no standardized test can assess better in a single day what you assess over a period of weeks.

Grades often result in a group of students being "winners" or "losers" from grade to grade. Indeed, one way in which teachers determine grades is by comparing students' performances, which might be referred to as norm-referenced grading. To paraphrase Robert Slavin: In the usual, competitive reward structure, the probability of one student's receiving a reward (or good grade) is negatively related to the probability of another student's receiving a reward.[33] Also, a demonstrable relationship exists between formal instruction and student performance at all grade levels, but constructing tests and grading accurately to reflect classroom tasks and intended learning are difficult for most teachers. Although teachers report that they feel they are able to interpret test results and transfer test scores into grades or grade equivalents, when teachers are tested on these abilities, the majority make some type of misinterpretation.[34]

Assigning grades to students' schoolwork is subjective. Teachers are required to make judgments, and few, if any, teachers are purely objective in making assessments. What test items should be included and how the items should be weighted are matters of judgment. Should points be deducted for partially wrong answers? How many As or Bs or Fs should be awarded? Will grading be on a curve or absolute? And what about all those special cases ("I lost my notebook") and problems ("I was sick last week")? Are students to be allowed to retake an exam because their results deviate from past performance? Should extra credit assignments be used to modify grades, and if so, to what extent? If test modification, additional tests, or extra credit assignments are permitted, teachers are forced into a more subjective role. But if a teacher fails to consider extraneous circumstances, possibly modifying the scoring results, then it can be argued that grades are being used as a weapon, certainly as a cold symbol of learning. It can also be argued that students are entitled to extra coaching and practice, but retaking exams or extra credit is unfair because it may improve the grades of some but not all students.

Homework is another consideration. Who should grade the homework: students or teacher? Prompt scoring by students enables the teacher to decide promptly what material needs further analysis. When the teacher grades the homework, his or her paper load is increased and feedback to students is delayed. Yet in the very act of grading homework, teachers add to their information about the specific thinking skills and problems of the students. Moreover, researchers point out that when the teacher takes time to write encouraging and constructive comments on the homework (or other student papers), it has positive measurable effects on achievement.[35]

Homework may be important in the learning process, but there is a question about whether it should be counted in the grading system. Some educators say no. There are similar questions about lowering grades for minor discipline problems (for example, chewing gum), not typing a paper, not doing an assignment on time, and coming to class late. A student whose behavior is unacceptable must be held accountable, but some educators are against reducing grades as a deterrent.[36] Many teachers, however, take another view, especially when classroom discipline is at stake.

There is also considerable disagreement about the value of using routine class activities, class participation, recitations, oral reading, chalkboard work, oral presentations, and even reports as part of the grade system. Although such practices broaden the base of information on student performance and also give students a chance to be evaluated on grounds other than tests, there are serious questions about the quality of information they provide. For example, some students "talk a good game" and know little, while others are introverted or shy but know the material. Other educators maintain that grades should be divided into primary measures of performance (unit tests, term papers) and secondary measures (homework, quizzes). The secondary measures are considered less important and are given less weight, since their purpose is to prepare students to achieve the primary learning outcomes.[37]

Regardless of what you think about grading, considerable evidence supports its efficacy for improving student learning, especially when the grading process is conducted in a fair and objective manner. E. D. Hirsch writes,

> It has been shown convincingly that tests and grades strongly contribute to effective teaching. This commonsense conjecture was confirmed by research conducted after the anti-grade, pass/fail mode of grading had become popular at colleges and universities in the 1960s and 70s. Quite unambiguous analysis showed that students who took courses for a grade studied harder and learned more than students who took the course for intrinsic interest alone.[38]

Traditional grading, as you can see, has subjectivity built into it. Much of that subjectiveness occurs as you compare one student's performance to that of others, as you assess a student's individual ability (How is the student working in comparison to personal potential?), and as you measure the student's individual progress over time. Based on all the data you collect, a judgment about a grade is made.

Clearly, traditional grading is what most preservice teachers will have experienced. There are other ways to assess students, however. One of those is more criterion-referenced, where student performance is measured against a defined standard.

Standards-Based Grading

We have examined the increased importance that educators are now placing on standards and on using them to assess student performance. Some teachers have begun to use criterion-referenced grading systems that they based on established standards. These standards-based grading systems involve measuring students' proficiency on well-defined course objectives.[39] Patricia Scriffiny argues that standards-based grading can be used to replace traditional point-based grades. Her arguments center on giving grades a new meaning and conclude with an emphasis on improving practice.[40] Table 9.4 compares traditional and standards-based grade books.

In **standards-based grading** systems there is a clear alignment among standards, assessment, and instruction. Such alignment should occur in traditional forms of grading, but it is often absent—that is, far too many teachers assign and grade individual assignments without really connecting the particular assignments to broader standards and learner expectations. Colby reports that several real advantages occur with standards-based grading. First, it is easier to quickly assess learner strengths and weaknesses. Second, it is easier to communicate to parents and students the specific nature of their learning progress. Third, the conferences between parents and teachers are more focused and less subjective.[41]

Table 9.4   Comparing Traditional and Standards-Based Grade Books

Traditional Grade Book

Name	Homework Average	Quiz 1	Chapter 1 Test
John	90	65	70
Bill	50	75	78
Susan	110	50	62
Felicia	10	90	85
Amanda	95	100	90

Standards-Based Grade Book

Name	Objective 1: Write an alternate ending for a story	Objective 2: Identify the elements of a story	Objective 3: Compare and contrast two stories
John	Partially proficient	Proficient	Partially proficient
Bill	Proficient	Proficient	Partially proficient
Susan	Partially proficient	Partially proficient	Partially proficient
Felicia	Advanced	Proficient	Proficient
Amanda	Partially proficient	Advanced	Proficient

Source: Patricia L. Scriffiny, "Seven Reasons for Standards-Based Grading: Expecting Excellence," *Educational Leadership* 66(2) (October 2008), 73. © 2008 by ASCD. Reprinted with permission. Learn more about ASCD at www.ascd.org.

There may be one other advantage: that students' performance is assessed in relation to a specific standard, not in relationship to how peers are performing. As we noted earlier, most grading systems are based on comparisons and not on an individual student's performance relative to a standard. Consider the grading systems that were used to assess you in school. Were you assessed based on a standard or based on how others performed?

Form of Grades

The most popular form in which grades are presented is the *letter grade*, which represents a translation from a number base resulting from a combination of test scores, ratings, and the like.

Good teachers use grades to show how well students have learned material in relationship to an established absolute criterion level—what the teacher intended them to learn. That's an appropriate form of grading. A much weaker (but frequently used) form is to compare students' performances and then to give grades based on those relative performances.

To some extent, the conversion from numbers to letters (*A, B, C*) distorts meaning and masks individual student differences. Because a letter represents a range of numbers, different students might receive the same letter grade from the same teacher for different levels of performance. Although the number system is more precise, often the difference between two or three points for a final grade is not that meaningful.

Most schools convert letters to an even more general statement of evaluation:

A = superior, excellent, outstanding, and firm command and mastery of content

B = good, above average, and mastery is evident in most but not all areas

C = fair, competent, average, and mastery is evident at basic but not at advanced levels

D = minimum passing, weakness or problems, and limited understanding of content

F = failure, serious weakness or problems, and little if any mastery of content

The standards on which grades are based vary considerably among school districts, so that a C student in one school may be an A student in another school. Schools and school districts eventually get reputations about how low or high standards are or about how rigorous their programs are.

One way in which states are beginning to deal with this "unevenness" in school districts is by creating *exit exams* or *end-of-course exams* that are administered on a statewide basis. A student taking Algebra I, for example, must take an exit exam, and his or her performance can be assessed against certain criterion levels of content mastery. In this way, the grade reflects what a student truly knows relative to a broader performance expectation as opposed to representing an assessment of a small group of students in a single class. It is helpful when you look at student grades to know whether absolute or relative standards have been used to make judgments about the level of student performance.

States are using exit exams more and more in areas such as science and social studies. State exit exams incorporate both traditional and open-ended types of questions. For example, many states now use some sort of essay writing in exit exams, and within the next few years more states will be using short-answer questions in their exit exams. All this effort is intended to ensure that a high school diploma means something to students and to employers. State legislators are trying to show the public that students are receiving a quality education, and one way they can do this is by requiring such exams.

Many critics argue that the exams will exacerbate problems for those in high-poverty areas.[42] Specifically, the tests will likely lead to higher dropout rates and will do little to ensure that high-need students receive the kind of educational experiences they need in order to be successful as learners.[43] At this point, the critics are losing the battle, and the No Child Left Behind legislation has resulted in even more testing requirements for students.[44] As a new teacher you will be confronting the reality of making certain that all your students learn. One of the ways in which that learning will be assessed is through mechanisms like exit exams. Some states have exit exams in place while others are in the process of developing them. The state of Alaska provides an example of how one state evaluates the worth of various state exit examinations against their own requirements. Based on the state of Alaska's exit standards, as of February 2010, twenty-six states required exit exams (see table 9.5). The research to either support or refute the power of exit exams is still quite mixed. The Center for Education Policy (Washington, DC) is documenting the impact on student achievement, dropout rates, and opportunities after high school. No clear and concise evidence on any of these variables is available, though it does appear that a relationship *may* exist between exit exams and higher dropout rates.[45]

Table 9.5   State High School Exit Exams

Accepted States*

State	Exam Name
Alabama	Alabama High School Graduation Exam
Arizona	Arizona's Instrument to Measure Standards
California	California High School Exit Examination
Georgia	Georgia High School Graduation Tests
Idaho	Idaho Standards Achievement
Indiana	Graduation Qualifying Examination
Louisiana	Graduation Exit Exam
Massachusetts	Massachusetts Comprehensive Assessment System
Minnesota	Basic Skills Test
Nevada	High School Proficiency Examination
New Jersey	High School Proficiency Assessment
New Mexico	New Mexico High School Competency Examination
New York	Regents Comprehensive Examinations
Ohio	Ohio Graduation Tests
South Carolina	High School Assessment Program
Texas	Texas Assessment of Knowledge and Skills
Washington	Washington Assessment of Student Learning *Note:* students with proficient scores in reading, writing, and mathematics from the WASL will be accepted. No coursework credits can be substituted for the mathematics WASL.

*The states shown here administer exit exams that fulfill the requirements for regulation 4 AAC 06.777 (students that have passed another state's competency examination).

Unaccepted States**

State	Reason
Arkansas	Content areas assessed are not comparable with the areas tested on the Alaska HSGQE [High School Graduation Qualifying Examination].
Florida	Reading and mathematics are the only content areas used to determine whether students graduate with a standard diploma.
Maryland	Content areas assessed are not comparable with the areas assessed on the Alaska HSGQE.

(continued)

State	Reason
Mississippi	Content areas assessed are not comparable with the areas assessed on the Alaska HSGQE.
North Carolina	Content areas assessed are not comparable with the areas assessed on the Alaska HSGQE.
Oklahoma	The flexibility of these exams are not compatible with Alaska's exit exam requirements. Students must take four of the seven end-of-instruction exams offered, but not as a graduation requirement.
Tennessee	Content areas assessed are not comparable with the areas tested on the Alaska HSGQE.
Virginia	Content areas assessed are not comparable with the areas tested on the Alaska HSGQE.

The states shown here **do not administer exit exams that fulfill the requirements for regulation 4 AAC 06.777 (students that have passed another state's competency examination.)

States and U.S. Territories without Exit Exams

American Samoa	Iowa	Nebraska	South Dakota
Colorado	Kansas	New Hampshire	Utah
Connecticut	Kentucky	North Dakota	Vermont
Delaware	Maine	Oregon	Virgin Islands
District of Columbia	Michigan	Pennsylvania	West Virginia
Hawaii	Missouri	Puerto Rico	Wisconsin
Illinois	Montana	Rhode Island	Wyoming

Source: State Exit Exams, Alaska Department of Education & Early Development, February 6, 2010. http://www.eed.state.ak.us/tls/Assessment/HSGQE/HSExitExams/2009_2010StateHighSchoolExitExams_0220

Absolute Grade Standards

Grades may be given according to fixed or **absolute standards**, as illustrated in table 9.6. One disadvantage of this approach is that the standards may be subject to the *error of leniency*—that is, if students have an easy grader, many As and Bs will be assigned; if they have a tough grader, many Cs and Ds will be assigned. Student scores also depend on the difficulty of the tests given. In some tests a score of 75 percent may be above average, but with an absolute or fixed standard as indicated in the table, this score would be a *D*. Many students who would be given a minimum passing grade under an absolute grading approach may benefit with a relative standard.

Despite these limitations, most teachers use this method of grading. It makes a great deal of sense as long as teachers have a firm idea of what students should be able to do, and as long as standards are realistic and fair. One of the most difficult aspects of being a new teacher is understanding the difficulties in developing tests. As you gain more experience it becomes easier to understand how to assess student learning fairly.

An absolute grading standard usually is imposed by teachers, school administrators, and boards of education in more traditional contexts. The process

---

Table 9.6   Examples of Absolute and Relative Standards of Grading*

Absolute Standard	Relative Standard Percent of Students
A = 95% or above	A = 7%
B = 86–94%	B = 24%
C = 78–85%	C = 38%
D = 70–77%	D = 24%
F = Below 70%	F = 7%

*Based on a normal curve.
Source: Adapted from Robert E. Slavin, *Educational Psychology: Theory into Practice,* 4th ed. (Needham Heights, MA: Allyn & Bacon, 1994).

---

assumes that the teacher can predict the difficulty level of his or her testing, thus predetermining the distribution of scores, so that a specified number of students will get *A*s, *B*s, *C*s, and so on. Not only is this task nearly impossible, but it also requires the teacher to play catch-up at the end of the semester, intentionally administering an easy or difficult test to get a more even distribution of grades, or to ignore an uneven distribution of grades skewed as too high or too low.[46]

Relative Grade Standards

Grades may be given according to how a student performs in relation to others. If a student scores 80 on an examination but most others score above 90, the student has done less-than-average work. Instead of receiving a *B* under the relative or norm-referenced method of grading, the student might receive a C. If a student scores 65 but most others score below 60, he or she has done well and might receive a *B* instead of a *D* or *F.*

Relative grading can be based on a curve, either a normal bell-shaped curve or a curve derived from a simple ranking system. In a normal curve few students receive *A*s or *F*s, the majority receive *C*s (the midpoint of the curve), and many receive *B*s and *D*s. This is also shown in table 9.6, which uses a 7–24–38–24–7 percent grade distribution. In a ranking system, which is more common, the teacher determines in advance the percentage equivalents for each letter grade (e.g., the top 25 percent will receive *A*, the next 30 percent *B*, the next 25 percent *C*, and the next 20 percent *D* or *F*). The grading on this curve is not always as precise as with the normal curve, and it tends to be a little easier for students to score higher grades.

Grading on a curve and other relative grading practices assure that grades will be distributed on the basis of scores in relation to one another, regardless of the difficulty of the test. It takes into consideration that the ability levels of students vary, and that tests vary in difficulty; thus, the distribution of scores or grades cannot be predicted. However, researchers contend this process can create competition among students and inhibit them from helping each other in class.[47] It can also have a negative effect on the students' desire to learn—highly competitive environments cause unnecessary comparisons that cause lower-ability students to lose interest in a task, and perhaps in school altogether.

Indeed, some educators argue that unnecessary comparisons could be the reason so many students decide to drop out of school, physically or psychologically.

Combining and Weighting Data

Although researchers generally agree that grading should be based on several indicators that are directly related to the instructional program, there is less agreement on what should be included, how the indicators should be weighted, and whether indicators not directly related to instruction, such as participation, effort, neatness, and conduct, are appropriate at all.[48]

Grades based on little information, such as only one or two tests, are unfair to students and are probably invalid. Assigning too much importance to term papers or homework is also invalid and unwise, because these indicators say little about whether the students have really learned the material. A heavier reliance on test data is preferred, especially at the secondary school level, as long as there are several quizzes or examinations and the tests are weighted properly. One of the reasons for using multiple measures (and different forms of assessment) is that it helps students clearly demonstrate what they know and helps protect teachers against various forms of bias, to which no human being is immune. Teachers can take measures to mitigate such biases (e.g., mask the identity of students or, with essays, grade all of the first-question responses at one time).

A number of problems exist related to combining several test scores into a single measure (or grade) for each student, including the fact that individual test scores may vary in significance level. For example, a teacher who wishes to combine scores on two separate tests might determine that each contributes 50 percent to the composite score. However, this rarely is the case, especially if one test was more difficult than the other; the composite score is a function not only of the mean but also of the standard deviation.

A question arises whether scores from different sources, representing different learning outcomes and levels of difficulty, can be combined into a composite score. Although there are arguments for and against this procedure, it is acceptable as long as the composite score is based on several sources that are independent of each other—see Tips for Teachers 9.3.

Contracting for Grades

A few schools permit teachers and students considerable flexibility in formulating grades. Teachers and students come to an agreement early in the term concerning grades for specific levels of performance or achievement on various tasks. Maximum, average, and minimum standards or performance levels are usually established. The teacher promises to award a specific grade for specified performance; in effect, teacher and student establish a contract. With this **contract grading** approach students know exactly what they have to do to receive a certain grade.

The plan seems suited to criterion-referenced learning and to teaching and learning by a set of objectives. The approach is not recommended for elementary school students because of their lack of maturity, their inability to engage in independent work for a sustained period of time, and their inability to follow through on individual activities. The contract can be implemented at the upper elementary level (grade 5 or higher) if great care is taken to match student maturity and abilities with performance requirements. Different standards will be needed for different students.

TIPS

F O R

T E A C H E R S

9.3

Advantages and Disadvantages of the Point System of Grading

Most teachers, especially from the middle grades onward, rely on a point system of grading that assigns points or percentages for various tests and class activities. Some teachers even post summaries at regular intervals so students can see their point totals as the term progresses. Special caution is recommended for its use. The point system has advantages and disadvantages.

Advantages

1. It is fair and objective. The teacher is not apt to be swayed by subjective factors, and the need for interpretation is minimized.

2. It is quantifiable, explicit, and precise. Students and teachers know exactly what the numbers are and what they represent.

3. It facilitates the weighting of tests and class activities (e.g., 10 points for each quiz, 25 points for a special project, 25 points each for the midterm and final).

4. It is cumulative. The final grade can be determined by a single computation at the end of the grading period.

5. It facilitates grading by establishing clear distinctions. Once categories are weighted and points totaled, assigning the grade for each student is a straightforward task.

Disadvantages

1. It emphasizes the objectivity of scoring, not learning. It conveys the message that learning is equivalent to the accumulation of points, not the acquisition of skills and knowledge.

2. It presents an illusion of objectivity. Every test or assignment results from a series of subjective decisions by the teacher (e.g., about what areas to cover and how to weight particular answers or aspects of performance).

3. It reduces a teacher's judgment. Point systems tend to be inflexible and minimize the teacher's professional input.

4. It leads to cumulative errors. A particular score or activity may not truly reflect the student's abilities or learning. The final total represents the *sum* of all such errors.

5. It is subject to misinterpretation. Without norms it is false to assume that a certain range (90 to 100) or number (93) represents a valid indicator (e.g., an *A*) of performance or that categories (breakpoints) can be decided in advance.

Source: Adapted from Ruben F. Madgic, "The Point System of Grading: A Critical Appraisal," *NASSP Bulletin* (April 1988): 29–34.

Revised contracts can be designed for students whose work is not satisfactory or who expected a higher grade than they received. This grading system provides more latitude for teachers in responding to unsatisfactory work and gives students a chance to improve their work and their grade. Good grade contracts take into account both the quality and quantity of student work.

You will find this contract approach used with some frequency in classrooms where there are specific performance measures for students so that they know what *products* they must produce and, if they produce those products, the grades they will receive.

Mastery and Continuous Progress Grading

Many elementary schools and a few middle grade and junior high schools now stress **mastery grading** and **continuous progress grading**, an outgrowth of the mastery learning approach. Both approaches require that teachers maintain specific records for each student and report on the student's progress. Schools using these approaches usually do not use grades but evaluate the student in terms of expected and mastered skills and behaviors.[49] Reports for the student and parents describe how the student is performing and progressing without any indication of how the student is doing in relation to others. Although a judgment is made about the student, the absence of a standard for comparison reduces some pressure related to grades. In mastery learning situations and continuous progress reporting, grades are usually based on criterion-referenced measurements.[50] Richard Arends describes how this approach might be used:

> For example, in spelling, the teacher might decide that the correct spelling of 100 specified words constitutes mastery. Student grades would then be determined and performance reported in terms of the percentage of the 100 words a student can spell correctly. A teacher using this approach might specify the following grading scale: A = 100 to 93 words spelled correctly; B = 92 to 85 words spelled correctly; C = 84 to 75 words spelled correctly; D = 74 to 65 words spelled correctly; and F = 64 or fewer words spelled correctly.[51]

Questions for Reflection 9.1

Grading is one of the most difficult aspects of the teaching–learning process. As you get to know students, you will develop natural biases based on their responsiveness in class or their behavior during your lessons. Some students will work hard and still not learn the material well. Others will hardly study, and yet their performance will be exceptional. As you observe all these different students, it is very human to want to reward students who are trying but still may not be learning. To what degree do you think effort should be considered as grades are awarded? Should you give a student a higher grade because that student has really worked hard? If not, how will you deal with these types of students, who may begin to "lose heart" because they are trying but still not succeeding?

Grading for Effort or Improvement

To what extent should teachers consider effort or improvement as part of the grade? This question surfaces for most teachers when they grade their students' work. Problems with considering effort are that bright students may show the least improvement and effort and that, by raising the grade or average of low-achieving students to reflect effort rather than achievement, you are to some extent lowering the value of the grade given to high-achieving students.[52] In addition, low-achieving students have more opportunity to improve by simple regression toward the mean (i.e., statistically they have a better chance to improve their scores than do other students whose scores are already above the mean).

Most teachers, especially in the elementary and middle grade schools, leave some room for judgment in grading. The more effort and improvement are considered in deciding on final grades, the more subjective the grades will be and the more biased they are likely to be. Teachers must examine their perceptions for accuracy. If a teacher feels strongly about a judgment, then the movement in a grade from a *B* to a *B*+ or an *A*– to an *A* is acceptable. A major change in a grade (say, from a *C* to an *A*), cannot be justified on the basis of the student's effort or teacher's hunches about the student.

Effort does become important in the teacher's efforts to communicate to parents and students about the way students approach their learning tasks. Are they working hard? Are they putting forth good effort and trying to do strong work? Such information sheds light on what a student is like as an individual and what interests and intrinsic motivation characterize the child. This information is important for parents to know, and for teachers to use as they work with students.

Regardless of whether you decide to "reward" effort by modifying a student's grade, you should place an emphasis on effort as you interact with your students. Why? Students can change their effort levels; they cannot change their innate abilities. In this regard, educators might learn something from the Japanese, who do place an emphasis on effort:

> In Asia, the emphasis on effort and the relative disregard for innate abilities are derived from Confucian philosophy. Confucius was interested above all in the moral perfectibility of mankind. He rejected categorization of human beings as good or bad, and stressed the potential for improving moral conduct through the creation of favorable environmental conditions. His view was gradually extended to all aspects of human behavior. Human beings were considered to be malleable, and like clay, subject to molding by the events of everyday life. Differences among individuals in innate abilities were recognized, for no one can claim that all people are born with the same endowments. But more important was the degree to which a person was willing to maximize these abilities through hard work.
>
> A typical example of Confucian position is found in the writings of the Chinese philosopher Hsun Tzu, who wrote, "Achievement consists of never giving up. . . . If there is no dark and doffed will, there will be no shining accomplishment; if there is no dull and determined effort, there will be no brilliant achievement." Lack of achievement, therefore, is attributed to insufficient effort rather than to a lack of ability or to personal or environmental obstacles.[53]

Records and Reports of Performance

The way student performance is recorded and reported is usually different between elementary and secondary school. Elementary teachers are usually more sensitive about the student's feelings, attitudes, and effort and are willing to consider these factors in reporting performance. Elementary school report cards often contain narratives, or a combination of grades and narratives, about the child's progress. The parents may be asked to write a reply instead of merely signing the report card, or to attend a conference perhaps two or three times a year at which they can discuss with the teacher the child's work.

Fewer middle grade and junior high schools have such elaborate reporting systems, and at the high school level this human (or social) dimension of reporting is almost nonexistent, partly because teachers have more students (perhaps 150 or more) and thus cannot easily write narratives and hold conferences with the parents of each student.

Report Cards

The teacher's judgments and scores on tests are communicated to students and parents by means of a report card. The reports should not come as a surprise to students. Both students and parents should know how marks or grades are computed and to what extent tests, class participation, homework, and other activities contribute to their overall grade. It is reasonable for students and parents to become anxious if they do not know the basis for the marks or grades on the report card.

At the lower elementary grade level (below grade 4) and to a lesser extent at the upper elementary and junior high school levels, the school may use a **mastery/progress report card** that gives a list of descriptors or for which the teacher checks off categories such as *outstanding* (O), *very good* (VG), *satisfactory* (S), *good* (G), *needs improvement* (NI), and *unsatisfactory* (U). Following is a list of common reading descriptors for which the teacher would assign accompanying progress options.

	O	VG	S	G	NI	U
1. Reads orally at appropriate level	—	—	—	—	—	—
2. Reads with comprehension	—	—	—	—	—	—
3. Identifies main ideas in stories	—	—	—	—	—	—
4. Recognizes main characters in stories	—	—	—	—	—	—
5. Finds details in stories	—	—	—	—	—	—
6. Draws conclusions from reading stories	—	—	—	—	—	—
7. Demonstrates appropriate vocabulary	—	—	—	—	—	—
8. Reads with appropriate speed	—	—	—	—	—	—
9. Finishes reading assignments on time	—	—	—	—	—	—
10. Persists even if understanding does not come immediately	—	—	—	—	—	—

Teachers can make up their own lists for any basic skill or subject. A mastery report might also involve individualized rather than standardized descriptions of progress or problems. At some levels and for some types of course content the list of descriptors or categories can be precise, with a date for achievement or mastery to be shown relative to some defined learning standard.

The approach fits with a criterion-referenced system of evaluation and is useful for schools that wish to eliminate grades and put more emphasis on progress or mastery. The same approach can be used for various subjects and grade levels. For example, eighth-grade math might consist of the following mastery items: (1) fractions and decimals, (2) solving equations, (3) geometric figures, (4) percentages and probability, (5) powers and roots, (6) areas and volumes, and (7) graphs and predictions. Space can also be provided for the teacher's comments—permitting in-depth analysis of the students' strengths and areas for improvement. See Tips for Teachers 9.4 for more ideas about mastery report cards and other reporting tools.

A traditional report card uses letter or numerical grades. At the elementary grade level, the emphasis is on reading and language skills, but there are also grades for citizenship or conduct, work habits or social habits, and absenteeism and tardiness. At the secondary level, the emphasis is on academic subjects (such as English, mathematics, and science), but provision is made for reporting on minor or elective subjects (such as music, art, or physical education). Most schools, regardless of grade level, should have a space on report cards for a parent's signature, teacher comments, and parent or teacher requests for a conference to discuss the report.

Electronic Recordkeeping/Virtual Recordkeeping

Teaching and learning has radically changed with advances in technology. Research has shown that the computer has become an effective tool for instruction and learning.[54] School districts have been purchasing computers and software for individual classrooms and are also using informational systems to manage student data (attendance, grades, homework, etc.). Online recordkeeping management is usually designed for administrative purposes, giving little if any attention to the developmental needs of young children. Recordkeeping plays an important role in the evaluation of students and also has financial and legal implications. With the assistance of a calculator, the average teacher takes 87 minutes to average and record grades for thirty students in a traditional record book. With a computerized record keeper, the same teacher takes 15 minutes to do the same work—a savings of 62 minutes for one class during a single grading period.[55]

The benefits of virtual recordkeeping are numerous. **Computerized recordkeeping** can generate school reports and parental reports, as well as customized letters and printout lists concerning student grades by numerous categories, in 10 to 20 seconds per report, compared to an average of 20 minutes per report required by traditional methods. Figuring on a minimum of one school report per week for 40 weeks and two customized letters or progress reports per year for 30 parents, the savings is another 33 hours.

TIPS FOR TEACHERS 9.4

Innovative Practices for Reporting Student Performance

In lieu of traditional report cards, teachers might experiment with new procedures for reporting on student performance and progress. A number of innovative ideas are listed here. Some are in practice in a few schools. Just how innovative you can be will depend, to a large extent, on your school's policy and philosophy about grading.

1. Consider more than a single grade or mark. Develop a progress report for each activity, detailing specific instructional tasks and student performance.

2. List more than cognitive development and specific subjects. Include social, psychological, and psychomotor behaviors and creative, aesthetic, and artistic learning as well as scientific and technical abilities.

3. Develop forms of report cards specifically suited to particular grade levels rather than using one form for the entire school. The absolute standards should be clearly defined so that the students understand what they need to know.

4. Grade students on the basis of both an absolute standard and a relative standard (especially in lower grades).

5. Report each student's progress. Feedback to students is critical to their academic growth.

6. In addition to or as a replacement for standard letter grades or categories (such as "excellent," "good," and "fair"), use new categories or written individual statements that clearly define what students know and need to learn.

7. Stress the strengths of the student. Include ways to share some of the student's best work with others in the class.

8. Point out only two or three weaknesses or problem areas, and specify ways for improving such areas.

9. Organize committees of students, teachers, and parents to meet periodically (every three or four years) to improve the school district's standard report card.

10. Supplement report cards with frequent informal letters to parents, parent-teacher conferences, and student-teacher conferences.

Source: Adapted from Allan C. Ornstein, "The Nature of Grading," *ClearingHouse* (April 1989): 65–69; David A. Payne, *Measuring and Evaluating Educational Outcomes* (New York: Macmillan, 1992).

Students have immediate access to their grades, and they can even read detailed feedback from essay exams online. *Online grade books* allow instructors to keep up-to-date records and communicate student progress to parents more effectively. Such systems automatically average students' grades and can keep track of grade averages and percentile scores. Grade books produce professional looking documents that can either be viewed online or be printed out for parents. They can also be used with authentic assessments, such as written portfolios that can be stored online. Teachers can also post grading rubrics and assessment checklists for students. The greatest advantage is the flexibility obtained in reporting student progress and the ability to compute and print individual and class averages; not to mention creating assignment sheets.[56]

Grade books do have faults, despite all of the positives. A major disadvantage is that they are geared to assessment on the secondary level and less useful on the primary level. Electronic grade books can work at the elementary level, if they are designed to meet the developmental needs and abilities of younger children. Early childhood teachers often document student progress through authentic assessments, such as student observational checklists or anecdotal records, rather than formal grades. For these teachers, using electronic grade books for numerical grades, means, and percentile scores is not realistic.[57]

The use of technology has become a prime component in education. A clear concept for educators to follow prior to purchasing a centralized informational system or an electronic grade book system is to examine students' developmental needs. Educators should also consider the cost of ongoing professional development and preparation for student and parent participation.

In this age of technology the pen-and-pencil method of recording data is dated. It has become essential to manage instruction and information professionally. Through the use of databases and spreadsheets for grading, evaluating, and reporting student performance, technology makes managerial efficiency possible.

Cumulative Records

Each student has a permanent record in which important data are filed during his or her entire school career. It contains information about subject grades, standardized test scores, family background, personal history, health, school service, parent and pupil interviews, special aptitudes, special problems (learning, behavioral, or physical), and absence/tardiness records.

The **cumulative record** is usually stored in the main office or guidance office. Teachers are permitted access to the cumulative records of the students in their classes to obtain information about them. They are also required to add to the information at the end of the term to keep the records complete and up to date.

Although the information found in cumulative records is extremely helpful, a major criticism is that they may prompt a teacher to make prejudgments about students before even meeting them in class. For this reason, some educators argue that a teacher should not look at cumulative records until a month or more after the school year begins. Each of us should consider whether the potential problems of teachers' "prior knowledge" warrant not looking at cumulative folders.

Since federal legislation permits the records of a child to be open to inspection and review by the child's parents, most educators are reluctant to write statements or reports that may be considered controversial or negative, unless supported with specific data. Sometimes important information is omitted. When parents review information in cumulative records, a qualified employee of the school (e.g., the principal's secretary or a guidance counselor) should be present to give assistance. Parents have the right to challenge any information contained in the cumulative record.

Salvia, Ysseldyke, and Bolt assert that there are three principles that should govern what is placed in a cumulative folder:

Principle 1: Include information in a folder only for the length of time that it is absolutely required.

Principle 2: Parents have the right to review, inspect, challenge, and even supplement information that is in a folder.

Principle 3: The cumulative records of students are classified information and should only be accessible to those school personnel who have a "need to know."[58]

Student Portfolios

Student portfolios (also discussed in chapter 8) can be used to exhibit students' work and their capabilities. Portfolios should show a range of students' work—to show a range of performance or the "best" pieces of work. Most portfolios expect students to show a variety of skills and the ability to improve performance. Portfolios tell an in-depth story, especially if they are maintained for the entire year and cut across domains or subjects. They may consist of a written autobiography; a statement about work (including a résumé); an essay on a particular subject or a series of essays; a special project, paper, or experiment; a series of photographs, drawings, or plans; or even a video, computer printout, or software developed by the student.[59]

Portfolios are becoming increasingly popular because they are considered an excellent way for the teacher to get to know the student. They are particularly useful in inclusion classrooms, in which students exhibit a wide range of needs and abilities. They help students (as well as teachers and parents) see the "big" picture, heightening the students' awareness of their own learning. Allowing students to select the contents of the portfolio also enables them to take an active role in their own instruction and assessment. The portfolio makes it possible to document instruction and learning over time and is an excellent resource for teacher, parent, and student when discussing overall school performance and progress. Portfolios portray a wide and rich array of what students know or can do. In effect, they capture multiple dimensions of learning, not only right answers or cognitive dimensions. They illuminate the process by which students solve problems, produce work, or perform in real-life contexts—what some educators call "authentic" assessment. Portfolios also help students integrate instruction and reflect on personal efforts.[60] As a tool for developing habits of reflection, they can lead to greater student confidence in their own learning, especially when they acquire information about their learning in ways that help them manage their learning.[61]

Despite the compelling reasons for using portfolios, certain potential problems accompany their use. Unless the portfolio system is designed carefully, accurate conclusions about what learning outcomes have been achieved cannot be made. The work in the portfolio may not be representative of what the student knows or can do, the criteria used to evaluate the product may not reflect relevant dimensions of the course content or skill, and the work that a student puts into the portfolio may not really be "authentic" or reflect the curriculum.[62]

With portfolios, defining selection and assessment criteria becomes crucial. The work assigned to students for the portfolio should match the behavior and content the teacher is trying to assess. For example, teachers cannot conclude the writing sample or research project in the portfolio is "typical" work for the student, if the student has selected only his or her "best" sample. The significance or value of the portfolio product also changes with the teacher analyzing it. Teacher bias and subjectivity in grading are much harder to control with this assessment system than with a short-answer test or when grading is based on right answers or a prescribed answer key.

Portfolios represent an assessment and grading strategy that can reveal much about a variety of learning outcomes; however, while most educators seem to favor their use, there is no single agreed-upon way to design a portfolio system. Effective use really depends on your intended purpose and audience, as well as your definition of a "good" portfolio. As a teacher, if you do not fully understand how portfolios can be developed and to what end, what content or skills should be assessed, and what criteria or standards should be used, then you are likely to become confused as you implement them as part of your assessment plan. Before beginning to use portfolios for assessment it is advisable to ask the questions formulated in box 9.3.

Box 9.3   Questions to Ask before Beginning a Portfolio System

1. **How will the portfolio be used?**
   - Period of time used for evaluation
   - All or part of students' work saved?
   - As part of a cumulative grade
   - Passed on (e.g., from one grade to the next)?
   - Sent home to parents
   - Reflective piece for students

2. **How should the pieces in the portfolio be selected?**
   - "Work in progress" or completed pieces
   - "Best" work or "typical" work
   - Teacher, student, or both in charge of selecting pieces
   - Should comments from teacher, peers be included?

3. **What specific pieces should be included?**
   - Homework
   - Class quizzes and tests
   - Peer-edited assignments
   - Group work
   - Logs, journals
   - Projects
   - Written work
   - Rough drafts
   - Video and audio recordings (cassettes, CDs, DVDs)
   - Graphic organizers
   - Self-assessments
   - Goals

(continued)

- Pictures
- Experiments
- Samples of artwork

4. **What are the evaluation options?**
   - A tool that is not graded
   - One grade on the entire portfolio
   - Each piece graded separately
   - Pieces (all or some) passed on to the next teacher
   - Used in interview process

5. **How can the portfolio be presented?**
   - Creative cover
   - Table of contents included
   - Contents arranged per table of contents
   - Written comment about each piece or item—why it was selected
   - Self-assessment of portfolio
   - Letter from teacher or parents with feedback, comments

6. **What are the options for conducting portfolio conferences?**
   - Student-teacher
   - Student-student
   - Cross-age
   - Student-parent
   - Student-parent-teacher
   - Exhibition

Source: Adapted from Raymond W. Lee, "Using Portfolios in Assessment" (January 7, 2005). http://www.harding.edu/dlee/portfolio.pdf

Guidelines for Grading Students and Reporting Student Progress

Here are some suggestions for deriving grades.

1. *Become familiar with the grading policy of your school and with your colleagues' standards.* Each school has its own standards for grading and procedures for reporting grades. Your standards and practices should not conflict with those of the school and should not differ greatly from those of your colleagues.

2. *Explain your grading system to the students.* To young students, explain your grading system orally and with concrete examples. Older students can read handouts that describe assignments, tests, test schedules, and grading criteria, although this information can also be explained orally.

3. *If possible, base grades on a predetermined set of standards.* For example, a student who is able to perform at a significantly higher performance standard than another student should receive a higher grade. Limit the degree to which student comparisons are used to determine grades.

4. *Don't count everything when calculating grades.* Teachers may decide to drop the weakest assignment or grade of each student. This is especially true if a lot of new and complex material is being taught.

5. *Base grades on a variety of data sources.* The more sources of information used and weighted properly, the more valid is the grade. Although most of the grade should be based on objective sources, some subjective sources should also be considered. For example, a student who frequently participates in class may be given a slightly higher grade than her test average.

6. *As a rule, do not change grades.* Grades should be determined after serious consideration, and only in rare circumstances should they be changed. Of course, an obvious mistake or error should be corrected, but if students think you will change grades they will start negotiating or pleading with you for changes.

7. *When failing a student, closely follow school procedures.* Each school has its own procedures to follow for failing a student. You may be required to have a warning conference, to send a pending failure notice to parents, and so forth.

8. *Record grades on report cards and cumulative records.* Report cards usually are mailed to parents or given to students to give to parents every six to eight weeks. Cumulative records are usually completed at the end of the school year.[63]

Remember to use the evaluation procedure as a teaching and learning device, to be fair in your evaluation of students, to interpret evaluative data properly, and to give students the benefit of the doubt.

Communication with Parents

The importance of parent involvement is well documented. How the teacher can help the parents improve the child's academic work and behavior is often the major concern among parents and teachers alike. According to Joyce Epstein, more than 85 percent of parents spend fifteen minutes or more helping their child at home when asked to do so by the teacher. Parents claim they can spend more time, 40 minutes on the average, if they are told specifically how to help, but fewer than 25 percent receive systematic requests and directions from teachers to assist their children with specific skills and subjects.[64] Epstein further notes that parents become involved most often with reading activities at the lower grades: reading to the child or listening to the child read, taking the child to the library, and helping with teaching materials brought home from school for practice at home.[65] Parents of older students (grade 4 and above) become more involved with specific homework and subject-related activities. One of the most important ways that parents can become involved with their children's learning is to assist with homework. A meta-analysis from 20 studies correlating parent involvement in homework and achievement-related outcomes reveals positive associations for elementary school and high school students; however, the type of involvement changes as children reach the higher grades.[66]

Parent involvement in children's learning and other school matters decreases with the level of schooling. Involvement and concern are considerable at the elementary school level, less at the middle school or junior high school level, and least at the high school level. Research also shows that children have an advantage in school when their parents support, participate, and communicate on a regular basis with school officials.[67] The No Child Left Behind Act mandated that schools increase parental involvement to help improve academic achievement, yet consensus on how best to accomplish this goal amidst the even greater challenge of higher academic standards imposed on schools remains elusive.[68] Table 9.7 shows the levels of parental involvement in various school activities.

Parent Conferences

Scheduling parent-teacher conferences is becoming increasingly difficult because an increasing number of children have only one adult living at home or have two parents in the workforce (including parents with more than one job). Few parents are able to attend school activities or conferences during normal school hours, and many have trouble scheduling meetings at all. Today's teacher must adjust to these new circumstances with greater efforts through letters, telephone calls, and e-mails to set up meetings and greater flexibility to accommodate the needs of the parents. Some schools are now setting up websites with parent chat rooms, bulletin boards, and even videoconferencing to enhance communication with parents.

> Computer communication can individualize interactions with parents. . . . Because messages to parents are accessible on their home computers, parents have 24-hour access, which sometimes frees them from having to leave work or [meet other] domestic obligations in the home to make school visits.[69]

Usually both teacher and parents are a little apprehensive before a conference, want to impress each other favorably, and don't know exactly what to expect. Teachers can reduce their anxiety by preparing for the conference, assembling in advance all the information pertinent to the student and the subject to be discussed with parents. This might include information regarding the student's academic achievement, other testing results, general health, attendance and lateness, social and emotional relations, work habits, special aptitudes, or other noteworthy characteristics or activities. If the conference is about subject grades, the teacher should assemble the student's tests, reports, and homework assignments. If it is about discipline, the teacher might have on hand detailed, hand-written accounts of behavior.

The conference should not be a time for lecturing parents. If the teacher asked for the conference, the teacher will set the agenda but should remain sensitive to the needs of the parents. The atmosphere should be unrushed and quiet. The information presented should be based on as many sources as possible, and it should be objective in content. See Tips for Teachers 9.5 (on p. 470) for suggestions on emphasizing objective communication of classroom management prob-

Table 9.7   Levels of Parental Involvement by Race, Ethnicity, School Type, and Economic Status: Learning Opportunities

		Participation in school activities by parent or other household member				
Characteristic	Number of students (in thousands)	Attended a general school or PTO/PTA meeting	Attended a regularly scheduled parent-teacher conference	Attended a school or class event	Volun-teered or served on a school committee	Participated in school fund-raising
All students	51,596	89.4	78.1	74.5	46.4	65.3
Grades K–8	**35,093**	**92.3**	**86.1**	**77.7**	**52.4**	**68.9**
Sex						
Male	18,442	92.1	87.1	74.8	50.5	69.6
Female	16,651	92.5	84.9	80.9	54.5	68.2
Race/ethnicity						
White	19,909	94.0	86.8	83.1	61.0	76.7
Black	5,372	90.4	81.8	68.7	40.9	62.0
Hispanic	7,054	88.6	86.2	68.0	36.5	53.6
Asian	1,057	94.8	89.3	74.8	49.4	62.3
Native Hawaiian/ Pacific Islander	‡	‡	‡	‡	‡	‡
American Indian/ Alaska Native	‡	‡	‡	‡	‡	‡
School type						
Public	30,505	91.7	85.1	76.2	48.6	66.7
Private	4,198	96.5	92.8	87.5	78.7	84.3
Poverty status						
Poor	7,163	84.2	83.9	60.8	31.5	49.4
Nonpoor	27,930	94.4	86.6	82.1	57.8	74.0
Grades 9–12	**16,503**	**83.4**	**61.0**	**67.6**	**33.6**	**57.4**
Sex						
Male	8,430	83.1	62.0	64.1	32.2	54.1
Female	8,072	83.6	60.1	71.2	34.9	60.8
Race/ethnicity						
White	9,921	84.9	59.6	73.9	40.5	64.0
Black	2,464	78.6	67.7	56.0	22.1	48.8
Hispanic	2,711	81.9	64.4	57.2	19.5	42.9
Asian	326	78.4	49.3	60.3	34.3	54.9
Native Hawaiian/ Pacific Islander	‡	‡	‡	‡	‡	‡
American Indian/ Alaska Native	‡	‡	‡	‡	‡	‡
School type						
Public	14,613	81.8	59.6	65.5	30.7	55.2
Private	1,798	95.9	73.1	83.9	56.0	76.2
Poverty status						
Poor	2,850	72.7	58.8	43.3	13.8	34.7
Nonpoor	13,653	85.6	61.5	72.6	37.7	62.2

‡Reporting standards not met (too few cases).
Note: Race categories excluded persons of Hispanic ethnicity. Detail may not sum to totals because of rounding.
Source: Table A-30-1, Percentage of students in grades K through 12 whose parents reported participation in school-related activities, by selected student, school, and family characteristics: 2007. US Department of Education Statistics, Parent and Family Involvement in Education Survey of the National Household Education Surveys Program (NHES), 2007.

TIPS FOR TEACHERS 9.5

Directing a Parent Conference

1. *Call a parent by the correct name.* If unsure, ask: "Are you Latoya's mother?"

2. *Identify yourself and provide a neutral focus for contact.* "I'm Mrs. Dawson, John's teacher, and I'm calling to talk about his behavior in math class."

3. *State the purpose for contact.* Describe the specific behavior(s) in *objective*—not *subjective*—terms. For example, in objective terms (what actually occurred) you'd say, "Today Rana grabbed a classmate's book and hid it." In subjective terms (your interpretation of what occurred) you might say, "Rana is very immature."

4. *Enlist parent support by stating the desired student behavior.* "I'm sure *you* want Clark to leave his classmates' property alone and concentrate on math."

5. *Identify the parent's responsibility.* "I believe it will help if you tell Mohammed to leave his classmates' property alone and concentrate on math."

6. *Ask the parent for additional ideas.* "What ideas do you have that might help me as I work with Keiko?"

7. *Reinforce parent and teacher responsibility.* "I believe it will help if you tell Angel to keep his hands, feet, and objects to himself and concentrate on math. Please remind him that failure to do so is the reason he must serve detention tomorrow. In addition, I will attempt to involve him in more group activities."

8. *State if and when a follow-up contact will occur.* "I will contact you next week to share how Emma is doing. With your help, Emma can correct her behavior."

9. *Finish contact on a cooperative note.* "Thank you for your time. Please don't hesitate to call me if you have questions or concerns."

Source: Adapted from a form developed by Charlene Sinclair, in Thomas J. Lasley, "Teacher Technicians: A 'New' Metaphor for New Teachers," *Action in Teacher Education* 16 (1): 11–19.

lems. It is advisable to begin and end on a positive note, even if a problem has to be discussed. The idea is to encourage parents. The teacher should not monopolize the discussion, should be truthful yet tactful and constructive, and should remain poised. The teacher should be cautious about giving too much advice, especially with regard to the child's home life. Unless there is an important problem, the average conference should last approximately 20 to 30 minutes.

The parent-teacher conference is helpful for both parties. Box 9.4 lists the ways in which the conference can help both teachers and parents.

Clark, Starr, and others also point out that the conference should examine how the student behaves in class (or school), how the student gets along with classmates, whether the student is working up to potential, the strengths of the student, the special abilities or interests of the student, ways for the student to improve, how the parent can help the student, and how the parent can help the teacher.[70]

Unfortunately, the data also reveals that teachers have a very narrow understanding of parent involvement. This understanding needs to be broadened if, indeed, we ever want to see parent involvement as a systemic, important foundation for student learning. Ferrara points out that teachers and parents have dis-

---

Box 9.4   Parent-Teacher Conferences

The parent-teacher conference helps teachers to:

- understand and clarify parents' impressions and expectations of the school program or particular classes,
- obtain additional information about the child,
- report on the child's developmental progress and suggest things the parents can do to stimulate development,
- develop a working relationship with parents, and
- encourage parents' support of the school.

According to some educators, the conference, in turn, helps parents to:

- gain a better understanding of the child's school program,
- learn about school activities that can enhance the child's growth and development,
- learn about the child's performance and progress,
- learn about the school's faculty and support staff,
- communicate concerns and ask questions about the child, and
- both provide and receive information that can benefit the child's development in school and at home.

---

similar views as to what constitutes parent involvement. The least vocal group in this discussion is the parent; the most vocal is the teacher. The conclusion of the study is that it is inherently important to provide training for pre-service and current teachers to help broaden the often myopic vision of parent involvement.[71]

Researchers have consistently found multiple positives for parent involvement in schools. Parent involvement increases students' academic achievement and, equally important, it promotes positive student attitudes and behaviors.[72] Researchers also found that when parents are involved in their children's education, there is an increase in students' school attendance and an increased sense of positive feelings of self.[73] (See Case Study 9.1 on appropriate procedures regarding parent conferences.)

The following case discusses the approaches teachers can adopt during parent-teacher conferences. It discusses teacher trepidations regarding irate parents and how they should be approached. The study spotlights the difficulties that sometimes occur in properly conducting a conference. When reading the study, compare and contrast the parents' views with those of the teachers. What role does student performance play for both parent and teacher?

Case Study 9.1
Parent-Teacher Conferences

Bob Jacobson was twenty-three years old, six feet two inches tall, rangy, bony, with knife-edge cheekbones, a long nose, blond hair worn unfashionably long, and pale blue eyes. His mother had always referred to him as an adorable Ichabod Crane. His friends called him Ichabod Jacobson. The name had stuck since he began working at the Sleepy Hollow Middle School.

Bob taught seventh-grade social studies in a school district that was obsessed with student performance and parent involvement. He was preparing himself for his first mid-year parent conference. To say that he was a little apprehensive would be an understatement. A better word might be frantic. He was trying to prepare his room according to the principal's directions. The principal, Dr. Gladstone, had suggested that teachers assemble information pertinent to each student prior to the parents' visit. He said they should include information regarding the student's academic achievement, testing results, attendance and tardiness, social and emotional behavior, work habits, and any other special characteristics.

Bob had assembled his students' tests, reports, and homework assignments on each student's desk so they corresponded to his marking book. He also had his behavior log, in which he kept handwritten, detailed accounts of behavior. In addition he had reviewed the list that Dr. Gladstone had advised the faculty to use when arranging parent meetings:

1. Make a specific appointment time for each parent.
2. Be courteous with parents. Stand up and welcome them.
3. Be sure they have a comfortable seat.
4. If parents are upset or emotional, let them express their feelings without interruptions. Do not become defensive; remain calm.
5. Be objective in analyzing the child's progress.
6. Show interest in the child's development, growth, and welfare.
7. Don't criticize another teacher or the principal. (Dr. Gladstone had insisted on that!)
8. Discuss cooperation between yourself and the parent.
9. Set up a follow-up conference, if needed.
10. End the conference on a positive note.

After all this planning, Bob still was not sure how he should deal with an irate parent. He had been told by his colleagues that parents held teachers accountable for student performance. A movement was afoot to tie salary increases to student grades. Bob felt that, although he could be sensitive to the needs of the parents, he was not going to accept responsibility for student grades. He would follow the school's guidelines and emphasize the need for establishing a friendly atmosphere, discussing his students' potential and limitations in an objective manner, avoiding arguments and remaining calm, and—most important of all—observing professional ethics.

Bob was as ready as he was ever going to be. His first parent was Mrs. Sanford, Cleo's mother. She started off by saying that Mr. Jacobson was too strict with her daughter. Her daughter had told her he favored the boys in the class, and she suggested that he graded unfairly. Bob remained calm and said, "I am sorry you feel that way. I would hope we could work together so that your daughter Cleo can raise her grades in the future."

The rest of the evening went fairly well until Mr. Hardgrave, Chad's father, said that his son had been treated in a hurtful fashion. Bob asked Mr. Hardgrave if he could be specific about exactly what he thought Bob had done. Mr. Hardgrave replied that Bob had made fun of his son in class because he had forgotten his homework. He also said that his son told him, "Mr. Jacobson is sarcastic with everyone in class." Bob said, "I am sorry you feel that way, but it's not true. Your son is not telling you the truth." At that point Mr. Hardgrave abruptly stood up and bolted out of the room, saying he was going to see the principal.

Discussion Topics and Questions to Ponder

1. How would you describe Bob's preparation for his parent conferences?

2. What suggestions would you give Bob?

3. Is there any evidence in this case study of Bob listening to gossip? Explain your answer.

4. Would you add or delete any of the items found on Dr. Gladstone's list?

5. Did Bob handle Mrs. Sanford and Mr. Hardgrave properly? Would you have done anything differently? If so, what?

What would you do if . . . ?

1. Dr. Gladstone said you could have been more respectful to Mr. Hardgrave.

2. Mr. Hardgrave said he wanted to visit your class and see your actions for himself.

3. Mrs. Sanford came back the following week and said you were now too easy with her daughter.

Letters to Parents

Letters to parents may be sent to make parents aware of, or invite them to participate in, certain classroom or school activities or functions. Letters may be sent out regularly, perhaps weekly or bimonthly, to keep parents up-to-date about their children's academic work and behavior. Parents are entitled to and appreciate this communication. Informing parents and seeking their input and support may help stop minor problems before they become serious. Letters may address specific problems, ask parents for their cooperation in one or more ways, or request a conference.

Guidelines for Communicating with Parents

Over the years many suggestions have been offered for teachers communicating with parents. The following guidelines elaborate upon Dr. Gladstone's list in Case Study 9.1. They emphasize the need for establishing a friendly atmosphere, discussing the child's potential and limitations in an objective manner, avoiding arguments and remaining calm, and observing professional ethics.

1. Begin on a positive note.

2. Be truthful and honest.

3. Accept the parent's feelings.

4. Emphasize the child's strengths.

5. Be specific about the student's learning difficulties—use objective, not subjective language (e.g., "Trent has not turned in homework for five straight days" rather than "Trent is irresponsible").

6. Have ready samples of the student's class work and homework as well as a record of his or her test scores, attendance, and so on.

7. Be receptive to the parent's suggestions.

8. Let the parent have the opportunity to talk about his or her concerns.

9. Avoid arguments; avoid pedantic language.

10. Provide constructive suggestions.

11. Be willing to explain activities or changes in the school curriculum that meet the needs of the child.

12. Close on a positive note, with a plan of action.[74]

Accountability

We have been focusing on how to set standards for student learning and then assess the degree to which students are learning the material taught. We have also discussed high-stakes (large-scale) testing (i.e., the type of tests students must pass in order to move to another grade level or to graduate). In the past such information would have been sufficient to capture the "state" of the assessment process. For good or bad, and the issue is highly debatable, your students' performance is now being used to hold you and your professional colleagues accountable, just as it is being used to hold students accountable. That accountability is evidenced at a number of different levels and has been punctuated in importance by the No Child Left Behind (NCLB) legislation of 2002 and the recent movement toward national standards. Accountability will be used as a means of reward or sanction with regard to school performance and as a way to benefit students.

In recent years, all 50 states have implemented accountability measures in response to the increasing concerns about the quality of American education. States have established clear guidelines for adequate yearly progress (AYP) for all students. These guidelines influence the climate within which teachers function. Specifically, here are some AYP components:

- A timeline to ensure all students reach proficiency by 2013–2014

- A baseline percentage of students meeting or exceeding the state's proficiency guidelines in each subject tested from which adequate yearly progress can be measured

- Intermediate goals that establish regular increases in the percentage of students meeting or exceeding proficiency guidelines

- Annual measurable assessment objectives

Accountability emboldens the idea of holding schools, districts, educators, and students responsible for results, and it creates threats as well as opportunities. The threats are being stressed by people like Alfie Kohn who argue that excessive testing reduces student intrinsic motivation.[75] Accountability has been employed as a two-edged sword that both rewards achievement and punishes failure in schools, all in the quest to ensure that children are getting a good education and that tax dollars aren't being wasted. In Florida an education bill is being considered that would eliminate tenure for new teachers and create a new pay scale linked to student performance. Critics suggest that students are simply being tested to death—in some school districts one-sixth of the school year is devoted to testing. Proponents of testing, on the other hand, assert that it is essential and offers opportunities for monitoring student progress. Tests help identify student weaknesses, allowing teachers to intervene, remediate, and create ways to ensure student success in a timely fashion.

You need realize that accountability is here to stay, at least for the foreseeable future. It will likely influence what and how you teach. You should try to find ways to create opportunities from what some would view as threats. Find ways to link teaching to assessment by understanding the academic standards (for your state) in your teaching area, then structure instruction and assessments around those standards. In this way your students will grow as responsible learners. This prescription sounds easy, but it will take great pedagogical skill on your part. (See Case Study 9.2 to explore the issue of teacher accountability.)

The following case discusses the issue of responsibility for student achievement. It discusses the idea that accountability can be seen as punitive by some in education. The study focuses on two questions: Is holding educators responsible for student performance appropriate, and does school accountability lead to improved student performance? The emphasis on accountability has put real pressure on teachers and school administrators. Reflect on both sides of the issue and see if you can arrive at a satisfactory solution.

Case Study 9.2
Accountability and the Relationship between
School and Student Performance

Neil King had always felt that his role as a teacher was to help students succeed, not only in school but for the rest of their lives. He wanted to build standards-based assessments for his classes to measure what they had learned. He favored using the data analysis provided by his school so that he could construct his lessons to meet specific student needs. Where he drew the line was on taking sole accountability for his students' achievement. He would not accept consequences for poor performance on his students' part that were punitive in nature. He realized that the National Assessment of Educational Progress had shown that accountability systems had a clear, positive impact on student achievement. He also knew that accountability systems had not led to any narrowing in the black–white achievement gap (though it had narrowed the Hispanic–white achievement gap). He just knew in his gut that it was wrong.

Barbara Sanchez, a friend of Neil's, asked him why he was such a sourpuss. He held up the local newspaper and said, "Haven't you read today's paper? US Secretary of Education Arne Duncan has released broad principles for renewing the Elementary and Secondary Education Act. He claims that the government is trying to address the perennial complaints that the law's current version, the No Child Left Behind Act, is inflexible and doesn't set a high enough bar for academic achievement."

Barbara said she knew they were working on developing core academic standards, not on changing the whole focus of the law. In the article Neil said that he found one item offensive in particular. "The old law had said that failing schools could continue to operate; the proposed revision says that the bottom 5 percent of schools must take action, including shutting down or mass firing of teachers. That's really going to motivate students to achieve! Secretary Duncan said, 'We've got to get accountability right this time so it actually drives improvement in student achievement.' I can't believe they think that's the road to student achievement. President Obama said, 'Through this plan, we are setting an ambitious goal: all students should graduate from high school prepared for college and a career—no matter who you are or where you come from.' Don't get me wrong: I have no problem with students achieving. I just don't think that by threatening to fire us, grades will go up."

Alyson Klein, a fifth-grade teacher, said, "I read that article too, and it said that Congress wanted to adopt college- and career-ready standards. I think that's a great objective. That's really the purpose of an education. The new vision would allow local and state authorities flexibility in determining what interventions were necessary to improve the schools. There would be consequences and rewards for districts and states as well as schools. Another shift would be that schools that failed to meet achievement targets would not be mandated to provide school choice or supplemental educational services, known as SES. Secretary Duncan said tutoring and public-school-choice provisions under NCLB were not acceptable to him."

Returning to his original point, Neil said, "But what about teacher accountability?" Alyson replied, "Randi Weingarten, the president of the American Federation of Teachers, said that the proposed law places 100 percent of responsibility on teachers for school success and gives them zero percent authority." Alyson said that since they were going to use "value-added" indicators to rate teachers and schools, tracking how much students learn throughout the school year under a given teacher, accountability would be easy and fair to assess.

Discussion Topics and Questions to Ponder

1. Should schools and teachers be accountable for student performance? Justify your answer.

2. What does accountability mean to Neil?

3. Do you agree or disagree with the following statement? Justify your response. "Accountability means you require teachers be evaluated by performance (not credentials), and use carrots (rewards) instead of sticks (punishments) to encourage progress."

4. Compare and contrast the arguments for and against teacher accountability.

5. Read the following statement and discuss its relevance to teacher accountability. "If a student were to start class work three grade levels behind and move up two by the end of the school year that would have counted as a victory. Now, it is rated a failure because the student is still behind."

What would you do if . . . ?

1. You were asked to delineate what you would be willing to be held accountable for.

2. Schools and teachers were being rewarded and students were still not on grade level.

3. Schools and teachers were being punished by being given less money because students were not on grade level.

School Performance

Helping parents understand the level of effectiveness of the schools that their children attend is a fundamental part of the NCLB legislation. That legislation requires that *all states* test the reading and mathematics skills of students in grades 3 through 8, although it does give discretion to the individual states regarding the types of tests used to make such assessments.

The NCLB legislation is proving to be extremely problematic for many states because, to be successful, schools must show that students from each racial and demographic group are succeeding and showing annual improvement. The fear is that with such an expectation, far too many of the nation's schools will be classified as failing.

The original hope of those who argued for the accountability movement and the NCLB legislation was that students and parents would end up with better school options—that is, through an analysis of the results of those tests, parents would have a better understanding of what students know and how much they have learned. Parents would also have a general sense of the overall effectiveness of a school. Those schools that are performing poorly would be singled out for either remedial action or suffer some other form of penalty.

On one level, the accountability movement is focusing on identifying those schools that may not be succeeding or are "low-performing." On another level, the movement is labeling districts based on their overall performance against certain state-defined criteria. On yet another level it is determining which schools remain open and whether teachers are retained.

Student Performance

Though a lot of attention has been given to the labeling of school districts and individual schools through the use of statewide standardized tests, other educators are beginning to look at how that same data can be used to foster student growth. Some are carefully examining standardized data to try to see student learning patterns that suggest areas of instructional focus. Some researchers have described how data can be used to create a data-driven school culture that attempts to create better learning opportunities for students.[76] Performance assessments that have been created in reading and writing have developed opportunities for teachers to provide assistance to students in skill areas where they experience problems or have academic weaknesses. Box 9.5 contains a model to help teachers focus on questions and data that will foster enhanced instructional effectiveness.

Questions for Reflection 9.2

The accountability emphasis has put real pressure on teachers and school administrators. The large-scale testing and accountability mania of the past decade has produced heated debate about the efficacy of testing—are teachers gearing instruction to just raise test scores, as Secretary of Education Arne Duncan implies, or are they really promoting student learning? That is, are teachers simply teaching to the test to make themselves look good? This question is drawing considerable discussion. What do you think? Is it wrong to teach to the test? Does such an emphasis limit or promote student learning?

Also being debated is whether the testing is causing some students to drop out of school altogether. Quite simply, many students who cannot deal with the high stakes may be coping by dropping out. Is this avoidable? If so, how?

Box 9.5   How Teachers Can Be Data Savvy

1. *Identify questions related to student performance.* You are likely to be most interested in information related to your classroom, but schoolwide, districtwide, and statewide patterns can also be informative.

2. *Identify data and gather necessary information.* Take into account demographic information, such as gender, race, eligibility for free or reduced lunch, and language spoken at home. Student responses to individual test questions tell you things that you can't learn from a single test score.

3. *Examine and use data.* Look at student performance in focused areas to target particular groups for assistance. Examine data from previous years. Regardless of how convincing patterns look, do not jump to conclusions. Look beneath the surface and ask more questions.

4. *Ask useful questions.*
   • How does performance for individuals and groups relate to state standards?
   • Is there variation across content areas?
   • How does the performance compare with that of other like groups, such as among students, schools, districts, states, and across the nation?
   • Are there data trends over time?
   • Are there existing initiatives in the school, district, or classroom that might help improve student performance? On the basis of what evidence?
   • What are the implications for your instructional practices or for your curriculum?
   • Do your findings suggest that you need more professional development?
   • How might other stakeholders benefit from this information?

Source: Adapted from Penny Noyce, David Preda, and Rob Traver, "Creating Data-Driven Schools," *Educational Leadership* (February 2000), 55.

Theory into Practice

We live in groups, and regardless of how noncompetitive we want others to be, we will always be evaluating people and making comparisons. As teachers you are expected to assess your students and give them a grade. You need to temper your judgments with balance and compassion. Give your students the benefit of the doubt, and try to reduce the anxiety and stress that often accompany the testing and grading process. Following are questions to consider for improving your own grading system.

1. Does your evaluation system coincide with your instructional objectives? Are those objectives clearly linked to your school district's curriculum guide and your state's academic content standards?

2. Do you make use of previous evaluation information for purposes of beginning instruction?

3. Is your grading system understood by your students?

4. Does your grading system adequately represent the content and skills you expect students to attain?

5. Are your grades derived from multiple sources (tests, quizzes, homework, papers, projects, class participation, and so forth)? Are these sources weighted according to their level of importance?

6. Do students know in advance how grades are to be determined?

7. Is your grading system fair and objective? Does it consider students' abilities, previous achievement, and maturity level?

8. Does your grading system enable students to demonstrate their progress and capabilities?

9. Do you use both formative and summative evaluation techniques? Are you willing to modify or reteach content, based on evaluation results?

10. Does your grading system coincide with school policy or school guidelines?

CONCLUSIONS

- The reasons for student evaluation include motivating students, providing feedback to students and teachers, informing parents, and making selection decisions.

- Four types of evaluation are placement, diagnostic, formative, and summative.

- Sources of information for evaluation in addition to tests and quizzes include classroom discussion and activity, homework, notebooks, reports, research papers, and peer evaluations.

- Grades are based on absolute or relative scales. Alternative grading practices include contracts, mastery grading, and grades for effort and progress.

- Portfolios provide another vehicle for showing what students have learned and how they are progressing.

- The conventional report card emphasizes basic subject areas and uses letters to designate grades; more contemporary methods of reporting include mastery and progress reports, statements about progress, and performance assessments.

- The cumulative record is a legal document that includes important data about the student's performance and behavior in school; it follows the student throughout his or her school career.

- Communication with parents takes place in the form of report cards, conferences, letters, and e-mail.

- Accountability systems are now in place for students, schools, and teachers.

KEY TERMS

absolute standards
accountability
computerized
 recordkeeping
continuous progress
 grading
contract grading

cumulative record
diagnostic evaluation
formal evaluation
formative evaluation
informal evaluation
mastery grading

mastery/progress report
 card
placement evaluation
quizzes
relative grading
standards-based grading
summative evaluation

DISCUSSION QUESTIONS

1. Can a teacher be objective in evaluating student performance? Explain.
2. How would you distinguish between placement, diagnostic, formative, and summative evaluation?
3. Compare your grading practices to that of teachers you had in school.
4. What are the differences between absolute and relative standards in grading? Which do you prefer? Why?
5. Why is it desirable to use several sources of data when arriving at a grade?
6. Describe instances when alignment between standards, assessment, and accountability are difficult if not possible.
7. What testing systems are mandated in the state in which you will teach? What accountability systems are in place?

MINI-CASES FROM THE FIELD

Case One: Types of Evaluation

Abdul Kali never realized how difficult it would be to evaluate the students in his fourth grade class. He had aligned his instruction to meet all of his state's mandated standards, yet he was still unable to determine whether the purpose of his evaluation should be for placement and diagnosis, or whether it should just be formative and summative. Abdul asked his friend, Judas Jones, if he had any suggestions. Judas said that he thought it all depended on what you were attempting to evaluate. "For example," said Judas, "if you were concerned about placement in a class group, you could use a standardized test. If you wanted to analyze your students' progress, you could use a teacher-made formative test or a standardized diagnostic test. If you were just concerned with a final grade on a topic or for the year, you should prepare a criterion-referenced summative test." Abdul thanked Judas for his advice, while thinking to himself that something was wrong with Judas' suggestions.

1. Was Abdul correct to question Judas's suggestions? Justify your explanation.
2. If Abdul was concerned about placement in a class reading group, did he need to give a standardized test? What could he have done instead?

3. What is the difference between a formative test and a standardized diagnostic test?

4. How should a criterion-referenced summative test be used?

5. Based on this mini-study, which of the four types of placement tests did Abdul need for his class? Explain the rationale for your answer.

Case Two: Evaluation Methods and Approaches

Mr. John Adams was asked by his principal, Mr. Nadler, to lead a committee in his social studies department to prepare the mid-year examinations. Mr. Adams felt that since all eight classes in the seventh grade had studied the same curriculum, only one test was needed. To be reliable and valid, the test needed only to be linked to the state standards for social studies. Adams decided that he had better not act alone in defiance of the principal's request. He decided to speak with the other seventh grade teachers to get their input on the type of test they felt could meet the standards. He would then go back and explain to Mr. Nadler that the department felt only one test was necessary. The responses from his colleagues ran the gamut, from short quizzes through authentic assessments such as observations of student work, group and peer evaluation and feedback, recitations, homework, reports, themes, research papers, discussions and debates, to written essay questions. It was obvious to Mr. Adams that each member of the department had very different ideas on how to develop a mid-year exam. Rather than clarify his approach, the attempt at collaboration had further muddied the waters.

1. Were Mr. Adams's actions appropriate for the development of an accurate performance assessment tool for a standards based curriculum? Explain.

2. How could Mr. Adams have gotten the teachers to agree on the type of mid-term examination to administer that would reflect a link to the standards?

3. Could authentic assessment be used on a mid-year examination? Justify your answer.

4. Was Principal Nadler correct in asking for different types of tests to judge mastery of standards? What do you think his reasoning was?

5. Describe the type of test that should have been prepared and the reason for its preparation.

Case Three: Records and Reports of Performance

Marla Thompson was aware of the importance of correct and truthful record keeping. She understood that an assessment process consisting of evaluation and measurement was worthless unless she kept records of performance that were accurate. She understood tests but was unclear about how report cards, electronic recordkeeping or (virtual recordkeeping), cumulative records, and student portfolios could be used in evaluating her students. How much weight should each carry? She decided to make a list of the various assessment procedures she was aware of. Her list included teacher-made tests, standardized tests, portfolios, observation, performance assessment, interviews, and questionnaires. Marla understood that the grades her assessments generated could be weighted and placed on a report card. What she didn't comprehend was how to use electronic recordkeeping, cumulative records, and portfolios. Marla was unsure of herself with regard to the worth of this type of record keeping.

1. Indicate which items on Marla's list are formal or informal.
2. How would you use student portfolios with electronic recordkeeping?
3. How could you combine the idea of performance assessment with a teacher-made test?
4. Why are your observations important in assessing student understanding?
5. When should a teacher consult a student's cumulative record? What types of materials should be entered in a cumulative record?

Case Four: Communication with Parents

Mrs. Olga Smyth couldn't believe that Mrs. Harridan had said that her child Laura never told a lie. Olga thought back to all the times she had caught Laura telling lies in class. She always said her dog ate her homework when she was unprepared. She was the type of child that had an excuse for everything. She didn't have a dental note because her dentist was sick. She couldn't study for the test she failed because her baby brother was making too much noise. Her father said she had to go to bed by eight o'clock; she therefore could not complete her report on time. It went on and on. Mrs. Smyth had finally written a letter explaining her concern with Laura's relentless lying. She had written that Laura's incessant lying had to stop. In her letter she had described numerous incidents and had asked for the parents' cooperation in resolving the problem. Yet the first thing out of Mrs. Harridan's mouth when the conference began was that Mrs. Smyth must be mistaken, her daughter never lies.

1. What would make Mrs. Harridan say her daughter never lies when she was confronted by Mrs. Smyth?
2. Who could Mrs. Smyth have asked for assistance in resolving this matter?
3. How could Mrs. Smyth have taken the initiative without being aggressive or accusatory?
4. How should Laura have been involved in this conference?
5. How could this conference be closed on a positive note? What plan of action should Mrs. Smyth consider?

Case Five: Accountability

Helen Brody was a sincere young teacher at the downtown urban campus of the Kemstort Elementary School, which was located in a low socioeconomic area. This was her second year with the same class. She had taught them in the third grade and now in the fourth grade. She had been told when she obtained the position that the Kemstort School had a very stringent accountability program, and looping classes for two years was part of their program. She knew that accountability was a concept that held schools, districts, educators, and students responsible for results. What exactly those results were she wasn't sure. Helen knew that the statewide standardized reading and mathematics tests were used to diagnose and foster student growth. On another level they were also used to identify schools that may not be succeeding or that were "low-performing." What she didn't understand was how she could be held personally accountable for the success of her students. They weren't all reading on grade level the first year she had them and they were still one to two years below grade level now.

1. Was Helen's definition of accountability correct? What might you add or delete from her description?

2. What is meant by the statement, "Accountability creates threats and opportunities?"

3. Should schools be held responsible for the success or failure of their students?

4. Describe your feeling regarding the following statement, "On one level accountability means determining which schools remain open and whether teachers are retained in their positions."

5. If you were a policy maker how would you develop an accountability program?

FIELD EXPERIENCE ACTIVITIES

1. Visit a school and ask staff members to list some examples of inappropriate evaluation techniques.

2. Prepare an outline of a grading procedure you expect to follow as a teacher, and explain how it would rectify the inappropriate evaluation techniques identified in question one.

3. Visit local schools, obtain sample report cards, and discuss their major characteristics in class. Analyze how various report cards differ.

4. Pretend you are about to have a general conference with a parent for the first time. Discuss with your classmates what topics might be important to include in a conference.

5. Examine the test scores for area school districts located near you. What are the high- and low-performing districts? Explore possible reasons for the differences in test scores between districts.

RECOMMENDED READING

Airasian, Peter, and Michael K. Russell. *Classroom Assessment: Concepts and Applications*, 6th ed. New York: McGraw-Hill, 2007.
Examines how assessment and grading procedures can be used to enhance instruction and learning.
Andrade, Heide, and Gregory J. Cizek (eds.). *Handbook of Formative Assessment*. New York: Routledge, 2009.
A discussion of key issues that dominate formative assessment policy and practice today, as well as those which are likely to affect research and practice in the coming years.

Barr, John R. *Parents Assuring Student Success*. Bloomington, IN: National Evaluation Service, 2000.

A wonderful resource that teachers can use to help parents understand how they can support a student's academic learning within the classroom.

Bloom, Benjamin S., J. Thomas Hastings, and George F. Madaus. *Handbook of Formative and Summative Evaluation of Student Learning*. New York: McGraw-Hill, 1971.

From some classic researchers in the field, a mammoth-sized text that can serve as an excellent source for technical questions about evaluation.

Burke, Kay. *Balanced Assessment: From Formative to Summative.* Bloomington, IN: Solution Tree, 2010.

Provides a comprehensive overview of the critical role that assessments, both formative and summative, play in today's classrooms.

Guskey, Thomas R., and Jane M. Bailey. *Developing Standards-Based Report Cards*. Thousand Oaks, CA: Corwin, 2010.

A guide for aligning assessment and reporting practices with standards-based education.

Hansen, David T., Mary E. Driscoll, René V. Arcilla, and Philip W. Jackson. *A Life in Classrooms: Philip W. Jackson and the Practice of Education*. New York: Teachers College Press, 2007.

Examines the full range of Philip W. Jackson's groundbreaking scholarship and teaching.

Miller, M. David, Norman E. Gronlund, and Robert L. Linn. *Measurement and Assessment in Teaching*, 10th ed. Upper Saddle River, NJ: Prentice-Hall, 2008.

Offers an appreciation of the advantages and disadvantages of various tests and evaluation procedures.

Johnson, Dale D., and Bonnie Johnson. *High Stakes: Children, Testing, and Failure in American Schools*. Lanham, MD: Rowman and Littlefield, 2002.

A thoughtful analysis of accountability and its impact on students in American schools.

Popham, W. James. *Educational Evaluation*, 3rd ed. Needham Heights, MA: Allyn & Bacon, 1992.

Presents various models and strategies for evaluating student outcomes. Popham is one of the most prolific writers in the area of assessment and evaluation.

Popham, W. James. *What Every Teacher Should Know About Educational Assessment*. Thousand Oaks, CA: Corwin, 2003.

Covers key understandings for school leaders, including validity, formative assessment, interpreting test results, and instructional sensitivity.

Popham, W. James. *Transformative Assessment.* Alexandria, VA: ASCD, 2008.

Clarifies what formative assessment really is, why it's right for your school or classroom, and how to use this approach to improve teaching, learning, classroom climate, teacher professional development, and school performance.

Popham, W. James. *Classroom Assessment: What Teachers Need to Know*, 6th ed. Upper Saddle River, NJ: Prentice-Hall, 2010.

A perfect guide to the basic information about assessment tools and their use in evaluation of students, covering the basics of authentic and standardized assessments

Tucker, Marc, and Judy B. Codding. *Standards for Our Schools*. San Francisco: Jossey-Bass, 2002.

A thoughtful analysis of standards, assessment, and accountability that describes both the political and practical implications of standards-based reform.

Part III

Preparing for Practice

In the first two sections of this text, we sketched the relationship between art and science as related to (Part I) perspectives on effective teaching performance, and (Part II) the practices and technical skills of teaching. In this part (chapter 10), we look to the future for you and for your profession. Effective teachers understand that good teaching practice is complex. To deal with this complexity we must find ways to advance academically and pedagogically; we must prepare for practice.

Professional growth in our practice requires understanding what your professional education experiences (your teacher education program) did and did not do for you. You must assess how you can grow so that your abilities are expanded, not encapsulated. We begin chapter 10 with a discussion of the problems of beginning teachers and the support available to them. Then we describe the variety of assessments that are now used. Finally, we close with a description of collegial associations. Most teachers think of these as the AFT or NEA, but other associations are just as important—in particular those that are related to the subject, grade level, or in some cases the students with special needs whom you are teaching.

Your professional preparation program provided you with many ideas, but for those ideas to have power, they need to be used. Similarly, this book documents a lot of what is now known about teaching. And even as this book is being written, new data is emerging. For example, in the 1960s, James Coleman argued that family socioeconomic status had the strongest influence on student achievement. In the 1990s and early 2000s, researchers began to challenge that notion. William Sanders (University of Tennessee) asserted that teachers are an equally important factor influencing student achievement. What you do in the classroom does make a difference for students. And, what you do to sustain your professional growth will ultimately influence how students view their own learning.

10

Preparing for Practice

FOCUS POINTS

1. Recognizing the need for teacher education and teacher professional status.
2. Discovering methods for improving support and learning opportunities during the first few years of teaching careers.
3. Utilizing self-evaluation and reflective methods to improve teacher practice.
4. Evaluating teachers by using peer and supervisory appraisals.
5. Discovering sources and products for teacher evaluation and professional growth.
6. Identifying professional organizations and teacher development.

OVERVIEW

This chapter explores the correlation (supported by research) between teacher effectiveness, professional growth, and improved learning outcomes. The goal of effective teacher practice is to facilitate learning and develop self-discipline for all students. An effective teacher is seen as a validated change agent[1] who gages success based on student achievement. The question is how best to achieve the goal?

Teaching practice can always be improved. The extent of improvement is related to how hard you work to meet your students' needs. Beginning (novice) teachers will always experience problems and frustrations. Your role is to learn from these encounters and improve your didactic classroom skills.

Effective teachers enjoy their work because they are well prepared and have acquired a variety of social skills for working with students, colleagues, supervisors, and parents. To be an effective teacher you must have a good educational background that includes content knowledge of your area, training in teaching methods, and experience with managing different types of students. Controversy exists about what qualities characterize effective teachers. There is, however, a general consensus that teachers who advance student achievement have high verbal ability, are well grounded in their disciplines, and can translate content into learning for students. The preceding chapters dealt with methods of teaching and the principles of practice that determine their use. This final chapter focuses on what it means to grow as a teacher and the resources available as you begin your professional journey.

Reforming Teacher Education

Professions have a monopoly on certain knowledge that separates their members from the general public and allows them to exercise control over those who are professionals. Indeed, years ago, one social critic observed that professions were nothing more than a conspiracy against the laity. Members of a profession have mastered a body of abstract knowledge that establishes their expertise and protects the public from quacks, untrained amateurs, and special interest groups. Further, they can use that abstract knowledge to deal with particular problems or cases.[2]

There is, however, no agreed-upon body of abstract knowledge that clearly constitutes what might be described as good education or teaching. Whereas the behavioral sciences, physical sciences, and professions such as law and medicine are guided by extensive rules of procedure and established methodologies, education has no agreed-upon set of procedures to guide teachers in the classroom as they diagnose student learning problems, make inferences about what to do, and then make decisions about how to proceed.[3]

As a result, many talk about education as if they were experts—resulting in a great deal of conflicting and sometimes negative conversation about teachers and the pedagogy of teaching. Another result of this ill-defined body of knowledge is that the content of teacher education courses varies from state to state, among teacher preparation institutions within states, and even within specific departments and schools of education. Thus, two students in the same program [at the same college or university] could end up with very different experiences.[4] Given such variation, what does it mean to be professionally prepared for the classroom? Do teacher education students (do you?) know how to diagnose the learning problems of students and then make informed decisions on how to proceed?

In short, there seems to be no overriding philosophy or body of defined abstract knowledge in teacher education programs, no agreed-upon pedagogy that must be learned by all candidates, and no set of criteria for making professional decisions in classrooms. This situation is clearly starting to change, but the diversity of views is still more common than consensus about what abstract knowledge teachers should use and apply. Nearly everyone has his or her own values, philosophy, and views about pedagogy. In far too many institutions, insight and intuition—what some call the "art of teaching or practice of teaching"—tend to rule rather than scientifically based procedures, as in the case of medicine, or professional procedures, as in the case of law.

Although most education departments and education schools continuously formulate committees to revise and improve teacher education and continuously debate the course content, far too many decisions are still made on the basis of personal ideologies and institutional politics. The result is often a hodgepodge of professional courses packaged together as a program, driven by state guidelines or faculty member interests, and varying from one teacher-training institution to another. Some might argue that this is an unfair criticism of teacher education, but mandates to improve and better coordinate teacher education efforts still largely go unheeded (although there are clear signs of change). Evidence of the problem can be seen in the *Improving Teacher Quality* report issued by *Education Week* in early 2003. In that report, no state was given an *A* grade for its overall approach to teacher quality, and well over half the states received grades of *C* or *D*.[5] Seven years later, more evidence of the problem appeared in "Quality Counts," another report issued by *Education Week* in early 2010. In that report only one state was given a grade of *A* for teacher quality, while still more than half received grades of *C* or *D* with two getting *F*s.[6] Though there are many reasons for the low grades, a primary reason relates to the lack of common abstract knowledge that educators can use to ground professional program content.

The debate over teacher preparation goes back to the 1960s when James Conant pointed out that professors of arts and science and professors of education were at war with each other over several important questions: the proper mix of courses, who should teach these courses (professors in content areas or professors of education), and even whether courses in pedagogy were worthwhile at all.[7] James Koerner described the problem further in his highly critical book *The Miseducation of American Teachers.* Koerner argued that, by requiring too many education courses—as many as 60 hours at some teacher colleges— and by making these courses too "soft," colleges of education were producing teachers versed in pedagogy at the expense of academic content.[8] Both critics argued that the academic quality of teachers needed to be upgraded.

Quality of teacher education was apparently a problem in the 1970s and 1980s, as a substantial percentage of prospective teachers were unable to demonstrate minimum competency on basic skills and writing tests. Critics argued that prospective teachers were weaker academically than their professional peers. Whether this "competency problem" is still manifest is now a matter of continued debate, but there are signs that teachers are just as academically able as others who attend college. For example, some reports suggest that the average SAT scores of prospective teachers were slightly above the national average for entering college students and that the performance of education and of noneducation students in general education coursework was quite similar.[9]

Critics suggest that certain factors are keeping good people out of teaching: pay, as compared to that of other "skilled" professions; rigid teacher education programs with many requirements; too little flexibility for employers to hire those persons they want to employ; and a compensation system that is based far too much on years of experience and advanced graduate work and far too little on the actual performance of teachers in terms of fostering student learning.

Even teacher education advocates such as John Goodlad and the authors of this book have pointed to a host of shortcomings in teacher education; namely, that departments and schools of education are fraught with instability, they lack institutional identity, their research base is limited, their programs often lack curricular cohesiveness, and professors of education too easily yield to personal ideology (rather than scientifically based research) to determine what constitutes good teaching.[10] In short, teacher education programs are not sufficiently in control of their own mission or policies. E. D. Hirsch wrote,

> The very thing which Horace Mann called upon teacher-training schools to do and which the American public assumes that such schools *are* doing—the teaching of effective pedagogy—is a domain of training that, according to both sympathetic and unsympathetic observers, gets short shrift in our education schools. Instead, it is mainly theory, and highly questionable theory at

that, which gets more attention in education-school courses. That point should be stated even more strongly: not only do our teacher-training schools decline to put a premium on nuts-and-bolts classroom effectiveness, but they promote ideas that actually run counter to consensus research into teacher effectiveness.[11]

In the 1980s and 1990s Goodlad proffered 19 recommendations, or what he called "postulates," for improving teacher education. They centered around screening candidates on the basis of moral and ethical decency, establishing well-defined program procedures and measurable outcomes, enhancing research and reflective practices, expanding the education faculty to include the entire university and public schools, resisting curriculum regulation by external authorities, and taking responsibility for the induction year of teaching.[12] Bold, new suggestions? Although there are differences in emphasis, much of what Goodlad advocates has been argued for before—from the time the findings of Conant and Koerner were published up to present-day reform movements such as the Carnegie Task Force on Teachers, the Holmes Group, and the National Network for Educational Renewal.[13]

The problem of teacher education is an ongoing national concern that needs to be addressed by establishing national standards for teacher preparation. The National Council for Accreditation of Teacher Education (NCATE) has set standards for professional content that outline the qualifications of the faculty who teach NCATE-accredited teacher education courses. However, by the early 2000s only half of the 1,200 colleges involved in preparing teachers were accredited by NCATE. As of 2009, 25 states have adopted or adapted NCATE unit standards as the state unit standards. NCATE's professional program standards have influenced teacher preparation in 48 states and the District of Columbia and Puerto Rico.[14]

Although many states have collaborative agreements with NCATE, teacher-training institutions can still receive state approval even if they are not accredited by NCATE. Moreover, the graduates of non-NCATE accredited institutions find jobs just as readily as graduates of accredited institutions. A former director of NCATE, Arthur Wise, hoped to remedy this confusing situation by making all teacher-education institutions measure up to more rigorous national standards through a single accrediting organization—and both the American Federation of Teachers and National Education Association supported this idea—which, almost twenty years later, has not come to fruition.[15] Nonetheless, the confusion will persist until educators reach greater agreement about the candidates most likely to succeed as teachers (What combination of variables predicts teacher success?), the basic body of professional knowledge that teachers need to learn (What foundations and pedagogical courses are needed in order to teach?), and the clinical and field experiences needed to prepare teachers for being thrust into the classroom on their own.

You should find out if the institution you attend is NCATE accredited. If it is not, it might hold Teacher Education Accreditation Council (TEAC) accreditation. Although the number of TEAC institutions is quite small, TEAC still represents an important alternative that, like NCATE, seeks to ensure that teachers prepared by institutions have the skills essential for teaching success. If your institution is not accredited, you might ask why not. Is it because of cost? Discuss with a faculty member the advantages and disadvantages of institutional accreditation.

As a step in the right direction, in October of 2010 NCATE and TEAC announced a merger, to take place within two years, into a new organization, the Council for Accreditation of Educator Preparation. The merger aims to make changes in the structure and substance of teacher-preparation accreditation. According to James G. Cibulka, current president of NCATE, "Our goal is not simply to bring together two organizations to do the same thing. . . . We really ought to have as our goal to raise the bar for quality educator preparation . . . and to speak with one voice about what that standard looks like, and how it should be implemented."[16]

The preparation of teachers tends to be very ideological. Everyone has an opinion on how to prepare teachers and on whether extensive teacher preparation is even necessary. During the late 1990s and early 2000s some new critics of teacher preparation programs emerged. None of those voices has been more prominent than that of Chester E. Finn, Jr., president of The Thomas B. Fordham Foundation.[17] Finn has attempted to cause policy makers to loosen, if not eliminate, extant requirements for those entering the field of education. To Finn, teaching has a weak knowledge base, and what teachers need is more content and less pedagogy, especially progressivist pedagogy. In essence, by opening up the field to all who want to teach, classrooms will be accessible to many intellectually capable people who now decide against teaching because of all the requirements. Further, some individuals will not be "force fed" progressivist ideology. Progressivist pedagogy includes ideas like constructivism, inquiry learning, and student-centered learning approaches that tend to be emphasized in teacher education programs. Finn and others, such as Jeanne Chall, argue that teacher-centered instruction, which this book describes more specifically as *direct instruction,* is the best way to foster enhanced academic results for students. They claim that direct instruction strategies are especially powerful for children who come from poor families or for "those [with] learning difficulties at all social and economic levels."[18]

Some of the people who may critique this book will argue for more constructivism (more student-centered strategies) because it is what they emphasize in their education classes. Critics like Finn would argue that young people don't need more progressivist ideas (because those show no real history of success), and instead they need more teacher-centered approaches and more content. We have tried to achieve a balance between progressivist and traditionalist ideas, but it is difficult to do. Where you teach, who you teach, and what you teach will dictate what approach makes sense. Good teachers know how and when to use constructivism and how and when to use direct instruction. They know how to be both traditional and progressive. How you teach depends on your goals for instruction. One size does not fit all students in all situations.

The voice of Linda Darling-Hammond, who is one of the staunchest and most articulate defenders of current teacher education programming, stands in stark contrast to the criticism of people like Koerner, Finn, and other conservative reformers. Darling-Hammond writes,

Other research confirms the effectiveness of teachers who comprehend their subject matter, understand student learning and development, know a wide range of teaching methods, and have developed their skills under expert guidance in clinical settings. Over two hundred studies illustrating the positive effects of teacher education contradict the long-standing myth that "teachers are born and not made." This research also makes it clear that teachers need to know much more than the subject matter they teach. Teachers who have had more opportunity to study the processes of learning and teaching are more highly rated and successful with students in fields from early childhood and elementary education to mathematics, science, and vocational education.[19]

The words of Darling-Hammond suggest that good teachers are both *born* and *made*. The more effective you are as a teacher, the more your students will learn in your classroom. You can make a difference. That is a scientifically based fact. And you make that difference by being well-read, knowing your subject, and using what you know about how students learn to foster enhanced achievement in what you are having them learn.

Helping the Beginning Teacher

What are the general needs of the beginning teacher? Most schools offer teacher orientation, but in spite of efforts to help teachers succeed, many of them still encounter adjustment problems. A review of the research on the problems of beginning teachers shows that feelings of isolation; poor understanding of what is expected of them; heavy workloads and extra assignments that they are unprepared to handle; lack of supplies, materials, or equipment; poor physical facilities; and lack of support or help from experienced teachers or supervisors contribute to their feelings of frustration and failure.[20] The result is that many potentially talented and creative teachers find teaching unrewarding and difficult, especially in inner-city schools, with approximately 11 percent leaving after one year of classroom experience and nearly 40 percent of newly hired teachers leaving the profession within five years.[21] The actual percentages vary by state and region. For example, teacher attrition tends to be a bit higher in Southern states than in Northern ones, but the attrition facts suggest that without proper support and positive working conditions, many teachers in all regions will decide to leave teaching.[22] A recent study found that for teachers in their first five years of employment, the attrition was substantially greater among beginning teachers with only some or no teacher preparation (13.7 percent) than among those with extensive preparation (8.6 percent), even after controlling for confounding variables.[23]

Problems of Education Students and Beginning Teachers

Over forty years ago, Frances Fuller suggested a progression in the type of concerns teachers have about teaching. Education students (at the preservice level) are characterized by "nonconcern"; student teachers are characterized by "increased concern"; beginning teachers are preoccupied with "survival concerns"; and experienced teachers focus on the tasks and problems of teachers (they have moved past initial survival) and are more involved with a variety of "self" concerns.[24] Similar concerns are still evident in more recent studies.[25]

A number of factors may contribute to the increasing concerns and anxieties student and beginning teachers have about the difficulty of teaching, beyond the fact that most people have concerns about the unknown when they start new jobs (especially their first jobs). Clearly, one factor is the content of and experiences associated with introductory teacher education courses, which do not seem to prepare teachers for the realities of the job, even if the course experiences are positive.[26] Another factor is that age and optimism may be inversely related. It takes a few years of seasoning to face reality, and college students at the pre-student teaching level tend to have confidence in their own abilities and to believe they are better equipped than others (older people) to be teachers. What young student cannot, after all, reasonably criticize many former teachers, thinking, "I can do a better job"? But once those same persons confront certain school and classroom realities, their optimism far too often evolves into pessimism—and a decision to leave teaching.

In a recent study, education students and beginning teachers were asked to rank problems they expected in the classroom. Although there was some agreement between the groups in the ranking of important problems, there was significant disagreement on the perceived difficulty of the problems. First-year teachers consistently ranked their perceived problems significantly more difficult than did preservice education students.[27] A logical deduction is that experience brought the "veterans" up against the challenges posed by day-to-day work in the classroom. The major problems they identified centered around workload, improving the academic performance of low-achieving students, dealing with misbehavior and maintaining control, and adapting materials to the needs and abilities of their students.

Numerous reports over the last several years document the new teacher's shock in the face of the realities of school and classrooms. Organized programs and internal support systems for beginning teachers are emerging, but they are still uneven in quality.[28] Mentor relations between experienced and beginning teachers and support from colleagues for continued learning and professional development are still exceptions, not the rule, even though they are being mandated by a large number of states and school districts.

Without question, the induction period—the first two or three years of teaching—is critical in developing teachers' capabilities. Beginning teachers should not be left alone to sink or swim. Over thirty states have recently developed induction programs for new teachers. Other states have increased staff development activities, and fifteen states have provided partial funding for such programs.[29] Most important for the professional development of new teachers are the internal support systems and strategies that many schools adopt—that is, the daily support activities and continual learning opportunities. Common causes of new teachers' failure need to be identified and addressed. Traditionally administrators have identified causes of failure that the schools should rectify:

1. *Assignment to difficult classes.* "Good" courses and "good" students are assigned to teachers on the basis of seniority; beginning teachers are given the "dregs" or "leftovers" to teach. A better balance is required (actually the opposite assignments) to permit beginning teachers to survive and learn from their mistakes in the classroom.

2. *Isolation of classrooms from colleagues and supervisors.* The classrooms farthest from the central office are usually assigned to beginning teachers. Isolating the new teacher from experienced teachers contributes to failure. Beginning teachers need to be assigned to rooms near the main office and near experienced teachers to encourage daily communication.

3. *Poor physical facilities.* Classrooms, room fixtures, and equipment are usually assigned on the basis of seniority. Providing the leftovers to new teachers is damaging to morale. A more equitable assignment of facilities is needed.

4. *Burdensome extra class assignments.* Extra class duties are cited as a source of ill feelings more than any other item. New teachers are often assigned burdensome or tough assignments that they are unprepared for and did not expect as teachers, such as yard patrol, hall patrol, cafeteria patrol, or study hall duties. Assignments given to beginning teachers should not be so burdensome that they affect the quality of their teaching.

5. *Lack of understanding of the school's expectations.* School officials should clarify the school's goals and priorities and the responsibilities of teachers early in the first term. Orientation sessions and written guides are usually provided; the problem seems to be the dearth of continuing communication and reinforcement as the teacher progresses through various stages of role acquisition.

6. *Inadequate supervision.* Most problems of beginning teachers could be either prevented or curtailed with proper supervision. Supervision often consists of only two or three formal visits to the classroom a year and possibly a few informal contacts and one or two meetings. The need is for increased supervisory contact, both formal and informal, so that assistance is provided regularly in the early stages of the teacher's career.[30]

In another study researchers identified a variety of reasons for high-ability teachers' decisions to leave the profession.[31] In the order identified by this select group of teachers, the reasons were family/motherhood, salary, career advancement, stress and demands of job, lack of support, student behavior, and lack of respect. In examining the causes of failure for new teachers and the reasons that more experienced teachers leave the profession, it is quite clear that students and student behavior are not the only (perhaps not even primary) reasons that most teachers exit the classroom. The quality-of-life issues that bother the "exiting" teachers relate to the lack of student respect and administrative support.

Interestingly, the nature of the problems that teachers confront in classrooms has changed little over time. Even though slight changes have occurred in the types of problems, the frequency and magnitude of the specific problems remain relatively stable. For years the *Phi Delta Kappan* poll highlighted areas such as student discipline as significant. Interestingly, in the 2007 poll, parents expressed more concern with how schools are funded and with No Child Left Behind than they did with issues such as discipline.[32] This fact highlights the notion that the types of problems that teachers will face are *contextually* specific and will not be significantly different from those evidenced in classrooms in the past.

The degree to which issues like student misbehavior or respect are problematic for you will likely be more a factor of *where* you teach. In schools in high-poverty areas, student misbehavior is an issue that impacts teacher perceptions of working conditions. Poverty influences many different aspects of school life, among them how the students act on their impulses and how responsive students are to the learning environment. There are great rewards to teaching in urban schools; there are also, quite candidly, real challenges. Knowing that those challenges are there is the first step toward identifying the theoretical and practical knowledge you need for success with high-need students.

Teaching Inner-City and Culturally Diverse Students

Teachers assigned to inner-city schools tend to feel significantly greater anxiety than those assigned to more affluent communities, and they even exhibit symptoms of exhaustion and battle fatigue. They may deal with classroom management and discipline problems, the inability of many of their students to grasp basic fundamentals (especially reading and writing), the nonresponsiveness or nonavailability of parents, and the lack of meaningful assistance from supervisors and administrators.

Several years ago, Ornstein and Levine summarized forty years of research aimed at understanding and overcoming the problems of teaching low-achieving and inner-city students. The problems are categorized into ten classroom realities, illustrated in box 10.1. The first five are teacher related and the remaining five are student or school related. The inference is that the finger of responsibility should not be pointed at any one group or one person. The researchers provide six teacher-education solutions for the teacher-related problems:

1. Increase the number of minority teacher-education students,
2. improve instructional strategies for low achievers (e.g., know how to use direct instruction),
3. permit student teachers more opportunity to work with an effective cooperating teacher,
4. promote greater assistance to teachers during the first three years (intern period) of teaching,
5. put greater emphasis on classroom management techniques (see chapter 7) during the preservice and intern periods, and
6. examine several different teacher effectiveness models in the preservice and intern stages of education.[33]

These and other "solutions" continue to be evidenced in the reports of commissions and researchers who are working on teacher quality issues.[34]

The increasingly rich diversity of American classrooms has created a challenge for teacher education. Many beginning teachers prefer to teach white middle-class students because they themselves are white and from middle-class communities, but the reality is that most of them will teach a very diverse group of students, even if they are in suburban teaching contexts. Even affluent subur-

---

Box 10.1   Realities of Teaching Inner-City, Low-Achieving Students

1. *Differences in teacher-student backgrounds.* Teachers with middle-class backgrounds may have difficulty understanding and motivating inner-city students; this may be particularly salient for white teachers working with minority students.

2. *Teacher perceptions of student inadequacy.* Many teachers working with inner-city students conclude from achievement test scores that large numbers are incapable of learning; hence the teachers may put less effort into improving student performance.

3. *Low standards of performance.* By the time many inner-city students reach middle or senior high school, low performance has become the norm, expected and accepted by both students and teachers.

4. *Ineffective instructional grouping.* Low achievers are frequently grouped into slow classes (or subgrouped in regular classes) where instruction proceeds at a slow rate.

5. *Poor teaching conditions.* As inner-city students fall further behind academically, and as both they and their teachers experience frustration and disappointment, classroom behavior problems increase and teachers find working conditions more difficult; the terms "battle fatigue," "battle pay," and "blackboard jungle" have been used in the literature to describe teaching conditions in inner-city schools.

6. *Differences between parental and school norms.* Differences between the way the inner-city home (physical punishment) and the school (internalization of norms) punish, shame, or control youngsters make it difficult for many students to follow school rules or for teachers to enforce them.

7. *Lack of previous success in school.* Lack of academic success in earlier grades hinders the learning of more difficult material and damages a student's perception of what he or she is capable of learning.

8. *Negative peer pressure.* High-achieving inner-city students are frequently ridiculed and rejected by peers for accepting the middle-class school norms.

9. *Inappropriate instruction.* As inner-city students proceed through school, academic tasks and concepts become increasingly more abstract, and many of these students fall further behind because their level of mastery is too rudimentary to allow for fluent learning.

10. *Delivery of services.* The tasks of delivering effective instruction and related services to students are increasingly more difficult in a classroom or school comprised mainly of lower-achieving, inner-city students (because their learning problems are more serious) than in a middle-class classroom or school that has a small percentage of lower-achieving inner-city students.

Source: Adapted from Allan C. Ornstein and Daniel U. Levine, "Social Class, Race, and School Achievement: Problems and Prospects," *Journal of Teacher Education* (September–October 1989), 17–23.

ban communities are more diverse than they were thirty to forty years ago. If preservice teachers are unprepared to deal with this diversity in the classroom, they will be unsuccessful. In California, almost 140 distinct cultural groups are represented in the classrooms. Nationally, of America's 53 million elementary and secondary students, 35 percent are from racial or ethnic minority groups, and 25 percent come from home environments characterized by poverty.[35] Present evidence suggests that current approaches in far too many institutions do not adequately prepare teachers—in terms of attitudes, behaviors, and teaching strategies—for dealing with this diverse student population.[36]

Legal immigration now accounts for up to one-half of the annual growth in the US population. From 1930 to 1950, 80 percent of the immigrants to the United States came from Western Europe and Canada. From 1970 through 1990, however, as many as 90 percent came from non-Western or Third World countries—chiefly and in rank order from Mexico, the Philippines, South Korea, Taiwan, Vietnam, Jamaica, India, the Dominican Republic, and Guatemala. Moreover, estimates of the illegal population, mainly from Latin America and the Caribbean, total about one million people in a given year (with approximately half establishing permanent residence).[37] According to the latest population count, more than 50 million Hispanics now live in the United States—about one-sixth of the total population. Most children in California are now of Hispanic origin, as are one in five children in public schools nationwide.

In 10 states and Washington, DC, the majority of people under 18 are now minorities, and 17 percent of kids live in mixed-race families. The date for when America will become "majority minority"—where no one ethnic group makes up more than half the population—is expected to be as early as 2042.[38]

Data on the US population were first collected in the 1850 decennial census. That year, there were 2.2 million foreign born in the United States, 9.7 percent of the total population. Between 1860 and 1920, immigrants as a percentage of the total population fluctuated between about 13 and 15 percent, peaking at 14.8 percent in 1890 mainly due to European immigration. By 1930, immigrants' share of the US population had dropped to 11.6 percent (14.2 million individuals). The share of foreign born in the US population continued to decline between the 1930s and 1970s, reaching a record low of 4.7 percent in 1970 (9.6 million individuals). However, since 1970, the percentage has risen rapidly, mainly due to large-scale immigration from Latin America and Asia. In 1980 the US Census Bureau reported that the foreign born represented 6.2 percent (14.1 million individuals) of the total US population. By 1990, their share had risen to 7.9 percent (19.8 million individuals) and, by the 2000 census, they made up 11.1 percent (31.1 million individuals) of the total US population.[39] As of 2008, immigrants comprised 12.5 percent (38.0 million) of the total US population (see figure 10.1). The average annual number of persons naturalizing increased from less than 120,000 during the 1950s and 1960s to 210,000 during the 1980s, 500,000 during the 1990s, and to 680,000 between 2000 and 2010.[40]

A significant number of these culturally diverse and immigrant families are "structurally poor," meaning that the family conditions are unstable or disorganized and the children have few chances to escape from poverty. The majority of

Figure 10.1   Foreign Born in the US Population

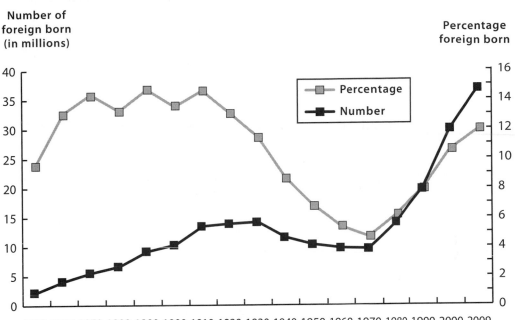

Number of foreign born (in millions)

Percentage foreign born

Legend: Percentage; Number

X-axis: 1850 1860 1870 1880 1890 1900 1910 1920 1930 1940 1950 1960 1970 1980 1990 2000 2009

minority children is at risk in school and lacks the requisite cognitive skills for learning because of poverty and lack of strong family structure. Such children are far too often labeled "learning disabled" or "slow" primarily because of cultural differences in learning styles and thinking patterns. This circumstance is regrettable.

Interestingly, the school performance of immigrant children suggests that, in almost all academic subjects, the immigrant students outperform native children who come from similar economic backgrounds.[41] Ironically, the longer immigrant students are in the United States, the more poorly they perform in school. Laurence Steinberg describes this phenomenon quite poignantly:

> We would hypothesize, therefore, that students born outside the United States would be doing worse in school than those who are native Americans, and that native Americans whose families have been in this country for several generations would be faring better than their counterparts who arrived more recently.
>
> Surprisingly, just the opposite is true: the longer a student's family has lived in this country, the worse the youngster's school performance and mental health. . . . Foreign-born students—who, incidentally, report significantly more discrimination than American-born youngsters and significantly more difficulty with the English language—nevertheless earn higher grades in school than their American-born counterparts. . . .
>
> It is not simply that immigrants are outperforming nonimmigrants on measures of school achievement. On virtually every factor we know to be correlated with school success, students who were not born in this country outscore those who were born here.[42]

In contrast to Steinberg's findings of 1996, in 2008, there were 31.9 million immigrants age 25 and older. Of those, 27.1 percent had a bachelor's degree or higher, while 32.5 percent lacked a high school diploma. Among the 168.2 million native-born adults age 25 and older, 27.8 percent had a bachelor's degree or higher and only 11.7 percent did not have a high school diploma.[43] The question is why the discrepancy exists for those not having a high school diploma. (See Case Study 10.1.)

Questions for Reflection

The Steinberg quote is a sad commentary on American education. It also suggests something about the nature of American culture. Assuming that Steinberg's argument is correct, what, if anything, can you as a teacher do to counteract this "diminished return" reality that he describes? Can you, as *one teacher*, really make a difference in mitigating the progression of weak performance of non-mainstream-culture (disadvantaged) students? What can you do that would really help non-mainstream students succeed?

Beginning teachers often do not learn to make modifications in their pedagogical efforts or in subject matter to adjust to culturally diverse learners. If you ask teachers (novice or experienced) about culturally diverse learners, you usually get socially acceptable responses since teachers may not want to admit to ignorance or biases. But responding to scenarios or questions in education classes or on job interviews is obviously not the same as teaching. Teacher education programs, as well as internship programs in the first three years of teaching, need to explore the attitudes that teachers have toward students who are culturally different from themselves, their attitude toward related learning and pedagogy issues, the teacher's role, and the effects of teacher expectations and behavior on the performance of minority students.

At the same time, it is imperative to explore the problem behaviors of at-risk student populations regardless of the racial, ethnic, or socioeconomic implications. To ignore the impact on schooling of such factors as early sexual activity, truancy, delinquency, and early use of drugs can result in the creation of educational underclasses under the guise of tolerance or political correctness. You need to know how to deal with "problem" students in order to empower them as learners. Identify a successful teacher in an urban school—someone who is not just surviving but whose students are academically thriving. Observe the person in a classroom lesson. What makes him or her unique?

The following case discusses an attempt by a teacher to meet the needs of a culturally diverse inner-city student population. The study documents the teacher's success as well as the hardships that success can bring due to bureaucratic misunderstanding. Evaluate the study and decide if the strategies used were appropriate for a multicultural school society.

Case Study 10.1
Culturally Diverse Inner-City Students

Barry Finkelman was faced with a problem that he had never dealt with during his professional training. His class at Baldwin Elementary contained the most diverse population he could ever have imagined. Essentially it reflected the makeup of the school community in which the school resided. His fifth-grade class took diversity to new heights, being composed of children of African, Asian, Hispanic, Russian, and Arabic origins. The only saving grace as Barry saw it was that the only common language was English, which he hoped to use as a focus for all class work.

Barry was especially fascinated with the variety of holidays celebrated in class. Aside from the traditional Christmas and Hanukah there was the African American Kwanza, the Chinese New Year, Mexican Independence Day, the Tet holiday for the Vietnamese, and Ramadan for Muslims. All students and their cultures were valued and respected. Barry hoped that this approach would establish a positive classroom environment. He used a variety of strategies and pedagogical approaches to achieve this objective. Children had been asked to place their pictures next to their country of origin on the class world map and write descriptions of their former homelands. This sharing of each child's background and cultural heritage added to his class's multicultural uniqueness. Barry described his own ancestral roots to highlight the similarities he and all the children shared. He explained that all immigrants shared the same dream and aspired to learn and prosper in their new country.

Barry reinforced his approach to multicultural education by expanding it to the rest of the curriculum. To encourage children to feel good about themselves, he asked them to count using their native languages as well as to sing various national songs. Despite all his efforts, this human relations approach apparently was not working. The children had not improved in reading and mathematics, and parents had not been heard from. Many of his colleagues said that was all he could expect "from such a class." To Barry's disappointment, students also argued and excluded each other from lunchtime games. Some insisted that their heritage was better than others'.

Barry's friend, Joan Velasquez, said that his feelings of despair were caused by his middle-class background, which made it difficult for him to understand and motivate multicultural inner-city kids; especially since he was a white teacher working with minority children.

Barry told Joan, "That's just not true! I care about my kids. I just can't get them to focus on learning. I'm going to try a new approach and write a grant for a community program." Joan said, "What are you talking about? How is a grant going to help you with your class?" "I'll tell you the problem as I see it," replied Barry, "It's not with what I've done but with what I haven't done. I've tried to meet my students' needs only in class through lessons, using a human relations approach—without getting the rest of our school community involved." Joan inquired, "How are you going to do that?"

Barry smiled and said he thought he would ask the principal to help fund an afternoon and summer program where children could come to learn and play. Only one proviso would be made. Each child must be escorted by a parent, legal guardian, or older sibling who would assist the children with their class work.

As it turned out, the program was a great success because of unintended consequences. Children were not taught by the parents; instead they assisted their non-English-speaking parents in learning English. Parents made cross-cultural friendships, experiencing the native foods and customs of other ethnic groups, and began to share in the American dream. Unfortunately, due to bureaucratic ineptness the program was not funded the following year.

Discussion Topics and Questions to Ponder

1. How would you describe Barry's strategy as it related to dealing with the inability of many students to grasp basic fundamentals, especially reading and writing, and the nonresponsiveness or unavailability of parents?

2. How do you feel about Joan's assertion that middle-class teachers can't understand or motivate inner-city kids?

3. Why did Barry feel that his stress on human relation activities had been ineffective?

4. Why has low performance become the norm, expected and accepted by both students and teachers in culturally diverse inner-city schools?

5. How did Barry's vision extend beyond any one classroom or subject matter and encompass the entire school community?

What would you do if . . . ?

1. Barry's approach was criticized because of its narrow view of diversity and its total disregard of the values and lifestyle of dominant American societal culture.

2. You were presented with the following teacher-education solutions and strategies and asked to evaluate them as positive, negative, or meaningless with regard to fostering multicultural education.
   - Increase the number of minority teacher-education students.
   - Improve instructional strategies for low achievers.
   - Promote greater assistance to beginning teachers.
   - Put greater emphasis on classroom management techniques during student teaching.
   - Use teaching strategies that build upon student strengths rather than weaknesses.
   - Stress the creation of environments that value and respect all students.

3. You were offered the following two descriptions of multicultural education and asked to choose and defend one.
   - Multicultural education offers an alternative way to achieve a common culture, while preserving traditional American values and making multiple traditions a reality.
   - Multicultural education rejects a common American culture. It celebrates the history and cultures of others, while pointing to faults in our society and ignoring its positive aspects.

How Beginning Teachers (Novices) Teach

The personal styles and images of beginning teachers, commonly called *novices,* tend to remain inflexible throughout their preservice training. Candidates tend to use the information provided in coursework to confirm rather than reconstruct their views about teaching. Further compounding the problem of adjusting to future classroom life, teacher candidates are often presented with contradictory and inconsistent views of teaching and learning in their coursework and while student teaching, with teacher education emphasizing one approach and a classroom teacher (in student teaching) encouraging another. As a result, novices come to their first job with an inadequate or conflicted notion of classroom practice and are unprepared to adjust their approach in response to varied problems of instruction, classroom management, and student learning. As beginning teachers acquire knowledge on the job, they must begin to use it to modify, adapt, and reconstruct their views and their teaching methods. Eventually, those who are successful move from focusing on their own behaviors to focusing on the performance of their students; they move from emphasizing classroom management to emphasizing instructional techniques and, finally, to the matter of how and whether students learn.

Many teacher educators oversimplify the reality of student teaching and ignore many complex teaching and learning variables that affect a teacher's classroom decisions. As a result, both student teachers and beginning teachers are expected to function at levels beyond their capacity; in fact, many possess only minimal survival skills. At issue is the failure of teacher educators to provide student teachers with sufficient procedural knowledge to deal with the unique requirements of students with special needs. Lacking sufficient knowledge when thrust into the classroom as beginning teachers, novices tend to rely on their own recent experiences as students—an approach that is inappropriate or insufficient for teaching younger pupils.[44]

Experience does not ensure future success. What you need is guided, purposeful experience that is built on the best available knowledge about what practices foster enhanced student success and that also entails involvement with a mentor teacher who has demonstrated success using those practices. (See the discussion of mentoring later in the chapter.) Consistency between what you learn from classroom experiences and what a mentor or cooperating teacher models has historically been a quandary. Although mastering procedural routines or generic teaching methods is important, one group of teacher educators contends that beginning teachers (or novices) must be concerned with learning how to teach content and helping students learn it.[45] This position stresses the importance of subject matter *and* subject-matter pedagogy—if there are any methods to learn, they are methods related to subject-matter delivery. This school of thought is rooted in the post-*Sputnik* era and in the old schism between professors of arts and science and professors of education over the centrality of disciplinary knowledge versus knowledge of pedagogy. As in the past, today's arts and science faculty continue to advocate the necessity of subject matter and are likely to remain skeptical of pedagogy.

Lee Shulman introduced the phrase *pedagogical content knowledge* and sparked a wave of scholarly articles on teachers' knowledge of their subject matter and the importance of this knowledge for successful teaching.[46] For the most part, content knowledge was ignored by researchers on teaching in the 1970s and 1980s when generic methods and principles of effective teaching were emphasized. In the early twenty-first century, interest has shifted toward specialized or content-based methods and toward enhanced teacher reflection relative to selected scientifically based practices—that is, toward an emphasis on techniques that research supports as effective in helping students learn.[47] Researchers began to examine specific strategies for teaching mathematics, science, or reading and to look for evidence that knowing how to teach something effectively is an important complement to possessing the requisite and essential disciplinary knowledge.

In Shulman's theoretical framework, teachers need to master two types of knowledge: (1) content, or "deep" knowledge of the subject itself, and (2) knowledge of curricular development. Content knowledge encompasses what Jerome Bruner would call the "structure of knowledge"—the theories, principles, and concepts of a particular discipline. Especially important is content knowledge that deals with the teaching process, including the most useful forms of representing and communicating content and how students best learn the specific concepts and topics of a subject.

Teachers' orientation to their subject matter influences their method of planning, choice of content, the use of textbooks, the supplementary materials they use, their pedagogical strategies, and their perceptions of students' instructional needs. Likewise, it determines the way teachers formulate, demonstrate, and explain the subject so that it is comprehensible to learners. All this suggests that beginning teachers need to integrate subject-matter content and pedagogy.[48] Teachers must know process *and* content. Research was conducted to determine the effects of teacher education coursework in subsequent professional practice. The researchers concluded that teachers who do and those who do not have teacher education backgrounds do teach differently.[49] More specifically, they make different assumptions about the students as learners. Pam Grossman describes six teachers (three with and three without formal teacher preparation):

> The six teachers in this study represent, in many ways, the best and the brightest of prospective teachers. All are well prepared in their subject matter; four of the six hold BAs in literature from prestigious colleges and universities, while one teacher was completing his doctorate in literature at the time of the study. . . . All six of the teachers were technically first-year teachers, although three of them had had prior experience as teaching interns or aides. Of the six teachers, three taught in suburban public schools and three taught in independent schools. Two of the teachers, one with and one without teacher education, taught at the same independent school, which provided opportunity for at least one cross-case analysis in which teaching context was controlled.
>
> The results of this study suggest that, in this case, subject specific coursework did make a difference in these beginning teachers' pedagogical content knowledge of English. The two groups of teachers differed in their conceptions of the purposes of teaching English, their ideas about what to teach in secondary English, and their knowledge of student understanding.[50]

If beginning teachers are to be successful, they must wrestle simultaneously with issues of specialized pedagogical content as well as issues of general pedagogy (or generic teaching principles). The authors of this book stress generic teaching principles, but specialized pedagogical approaches and generic teaching principles are not mutually exclusive. You will use some generic principles to learn to teach reading; for example, you will also need more highly defined skills for phonetics instruction. Only by integrating both forms of pedagogy can a teacher personally define and understand the purpose of teaching, understand students' learning, and develop realistic curricular and instructional strategies.

In the ideal, you will have matriculated through a program that combines theory and practice (and general and specialized methods) in ways that help you see the connections between what is known and how that known knowledge can be applied. You should be able to negotiate the problems of teaching in ways that improve your practice and foster enhanced opportunities for your students, and be able to mitigate some of the common problems that often plague novice teachers. You will develop your own artful twist on the known science of teaching. This vision of success is only possible if you have had long-term exposure to teacher education content through your own long-term professional development and growth. In essence, you will always be on a professional journey, and though you may find accomplishment, you may never feel as though you have reached your goal. Teachers cannot and should not "short-course." Some evidence is emerging to suggest that although good intentions are necessary, they are not a sufficient condition for success. Such anecdotal evidence comes from an analysis of teachers who have been "short-coursed" into the classroom:

> Even very bright people who are enthusiastic about teaching find that they cannot easily succeed without preparation, especially if they are assigned to work with children who need skillful teaching. Perhaps the best example of the limitations of the "bright person" myth about teaching is Teach for America (TFA), a program created to recruit talented college graduates to disadvantaged urban and rural classrooms for two years en-route to careers in law, medicine, and other professions. If anyone could prove that teachers are born and not made, these bright, eager students, many of them from top schools, might have been the ones to do it. Yet four separate evaluations found that TFA's three-to-eight-week training program did not prepare candidates to succeed with students.
>
> Many recruits know that their success, and that of their students, had been compromised by their lack of access to the knowledge needed to teach. Yale University graduate Jonathan Schorr was one of the many to raise this concern. He wrote:
>
> "I—perhaps like most TFAers—harbored dreams of liberating my students from public school mediocrity and offering them as good an education as I had received. But I was not ready. . . . As bad as it was for me, it was worse for the students. Many of mine . . . took long steps on the path toward dropping out. . . . I was not a successful teacher and the loss to the students was real and large."[51]

Support from Colleagues

In general, having to learn by trial and error without support and supervision has been the most common problem faced by new teachers. Expecting teachers to function without support is based on the false assumptions that (1) teachers are well prepared for their initial classroom and school experiences, (2) teachers can develop professional expertise on their own, and (3) teaching can be mastered in a relatively short period of time. Researchers find that there is little attempt to lighten the class load and limit extra class assignments to make the beginning teacher's job easier. In the few schools that do limit these activities, teachers have reported that they have had the opportunity to "learn to teach."[52]

Unquestionably, new teachers need the feedback and encouragement experienced teachers and professional peers can provide. The exchange of ideas can take place in school and out, such as while sharing a ride to a local meeting. Experienced teachers must be willing to open their classrooms to new teachers. Because of the desire for autonomy in the classrooms, there is seldom sufficient communication or visitation between classrooms. No matter how successful individuals are as student teachers and how good their preservice training is, they can benefit from the advice and assistance of experienced colleagues. Talking to other teachers gives novices the chance to sound out ideas and assimilate information. **Peer coaching** and **mentoring** are nothing more than purposeful faculty collaboration where you, as a new teacher, work with colleagues to share ideas about instruction and student learning. Mentoring and peer coaching are two important components of a successful induction program.[53]

Teachers expect to learn from one another when the school provides opportunities for them to talk routinely to one another about teaching, be observed regularly in the classroom, and jointly participate in planning and lesson preparation. Teachers who are given opportunities to develop and implement curriculum ideas, join study groups about implementing classroom practices, or experiment in new skills and training feel more confident in their individual and collective ability to perform their work.[54]

During peer coaching or mentoring, classroom teachers observe one another, provide feedback concerning their teaching, and together develop (or reflect upon) instructional plans. New teachers should look for techniques of teaching and lesson planning that are unfamiliar to them, that coincide with their teaching style, and that are an improvement over what they are doing. Mentor programs are in place in a number of states. These programs were established to help new teachers be successful and to reduce high teacher attrition rates.[55]

An experienced teacher who acts as a peer coach or mentor teacher for an inexperienced teacher performs five functions: (1) *companionship*, or discussing ideas, problems, and successes; (2) *technical feedback*, especially related to lesson planning and classroom observations; (3) *analysis of application*, or integrating what happens or what works into the beginning teacher's repertoire; (4) *adaptation*, or helping the beginning teacher adjust to particular situations; and (5) *personal facilitation*, or helping the teacher feel good about himself or herself after trying new strategies.[56]

Similar data have been reported by Neubert and Bratton. They studied visiting mentor teachers in Maryland school districts who, rather than observe classroom teachers, teach alongside them. From this study they identified five characteristics of resource teachers that promote an effective coaching relationship: *knowledge*—more knowledge about teaching methods than the classroom teacher; *credibility*—demonstrated success in the classroom; *support*—a mix of honest praise and constructive criticism; *facilitation*—recommending and encouraging rather than dictating, assisting rather than dominating in the classroom; and *availability*—accessibility to the classroom teacher for planning, team teaching, and conferences.[57]

In one Pennsylvania school district, a "buddy system" has been developed for beginning and experienced teachers who need additional assistance. Continuous peer support is provided, with teachers who are teamed together by same subject or grade level. The teacher "coaches" who are selected work full-time (and often after school) helping their less-experienced colleagues become better teachers.[58]

Data suggest, however, that beginning teachers are selective about whom they ask for help. They seek help from experienced teachers whom they perceive as "knowledgeable," "friendly," and "supportive," independent of whether the teachers are formally recognized as their "mentors" or "coaches." In a study of 128 teachers in 90 different schools, 75 percent sought help from teachers who were not their assigned mentors; only 53 percent were generally satisfied with the mentors they were assigned.[59]

Although mentors are usually comfortable offering help to their inexperienced colleagues, the success of any mentoring program hinges on whether inexperienced teachers are comfortable seeking help from their experienced counterparts. The decision for adults to seek help and then to accept it is influenced by numerous variables. The tension that impacts the decision process about asking for help is the tension between the embarrassment of continued failure without help and the embarrassment of asking for help to solve a problem. Indeed, the staggering number of teachers who leave the profession after only a few years of service suggests the need to be sensitive to the concerns of beginning teachers and the need to improve mentoring programs, which is why in the early 21st century so many states are developing more formalized mentoring systems for their new teachers.

Some educators, such as James Stigler and James Hiebert, outline new ways for teachers to help teachers by relying on models used in Japan for professional development. The *jugyoukenkynu* (or Japanese study lesson) takes different forms but often includes a group of teachers collaborating to develop lesson plans—they essentially plan together.[60] One "appointed" teacher then teaches the lesson, and professional colleagues from the planning group watch and take notes on a variety of classroom dynamics, especially the students' reactions to the lesson. After the lesson, they hold a general discussion about what happened and how the students responded (what they learned). This model is quite unique, but some American schools are trying it with the goal of making teachers less isolated and more focused on working with others to improve teaching performance. Even if the school where you eventually teach has no such program (and it likely will not), find someone to talk to about your teaching and find ways to have him or her watch you teach—whether in person or on a video recording.

Support from Other Beginning Teachers

The **induction period**—the first two or three years of teaching—is critical in developing teachers' capabilities. The internal support systems that schools adopt are vital for the professional development of new teachers. In the words of Harry Wong, "If you are a potential new teacher, the most important question you need to ask during the interview is 'Does the district have an induction program?' Your success as a teacher may depend on it."[61] (See, for example, the Institute for Teacher Renewal and Growth in Tucson, Arizona, which produced 12 finalists for Teacher of the Year.[62])

Unfortunately, some schools (and school districts) do not respond adequately to the needs of their new teachers and expect too much from them in terms of expertise. One supplementary activity is for beginning in-service teachers to share classroom experiences, to tell their stories, and to reflect on ways of addressing problems within the structure of a college course or as part of a staff development program at the school district level.[63] Beginning teachers from various schools can share, organize, and apply what they know about teaching in a sort of self-help process.[64] Preservice teachers, especially student teachers, have been doing this for years, returning from their field experiences to meet in groups with a supervisor. Such sharing of personal stories and experiences, with feedback and interpretation from peers, can have a nurturing effect and help change and improve the lives of teachers at many stages of their professional growth.

Still another method for supporting beginning teachers is computer networking. Across the country in various schools and colleges, teachers, administrators, professors, and even students frequently communicate with each other electronically.[65]

> Cyber-enabled networks hold great promise for supporting teachers' development of new knowledge and practices. . . . Studies have shown that, online, teachers can, under certain conditions, interact more frequently, build more diverse networks, and gain more equitable access to human and information resources not available locally. In addition, the quality of dialogue online has been shown to be equivalent to and in some cases better than face to face.[66]

One network is the Beginning Teacher Computer Network (BTCN), initiated at Harvard University to help its first-year teacher graduates, now based in schools across the country, stay in touch with each other.[67] Unlike larger computer conferencing systems such as Bitnet or Prodigy, the BTCN network is small and relies on personal computers. It is an inexpensive way for teachers to work out small problems; to offer peer diagnosis, rather than expert or supervisor analysis; and to provide nonevaluative feedback. The network provides support, collegiality, and opportunity for professional growth; participants know that a friend and former classmate are close at hand to listen and offer ideas and advice. Beginning teachers who graduate from any teacher education program can form their own networks with or without the assistance of their professors or principals.

Guidelines for Improving Support for Beginning Teachers

Whatever the existing policies regarding the induction period for entry teachers, there is a need to improve provisions for continued professional development, to make the job easier, to make new teachers feel more confident in the classroom and school, to reduce the isolation of their work settings, and to enhance interaction with colleagues. Following are some recommendations written from the perspective of those providing assistance. They suggest what you, as a new teacher, might expect.

1. Appoint someone to help beginning teachers set up their rooms. Beginning teachers should actively seek a good mentor.

2. Pair beginning teachers with master teachers to meet regularly to identify general problems before they become serious. Beginning teachers should identify teachers with whom they can discuss content and instructional process.

3. Provide coaching groups, tutor groups, or collaborative problem-solving groups for all beginning teachers to attend. Beginning teachers can teach each other just as they can learn from master teachers.

4. Provide for joint planning, team teaching, committee assignments, and other cooperative arrangements between new and experienced teachers. Beginning teachers should find professional partners to support them.

5. Plan special and continuous in-service activities with topics directly related to the needs and interests of beginning teachers. Eventually, integrate beginning staff development activities with regular staff development activities. Beginning teachers should communicate common problem areas to those responsible for staff development.

6. Carry out regular evaluation of beginning teachers; evaluate strengths and weaknesses, present new information, demonstrate new skills, and provide opportunities for practice and feedback. Beginning teachers should expect administrator evaluation and should engage in personal self-evaluation.[68]

Preparing Teachers for the Real Classroom

There are essentially two questions that have to be asked and answered regarding teacher preparation programs. (1) What are the characteristics of teacher preparation programs that are most likely to prepare teachers for the realities of K–12 classroom teaching? (2) Where are these programs found?

Good teachers matter more than anything; they are the key to student success. Having a good teacher is far more important than being in small classes or going to a good school staffed with mediocre teachers. The present methods used to screen potential teachers to determine their effectiveness just do not work. Studies show that there are no correlations between teacher certification programs and teacher effectiveness and the amount of course work that teachers received as part of their alternative or traditional teacher training programs.[69] Throwing more money at the same ineffective practices is surely a foolish approach to developing effective teachers.

One approach to rectifying this problem is to create a model institute to support new teachers for the purpose of preparing them for the real classroom. Approximately one half of all new teachers leave teaching within their first years of service. The statistics for turnover among new teachers are startling. Nearly a quarter of all new hires leave the classroom within three years.[70] In urban districts, the numbers are worse; close to 50 percent of newcomers flee the profession during the first five years of teaching.[71] Research shows that, although it takes between five and seven years to develop an effective teacher, the attrition rate of teachers in urban schools indicates that over half leave before they are fully developed.[72] According to the United Federation of Teachers, in New York City 40 percent of teachers leave after three years, and 48 percent will be gone after five years.[73] Teachers say they are overwhelmed by expectations and the scope of the job. This is due in part to their inability to meet the stress of the job and inability to manage classes. Novice teachers cite "a lack of appreciation and professional recognition from students and from the public," as well as a "lack of collaborative and supportive ambience" as a cause of burnout.[74] A typical list of why teachers say they leave always includes stress of disruptive students. This is the most commonly cited reason given for leaving teaching. Research shows that lack of discipline and motivation was the primary source of teacher stress and most significant predictor of burnout.[75]

Brownell and colleagues identified new special education teachers' basic problem as an inability to provide instruction because of their inability to handle discipline. Teachers most commonly attempted to suppress problems rather than resolve them.[76] Abel and Sewell further found that urban teachers attributed greater stress to student discipline and behavior problems than did rural teachers.[77] The constant and increasing pressure on teachers as a result of test accountability has been considered a primary cause of teacher stress; nevertheless, the preponderance of studies still point to lack of discipline and classroom management as the primary cause of teacher stress and burnout.[78]

Hundreds of thousands of dollars can be saved annually by reducing teacher turnover. A school system with roughly 10,000 teachers and an estimated turnover rate of 20 percent would stand to save approximately $500,000 per year by reducing turnover by 1 percentage point.[79]

Recently, the *Chicago Sun-Times* reported that 1,116 non-tenured teachers struggling to control their classrooms were let go. According to the reasons cited by principals, more than half those bumped had problems with classroom management or teacher-pupil relationships, and nearly half struggled with instruction (see the breakdown below).[80]

Why Teachers Were Fired

Reasons checked by principals	% of teachers fired
Classroom failings (Management, teacher-pupil relationships)	55%
Poor Instruction (Planning, methods, knowledge of subject)	46%
Lack of responsibility (Attendance, tardiness, professional judgment)	38%
Poor communication (Parent conferences, staff relations)	24%
Attitude (Lack of cooperation, respect for others)	20%
Other	26%

It bears repeating that nearly half of all new teachers in our inner cities leave teaching within their first five years of service. Pre-service and new teachers need well designed and extensive clinical experiences to prepare for the issues and challenges of effective teaching, particularly through their acquisition of classroom management skills.[81] It should be noted that the nature of teacher preparation has changed tremendously in the past few years. Fewer new teachers are prepared in traditional undergraduate programs, and more are being prepared in alternative certification and post-baccalaureate programs.

For example, former Chancellor Michelle Rhee of Washington DC has spoken of a model mentor program, based on the best researched educational practices and built around a system of school-based mentors and coaches, working to improve teacher instructional effectiveness. She wants to utilize the services of consulting firms to assist in developing a mentor model for improving teachers' skills. At the same time the school system's direct support for instructors seeking National Board for Professional Teaching Standards certification will be terminated because of a lack of evidence that the training improves student achievement. Training left to individual schools and their principals has also shown limited success. Courses sponsored by the District Union have not provided a coherent program that amplifies instruction.[82]

In recent years, value-added studies have shed some light on how to evaluate what makes an effective teacher. The method ties teacher qualifications to actual classroom results by analyzing year-to-year gains on standardized tests.[83] In another recent research report, R. C. Wei and others established an overall picture of the nation's professional development by linking a review of the research literature on staff training with data from a nationally representative survey of teachers. It incorporated information on the staff-development practices of countries around the world. Wei and colleagues reviewed dozens of studies and other analyses of professional development using the most scientifically rigorous methodologies. They found that training programs that contained 30 to 100 hours of time over six months to a year influenced student achievement positively, while those with fewer than 14 hours had little effect. The report drew on qualitative research to outline common features of professional development that appear to improve teacher effectiveness, including a curriculum connected to teachers' classroom practice, with a focus on content, alignment with school goals, and collaboration among faculty.[84]

Learning to teach is a career-long, developmental process, and teacher learning best occurs in collaborative environments. New teachers must be encouraged to focus on self-assessment and self-prescription to effectively manage the instructional and behavioral problems that are the cause of most teacher dissatisfaction. It would appear that teachers have forgotten that the purpose of education is to facilitate student learning. We need to refocus on learning critical comprehensive end products, advancing reading and writing as tools that create literate, critical-thinking young people.

Literate Critical Thinking

To prepare for the real classroom teachers must understand that literate critical thinking is a process of gaining and sharing information and the ability to analyze that information in all its forms. This process is not an outcome in itself. It utilizes all forms of communication, and it is the type of thinking needed to succeed in life. To be considered literate in the age of technology requires learning the kind of thinking skills that will be useful in making important decisions in our lives. Literate critical thinking involves the ability to use language and thought, combined with the ability to access, analyze, evaluate, and communicate information. It involves feelings as well as reasons. We learn from our experiences, which by definition include our senses and feelings. Understanding these concepts as well as practicing them prepares teachers for the reality of classroom teaching.

There are six essential ingredients for literate critical thinking to take place. We should be *skeptical,* questioning the accuracy, authenticity, and plausibility of what is presented. Determine the criteria for making judgments and insist that these *conditions* be met. Critical thinking is supporting proposition with *argument* that provides evidence based on reasoning. *Reasoning* becomes the cement that binds an argument. *Opinions* based on experiences should come from different sources to achieve a broader point of view. While there are no general *procedures* for literate critical thinking, these six elements provide a basis for comprehension.

The literate critical thinking approach involves asking questions and making judgments based on specific conditions related to content; literate critical thinking should be considered a way of learning content and not an esoteric exercise. When students are taught to think logically, to analyze and compare, to question and evaluate in *all* content areas, they are prepared to face the realities of life. If these skills are taught in isolation, students only learn remote skills that have little relevance to life. The essential outcome of the literate critical thinking approach is critical inquiry.

Critical thinking strategies should be taught in conjunction with subject matter and presented to students in the form of real-life problems. Case studies and stories with moral perspectives offer ample opportunities to do so. Critical thinking is essentially a novel way of instruction that differs from traditional instruction, in which teachers introduce materials and diversify instructional approaches. In contrast, it provides students with applications to be completed independently with teacher assistance when needed. Critical thinking instruction consists of providing a focus question or problem and dividing the class into cooperative groups to solve it. Each group solves their problem and defends their solution. The teacher provides students with a summary and an opportunity to reflect on various solutions.

IOSIE Method

A critical thinking strategy that amplifies this problem-solving approach is the IOSIE method (mentioned in chapter 1), a user-friendly five-step process that can be used in reflecting on most educational situations.[85] The letters in IOSIE represent a mnemonic that can be used when critically analyzing any problem that requires prior reflection to resolve. The method is a commonsense approach to dealing with analysis that fosters critical thinking. The first steps involve *identifying* a problem's cause and determining the *objectives* you wish to achieve by solving it. *Solutions* are achieved by utilizing the six essential elements of literate critical thinking. The final steps involve *implementing* the solution and *evaluating* its success. This five-step strategy can be used in most problem-solving situations. It consists of identifying the problem, deciding on objectives, developing a potential solution, implementing it, and evaluating the results.[86]

An Alternative: A Mentoring Model

The Leadership Learning Lab, an organization that prepares teachers for the real-life situations that occur in the classroom, has been providing interactive professional development to school personnel in the New York City area for over 35 years. It advocates an internship model for developing and working with educational professionals who are in active practice. Trainees are enrolled in a variety of focused and researched-based training activities funded under the federal Eisenhower Title II Professional Development Program. In cooperation with the college community it has attempted to provide the missing link to effective teacher development by focusing on a particular shortfall in educational preparation: how to deal with situations that actually arise in the classroom. The Lab's institutes provide teachers with cutting-edge, environmentally friendly strategies (e.g., proper lighting for reading instruction) and instructional management that allow teachers to develop effective instructional and behavioral management plans.

The program requires successful completion of a 100-hour staff development program and participation in follow-up workshops. Teachers take a systematic look at their own educational practices and record what was done, and why. Field advisors assist them in collecting and analyzing data, which is then reflected upon. The results of these action research projects are presented with an eye toward the impact on developing literate critical thinking learners. Participants describe real classroom cases and explain how each was managed. Lab field advisors conduct follow-up consultations and observations and deal with immediate management problems.

This organization has a slightly different take on the situation of retaining teachers. It acts as a catalyst to improve the quality of the teachers it works with by building a sense of professionalism and loyalty among its volunteer network of support. It addresses needs for quality education by development of quality teaching. The program highlights what an educator can do with the right tools. It encourages educators to educate themselves in order to prepare for life in the real classroom. The program claims to remedy problems of training, finding, and retaining effective teachers.[87]

Something must be done to stem the flood of teachers from the classroom. It is quite obvious that at present no single entity has taken responsibility for developing and retaining effective teachers. We've already noted that hundreds of millions of dollars can be saved annually by reducing teacher turnover. This begs the question of why it hasn't been done. The answer is that schools, unions, and colleges have not been successful in finding, developing, and retaining teachers because they believe (correctly) that it is not their job or their true purpose. Schools wish to educate students, unions are concerned with their members' welfare, and colleges of education are concerned with training teachers prior to their movement into the classroom. The role of preparing teachers for the real classroom has to be undertaken by new entities, whose sole purpose is to improve teacher quality, effectiveness, and retention rate.

Self-Evaluation

Teaching presents ample opportunities for self-evaluation. The teacher who does a good job and knows it has the satisfaction of seeing students grow, being rewarded by their respect and affection, and obtaining the recognition of colleagues, parents, and the community.

Self-evaluation by the teacher can contribute to professional growth. This idea is a logical outgrowth of the modern belief in the value of teacher-supervisor cooperation. If teacher evaluations are accepted as an integral part of an effective supervisory situation for professional development, then teachers should be involved in the clarification and continual appraisal of their goals and effectiveness. Part of that clarification process is the teacher's ability to identify areas of need in terms of his or her own teaching skills or to add information to data that might be collected by a mentor or administrator. Self-assessments have embedded problems (some self-evaluations are not especially accurate), but they are important for professional growth.[88]

According to Good and Brophy, one of the first steps to improve your teaching is to evaluate your current professional strengths and weaknesses. In order to do so, you must decide what you want to do and how to determine whether your plans are working. In their words, "Resolutions [to improve teaching] are more likely to be fulfilled when . . . [teachers] specify the desired change: 'I want to increase the time I spend in small-group and project-based work by 25 percent.'"[89]

There are good and practical reasons for thoughtful self-evaluation and for seeking out mentor support. Several years ago a US government survey of 10,000 secondary teachers and 400 schools revealed that about one-fourth (26 percent) of the respondents were never evaluated by their building principal or supervisor the previous year, and another 27 percent had received only one visit. When teachers were asked how many times they visited other teachers to observe or discuss teaching techniques, 70 percent said, "Never."[90]

Some school districts have established their own intern/new teacher evaluation process. In the Toledo Public Schools, for example, all newly hired teachers are mentored for two semesters. They are assigned a consulting (mentor) teacher who works with them to determine their progress and success in meeting the school district's teacher development performance standards. The mentor teacher has the final responsibility for each semester's evaluation, which is based on mutually defined teacher goals. At the last evaluation date, the mentor teacher's recommendations to an Intern Board of Review determine the future employment status of the novice teacher.[91] The Toledo system has resulted in the termination of some teachers and the nonrenewal and resignation of others.

Clearly, evaluation systems like Toledo's are making a difference in improving teacher quality, but they still represent an exception rather than the rule. As a consequence, you must be able to self-assess your own teaching, and you will need to continue the self-evaluation process throughout your career. Few school districts have the type of evaluation and supervisory systems needed for ongoing professional growth.

Far too many teachers operate with virtual autonomy in the classroom and receive minimal assistance from supervisors or colleagues. It follows, therefore, that a thoughtful self-evaluation may be more useful and possibly less biased than an outside evaluation based on one or two visits from an administrator who is rushed or going through motions to satisfy some school policy.

What is thoughtful self-evaluation? Some self-evaluation involves *reflection in action.* The teacher is thinking about the teaching act *as it occurs.* New teachers may find this difficult to do because they are still trying, all too often, to survive the moment. As a result they may engage more in *reflection on action,* which is reflection *after the teaching occurs.*

There are basically two forms of reflection on action. With the first form, teachers can assess themselves on their teaching methods at the classroom level by using some type of self-evaluation form. This form can be developed by the teacher, a group of teachers, the school district, or researchers. Teachers should have input either in devising the instrument (to build acceptance of the process) or in selecting a previously developed instrument that may be in use in another school district and then modifying it according to their own purposes. The point is that teachers should feel comfortable with (and understand) the evaluation instrument. One type (shown in box 10.2) is general in nature, focusing on general instructional effectiveness and determining only the presence of a teaching behavior.

In the second form of reflection on action, teachers can rate themselves on their professional responsibilities at the school and community levels. According to administrators, this form might include classroom climate, student learning, contractual responsibilities, service to school, and professional development.[92] To this list might be added relations with students, parents, and colleagues, as well as service to the community. Beginning teachers need to be conscious of both what students are learning and the environment within which that learning occurs.

How you self-evaluate will be dictated by how and what you teach. A teacher who uses step-by-step (teacher-centered) direct instruction (see box 10.3 on p. 517) will look at a lesson on teaching fractions in a much different way than will a constructivist teacher whose students are engaged in exploring the same concept. To complicate matters, that constructivist teacher might be a rational constructivist (Piagetian) or a dialectical constructivist (Vygotskian): If the former, the teacher will be guiding students toward a more complete understanding of the concept; and if the latter, the teacher and student will be co-constructing the knowledge—that is, the students might develop personal representations of a concept that differ from but are equally valid to those identified by a teacher.[93] Both teachers have a common goal: student understanding of fractions. The question for self-evaluation is whether that goal was achieved.

Reflection

The terms **reflection** and **reflective practice** are partially based on the works of Carl Rogers and Donald Schon, who studied the actions and thoughts of workers in a variety of fields in which reflection is needed for personal development and day-to-day practice. They believe that each person is capable of asking questions and analyzing the answers about their own professional performance for the purpose of improvement. Through open-mindedness and matu-

---

Box 10.2   General Instructional Effectiveness

This evaluation form is used to assess whether a teacher is presenting content in a clear, logical way to students. It evaluates the presence of certain salient teacher behaviors.

Establishing the Purpose of a Lesson	Yes	No
1. Teacher states purpose of lesson	____	____
2. Teacher lists objectives on board	____	____
3. Teacher ties objectives to defined content standards	____	____
4. Teacher provides students with some type of advanced organizer	____	____

Presenting the Lesson

	Yes	No
1. Teacher begins lesson promptly	____	____
2. Teacher has materials ready for student use	____	____
3. Teacher speaks clearly and fluently	____	____
4. Teacher is enthusiastic in presenting content	____	____
5. Teacher defines or clarifies abstract terms	____	____
6. Teacher presents material in step-by-step fashion	____	____
7. Teacher provides time for students to ask questions	____	____
8. Teacher requires students to demonstrate that they understand content	____	____
9. Teacher provides feedback to students during lesson as students demonstrate their knowledge	____	____
10. Teacher paces lesson to fit student learning needs	____	____

Closing the Lesson

	Yes	No
1. Teacher summarizes content covered	____	____
2. Teacher provides students with an opportunity to do their own summary	____	____
3. Teacher allows students an opportunity to ask questions	____	____
4. Teacher provides meaningful independent practice	____	____

Source: Adapted from Thomas J. Lasley, II, Thomas J. Matczynski, and James Rowley, *Instructional Methods: Strategies for Teaching in a Diverse Society* (Belmont, CA: Wadsworth, 2002), 288–289.

---

rity and with the help of colleagues, individuals can discover new ideas that illuminate what they already understand and know how to do.[94] According to one researcher,

> When teachers become reflective practitioners, they move beyond a knowledge base of discrete skills to a stage where they integrate and modify skills to fit specific contexts, and eventually, to a point where the skills are internalized, enabling them to invent new strategies. They develop the necessary sense of self-efficacy to create personal solutions to problems. . . . Unless

Box 10.3   Direct-Instruction Assessment

	Not Evident	Somewhat Evident	Clearly Evident
Phase I: Review			
1. The teacher reviews ideas from the previous day's lessons.	_____	_____	_____
2. The teacher reteaches content material that students had difficulty understanding.	_____	_____	_____
Phase II: Presenting New Material			
1. The teacher clearly states the objectives for the lesson.	_____	_____	_____
2. The teacher teaches the skill or action sequence in a step-by-step fashion.	_____	_____	_____
3. The teacher lets students see the standard connected to the objective.	_____	_____	_____
Phase III: Guided Practice			
1. The teacher frequently asks questions to assess student understanding.	_____	_____	_____
2. The teacher calls on both volunteers and nonvolunteers.	_____	_____	_____
3. All students have an opportunity to respond to the teacher's questions.	_____	_____	_____
4. Students successfully respond to the teacher's questions (at approximately an 80 percent rate of success).	_____	_____	_____
5. The teacher continues to practice the skill until student understanding appears firm.	_____	_____	_____
Phase IV: Feedback and Correctives			
1. The teacher provides specific feedback to students when their responses are hesitant.	_____	_____	_____
2. The teacher reteaches material when student responses are incorrect.	_____	_____	_____
Phase V. Independent Practice			
1. The teacher provides an appropriate number of problems for independent practice.	_____	_____	_____
2. Students are assigned homework that is meaningful and appropriate.	_____	_____	_____
3. Students appear to know how to do the homework successfully.	_____	_____	_____

Source: Adapted from Thomas J. Lasley II, Thomas J. Matczynski, and James Rowley, *Instructional Methods: Strategies for Teaching in a Diverse Society* (Belmont, CA: Wadsworth, 2002), 288–289.

teachers develop the practice of critical reflection, they stay trapped in unexamined judgments, interpretations, assumptions and expectations.[95]

Reflection can help beginning and experienced teachers alike, and it can be incorporated into preservice, internship, and in-service or staff development programs. Most participants are resistant in the initial stage of the process and usually express some ambivalence or confusion about what is required, especially as unsettling questions about their teaching are examined. But more often than not, teachers' reflection results in more questions, clearer perceptions of themselves, and better plans for solving individual problems.[96]

One of the more sophisticated tools for analyzing teachers' reflective thoughts at the preservice level was developed by Dorene Ross, who contends that reflection becomes increasingly complex with greater maturity and perception of safety in expressing one's views. Ross identifies three levels of complexity in the reflection process: (1) describing a teacher's practice with little detailed analysis and little insight into the reasons behind teacher or student behaviors; (2) providing a cogent critique of a practice from one perspective but failing to consider multiple factors; and (3) analyzing teaching and learning from multiple perspectives and recognizing that teachers' actions have a pervasive impact beyond the moment of instruction.[97]

In the later stages of reflection, individuals come to realize that behaviors (and feelings) are contextually based. Rather than dealing in absolutes, they begin to deal in relative pedagogical truths and points of view. In the second stage, people are open to more change and willing to admit that they don't always know the answer. The third stage suggests the presence of considerable professional experience and maturity. It can be inferred that beginning teachers operate at the lower levels of reflection and, therefore, are more singular in their approaches and unwilling to accept other viewpoints about their teaching. This is only an educated inference, yet it does conform to research data that suggest that only one out of five preservice teachers function above the second stage and then only for particular topics.[98]

Through reflection, teachers focus on their concerns, come to better understand their own teacher behavior, and help themselves and their colleagues improve as teachers. Through reflective practices in a group setting, or forums, teachers learn to listen carefully to each other, which also helps provide insight into their own work. In turn, as researchers hear teachers reflect on their practices in the classroom and the basis for those actions, they are in the position to translate the teachers' practical knowledge and particular points of view into theoretical knowledge and to integrate it with other viewpoints.

As you reflect on practice, don't select only exceptional events for guided reflections—the ordinary and the extraordinary offer equally useful opportunities to think in more depth about teaching. Hole and McEntree articulate a four-step process that consists of asking critically reflective questions:[99] Select a classroom event (e.g., students excitedly working on a project but then ignoring teacher calls for their attention, or students playing a game such as "around the world" and then getting angry when a high-performing student wins the game, *again*) and then focus on the following questions about the event to foster your personal reflection on what occurred. This guided reflection should suggest ways of rethinking or modifying practice.[100]

Step 1: What happened? Be specific and detailed in describing the "critical incident."

Step 2: Why did it happen? Look at both the surface and hidden contextual clues to explain the critical event.

Step 3: What might it mean? What is the potential or real meaning of the event?

Step 4: What are the implications for my practice?

The Hole and McEntree Guided Reflection Protocol is a way to help you think through the classroom events you experience. At times, there is simply no colleague with whom you can discuss a classroom event. The key to this protocol is that it moves you from classroom instruction *as it is* to envisioning how it *might be.*

As teachers probe and further examine specific teaching situations, a language of practice can emerge that allows you to better understand how you cope and deal with the complexity of your work. The goal of such self-reflection is to make sense of what happens in a classroom, to clarify and elaborate particular scripts or situations, and to delineate the meaning these reflections have for you and for students.

Guidelines for Self-Evaluation and Reflection

Self-evaluation can serve as the initial step in an ongoing attempt to improve teaching and instructional procedures. A written self-evaluation instrument focuses your attention on specific aspects of your teaching and ensures that you do not overlook anything important. Reflection, because it involves no instrumentation, keeps you open to probing deeper and deeper as you discover more about your teaching. Follow these guidelines when reflecting on and evaluating your own teaching:

1. The teacher's ability to assess his or her weaknesses and strengths is important for self-improvement. This ability can be enhanced through good relations and communication between the teacher and supervisor.

2. If professional growth contracts are used in a school, self-evaluations may be included as part of the contract or formal evaluation process.

3. Self-ratings should be compared with student ratings if the same items are included in the forms. Discrepancies between the ratings should be interpreted or analyzed.

4. Self-evaluations can be used as a starting point for the formal supervisor evaluation of the teacher.

5. Teachers wishing to focus on specific behaviors or instructional activities should make a video recording of a particular lesson in conjunction with the self-evaluation of that lesson. The same videotape can be used for the purpose of reflection. You can use forms such as those in boxes 10.2 and 10.3 to focus your analysis of a video-recorded lesson you teach.

6. Reflection takes place when teachers volunteer to collaborate and exchange ideas with colleagues about shared pedagogical concerns.

7. Through reflection teachers can come to better understand their strengths and weaknesses.

8. The key to reflection is the ability to be honest with yourself and with colleagues or peers and to listen to and dialogue with them as they help you analyze your own teaching.

---

classic professional viewpoint **10.1**   **Becoming a Teacher**

Julian C. Stanley

I entered teaching during the Great Depression, perhaps chiefly because of having graduated from a state teacher's college. The year was 1937, and I was barely nineteen years old. Teaching positions for high school chemistry teachers were not scarce, but the ones offered me paid little: $75 per month for seven months in a Georgia village, and the munificent sum of $120 per month for ten months in the county surrounding Atlanta. Of course, those dollars were worth far more than they are now. I began in the lowest socio-economic-level high school the Atlanta area had—with only white students.

Imagine my surprise when, shortly before school started, the assistant principal told me I would be teaching commercial arithmetic (which I, who had graduated in the "classical" curriculum from another high school in the same Fulton County system, had never heard of) to ninth graders and general business training to eighth graders. Other teachers "owned" chemistry and physics. I was even more disconcerted to discover that about two-thirds of my arithmetic students had failed the subject the preceding year.

I somehow managed to survive the nine months (including five classes, management of large study halls, and many other duties). During my four-and-a-half-year high school teaching career, which ended when World War II called me into service, I taught ten different subjects, including spelling, remedial mathematics, and English.

Other aspects of teaching were strange at that time. We had only six days of sick leave each school year at half pay, so my only absence in 810 days was for three consecutive days of influenza. Women could not teach in high school initially unless they were in home economics or library science; they had to start in elementary schools, no matter what their college major had been. One I knew served six years there, at far less pay than high school teachers received, before getting to teach mathematics in the same high schools that had hired me straight out of college. Women could not even get married and continue to teach in this school system. Fortunately, these totally sexist rules were changed after the war.

Maybe in the "good old days" discipline was considerably easier than it is in some schools nowadays, but in many respects teaching is more attractive now than then. Also, the type of college I attended, which prepared only for teaching, has virtually vanished. You have more choices. Consider them well!

Supervision and Evaluation

Beginning teachers should welcome evaluation as a means to develop professionally. In general, evaluations take two forms: formative and summative (similar to student evaluations). They are primarily intended to reassure new teachers that they can succeed and foster student growth. They are also intended to help teachers know how they are performing relative to the specific criteria of a school district's evaluation system.[101] From your supervisor (i.e., your principal), determine how you will be evaluated and who will be doing the evaluation. Alternatively, if you are currently involved in a field experience, ask your cooperating teacher to review with you the process that is followed to evaluate teacher performance of regular classroom teachers. Is that process different for new teachers than it is for experienced teachers?

Evaluation systems take on many different forms. As you review the evaluation procedures used in different school districts, several models will emerge. Some of those models will be relatively ineffective in helping you grow professionally or in identifying specific areas needed for professional growth. Peterson describes several evaluative models that are ineffective:

- *Testimonials,* or the use of third-party claims about a teacher's abilities or expertise;

- *Student assessments,* in which students who have worked with a particular teacher assess his or her abilities; and

- *Competency-based approaches,* which use highly specific descriptions of teacher behavior that do not take into account the context within which you teach.[102]

Peterson does argue that standard-based systems can be problematic because they have not yet demonstrated a clear relationship to student achievement. Although this is true, such systems are based on a body of research that *does* relate teacher behaviors and student achievement. These models are problematic only when they become selected methods for assessing teacher performance rather than parts of a broad system of teacher assessment. No one type of supervision is used by all school districts. The options are too numerous to discuss, but we will consider two relatively common options.

A relatively small number of school districts (and teacher education institutions) use a form of supervision known as clinical supervision, which is the more collaborative of the two options. In **clinical supervision**, members of the supervisory and administrative staff create a partnership with the new teacher focused on inquiry into the instructional process. As the school year gets under way, a grade-level or subject-related supervisor works with the novice to plan lessons, discuss appropriate materials and media, and dialogue about curriculum suggestions. Ideally, he or she informally visits the class for short periods of time to learn about the new teacher's style, abilities, and needs. Later, at the teacher's invitation or by mutual agreement, the supervisor observes a complete lesson. Such a visit is often formally planned in conjunction with a preobservation conference to talk over the plans for the lesson and a postobservation conference to discuss the observation and evaluation of the lesson. Clinical supervision is a demanding, time-consuming process for the supervisor and the novice teacher, and it can be either directive or nondirective.

The three-step clinical process (preobservation conference, observation, and postobservation conference) has been expanded to eight phases by Morris Cogan, a major theorist in the area of supervision of teachers: (1) establishing the teacher-supervisor relationship, (2) planning the lesson with the teacher, (3) planning the strategy of observation, (4) observing instruction, (5) analyzing the teaching–learning process, (6) planning the strategy of the conference, (7) holding the conference, and (8) renewed planning.[103]

Robert Goldhammer, a student of Cogan, developed a similar model consisting of five stages: preobservation conference, observation, analysis and strategy, supervision conference, and postconference analysis. In both of these models the teacher's behavior and techniques are observed, analyzed, and interpreted, and decisions are made in order to improve the teacher's effectiveness.[104]

According to Ben Harris, the teacher can learn to assume increasing responsibilities for each step in the process. As teachers learn to analyze and interpret observational data and confront their own concerns and needs, they should become less dependent on the supervisor and more capable of reflection and self-analysis.[105]

Obviously, several observations and conferences are needed before any formal judgment is made about a teacher's performance. However, even one or two observations by a skilled supervisor can be helpful to the teacher, especially for the new teacher who lacks practical experience in the classroom. There is also evidence that beginning (as well as experienced) teachers value supervisory feedback and appreciate supervisors' and principals' input in diagnosing, prescribing, and recommending teaching strategies and skills. The input helps teachers learn to teach and to understand the expectations of the school district.[106] This type of support is considered important in view of the fact that the turnover among new teachers (those with fewer than three years of experience) may be as high as 40–50 percent.

The second form of supervision discussed in this chapter is **technical coaching**, which is the more structured and directive of the two—that is, the coach or mentor is more specific about the teaching behaviors that the novice needs to use. Technical coaching assists teachers in developing new teaching strategies and skills over longer time periods. Technical coaching, however, tends to inhibit professional dialogue and peer exchange because the focus is on teacher acquisition of a particular teaching skill, such as how to teach fractions using inquiry or how to teach the same concept using direct instruction. Discussions often focus on the presence or absence of a particular behavior or teaching skill rather than on its development.

Technical coaching assumes that objective feedback, given in a nonthreatening and constructive climate, can improve teaching, especially if a novice teacher understands the theory behind a particular approach that is used and then has opportunities to view its use by an expert and subsequently to practice the teaching skill on his or her own.

Whether a clinical or technical approach is best for you may depend on how you think about teaching. Carl Glickman distinguishes between teachers who think in concrete terms and those who think in abstract terms. Both teacher types are willing to accept feedback and evaluation. However, concrete types (to whom Glickman attributes low conceptual professional thought patterns) are confused about their instructional problems, lack ideas about what to do, and need assistance in clarifying such issues—they profit from specific and highly structured recommendations. They want answers, and technical approaches may be good ways to start. Highly conceptual, abstract recommendations from their supervisor or mentor will only confuse them. The second type of teacher (who functions at a high conceptual level) can identify instructional problems and seek and generate multiple sources of ideas about what can be done; these teachers can visualize and verbalize the consequences of various choices or actions and easily make modifications to their teaching. A subtle, more generalized clinical approach to supervision is more likely to succeed with them. In practice, a good number of teachers are moderately abstract and fall between the two groups.[107]

Teachers move through different stages of development, in part due to experience and age and in part because of different thresholds or levels of willingness to accept recommendations for change. Different supervisory approaches—from directive (technical) to collaborative or nondirective (clinical)—should be considered in the context of the developmental stage and thinking pattern of the teacher to enhance positive changes in teaching. Certainly, an experienced and/or older teacher needs different types of coaching than does an inexperienced and/or younger teacher. As a new teacher, you may prefer a more directive style, but your professional goal should be to collaborate with mentors and colleagues for your own personal development—and that will mean developing comfort with a more nondirective approach.

New Forms of Evaluation

Some school districts and states are experimenting with new forms of evaluation. These were limited in use until the early 1990s, but since that time many schools and institutions have been exploring how to use them effectively.

Authentic Evaluation

Authentic evaluation relies on a variety of different artifacts of the teaching process. **Artifacts of teaching** are sources of data for teacher reflection and growth. These products offer teachers prime examples of their teaching performance and of student learning:

1. *Lesson plans and unit plans.* Examination of lesson plans and unit plans should reveal whether the curriculum or course syllabus is being taught, whether the teacher's pace and focus are appropriate, how individual student differences are provided for, whether the instructional objectives are clear, whether the activities are appropriate, and whether study and homework exercises are adequate.

2. *Assessments.* Do quizzes and examinations reflect the important objectives and learning outcomes? Are the test questions appropriately written? Are there different types of assessments being used?

3. *Laboratory and special projects.* Handouts for these projects should be examined for clarity, spelling, punctuation, and appropriateness. They should coincide with the important objectives and content of the course and serve to motivate students and enrich their learning experiences.

4. *Materials and media.* The quality and appropriateness of materials and media and the way they are incorporated into the instructional process can reveal the teacher's knowledge, skills, and effort to facilitate student learning.

5. *Reading lists and bibliographies.* These current lists should accommodate varied student abilities, needs, and interests.

6. *Student outcomes.* Student product will evidence mastery of skills and content. Teachers can use this information to determine if their objectives have been met.

7. *Teacher portfolios.* Portfolios, although difficult to construct and vulnerable to misrepresentation, provide a rich portrayal of the teacher's performance. Such materials as video recordings, lesson plans, teacher logs or personal commentaries, student work (e.g., writing samples, laboratory exercises), and records of teacher observations can be used for purposes of documentation, assessment, and/or reflective analysis.

You may be fortunate enough to work in a school district or be in a teacher education program that has a fairly comprehensive perspective on evaluation and uses authentic evaluation. Certain principles of practice will be evidenced in such authentic systems.

Principle 1: Authentic teacher evaluation enables teachers to collect and show real artifacts of student learning. The focus is on whether students (*all* students) are learning the requisite content. What examples can you provide that suggest specifically what your different students are learning and document the extent of their learning? Can you connect that learning to defined state and national standards?

Principle 2: The authentic representations of student learning can be illustrated through teacher-developed portfolios of student work. These portfolios should include examples of student work (e.g., assignments, tests, homework, projects) and of the teacher's work (e.g., lesson plans, video recordings of lessons).

Clearly, these authentic representations are not perfect. They work only if teachers make good decisions about what to include in the portfolios and if supervisors comment on and discuss them. If you know how to do these things, you will almost assuredly be successful. Even with such knowledge, however, there is room for growth. One of the most acknowledged approaches to continued professional growth is National Board Certification.

National Board Certification

Founded in 1987, the **National Board for Professional Teaching Standards** (NBPTS) launched a massive research and development program to improve teacher certification and teacher assessment. Its mission is to develop a voluntary (advanced) certification system that establishes high standards of what teachers should know and be able to do and identifies a governing board (comprised mainly of teachers) to enforce these standards. The specific mission of the NBPTS can be reviewed by visiting its website (www.nbpts.org). In general its goals are:

- Maintaining high and vigorous standards for what accomplished teachers should know and be able to do.

- Providing a voluntary certification system for those who meet those standards.

- Advocating related education reforms to integrate National Board Certification into American education.

The National Board Certification process emphasizes the APPLE criteria, which require that assessments be **A**dministratively feasible, **P**rofessionally acceptable, **P**ublicly credible, **L**egally defensible, and **E**conomically affordable.

The NBPTS certification process is not inexpensive. It costs $2300 to secure a certificate valid for ten years. It is available for anyone who holds a baccalaureate degree and has three years of teaching experience in a public or private school.

The process is also not without controversy. A very high percentage of teachers who pursue NBPTS are not successful, and critics argue that there is simply no good evidence to show that teachers who hold NBPTS certificates create greater learning gains in the students they teach. Current research is being undertaken to determine whether NBPTS certification does make a "value-added" learning difference for students, but that research will likely not resolve the controversy completely. NBPTS has conducted research attempting to prove that those who hold NBPTS certificates do perform better on a variety of performance indicators, but critics often argue that the key variable is student learning. Do NBPTS teachers create enhanced student learning? The answer is not known. What is known is that the NBPTS teachers believe that the process does benefit them the most but also benefits their students with their enhanced pedagogical skill. Even though NBPTS teachers receive salary incentives in most states, most do not cite that as a motivation for pursuing advanced certification. They argue that the personal challenge coupled with the enhanced professional development provides the incentive for pursuing the NBPTS certificate.[108]

The new NBPTS "advanced" certification system consists of over thirty different teaching certificates (developed or underdeveloped) that consider two dimensions: (1) developmental level of students (*how* they should be taught) and (2) subject matter (*what* should be taught). In the developmental-level dimension there are four categories: early childhood (ages 3–8), middle childhood (ages 7–12), early adolescence (ages 11–15), and adolescence/young adulthood (ages 14–18+). This structure differs from traditional practices of state licensing by school grade level. In the subject-matter dimension there are teaching certificates for generalists (e.g., early and middle childhood generalists) and subject specialists (e.g., early adolescent English/language arts, adolescent and young adult math). The National Board has also developed certificates for exceptional needs, English as a new language, and world languages other than English.

The number of National Board Certified teachers is still quite limited. In early 2003, North Carolina and Florida had the highest number of Board Certified teachers in the country, 5,111 and 3,489, respectively. Closely behind were South Carolina (2,358), California (1,960), and Ohio (1,771). All states have some Board Certified teachers, though in some states the actual numbers are quite small (e.g., North Dakota, 13, and Pennsylvania, 225). Nearly 7,800 teachers achieved National Board Certification in 2006, which brings the total to more than 55,000. As of 2010, more than 80,000 teachers have achieved National Board Certification status.[109]

Professional Associations and Activities

Membership in professional organizations and participation in meetings, research, and advanced study can contribute to your practice and professional growth while helping improve conditions for teachers.

Teacher Associations

There are two major teacher associations, the American Federation of Teachers (AFT) and the National Education Association (NEA). In most school districts teachers vote on which of the two associations all the teachers will join. In some school districts, the choice of joining or not joining a local chapter of the AFT or a state affiliate of the NEA is left to the individual. If you have a choice, you should not be rushed into making a decision. Keep in mind, however, that both organizations have helped improve salaries, benefits, and working conditions for teachers and that you should probably join one of them. At present over three-quarters of all public school teachers belong to either the AFT or the NEA.[110]

The AFT has approximately one million members and is organized in local chapters, mainly in cities. The AFT advocates a wide variety of reforms including

- High academic standards and vigorous curricula
- Solid school discipline policies
- Higher standards for teacher certification
- Peer review to ensure a high-quality teacher corps
- Well-crafted charter schools
- Voluntary advanced teacher certification

The AFT is affiliated with the AFL-CIO and bills itself as one of the country's oldest advocates of "free public education" (see www.AFT.org).

Disproportionately suburban and rural, the National Education Association (NEA) membership is served by a large network of affiliates in every state, Puerto Rico, and the District of Columbia. There are 13,000 local affiliate groups, but unlike the AFT (in which local affiliates are powerful), most of the NEA's power is derived from the state affiliates. In terms of actual numbers, the NEA represents the second largest lobby force in the country, trailing only behind the Teamsters. There are nearly 3.2 million current NEA members. Founded in 1857, it is also committed to advancing public education.

Although the two organizations occasionally take different positions on educational matters and battle over membership, "no raid" efforts (meaning that AFT and NEA don't attempt to "steal" each other's members) have been discussed at the state level. Most important, both organizations seek to improve the status of the teaching profession, agree on many issues concerning teachers and schools, and sometimes join forces on policy matters.

The American Federation of Teachers (AFT) is the second largest education union in America with 856,000 members as of fall 2008. The National Education Association (NEA) has a membership of 3.2 million as of 2010 and unlike the AFT is not affiliated with the AFL-CIO. These two leading educational organizations had proposed to merge in 1998 but the membership of the NEA voted against it. However, in 2000 they did form a NEA-AFT partnership as separate organizations committed to nurturing and improving public education above all.[111]

Advantages of Membership in Professional Organizations

At the working level of the classroom, the professional organization of greatest academic benefit to a teacher (and preservice teacher) is usually one that focuses on his or her major field. Each professional association provides a meeting ground for teachers of similar interests. The activities of these professional organizations usually consist of regional and national meetings and publication of a monthly or quarterly journal that describes accepted curriculum and teaching practices.

Some organizations are subject centered, such as the National Council for the Social Studies, the National Council of Teachers of English, the Modern Language Association, the National Science Teachers Association, and the National Council of Teachers of Mathematics. Others focus on the needs of specific groups of students, such as the Council for Exceptional Children, the National Association for Bilingual Children, the National Association for the Education of Young Children, and the National Scholarship Service and Fund for Negro Students. Such associations are organized to ensure that specific children and youth are served by well-prepared school personnel and to improve specialized teaching techniques.

Still another type of professional organization cuts across subjects and student types. These organizations tend to highlight innovative teaching and instructional practices in general. Articles in their journals describe new trends and policies that affect the entire field of education; they have a wide range of membership including teachers, administrators, and professors; and they work for the advancement of the teaching profession in general.

Perhaps the best known organization of this type is Phi Delta Kappa (www.pdkintl.org), which includes 649 local chapters in the United States, Canada, and abroad. Its membership is available to graduate students, administrators, and grade-school and college-level teachers. Even undergraduates may join if they are pursuing teacher certification. The membership is approximately 120,000. Originally open only to men, it opened its membership to women in 1974. The purpose of the organization is to promote quality and equality in education, with particular emphasis on public education. Members receive *Phi Delta Kappan,* a highly respected journal that is published ten times a year, and the fraternity newsletter. Paperback (Fastback) publications of interest are available at reduced rates for members and are published on a variety of topics, including *Portfolio Development for Preservice Teachers* and *Student Literacy: Myths and Realities.*

Professional Journals

Almost any professional organization you join should have a monthly or quarterly journal. The journal that will have the most immediate value for you is the one that focuses on your subject and grade level. For example, reading teachers might subscribe to the *Journal of Reading, Reading Teacher,* or *Reading Today.* Math teachers might want to subscribe to *Teaching Children Mathematics* or *Mathematics,* and social studies teachers would do well to read *Social Education and the Social Studies.* Elementary teachers who are more tuned to their grade level might subscribe to *Childhood Education* or *Young Education* and high school teachers might want *Middle Ground* or *High School Journal.*

There are many professional journals in education. Pick and choose wisely because of the amount of time it takes to read journals and the cost of subscriptions. The answers to two questions can help determine your reading and subscription focus: "Do I want practical advice and easy-to-read articles or theoretical and in-depth reading?" and "Do I want to focus on subject or grade-level issues, or do I want a broad discussion of education issues?" Practitioner journals such as *Instructor* will have easy-to-read, practical articles, while journals such as *Educational Researcher* will have more complex, research-based articles.

In addition to reading books and journals, you might also want to subscribe to virtual services that provide daily updates on significant issues relevant to classroom practices. One of the very best is ASCDBrief, which can be contacted at ASCD@Smartbrief.com. The ASCDBrief offers daily information on a wide variety of topics, with links to specific stories of interest. On any given day, you will find information on topics ranging from special education to high-stakes testing.

Meetings

The two major teacher organizations—the American Federation of Teachers and the National Education Association—meet annually in different cities. If you become a member of one of these organizations, it would be beneficial to become an active participant and attend the annual meeting. The various subject-related associations and specialized student associations also have local and regional conferences. Keep an eye on your local colleges and universities; their departments or schools of education often sponsor professional meetings and short seminars that are excellent for updating your knowledge about teaching and for meeting other professionals in the local area. State departments of education and local school districts frequently organize in-service workshops and one- or two-day conferences on timely educational topics and teaching techniques.

Choose wisely which meetings and conferences best serve your professional needs and interests and organize your schedule so you can attend them. Become acquainted with the scheduling and travel policy of your school district. If the meetings take place during the school year, you will need special permission to attend. Some school districts give travel reimbursement for certain meetings. Local meetings sponsored by colleges or universities, state departments, regional education agencies, or local school districts often occur after school hours or on weekends. These sessions are easier to attend in terms of scheduling, time, and cost.

Coursework

You should take advantage of university coursework and programs that lead to graduate degrees and state certification in a field of study. You may also attend summer sessions, workshops, special institutes, and in-service courses conducted by a local university or the school district.

Check to see whether special stipends, scholarships, or grants are available through the school district or state in which you teach. Several states offer monetary incentives for enrolling in programs in special fields, especially science education, math education, and special education. Many school districts offer partial or full reimbursement for graduate work.

Although many of the recent reports on excellence in education recommend reducing the role of teacher-training institutions in the preparation and certification of teachers by limiting the number of professional educational courses, others, such as the Carnegie Report *A Nation Prepared* and the National Commission on Excellence in Education, call for increased professional education and field experiences.

You might find it useful to consider how you want to focus your future professional growth experiences. Here are some prescriptions that are logical extensions of research reported in *Teaching Quality Research Matters*. These ideas have real relevance to whatever pedagogical experiences you participate in as a prospective teacher.

1. Professional development experiences that are very focused on acquisition of a particular pedagogical practice are predictive of a teacher's use of that practice. Learning a lot about everything will likely limit what you use correctly. To develop skill in *direct instruction* or *constructivist teaching* requires focus and practice. Watch others who use an approach and then engage in that practice and try to receive feedback on your practice.

2. Technology related to professional development that involves teachers with similar backgrounds and teaching interests (even grade-level focus) results in better outcomes instructionally.

3. Find a mentor or a study group to work with as you develop your professional skills. Good teachers do not isolate themselves; they collaborate.[112]

Researcher-Teacher Collaboration

In what is often called the **collaborative research model,** university researchers increasingly join with schools in an effort to deal with a range of educational problems by involving teachers in the solutions to these problems. The model has spread because of the belief that cooperative problem solving allows researchers to get a better grasp of practitioners' problems and develop strategies that improve teaching and benefit teachers and schools. In fact, a large portion of the new research on teacher effectiveness is derived from such cooperative efforts. The new collaborative centers (sometimes called *R&D education centers* or *laboratory research centers*) tend to focus less on theory and what researchers want to study and more on practical and enduring problems of teachers.

Decisions regarding research questions, data collection, and reporting are jointly determined by the university and the school. Collaboration between teachers and researchers is stressed, with both groups working together to improve the theory and practice of education. Researchers are learning to respect teachers and to conduct research of practical value, and teachers are learning to appreciate the work of researchers and to do research.[113]

A most interesting development in collaborative relationships is that many teachers no longer want anonymity in the studies conducted by researchers. In the old relationship, the desire was to protect the rights and anonymity of "informants" or "respondents." Now teachers often seek full partnership in the research, so they can share in the recognition when it is published. This is an ethical issue that has not been pressed in the past and may very well become an issue as experienced teachers develop relationships with researchers—and perceive only the researchers' benefit when the materials are published. This issue involves teachers' sense of ownership and empowerment as well as teacher-researcher relations. To better blend theory and practice in the future these relations need to be improved.[114] Some teachers have taken research a step further and conduct their own research, either alone or in collaboration with other teachers, university professors, and doctoral students. The topic of the research is something they themselves choose, and it applies directly to some aspect of classroom practices that interests them personally. If the results are written up and published in professional journals, the teachers are full coauthors and receive credit for their work.[115]

It is important for you to realize that teaching can be both difficult and rewarding. True, there are problems, but few professions are more exciting and more important than teaching. When competent teachers work with young children, there is rarely a dull moment. Through their students, teachers can contribute to the shaping and growth of the community and the nation; the teachers' impact is long-term—and we are unable to determine when the influence ceases. Teaching is a proud profession, and professional growth and development is an important part of the life of a teacher. Unfortunately, it is likely that you will not receive all the professional development that you need to be successful. Most American teachers do not. Interestingly, Japanese teachers receive almost twenty days of in-service training during their first year of teaching. You will be lucky to receive more than a couple, which leads us to a final point for this chapter.

As you begin the practice of teaching, be aware of two negative realities that are in large part not your fault, but rather by-products of the structure of American education. One is burnout; the other is a lack of personal and professional self-esteem. Both are caused, directly or indirectly, by a lack of personal and professional growth. Specifically, you will be placed in classrooms and expected to do too much, too soon, with too little. The best way for you to counter the potential negative realities is to identify ways to continue to extend your own skills (through computer networking) and to understand the complexity of teaching. Jennifer Bradford, an experienced teacher, also offers some "fun" lessons for you to consider when you need renewal:

- Get a massage. Find a way to relax.
- Exercise.
- Get a dog, or at least some perspective.
- Don't expect "outsiders" to understand.
- Realize that schools have many faculty members for a reason.
- Vacation means vacate. Find ways to "recharge."[116]

A book such as this one necessarily examines teaching practices. As a teacher who grows professionally, you must be able to see how the different practices can be commingled to address the inherent complexity of the teaching–learning process. But for now, or very soon, you will need to consider how to make sense of all the "parts" of teaching to prepare for interviews. (See Case Study 10.2 to evaluate how one prospective teacher prepares to be interviewed.) We hope this book helps you as you prepare for those interviews. You will be asked questions about:

- Your philosophy of teaching to bring together the science and art of professional practice.
- Your ability to create meaningful instruction around the academic content standards in your state and school district.
- Your approach to adapting instruction to address the multiple learning needs of students.
- Your approach to classroom management and discipline.
- Your own professional short- and long-term goals.

The following case discusses the last thing a prospective teacher faces and the first thing she must do: find a position. This study focuses on appropriate strategies that can be used in preparing for that first important job interview. Evaluate the study and decide whether the strategies described will be useful to you in organizing your thoughts about obtaining a teaching position.

Case Study 10.2
Helping the Beginning Teacher Prepare for a Job Interview

Esther Miller was a young single mother of two who had gone back to school in order to become a teacher. It had been a difficult road for Esther, but through perseverance and hard work she was on the verge of triumph. As she sat in Dr. Mosby's outer office, quietly reviewing her notes and thinking about how she was going to handle this job interview, she began to fixate on her appearance. She had a short, no-nonsense hairdo which she felt projected an air of efficiency. She wore a businesslike blue suit, as close in style to a man's as she could get without being obvious about it. In place of a tie she wore a cobalt and gold silk scarf, and an imitation diamond designer-look pin graced her lapel. Esther believed that she had dressed in a way that would present her in the best light during a short interview. She felt a first impression was vital to securing any position.

Esther remembered her university supervisor's comment that certain characteristics distinguished a teacher interview from a general business interview: "The person who interviews you will be looking for diplomacy, poise, and most of all, teaching personality. They will, of course, also be interested in your mastery of content, your classroom management skills, and your understanding of instructional methods."

Esther had gone over her notes with her friend Charlene Dewars. They understood that preparing for tough interview questions would take a certain amount of thought. Esther wanted to convey a positive image that spotlighted the strengths she possessed.

Charlene reminded Esther of what they had been taught in class: The typical interview format for beginning teachers would consist of an introductory stage where rapport and impressions were created. The second stage would be a general discussion of background and interests in order to sift out qualifications. This would be followed by the interviewer matching the prospective teacher's qualifications and interests to the available opening. The final step, Charlene grinned, was to find out if you would be hired!

Esther was finally called into Dr. Mosby's office, where he offered her a seat and asked for a copy of her resume. He also asked her to tell him something about her background and why she wanted to work at his school.

Esther was startled by such an open-ended question. She finally responded in a controlled and professional way that she had always wanted to be a teacher, and now—with children of her own—she felt she had a calling. That was why she had gone back to school.

Dr. Mosby asked Esther to tell him about any specific strength she had. Esther said that she had been a good student with a 3.9 index. She explained that she had been president of her school's drama club and part-time editor of the school newspaper. She also had played on the girls' volleyball team.

Dr. Mosby said that while those accomplishments were very impressive, he would like to know if she had any experience working with elementary school children. Esther said that all her experience had been during her student teaching, when she had been assigned to a second- and a fifth-grade class for six months or half a semester.

Dr. Mosby requested that Esther describe her experience. Esther said, "It was great. I hated to leave the children. I became so attached to them."

Dr. Mosby then asked, "Why do you want to work at our school if you loved your other school so much?" She responded that there were no openings there.

He then asked her what her greatest weakness was. Esther responded immediately, "As you can see, I am very honest."

Dr. Mosby's final question was why he should hire her. Esther said, "Because I would be the best person for the job."

Discussion Topics and Questions to Ponder

1. Did Esther present herself properly? Explain your answer.

2. How did Esther analyze her teaching experience?

3. Was Dr. Mosby satisfied with Esther's response regarding her specific strengths?

4. Based on this interview, could Dr. Mosby have rated Esther with regard to her management skills or her knowledge of instructional methods?

5. How would you have rated Esther? Justify your response.

What would you do if . . . ?

1. You were asked to describe a situation that you resolved during your internship.

2. You were asked to explain your approach to classroom management if a child was using foul language.

3. You were handed the following assessment tool and asked to complete it based on Esther's interview.

Assessment Scale for Job Interview

Rate the interview on the following scale:
5 Superior, 4 Above average, 3 Average, 2 Satisfactory, 1 Unsatisfactory.

		Rating
1.	Applicant introduced self appropriately	_____
2.	Position sought was clear	_____
3.	Presentation was logically organized	_____
4.	Explanation of qualifications for position was clear	_____
5.	Applicant indicated understanding and enthusiasm	_____
6.	Applicant's educational philosophy was clear and concise	_____
7.	Applicant stressed achievement	_____
8.	Applicant effectively used pauses and evidenced proper body language	_____
9.	Applicant was professional	_____
10.	Applicant concluded interview on a positive note	_____

Points Scored _____
(Maximum is 50)

Our goal in this text was not to give you answers to all areas of concern but rather to give you information to use to shape your answers! We hope your professional journey in the practice of teaching for the next 20 to 30 years is rewarding. To become an effective teacher is to make a difference in children's lives. It will also make a difference in how you feel about yourself as a professional practitioner of teaching.

Box 10.4   Secrets for Success in the Practice of Teaching

Investor's Business Daily has spent years analyzing leaders and successful people in all walks of life. Most were found to have traits that when combined turned dreams into reality and lead to ultimate success. These same traits are not unlike the traits needed for success in the practice of teaching.

1. Be positive in your thoughts; think about success (not failure) in achieving your goals.
2. Determine specific goals and objectives and prepare a plan to arrive at them.
3. Be decisive; don't be afraid to take action where necessary.
4. Never stop developing professionally. Read, attend conferences, go back to school.
5. Be relentless; never give up the vision of true success in your teaching practice.
6. Focus on the details necessary to implement your plans. Learn from your mistakes.
7. Be centered on your goals, objectives, and standards. Don't let other things distract you.
8. Be innovative, be different, and think outside the box. Being a follower only leads to mediocrity.
9. Communicate and deal with the school community of students, parents, and administrators honestly and effectively.
10. Take responsibility for your actions: otherwise numbers one to nine won't matter.

Cord Cooper, "IBD'S 10 Secrets to Success: Decide Upon Your True Dreams and Goals," *Investor's Business Daily* (February 23, 2010), A3. © 2010–2011 Investor's Business Daily, Inc. Used with permission.

Theory into Practice

This chapter has focused on how teachers are prepared and how they subsequently develop as professionals. We conclude with one of the most troubling issues: How do schools keep good teachers? This question is at the nexus of theory and practice. There are theories about how to prepare teachers, but in practice many of those "prepared" teachers decide to leave the profession.

Research is mixed about why teachers drop out of teaching. Clearly, some drop out for very common reasons (e.g., to start families) while others drop out because they simply feel unsupported and unfulfilled.[117] William Sanders believes that teachers reach their peak effectiveness between their seventh and twenty-fifth years of practice.[118] He believes that teachers develop skills (years 1 to 7), attain proficiency (years 7 to 25), and then begin to diminish in effectiveness. That pattern is not always the norm, however. For some, the decline never occurs; for others, the "decline" in performance may occur early in a career or may be evident only during a particular year. In order to prevent this decline, teachers need challenging and practical programs. Each school has to concentrate on a few of its most serious problems and then develop in-service programs to meet these problems. In-service programs can be vastly improved if the staff of teacher education institutions and school districts work together to identify and focus on serious problems.

If you expect to be an effective teacher, you will need to be able to cope with the frustrations and problems that arise on the job. Regardless of the amount of satisfaction you obtain from teaching, there will be dissatisfying aspects of the job. What follows is a list of **mental health strategies**—keys to professional well-being in the form of questions that are a mix of common sense and psychology for self-understanding. They are intended to help you deal with problems or dissatisfactions that may arise on the job.

- *Key 1.* Are you aware of your strengths and weaknesses? The ability to make realistic self-estimates is crucial, given the fact that your students and colleagues will observe and make judgments about your behavior, attitude, and abilities. Learn to see yourself as others see you and to compensate for or modify areas that need to be improved.

- *Key 2.* Are you aware of your social and personal skills? You need to understand the attitudes and feelings of your students, colleagues, and supervisors; how to adapt to and interact with different persons; how to learn from them; and how to work cooperatively with them.

- *Key 3.* Can you function in a bureaucratic setting? Schools are bureaucracies, and you must learn the rules and regulations, as well as the norms and behaviors of the school. As a teacher, you are an employee of an organization that has certain expectations of you and all its employees.

- *Key 4.* Can you cope with school forms and records? Schools expect teachers to complete a host of forms, reports, and records accurately and on time. The more quickly you become familiar with this work, the smoother it will be for you. At first the various forms, reports, and records may seem burdensome, yet neither you, your supervisors, nor the school can function without them.

- *Key 5.* Can you study and learn from someone else with similar problems? It helps to assess people with similar problems to see what they are doing wrong to avoid making the same mistakes.

- *Key 6.* Do you look for help on specific questions? Often teacher dissatisfaction pertains to a specific problem, such as the inability to maintain discipline. Consulting with an experienced colleague or supervisor sometimes helps.

- *Key 7.* Do you take out your frustrations in class? Don't vent your dissatisfactions on your students. It solves nothing and only adds to your teaching problems.

- *Key 8.* Do you understand your roles as a teacher? The teacher's role goes far beyond teaching a group of students in class. Teaching occurs in a particular social context, and much of what you do and are expected to do is influenced by this context. Different students, supervisors, administrators, parents, and community members expect different things from you. You must expect to perform varied roles depending on the realities, demands, and expectations of a school's culture.

- *Key 9*. Are you able to organize your time? There are only so many hours in a day, and many demands and expectations are imposed on you as a person and a professional. You will need to make good use of time, set priorities, plan, and get your work done.

- *Key 10*. Can you separate your job from your personal life? Never let the teaching job (or any job) overwhelm you to the point that it interferes with your personal life. There are times when you may have to spend a few extra hours in school helping students or working with colleagues, and there are times when you will have to spend extra after-school hours grading papers and tests, preparing lessons, and performing clerical tasks, but for your own mental health be sure you have time left for your private, family, and social life.

The professional mental health of many teachers is being influenced by things like the No Child Left Behind legislation. Tye and O'Brien discuss a number of the reasons teachers have left the profession during the past several years. The reasons they list include accountability, increased paperwork, student attitudes, no parent support, unresponsive administration, low status of the profession, and salary considerations.[119] Of particular interest is the concern of teachers relative to accountability and increased paperwork. Teachers are now required to do more testing and more curriculum development work that relates to that testing. What appears to be especially problematic is that teachers are not given the time to really think through many of the curriculum instruction issues that they will confront. American teachers have less time to plan and are in front of students more than teachers in many other countries. Without adequate planning time teachers are at a disadvantage in terms of their overall effectiveness. Although the increased accountability focus may have positive aspects, it will be limited in its effectiveness unless teachers are given the professional time to plan and think about their teaching.

CONCLUSIONS

- Little agreement exists on a national level regarding the number and mix of educational courses for teacher preparation.

- Beginning teachers need support and assistance to ease into their position and improve their instructional skills.

- To become a master teacher, you need to continually improve your teaching abilities and focus your professional development. People closely associated with your teaching and instruction, including peers and supervisors, are best able to provide feedback and evaluation.

- Several different types of formative and summative evaluations will help you assess your progress as a teacher.

- A variety of associations are available for teachers to join; the two largest ones and the ones that have probably done the most to improve teacher salaries and working conditions are the American Federation of Teachers and the National Education Association.

- Several opportunities exist to help teachers grow as professionals, including reading the professional literature, attending conferences, taking courses, and collaborating with researchers.

KEY TERMS

artifacts of teaching
authentic evaluation
clinical supervision
collaborative research model
induction period
mental health strategies

National Board for
   Professional Teaching Standards
peer coaching/mentoring
reflection/reflective practice
technical coaching

DISCUSSION QUESTIONS

1. Why should you begin now, as a preservice teacher, to consider ways for improving your skills as a regular classroom teacher?

2. What are some ways for coping with problems or concerns related to the job of teaching?

3. Which of your experiences as a preservice teacher do you think will help you as a beginning teacher? In what ways has your teacher education program focused your acquisition of important teaching skills and dispositions?

4. Of the following evaluation alternatives—student, peer, self, and supervisory—which would you prefer as a beginning teacher? As an experienced teacher? Explain your answers.

5. Name two or three professional organizations you expect to join as a teacher. Go to their websites and review the qualifications for membership. Are preservice teachers permitted to join? How do you expect to benefit from membership in these organizations? What is the explicitly stated mission of each association?

MINI-CASES FROM THE FIELD

Case One: Support from Colleagues for Beginning Teachers

Jonathon Hobbs was an innovative principal. He had decided long ago that the way to support the professional growth of new teachers was to empower teachers to determine for themselves the best approach to take. A mentor program had been established that teamed veteran teachers with new teachers for their first two years. Mr. Hobbs had been a proponent of teacher empowerment as a tool for educational change and improved student learning. He reasoned that the mentor program would help his new teachers grow and therefore improve student outcomes.

The program had worked well for the first three years until an impasse with the faculty steering committee brought the program to a shuddering halt. It ran smoothly in those initial years, when enthusiasm was high and objectives were being developed. But now veteran teachers just saw the term *teacher empower-*

ment as a way to get more for new teachers without considering pay increases, vacation time, and the additional work regarding their staff-development activities. Mr. Hobbs was on the verge of dropping the mentor program and going back to a top-down type of organization in which his assistants would provide support to beginning teachers.

1. How could Mr. Hobbs respond to the teachers' arguments that the mentor program was just a way to help new teachers at the expense of veteran teachers?

2. Describe a possible negotiating position that the school district could implement to resolve the issues that concern the veterans.

3. What would happen if those issues were resolved?

4. Are there any other issues that could stop teacher empowerment from succeeding? Include your definition of teacher empowerment in your response.

5. Do you think there is a causal relationship between staff development and improved student outcomes?

Case Two: Preparing Teachers for the Real Classroom

Connie Jameson wondered if it were true that effective teachers were really the key to student success. Connie had read in a professional journal that having a good teacher in a classroom was more important than smaller class size. She had also read that there was no correlation between teacher certification programs, teacher effectiveness, and the amount of course work that teachers received as part of their alternative or traditional teacher training programs. In a way, Connie agreed with what she had read. Her reservations had to do with teacher personality. She had always believed that effective teachers possessed a special teaching personality.

Connie's colleagues thought that she lived in a dream world. They claimed that the only thing that determined teacher effectiveness was whether you could teach an effective lesson in a real classroom where students learned. Connie told her friends that she agreed that student learning was a hallmark of a teacher's effectiveness, but that practice and outcomes would be improved in a class were the instructor had an effective teaching personality.

1. Why would Connie's colleagues ignore personality as a factor for teacher effectiveness?

2. Describe your feelings with regard to the position taken by Connie.

3. How do you feel about the statement that no correlation exists between teacher training programs and teacher effectiveness?

4. Discuss the argument regarding class size and teacher effectiveness.

5. Can effective teaching personality be objectively determined? If so, how?

Case Three: IOSIE Method

Carol Keys appreciated the value of mnemonics—a short rhyme, phrase, or other mental technique for making information easier to memorize. What Carol didn't understand was why Mrs. Greene had asked her to use the mnemonic IOSIE to analyze her classroom situation. Mrs. Greene said that the IOSIE method could be used when critically analyzing any problem that required prior reflection to resolve. This method was a commonsense approach to dealing with behavioral analysis. It essentially consisted of identifying the problem, deciding on objectives, developing a potential solution, implementing it, and evaluating the results. Although Carol liked it in theory, she didn't understand how to use it with the problems she was facing in her tenth-grade class: tardiness, homework not being turned in, calling out in class, and lack of parental support. If that weren't enough, her students had told her that they hated her math class because she spoke so fast that they didn't understand anything she said.

Use a brief version of the IOSIE method to describe how Carol could resolve her problems with:

1. student tardiness,
2. no homework,
3. disruptive behavior,
4. parent cooperation, and
5. student attitude toward the teacher.

Case Four: Supervision and Evaluation

Marion Lish was a beginning teacher who had been told that she should welcome evaluation as a means to develop professionally. Marion had a problem with the concept that an evaluation should be considered an opportunity to enhance professional growth. For Marion, supervision and evaluation had always been activities to fear. She understood that in general, evaluations took two forms, formative and summative, similarly to student evaluations. She had been told that their purpose was twofold: to reassure her that she could succeed in helping students to learn, and to assist her in evaluating her own performance. Marion wanted to be a good teacher. She had heard that clinical supervision was effective, despite being time consuming for both the teacher and supervisor. It was a three-step clinical process consisting of a pre-observation conference, the observation, and a post-observation conference. Marion was still fearful. Could a technical coaching program offer her more security?

1. Were Marion's fears justified? Explain your answer.
2. How could evaluation help a teacher to develop professionally?
3. Describe other ways that Marion could be evaluated.
4. Compare clinical supervision to a portfolio system utilizing authentic assessments.
5. Describe how you would like to be evaluated. Explain your reasons.

Case Five: Secrets for Success in the Practice of Teaching

Philip Carr wanted to be an effective teacher. He knew he had a teaching personality by the way his students reacted to him. He decided to do some research and look into what leaders and successful people were really like. In the literature he discovered that most effective teachers had similar traits that, when combined, led to success: Be positive in your thoughts, and think about success (not failure) in achieving your goals. He knew that he was decisive and would never stop growing professionally. Philip figured he had the answer to success. The key was to be relentless in pursuit of his goals and objectives. When Phil attempted to explain his beliefs regarding success to Mary, she exclaimed critically, "Aren't you full of yourself!"

1. What exactly did Philip believe the key to success was?
2. Do character traits such as personality relate to effective teaching? If so, how?
3. Was Philip really "full of himself"? Explain your answer.
4. What are your goals and objectives for your future career as a teacher?
5. How will they be achieved?

FIELD EXPERIENCE ACTIVITIES

1. Survey class members (in the course you are taking) on problems they anticipate as potential new teachers. Rank order all responses. Discuss in class how problems considered important (top five) can be addressed through preparation experiences. For example, if classroom management is an anticipated problem, what specific steps can you take to deal with that problem?

2. Evaluate a class member's teaching of a sample lesson geared for a particular grade level. Evaluate the lesson in terms of instructional methods, use of media, and organization of subject matter.

3. Invite a representative of the AFT and NEA to your class to discuss each organization's purposes and mission. What are their views on specific topics (e.g., class size, high-stakes testing)? Do you think their views are consistent with the best interests of students?

4. This book discusses several professional organizations and professional journals. Identify the ones that offer potential for your professional development. Explain the reasons to the class.

5. Obtain the evaluation instrument for your student teaching experience. On what standards is it based?

RECOMMENDED READING

Beerens, Daniel. *Evaluating Teachers for Professional Growth.* Thousand Oaks, CA: Corwin Press, 2000.
    A thoughtful analysis of all the different ways to evaluate teaching practice.
Boreen, Jean, Donna Niday, Joe Potts, and Mary K. Johnson. *Mentoring Beginning Teachers: Guiding, Reflecting, Coaching,* 2nd ed. Portland, ME: Stenhouse, 2009.
    The latest findings on all aspects of mentoring—from preparing to be a mentoring guide or coach to school culture and parent outreach.
Darling-Hammond, Linda. *Professional Development Schools.* New York: Teachers College Press, Columbia University, 1994.
    A discussion concerning how to improve teacher education and schools of education.

Hill-Jackson, Valerie, Chance W. Lewis, and Peter McLaren. *Transforming Teacher Educa-tion: What Went Wrong with Teacher Training, and How We Can Fix It.* Sterling VA: Stylus 2010.
Twelve distinguished scholars provide a hard-hitting, thoroughly researched, histori-cal and theoretical critique of our schools of education and offer clear recommenda-tions on what must be done to ensure all children can achieve their potential and contribute to a vibrant, democratic society.

Ladson-Billings, Gloria. *Crossing Over to Canaan.* San Francisco: Jossey Bass, 2001.
Outlines the experiences of eight novice teachers learning how to teach for diversity.

Laine, Sabrina W., Molly Lasagna, and Ellen Behrstock-Sherratt. *Improving Teacher Qual-ity: A Guide for Education Leaders.* San Francisco: Jossey-Bass, 2011.
Illustrative examples, the most current research, and a proven process for improving teacher quality, with innovative strategies based on best practices that are at once proactive, strategic, and coordinated.

Marzano, Robert J. *What Works in Schools: Translating Research into Action.* Alexandria, VA: ASCD, 2003.
A description of packages that teachers and schools can use to enhance student success.

Meeting the Highly Qualified Teachers Challenge. Washington DC: US Department of Edu-cation, 2002.
A monograph released by the government that highlights information about how states need to address the issue of having highly qualified teachers in every class-room, which is a requirement of the No Child Left Behind legislation of 2002.

No Dream Denied: A Pledge to America's Children. Washington, DC: National Commission on Teaching and America's Future, 2003.
An analysis of the state of the teaching profession and a description of promising practices to ensure a highly qualified teacher in each classroom.

Nolan, James Jr., and Linda A. Hoover. *Teacher Supervision and Evaluation.* Hoboken, NJ: Wiley, 2011.
Equips teachers with the knowledge and skills needed to transform teacher supervi-sion and evaluation into a powerful vehicle for maximizing growth and enhancing student learning.

Portner, Hal. *Mentoring New Teachers.* Thousand Oaks, CA: Corwin, 2008.
Draws upon research to illustrate essential mentoring behaviors and provides useful tools, such as classroom observation methods, teacher mentor standards, and learn-ing styles assessment.

Ryan, Kevin, and James M. Cooper (Eds.). *Kaleidoscope: Contemporary and Classic Read-ings in Education,* 12th ed. Belmont, CA: Wadsworth, 2010.
A comprehensive collection of high-interest readings drawn from a wide range of sources (from the classic John Dewey and Carl Rogers to the contemporary Diane Ravitch, Elliot Eisner, Linda Darling-Hammond, and Alfie Kohn), with topics that include students and teachers; schools and instruction; curriculum and standards; foundations, philosophy, and reform; educational technology; and diversity and social issues.

Strong, Michael. *Effective Teacher Induction and Mentoring: Assessing the Evidence.* New York: Teachers College Press, 2009.
A detailed and well-balanced appraisal of the empirical evidence on the impact of teacher mentoring and induction programs.

Testing Teacher Candidates. Washington, DC: National Academy Press, 2001.
A thorough analysis of practices and policies related to teacher licensure in the United States.

Endnotes

Chapter 1

1 Susan M. Johnson, *Teachers at Work* (New York: Basic Books, 1990); Ann Liberman and Lynne Miller, *Teachers—Their World and Their Work* (New York: Teachers College Press, Columbia University, 1992); Studs Terkel, *Hope Dies Last: Making a Difference in an Indifferent World* (London: Granta Books, 2005).

2 Larry Cuban, *How Teacher Taught*, 2nd ed. (New York: Teachers College Press, Columbia University, 1993); John I. Goodlad, *Teachers for Our Nation's Schools* (San Francisco: Jossey-Bass, 1994); Carol Chmelynski, *Education Leaders Look for Ways to Get More Men into Teaching* (National School Board Association, 2005), http://www.nsba.org/HPC/Features/AboutSBN/SbnArchive/2005/October2005/Education leaderslookforwaystogetmoremenintoteaching.aspx.

3 *The Condition of Education, 2001*, Tables 70, 80 (Washington, DC: Government Printing Office, 2001); *Digest of Education Statistics 2000*, Tables 70, 79 (Washington, DC: Government Printing Office, 2001); Thomas S. Dee, *Teachers and the Gender Gaps in Student Achievement*, Swarthmore College, Economics Department; National Bureau of Economic Research (NBER) (October 2005), NBER Working Paper No. W11660; *National Board Certification Statistics*, National Board for Professional Teaching Standards, http://www.nbpts.org/about_us/national_board_certifica1/national_board/certifica?print=on.

4 "Measures to Woo Men to Teaching Jobs: Low Pay, Hard Work Cited for Declining Numbers," http://fyi.cnn.com/2002/fyi/teachers.ednews/07/05/male.teachers.ap/index.html; *Digest of Education Statistics, 2000*, Tables 70, 79; *Education Secretary Appeals for Extraordinary Teachers*, http://www.ed.gov/index.jhtml; Tamara Snyder, "Male Call: Recruiting More Men to Teach Elementary School," *Edutopia: What Works in Education* (April 28, 2008), http://www.edutopia.org/print/node/5445.

5 Benjamin D. Wright and Shirley A. Tuska, "From a Dream to Life in the Psychology of Becoming a Teacher," *School Review* (September 1968), 259–393.

6 Dan Lorte, "Observations on Teaching as Work," in R. M. Travers (ed.), *Second Handbook of Research on Teaching* (Chicago: Rand McNally, 1973), 474–497; Lortie, *School Teacher: A Sociological Study*, 2nd ed. (Chicago: The University of Chicago Press, 2002).

7 Allan C. Ornstein, Daniel U. Levine, and Gerry Gutek, *Foundations of Education*, 11th ed. (Boston: Wadsworth, 2003); Nathalie J. Gehrke, *On Being a Teacher* (West Lafayette, IN: Kappa Delta Pi, 1987).

8 Allan C. Ornstein and F. P. Hunkins, *Curriculum: Foundations, Principles, and Issues*, 5th ed. (New York: Allyn & Bacon, 2008).

9 William Glasser, *Choice Theory: A New Psychology of Personal Freedom* (New York: Harper Collins, 1999).

10 Judy Reinhartz and Don Beach, *Teaching and Learning in the Elementary School: Focus on Curriculum* (Columbus OH: Merrill, 1997).

[11] John Flavell, Patricia H. Miller, and Scott A. Miller, *Cognitive Development*, 4th ed. (Englewood Cliffs, NJ: Prentice-Hall, 2001); Robert Glaser, *Advances in Instructional Psychology, Vol. 5: Educational Design and Cognitive Science* (Hillside, NJ: Erlbaum, 2000).

[12] Gaea Leinhardt, "What Research on Learning Tells Us about Teaching," *Educational Leadership* (April 1992), 20–25.

[13] Charles Letteri, "Teaching Students How to Learn," *Theory into Practice* (Spring 1985), 112–122; Richard E. Mayer, "Models for Understanding," *Review of Educational Research* (Spring 1988), 43–64; Richard S. Prawat, "The Value of Ideas," *Educational Researcher* (August–September 1993), 5–16.

[14] James Stronge, *Qualities of Effective Teachers*, 2nd ed. (Washington, DC: ASCD, 2007), 17.

[15] Olaf Jorgenson and Rick Vanosdall, "The Death of Science?" *Phi Delta Kappan* (April 2002), 601–605.

[16] Gerald G. Duffy, "Rethinking Strategy Instruction," *Elementary School Journal* (January 1993), 231–248; Alan H. Schoenfield, "Teaching Mathematical Thinking and Problem Solving," in L. B. Resnick and L. E. Klopfer (eds.), *Toward the Thinking Curriculum* (Alexandria, VA: ASCD, 1989), 83–103.

[17] Jerome Bruner, *The Process of Education* (Cambridge, MA: Harvard University Press, 1960).

[18] Lauren Resnick, *Education and Learning to Think* (Washington, DC: National Academy Press, 1987).

[19] Justin Brown and Ellen Langer, "Mindfulness of Intelligence: A Comparison," *Educational Psychologist* (Summer 1990), 305–36; David Perkins, Eileen Jay, and Shari Tishman, "New Conceptions of Thinking," *Educational Psychologist* (Winter 1993), 67–75.

[20] Bruner, *The Process of Education*.

[21] John Goodlad, *Romance with Schools: A Life in Education* (New York: McGraw-Hill, 2004).

[22] Burrhus F. Skinner, *Walden Two* (Upper Saddle River, NJ: Prentice-Hall, 1948); Skinner, *The Technology of Teaching* (New York: Appleton Century Crofts, 1968).

[23] Ibid., 64.

[24] Ibid., 10.

[25] Einar T. Ingvorsson and Edward Morris, "Post Skinnerian, Post Skinner, or Neo Skinnerian?" *Psychological Record*, 54 (2004), 97.

[26] Gary S. Belkin and Jerry L. Gray, *Educational Psychology: An Introduction* (Dubuque, IA: William C. Brown, 1977), 59.

[27] Catherine T. Fosnot (ed.), *Constructivism: Theory, Perspectives and Practice*, 2nd ed. (New York: Teachers College Press, 2005).

[28] George W. Gagnon and Michelle Collay, "Constructivist Learning Design," paper presented on the Internet, www.prainbow.com/cld/cldp.html (n.d.).

[29] Jean Piaget, *The Origins of Intelligence* (New York: International Universities Press, 1952).

[30] Richard T. Scarpaci, *A Case Study Approach to Classroom Management* (New York: Allyn & Bacon, 2007).

[31] Robert Barr and John Tagg, "From Teaching to Learning," *Change* (June 1995), 16.

[32] Theodore R. Sizer, *Horace's School: Redesigning the American High School* (Boston: Houghton Mifflin, 1992).

[33] William L. Sanders and June C. Rivers, *Cumulative and Residual Effects of Teachers on Future Student Academic Achievement* (Knoxville: University of Tennessee Value-Added Research and Assessment Center, 1996).

[34] Dale Ballou, "Sizing Up Test Scores," *Education Next* (Summer 2002), 10–15.

[35] Harold Stevenson and James Stigler, *The Learning Gap* (New York: Summit, 1992).

[36] Ibid.

[37] Barry Beyer, *Critical Thinking* (Bloomington IN: Phi Delta Kappa Educational Foundation, 1995).

[38] Randall J. Ryder and Michael F. Graves, *Reading and Learning in Content Areas* (New York: Macmillan, 1994).

[39] Beyer, *Critical Thinking*, 1995.

[40] Mortimer J. Adler, *The Paideia Proposal: An Educational Manifesto* (New York: Collier Books, 1983).

[41] Cathy C. Block, Sheri P. Rains, and Lesley M. Morrow, *Comprehension Instruction*, 2nd ed. (New York: Gilford, 2008).

[42] Matthew Lipman, "The Culturation of Reasoning through Philosophy," *Educational Leadership* (September 1984), 51–56.

[43] Matthew Lipman, *Philosophy for Children*, 2nd ed. (Philadelphia: Temple University Press, 1980); Lipman, *Philosophy Goes to School* (Philadelphia: Temple University Press, 1988).

[44] Matthew Lipman, "Critical Thinking—What Can It Be?" *Educational Leadership* (September 1988), 38–43.

[45] Robert J. Sternberg, "How Can We Teach Intelligence?" *Educational Leadership* (September 1984), 38–48; Sternberg, "Practical Intelligence for Success in School," *Educational Leadership* (September 1990), 35–39.

[46] Robert H. Ennis, "A Logical Basis for Measuring Critical Thinking Skills," *Educational Leadership* (October 1985), 44–48; Ennis, "Critical Thinking and Subject Specificity," *Educational Researcher* (April 1989), 4–10.

[47] William A. Sadler, Jr., and Arthur Whimbey, "A Holistic Approach to Improving Thinking Skills," *Phi Delta Kappan* (November 1985), 200.

[48] Fred Newmann, "Beyond Common Sense in Educational Restructuring: The Issues of Content and Linkage," *Educational Researcher* (March 1993), 4–13.

[49] Robert J. Sternberg, "Teaching Critical Thinking: Possible Solutions," *Phi Delta Kappan* (December 1985), 277. Also see Robert J. Sternberg and Peter A. French, *Complex Problem Solving* (Hillsdale, NJ: Erlbaum, 1991).

[50] Ennis, "A Logical Basis for Measuring Critical Thinking Skills."

[51] Allan C. Ornstein, *Teaching and Schooling in America: Pre- and Post-September 11* (Boston: Allyn & Bacon, 2003).

[52] Mihaly Csikszentmihalyi, *Creativity: Flow and the Psychology of Discovery and Invention* (New York: Harper Collins, 1996), 8.

[53] Howard Gardner, *Creating Minds: An Anatomy of Creativity Seen through the Lives of Freud, Einstein, Picasso, Stravinsky, Eliot, Graham, and Gandhi* (New York: Basic Books, 1994); Csikszentmihalyi, *Creativity.*

[54] Robert J. Sternberg, "Intelligence, Wisdom, and Creativity: Three Is Better than One," *Educational Psychologist* (Summer 1986), 175–190.

[55] Carl Rogers, "Toward a Theory of Creativity," in M. Barkan and R. L. Mooney (eds.), *Conference on Creativity: A Report to the Rockefeller Foundation* (Columbus: Ohio State University Press, 1953), 73–82.

[56] Paul Bloom, *How Children Learn the Meanings of Words* (Cambridge: MIT Press, 2000); Robert Marzano, *Dimensions of Learning* (Alexandria, VA: ASCD, 1991).

[57] Jerome S. Bruner, *The Process of Education* (Cambridge, MA: Harvard University Press, 1960), 57.

[58] Richard D. Kellough, *A Resource Guide for Teaching K–12* (Upper Saddle River, NJ: Merrill/Prentice-Hall, 2004).

[59] Penelope L. Peterson, "Direct Instruction Reconsidered," in P. L. Peterson and H. J. Walberg (eds.), *Research on Teaching: Concepts, Findings, and Implications* (Berkeley, CA: McCutchan, 1979), 57–69.

[60] Ronald Lippitt and Ralph K.White, "The Social Climate of Children's Groups," in R. G. Barker and J. S. Kounin (eds.), *Child Behavior and Development* (New York: McGraw-Hill, 1943), 485–508.

[61] Edmund T. Emmer, Carolyn M. Evertson, and Linda M. Anderson, "Effective Classroom Management at the Beginning of the School Year," *Elementary School Journal*, vol. 5 (1980), 219–223.

[62] Ned A. Flanders, *Teacher Influence, Pupil Attitude, and Achievement* (Washington, DC: Government Printing Office, 1965); Flanders, *Analyzing Teaching Behavior* (Reading MA: Addison-Wesley, 1970).

[63] Edmund J. Amidon and Ned A. Flanders, *The Role of the Teacher in the Classroom* (St. Paul, MN: Amidon & Associates, 1971). Also see Allan Ornstein, "Analyzing and Improving Teachers," in Hersholt S. Waxman and Herbert J. Walberg (eds.), *New Directions for Teaching* (Berkeley, CA: McCutchan, 1999), 17–62.

[64] Herbert A. Thelen, *Classroom Grouping for Teachability* (New York: Wiley, 1967).

[65] Donald M. Medley, *Teacher Competence and Teacher Effectiveness: A Review of Process-Product Research* (Washington, DC: American Association of Colleges for Teacher Education, 1977); Medley, "The Effectiveness of Teachers," in P. L. Peterson and H. J. Walberg (eds.), *Research on Teaching: Concepts, Findings, and Implications* (Berkeley, CA: McCutchan, 1979), 11–27.

[66] Allan C. Ornstein, "How Good Are Teachers in Affecting Student Outcomes?" *NASSP Bulletin* (December 1992), 61–70; Michael S. Knapp and Patrick M. Shields, "Reconceiving Academic Instruction for the Children of Poverty," *Phi Delta Kappan* (June 1990), 753–758.

[67] Hersh C. Waxman, "Classroom Observation," *Encyclopedia of Education* (The Gale Group Inc. 2003); Encyclopedia.com, http://www.encyclopedia.com/doc/162-3403200114.html.

[68] Martin Haberman, *Star Teachers of Children in Poverty* (West Lafayette, IN: Kappa Delta Pi, 1995).

[69] Jeanne Ellis Ormrod, *Human Learning* (Upper Saddle River, NJ: Merrill, 1999); Virginia Richardson, *Handbook of Research on Teaching*, 4th ed. (Washington, DC: American Educational Research Association, 2001).

[70] Thomas L. Good and Jere Brophy, *Educational Psychology*, 5th ed. (New York: Longman, 1995), 180.

[71] Wayne K. Hoy and Cecil E. Miskel, *Educational Administration: Theory Research and Practice*, 6th ed. (Boston: McGraw-Hill, 2001).

[72] Kenneth T. Henson, *Curriculum Planning: Integrating Multiculturalism, Constructivism, and Education Reform*, 4th ed. (Long Grove, IL: Waveland, 2010).

[73] Ken Macrorie, *Twenty Teachers* (London: Oxford University Press, 1990), 147.

Chapter 2

[1] Eric D. Hirsch, Jr., *The Schools We Need* (New York: Anchor Books, 1999).

[2] Hilda Taba, *Curriculum Development: Theory and Practice* (New York: Harcourt Brace Jovanovich, 1962), 197.

[3] Ibid.

[4] Commission on the Reorganization of Secondary Education, *Cardinal Principles of Secondary Education* (Washington, DC: Government Printing Office, 1918).

[5] National Commission on Excellence in Education, *A Nation at Risk: The Imperative for Reform* (Washington, DC: Government Printing Office, 1983).

[6] Peter E. Oliva, *Developing the Curriculum*, 3rd ed. (New York: Harper Collins, 1992), 265.

[7] Kenneth T. Henson, *Curriculum Planning: Integrating Multiculturalism, Constructivism, and Education Reform*, 4th ed. (Long Grove, IL: Waveland, 2010); Shirley M. Hufstedler, "The Once and Future K–12," *Phi Delta Kappan* (May 2002), 684–89; Allan C. Ornstein, "The National Reform of Education," *NASSP Bulletin* (September 1992), 89–105.

[8] Pete Plastrik, *Decoding Duncan: "A" Is for Accountability, But What Comes After That?* http://www.nupolis.com/public/item/230727.

[9] James A. Banks, *Teaching Strategies for Ethnic Studies*, 8th ed. (Boston: Allyn & Bacon, 2008); Henson, *Curriculum Planning*; Allan C. Ornstein and Francis P. Hunkins, *Curriculum: Foundations, Principles and Issues*, 5th ed. (Boston: Allyn & Bacon, 2009).

[10] Henson, *Curriculum Planning*; George J. Posner, *Analyzing the Curriculum*, 3rd ed. (New York: McGraw-Hill, 2003); George J. Posner and Alan N. Rudnitsky, *Course Design: A Guide to Curriculum Development for Teachers*, 7th ed. (New York: Allyn & Bacon, 2005); Kevin B. Zook, *Instructional Design for Classroom Teaching and Learning* (Boston: Allyn & Bacon, 2001).

[11] Henson, *Curriculum Planning*; Ronald C. Doll, *Curriculum Improvement: Decision Making and Process*, 10th ed. (Needham Heights, MA: Allyn & Bacon, 1997); Ornstein and Hunkins, *Curriculum*.

[12] W. James Popham, *Modern Educational Measurement*, 3rd ed. (Needham Heights, MA: Allyn & Bacon, 1999); Robert E. Slavin, *Educational Psychology: Theory into Practice*, 3rd ed. (Needham Heights, MA: Allyn & Bacon, 1992).

[13] Ralph Tyler, *Basic Principles of Curriculum and Instruction* (Chicago: University of Chicago Press, 1949).

[14] Ibid., 34.

[15] Ibid., 41.

[16] Grant Wiggins and Jay McTighe, *Understanding by Design*, expanded 2nd ed. (Upper Saddle River, NJ: Prentice-Hall, 2005).

[17] Grant Wiggins, *Assessing Student Performance* (San Francisco: Jossey-Bass, 1999).

[18] Jeanne Chall, *The Academic Achievement Challenge* (New York: Guilford, 2000).

[19] Henson, *Curriculum Planning*; John Bransford, Nancy Nye, and Helen Bateman, "Creating High Quality Learning Environments: Guidelines from Research on How People Learn," presentation to the National Governor's Association, San Francisco, CA, July 2002.

[20] Benjamin S. Bloom et al., *Taxonomy of Educational Objectives. Handbook I: Cognitive Domain* (New York: David McKay, 1956).

21 David R. Krathwohl, Benjamin S. Bloom, and Bertram Masia (eds.), *Taxonomy of Educational Objectives. Handbook II: Affective Domain* (New York: David McKay, 1964).

22 Ibid.

23 Anita J. Harrow, *Taxonomy of the Psychomotor Domain: A Guide for Developing Behavioral Objectives* (New York: McKay, 1972).

24 Norman E. Gronlund, *How to Write and Use Instructional Objectives*, 5th ed. (New York: Macmillan, 1995), 21, 52–53; Norman E. Gronlund and Robert L. Linn, *Measurement and Evaluation in Teaching*, 7th ed. (New York: Macmillan, 1995), 41–42.

25 Norman E. Gronlund and C. Keith Waush, *Assessment of Student Achievement*, 9th ed. (Boston: Allyn & Bacon, 2008).

26 Ibid.

27 Robert F. Mager, *Preparing Instructional Objectives*, rev. ed. (Belmont, CA: Fearon, 1984). The examples of each component are derived from the authors.

28 Ornstein and Hunkins, *Curriculum*.

29 Lorin W. Anderson and David R. Krathwohl, *A Taxonomy for Learning, Teaching and Assessing* (Boston: Allyn & Bacon, 2001); Popham, *Modern Educational Measurement*; Charles K. West, James A. Farmer, and Philip M. Wolff, *Instructional Design* (Needham Heights, MA: Allyn & Bacon, 1991).

30 Lynn L. Morris and Carol T. FitzGibbon, *How to Deal with Goals and Objectives* (Beverly Hills, CA: Sage, 1978); Michael Fullan, *The New Meaning of Change* (New York: Teachers College Press, 2001).

31 Hirsch, *The Schools We Need*.

32 Donald C. Orlich, Robert J. Harder, Richard C. Callahan, Michael S. Trevisan, and Abbie H. Brown, *Teaching Strategies: A Guide to Effective Instruction*, 9th ed. (Belmont, CA: Cengage, 2009).

33 Ángel Gutiérrez and A. Jaime, "On the Assessment of the Van Hiele levels of Reasoning," *Focus on Learning Problems in Mathematics* 20, nos. 2–3 (1998), 27–46; Douglas H. Clements, Sudha Swaminathan, Mary Ann Zeitler Hannibal, and Julie Sarama, "Young Children's Concepts of Shape," *Journal for Research in Mathematics Education* 30, no. 2 (March 1999), 192–212.

34 Wiggins and McTighe, *Understanding by Design*.

35 Mark W. Conley, *Connecting Standards and Assessments through Literacy* (New York: Pearson, 2005).

36 Common Core State Standards Initiative, http://www.corestandards.org/in-the-states.

37 Ibid., *National Governors Association and State Education Chiefs Launch Common State Academic Standards*, http://www.corestandards.org/articles/8-national-governors-association-and-state-education-chiefs-launch-common-state-academic-standards.

38 Barack Obama, "A More Perfect Union" (full speech), http://tpmtv.talkingpointsmemo.com/?id=3030894.

39 *National Board Certification Statistics*. National Board for Professional Teaching Standards (TBPTS). http://www.nbpts.org/about_us/national_board_certifica1/national_board_certifica?print=on.

40 *Standards Based Classroom Operator's Manual* (Alexandra, VA: Just Ask Publications and Professional Development, 2002).

41 Mark R. O'Shea, *From Standards to Success* (Alexandria, VA: ASCD, 2005).

Chapter 3

1 Eric D. Hirsch, *Cultural Literacy: What Every American Needs to Know* (Boston: Houghton Mifflin, 1987).

2 Terry J. Foriska, *A Toolkit for Developing Curriculum and Assessment* (Mankato, MN: Ten Sigma, 1997; Foriska, *Restructuring around Standards: A Practitioner's Guide to Design and Implementation* (Thousand Oaks, CA: Corwin, 1998).

3 Paul V. Bredeson, *Designs for Learning* (Thousand Oaks, CA: Corwin, 2003); Pamela G. Grossman, "Why Models Matter," *Review of Educational Research* (Summer 1993), 171–80; John Solas, "Investigating Teacher and Student Thinking about the Process of Teaching and Learning," *Review of Educational Research* (Summer 1992), 205–225.

4 Craig D. Jerald and Richard M. Ingersoll, "All Talk, No Action: Putting an End to Out-of-Field Teaching" (Washington, DC: Education Trust, 2002).

5 John A. Zahorik, "Teachers' Planning Models," *Educational Leadership* (November 1975), 134–139.

6 Christopher Clark, "Real Lessons from Imaginary Teachers," *Journal of Curriculum Studies* (September–October 1991), 429–434; Penelope L. Peterson, Christopher W. Marx, and Ronald M. Clark, "Teacher Planning, Teacher Behavior, and Student Achievement," *American Educational Research Journal* (Summer 1978), 417–432.

7 Elliot W. Eisner, *The Educational Imagination*, 3rd ed. (New York: Prentice-Hall, 2001).

8 Carol Ann Tomlinson, *The Differentiated Classroom* (Alexandria, VA: ASCD, 1999), 40.

9 Deborah S. Brown, "Twelve Middle School Teachers' Planning," *Elementary School Journal* (September 1988), 69–87; Brown, "Descriptions of Two Novice Secondary Teachers' Planning," *Curriculum Inquiry* (Spring 1993), 34–45.

10 Robert J. Yinger, "A Study of Teacher Planning," *Elementary School Journal* (January 1980), 107–127.

11 William Sanders, "Value-Added Teaching," Presentation to the Governor's Commission on Teaching Success (Columbus, OH, 2002).

12 Gail McCutcheon, "How Do Elementary School Teachers Plan?" *Elementary School Journal* (September 1980), 4–23.

13 Jacqueline Jordon Irvine and Beverly Jeanne Armento, *Culturally Responsive Teaching* (Boston: McGraw-Hill, 2001).

14 Beverly Jeanne Armento, "Principles of a Culturally Responsive Classroom," in Jacqueline Irvine and Beverly J. Armento (eds.), *Culturally Responsive Teaching* (Boston: McGraw-Hill, 2001), 19–32.

15 Kenneth T. Henson, *Curriculum Planning: Integrating Multiculturalism, Constructivism, and Education Reform*, 4th ed. (Long Grove, IL: Waveland, 2007), 51–52.

16 James A. Banks, *Race, Culture, and Education: The Selected Works of James A. Banks* (London & New York: Routledge, 2006).

17 Allan C. Ornstein, "Effective Course Planning by Mapping." *Kappa Delta Pi Record* (Fall, 1990), 24–26; Ornstein, *Educational Administration: Concepts and Practices*, 5th ed. (Belmont, CA: Wadsworth, 2007).

18 Eric D. Hirsch, Jr., *The Schools We Need and Why We Don't Have Them* (New York: Doubleday, 1996), 30.

19 Tomlinson, *The Differentiated Classroom*, 81–82. See also Howard Gardner's video, *MI: Millennium* (Los Angeles: Into the Classroom Media, 2002).

20 W. James Popham, "Can High-Stakes Tests Be Developed at the Local Level?" *NASSP Bulletin* (February 1987), 77–84; Thomas R. Guskey, "Helping Standards Make the Grade," *Educational Leadership* (September 2001), 20–27.

21 Deborah J. Stipek, *Motivation to Learn*, 2nd ed. (Needham Heights, MA: Allyn & Bacon, 1993); Martin V. Covington, *Making the Grade: A Self-Worth Perspective on Motivation* (New York: Cambridge University Press, 1992).

22 Thomas L. Good and Jere E. Brophy, *Looking in Classrooms*, 10th ed. (Upper Saddle River, NJ: Pearson Education, 2008), 141–144.

23 Paul Chance, "The Rewards of Learning," *Phi Delta Kappan* (November 1992), 204.

24 Allan C. Ornstein and Francis P. Hunkins, *Curriculum: Foundations, Principles, and Issues*, 5th ed. (Boston: Pearson, 2009).

25 Peter C. Murrell, Jr., *African-Centered Pedagogy* (Albany: SUNY Press, 2002), 46.

26 Ibid.

27 Donald A. Bligh, *What's the Use of Lectures?* (San Francisco: Jossey-Bass, 2000), 282.

28 Kenneth A. Kiewra, "Aids to Lecture Learning," *Educational Psychologist* (Winter 1991), 37–53; Elizabeth Perrott, *Effective Teaching: A Practical Guide to Improving Your Teaching* (New York: Longman, 1982).

29 Henson, *Curriculum Planning*, 174.

30 Ibid.

31 Paul A. Schutz, "Goals in Self-Directed Behavior," *Educational Psychologist* (Winter 1991), 55–67; Kathryn R. Wentzel, "Social Competence at School: Relationship between Social Responsibility and Academic Achievement," *Review of Educational Research* (Spring 1991), 1–24.

32 Henson, *Curriculum Planning*, 249–250.

33 Jerome S. Bruner, *Toward a Theory of Instruction* (Cambridge, MA: Harvard University Press, 1966).

34 Kurt W. Fischer and L. Todd Rose, "Webs of Skill: How Students Learn," *Educational Leadership* (November 2001), 6–13; Steven Zemelman, Harvey Daniels and Arthur Hyde, *Best Practice: New Standards for Teaching and Learning in America's Schools* (Portsmouth, NH: Heinemann, 1998).

35 Vito Perrone, "How to Engage Students in Learning," *Educational Leadership* (February 1994), 11–13; Frank Smith, "Learning to Read: The Never-Ending Debate," *Phi Delta Kappan* (February 1992), 432–441.

36 Good and Brophy, *Looking in Classrooms*.

37 Paul R. Burden and David M. Byrd, *Methods for Effective Teaching*, 5th ed. (Boston: Allyn & Bacon, 2009).

38 Ruth Garner, "When Children Do Not Use Learning Strategies," *Review of Educational Research* (Winter 1990), 517–530; Donna M. Kagan and Deborah J. Tippins, "Helping Student Teachers Attend to Student Cues," *Elementary School Journal* (March 1991), 343–356; Marge Scherer, "Do Students Care about Learning?" *Educational Leadership* (September 2002), 12–17.

39 Alfie Kohn, "Abusing Research: The Study of Homework and Other Examples," *Phi Delta Kappan* 18(1) (2006), 15, http://www.alfiekohn.org/teaching/research.htm.

40 Lyn Corno and Jianzhong Xu, "Homework as the Job of Childhood," *Theory into Practice* 43, no. 3 (2004), 227–33; P. M. Coutts, "Meanings of Homework and Implications for Practice," *Theory into Practice* 43, no. 3 (2004), 182–188.

41 Harris Cooper, "Homework for All—in Moderation," *Educational Leadership* 58 (2001), 34–38; Cooper, "Duke Study: Homework Helps Students Succeed in School, as Long as There Isn't too Much," *Dukenews*, http://www.dukenews.duke.edu/2006/03/homework.html.

Chapter 4

1 John Bransford, Nancy Vye, and Helen Bateman, "Creating High Quality Learning Environments: Guidelines from Research on How People Learn," paper presented at the National Governor's Association, San Francisco, July 2002.

2 Ibid.

3 Ibid.

4 Wilbert J. McKeachie, "Learning, Thinking, and Thorndike," *Educational Psychologist* (Spring 1990), 127–141; Richard M. Wolf, "In Memoriam—Robert Thorndike," *Educational Researcher* (April 1991), 22–23.

5 Carl Bereiter, "Implications of Connectionism and Thinking about Rules," *Educational Researcher* (April 1991), 10–16; Nicola Findley, "In Their Own Ways," *Educational Leadership* (September 2003), 60–63.

6 Thomas L. Good, Douglas A. Grouws, and Howard Ebermeier, *Active Mathematics Teaching* (New York: Longman, 1983); Leslie Steffe and Terry Woods, *Transforming Children's Mathematics Education* (Hillsdale, NJ: Erlbaum, 1990).

7 Robert J. Marzano, Debra J. Pickering, and Jane E. Pollock, *Classroom Instruction That Works* (Alexandria, VA: ASCD, 2001), 128–129.

8 Robert Glazer, *Adaptive Education: Individual Diversity and Learning* (New York: Holt, Rinehart and Winston, 1977), 77.

9 Paul R. Burden and David M. Byrd, *Methods for Effective Teaching*, 5th ed. (New York: Allyn & Bacon, 2009).

10 James H. Block, Helen E. Efthim, and Robert B. Burns, *Building Effective Mastery Learning Schools* (New York: Longman, 1989).

11 Benjamin Bloom, *Human Characteristics and School Learning* (New York: McGraw-Hill, 1976), 35; Arthur Costa (ed.), *Developing Minds* (Alexandria, VA: ASCD, 1991).

12 Thomas L. Good and Jere E. Brophy, *Looking in Classrooms*, 10th ed. (Upper Saddle River, NJ: Pearson Education, 2008); Richard S. Marliave and Nikola N. Filby, "Success Rate: A Measure of Task Appropriateness," in Charles W. Fisher and David C. Berliner (eds.), *Perspectives on Instructional Time* (New York: Longman, 1985), 217–236.

13 James A. Kulik and Chen-Lin C. Kulik, "Timing and Feedback and Verbal Learning," *Review of Educational Research* (Spring 1988), 79–97; James A. Kulik, Chen-Lin C. Kulik, and Robert L.

Bangert-Drowns, "Effectiveness of Mastery Learning Programs: Meta-Analysis," *Review of Educational Research* (Summer 1990), 265–299.

[14] The ten recommendations for practice and drill are based on Allan C. Ornstein, "Practice and Drill: Implications for Instruction," *NASSP Bulletin* (April 1990), 112–116. See also Jeanne Ellis Ormrod, *Human Learning*, 3rd ed. (Upper Saddle River, NJ: Merrill Prentice-Hall, 1999).

[15] Francis P. Hunkins, *Effective Questions, Effective Thinking*, 2nd ed. (Needham Heights, MA: Gordon Publishers, 1994); Walter Dick, Lou Carey, and James Carey, *The Systematic Design of Instruction*, 7th ed. (New York: Allyn & Bacon, 2008); Neal A. Glasgow and Cathy Hicks, *What Successful Teachers Do* (Thousand Oaks, CA: Corwin, 2003).

[16] Carl Bereiter and Siegfried Englemann, *Teaching Disadvantaged Children in the Preschool* (Englewood Cliffs, NJ: Prentice-Hall, 1966); George H. Wood, *Schools That Work* (New York: Dutton, 1992); Patricia Davenport and Gerald Anderson, *Closing the Achievement Gap* (Houston, TX: American Productivity and Quality Center, 2002).

[17] Jeanne Chall, *The Academic Achievement Challenge* (New York: Guilford, 2000).

[18] Walter Doyle, "Effective Teaching and the Concept of the Master Teacher," *Elementary School Journal* (September 1985), 27–34; Ronald F. Ferguson; "Closing the Achievement Gap," Presentation at Ohio's Invitational Conference: Narrowing the Achievement Gap, Columbus, OH, September 2002; Katherine G. Simon, "The Blue Blood is Bad, Right?" *Educational Leadership* (September 2002), 24–29.

[19] James H. Stronge, *Qualities of Effective Teaching* (Alexandria, VA: ASCD, 2002), 75.

[20] Benjamin Bloom (ed.), *Taxonomy of Educational Objectives, Handbook I: Cognitive Domain* (New York: Longman-McKay, 1956), 28.

[21] Al Andrade, *The Thinking Classroom*, Harvard Zero Project, http://learnweb.harvard.edu/alps/thinking/ways.cfm.

[22] Arthur T. Jersild, *When Teachers Face Themselves* (New York: Teachers College Press, 1955).

[23] Barry K. Beyer, *Teaching Thinking Skills* (Needham Heights, MA: Allyn & Bacon, 1991); Lauren B. Resnick and Leopold E. Klopfer (eds.), *Toward the Thinking Curriculum: Current Cognitive Research, 1989 ASCD Yearbook* (Alexandria, VA: ASCD, 1989).

[24] James T. Dillon, "Research on Questioning and Discussion," *Educational Leadership* (November 1984), 50–56; George D. Nelson, "Choosing Content That is Worth Teaching," *Educational Leadership* (October 2001), 12–16.

[25] Jules Henry, "Docility, or Giving Teacher What She Wants," in John H. Chilcott, Norman C. Greenberg, and Herbert B. Wilson (eds.), *Readings in the Socio-Cultural Foundations of Education* (Belmont, CA: Wadsworth, 1969), 249.

[26] John Holt, *How Children Fail* (New York: Pitman, 1964), 12.

[27] Allan C. Ornstein, "Questioning: The Essence of Good Teaching: Part I," *NASSP Bulletin* (May 1987), 71–79; Stephen T. Peverly, "Problems with Knowledge-Based Explanation of Memory and Development," *Review of Educational Research* (Spring 1991), 71–93.

[28] Mary B. Rowe, "Wait-Time and Reward as Instructional Variables," *Journal of Research in Science Teaching* (February 1974), 81–97.

[29] Paulette P. Harris and Kevin J. Swick, "Improving Teacher Communications: Focus on Clarity and Questioning Skills," *Clearing House* (September 1985), 13–15; James Hiebert and Diana Wearne, "Instructional Tasks, Classroom Discourse, and Students' Learning," *American Educational Research Journal* (Summer 1993), 393–425; Kenneth Tobin, "Effects of Teacher Wait-Time on Discourse Characteristics in Mathematics and Language Arts Classes," *American Educational Research Journal* (Summer 1986), 191–200.

[30] Carolyn Evertson, Edmund T. Emmer, and Murray E. Worsham, *Classroom Management for Elementary Teachers*, 7th ed. (Boston: Addison Wesley, 2006).

[31] Clark A. Chinn, "Situated Actions During Reading Lessons: A Microanalysis of Oral Reading Error Episodes," *American Educational Research Journal* (Summer 1993), 361–392; Linda M. Anderson, Carolyn Evertson, and Jere E. Brophy, "An Experimental Study of Effective Teaching in First Grade Reading Groups," *Elementary School Journal* (March 1979), 193–223; Vickie Gill, *The Eleven Commandments of Good Teaching*, 3rd ed. (Thousand Oaks, CA: Corwin, 2009).

[32] Donna M. Kagan, "How Schools Alienate Students at Risk," *Educational Psychologist* (Spring 1990), 105–125; Alexis L. Mitman and Andrea Lash, "Students' Perceptions of the Academic Learning and Classroom Behavior," *Elementary School Journal* (September 1988), 55–68.

[33] Jere E. Brophy and Carolyn Evertson, *Learning from Teaching: A Developmental Perspective* (Boston: Allyn & Bacon, 1976); Nathaniel L. Gage, *The Scientific Basis of the Art of Teaching* (New York: Teachers College Press, Columbia University, 1978); Vincent R. Ruggiero, *Teaching Thinking across the Curriculum* (New York: HarperCollins, 1992).

[34] Robert Marzano, *A Different Kind of Classroom: Teaching with Dimensions of Learning* (Alexandria, VA: ASCD, 1992); Kathy Comfort, Tamara Kushner, Jane Delgado, and Derek Briggs, "The Achievement Gap: How We Know if Reform Efforts Are Leading to High Achievement by All Students in Science" (San Francisco: WestEd, 2000).

[35] Michael J. Dunkin and Bruce J. Biddle, *The Study of Teaching* (Washington, DC: University Press America, 1982); Lance T. Isumi, *They Have Overcome: High Poverty, High-Performing Schools in California* (San Francisco: Pacific Research Institute, 2002).

[36] Jere E. Brophy, "Teacher Praise: A Functional Analysis," *Review of Educational Research* (Spring 1981), 5–32; Brophy, "On Praising Effectively," *Elementary School Journal* (May 1981), 269–280; Good and Brophy, *Looking in Classrooms*, 141–144.

[37] James T. Dillon, "A Norm against Student Questioning," *Clearing House* (November 1981), 136–139; Kieran Egan, "Start with What the Student Knows," *Phi Delta Kappan* (February 2003), 443–445.

[38] Myra Pollack Sadker and David Miller Sadker, *Teachers, Schools and Society*, 5th ed. (Boston: McGraw-Hill, 2000); Thomas L. Good, Bruce J. Biddle, and Jere E. Brophy, *Teachers Make a Difference* (New York: Holt, Rinehart and Winston, 1975).

[39] Robert M. W. Travers, *Essentials of Learning*, 5th ed. (New York: Macmillan, 1982), 436.

[40] Elizabeth Perrott, *Effective Teaching: A Practical Guide to Improving Your Teaching* (New York: Longman, 1981); Alane J. Starko, Georgea M. Sparks-Langer, Marvin Pasch, Lisa Franks, Trevor G. Gardner, and Cristella D. Moody, *Teaching as Decision Making: Successful Practices for the Elementary Teacher* (Upper Saddle River, NJ: Prentice-Hall, 2002).

[41] Gerald G. Duffy, "Conceptualizing Instructional Explanation," *Teaching and Teacher Education*, no. 2 (1986), 197–214.

[42] David P. Ausubel, "In Defense of Advanced Organizers: A Reply to the Critics," *Review of Educational Research* (Spring 1978), 251–259; Nathaniel L. Gage and David C. Berliner, *Educational Psychology*, 6th ed. (Boston: Houghton Mifflin, 1998).

[43] Robert Garmston and Bruce Wellman, "How to Make Presentations," *Educational Leadership* (February 1994), 88–89.

[44] Kenneth A. Kiewa, "Aids to Lecture Learning," *Educational Psychologist* (Winter 1991), 37–53.

[45] Cecilia Heyes and Ludwig Huber, *The Evolution of Cognition* (Cambridge, MA: MIT Press, 2000); Allen Newell and Herbert Simon, *Human Problem Solving* (Englewood Cliffs, NJ: Prentice-Hall, 1972).

[46] John Dewey, *How We Think* (Lexington, MA: Heath, 1910).

[47] John Bransford and Barry Stein, *The IDEAL Problem Solver*, 2nd ed. (New York: Worth, 1993).

[48] Morris L. Bigge, *Learning Theories for Teachers*, 6th ed. (New York: Allyn & Bacon, 2003); Richard E. Mayer, *Thinking, Problem Solving and Cognition* (San Francisco: Freeman, 1983); Kati Haycock, "Closing the Achievement Gap," *Educational Leadership* (March 2001), 6–11.

[49] Cecilia Heyes and Ludwig Huber, *The Evolution of Cognition* (Cambridge, MA: MIT Press, 2000); Allen Newell and Herbert Simon, *Human Problem Solving* (Englewood Cliffs, NJ: Prentice-Hall, 1972).

[50] Bruce Joyce and Beverly Showers, *Student Achievement through Staff Development*, 3rd ed. (Alexandria, VA: ASCD, 2003).

[51] Linda Darling-Hammond, *Redesigning Schools: What Matters and What Works* (Stanford, CA: School Redesign Network, 2002), http://www.schoolredesign.net.

[52] Paul Cobb et al., "Characteristics of Classroom Mathematics Traditions," *American Educational Research Journal* (Fall 1992), 573–604; Penelope Peterson, Elizabeth Fennema, and Thomas Carpenter, "Using Knowledge of How Students Think about Mathematics," *Educational Leadership* (December 1988–January 1989), 42–46.

[53] Benjamin Bloom and Lois J. Broder, "Problem Solving Process of College Students," *Supplementary Education and Monograph*, no. 73 (Chicago: University of Chicago Press, 1950).

[54] Jere E. Brophy, "Research Linking Teacher Behavior to Student Achievement," *Educational Psychologist* (Summer 1988), 235–286; Joe Becker and Maria Varelas, "Piaget's Early Theory of the

Role of Language in Intellectual Development: A Comment on Devrie's Account of Piaget's Social Theory," *Educational Researcher* (August/September 2001), 22–23; John Woodward, "Effects of Curriculum Discourse Style on Eighth Graders' Recall and Problem Solving in Earth Science," *Elementary School Journal* (January 1994), 299–314.

55 Ruth Garner, "When Children and Adults Do Not Use Learning Strategies," *Review of Educational Research* (Winter 1990), 517–529; Michael S. Knapp and Patrick M. Shields, "Reconceiving Academic Instruction for Children of Poverty," *Phi Delta Kappan* (June 1990), 752–758; Kenneth E. Vogler and Robert J. Kennedy, "A View from the Bo Hum," *Phi Delta Kappan* (February 2003), 444–448.

56 Jean Piaget, *The Origins of Intelligence in Children* (New York: International Universities Press, 1952); Jean Piaget and Barbel Inhelder, *The Early Growth of Logic in the Child* (London: Routledge & Kegan Paul, 1963).

57 Robert J. Sternberg et al., "Practical Intelligence for Success in School," *Educational Leadership* (September 1990), 35–39.

58 Thomas L. Good and Douglas A. Grouws, "Increasing Teachers' Understanding of Mathematical Ideas through In-Service Training," *Phi Delta Kappan* (June 1987), 778–783.

59 Alan H. Schoenfeld, "Teaching Mathematical Thinking and Problem Solving," in Lauren B. Resnick and Leopold E. Klopfer (eds.), *Toward the Thinking Curriculum* (Alexandria, VA: ASCD, 1989), 83–103.

60 John Goodlad, *A Place Called School*, 2nd ed. (New York: McGraw-Hill, 2004).

Chapter 5

1 Richard Allington, "You Can't Learn Too Much from Books You Can't Read," *Educational Leadership* 60, no. 3 (2002), 16–19.

2 Elliot W. Eisner, "Why the Textbook Influences Curriculum," *Curriculum Review* (January–February 1987), 11–13; Eisner, "Who Decides What Schools Should Teach?" *Phi Delta Kappan* (March 1990), 523–526.

3 Linda G. Fielding and David R. Pearson, "Synthesis of Research: Reading Comprehension—What Works," *Educational Leadership* (February 1994), 62–68; Maureen McLaughlin and MaryBeth Allen, *Guided Comprehension: A Teaching Model for Grades 3–8* (Newark, DE: International Reading Association, 2002).

4 James H. Block, Helen E. Efthim, and Robert B. Burns, *Building Effective Mastery Learning in Schools* (New York: Longman, 1989); Thomas L. Good and Jere E. Brophy, *Looking in Classrooms*, 10th ed. (Upper Saddle River, NJ: Pearson Education, 2008).

5 Paul Burden and David M. Byrd, *Methods for Effective Teaching*, 3rd ed. (Needham Heights, MA: Allyn & Bacon, 2003).

6 Trent Toone, "Creativity, Imagination Churned Out through Teachers' Machine" (Ogden, Utah: *Standard-Examiner*, 2009), http://www.standard.net/topics/featured/2009/12/23/creativity-imagination-churned-out-through-teachers-machine.

7 Cathy Newsome, *A Teacher's Guide to Fair Use and Copyright: Modeling Honesty and Resourcefulness* (1997), http://home.earthling.net/~cnew/research.htm; Kenneth T. Murray, "Copyright and the Educator," *Phi Delta Kappan* (March 1994), 552–555; Kenneth Crews, *Copyright Law for Librarians and Educators* (Atlanta, GA: American Library Association ALA Editions, 2005).

8 Crews, *Copyright Law for Librarians and Educators*.

9 Brad Templeton, *10 Big Myths about Copyright Explained* (October, 2008), http://www.templetons.com/brad/copymyths.html.

10 Amy Seely Flint, *Literate Lives: Teaching Reading and Writing in Elementary Classrooms* (Hoboken, NJ: Wiley, 2008); Rebecca Barr, *Teaching Reading in Elementary Classrooms* (New York: Longman, 1991); Elfrieda H. Hiebert and Barbara M. Taylor, *Getting Reading Right from the Start* (Needham Heights, MA: Allyn & Bacon, 1994).

11 Robert C. Calfee, "Organizing for Comprehension and Composition," in R. Dowler and W. Ellis (eds.), *Whole Language and the Creation of Literacy* (Baltimore: Dyslexia Society, 1991), 111–

129; Patricia G. Mathes and Joseph K. Torgensen, "A Call for Equity in Reading Instruction for All Students: A Response to Allington and Woodside-Jiron," *Educational Researcher* (August–September 2000), 4–15.

12 Allan C. Ornstein and Francis P. Hunkins, *Curriculum: Foundations, Principles, and Issues*, 4th ed. (Boston: Allyn & Bacon, 2003).

13 Des Hewett, *Understanding Effective Learning: Strategies for the Classroom* (New York: McGraw-Hill, 2008); Gaea Leinhardt, "What Research on Learning Tells Us about Teaching," *Educational Leadership* (April 1992), 20–25; Claire E. Weinstein et al., "Helping Students Develop Strategies for Effective Learning," *Educational Leadership* (December–January 1989), 17–19; McLaughlin and Allen, *Guided Comprehension.*

14 George J. Posner and Alan N. Rudnitsky, *Course Design: A Guide to Curriculum Development for Teachers*, 6th ed. (Boston: Allyn & Bacon, 2001); Jon Wiles, *Curriculum Essentials* (Boston: Allyn & Bacon, 1999).

15 Thomas J. Lasley II, Thomas J. Matczynski, and James Rowley, *Instructional Models: Strategies for Teaching in a Diverse Society*, 2nd ed. (Belmont, CA: Wadsworth, 2002).

16 Thomas L. Good and Jere Brophy, *Educational Psychology*, 5th ed. (New York: Longman, 1995), 531.

17 Eisner, "Why the Textbook Influences Curriculum," 111.

18 Myra Pollock Sadker and David Miller Sadker, *Teachers, Schools and Society*, 5th ed. (Boston: McGraw-Hill, 2000); Educational Products Information Exchange, *Report on a National Study of the Nature and Quality of Instructional Materials Most Used by Teachers and Learners* (New York: EPIE Institute, 1977).

19 Arthur Woodward and David L. Elliott, "School Reform and Textbooks," *Educational Horizons* (Summer 1992), 176–180; Colleen Fairbanks, "Teaching and Learning beyond the Text," *Journal of Curriculum Supervision* (Winter 1994), 155–173. Also see Randi Stone, *Best Practices for High School Classrooms* (Thousand Oaks, CA: Corwin, 2001).

20 John S. Simmons and Eliza T. Dresang, *School Censorship in the 21st Century* (Newark, DE: International Reading Association, 2001); Harriet Tyson Bernstein, *America's Textbook Fiasco: A Conspiracy of Good Intentions* (Washington, DC: Council for Basic Education, 1988); Joan DelFattore, *What Johnny Shouldn't Read: Textbook Censorship in America* (New Haven CT: Yale University Press, 1992); Kris Axtman, "Texas Wrangles over Bias in School Textbooks," *Christian Science Monitor* (July 22, 2002), www.csmonitor.com/2002/0722/p03501–ussc.html.

21 Sadker and Sadker, *Teachers, Schools, and Society.*

22 Cleo H. Cherryholmes, "Readers' Research," *Journal of Curriculum Studies* (January–February 1993), 1–32; Allan C. Ornstein, "The Textbook Curriculum," *Educational Horizons* (Summer 1992), 167–169.

23 Mario D. Fantini and Gerald Weinstein, *The Disadvantaged: Challenge to Education* (New York: Harper & Row, 1968), 133. See also Chris Stray, "Paradigms Regained: Towards a Historical Sociology of the Textbook," *Journal of Curriculum Studies* (January–February 1994), 1–30.

24 Allan C. Ornstein, "The Irrelevant Curriculum: A Review from Four Perspectives," *NASSP Bulletin* (September 1988), 26–32. See also Elaine K. McEwan, *Teach Them All to Read* (Thousand Oaks, CA: Corwin, 2002).

25 Nathan Glazer, *We Are All Multiculturalists Now* (Cambridge, MA: Harvard University Press, 1997); Henry A. Giroux, "Curriculum, Multiculturalism, and the Politics of Identity," *NASSP Bulletin* (December 1992), 1–11.

26 Christine E. Sleeter and Carl A. Grant, "Race, Class, Gender and Disability in Current Textbooks," in Eugene F. Provenzo, Jr., Annis N. Shaver, and Manuel Bello (eds.), *The Textbook as Discourse: Sociocultural Dimensions of American Schoolbooks* (New York: Routledge, 2010). See, for example, the article "Former Professor Claims Nursing Textbook Contains Racial Stereotypes," *AFRO Black History Archives* (November 27, 2010), http://www.afro.com/sections/news/afro_briefs/story.htm?storyid=3314; Dennis Doyle, "The Unsacred Text," *American Education* (Summer 1984), 3–13; Connie Muther, "What Every Textbook Evaluator Should Know," *Educational Leadership* (April 1985), 4–8; Allan C. Ornstein, "The Textbook Driven Curriculum," *Peabody Journal of Education* (Spring 1994), 70–85.

27 Jeannie Oakes and Martin Lipton, *Teaching to Change the World* (Boston: McGraw-Hill, 1999), 169–170.

28 Connie Muther, "What Every Textbook Evaluator Should Know," *Educational Leadership* (April, 1985), 7. Also see Connie Muther, "Reflections on Textbooks and Teaching," *Educational Horizons* (Summer 1992), 194–200.

29 *The Classics, Oddly . . .* ; blog entry by Elliott Back, January 7, 2011, http://books.elliottback.com/new-edition-of-mark-twains-huck-finn-replaces-nigger-with-slave/.

30 Ibid.

31 Allan C. Ornstein, *Teachers and Schooling in America: Pre and Post September 11* (Boston: Allyn & Bacon, 2003), xiv–xv.

32 Richard T. Vacca, JoAnne L. Vacca, and Maryanne E. Mraz, *Content Area Reading: Literacy and Learning across the Curriculum*, 10th ed. (Boston: Allyn & Bacon, 2010); Harold L. Herber and Joan N. Herber, *Teaching in Content Areas* (Needham Heights, MA: Allyn & Bacon, 1993); Michael C. McKenna and Richard D. Robinson, *Teaching through Text: Reading and Writing in the Content Areas* (Boston, Allyn & Bacon, 2008); D. Fisher and N. Frey, *Improving Adolescent Literacy: Content Area Strategies at Work*, 3rd ed. (Boston: Allyn & Bacon, 2011).

33 Edward Fry, "Fry's Readability Graph: Clarification, Validity, and Extension to Level," *Journal of Reading* (December 1977), 242–252; Fry, "Readability versus Leveling," *The Reading Teacher* (November 2002), 286–291.

34 Irene C. Fountas and Gay Su Pinnell, *Leveled Books, K–8: Matching Texts to Readers for Effective Teaching* (Portsmouth, NH: Heinemann, 2005); Alton L. Raygor and George B. Schick, *Reading at Efficient Rates*, 2nd ed. (New York: McGraw-Hill, 1980).

35 James P. Byrnes, *Cognitive Development and Learning in Instructional Contexts*, 2nd ed. (Boston: Allyn & Bacon, 2001); Alice Davidson, "Readability—Appraising Text Difficulty," in Richard C. Anderson, Joan Osborn, and Robert J. Tierney (eds.), *Learning to Read in American Schools* (Hillsdale, NJ: Erlbaum, 1984), 121–139; Robert J. Tierney, John E. Readence, and Ernest K. Dishner, *Reading Strategies and Practices*, 3rd ed. (Needham Heights, MA: Allyn & Bacon, 1990).

36 Harriet T. Bernstein, "The New Politics of Textbook Adoption," *Education Digest* (December 1985), 12–15; Bernstein, "The Academy's Contribution to the Impoverishment of America's Textbooks," *Phi Delta Kappan* (November 1988), 193–198; Marie Carbo, "Eliminating the Need for Dumbed-Down Textbooks," *Educational Horizons* (Summer 1992), 189–193; Jess E. House and Rosemary T. Taylor, "Leverage on Learning: Test Scores, Textbooks and Publishers," *Phi Delta Kappan* (March 2003), 537–541.

37 Robert A. Pavlik, "Tips on Texts," *Phi Delta Kappan* (September, 1985), 86.

38 Michael L. Miles and Bruce S. Cooper, "Reimagining the Textbook: The Risks and Rewards of Electronic Reading Devices," *Education Week* 29, no. 11 (November 11, 2009), 24–25.

39 Bernstein, "The New Politics of Textbook Adoption"; Peter W. Foltz and Walter Kintsch, "Readers' Strategies and Comprehension in Linear Text and Hyper Text," paper presented at the annual meeting of the American Educational Research Association, Atlanta, GA, April 1993.

40 Rebecca Barr, Marilyn Sadow, and Camille Blachowicz, *Reading Diagnosis for Teachers*, 2nd ed. (New York: Longman, 1990); Robert Glaser (ed.), *Advances in Instructional Psychology*, vol. 4 (Hillsdale, NJ: Erlbaum, 1993).

41 Neville Bennett and Clive Carré, *Learning to Teach* (New York: Routledge, 1991).

42 Ezra Bowen, "Flunking Grade in Math," *Time* (June 20, 1988), 79. Also see Anne L'Hafner, "Teaching-Methods Scales and Mathematics-Class Achievement," *American Educational Research Journal* (Spring 1993), 71–94; Jian jun Wang, "TIMSS Primary and Middle School Data," *Educational Researcher* (August–September 2001), 17–21.

43 Harriet Tyson, *Who Will Teach the Children?* (San Francisco: Jossey-Bass, 1994), 10.

44 Geoff Ruth, *No Books, No Problem: Teaching without a Text* (2005), http://www.edutopia.org/teaching-without-text; Monya Baker, *How To: Toss the Text* (2005) http://www.edutopia.org/how-toss-text.

45 Richard L. Allington, "What I've Learned about Effective Reading Instruction," *Phi Delta Kappan* (June 2002), 740–747; Richard E. Mayer, "Aids to Text Comprehension," *Educational Psychologist* (Winter 1984), 30–42; Philip H. Winne, Lorraine Graham, and Leone Prock, "A Model of Poor Readers' Text-Based Inferencing," *Reading Research Quarterly* (January 1993), 52–69.

46 Jason Wermers, "Virginia Becoming Textbook Power," *Richmond Times Dispatch* (November 1, 2002), www.timesdispatch.com.

47 Ibid.

48 Guy M. Whipple (ed.), "Report on the National Committee on Reading: 24th Yearbook of the National Society for the Study of Education." Bloomington, IL: *Public School Publishing* 6, 1925.

49 Vicki A. Jacobs, "Adolescent Literacy: Putting the Crisis in Context," *Harvard Educational Review* 78, no. 1 (Spring 2008), 7–9.

50 Deborah Menke and Beth Davey, "Teachers' Views of Textbooks and Text Reading Instruction," *Journal of Reading* (March 1994), 464–470.

51 Sigmund A. Boloz and Donna H. Muri, "Supporting Literacy Is Everyone's Responsibility," *Reading Teacher* (February 1994), 388–391; Rebecca B. Sammons and Beth Davey, "Assessing Students' Skills in Using Textbooks," *Journal of Reading* (December–January 1994), 280–287.

52 McLaughlin and Allen, *Guided Comprehension.*

53 Ibid.; see also Bonnie B. Armbruster, "Schema Theory and the Design of Content Area Textbooks," *Educational Psychologist* (Fall 1986), 253–268; Stephen Krashen, "Whole Language and the Great Plummet of 1987–92," *Phi Delta Kappan* (June 2002), 748–753; Richard F. West, Keith E. Stanovich, and Harold R. Mitchell, "Reading in the Real World and its Correlates," *Reading Research Quarterly* (January 1993), 34–51.

54 Amy Driscoll, *Psychology of Learning and Instruction*, 2nd ed. (Boston: Allyn & Bacon, 2001); Dolores Durkin, *Teaching Them to Read*, 6th ed. (Needham Heights, MA: Allyn & Bacon, 1993); Anne P. Sweet and Judith I. Anderson, *Reading Research into the Year 2000* (Hillsdale, NJ: Erlbaum, 1993).

55 Sara Bernard, *Science Shows Making Lessons Relevant Really Matters* (2010), http://www.edutopia.org/neuroscience-brain-based-learning-relevance-improves-engagement.

56 David P. Ausubel, "In Defense of Advance Organizers: A Reply to the Critics," *Review of Educational Research* (Spring 1978), 251–257.

57 David G. Armstrong, Kenneth T. Henson, and Tom V. Savage, *Teaching Today*, 8th ed. (Upper Saddle River, NJ: Pearson, 2009).

58 Henson, *Curriculum Planning.*

59 Peter H. Johnson, *Constructive Evaluation of Literate Activity* (New York: Longman, 1992); McKenna and Robinson, *Teaching through Text.*

60 Livingston Alexander, Ronald G. Frankiewicz, and Robert E. Williams, "Facilitation of Learning and Retention of Oral Instruction Using Advance and Post Organizers," *Journal of Educational Psychology* (October 1979), 701–707; Mayer, "Aids to Text Comprehension"; Elizabeth U. Saul et al., "Students' Strategies for Making Text Make Sense," paper presented at the annual meeting of the American Educational Research Association, Atlanta, GA, April 1993.

61 John A. Ellis et al., "Effect of Generic Advance Instructions on Learning a Classification Task," *Journal of Educational Psychology* (August 1986), 294–299; James Harley and Ivor K. Davies, "Preinstructional Strategies: The Role of Pretest, Behavioral Objectives, Overviews, and Advance Organizers," *Review of Educational Research* (Spring 1976), 239–265.

62 Joanna P. Williams, Kendra M. Hall, Kristen D. Laure, K. Brooke Stafford, Laura A. DeSisto, and John S. deCani, "Expository Text Comprehension in the Primary Grade Classroom," *Journal of Educational Psychology*, 97, no. 4 (November 2005), 538–550; Rachel Best, Yasujiro Ozuru, Randy G. Floyd, and Danielle S. McNamara, *Children's Text Comprehension: Effects of Genre, Knowledge and Text Cohesion* (2006), proceeding of the ICLS 7th International Conference on Learning Sciences; Bonnie B. Armbruster, Thomas H. Anderson, and Joyce Ostertag, "Teaching Text Structure to Improve Reading," *Reading Teacher* (November 1989), 130–137; Marilyn M. Ohlhausen and Cathy M. Roller, "The Operation of Text Structure and Content Schema in Isolation and in Interaction," *Reading Research Quarterly* (Winter 1988), 70–88; Raymond E. Wright and Sheldon Rosenberg, "Knowledge of Text Coherence and Expository Writing: A Developmental Study," *Journal of Educational Psychology* (March 1993), 152–158.

63 Bernstein, "The Academy's Contribution to the Impoverishment of America's Textbooks"; Susan M. Hubbuch, "The Trouble with Textbooks," *High School Journal* (April–May 1989), 203–210; Allan C. Ornstein, "The Censored Curriculum: The Problems with Textbooks Today," *NASSP Bulletin* (November 1992), 1–9.

64 McLaughlin and Allen, *Guided Comprehension*; Richard L. Allington and Peter H. Johnston, *Reading to Learn* (New York: Guilford, 2002).

65 *Reconsidering the Textbook*, An invitation-only workshop for NSF DTS and CAREER awardees, National Academy of Sciences, Washington, DC, May 24–26, 2006, http://serc.carleton.edu/textbook/index.html.

66 Miriam J. Metzger and Andrew J. Flanagin (eds.), *Digital Media, Youth, and Credibility* (Cambridge, MA: MIT Press).

67 Lauren A. Sosniak and Susan S. Stodolsky, "Teachers and Textbooks: Materials Use in Four Fourth-Grade Classrooms," *Elementary School Journal* (January 1993), 249–276.

68 Marie Carbo, "Match the Style of Instruction to the Style of Reading," *Phi Delta Kappan* 90, no. 5 (January 2008), 373–378; Richard L. Allington and Anne McGill-Franzen, "School Response to Reading Failure," *Elementary School Journal* (May 1989), 529–542; Ruth Gardner and Patricia A. Alexander, "Metacognition: Answered and Unanswered Questions," *Educational Psychologist* (Spring 1989), 143–158; Michael McKenna, *Help for Struggling Readers* (New York: Guilford, 2002); Alan E. Farstrup and S. Jay Samuels, *What Research Has to Say about Reading Instruction* (Newark, DE: International Reading Association, 2002).

69 Paul R. Burden and David Byrd, *Methods for Effective Teaching*, 3rd ed. (Boston: Allyn & Bacon, 2003).

70 Jack W. Humphrey, "There's No Simple Way to Build a Middle School Reading Program," *Phi Delta Kappan* (June 2002), 754–757; David R. Olson and Janet W. Astington, "Thinking about Thinking," *Educational Psychologist* (Winter 1993), 7–24; Arthur Woodward, "Over-Programmed Materials: Taking the Teacher Out of Teaching," *American Educator* (Spring 1986), 26–31.

71 Patricia M. Cunningham, "What Would Make Workbooks Worthwhile?" in Richard C. Anderson, Jean Osborn, and Robert J. Tierney (eds.), *Learning to Read in American Schools* (Hillsdale, NJ: Erlbaum, 1984), 113–120; Bonnie J. Meyer, "Text Dimensions and Cognitive Processing," in Heinz Mandl, Nancy L. Stein, and Tom Trabasso (eds.), *Learning and Comprehension of Text* (Hillsdale, NJ: Erlbaum, 1984), 3–52; Edward P. St. John, Siri Ann Loescher, and Jeff S. Bardzell, *Improving Reading and Literacy in Grades 1–5* (Thousand Oaks, CA: Corwin, 2003).

72 Uma N. Iyer, "Using Workbooks in Classrooms—An Old-Fashioned Approach to Teaching," *Mathematics Teaching—Research Journal Online* 4, no. 1 (August 2010), http://www.hostos.cuny.edu/departments/math/mtrj.

73 Jean Osborn, "The Purpose, Uses, and Contents of Workbooks," in R. C. Anderson, J. Osborn and R. J. Tierney (eds.), *Learning to Read in American Schools* (Hillsdale, NJ: Erlbaum, 1984), 45–111.

74 The North American Association for Environmental Education, *Guidelines for Environmental Educational Materials* (2004), http://naaee.org/npeee/materials.php.

75 Donald C. Olrich et al., *Teaching Strategies: A Guide to Better Instruction*, 3rd ed. (Lexington, MA: Heath, 1990); Charles K. West, James A. Farmer, and Philip M. Wolff, *Instructional Design: Implications from Cognitive Science* (Needham Heights, MA: Allyn & Bacon, 1991).

76 Association of Teachers of Social Studies in the City of New York, A *Handbook for the Teaching of Social Studies*, 4th ed. (Boston: Allyn & Bacon, 1977), 127.

77 Thomas C. Gee, Mary W. Olson, and Nora J. Forester, "Classroom Use of Specialized Magazines," *Clearing House* (October 1989), 53–55.

78 Ibid.

79 Kenneth T. Henson, *Curriculum Planning: Integrating Multiculturalism, Constructivism, and Education Reform*, 4th ed. (Long Grove, IL: Waveland, 2010).

80 Tom March, "The Learning Power of WebQuests," *Educational Leadership*, 61, no 4 (2003/2004), 42–47.

81 Fengfeng Ke, "Computer Games Application within Alternative Classroom Goal Structures: Cognitive, Metacognitive, and Affective Evaluation, *Educational Technology Research and Development* 56, no. 5/6 (2008), 539–556; Marina Papastergiou, "Digital Game-Based Learning in High School Computer Science Education: Impact on Educational Effectiveness and Student Motivation, *Computers and Education* 52, no. 1 (2009), 1–2; Hakan Tüzün, Meryen Yilmaz-Soylu, Türkan Karakus, Yavuz Inal, and Gonca Kizilkaya, "The Effects of Computer Games on Primary School Students' Achievement and Motivation in Geography Learning," *Computers and Education* 52, no. 1 (2009), 68–77; Mable B. Kinzie and Dolly R. D. Joseph, "Gender Differences in Game Activity Preferences of Middle School Children: Implications for Educational Game Design," *Educational Technology Research and Development* 56, no. 5/6 (2008), 643–663.

82 *Discover Babylon*™, a joint project of the Federation of American Scientists Learning Technologies Project, UCLA's Cuneiform Digital Library Initiative, Escape Hatch Entertainment, and the Walters Art Museum, http://fas.org/babylon/.

83 Edmund Sutro, "Full-Dress Simulations: A Total Learning Experience," *Social Education* (October 1985), 634.

84 K. Platoni, *Top Issue-Oriented Computer Simulations*, 2009, http://www.edutopia.org/serious-games-computer-simulations-examples.

85 R. Van Horn, "Educational Games," *Phi Delta Kappan* 89, no. 1 (2007), 73–74.

86 Penelope Semrau and Barbara A. Boyer, *Using Interactive Video in Education* (Needham Heights, MA: Allyn & Bacon, 1994); Lillian Stephens, *Developing Thinking Skills through Real-Life Activities* (Boston: Allyn & Bacon, 1988).

87 Harry Jenkins, "Getting into the Game, *Educational Leadership* 62, no. 7 (2005), 48–51.

88 Mable B. Kinzie and Dolly R. D. Joseph, "Gender Differences in Game Activity Preferences of Middle School Children: Implications for Educational Game Design, *Educational Technology Research and Development* 56, no. 5/6 (2008), 643–663.

Chapter 6

1 "Students Get More Face Time with Average Results," *USA Today* (October 30, 2002), http://www.usatoday.com/news/education/2002–10–30–students-average_xihtm; Herman G. Van de Werfhorst, "Achievement Inequality and the Institutional Structure of Educational Systems: A Comparative Perspective," *Annual Review of Sociology* 36 (2010), 407–428.

2 Raymond S. Adams and Bruce J. Biddle, *Realities of Teaching* (New York: Holt, Rinehart and Winston, 1970).

3 Edmund T. Emmer, Carolyn Evertson, and Murray Worsham, *Classroom Management for Secondary Teachers*, 6th ed. (Boston: Allyn & Bacon, 2003); Carolyn Evertson, Edmund T. Emmer, and Murray E. Worsham, *Classroom Management for Elementary Teachers*, 7th ed. (Addison Wesley, 2006).

4 Thomas L. Good and Jere E. Brophy, *Looking in Classrooms*, 10th ed. (Upper Saddle River, NJ: Pearson Education, 2008).

5 Larry Cuban, *Why Is It So Hard to Get Good Schools?* (New York: Teachers College Press, 2003); Larry Cuban, *How Teachers Taught* (New York: Teachers College Press, Columbia University, 1993).

6 Joseph P. Robinson, "Evidence of a Differential Effect of Ability Grouping on the Reading Achievement Growth of Language-Minority Hispanics," *Educational Evaluation and Policy Analysis* 30, no. 2 (June 2008), 141–180; Mido Chang, "Teacher Instructional Practices and Language Minority Students: A Longitudinal Model," *The Journal of Educational Research* 102, no. 2 (November–December 2008), 83–98.

7 Eugene Garcia, "Effective Instruction for Language Minority Students: The Teacher," in Antonio Darder, Roldolfo D. Torres, and Henry Gutierrez (eds.), *Latinos and Education* (New York: Routledge, 1997), 368.

8 Timothy A. Hacsi, *Children as Pawns* (Cambridge, MA: Harvard University Press, 2002).

9 Melvin Borland, Roy Howsen, and Michelle Trawick, "An Investigation of the Effect of Class Size on Student Academic Achievement," *Education Economics* 13, no. 1 (March 2005), 73–83; Ronald G. Ehrenberg, Dominic J. Brewer, Adam Gamoran, and J. Douglas Willms, "Class Size and Student Achievement," *Psychological Science in the Public Interest* 2, no. 1 (May 2001), 1–30.

10 Eric A. Hanushek, "The Impact of Differential Expenditures on School Performance," *Educational Researcher* (May 1989), 45–51, 62.

11 Christopher Jepsen and Steven Rivkin, "Class Size Reduction and Student Achievement: The Potential Trade-off between Teacher Quality and Class Size," *Journal of Human Resources* 44, no. 1 (2009), 223–250.

12 Robert E. Slavin, "Class Size and Student Achievement: Small Effects of Small Classes," *Educational Psychologist* (Winter 1989), 99–110; Robert Slavin, "Putting the School Back in School Reform," *Educational Leadership* (January 2001), 22–27.

13 Robert E. Slavin, "Chapter 1: A Vision for the Next Quarter Century," *Phi Delta Kappan* (April 1991), 586–589.

[14] Northwestern University, "Class Size Alone Not Enough to Close Academic Achievement Gap," *ScienceDaily* (March 1, 2008), http://www.sciencedaily.com/releases/2008/02/080228112004.htm.

[15] University of Chicago Press Journals, "Small Classes Give Extra Boost to Low-Achieving Students." *ScienceDaily* (October 19, 2009), http://www.sciencedaily.com/releases/2009/10/091014122045.htm.

[16] Kirk A. Johnson, "Do Small Classes Influence Academic Achievement? What the National Assessment of Educational Progress Shows," *The Heritage Foundation* (June 9, 2000), http://www.heritage.org/Research/Education/CDA00-07.cfm.

[17] Bruce J. Biddle and /David C. Berliner, "Small Class Size and Its Effects," *Journal of Educational Leadership* 59, no. 5 (2002), 12–23; Elizabeth Graue, Denise Oen, Kelly Hatch, Kalpana Rao, and Erica Fadali, "Perspectives on Class Size Reduction," a paper presented at the symposium *Early Childhood Policy in Practice: The Case of Class Size Reduction* at the annual meeting of the American Educational Research Association, April 12, 2005, Montreal, Canada, http://varc.wceruw.org/sage/Perspectives_on_Class_Size_Reduction.pdf.

[18] Gene V. Glass and Mary Lee Smith, "Meta-Analysis of Research on the Relationship of Class Size and Achievement," *Educational Evaluation and Policy Analysis* 1, no. 1 (Jan.–Feb., 1979), 2–16; Glen E. Robinson, "Synthesis of Research on the Effects of Class Size," *Educational Leadership* (April 1990), 80–90. Also see Stanley Pogrow, "The Unsubstantiated 'Success' of Success for All," *Phi Delta Kappan* (April 2000), 596–600.

[19] Harris M. Cooper, "Does Reducing Student-to-Instructor Ratios Affect Achievement?" *Educational Psychologist* (Winter 1989), 79–88.

[20] Kirk A. Johnson, "The Downside to Small Class Policies," *Educational Leadership* (February 2002), 27–29; Table 411 in *Digest of Education Statistics*, 2000 (Washington, DC: United States Government Printing Office, 2001).

[21] Ibid., 29.

[22] Derrick L. Campbell, "Student Input Is the Key to Effective Classroom Management," *Leadership for Educational and Organizational Advancement* 1, no. 7 (February 1, 2009); Martin Agran and Carolyn Hughes, "Asking Student Input: Students' Opinion Regarding Their Individualized Education Program Involvement," *Career Development for Exceptional Individuals* 31, no. 2 (2008), 69–76; Ronald W. Marx and John Walsh, "Learning from Academic Tasks," *Elementary School Journal* (January 1988), 207–219; Stephen T. Peverly, "Problems with the Knowledge-Based Explanation of Memory and Development," *Review of Educational Research* (Spring 1991), 71–93.

[23] Deborah Meier, "Standardization versus Standards," *Phi Delta Kappan* (November 2002), 190–198; Jacques S. Benninga et al., "Effects of Two Contrasting School Task and Incentive Structures on Children's Social Development," *Elementary School Journal* (November 1991), 149–168.

[24] Nancy S. Cole, "Conceptions of Educational Achievement," *Educational Researcher* (April 1990), 2–7.

[25] C. A. Tomlinson and M. B. Inbeau, *Leading and Managing a Differentiated Classroom* (Alexandria, VA: ASCD); M. Byra and J. Jenkins, "Matching Instructional Tasks with Learner Ability: Inclusion Style of Teaching," *Journal of Physical Education, Recreation, and Dance* 71, no. 3 (2000), 26–30; Neville Bennett et al., "Task Processes in Mixed and Single Age Classes," *Education* (Fall 1987), 43–50; Neville Bennett and Clive Cane, *Learning to Teach* (New York: Routledge, 1993); also see Weldon Zenger and Sharon Zenger, "Why Teach Certain Material at Specific Grade Levels?" *Phi Delta Kappan* (November 2002), 212–214.

[26] Paul J. Vermette, *Making Cooperative Learning Work* (Upper Saddle River, NJ: Merrill/Prentice-Hall, 1998).

[27] Thomas J. Lasley II, Thomas J. Matczynski, and James Rowley, *Instructional Models: Strategies for Teaching in a Diverse Society*, 2nd ed. (Belmont, CA: Wadsworth, 2002).

[28] Brandi Simonsen, Sarah Fairbanks, Amy Briesch, Diane Myers, and George Sugai, "Evidence–Based Practices in Classroom Management: Considerations for Research to Practice," *Education and Treatment of Children* 31, no. 3 (2008), 351–380.

[29] Robert E. Slavin, "A Theory of School and Classroom Organization," *Educational Psychologist* (Spring 1987), 89–128.

[30] Benjamin S. Bloom, "The 2 Sigma Problem: The Search for Methods of Group Instruction as Effective as One-to-One Tutoring," *Educational Researcher* (June–July 1984), 4–16.

[31] Ibid., 6. Also see Benjamin Bloom, "Helping All Children Learn," *Principal* (March 1988), 12–17.

[32] Good and Brophy, *Looking in Classrooms*, 456.

[33] Robert J. Marzano, *A New Era of School Reform: Going Where the Research Takes Us* (Aurora, CO: Mid-Continent Research for Education and Learning, 2000).

[34] Robert J. Marzano, *A Theory-Based Meta-Analysis of Research on Instruction* (Aurora, CO: Mid-Continental Regional Educational Laboratory, 1998), 62.

[35] Robert J. Marzano, *What Works in Schools: Translating Research into Action* (Alexandria, VA: ASCD, 2003).

[36] David Johnson and Frank P. Johnson, *Joining Together: Group Theory and Group Skills*, 10th ed. (Boston: Pearson, 2008); Robert E. Slavin, "Student Teams and Comparison among Equals: Effects on Academic Performance and Student Attitudes," *Journal of Educational Psychology* (August 1978), 532–538; Noreen M. Webb, "Verbal Interaction and Learning in Peer-Directed Groups," *Theory into Teaching* (Winter 1985), 32–39.

[37] Beth C. Rubin, "Detracking in Context: How Local Constructions of Ability Complicate Equity-Geared Reform," *Teachers College Record* 110, no. 3 (March 2008), 646–699; Rubin, "Tracking and Detracking: Debates, Evidence, and Best Practices for a Heterogeneous World," *Theory Into Practice* 45, no. 1 (2006), 4–14; Jomills H. Braddock and James M. McPartland, "Alternatives to Tracking," *Educational Leadership* (April 1990), 76–79; Jeannie Oakes and Martin Lipton, "Detracking Schools: Early Lessons from the Field," *Phi Delta Kappan* (February 1992), 448–454.

[38] Janet W. Schofield, "International Evidence on Ability Grouping with Curriculum Differentiation and the Achievement Gap in Secondary Schools," *Teachers College Record* 12, no. 5 (2010), 1492–1528; Judith Ireson and Susan Hallam, "Academic Self-Concepts in Adolescence: Relations with Achievement and Ability Grouping in Schools," *Learning and Instruction* 19, no. 3 (2009), 201–213; Maureen Neihart, "The Socioaffective Impact of Acceleration and Ability Grouping: Recommendations for Best Practice," *Gifted Child Quarterly* 51, no. 4 (2007), 330–341; Thomas L. Good, "Two Decades of Research on Teacher Expectations," *Journal of Teacher Education* (July–August 1987), 32–47. Cloyd Hastings, "Ending Ability Grouping Is a Moral Imperative," *Educational Leadership* (October 1992), 14–18.

[39] Christy Lleras and Claudia Rangel, "Ability Grouping Practices in Elementary School and African American/Hispanic Achievement," *American Journal of Education* 115, no. 2, 279–304; Robinson, "Evidence of a Differential Effect of Ability Grouping."

[40] Jacqueline Jordon Irvine, *Educating Teachers for Diversity* (New York: Teachers College Press, 2003); Oakes and Lipton, "Detracking Schools"; Anne Wheelock, "The Case for Untracking," *Educational Leadership* (October 1992), 14–18.

[41] Adam Gamoran, *The Variable Effects of High School Tracking* (Madison, WI: Center on Organization and Restructuring of Schools, University of Wisconsin–Madison, 1992); Ralph Scott, "Untracking Advocates Make Incredible Claims," *Educational Leadership* (October 1993), 79–81.

[42] Lleras and Rangel, "Ability Grouping Practices"; Robinson, "Evidence of a Differential Effect of Ability Grouping," 141–180.

[43] Robert E. Slavin, "Grouping for Instruction in the Elementary School," *Educational Psychologist* (Spring 1987), 12.

[44] John Goodlad, *A Place Called School*, 2nd ed. (New York: McGraw-Hill, 2004); Jeannie Oakes, *Keeping Track: How Schools Structure Inequality* (New Haven, CT: Yale University Press, 1985).

[45] Adam Gamoran, "Synthesis of Research: Is Ability Grouping Equitable?" *Educational Leadership* (October 1992), 11–14; De Wayne A. Mason et al., "Assigning Average-Achieving Eighth Graders to Advanced Mathematics Classes in an Urban Junior High," *Elementary School Journal* (May 1992), 587–599.

[46] Prihadi Kususanto, Hiral Nizam Ismail, and Hazri Jamil, "Students' Self-Esteem and Their Perception of Teacher Behavior: A Study of Between-Class Ability Grouping," *Electronic Journal of Research in Educational Psychology* 8, no. 2 (2010), 707–724, http://www.intestigacion-psicope-digogica.org/revista/new/English/ContadorArticulo.php?457.

[47] Good and Brophy, *Looking in Classrooms*, 278.

[48] Herman G. Van de Werfhorst, "Achievement Inequality and the Institutional Structure of Educational Systems: A Comparative Perspective," *Annual Review of Sociology* 36 (August 2010), 407–428.

[49] Anthony Buttaro, Jr., Sophia Catsambis, Lynn M. Mulkey & Lala Carr Steelman, "An Organizational Perspective on the Origins of Instructional Segregation: School Composition and Use of Within-Class Ability Grouping in American Kindergartens," *Teachers College Record* 112, no. 5 (2010), 1300–1337.

[50] Adam Gamoran, "Synthesis of Research: Is Ability Grouping Equitable?" *Educational Leadership* (October 1992), 11–13; Jeanne Oakes, "Tracking in Secondary Schools," *Educational Psychologist* (Spring 1987), 129–153; De Wayne A. Mason and Thomas L. Good, "Effects of Two-Group and Whole-Class Teaching on Regrouped Elementary Students' Mathematics Achievement," *American Educational Research Journal* (September 1993), 328–360.

[51] Elfrieda Heibert, "An Examination of Ability Grouping in Reading Instruction," *Reading Research Quarterly* (Winter 1983), 231–255.

[52] Robert E. Slavin, "Ability Grouping and Student Achievement in Secondary Schools," *Review of Educational Research* (Fall 1990); Joseph S. Yarworth et al., "Organizing for Results in Elementary and Middle School Mathematics," *Educational Leadership* (October 1988), 61–67.

[53] Good and Brophy, *Looking in Classrooms*, 275–281.

[54] Jeanne Ellis Ormrod, *Human Learning*, 5th ed. (Upper Saddle River, NJ: Prentice-Hall, 2008).

[55] Robert E. Slavin, "Mounting Evidence Supports the Achievement Effects of Success for All," *Phi Delta Kappan* (February 2002), 469–471; Theresa A. Thorkildsen, "Those Who Can, Tutor," *Journal of Educational Psychology* (March 1993), 82–190.

[56] Marilyn J. Adams, *Beginning to Read* (Cambridge, MA: MIT Press, 1996); Penelope L. Peterson et al., "Ability X Treatment Interaction Effects on Children's Learning in Large-Group and Small-Group Approaches," *American Educational Research Journal* (Winter 1981), 453–473.

[57] David Johnson and Roger Johnson, *Learning Together and Alone: Cooperative, Competitive and Individualistic Learning*, 5th ed. (Boston: Allyn & Bacon, 1998).

[58] Susan R. Swing and Penelope L. Peterson, "The Relationship of Student Ability and Small-Group Interaction to Student Achievement," *American Educational Research Journal* (Summer 1982), 259–274; Noreen M. Webb, "Predicting Learning from Student Interaction: Defining the Interaction Variables," *Educational Psychologist* (Spring 1983), 33–41.

[59] Nicola Findley, "In Their Own Ways," *Educational Leadership* (September 2002), 60–63; Panayota Mantzicopoulous et al., "Use of Search/Teach Tutoring Approach with Middle-Class Students at Risk for Reading Failure," *Elementary School Journal* (May 1992), 573–586.

[60] Christine E. Neddenriep, Christopher H. Skinner, Monica A. Wallace, and Elizabeth McCallum, "Class-Wide Peer Tutoring: Two Experiments Investigating the Generalized Relationship between Increased Oral Reading Fluency and Reading Comprehension," *Journal of Applied School Psychology* 25, no. 3 (2009), 244–269.

[61] Lynn S. Fuchs et al., "The Nature of Student Interactions during Peer Tutoring with and without Peer Training and Experience," *American Educational Research Journal* (Spring 1994), 75–103; Noreen M. Webb, "Peer Interaction and Learning in Small Groups," *International Journal of Educational Research* (Spring 1989), 211–224.

[62] William S. Carlsen, "Questioning in Classrooms: A Sociolinguistic Perspective," *Review of Educational Research* (Summer 1991), 157–178.

[63] Benjamin Bloom, "Helping All Children Learn in Elementary School—and Beyond," *Principal* (March 1988), 12–17; Bloom, "The 2 Sigma Problem."

[64] Peter A. Cohen, James A. Kulik, and Chen-Lin C. Kulik, "Educational Outcomes of Tutoring: A Meta-Analysis of Findings," *American Educational Research Journal* (Summer 1982), 237–248; Darrell Morris, Beverly Shaw, and Jan Perney, "Helping Low Readers in Grades 2 and 3: An After-School Volunteer Tutoring Program," *Elementary School Journal* (November 1990), 133–150; Linda Devin-Sheehan, Robert S. Feldman, and Vernon I. Allen, "Research on Children Tutoring Children: A Critical Review," *Review of Educational Research* (Summer 1976), 355–385.

[65] *What Works: Research about Teaching and Learning* (Washington, DC: US Government Printing Office, 1987), 36.

[66] James W. Keefe and John W. Jenkins, "Personalized Instruction," *Phi Delta Kappan* (February 2002), 440–448; Robert E. Slavin, "Synthesis of Research on Cooperative Learning," *Educational Leadership* (February 1991), 71–82.

[67] Alfie Kohn, "Group Grade Grubbing versus Cooperative Learning," *Educational Leadership* (February 1991), 83–87; Marian Matthews, "Gifted Students Talk about Cooperative Learning," *Educational Leadership* (October 1992), 48–50; Chip Wood, "Changing the Pace of School," *Phi Delta Kappan* (March 2002), 545–550.

[68] Robyn Gillies and Michael Boyle, "Teachers' Reflections of Cooperative Learning (CL), A Two-Year Follow-Up," *Teaching Education* 22, no. 1 (2011), 63–78; R. Gillies, *Cooperative Learning: Integrating Theory and Practice* (Thousand Oaks, CA: Sage, 2007).

[69] David Johnson and Frank P. Johnson, *Joining Together: Group Therapy and Group Skills*, 10th ed. (Needham Heights, MA: Pearson, 2008); Robert E. Slavin, *Cooperative Learning: Theory, Research, and Practice*, 2nd ed. (Boston: Allyn & Bacon, 1994).

[70] Slavin, "Synthesis of Research on Cooperative Learning"; see also Gayle H. Gregory and Carolyn Chapman, *Differentiated Instructional Strategies: One Size Doesn't Fit All*, 2nd ed. (Thousand Oaks, CA: Corwin, 2006).

[71] Michael S. Meloth and Paul D. Deering, "Task Talk and Task Awareness under Different Cooperative Learning Conditions," *American Educational Research Journal* (Spring 1994), 139.

[72] Richard T. Scarpaci, *Resource Methods for Managing K–12 Instruction: A Case Study Approach* (Boston: Allyn & Bacon, 2009).

[73] Robert E. Slavin, *Using Student Team Learning*, 3rd ed. (Baltimore: Johns Hopkins University Press, 1986).

[74] Robert E. Slavin, *School and Classroom Organization* (Hillsdale, NJ: Erlbaum, 1988); Slavin, "Synthesis of Research."

[75] J. Clark, "Pieces of the Puzzle: The Jigsaw Method," in Schlomo Sharan (ed.), *Handbook of Cooperative Learning Methods* (Westport, CT: Greenwood, 1994); Elliot Aronson, Nancy Blaney, Cookie Stephin, Jev Sikes, and Matthew Snapp, *The Jigsaw Classroom* (Beverly Hills, CA: Sage Publications, 1978).

[76] Lynda A. Baloche, *The Cooperative Classroom* (Columbus, OH: Prentice-Hall, 1998), 100–101.

[77] Stanley Kagan, "The Structural Approach to Cooperative Learning," *Educational Researcher* (December–January 1989–1990), 13.

[78] Thomas J. Lasley, Thomas J. Matczynski, and James Rowley, *Instructional Models: Strategies for Teaching in a Diverse Society* (Belmont, CA: Wadsworth, 2002), 315.

[79] Robert J. Marzano, Debra J. Pickering, and Jane E. Pollock, *Classroom Instruction That Works* (Prentice-Hall, 2004), 89–90.

[80] Richard T. Scarpaci, *Resource Methods for Managing K–12 Instruction: A Case Study Approach* (Boston: Allyn & Bacon, 2009).

[81] Ibid., 80; David Johnson and Roger Johnson, *Learning Together and Alone: Cooperative, Competitive and Individualistic Learning*, 5th ed. (Boston: Allyn & Bacon, 1998).

[82] Roger Johnson and David Johnson, "Toward a Cooperative Effort," *Educational Leadership* (April 1989), 80–81.

[83] Roger Johnson and David Johnson, "Gifted Students Illustrate What Isn't Cooperative Learning," *Educational Leadership* (March 1993), 60–61; John A. Ross and Dennis Raphael, "Communication and Problem Solving Achievement in Cooperative Learning," *Journal of Curriculum Studies* (March–April 1990), 149–164.

[84] Robert Glaser and Lauren B. Resnik, "Instructional Psychology," *Annual Review of Psychology* 23 (1972), 207–276; also see Glaser (ed.), *Advances in Instructional Psychology* (Hillsdale, NJ: Erlbaum, 1978); Lorrie Shepard, "The Role of Classroom Assessment in Teaching and Learning," in Virginia Richardson (ed.), *Handbook of Research on Teaching*, 4th ed. (Washington, DC: American Educational Research Association, 2001), 1066–1011.

[85] Herbert J. Klausmeier and Richard E. Ripple, *Learning and Human Abilities*, 3rd ed. (New York: Harper & Row, 1971); also see Beverly A. Parsons, *Evaluative Inquiry: Using Evaluation to Promote Student Success* (Thousand Oaks, CA: Corwin, 2002).

[86] Fred S. Keller, "Good-Bye Teacher," *Journal of Applied Behavioral Analysis* (April 1968), 79–84.

[87] Margaret C. Wang and Herbert J. Walberg (eds.), *Adapting Instruction to Individual Differences* (Berkeley, CA: McCutchan, 1985); also see Margaret C. Wang (ed.), *The Handbook of Adaptive Instruction* (Baltimore: Paul Brooks, 1992).

88 Mary A. Gunter, Thomas H. Estes, Jan Schwab, and Christine Hasbrouck Chaille, *Instruction: A Models Approach*, 4th ed. (Boston: Allyn & Bacon, 2003); Deborah B. Strother, "Adapting Instruction to Individual Needs," *Phi Delta Kappan* (December 1985), 308–311; also see Robert E. Slavin et al., *Preventing Early School Failure* (Needham Heights, MA: Allyn & Bacon, 1993).

89 Marsha Ironsmith and Marion A. Eppler, "Mastery Learning Benefits Low-Aptitude Students," *Teaching of Psychology* 34, no. 1 (2007), 28–31; John B. Carroll, "A Model of School Learning," *Teacher's College Record* (May 1963), 723–733.

90 John B. Carroll, "The Carroll Model: A 25-Year Retrospective and Prospective View," *Educational Researcher* (January–February 1989), 26–31; Robert E. Slavin, "Mastery Learning Reconsidered," *Review of Educational Research* (Summer 1987), 175–214.

91 James H. Block, *Mastery Learning: Theory and Practice* (New York: Holt, Rinehart and Winston, 1971); Benjamin Bloom, *Human Characteristics and School Learning* (New York: McGraw-Hill, 1976); Benjamin Bloom, *All Our Children Learning* (New York: McGraw-Hill, 1981).

92 James Block and Robert Burns, "Mastery Learning," in Lee S. Shulman (ed.), *Review of Research in Education, volume 4* (Itasca, IL: Peacock, 1976), 118–145; also see James Block, Helen Efthim, and Robert Burns, *Building Effective Mastery Learning Schools* (New York: Longman, 1989).

93 Marsha Ironsmith and Marion A. Eppler, "Mastery Learning Benefits Low-Aptitude Students," *Teaching Psychology* 34, no. 1 (2007), 28–31; Thomas R. Guskey, "Helping Students Make the Grade," *Educational Leadership* (September 2001), 20–27; Daniel U. Levine, "Creating Effective Schools," *Phi Delta Kappan* (January 1991), 394–397; Daniel U. Levine and Allan C. Ornstein, "Reforms That Can Work," *American School Board Journal* (June 1993), 31–34.

94 Mary Ann Raywid, "Accountability: What's Worth Measuring?" *Phi Delta Kappan* (February 2002), 433–436; Allan C. Ornstein, "Comparing and Contrasting Norm-Reference Tests and Criterion-Reference Tests," *NASSP Bulletin* (October 1993), 28–39; Blaine R. Worthen and Vicki Spandel, "Putting the Standardized Test Debate in Perspective," *Educational Leadership* (February 1991), 65–70.

95 Marshal Arlin, "Time, Equality, and Mastery Learning," *Review of Educational* Research (Spring 1984), 65–86; Arlin, "Time Variability in Mastery Learning," *American Educational Research Journal* (Spring 1984), 103–120; Kevin Castner, Lorraine Costella, and Steven Hass, "Moving from Seat Time to Mastery," *Educational Leadership* (September 1993), 45–50.

96 Arthur K. Ellis and Jeffrey T. Fouts, *Research on Educational Innovations* (Larchmont, NY: Eye on Education, 1997).

Chapter 7

1 Richard T. Scarpaci, *Resource Methods for Managing K–12 Instruction: A Case Study Approach* (Boston: Allyn & Bacon, 2009).

2 The annual poll is published in the September or October issue of *Phi Delta Kappan*.

3 *Public and K–12 Teacher Members*, Washington, DC: National Education Association, 1993.

4 *Teaching Interrupted: Do Discipline Policies in Today's Schools Foster the Common Good?* (May, 2004). Prepared by Public Agenda with support from Common Good, http://www.publicagenda.org.

5 Ibid.

6 Daniel L. Duke and Adrienne M. Meckel, *Teacher's Guide to Classroom Management* (New York: Random House, 1984), 23; Ronald C. Martella, J. Ron Nelson, Nancy E. Marchand-Martella, and Ronald Nelson, *Managing Disruptive Behavior in the Schools: A Schoolwide, Classroom and Individualized Social Learning Approach* (Boston: Allyn & Bacon, 2002).

7 Paul Chance, *The Teacher's Craft: The 10 Essential Skills of Effective Teaching* (Long Grove, IL: Waveland), 131.

8 Lee Canter and Marlene Canter, *Assertive Discipline: Positive Behavior Management for Today's Classroom* (Bloomington, IN: Solution Tree Press, 2010). See also Lee Canter et al., *First Class Teacher: Success Strategies for New Teachers* (Santa Monica, CA: Canter and Associates, 1998).

9 Thomas J. Lasley, "A Teacher Development Model for Classroom Management," *Phi Delta Kappan* (September 1989), 36–38.

10 Canter and Canter, *Assertive Discipline*.

11 Chance, *The Teacher's Craft*; Scarpaci, *A Case Study Approach to Classroom Management*.

[12] Carolyn M. Evertson et al., *Classroom Management for Elementary Teachers* (Boston: Allyn & Bacon, 2006); Edmund T. Emmer et al., *Classroom Management for Secondary Teachers* (Boston: Allyn & Bacon, 2003).

[13] Ibid.; Chance, *The Teacher's Craft.*

[14] Johns, E., Beverly, H., Crowley, Paula, and Guetzloe, Eleanor, "Engaged Time in the Classroom," *Focus on Exceptional Children* 4, no. 4 (December 2008).

[15] Allan C. Ornstein, "Emphasis on Student Outcomes Focuses Attention on Quality of Instruction," *NASSP Bulletin* (January 1987), 88–95; Allan C. Ornstein, "Teacher Effectiveness Research: Theoretical Considerations," in H. Waxman and H. J. Walberg (eds.), *Effective Teaching: Current Research* (Berkeley, CA: McCutchan, 1991), 63–80.

[16] Ibid.

[17] Chance, *The Teacher's Craft*, 129.

[18] Scarpaci, *A Case Study Approach to Classroom Management.*

[19] Paul Chance, *First Course in Applied Behavioral Analysis* (Long Grove, IL: Waveland, 2006); Albert Bandura, *Principles of Behavioral Modification* (New York: Holt, Rinehart and Winston, 1969); Albert Bandura, *Social Foundations of Thought and Action: A Social-Cognitive Theory* (Englewood Cliffs, NJ: Prentice-Hall, 1986).

[20] Burrhus F. Skinner, "The Evolution of Behavior," *Journal of Experimental Analysis of Behavior* (March 1984), 217–222; B. F. Skinner, "Cognitive Science and Behaviorism," *British Journal of Psychology* (August 1985), 291–301.

[21] Paul R. Burden, *Classroom Management: Creating a Successful K–12 Learning Community* (New York: John Wiley, 2009); Paul A. Schutz, "Facilitating Self-Regulation in the Classroom," paper presented at the annual meeting of the American Educational Research Association, New Orleans, April 1994.

[22] Jack Snowman, Robert F. Biehler, and Curtis J. Bank, *Psychology Applied to Teaching* (Boston: Houghton Mifflin, 2000).

[23] Carol M. Charles, *Building Classroom Discipline* (New York: Longman, 1999).

[24] Albert Bandura et al., "Representing Personal Determinants in Causal Structures," *Journal of Personality and Social Psychology* (June 1985), 406–414; Virginia W. Benninger and Robert D. Abbott, "The Unit of Analysis and the Constructive Process of the Learner," *Educational Psychologist* (Winter 1992), 223–242; B. F. Skinner, "The Evaluation of Verbal Behavior," *Journal of Experimental Analysis of Behavior* (January 1986), 115–122.

[25] Raymond G. Miltenberger, *Behavior Modification Principles and Procedures* (Belmont, CA: Wadsworth, 2007).

[26] Jacob S. Kounin, *Discipline and Group Management in Classroom* (New York: Holt, Rinehart and Winston, 1970); Kounin, *Discipline and Classroom Management* (New York: Holt, Rinehart and Winston, 1977).

[27] Paul R. Burden, *Classroom Management: Creating a Successful K–12 Learning Community* (New York: John Wiley, 2009).

[28] Scarpaci, *A Case Study Approach to Classroom Management.*

[29] Rudolph Dreikurs, *Psychology in the Classroom* (New York: Harper & Row, 1968); Rudolph Dreikurs and Pearl Cassel, *Discipline without Tears* (New York: Dutton, 1988).

[30] Rudolph Dreikurs, Bernice B. Grunwalk, and Floyd C. Pepper, *Maintaining Sanity in the Classroom* (New York: Harper & Row, 1982); Rudolph Dreikurs and Loren Grey, *The New Approach to Discipline: Logical Consequences* (New York: Dutton, 1988); Rudolph Dreikurs, *Children: The Challenge* (New York: Plume/Penguin, 1993).

[31] Scarpaci, *A Case Study Approach to Classroom Management.*

[32] William W. Glasser, *Reality Therapy: A New Approach to Psychiatry* (New York: Harper & Row, 1965); William W. Glasser, *The Quality School: Managing Students without Coercion* (New York: HarperCollins, 1998).

[33] Scarpaci, *A Case Study Approach to Classroom Management.*

[34] William W. Glasser, *School without Failure* (New York: Harper & Row, 1969); Glasser, *The Quality School.*

[35] William W. Glasser, *Counseling with Choice Theory: The New Reality Therapy* (Chatsworth, CA: Black Forest Press, 2001); The William Glasser Institute website (http://www.wglasser.com).

[36] William W. Glasser, *Control Theory in the Classroom* (New York: Harper & Row, 1986).

[37] Ibid.

[38] Glasser, *The Quality School*; Glasser, *Every Student Can Succeed* (Chatsworth, CA: Black Forest Press, 2000).

[39] Evertson et al., *Classroom Management for Elementary Teachers.*

[40] Burden, *Classroom Management.*

[41] Vernon F. Jones and Louise S. Jones, *Comprehensive Classroom Management: Creating Positive Learning Environments for All Students* (New York: Prentice-Hall, 2010).

[42] Thomas L. Good and Jere E. Brophy, *Contemporary Educational Psychology* (New York: Longman, 1995); Good and Brophy, *Looking in Classrooms,* 10th ed. (Upper Saddle River, NJ: Pearson Education, 2008).

[43] Bob Algozzine and Pam Kay, *Preventing Problem Behavior* (Thousand Oaks, CA: Corwin, 2002); Tom V. Savage, *Teaching Self-Control through Management and Discipline* (Needham Heights, MA: Allyn & Bacon, 1999).

[44] Merlin C. Wittrock, Christopher M. Clark, and Penelope L. Peterson, *Students' Thought Processes/ Teachers' Thought Processes* (New York: Macmillan, 1990); Christopher M. Clark and Penelope L. Peterson, "Teachers' Thought Processes," in M. C. Wittrock (ed.), *Handbook of Research on Teaching* (New York: Macmillan, 1986), 255–296; Bud Wellington, "The Promise of Reflective Practice," *Educational Leadership* (March 1991), 4–5.

[45] Ornstein, "Techniques and Fundamentals for Teaching the Disadvantaged"; Ornstein, "Teaching the Disadvantaged"; Allan C. Ornstein, "A Difference Teachers Make: How Much?" *Educational Forum* (Fall 1984), 109–117. Also see Joseph E. Williams, "Principles of Discipline," *American School Board Journal* (February 1993), 27–209.

[46] David W. Johnson, *Reaching Out: Interpersonal Effectiveness and Self-Actualization* (Needham Heights, MA: Allyn & Bacon, 2008).

[47] Chance, *The Teacher's Craft,* 71.

[48] Anne Gregory and Michael B. Ripski, "Adolescent Trust in Teachers: Implications for Behavior in the High School Classroom," *School Psychology Review* 37, no. 3, 337–353.

[49] Katherine C. Powell and Cody J. Kalina, "Cognitive and Social Constructivism: Developing Tools for an Effective Classroom," *Education* 130, no. 2 (2009), 241–250; Thomas S. C. Farrell, *Talking, Listening, and Teaching: A Guide to Classroom Communication* (Thousand Oaks, CA: Corwin, 2009).

[50] Johnson, *Reaching Out.*

[51] Elliot Aronson, *Nobody Left to Hate* (New York: Holt Paperbacks, 2001).

[52] ABC News, *Prime Time Live* (April 4, 1998).

[53] John Kehe, "It's 8 A.M., and Everything Is Not Under Control," *Christian Science Monitor* (October 8, 2002), http://ccmonitor.com/2002/1008/14s01-lecl.html.

Chapter 8

[1] See Common Core State Standards Initiative, http://www.corestandards.org/

[2] Ibid.

[3] E. D. Hirsch, "First Do No Harm," *Education Week* 29, no. 17 (January 14, 2010), 29.

[4] E. D. Hirsch, *The Making of Americans: Democracy and Our Schools* (Yale University Press, 2009).

[5] Matthew Gandal and Jennifer Vranek, "Standards: Here Today, Here Tomorrow," *Educational Leadership* (September 2001), 7–13.

[6] Ibid.

[7] See, for example, Marge Scherer, "How and Why Standards Can Improve Student Achievement," *Educational Leadership* (September 2001), 14–18.

[8] Ibid.

[9] Diane Ravitch, "We've Always Had National Standards," *Education Week* 29, no. 17 (January 14, 2010), 28.

[10] Stanley Pogrow, "Teaching Content Outrageously," in Allan C. Ornstein, Edward F. Pajak, and Stacey B. Ornstein (eds.), *Contemporary Issues in Curriculum,* 5th ed. (Upper Saddle River, NY: Pearson, 2011); Donald C. Orlich, Robert J. Harder, Richard C. Callahan and Michael S. Trevisan,

Teaching Strategies: A Guide to Effective Instruction (Boston: Wadsworth/Cengage, 2010); Robert Sternberg, Bruce Torff, and Elena Grigorenko, "Teaching for Successful Intelligence Raises Achievement," *Phi Delta Kappan* (May, 1998), 667–669.

[11] David R. Krathwohl, *Methods of Educational and Social Science Research*, 3rd ed. (Long Grove, IL: Waveland, 2009).

[12] Ibid.

[13] Jum C. Nunnally, "Reliability of Measurement," in M. C. Wittrock (ed.), *Encyclopedia of Educational Research*, 5th ed. (New York: Macmillan, 1982), 1589–1601; Ross E. Traub and Glenn L. Rowley, "Understanding Reliability," *Educational Measurement* (Spring 1991), 37–45.

[14] John Sylvia and James Ysseldyke, *Assessment*, 11th ed. (Belmont, CA: Wadsworth, 2009).

[15] William A. Mehrens and Irvin J. Lehmann, *Using Standardized Tests in Education* (New York: Longman, 1987), 64–65.

[16] Richard T. Scarpaci, *Resource Methods for Managing K–12 Instruction: A Case Study Approach* (Boston: Pearson, 2009).

[17] James H. McMillan, *Assessment Essentials for Standards-Based Education* (Thousand Oaks, CA: Corwin, 2008); Robert L. Brennan, *Educational Measurement*, 4th ed. (Lanham, MD: Rowman & Littlefield, 2006); Samuel Messick, "Validity," in Robert L. Linn (ed.), *Educational Measurement*, 3rd ed. (New York: Macmillan, 1989), 13–103; Pamela A. Moss, "Shifting Conceptions of Validity in Educational Measurement," *Review of Educational Research* (Fall, 1992), 229–258.

[18] M. David Miller, Robert L. Linn and Norman E. Gronlund, *Measurement and Assessment in Teaching*, 10th ed. (Upper Saddle River, NJ: Prentice-Hall, 2008); Tom Kubiszyn and Gary Borich, *Educational Testing and Measurement: Classroom Application and Practice*, 9th ed. (New York: John Wiley and Sons, 2007).

[19] Robert M. Thorndike and Tracy M. Thorndike-Christ, *Measurement and Evaluation in Psychology and Education*, 8th ed. (Needham Heights, MA: Allyn & Bacon, 2010); Miller, Linn and Gronlund, *Measurement and Assessment in Teaching*.

[20] N. L. Gage and David C. Berliner, *Educational Psychology*, 6th ed. (Boston: Houghton Mifflin, 1998).

[21] Peter W. Airasian, "Perspectives on Measurement Instruction," *Educational Measurement* (Spring 1991), 13–16; Herbert C. Rudman, "Classroom Instruction and Tests," *NASSP Bulletin* (February 1987), 3–22; Robert E. Stake, "The Teacher, Standardized Testing and Prospects of Revolution," *Phi Delta Kappan* (November 1991), 241–247; Lorrie R. Gay, Peter W. Airasian, Peter Airasian, and Geoff Mills, *Educational Research: Competencies for Analysis and Applications* (Upper Saddle River, NJ: Prentice-Hall, 2008).

[22] Scarpaci, *Resource Methods for Managing K–12 Instruction*, 217.

[23] Ronald K. Hambleton et al., "Criterion-Referenced Testing and Measurement: A Review of Technical Issues and Developments," *Review of Educational Research* (Winter 1988), 1–47; Robert L. Linn, "Educational Testing and Assessment," *American Psychologist* (October 1985\6), 1153–1160; Grant Wiggins, "Creating Tests Worth Taking," *Educational Leadership* (May 1992), 26–34.

[24] Norman E. Gronlund and Robert L. Linn, *Measurement and Evaluation in Teaching*, 10th ed. (Upper Saddle River, NJ: Prentice-Hall, 2008).

[25] Sylvia and Ysseldyke, *Assessment*.

[26] See http://nces.ed.gov./nationsreportcard/about/state.asp 12/4/2002.

[27] Ibid.

[28] Peter W. Airasian, "Teacher Assessments," *NASSP Bulletin* (October 1993), 55–65; Allan C. Ornstein, "Accountability Report from the USA," *Journal of Curriculum Studies* (December 1985), 437–439; Allan C. Ornstein, "Teaching and Teacher Accountability," in Allan C. Ornstein et al., *Contemporary Issues in Curriculum* (Boston: Allyn & Bacon, 2003), 248–261.

[29] Robert J. Drummond, *Appraisal Procedures for Counselors and Helping Professionals* (Upper Saddle River, NJ: Merrill/Prentice-Hall, 2000).

[30] W. James Popham, *Modern Educational Measurement*, 3rd ed. (Needham Heights, MA: Allyn & Bacon, 1999).

[31] William A. Mehrens, "Educational Tests: Blessing or Curse?" Unpublished manuscript, 1987; Mehrens, "Facts About Samples, Fantasies, and Domains," *Educational Measurement* (Summer 1991), 23–25.

32 Claudia Meek, "Classroom Crisis: It's About Time," *Phi Delta Kappan* 84, no. 8 (April, 2003), 592–595; William A. Mehrens and Irvin J. Lehmann, "Using Teacher-Made Measurement Devices," *NASSP Bulletin* (February 1987), 36–44; W. James Popham, "Can High-Stakes Tests Be Developed at the Local Level?" *NASSP Bulletin* (February 1987), 77–84.

33 Margaret Fleming and Barbara Chambers, "Teacher-Made Tests: Windows in the Classroom," in W. E. Hathaway (ed.), *Testing in Schools* (San Francisco: Jossey-Bass, 1983), 29–38; Richard J. Stiggins, "Relevant Classroom Assessment Training for Teachers," *Educational Measurement* 10, no. 1 (March, 1991), 7–12.

34 Scarpaci, *Resource Methods for Managing K–12 Instruction.*

35 Thorndike and Thorndike-Christ, *Measurement and Evaluation in Psychology and Education*; Robert L. Ebel and David A. Frisbie, *Essentials of Educational Measurement*, 5th ed. (Needham Heights, MA: Allyn & Bacon, 1991).

36 William A. Mehrens and Irvin J. Lehmann, *Measurement and Evaluation in Education and Psychology.* The fifth point is mainly based on the author's ideas about testing students at various ages.

37 John Painter, *Writing and Reviewing Assessment Items: Guidelines and Tips*, Family and Children's Resource Program, University of North Carolina–Chapel Hill, 2004, http://www.unc.edu/~painter/docs/TestPreparation.pdf.

38 Ibid.

39 David A. Payne, *Measuring and Evaluating Educational Outcomes* (New York: Macmillan, 1992).

40 Thorndike and Thorndike-Christ, *Measurement and Evaluation in Psychology and Education*; Kenneth D. Hopkins, Julian C. Stanley, and B. R. Hopkins, *Educational and Psychological Measurement and Evaluation*, 8th ed. (Needham Heights, MA: Allyn & Bacon, 1998).

41 Benjamin S. Bloom, J. Thomas Hastings, and George F. Madaus, *Evaluation to Improve Learning* (New York: McGraw-Hill, 1981); George K. Cunningham, *Educational and Psychological Measurement*, 2nd ed. (New York: Macmillan, 1992).

42 Robert L. Ebel and David A. Frisbie, *Essentials of Educational Measurement*, 5th ed. (Upper Saddle River, NJ: Prentice-Hall, 1991), 164–165.

43 Gage and Berliner, *Educational Psychology*; W. James Popham, *Educational Evaluation*, 3rd. ed. (Needham Heights, MA: Allyn & Bacon, 1993).

44 Bruce W. Tuckman, "Evaluating the Alternative to Multiple-Choice Testing for Teachers," *Contemporary Education* (Summer 1991), 299–300.

45 Allan C. Ornstein, "Questioning: The Essence of Good Teaching," *NASSP Bulletin* (February 1988), 72–80; Barak V. Rosenshine and Carla Meister, "The Use of Scaffolds for Teaching Higher-Level Cognitive Strategies," *Educational Leadership* (April 1992), 26–33.

46 Penelope L. Peterson, "Toward an Understanding of What We Know about School Learning," *Review of Educational Research* (Fall 1993), 319–326; Francis P. Hunkins, *Teaching Thinking through Effective Questioning*, 2nd ed. (Needham Heights, MA: Gordon, 1995).

47 Gronlund and Linn, *Measurement and Evaluation in Teaching.*

48 Peter W. Airasian, *Classroom Assessment: Concepts and Applications*, 6th ed. (Boston: McGraw-Hill, 2007).

49 Gavin T. L. Brown, "The Validity of Examination Essays in Higher Education: Issues and Responses," *Higher Education Quarterly* 64, no. 3 (July 2010), 276–291; James Hartley, Mark Trueman, Lucy Betts, and Lauren Brodie, "What Price Presentation? The Effects of Typographic Variables on Essay Grades," *Assessment & Evaluation in Higher Education* 31, no. 5 (October 2006), 523–534; Ray Bull and Julia Stevens, "The Effects of Attractiveness of Writer and Penmanship on Essay Grades," *Journal of Occupational Psychology* (April 1979), 53–59; Jon C. Marshall and Jerry M. Powers, "Writing Neatness, Composition Errors, and Essay Grades," *Journal of Educational Measurement* (Summer 1969), 97–101.

50 Bruce W. Tuckman, "The Essay Test: A Look at the Advantages and Disadvantages," *NASSP Bulletin* (October 1993), 20–27.

51 Robert Sommer and Barbara A. Sommer, "The Dreaded Essay Exam," *Teaching of Psychology* 36 (2009), 197–199.

52 Most authorities (e.g., Ebel, Gronlund, and Payne) recommend that students answer all questions and that no choice be provided because a common set of questions tends to increase reliability in scoring, while options tend to distort results. However, weighed against this advantage is the fact

that being able to select an area they know well increases students' morale, reduces test anxiety, and gives them a greater chance to show they can organize and interpret the subject matter.

53 Gunter Maris, "Detecting Halo Effects in Performance-Based Examinations," *Applied Psychological Measurement* (July 16, 2010); Benoit Dompnier, Pascal Pansu, and Pascal Bressour, "An Integrative Model of Scholastic Judgments: Pupil's Characteristics, Class Context, Halo Effect and Internal Attributions," *European Journal of Psychology of Education* 21, no. 2, 119–133.

54 Pennsylvania State University, Guidelines for Question Writing (2008), http://ets.tlt.psu.edu/learningdesign/effective_questions/minute_essay.

55 L. Darling-Hammond, "The Implications of Testing Policy for Quality and Equality, *Phi Delta Kappan* 73, no. 3 (November, 1991), 220–225; George F. Madaus, "The Effects of Important Tests on Students," *Phi Delta Kappan* 73, no. 3 (1991), 226–231.

56 Jim Knight, *Coaching: Approaches and Perspectives* (Thousand Oaks, CA: Corwin, 2009); Henry S. Dyer, "The Effects of Coaching for Scholastic Aptitude," *NASSP Bulletin* (February 1987), 46–53; Samuel Messick, "Issue and Equity in the Coaching Controversy: Implications for Educational Testing and Practice," *Educational Psychologist* (Summer 1982), 67–91.

57 Stephen N. Elliot, Jeffrey P. Braden, Jennifer L. White, *Assessing One and All* (Arlington, VA: Council for Exceptional Children, 2001), 115.

58 Ibid.

59 Patricia Davenport and Gerald Anderson, *Closing the Achievement Gap: No Excuses* (Houston, TX: American Productivity and Quality Center, 2002), 88.

60 Dale D. Johnson and Bonnie Johnson, *High Stakes: Children, Testing, and Failure in American Schools* (Lanham, MD: Rowman and Littlefield, 2002); Jane Canner, "Regaining the Public Trust: A Review of School Testing Programs, Practices," *NASSP Bulletin* (September 1992), 6–15.

61 Thomas J. Huberty, "Test and Performance Anxiety," *Education Digest* 75, no. 9 (May 2010), 34–38; Adelaide M. Nicholson, "Effects of Test Anxiety on Student Achievement (ACT) for College Bound Students," PhD diss., Trevecca Nazarene University, 2009; Michael T. Miesner and Ruth H. Maki, "The Role of Test Anxiety in Absolute and Relative Metacomprehension Accuracy," *The European Journal of Cognitive Psychology* 19, no. 4–5, 650–670.

62 M. Zeidner, "Test Anxiety in Educational Contexts: Concepts, Findings, and Future Directions," in Paul A. Schutz and Reinhard Pekrun (eds.), *Emotion in Education* (San Diego, CA: Academic Press, 2007), 165–184.

63 Ray Hembree, "Correlates, Causes, Effects and Treatments of Test Anxiety," *Review of Educational Research* (Spring 1988), 47–77.

64 Susan B. Nolan, Thomas M. Haladyna, and Nancy S. Hass, "Uses and Abuses of Achievement Tests," *Educational Measurement* (Summer 1992), 9–15.

65 Dubi Lufi, Susan Okasha, and Aric Cohen, "Test Anxiety and its Effect on the Personality of Students with Learning Disabilities," *Learning Disability Quarterly* 27, no. 3 (2004), 176–184.

66 Robert Sommer and Barbara A. Sommer, "The Dreaded Essay Exam," *Teaching of Psychology* 36 (2009), 197–199.

67 Gregory J. Cizek and Samantha S. Burg, *Addressing Test Anxiety in a High-Stakes Environment: Strategies for Classrooms and Schools* (Thousand Oaks, CA: Corwin, 2005).

68 Nancy S. Hass, *Standardized Testing in Arizona*, Technical Report 89-3 (Phoenix: Arizona State University West, 1989).

69 Cizek and Burg, *Addressing Test Anxiety in a High-Stakes Environment.*

70 Marshall L. Smith et al., "Put to the Test: The Effects of External Testing on Teachers," *Educational Researcher* (November 1991), 8–11; Nolan, "Uses and Abuses of Achievement Tests."

71 Hembree, "Correlates, Causes, Effects and Treatments of Test Anxiety."

72 Heidi A. Larson, Mera K. El Ramahi, Steven R. Conn, et al., "Reducing Text Anxiety among Third Grade Students through the Implementation of Relaxation Techniques," *Journal of School Counseling* 8 (2010), 1–19; Gina Paul, Barb Elam, and Steven J. Verhulst, "A Longitudinal Study of Students' Perceptions of Using Deep Breathing Mediation to Reduce Testing Stresses," *Teaching and Learning in Medicine* 19, no. 3, (2007), 287–292.

73 Jeanne Ellis Ormrod, *Educational Psychology: Developing Learners,* 7th ed. (Boston: Allyn & Bacon, 2011).

74 Linda Darling-Hammond, *Performance Counts: Assessment Systems that Support High-Quality Learning* (Washington, DC: Council of Chief State School Officers, 2010), http://www.ccsso.org/Documents/2010/Performance_Counts_Assessment_Systems_2010.pdf; Darling-Hammond, "The Case for Authentic Assessment," *NASSP Bulletin* (November 1993), 18–26; Lorrie A. Shepard, "Psychometrician's Beliefs about Learning," *Educational Researcher* (October 1991), 2–15.

75 Daniel Koretz, *Measuring Up: What Educational Testing Really Tells Us* (Cambridge, MA: Harvard University Press, 2008); Grant Wiggins, "Teaching to the (Authentic) Test," *Educational Leadership* (April 1989), 41–47; Wiggins, "Creating Tests Worth Taking," Wiggins, *Assessing Student Performance: Exploring the Purpose and Limits of Testing* (San Francisco: Jossey-Bass, 1999).

76 Kenneth T. Henson, *Curriculum Planning: Integrating Multiculturalism, Constructivism, and Education Reform*, 4th ed. (Long Grove, IL: Waveland, 2010).

77 John Zubizarreta and Barbara J. Mills, *The Learning Portfolio: Reflective Practice for Improving Student Learning* (New York: John Wiley and Sons, 2009); F. Leon Paulson, Pearl R. Paulson, and Carol A. Meyer, "What Makes a Portfolio a Portfolio," *Educational Leadership* (February 1991), 60–63.

78 Kay Burke, *How to Assess Authentic Learning*, 5th ed. (Thousand Oaks, CA: Corwin, 2009).

79 Elizabeth Meyer, Philip C. Abrami, C. Anne Wade, et al., "Improving Literacy and Metacognition with Electronic Portfolios," *Computers & Education* 5, no. 1 (August 2010), 84–91. See also Helen C. Barrett, "Researching Electronic Portfolios and Learner Engagement: The REFLECT Initiative, *Journal of Adolescent & Adult Literacy* 50, no. 6 (March, 2007), 436–439; Pete Adamy and Natalie B. Milman (eds.), *Evaluating Electronic Portfolios in Teacher Education* (Charlotte, NC: Information Age, 2009).

80 Ted Sizer, *Horace's School* (Boston: Houghton Mifflin, 1992), 25.

81 Edutopia staff, "Why Teach with Project-Based Learning?: Providing Students with a Well-Rounded Classroom Experience" (2008), http://www.edutopia.org/project-learning-introduction.

82 Ibid.

83 Burke, *How to Assess Authentic Learning*, 169–170.

84 Marc Tucker and Judy B. Codding, *Standards for Our Schools* (San Francisco, CA: Jossey-Bass, 2002).

Chapter 9

1 Kay Burke, *How to Assess Authentic Learning*, 5th ed. (Thousand Oaks, CA: Corwin, 2009).

2 Philip W. Jackson, *Life in Classrooms,* 2nd ed. (New York: Teachers College Press, Columbia University, 1990), 19.

3 Richard D. Kellough, *A Resource Guide for Teaching K–12,* 5th ed. (Needham Heights, MA: Allyn & Bacon, 2010).

4 Richard T. Scarpaci, *Resource Methods for Managing K–12 Instruction: A Case Study Approach* (Boston: Allyn & Bacon, 2009), 214.

5 Bruce W. Tuckman, *Measuring Educational Outcomes*, 2nd ed. (San Diego: Harcourt Brace Jovanovich, 1985), 300; also see Bruce W. Tuckman, "The Essay Test: A Look at the Advantages and Disadvantages," *NASSP Bulletin* (October 1993), 20–27.

6 M. David Miller, Robert L. Linn, and Norman E. Gronlund, *Measurement and Evaluation in Teaching*, 10th ed. (Upper Saddle River, NJ: Prentice-Hall, 2008).

7 Jeanne Ellis Ormrod, *Essentials of Educational Psychology,* 7th ed. (Upper Saddle River, NJ: Prentice-Hall, 2010); Ormrod, *Educational Psychology: Developing Learners*, 7th ed. (Boston: Allyn & Bacon, 2011).

8 Michael Scriven, "The Methodology of Evaluation," in R. W. Tyler, R. Gagne, and M. Scriven (eds.), *Perspectives on Curriculum Evaluation* (Chicago: Rand McNally, 1967), 39–83.

9 Benjamin S. Bloom, J. Thomas Hastings, and George F. Madaus, *Handbook on Formative and Summative Evaluation of Student Learning* (New York: McGraw-Hill, 1971), 20.

10 Paul Black and Dylan Wiliam, "Developing the Theory of Formative Assessment," *Educational Assessment, Evaluation and Accountability* 21, no. 1 (2008), 5–31; Black and Wiliam, "Inside the Black Box: Raising Standards through Classroom Assessment," *Phi Delta Kappan* (October 1998), 140.

[11] Robert M. Thorndike and Tracy M. Thorndike-Christ, *Measurement and Evaluation in Psychology and Education*, 8th ed. (Needham Heights, MA: Allyn & Bacon); Norman E. Gronlund, *How to Make Achievements Tests and Assessments*, 5th ed. (Needham Heights, MA: Allyn & Bacon, 1993).

[12] Nancy S. Cole, "Conceptions of Educational Achievement," *Educational Researcher* (April 1990), 2–7; Penelope L. Peterson, "Toward an Understanding of What We Know about School Learning," *Review of Educational Research* (Fall 1993), 319–326; W. James Popham, "Why Standardized Tests Don't Measure Educational Quality," *Educational Leadership* (March 1999), 8–15.

[13] James H. McMillan and Jessica Hearn, "Student Self-Assessment; The Key to Stronger Student Motivation and Higher Achievement," *Educational Horizons* 87, no. 1 (Fall 2008), 40–49.

[14] Benjamin S. Bloom, George F. Madaus, and J. Thomas Hastings, *Evaluation to Improve Learning* (New York: McGraw-Hill, 1981); Tom Kubiszyn and Gary Borich, *Educational Testing and Measurement*, 9th ed. (Hoboken, NJ: Wiley, 2009); Merlin C. Wittrock and Eva L. Baker, *Testing and Cognition* (Needham Heights, MA: Allyn & Bacon, 1991).

[15] Vicki Todd and Jerry C. Hudson, "Using Graded Peer Evaluation to Improve Students' Writing Skills, Critical Thinking Ability, and Comprehension of Material in a Principles of Public Relations Course," *Journal of College Teaching & Learning* 4, no. 10 (2007).

[16] Jan La Bonty and Kathy Everts-Danielson, "Alternative Assessment and Feedback in Methods Courses," *Clearing House* (January–February 1992), 186–190; Allan C. Ornstein, "Assessing Without Testing," *Elementary Principal* (January 1994), 16–18.

[17] David W. Johnson, David R. Johnson, and Frank P. Johnson, *Joining Together: Group Theory and Group Skills*, 10th ed. (Upper Saddle River, NJ: Merrill, 2009).

[18] Black and Wiliam, "Inside the Black Box," 143–144.

[19] Herbert J. Walberg, "Homework's Powerful Effects on Learning," *Educational Leadership* (April 1985), 75–79; Melanie F. Sikorski, Richard P. Niemiec, and Herbert J. Walberg, "Best Teaching Practices," *NASSP Bulletin* (April 1994), 50–54.

[20] Thomas L. Good and Jere E. Brophy, *Looking in Classrooms*, 10th ed. (Upper Saddle River, NJ: Pearson Education, 2008).

[21] Harris Cooper, *The Battle Over Homework: Common Ground for Administrators, Teachers, and Parents*, 3rd ed. (Thousand Oaks, CA: Corwin, 2007).

[22] Alfie Kohn, *The Homework Myth: Why Our Kids Get Too Much of a Bad Thing* (Cambridge: Da Capo, 2006); Richard J. Marzano and D. J. Pickering, "The Case For and Against Homework," *Educational Leadership* 64, no. 6 (March 2007), 74–79; Kohn, "Abusing Research: The Study of Homework and Other Examples," *Phi Delta Kappan* 88, no. 1 (September 2006), 8–22; Marzano and Pickering, "Errors and Allegations about Research on Homework," *Phi Delta Kappan* 88, no. 7 (March 2007), 507–513.

[23] Carol Ann Tomlinson, "Invitations to Learn," *Educational Leadership* (September 2002), 6–11; Mary Ross Moran, Brenda Smith Myles, and Marilyn S. Shank, "Variables in Eliciting Writing Samples," *Educational Measurement* (Fall 1991), 23–26.

[24] Kenneth A. Kiewra, "Providing the Instructor's Notes: An Effective Addition to Student Note-Taking," *Educational Psychologist* (Winter 1985), 33–39; Kiewra, "Aids to Lecture Learning," *Educational Psychologist* (Winter 1991), 37–53.

[25] Maureen McLaughlin and Mary Beth Allen, *Guided Comprehension: A Teaching Model for Grades 3–8*, 2nd ed. (Newark, DE: International Reading Association, 2009).

[26] Kieran Egan, "Start With What the Student Knows or With What the Student Can Imagine," *Phi Delta Kappan* (February 2003), 443–445; Allison Zmuda and Mary Tomaino, "A Contract for the High School Classroom," *Educational Leadership* (March 1999), 59–61.

[27] Zmuda and Tomaino, 60.

[28] David W. Johnson and Roger J. Johnson, *Learning Together and Alone*, 5th ed. (Boston: Allyn & Bacon, 1998).

[29] Michelle K. Smith, William B. Wood, et al., "Why Peer Discussion Improves Student Performance on In-Class Concept Questions," *Science Magazine* 323, no. 59 (January, 2009), 122–124; Elizabeth G. Cohen, *Designing Groupwork* (New York: Teachers College Press, Columbia University, 1994); Peter M. Martorella, *Elementary Social Studies* (Boston: Little Brown, 1985). Also see Alfie Kohn, *What to Look for in a Classroom* (San Francisco: Jossey-Bass, 2000).

[30] Robert L. Ebel and David A. Frisbie, *Essentials of Educational Measurement*, 5th ed. (Needham Heights, MA: Allyn & Bacon, 1991), Gary Natriello and James McPartland, *Adjustments in High School Teachers' Grading Criteria* (Baltimore: Johns Hopkins University Press, 1988).

[31] Ellis D. Evans and Ruth A. Engleberg, "Student Perceptions of School Grading," *Journal of Research and Development in Education* (Winter 1988), 45–54; Mary A. Lundeberg and Paul W. Fox, "Do Laboratory Findings on Test Expectancy Generalize to Classroom Outcomes?" *Review of Educational Research* (Spring 1991), 94–106.

[32] Deborah Meier, "Standardization Versus Standards," *Phi Delta Kappan* (November 2002), 190–198; William W. Cooley, "State-Wide Student Assessment," *Educational Measurement* (Winter 1991), 3–6.

[33] Robert E. Slavin, "Classroom Reward Structure: An Analytical and Practical Review," *Review of Educational Research* (Fall 1977), 633–650; Slavin, "Synthesis of Research on Cooperative Learning," *Educational Leadership* (February 1991), 71–82.

[34] Neville Bennett and Charles Desforges, "Matching Classroom Tasks to Students' Attainments," *Elementary School Journal* (January 1988), 221–234; W. James Popham, "Appropriateness of Teachers' Test-Preparation," *Educational Measurement* (Winter 1991), 12–15; Robert E. Stake, "The Teacher, Standardized Testing, and Prospects of Revolution," *Phi Delta Kappan* (November 1991), 243–247.

[35] Marge Scherer, "Do Students Care about Learning?" *Educational Leadership* (September 2002), 12–17; Robert L. Bangert-Drowns, "The Instructional Effect of Feedback in Test-Like Events," *Review of Educational Research* (Summer 1991), 213–238; Gary Natriello and Edward L. McDill, "Performance Standards, Student Effort on Homework and Academic Achievement," *Sociology of Education* (January 1986), 18–31; Alvin C. Rose, "Homework Preferences," *NASSP Bulletin* (March 1994), 65–75.

[36] Gary Natriello, "The Impact of Evaluation Processes on Students"; Mary Nottingham, "Grading Practices—Watching Out for Land Mines," *NASSP Bulletin* (April 1988), 24–28.

[37] Robert F. Madgic, "The Point System of Grading: A Critical Appraisal," *NASSP Bulletin* (April 1988), 29–34; Margot A. Olson, "The Distortion of the Grading System," *Clearing House* (November–December 1990), 77–79.

[38] Eric Donald Hirsch, *The Schools We Need* (New York: Doubleday, 1996), 181–182.

[39] Carol Tomlinson and Jay McTighe, *Integrating Differentiated Instruction and Understanding by Design* (Alexandria, VA: ASCD, 2006).

[40] Patricia L. Scriffiny, "Seven Reasons for Standards-Based Grading: Expecting Excellence," *Educational Leadership* 66, no. 2 (October 2008).

[41] Susan A. Colby, "Grading in a Standards-Based System," *Educational Leadership* (March 1999), 52–55.

[42] Debra Vladero, "Scholars Probe Diverse Effects of Exit Exams: State Graduation Tests Found to Hit Certain Groups Harder," *Education Week* 28, no. 30 (April 2009), 1, 1–11.

[43] Gerald W. Bracey, "Mandatory Exit Exams Discourage Graduation," *Phi Delta Kappan* 91, no. 3 (November 2009), 88–89.

[44] Paul S. George, "A+ Accountability in Florida?" *Educational Leadership* (September 2001), 28–32.

[45] State Exit Exams, Alaska Department of Education & Early Development, *State High School Exams: A Baseline Report* (Washington, DC: Center on Education Policy, 2002), February 6, 2010, http://eed.alaska.gov/tls/assessment/HSGQE/HSExitExams/06StateHighSchoolExams.pdf.

[46] William A. Mehrens and Irvin J. Lehmann, *Measurement and Evaluation in Education and Psychology*, 4th ed. (Fort Worth, TX: Holt, Rinehart, and Winston, 1991); David A. Payne, *Measuring and Evaluating Educational Outcomes* (New York: Macmillan, 1992).

[47] Carole Ames, "Motivation: What Teachers Need to Know," *Teachers College Record* (Spring 1991), 409–421; Pamela A. Moss, "Shifting Consequences of Validity in Educational Measurement," *Review of Educational Research* (Fall 1992), 229–258; Lynda A. Baloche, *The Cooperative Classroom* (Columbus, OH: Prentice-Hall, 1998).

[48] Payne, *Measuring and Evaluating Educational Outcomes.*

[49] Benjamin S. Bloom, "The 2 Sigma Problem: The Search for Methods of Instruction as Effective as One-to-One Tutoring," *Educational Researcher* (June–July 1984), 4–16; Robert E. Slavin, "Group-

ing for Instruction in the Elementary School," *Educational Psychologist* (Spring 1987), 109–128; Slavin, "On Mastery Learning and Mastery Teaching," *Educational Leadership* (April 1989), 77–79.

50 James P. Lalley and J. Ronald Gentile, "Classroom Assessment and Grading to Assure Mastery," *Theory Into Practice* 48, no. 1 (January 2009), 28–35.

51 Richard Arends, *Learning to Teach*, 8th ed. (Boston: McGraw-Hill, 2009).

52 S. Alan Cohen and Joan S. Hyman, "Can Fantasies Become Facts?" *NASSP Bulletin* (Spring 1991), 20–23; George F. Madaus, "The Effect of Important Tests on Students," *Phi Delta Kappan* (November 1991), 226–231.

53 Harold Stevenson and James W. Stigler, *The Learning Gap* (New York: Summit Books, 1992), 97–98.

54 Nicholas J. Migliorino and Jeffrey Maiden, "Educator Attitudes toward Electronic Grading Software," *Journal of Research on Technology in Education* 36, no. 3 (2004), 193–212.

55 Edward L. Vockell and Donald Kopenec, "Record Keeping without Tears," *Clearing House* (April 1989), 355–359.

56 Linda Anglin, Kenneth Anglin, Paul L. Schumann, and John A. Kaliski, "Improving the Efficiency and Effectiveness of Grading through the Use of Computer-Assisted Grading Rubrics," *Decision Sciences Journal of Innovative Education* 6, no. 1 (January 2008), 51–73; Jan Lacina, "Virtual Record Keeping: Should Teachers Keep Online Grade Books?" *Child Education* (June 22, 2006), http://www.thefreelibrary.com/Virtual+record+keeping%3a+should+teachers+keep+ onli ne+grade+books%3f-a0145388358.

57 Lacina, "Virtual Record Keeping."

58 John Salvia, James Ysseldyke, and Sara Bolt, *Assessment*, 11th ed. (Belmont, CA: Wadsworth, 2009).

59 Conn Thomas, Pat Britt et al., "Portfolio Assessment: A Guide for Teachers and Administrators," *National Forum of Educational Administration and Supervision Journal–Electronic*, 2004–2005; F. Leon Paulson, Pearl R. Paulson, and Carol A. Meyer, "What Makes a Portfolio a Portfolio?" *Educational Leadership* (February 1991), 60–64; Richard J. Shavelson and Gail P. Baxter, "What We've Learned about Assessing Hands-On Science," *Educational Leadership* (May 1992), 20–25.

60 Helen C. Barrett, "Researching Electronic Portfolios and Learner Engagement: The REFLECT Initiative," *Journal of Adolescent & Adult Literacy* 50, no. 6 (March 2007), 436–499; Judith A. Arter and Vicki Spandel, "Using Portfolios of Student Work in Instruction and Assessment," *Educational Measurement* (Spring 1992), 36–44; Doris Sperling, "What's Worth an 'A'?: Setting Standards Together," *Educational Leadership* (February 1993), 73–75; Baloche, *The Cooperative Classroom*.

61 Barrett, "Researching Electronic Portfolios and Learner Engagement"; Stephen Chappuis and Richard J. Stiggins, "Classroom Assessment for Learning," *Educational Leadership* (September 2002), 40–44; Darlene M. Frazier and F. Leon Paulson, "How Portfolios Motivate Reluctant Workers," *Educational Leadership* (May 1992), 62–65.

62 Arter and Spandel, "Using Portfolios of Student Work in Instruction and Assessment"; Richard J. Stiggins, "Relevant Classroom Assessment Trainers for Teachers," *Educational Measurement* (Spring 1991), 7–12.

63 Allan C. Ornstein, "The Nature of Grading," *Clearing House* (April, 1986), 365–369.

64 Joyce L. Epstein, "Parents' Reactions to Teacher Practices of Parent Involvement," *Elementary School Journal* (January 1986), 277–294; Joyce L. Epstein, "School/Family/Community Partnerships: Caring for the Children We Share," *Phi Delta Kappan* (May 1995), 701–712.

65 Joyce L. Epstein, "How Do We Improve Programs for Parent Involvement?" *Educational Horizons* (Winter 1988), 58–59; Joyce L. Epstein, "Parent Involvement: What Research Says to Administrators," *Education and Urban Society* (February 1987), 119–36.

66 Erika A. Patall, Harris Cooper, and Jorgianne C. Robinson, "Parent Involvement in Homework: A Research Synthesis," *Review of Educational Research* 78, no. 4 (December 2008), 1039–1101.

67 Kellie J. Anderson and Kathleen M. Minke, "Parent Involvement in Education: Toward an Understanding of Parents' Decision Making, "*The Journal of Educational Research* 100, no. 5 (May–June 2007), 311–323; James P. Comer and Norris M. Haynes, "Parent Involvement in Schools," *Elementary School Journal* (January 1991), 271–277; Anne T. Henderson, "An Ecologically Balanced Approach to Academic Improvement," *Educational Horizons* (Winter 1988), 60–62; Judith A. Vandegrift and Andrea L. Greene, "Rethinking Parent Involvement," *Educational Leadership* (September 1992), 57–59; Marilyn Price-Mitchell, "Implications for Building Parent-School Partnerships," *The School Community Journal* 19, no. 2 (Fall/Winter 2009).

68 Marilyn Price-Mitchell, "Implications for Building Parent-School Partnerships," 9–11.

[69] Kenneth T. Henson, *Curriculum Planning: Integrating Multiculturalism, Constructivism, and Education Reform*, 4th ed. (Long Grove, IL: Waveland, 2010), 81–82.

[70] Leonard H. Clark and Irving S. Starr, *Secondary and Middle School Teaching Methods*, 7th ed. (New York: Prentice-Hall, 1995); Richard Kindsvatter, William Wilen, and Margaret Ishler, *Dynamics of Effective Teaching*, 4th ed. (New York: Longman, 1999).

[71] Margaret M. Ferrara, "Broadening the Myopic Vision of Parent Involvement," *The School Community Journal* (Fall/Winter 2009),127–143.

[72] William H. Jeynes, "The Relationship between Parental Involvement and Urban Secondary School Student Academic Achievement: A Meta-Analysis." *Urban Education* 42, no. 1 (2007), 82–110.

[73] Eugenia H. Berger, *Parents as Partners in Education: The School and Home Working Together*, 7th ed. (Upper Saddle River, NJ: Merrill, 2008).

[74] Allan C. Ornstein, "Parent Conferencing: Recommendations and Guidelines," *Kappa Delta Pi Record* (Winter 1990), 55–57.

[75] Alfie Kohn, "Offering Challenges, Creating Cognitive Dissonance," in J. Cynthia McDermott (ed.), *Beyond the Silence* (Portsmouth, NH: Heinemann, 1999).

[76] Penny Noyce, David Perda, Rob Traver, "Creating Data Driven Schools," *Educational Leadership* (February 2000), 52–55.

Chapter 10

[1] Kenneth T. Henson, *Curriculum Planning: Integrating Multiculturalism, Constructivism, and Education Reform*, 4th ed. (Long Grove, IL: Waveland, 2010); Richard T. Scarpaci, *Resource Methods for Managing K–12 Instruction: A Case Study Approach.* (Boston: Allyn & Bacon, 2009), 234–235.

[2] Robert J. Yinder and Amanda L. Nolen, "Surviving the Legitimacy Challenge," *Phi Delta Kappan* (January 2003), 386–390.

[3] Linda Darling-Hammond, "Teacher Education and the American Future," *Journal of Teacher Education, 61*(1-2) (2010), 35–47.

[4] Kenneth A. Sirotnik, "On the Eroding Foundations of Teacher Education," *Phi Delta Kappan* (May 1990), 714.

[5] "Improving Teacher Quality: The State of the States," *Education Week* (January 9, 2003), 90.

[6] "Quality Counts: Fresh Course, Swift Current," *Education Week* (January 14, 2010), 42.

[7] James B. Conant, *The Education of American Teachers* (New York: McGraw-Hill, 1964).

[8] James D. Koerner, *The Miseducation of American Teachers* (Boston: Houghton Mifflin, 1963).

[9] Susan Chira, "In the Drive to Revive Schools: Better Teachers but Too Few," *The New York Times* (August 2, 1990), Al, Al2; "School Administrators Report New Teachers Are Better Prepared Than Predecessors," *AACTE Briefs* (13 May 1991), 1, 8; Greg Toppo, "Teacher Qualifications Improve in the Past Decade," *USA Today* (December 12, 2007), http://www.usatoday.com/news/education/2007-12-11-teacher-qualifications_N.htm.

[10] John I. Goodlad, Roger Soder, and Kenneth Sirotnik, *Places Where Teachers Are Taught* (San Francisco: Jossey-Bass, 1990).

[11] Eric D. Hirsch, Jr., *The Schools We Need and Why We Don't Have Them* (New York: Doubleday, 1995).

[12] John I. Goodlad, *Teachers for Our Nation's Schools* (San Francisco, Jossey-Bass, 1990); Goodlad, *Educational Renewal* (San Francisco: Jossey-Bass, 1998); Linda Darling-Hammond and John Bransford (eds.), *Preparing Teachers for a Changing World* (New York: Wiley, 2005).

[13] James W. Fraser, "Preparing Teachers for Democratic Schools: The Holmes and Carnegie Reports Five Years Later," *Teachers' College Record* (Fall 1992), 7–39; James Hiebert, Anne K. Morris, Dawn Berk, and Amanda Jansen, "Preparing Teachers to Learn from Teaching," *Journal of Teacher Education* 58, no. 1 (January/February 2007), 47–61.

[14] The National Council for Accreditation of Teacher Education (NCATE), "The Standards of Excellence in Teacher Preparation," http://ncate.org/Public/AboutNCATE/QuickFacts/tabid/343/Default.aspx.

[15] Linda Darling-Hammond, "Teacher Education and the American Future"; "Meeting Teaching's Toughest Critic," *NEA Today* (April 1991), 8–9; Telephone conversation with Arthur E. Wise, Director of NCATE, March 1, 1993.

16 "Teacher-Prep Accrediting Groups to Merge," *AACTE in the News* (October 25, 2010), http://aacte.org/index.php?/Media-Center/AACTE-in-the-News/.

17 Thomas J. Lasley, II, William L. Bainbridge, and Barnett Berry, "Improving Teacher Quality: Ideological Perspectives and Policy Prescriptions," *Educational Forum* (Fall 2002), 14–25.

18 Jeanne S. Chall, *The Academic Achievement Challenge* (New York: Guilford, 2000), 182.

19 Linda Darling-Hammond, "Educating Teachers," *Academe* (January–February 1999), 29. See also Linda Darling-Hammond, D. J. Holtzman, S. J. Gatlin, & V. Heilig, *Does Teacher Preparation Matter? Evidence about Teacher Certification, Teach for America, and Teacher Effectiveness* (2005), http://www.stanford.edu/~ldh/publications.html.

20 Hilda Borko, "Research on Learning to Teach," in A. Woolfolk (ed.), *Research Perspectives on the Graduate Preparation of Teachers* (Englewood Cliffs, NJ: Allyn & Bacon, 1989), 69–87; Simon Veenman, "Perceived Problems of Beginning Teachers," *Review of Educational Research* (Summer 1984), 143–178; Sylvia M. Yee, *Careers in the Classroom: When Teaching Is More Than a Job* (New York: Teachers College Press, Columbia University, 1990).

21 The research of Richard M. Ingersoll effectively documents the teacher attrition problem. See, for example, Richard M. Ingersoll, "Teacher Turnover and Teacher Shortages," *American Educational Research Journal* (Fall 2001), 449–534.

22 Bridget Curran and Liam Goldrich, *Mentoring and Supporting New Teachers* (Education Policy Studies Division, National Governor's Association Center for Best Practices, 2002). For copies of the report contact bccurran@nga.org.

23 Erling E. Boe, Lynne H. Cook, and Robert J. Sunderland, "Attrition of Beginning Teachers: Does Teacher Preparation Matter?" *Research Report No. 2006–TSDQ2* (Center for Research and Evaluation in Social Policy, Graduate School of Education University of Pennsylvania, July 7, 2006), http://www.monarchcenter.org/pdfs/attritionboe_06.pdf.

24 Frances F. Fuller, "Concerns for Teachers," *American Educational Research Journal* (March 1969), 207–226.

25 Michael Hansen, "Career Concerns, Incentives, and Teacher Effort," University of Washington and Center on Reinventing Public Education (November 2008), www.aeaweb.org/annual_mtg_papers/2009/retrieve.php?pdfid=343.

26 Arne Duncan, "Teacher Preparation: Reforming the Uncertain Profession," *Education Digest* 75, no. 5 (2010), 13–22.

27 Carol S. Weinstein, "Preservice Teachers' Expectations About the First Year of Teaching," *Teaching and Teacher Education* 1 (1988), 31–40; Weinstein, "Prospective Elementary Teachers' Beliefs about Teaching," *Teaching and Teacher Education* 6 (1990), 279–290; Dan Brown, *The Great Expectations School: A Rookie Year in the New Blackboard Jungle* (New York: Arcade, 2007).

28 Marilyn Cochran-Smith and Susan Lytle, "Research on Teaching and Teacher Research," *Educational Researcher* (March 1990), 2–11.

29 Scott Joftus, *New Teacher Excellence: Retaining Our Best* (Washington, DC: Alliance for Excellent Education, 2002).

30 Kenneth T. Henson, *Supervision: A Collaborative Approach to Instructional Improvement* (Long Grove, IL: Waveland, 2010); William H. Kurtz, "How the Principal Can Help Beginning Teachers," *NASSP Bulletin* (January 1983), 42–45; also see Thomas J. Sergiovanni, *Building Communities in Schools* (San Francisco: Jossey-Bass, 1999).

31 Donald Boyd, Pam Grossman, Hamilton Lankford, Susanna Loeb, and James Wyckoff, "Who Leaves? Teacher Attrition and Student Achievement," *Calder Working Paper* 23 (March 2009); Diane Davis and Marjorie Leppo, *A First Class Look at Teaching* (Washington DC: Sallie Mae Education Institute, 1999).

32 Lowell C. Rose and Alec M. Gallup, "The 39th Annual Phi Delta Kappa/Gallup Poll of the Public's Attitudes toward the Public Schools," *Phi Delta Kappan* (September 2007), 33–45.

33 Allan C. Ornstein and Daniel U. Levine, "Social Class, Race, and School Achievement Problems and Prospects," *Journal of Teacher Education* 40, no. 5 (September 1989), 17–23.

34 Jennifer H. Waddell, "Fostering Relationships to Increase Teacher Retention in Urban Schools," *Journal of Curriculum and Instruction* 4, no. 1 (May, 2010), 70–85; Antonio J. Castro, John Kelly, and Minyi Shih, "Resilience Strategies for New Teachers in High-Needs Areas," *Teaching and Teacher Education* 26, no. 3 (April 2010), 622–629.

[35] Mary H. Futrell, Joel Gomez, and Dana Belden, "Teaching the Children of a New America: The Challenge of Diversity," *Phi Delta Kappan* (January 2003), 381–385; Maria Enchautequi, *Immigration and County Employment Growth* (Washington, DC: Urban Institute, 1992); Jason Juffus, *The Impact of the Immigration Reform and Control Act of Immigration* (Washington, DC: Urban Institute, 1992).

[36] Ibid.

[37] Michael Fix and Wendy Zimmermann, *Educating Immigrant Children* (Washington, DC: Urban Institute, 1993).

[38] "Census Data Reveals Dramatic Population Increase among Minority Groups," *PBS News Hour* (April 11, 2011), http://www.pbs.org/newshour/extra/features/us/jan-june11/census_04-01.html.

[39] *Census 2000*, http://www.census.gov/main/www/cen2000.html.

[40] James Lee, "U.S. Naturalizations: 2010," *Annual Flow Report* (Department of Homeland Security, Office of Immigration Statistics, April, 2011).

[41] Laurence Steinberg, *Beyond the Classroom* (New York: Simon and Schuster, 1996).

[42] Ibid., 97.

[43] Aaron Terrazas and Jeanne Batalova, "Frequently Requested Statistics on Immigrants and Immigration in the United States," *Migration Policy Institute* (October 2009), http://www.migrationinformation.org/feature/display.cfm?ID=747#2i.

[44] F. Michael Connelly and Jean Clandinin, *Shaping a Professional Identity* (New York: Teachers College Press, 1999); Margaret Eisenhart, Linda Behm, and Linda Romagnano, "Learning to Teach: Developing Expertise or Rite of Passage?" *Journal of Education for Teaching* (January 1991), 51–71; Anne Reynolds, "What Is Competent Beginning Teaching?" *Review of Educational Research* (Spring 1992), 1–36.

[45] Donald P. Kauchak and Paul D. Eggen, *Learning and Teaching: Research Based Methods*, 5th ed. (Boston: Allyn & Bacon, 2007); Pamela Grossman, "Why Models Matter: An Alternative View on Professional Growth in Teaching," *Review of Educational Research* (Summer 1992), 171–179.

[46] Lee Shulman, "Those Who Understand: Knowledge Growth in Teaching," *Educational Researcher* (March–April, 1986), 4–14; Shulman, "Knowledge and Teaching: Foundations of the New Reform," *Harvard Educational Review* (February 1987), 1–22; Shulman, "Ways of Seeing, Ways of Knowing, Ways of Teaching, Ways of Learning about Teaching," *Journal of Curriculum Studies* (September–October 1992), 393–96; Shulman, *The Wisdom of Practice: Essays on Teaching, Learning, and Learning to Teach* (San Francisco: Jossey-Bass, 2004).

[47] Susan E. Wade, *Preparing Teachers for Inclusive Education* (Mahwah, NJ: Erlbaum, 2000).

[48] Sigrun Gudmundsdottir, "Values in Pedagogical Content Knowledge," *Journal of Teacher Education* (May–June 1991), 44–52; Rick Marks, "Pedagogical Content Knowledge: From a Mathematical Case to a Modified Conception," *Journal of Teacher Education* (May–June 1990), 3–11; Barbara Scott Nelson, "Teachers' Special Knowledge," *Educational Researcher* (December 1992), 32–33.

[49] Robert Kunzman, "From Teacher to Student: The Value of Teacher Education for Experienced Teachers," *Journal of Teacher Education* (May–June 2003), 241–253; Pamela L. Grossman, "A Study in Contrast: Sources of Pedagogical Content Knowledge in Secondary English," *Journal of Teacher Education* (September–October 1989), 24–32.

[50] Grossman, "A Study in Contrast," 25–26.

[51] Linda Darling-Hammond, "Educating Teachers," 30.

[52] Lisa Renard, "Setting New Teachers Up for Failure . . . or Success," *Educational Leadership* 60, no. 8 (May 2003), 62–64; Karen Carter, "Teachers' Knowledge and Learning to Teach," in W. Robert Houston (ed.), *Handbook of Research on Teacher Education* (New York: Macmillan, 1990), 291–310; Daniel L. Duke, "How a Staff Development Program Can Rescue At-Risk Students," *Educational Leadership* (December–January 1993), 28–30.

[53] Harry K. Wong, "Producing Educational Leaders through Induction Programs," *Kappa Delta Pi Record* (Spring 2004), 100–111.

[54] Henson, *Curriculum Planning*; Thomas D. Bird, "Early Implementation of the California Mentor Teacher Program," paper presented at the annual meeting of the American Educational Research Association, San Francisco, April 1986; Auroro Chase and Pat Wolfe, "Off to a Good Start in Peer

Coaching," *Educational Leadership* (May 1989), 37–38; Donna Gordon and Margaret Moles, "Mentoring Becomes Staff Development," *NASSP Bulletin* (February 1994), 62–65.

55 Wong, "Producing Educational Leaders"; Jean Boreen, Donna Niday, and Mary K. Johnson, *Mentoring Beginning Teachers: Guiding, Reflecting, Coaching*, 2nd ed. (Portland, ME: Stenhouse, 2009); Curran and Goldrich, *Mentoring and Supporting New Teachers*.

56 Bruce Joyce and Beverly Showers, *Student Achievement Through Staff Development*, 3rd ed. (Alexandria, VA: ASCD, 2002); Joyce and Showers, *Power in Staff Development through Research in Training* (Alexandria, VA: ASCD, 1983).

57 Gloria A. Neubert and Elizabeth C. Bratton, "Team Coaching: Staff Development Side by Side," *Educational Leadership* (February 1987), 29–32.

58 Judith T. Witmer, "Mentoring One District's Success Story," *NASSP Bulletin* (February 1993), 71–78.

59 Kip Tellez, "Mentors by Choice, Not Design," *Journal of Teacher Education* (May–June 1992), 214–221.

60 Tad Watanabe, "Learning from Japanese Lesson Study," *Educational Leadership* (March 2002), 36–39.

61 Wong, "Producing Educational Leaders."

62 Ibid.

63 Henson, *Supervision*.

64 Mary R. Jalongo, "Teachers' Stories: Our Ways of Knowing," *Educational Leadership* (April 1992), 68–73.

65 E. Ryymin, T. Palonen, and K. Hakkarainen, "Networking Relations of Using ICT within a Teacher Community," *Computers & Education* 51, no. 3 (November, 2008).

66 Mark S. Schlager, Umer Farooq, et al., "Analyzing Online Teacher Networks: Cyber-Networks Require Cyber-Research Tools," *Journal of Technology Education* 60, no. 1 (January–February 2009), 88.

67 Katherine K. Merseth, "First Aid for First-Year Teachers," *Phi Delta Kappan* (May 1992), 678–83.

68 Allan C. Ornstein and Thomas J. Lasley, *Strategies for Effective Teaching*, 4th ed. (New York: McGraw-Hill, 2004), 569.

69 The United States Department of Education Institute of Education Sciences, *Teacher Quality under NCLB: Final Report* (2009), www.ed.gov/about/offices/opepd/ppss/reports.htm/.

70 Boyd, Grossman, et al., "Who Leaves?"

71 National Education Association (NEA), "Attracting and Keeping Quality Teachers" (2005), http://www.nea.org/teacher shortage/index.html.

72 Wong, "Save Millions—Train and Support New Teachers," *School Business Affairs* (November, 2003), 19–20.

73 NEA, *Attracting and Keeping Quality Teachers*.

74 Bella Gavish and Isaac A. Friedman, "Novice Teachers' Experience of Teaching: A Dynamic Aspect of Burnout," *Social Psychology of Education* 13, no. 2 (June 2010), 141–167.

75 Costas N. Tsouloupas, Russell L. Carson, Russell Matthews, Matthew J. Grawitch, and Larissa K. Barber, "Exploring the Association between Teachers' Perceived Student Misbehaviour and Emotional Exhaustion: The Importance of Teacher Efficacy Beliefs and Emotion Regulation," *Educational Psychology* 30, no. 2 (2010), 173–189, http://www.informaworld.com/smpp/section?content=a918855037&fulltext=71340928; M. A. Gonzalez, "Study of the Relationship of Stress, Burnout, Hardiness, and Social Support in Urban Secondary School Teachers," (Temple University, Unpublished Ph.D. Dissertation, 1997).

76 Mary T. Brownell, Stephen Smith, Janet Mc Nellis, and Linda Lenk, "Career Decisions in Special Education: Current and Former Teachers Personal Views," *Exceptionality* 5, no. 2 (1994) 83–102.

77 Millicent H. Abel and Joanne Sewell, "Stress and Burnout in Rural and Urban Secondary School Teachers," *Journal of Educational Research* 92, no. 5 (1999) 287–293.

78 Linda Darling-Hammond and G. Sykes, *Wanted: a National Manpower Policy for Education* (Denver: Education Commission of the States, 2003).

79 A. D. Benner, "The Cost of Teacher Turnover," Texas Center for Educational Research (2000), http://www.tcer.org/research/documents/teacher_turnover_full.doc.

80 Rosaline Rossi, "1,116 City Teachers Flunk Out," *Chicago Sun-Times* (April 15, 2005), http://www.lib.usm.edu/~instruct/guides/apa.html.

[81] American Productivity and Quality Center, *Teacher Education and Preparation* (Northeast Ohio Council of Higher Education, 2003), http:// www.Noche.org/pdfs/tep_report.pdf.

[82] Bill Turque, "Rhee Plans Shake-up of Teaching Staff, Training: Career Development Would Change for Those who Remain," *The Washington Post* (January 5, 2009), B1.

[83] Debra Viadero, "Charters Seen as Lab for Report's Ideas on Teachers," *Education Week* (February 25, 2009), 17–18.

[84] Ruth Chang Wei, Linda Darling-Hammond, Alethea Andree, Nikole Richardson, Stelios Orphanos, *Professional Learning in the Learning Profession: A Status Report on Teacher Development in the United States and Abroad* (Dallas, TX: National Staff Development Council, 2009), http:// www.srnleads.org/resources/publications/pdf/.

[85] Richard T. Scarpaci, *A Case Study Approach to Classroom Management* (New York: Allyn & Bacon, 2007), 10–13.

[86] Richard T. Scarpaci, "IOSIE: A Method for Analyzing Student Behavioral Problems," *The Clearing House* (January/February, 2007), 111–116.

[87] Robin Mumford (Executive Director of the Learning Leadership Lab), interviewed by author, May, 2009.

[88] Kenneth D. Peterson, *Teacher Education*, 2nd ed. (Thousand Oaks, CA: Corwin, 2000).

[89] Thomas L. Good and Jere E. Brophy, *Looking in Classrooms*, 10th ed. (New York: Harper & Collins, 2007).

[90] National Institute for Education Sciences, *High School and Beyond: Teacher and Administrator Survey* (Washington, DC: National Center for Education Statistics, 1985), http://nces.ed.gov/pubsearch/getpubcats.asp&sid=022#.

[91] "Intern Intervention Evaluation: The Toledo Plan." (Toledo, OH: Toledo Public Schools, 2001).

[92] Carol A. Dwyer, "Teaching and Diversity: Meeting the Challenges for Innovative Teacher Assessment," *Journal of Teacher Education* (March–April 1993), 119–129; Carolyn J. Wood, "Toward More Effective Teacher Evaluation," *NASSP Bulletin* (March 1992), 52–59.

[93] Wayne K. Hoy and Cecil G. Miskel, *Educational Administration*, 6th ed. (Boston: McGraw-Hill, 2001).

[94] Carl Rogers, *A Way of Being* (Boston: Houghton Mifflin, 1980); Donald A. Schon, *The Reflective Practitioner: How Professionals Think in Action* (New York: Ashgate Publishing, 1995); Donald A. Schon (ed.), *The Reflective Turn* (New York: Teachers College Press, Columbia University, 1991).

[95] Barbara Larrivee, "Transforming Teaching Practice: Becoming the Critically Reflective Teacher," *Reflective Practice* 1, no. 3 (2000), 294.

[96] Linda Darling-Hammond and Gary Sykes (Eds.), *Teaching as the Learning Profession* (San Francisco: Jossey-Bass, 1999).

[97] Dorene D. Ross, "First Steps in Developing a Reflective Approach," *Journal of Teacher Education* (March–April 1989), 22–30.

[98] Ibid.

[99] Simon Hole and Grace Hall McEntree, "Reflections in the Heat of Practice," *Educational Leadership* (May 1999), 34–37.

[100] Ibid.

[101] Kenneth D. Peterson, *Teacher Education*, 2nd ed. (Thousand Oaks, CA: Corwin, 2000).

[102] Ibid.

[103] Morris Cogan, *Clinical Supervision* (Boston: Houghton Mifflin, 1973).

[104] Robert Goldhammer, Robert H. Anderson, and Robert J. Krajewski, *Clinical Supervision: Special Methods for the Supervision of Teachers*, 3rd ed. (Fort Worth, TX: Harcourt Brace Jovanovich, 1993.

[105] Ben M. Harris, *In-Service Education for Staff Development* (Needham Heights, MA: Allyn & Bacon, 1989); Ben M. Harris, *Personnel Administration in Education* (Needham Heights, MA: Allyn & Bacon, 1992).

[106] Allan A. Glatthorn, *Supervisory Leadership* (New York: Harper Collins, 1990); Arthur E. Wise et al., *Effective Teacher Selection: From Recruitment to Retention* (Santa Monica, CA: Rand Corporation, 1987).

[107] Carl D. Glickman, *Supervision of Instruction: A Developmental Approach*, 4th ed. (Needham Heights, MA: Allyn & Bacon, 1997); Mary D. Phillips and Carl D. Glickman, "Peer Coaching: Developmental Approach to Enhance Teacher Thinking," *Journal of Staff Development* (Spring

1991), 20–25; Jeanne Swafford, "Teachers Supporting Teachers through Peer Coaching," *Support for Learning* (Jan, 7, 2003), 54–58.

108 *Teaching Quality Research Matters*, Issue 2 (Chapel Hill, NC: The Southwest Center for Teaching Quality, November 2002).

109 eHow.com, "Board Teacher Certification," http://www.ehow.com/about_6519157_ board-teacher-certification.html#ixzz1JiQJvZ3B.

110 Allan Ornstein and Daniel Levine, *Introduction to the Foundations of Education*, 9th ed. (Boston: Houghton Mifflin, 2006).

111 NEA–AFT Partnership (2010), http://www.nea.org/home/11204.htm.

112 *Teaching Quality Research Matters.*

113 Henson, *Supervision*; Christopher Clark, "Teacher Preparation: Contributions of Research on Teacher Thinking," *Educational Researcher* (March 1988), 5–12; Michael O'Loughlin, "Engaging Teachers in Emancipatory Knowledge Construction," *Journal of Teacher Education* (November– December 1992), 42–48.

114 Judith H. Shulman, "Now You See Them, Now You Don't," *Educational Researcher* (August–September 1990), 11–15.

115 Henson, *Supervision*.

116 Jennifer J. Bradford, "How to Stay in Teaching (When You Really Feel Like Crying)," *Educational Leadership* (May 1999), 67–68.

117 Boyd, Grossman, et al., "Who Leaves?"

118 William Sanders, Presentation to the Governor's Commission on Teaching Success (Columbus, OH: July, 2002).

119 Barbara Benham Tye and Lisa O'Brien, "Why Are Experienced Teachers Leaving the Profession?" *Phi Delta Kappan* (September 2002), 24–32.

Name Index

Abel, M., 510
Adams, R. S., 272
Adler, M., 13
Airasian, P., 436
Allen, M., 246
Amidon, E. J., 42
Anderson, G., 310
Anderson, L. W., 83, 84
Anderson, R. C., 223
Andrade, A., 182
Arends, R., 458
Aristotle, 14
Armento, B. J., 123, 124
Armstrong, D. G., 247
Aronson, E., 362
Ausubel, D. P., 247

Baker, M., 240
Baloche, L., 303
Bandura, A., 332
Banks, J. A., 124
Barr, R., 9
Beach, D., 12
Beaty, J., 441
Bennett, N., 239
Bernard, S., 245
Biddle, B. J., 272, 282
Bligh, D. A., 145
Block, J. H., 311, 312, 313
Bloom, B. S., 68, 80, 182, 211, 286, 294, 311, 312, 314, 435
Bogad, C., 5
Bolt, S., 463
Braddock, J. H., 291

Bradford, J., 531
Bransford, J., 172, 205
Bratton, E. C., 506
Brennan, R. L., 386
Brophy, J., 137, 149, 228, 286, 290, 291, 357, 445, 514
Brown, H., 302
Brownell, M. T., 510
Bruner, J. S., 14, 36, 503
Burden, P. R., 354, 356
Burke, K., 419
Burns, R., 313
Bush, G. H. W., 95

Canter, L., 327
Canter, M., 327
Carroll, J. B., 311, 312
Chall, J., 77, 125, 492
Chance, P., 143, 327, 330, 360
Cibulka, J. G., 492
Ciuffetelli, D. C., 302
Clark, C., 119
Clark, L. H., 470
Clinton, W. J., 95
Cogan, M., 522
Colby, S. A., 450
Collay, M., 19
Conant, J. B., 490
Cooper, C., 534
Cooper, H., 163, 445
Csikszentmihalyi, M., 34

Darling-Hammond, L., 205, 492, 493
Darwin, C., 15

Davenport, P., 310
Descartes, R., 14
Dewey, J., 204, 296
Dreikurs, R., 341, 342, 343
Duke, D. L., 326, 365
Duncan, A., 67

Eisenhard, S., 333
Eisner, E. W., 119, 314
Elder, L., 29
Emmer, E. T., 37, 44, 328, 330, 331
England, D. A., 445
Ennis, R. H., 32, 33
Epstein, J. L., 467
Evertson, C. M., 44, 191, 325, 328, 330, 331

Fantini, M. D., 231
Feurestein, R., 13
Finn, C. E., Jr., 98, 492
Flanders, N. A., 41, 42, 43
Flatley, J. K., 445
Fosnot, C. T., 19
Fry, E., 233, 234
Fuller, F. F., 493

Gagne, N. L., 25, 137
Gagnon, G. W., 19
Garcia, E., 280
Gardner, H., 34, 134
Gay, G., 48
Gehrke, N. J., 5
Glasser, W. W., 344, 345, 346, 347, 348

Glazer, N., 231
Glickman, C. D., 523
Goldhammer, R., 522
Good, T. L., 137, 149, 210, 286, 290, 291, 357, 445, 514
Goodlad, J. I., 14, 65, 66, 490, 491
Graves, M. F., 245
Gregory, A., 360
Gronlund, N. E., 85, 87, 90, 91, 92, 384, 402, 404, 412, 435, 436
Grossman, P., 504
Grouws, D. A., 137, 210

Haberman, M., 45, 437
Hambleton, R. K., 386
Harris, B. M., 522
Harrow, A. J., 81, 89
Henry, J., 186
Henson, K. T., 124, 145, 147, 247, 257
Hiebert, J., 507
Hilgard, E. R., 309
Hirsch, E. D., Jr., 12, 95, 128, 375, 450, 490
Hole, S., 518, 519
Holloway, J. H., 305
Holt, J., 187
Hunkins, F. P., 94, 144
Hunter, M., 137, 145

Irvine, J. J., 124

Jackson, P. W., 432
Johnson, D., 293, 296, 301, 302, 359, 447
Johnson, K. A., 283
Johnson, R., 293, 296, 301, 302, 447
Judd, C., 204

Kellough, R. D., 37
Kinnucan-Welsch, K., 23
Kirsner, D. A., 87, 88
Klieband, H. M., 174
Koerner, J. D., 490
Kohn, A., 162, 445, 474
Kounin, J. S., 336, 337, 338, 339

Krathwohl, D. R., 81, 82, 83, 84

Ladson-Billings, G., 125
Lasley, T. J., II, 470, 516, 517
Lee, R. W., 466
Lehmann, I. J., 393
Levine, D. U., 496, 497
Linn, R. L., 384, 402, 404, 435, 436
Lipham, M., 13
Lipman, M., 29, 32, 33
Lippitt, R., 37, 42
Lipton, M., 231, 232, 291
Lortie, D., 5
Lowery, L. F., 76

Madgic, R. F., 457
Mager, R. F., 90, 91, 92
March, T., 259
Marzano, R. J., 175, 286, 300, 376, 446
Matczynski, T. J., 516, 517
McCutcheon, G., 123
McEntree, G. H., 518, 519
McLaughlin, M., 246
McPartland, J. P., 291
McTighe, J., 77, 78
Meckel, A. M., 326, 365
Medley, D. M., 44, 45
Mehrens, W. A., 393
Mertler, C. A., 386
Metfessel, N. S., 87, 88
Michael, W. B., 87, 88
Miller, M. D., 402, 404, 436
Miltenberger, R. G., 335
Murrell, P. C., 144
Mussell, M., 436
Muther, C., 232

Neubert, G. A., 506
Newell, A., 205
Newmann, F., 33
Noyce, P., 478

Oakes, J., 231, 232, 291
Obama, B. H., 100, 101
O'Brien, L., 536
Oliva, P. E., 65
Ormrod, J. E., 293, 358, 394

Ornstein, A. C., 94, 137, 144, 183, 189, 222, 244, 252, 330, 358, 386, 404, 462, 496, 497
Osborn, J., 223
O'Shea, M. R., 105

Paul, R. W., 29
Pavlov, I., 18
Payne, D. A., 462
Peterson, K. D., 521
Peterson, P. L., 36, 37, 119
Peterson, R., 130
Piaget, J., 8, 19, 20, 21, 208
Pickering, D., 446
Pitoniak, M., 386
Popham, W. J., 388
Powers, W. T., 345
Preda, D., 478

Ravitch, D., 239
Raygor, A. L., 234
Redding, N., 439
Reeves, D. B., 383
Reinhartz, J., 12
Rhee, M., 511
Rice, J. M., 174
Ripski, M. B., 360
Rogers, C., 35, 515
Rosenshine, B. V., 177, 227, 279
Rothman, R., 415
Rowe, M. B., 187
Rowley, J., 516, 517
Ruth, G., 240
Ryder, R. J., 245

Sadler, W. A., Jr., 33
Salvia, J., 463
Sanders, W., 27, 122, 534
Scarpaci, R. T., 8, 17, 20, 25, 30, 40, 139, 185, 271, 292, 298, 348, 391
Schoenfeld, A. H., 211
Schon, D. A., 515
Schorr, J., 505
Scriffiny, P. L., 450, 451
Scriven, M., 435
Sewell, J., 510
Shanker, A., 136
Shulman, L., 503

Simon, H. A., 205
Simonsen, B., 285
Sinclair, C., 470
Sizer, T. R., 417, 418
Skinner, B. F., 15, 16, 332
Slavin, R. E., 286, 290, 296, 299, 312, 455
Stanley, J. C., 520
Starr, I. S., 470
Stein, B., 205
Steinberg, L., 499, 500
Sternberg, R. J., 28, 32, 33, 34, 35, 208
Stevenson, H., 27
Stigler, J., 27, 507
Stronge, J. H., 147, 148
Stufflebeam, D. L., 434

Taba, H., 63, 72, 206
Tagg, J., 9

Thelen, H. A., 43
Thomas, C., 383
Thorndike, E., 204
Tierney, R. J., 223
Tomaino, M., 447
Tomlinson, C. A., 120
Torrance, E. P., 49
Traver, R., 478
Tuckman, B. W., 395, 435
Tuska, S. A., 5
Tye, B. B., 536
Tyler, R. W., 68, 74, 160
Tyson, H., 240

van Hiele, P., 98
van Hiele-Geldof, D., 98
Vygotsky, L., 8

Walberg, H. J., 68
Watson, J. B., 15, 18

Wei, R. C., 511
Weinstein, G., 231
Whimbey, A., 33
White, R. K., 37, 42
Wiggins, G., 77, 78, 94, 98
Wolfgang, C. H., 40
Wong, H., 507
Woolfolk, A. E., 409, 412
Worsham, M. E., 44
Wright, B. D., 5

Yager, R. E., 390
Yinger, R. J., 122
Ysseldyke, J., 463

Zahorik, J. A., 119
Zmuda, A., 447

Subject Index

Ability
  instructional materials
    and, 221
  intelligence and, 21
Ability grouping
  between-class, 289–290
  heterogeneous grouping
    vs., 292, 319–320
  within-class, 290–292
Absolute grade standards,
  454–455
*Academic Achievement Chal-
  lenge, The* (Chall), 125
Academic standards. *See*
  Standards
Academic Standards for Chicago Public Schools website, 68
Acceptance approach to discipline, 341, 343–344
Accountability
  in cooperative groups,
    297–298
  individual, in cooperative
    learning, 298, 301
  relationship between
    school and student per-
    formance, 475–476
  value-added focus on
    learning and, 27
Accountability movement,
  474, 477, 482–483
Accreditation, 491–492. *See
  also* Certification

Achievement
  impact of class size on,
    280–283, 305
  impact of peer tutoring
    on, 294
  mastery learning and, 294
  teacher-level variables
    that raise, 286–287
Achievement gap, 228–229,
  290
Achievement tests, 386–387
Action system (pedagogical)
  knowledge, 119
Action zone, 272
Adaptation process model, 21
Adaptive pedagogy, 228
Adequate Yearly Progress
  (AYP), 100, 474
Affective domain, 81, 88
Age, grouping by, 270–271
Aims
  definition of, 62
  goals and objectives vs.,
    110
  history of, 64–65
  relationship with goals
    and objectives, 64
  in traditional lesson plans,
    141
Alameda Unified School Dis-
  trict's "New Basics,"
  67–69
Alerting activities and group
  focus, 339

Alterable environments/
  instructional variables,
  286–287
Alternative assessment
  authentic, 415–419
  criteria for, 439
  portfolios, 415–416,
    465–466
*America 2000: An Education
  Strategy* (US Dept. of
  Education), 95
American College Testing program (ACT) exam, 387
American Federation of
  Teachers (AFT), 61, 491,
  526–527
AMMCASH, 138–139,
  152–153
Analysis, in cognitive
  domain, 80, 85
Application, in cognitive
  domain, 80, 85
Applied science approach to
  classroom management,
  328–332
Aptitude tests, 387–388
Assertive disciplinary
  method, 326–328
Assessment
  alternative, 415–417, 439,
    465–466
  authentic, 415, 418–419
  in cooperative learning
    lessons, 301–303

definition of, 377
direct instruction, 517
homework as tool of, 427
improving procedures for, 382–383
lesson planning and, 117–119, 162
performance, 417
personal, of work in groups, 303
portfolio, 415–417
purpose of, 421–422
in unit planning, 128, 131
See also Evaluation
Assimilation/accommoda-tion, and adaptation, 21
Associations, professional, 526–528
Atomistic teaching/learning structures, 9
ATOS Grade Level formula, 234
Attention getting, 341
Attitudinal scales, 388
Authentic assessment
performance-based, 417–418
portfolios, 415–416, 464–465
project work, 418
teacher-made tests and, 419–421

Beginning Teacher Computer Network (BTCN), 508
Beginning teachers
inadequate/conflicted notions of classroom practice, 502–505
job interview preparation, 532–533
national board certifica-tion of, 525
preparing for the real classroom, 509–520
problems of, 493–496
professional development of, 526–531
providing support for, 493–509

supervision/evaluation of, 521–524
Behavior modification
approach to classroom management, 332–336, 369
plan for shaping, 16–17
rewards and punishment in, 17–18
Behavioral reinforcers
neo-Skinnerian model of, 16, 18
positive and negative, 332, 334
Behaviorism, 8, 11, 14–18
Behaviors
classroom, formal classifi-cation of, 37
direct vs. indirect, 42
Beliefs and style, 38
Best practices, 111–112
Betts Levels formula for oral reading, 234
Between-class ability group-ing, 289–290
Block scheduling, 135
Brainstorming, 198, 304
Bridge classes, combined grades in, 271
Burnout, 510, 531
Buzz sessions for small groups, 304

California Standards for Pub-lic Schools website, 68
Cardinal Principles of Sec-ondary Education, 64
Case studies, advantages of, 199
Cause-effect relationships, 250
Certification, 101, 509–511, 525–526, 528–529. *See also* Accreditation
Child-centered learning, 215
Choice theory, 345–347, 370
Chunking strategies, 204
Clarity, instructional, 12
Class size
impact on instruction, 280–283

impact on student achievement, 305
Classification/sorting, 31
Classroom(s)
culturally responsive, 123–125, 353
design, factors to con-sider in arranging, 277–278
instruction, curriculum model for, 117–118
instructional tasks in, 283–285
seating arrangements in, 272–273
self-contained, 270
Classroom Interaction Analy-sis Scale (Flanders), 42
Classroom management
acceptance approach, 341–344, 369–370
alternative approaches to, 351–355
applied science approach, 328–332
assertive approach, 326–328, 368–369
behavior modification approach, 332–336, 369
"catch them being good" approach, 335
checklist for, 366–367
choice theory/reality therapy (success approach), 344–345
contingency management approach, 335
contracting approach, 336
control over classroom tasks, 283–285
first-day procedures, 333
Glasser's theories applied to, 345–349
group managerial approach, 336–341
high intervention levels of, 326–336
instructional practice approach, 328–332

Kounin's behaviors/categories for observing, 337

Learning Team Model, 347–348

logical consequences approach, 341–344, 369–370

moderate intervention levels of, 336–349

overview of models, 352

politically expedient interventions, 362

practical suggestions for, 340

principle of least intervention, 356

proactive vs. remedial, 325

punishment, guidelines for using, 357–359, 370–371

quick-fix solutions, 362

rules-ignore-praise/rules-reward-punishment approaches, 335

strategies for managing problem students, 358

success approach, 370

tips for preventing student misbehavior, 365

traditional methods of, 331

twelve beliefs leading to effective management strategies, 349, 351

Classroom objectives, 70, 72–73, 94

Classroom tasks, 283–285

Clinical supervision, 521

Cloze method of ranking books, 234

Coaching
peer, 506–507
technical, 522

Cognition
definition of, 21
metacognition/metacognitive skills, 27, 207–208

sociocultural theory of cognition, 20

Cognitive development, Piaget's stages of, 20–22

Cognitive domain
analysis and application in, 80, 85

eliciting questions for cognitive tasks, 206

key words for objectives in, 86–87

levels of questions in, 206

objective levels in, 80

questioning levels related to, 182

sample questions by category, 183

sample thought questions for, 404

Cognitive process dimension, six categories of, 84

Cognitive psychologist's approach to teaching and learning, 14

Cognitive skills, inclusion in unit plans, 79, 128

Cognitive structures, 12–13

Cognitive theory and constructivism, 19

Collaborative research model, 530

Collection, and information overload, 251

Common Core State Standards, 69, 375

Communicating
effectively, 361–362
with parents, 467–474, 482

Comparison-contrast structure, 250–251

Competition among groups, 296, 298

Completion tests, 399

Comprehensibility vs. readability in textbooks, 235

Comprehension, in cognitive domain, 80, 85

Computer networking, 508, 531

Computer-assisted instruction (CAI), 15, 174

Computerized recordkeeping, 461–463

Concept formation/development, 208, 210, 285

Conceptual frameworks, 204

Conditioned reinforcers, 17

Constructed response/free-response tests. *See* Essay tests

Constructivism
approach to teaching and learning, 14

cognitive theory and, 19

concept/design of constructivist learning, 18–19

constructivist view of teaching, 148–150

developmental, 20

key assumptions of, 24

lesson planning and, 168–169

methods/procedures in, 22–23, 148–150

social construction of knowledge in, 149

social vs. developmental, 20–22

teacher's role in, 8

teaching practices for, 22–23

theories of, 18–22

Content
enrichment, 256–257

explanations of, in instructional practices, 201–204

grade-level standards, 60

mastery of knowledge about, 12

standards, 75–76, 376

student construction of, 205

student-facilitated delivery of, 148, 150

summarizing, 203–204

teacher-centered delivery of, 145, 148

in unit planning, 12
validity, 379, 390
Content area reading instruction, 245, 248–249
Contingency management approach to discipline, 335
Continuous progress grading, 458
Contract grading approach, 456, 458
Control theory systems, 345
Convergent questions, 184–186
Cooperative learning
advantages of, 298
checklist for, 297
competition among groups in, 296, 298
drawbacks of, 198
guidelines for, 301–302
informal, 299–300
lesson activities for, 300–301
"numbered heads together" method, 300
peer pairing, 293
small group instruction and, 296–301, 318
think-pair-share, 300
Council for Exceptional Children, 527
Course objectives
scope, continuity, and sequence in, 70
stating as topics and concepts, 71
Courses of study, 125–163
Creative thinking, 34–36, 511–512
Criterion-referenced tests, 382–386
Critical thinking
creativity and, 34–36
essential elements of, 29
in the everyday world, 28
importance of, 27–29
indirect instructional practices for, 197–199

IOSIE analysis model, 29–30
promoting through questioning, 182, 184
research on, 32–34
seminar model of, 30–32
skills development for, 31
strategies for teaching, 29–32
student-centered learning and, 204–211
types of, 34–36
Criticism/negative comments, 193
Culturally diverse learners, 496–500, 502
Culturally responsive classrooms, 123–125, 353
Cumulative records, 380, 463–464, 482
Curricular validity, 379
Curriculum
culturally responsive principles of, 124
defining, 117–119, 166
guides/courses of study, 125–163
model for classroom instruction, 117–119
Curriculum Frameworks (New York), 96–97
Cyber-enabled computer networking, 508

Daily plans. See lesson plans
Data, standardized, understanding student learning patterns through, 477
Debates, 304, 447
Decision making
teacher planning and, 119
about textbooks, 246
Deductive reasoning, 184
Democracy and Education (Dewey), 296
Democratic model of teaching, 347
Demonstrations, instructional method of, 146–147

Departmentalization, 270
Desist behaviors/techniques, 338, 354
Developmental constructivism, 20
Developmental theory of cognition, 20
Deviancy, 337
Diagnostic evaluation, 387, 435
Differentiated instruction
with field dependent/independent learners, 227–228
grouping for language minority students, 280
lesson planning and, 160–161
teacher planning for, 122
Direct instruction
assessment form, 517
components of, 279
direct teaching method, 195–196
explanation combined with discussion, 197
lecture/explanation method, 196
lesson objectives for, 174, 177
with low-achieving students, 45
methods from authorities, 136–138
practice and drill in, 176–177
practices of, 195–197
strategies for, 215
teacher/centered practices, 145, 177, 199, 492
transmission model, 177
unscripted (explicit), 175–177
Discipline, approaches to, 325–329. See also Classroom management
Discovery teaching, 179, 181
Discussion, 197, 447
Divergent questions, 184–186

Diversity
  in American classrooms,
    353, 497, 499
  common academic stan-
    dards required for, 13
  See also Cultural respon-
    siveness
Dreamkeepers, The (Ladson-
  Billings), 125
Drill (fact) questions, 184
DRP units, 234
Duplication of educational
  materials, 222

Eclectic approach to learning,
  14, 24–25
Edible reinforcers, 17
Education students, problems
  of, 493–496
Effective teachers, defining,
  46–48
Effective teaching
  behaviors of, 11–12, 25
  eight behaviors for, 12
  keys to, 7–11, 52
  new paradigm for under-
    standing, 45–48
  styles of, 37–38
Elaborating, 226
Electronic reading devices/
  e-books, 235–238, 251,
  264–265
Electronic recordkeeping,
  461–463, 481
Electronic workbooks, 255
Enthusiasm, 12
Environmental theory, 20
Equity pedagogy, 125
Essay questions, 403–407
Essay tests, 391–393
Evaluation
  of beginning teachers,
    521–524
  in cognitive domain, 80,
    85
  definition of, 377
  diagnostic, 435
  of discussions/debates,
    447
  formative, 435–436

general instructional
    effectiveness form, 516
  group/peer, 440, 443
  homework, 443–446
  learning prescription
    form, 441
  lesson planning and, 162
  measurement through
    testing. *See* Tests
  methods and approaches,
    437–447, 481
  notebooks as tool for, 446
  observation of student
    work, 440–442
  peer judgment/self-judg-
    ment, 438
  placement, 433–434
  quizzes, 438, 440
  reasons for, 434
  recitation, 443
  reports/themes/research
    papers, 447
  self-evaluation, 514–515
  summative, 436–437
  types of, 436, 480–481
  in unit planning, 128, 131
  See also Assessment; Grad-
    ing
Exhibitions (performance
  from memory), 417–418
Exit exams, state (high
  school), 453–454
Experiments, instructional
  method of, 146–147
Explanation
  combined with discus-
    sion, 197
  in demonstrations/experi-
    ments, 146–147
  enhancing, 196
  of instructional materials,
    226
  in lectures, 145–146, 196
Explicit direct instruction,
  176, 279
Expository text, 228, 249–250
Extensive curriculum, 117
Extinction, behavioral reinforcer of, 17
Extrinsic motivation, 142–143

Face-to-face interaction, in
  cooperative learning,
  301
Feedback
  in applied science
    approach to discipline,
    329–330
  group/peer evaluation,
    440, 443
  preventing misbehaviors
    through, 359–360
  on student tests, 414
Field dependent/indepen-
  dent learners, 227–228
Final summaries/conclusions,
  151, 203–204
Fish bowl technique for small
  groups, 304
Flesch-Kincaid Formula, 234
Flexibility
  diverse developmental
    needs and, 122
  in lesson planning,
    154–155, 161
Formal planning, 123
Formal vs. informal evaluation, 437
Formative evaluation,
  435–436
Fragmentation, 338
Fry Readability Graph, 234
Fundamental movements, in
  psychomotor domain, 81

Games, simulations, and
  technology, 257–262
General instructional objectives. *See* Objectives
General Objectives (Gron-
  lund's model), 85–91
Generalizations, 251
Goals
  of American schools, 66
  criteria for setting, 67
  definition of, 62–63
  New Basics (Alameda Uni-
    fied School District),
    69
  New Compact for Learn-
    ing, 97

relationship with aims and objectives, 64
trends in, 65–68
Tyler's model for developing, 74–77
writing one's own, 92–95
Goals 2000: Educate America Act, 95–96
Grade books, traditional vs. standards-based, 451
Grading
absolute, 455
considering student effort in, 458
cumulative records, 463–464
electronic recordkeeping, 461, 463
guidelines for reporting student progress, 466–467
point system, 457
portfolios as strategy for, 464–465
purpose of, 448–450
records and reports of performance, 460–467, 481–482
relative, 455
report cards, 460–461
standards-based, 450–459
Graduate Record Examination (GRE), 387
Graphic organizers, 203
Group managerial approach to discipline, 336–341
Groups/grouping
ability grouping, 319–320
activities for, 304
by age, 271
basic ways of, 270
brainstorming, 198
classroom seating arrangements, 272
competition among, 296
cooperative learning, 198, 318
evaluation in, 440, 443
flexible grouping lesson plan, 154–155

focus and alerting activities, 339
group seating formations, 277
heterogeneous, 292, 319–320
homogeneous, 292
large-group instruction, 270
for learning, 306–307
learning distinct skills or processes with, 279
numbering as method of forming, 300
personal assessment of work in, 303
recommended practices for, 291
situational, 292
small-group instruction, 288–306, 319
structural vs. situational, 292
whole-group instruction, 270, 278–288, 318–319
Guest speakers, 197
Guided discovery, 181

Heterogeneous grouping, 292, 319–320
Heuristic thinking, 205
Hidden curriculum, 48, 125
Higher-achieving students
ability grouping and, 292, 319
alternatives to grouping for, 291
higher-level questions for, 184
influence on lower-achieving students, 320
mastery learning and, 313
varying instructional time for, 312
High-level questions, 181–182
High-level thinking and metacognitive skills, 12–13, 27, 207–208
Holistic teaching/learning structures, 9

Homework
as assessment tool, 427
do's and don'ts, 444–445
grading, 449
lesson planning and, 152
research-based guidelines for, 446
varying perspectives on, 162–163
Homogeneous grouping, 292
Horizontal relationships, 226

Immediate summary, in lesson planning, 151
Immigrant students, 498–499
Indirect instruction, 197–199, 215. See also Student-centered instruction
Individualized instruction, 270–271, 308–314, 320
Induction period, 507
Inductive reasoning, 184
Informal cooperative learning, 299–300
Informal vs. formal evaluation, 437
Inner-city schools
beginning teachers in, 493
disciplinary problems in, 325
teaching challenges in, 496–500, 502
Inquiry, critical. See Critical thinking
Inquiry-based learning, 210–211
Instruction
behaviors, 137
computer-assisted, 15
in critical thinking, 29–32
curriculum model for, 117–118
direct. See Direct instruction
grouping for. See Groups/grouping
indirect. See Student-centered learning
individualized, 308–314

methods. *See* Instructional methods
planning by level of, 121–125
practices. *See* Instructional practices
psychology of, 309
Instructional aids, 150
Instructional clarity, 12
Instructional design, lesson plan for, 137
Instructional methods, 172–213
combining materials and strategies, 203
constructivist view of, 148–150
direct. *See* Direct instruction
indirect instruction, 197–199. *See also* Student-centered learning
lectures, 145–146, 196, 204
practice and drill, 173–179
questioning, 179–193
selecting with an if–then relationship, 173
teacher centered. *See* Direct instruction
transmission view of, 145–148
See also Instructional practices
Instructional objectives. *See* Objectives
Instructional paradigm, 8–9, 26
Instructional practices
explanations of content, 201–204
lecture, 145–146, 196, 204
in US vs. other countries, 211
See also Instructional methods
Instructional resources
appropriate selection of, 220, 222–225
copyrighted materials, 224–225

duplicating materials, 222
effective teaching with, 12
explaining instructional materials, 226, 264
journals, magazines, and newspapers, 256–257
lesson planning with, 150
materials and media, 150
presenting instructional materials, 225–227
simulations, games, and technology, 257–262
teacher-made, 223–224
textbooks, 229–253
in unit planning, 128
workbooks, 253–256
Instructional strategies. *See* Instructional methods
Instructional variables/alterable environments, 286–287
Intelligence tests, 386
Intensive curriculum, 117
Internal summaries, 203–204
Internet
cyber-enabled computer networking, 508
online student portfolios, 417
WebQuests, 259
See also Websites
Interventions, 362
Intrinsic motivation, 142
Intuitive thinking, 36
IOSIE Analysis Model, 29–30, 350, 363–364, 512
Iowa Test of Basic Skills (ITBS), 386

Jigsaw, 299
Job interview, preparation for, 532–533
Joint strategy of problem solving, 206
Journals
guidelines for using, 258
as instructional resource, 256–257
professional, 528

Jugyoukenkynu (Japanese study lesson), 507

Keller plan, 309
K-i-s-s (keep it short and simple) principle, 203
Knowledge
in cognitive domain, 80, 83–85
about content, 12
transmission view vs. constructivist view of, 149
Knowledge base, 12–13

Laboratory research centers, 530
Large-group instruction, 270. *See also* Whole-group instruction
Leadership Learning Lab, 513
Learning
activities, in unit planning, 128
behaviorist concept/theory of, 8, 11, 14–18
concepts of, 11–25
constructivist concept of, 18–19, 22. *See also* Constructivism
eclectic approach to, 24–25
expectations, establishing, 12
field dependent/independent learners, 227–228
Gardner's "entry points" to, 134
levels of, 120–121
outcomes, specific, 91
planning instruction for, 116–165
project-based, 418–419
student-centered. *See* Student-centered learning
teaching style and, 43–44
Learning paradigm, 7–9, 26–27
Learning prescription, 441
Learning-to-learn skills, 13–14
Lectures, 145–146, 196, 204

Lesson planning/design
AMMCASH approach to, 138–139, 152
assessment/evaluation in, 162
by authorities, 136–138
best practices, 105–108
"big picture" approach to, 78
case studies on, 167–169
checklist for, 164–165
components of, 137
cooperative learning activities for, 300–301
as course of study, 135
culturally responsive, 123
direct instruction objectives for, 177
enhancing lectures/explanations in, 196
flexible grouping and, 154–155
good questioning strategies for, 148
guidelines for implementing, 160–163
homework assignments in, 162–163
importance of, 152–153
instructional resources for, 150, 225–227
integrating real-life experiences, 160
mastery learning, 158–159
media and materials used in, 150
objectives, 72–73
online lesson/unit builders, 164
organizing/implementing, 163
parameters of, 135
professionalism in, 136
sample, 154–159
SAPC's five-step process for, 105
standards-based, 104–105, 112, 140–141
for student participation/understanding, 161–162
successful, key ingredients for, 116
summaries in, 150–152
Taba's classic approach for, 72
thinking skills, 156–157
time constraints considered in, 161
traditional, how to write, 138–144
variety in teaching procedures, 145–150
Leveling, 234
Lexiles, 234
Literate critical thinking, 511–512
Lix and Rix readability formula, 234
Logical consequences approach to discipline, 341–344
Low-achieving students
ability grouping and, 292, 319
challenges in teaching, 496–497
direct instruction with, 45
higher-achieving students' influence on, 320
non-mainstream-culture, 500
task development for, 285
teaching tips for, 44
varying instructional time for, 312
Low-level questions, 181–182, 184

Magazines, as instructional resource, 256–258
Mastery grading, 458
Mastery learning
achievement levels and, 294
basic components of, 314
direct or indirect instruction, 315–316
lesson plan for, 137, 158–159
practice and drill in, 175–176
Matching tasks to student learning needs, 283–285
Matching tests, 398–399
Material reinforcers, 17
Materials, instructional. *See* Instructional resources
Meaning, construction of, 21, 23
Media, using in lesson planning, 150
Medial summaries, 151, 204
Mental planning, 123
Mentioning phenomenon, 230, 239
Mentoring, 506–507, 513
Metacognition/metacognitive skills, 27, 207–208
Miller Analogies Test (MAT), 387
Misbehavior, preventing, 356, 365. *See also* Classroom management
Miseducation, 490
Miseducation of American Teachers, The (Koerner), 490
Modeling, 335–336
Modern Language Association, 527
Momentum, 338–339
Motivation
extrinsic, 142–143
instructional materials for, 226–227
intrinsic, 142
through relevance, 202
strategies/methods for, 10
theories of, 10
in traditional lesson plans, 142–143
Movement management, 338
Multi-age grouping, 271
Multicultural education, 124. *See also* Culturally responsive classrooms

Multimedia and technology, 198–199
Multiple-choice questions, 396–398

Narrative text structure, 249–250
Nation at Risk, A, 65
National Assessment of Educational Progress (NAEP) exams, 282–283, 386–387
National Association for Bilingual Children, 527
National Association for the Education of Exceptional Children, 527
National board certification, 525–526
National Core Standards, 95
National Council for Accreditation of Teacher Education (NCATE), 491–492
National Council of Teachers of English, 527
National Council of Teachers of Mathematics (NCTM), 75, 123
National Education Association (NEA), 491, 526–527
National Geographic Xpeditions, 259–260
National Science Teachers Association (NSTA), 75–76, 123, 527
National Scholarship Service and Fund for Negro Students, 527
Negative reinforcement, 16, 332
Neo-Skinnerian model for reinforcement, 16
Networking, computerized, 508
New Compact for Learning, 97
New Dale-Chall Readability Formula, 234
New York's Curriculum Frameworks, 97

Newspapers, as instructional resource, 256–258
No Child Left Behind (NCLB) legislation
  accountability movement and, 474, 477
  as aim of education, 65
  NAEP testing requirements, 387
Nondiscursive communication, in psychomotor domain, 82
Non-mainstream-culture (disadvantaged) students, weak performance of, 500
Nonstandardized tests, 381
Norm-referenced tests, 381, 383–386
Note taking, 203, 446
Novices. *See* Beginning teachers

Objectives
  creating, 70–95
  definition of, 63
  general (Gronlund's model, 85–90, 91
  instructional, characteristics at the classroom level, 72
  lesson-planning, 72–73, 141, 177
  necessity of, 110–111
  relationship with aims and goals, 64
  specific learning outcomes and, 91
  specific objectives (Mager's model), 90–92
  taxonomy of. *See* Taxonomy of educational objectives
  teachers' checklists for, 108–109
  Tyler's method for formulating, 74
  types of, 70–72
  in unit planning, 72–73, 126
  writing one's own, 92–95

Observation instruments
  direct-instruction assessment, 517
  general instructional effectiveness, 516
  learning prescription, 441
  student behavior observation/skills checklists, 442
Occupational attitudinal tests, 388
One-minute essay questions, 407
Open classroom seating patterns, 276
Operant behavior, 16
Oral tests, 391
Organization, in affective domain, 81
Overdwelling, 338

Pacing, 226
Paideia Program (Adler), 13
Panel discussions for small groups, 304
Parallel forms method, 378
Parental involvement, levels of, 469
Parents, communication with, 467–474, 482
Parent-teacher conferences, 468, 470–474
Part-part-whole strategy of problem solving, 206
Pedagogical aids, 241–243
Pedagogical content knowledge, 503
Peer coaching, 506–507
Peer judgment, 438
Peer tutoring, 292, 294–296
Perceptual abilities, in psychomotor domain, 81
Performance objectives, 79, 140
Performance standards, 60
Performance-based assessment, 417–418
Personality tests, 388
Personalized System of Instruction (PSI), 309

Philosophy for Children (Lipham), 13
Physical abilities, in psycho-motor domain, 81
Piaget's stages of cognitive development, 20–22
Placement evaluation, 433–434
Plan-Do-Check-Act instructional cycle (PDCA), 310
Planning
  by level of instruction, 121–125
  mental vs. formal, 123
  reflective thinking and, 123
  sources of knowledge influencing, 122
  weekly, factors influencing, 122
  See also Lesson planning/design; Unit plans/unit planning
Point system of grading, 457
Politically expedient interventions, 362
Portfolios, 415–416
  definition/content/types of, 415–417
  preparation of, 416
  questions to ask before beginning a portfolio system, 465–466
  recordkeeping through, 464–465
Positive interdependence, 301
Positive reinforcement, 16, 332
Post-organizers, 203
Poverty
  at-risk children resulting from, 452, 498–499
  inner-city schools and, 325, 493, 496–500, 502
  parental involvement levels and, 469
  student misbehavior and, 496

Power seeking, 341–342
Practice and drill
  applications of, 173–175
  as direct instruction method, 176–177
  implementing, 177–179
  importance of, 147–148
  as mastery learning method, 175–176
  persistence of, 174
  recommendations for improving, 180
  strengths and weaknesses of, 214
Praise/praising, 42, 192, 342
Pre-assessment/placement evaluation, 433–434
Predictive validity, 379–380
Prejudice reduction, 124
Preparing Instructional Objectives (Mager), 90
President's Goals 2000, 67
Principle of least intervention, 356
Problem solving
  experiential/inquiry approach to, 210–211
  with IOSIE method, 512
  metacognitive skills in, 207–208
  part-part-whole strategy of, 206
  separate strategy of, 206
  strategies for, 204–208
  students as problem solvers, 205–208
Professional associations, 526–528
Professional development
  attending annual meetings, 528–529
  collaborative research, 530
  coursework for graduate degrees/state certification, 529
  journals as means of, 528
  teacher associations, 526–528
Proficiency tests, 387

Program objectives, 70
Progressivist pedagogy, 492
Project-based assessment, 418–419
Project-based learning, 300
Psychology of instruction vs. psychology of learning, 309
Psychomotor domain, 81–82, 89
Punishment
  behavior modification and, 16–17, 22
  guidelines for using, 357–359, 370–371
  for inappropriate behavior, 352–353
  judicious/minimal use of, 334
  as negative reinforcement, 16

Questions/questioning
  asking questions correctly, 187–193
  bad habits to avoid in, 188–189
  checklist for, 189–190
  cognitive taxonomy-related, 182–183
  completion, 399
  designing, 184
  discovery teaching based on, 179, 181
  divergent and convergent, 184–186
  effective, 184–185, 189–190
  essay, 403–407
  good strategies for, 148
  high- and low-level questions, 181–182
  instructional method of, 147
  for learning, 182, 184
  lesson planning and, 214–215
  levels, and cognitive operations, 206
  matching, 398–399

multiple-choice, 396–398
"right-answer" orienta-
tion, 186–187
short-answer, 402–403
Socratic, 33
strategies and techniques
for, 148, 193, 195
with students of low socioeconomic status, 44
thinking promoted by,
182, 184
true-false, 400–402, 404
types of, 181–185
in whole-classroom set-
tings, 294
Quizzes, 438, 440

Reactive thinking, 35
Readability/reading formulas, 233–235
Reading
achievement and socio-
economic status,
228–229
content area instruction,
243, 245–249
metacognition and text
structure, 249
Reality therapy, 344–345,
347, 370
Reasoned judgments/means,
27
Reasoning
in affective domain, 81
deductive/inductive, 184
Recitations, 443
Recordkeeping
cumulative records,
463–464
electronic/virtual, 461–463
reports of performance
and, 460–467, 481–482
student portfolios,
464–465
Reductionism, 24, 33
Reflective thinking
in the planning process,
123
problem solving and,
204–205

reflective practice,
515–519
Reflex movements, in psychomotor domain, 81
Reform
standards-based, 69,
95–97, 99
of teacher education,
488–493
Reinforcement, 16–17, 174
Relative grade standards,
455–456
Relevance, motivation
through, 202
Reliability, 377–378
Report cards, 460–461
Reports/themes, 447
Research
on class size, 280
critical thinking, 32–34
papers, 447
surveys, 198
teacher collaboration in,
530
on teaching style, 41–43
value-added emphasis of,
26–27
Resources. See Instructional
resources
Responding, in affective
domain, 81
Response structure, in textbooks, 250
Response-cost procedures,
17
Responsibility training,
345–347
Revenge seeking, 342
Rewards, and behavior modification, 17–18
Rix and Lix Readability Formula, 234
Role playing, 199
Room arrangements. See
Classroom seating
arrangements
Root-cause/peripheral interventions, 362
Round table technique for
small groups, 305

SAPC. See Standards Achieve-
ment Planning Cycle
SCARPO acronym for ele-
ments of critical think-
ing, 28–29
Schema, definition of, 21
Scholastic Aptitude Tests
(SATs), 387, 379
Scorer reliability, 378–379
Scripturally implicit instruction, 240
Seating arrangements,
272–277
Selected response/objective
tests. See Short-answer
tests
Self-contained classrooms,
270
Self-evaluation, 514–515
Self-judgment, 438
Seminar model of critical
thinking, 30–32
Separate strategy of problem
solving, 206
Short-answer tests
advantages/limitations of,
402
criteria for selecting, 393
essay tests vs., 391–392
preparing, 393–395
questions in, 402–403
rules of thumb for taking,
395–396
Simulations, games, and
technology, 257–262,
266
Situational grouping, 292
Skilled movements, in psychomotor domain, 81
Small groups
activity guidelines for,
305–306
projects and activities for,
303–304
teaching/learning tech-
niques for, 304–305
Small-group instruction,
288–306
ability grouping, 289–292
checklist for, 317

cooperative learning, 296–301

definition of, 270

peer tutoring, 292–296

whole-group instruction vs., 319

SMART Objectives, 79, 140

Social constructivism, 20

Social promotion (continuous progress) grouping, 271

Social skills

in cooperative learning, 301

inclusion in unit plans, 79, 128

Sociocultural theory of cognition, 20

Socioeconomic status and reading achievement, 228–229

Sorting/classification, 31

Specific learning outcomes, 91

Specific objectives (Mager's model), 90–92

Split-half reliability method, 378

Standardized tests

administering, 428

criteria for selecting, 388–389

definition/purpose of, 380–381

types of, 386–388

Standards

arguments for and against, 377

clarity and parsimony of, 376

Common Core State Standards, 69

culturally responsible lesson planning with, 123

current status of, 100–101

definition/types of, 60–61

determining what is worthy of understanding, 77–78

educational, 60–68

evaluation, 102

honor roll vs., 106–107

learning vs., 103–104

making a difference with, 376–377

national standards for teachers, 101–102

necessity of, 110–111

planning by levels of learning, 120–121

purpose of, 375

for reading progress, 426

significance of, 376

state, 61, 97–99

student performance standards, 102

types of, 60

writing lessons to achieve, 105

Standards Achievement Planning Cycle (SAPC), 104–105

Standards-based grading, 450–459

absolute, 454–455

combining/weighting data, 456

contracting for grades, 456, 458

for effort or improvement, 459

mastery/continuous progress grading, 458

relative, 455–456

types/forms of, 451–453

Standards-based design/lesson planning, 104–105, 112

Stanford Achievement Test (SAT), 386

Stanford Diagnostic Reading Test 4 (SDRT4), 387

Stanford-Binet (SB) intelligence test, 386

State standards, 61, 97–99

Statements of topic aims, 62

Structural grouping, 292

Structure/sequence, establishing, 202

Structured explanation, criteria for, 202

Student behavior observation checklist, 442

Student evaluation. *See* Assessment; Evaluation; Grading

Student performance

innovative practices for reporting, 462

standards for, 102

Student skill checklist, 442

Student Teams-Achievement Divisions (STAD), 298–299

Student-centered learning

child-centered, 215–216

indirect instruction, 197–199, 215

informal seating patterns for, 199, 273

inquiry-based, 210–211

instructional approaches to, 204–211

problem solving, 204–208

Student-facilitated content delivery, 148, 150

Students

culturally diverse, 160–161, 496–500, 502

difficult, strategies for managing, 358

establishing rapport with, 202

immigrant, 498–499

inner-city, challenges in teaching, 325, 496–500, 502

motivation strategies for, 10, 202

peer tutoring by, 292, 296

as problem solvers, 205–208

Study of Schooling (Goodlad), 65

Style(s)

defining, 36–45

determining one's own, 38–41

personality, beliefs, and practices inventory, 39–40

research on, 41–43
student learning and,
43–44
teaching skills/practices
and, 38
Subject exit tests, 387
Subject-matter (content)
knowledge, 119
Subject-matter pedagogy, 503
Success approach to discipline, 344–349
Summaries, 150–152,
203–204
Summative evaluation,
436–437
Supervision of beginning
teachers, 521–524
Synthesis, in cognitive
domain, 80, 85

Tasks, matching to student
learning needs, 283–285
Taxonomic approach to unit
planning, 130–131
Taxonomy of educational
objectives, 79–85
affective domain, 81, 88
cognitive domain, 80,
85–87, 182–183, 206,
404
definition/purpose of,
79–80
establishing objectives,
83–94
knowledge dimension/
cognitive process
dimension of, 83–84
modifying the frame-
works of, 82–83
psychomotor domain,
81–82, 89
using, 82–83
Teach for America, 7
Teachable moments, 124,
161
Teacher attrition, 493, 495,
506, 509–510
Teacher Education Accreditation Council (TEAC),
491–492

Teacher education reform,
488–493
Teacher evaluation observation form, 516
Teacher-centered instruction
content delivery, 145,
148
effectiveness for students
from impoverished
backgrounds, 492
guided discovery, 181
types of, 199
See also Direct instruction
Teacher-made tests, 381,
389–407, 419–421
Teachers
concrete vs. abstract
thinkers, 523
essential skills and behaviors for, 355
novice. See Beginning
teachers
planning and decision
making by, 119–120
Teaching
art and science of, 25–27
constructivist, 22–23,
148–150
culturally responsive, 125
democratic model of, 347
direct. See Direct instruction
effective. See Effective
teaching
during the Great Depres-
sion, 520
indirect. See Student-centered learning
long-term professional
commitment to, 7
lower-achieving students,
44
methods/procedures. See
Instructional methods
preparing for practice,
488–536
reasons for, 4, 5–7, 52
style, 36–45
ten secrets for success in,
534

transmission view of,
145–148
variation in, 12
why, what, how, and who
of, 9
Teaching to the test, 422–423
Team learning approaches
Jigsaw, 299
Student Teams-Achieve-
ment Divisions (STAD),
298–299
Teams-Games-Tourna-
ments (TGT), 299
Technical coaching, 522
Technology
electronic reading
devices/e-books, 251
multimedia instructional
methods, 198–199
simulations and games,
257–262, 266
See also Internet
Technology of Teaching (Skinner), 16
Test anxiety, 413–414
Test-retest method of reliability, 378
Tests
administering and return-
ing, 407–414, 410–411
authentic assessment and,
415
basic testing practices,
391
checklist for constructing,
424
completion, 399
criteria for selecting,
377–380, 426–427
criterion-referenced,
382–386
diagnostic, 387, 435
essay, 391–393, 403–407
as feedback tool, 414
matching, 398–399
multiple-choice, 396–398
nonstandardized, 381
norm-referenced, 381,
383–386
oral, 391

purpose of, 422–423
questions to consider in
selecting, 388–389
quizzes, 438, 440
reliability of, 378–379
sample thought questions
for, 404
short-answer, 391–396,
402
skills for test taking,
408–410
standardized, 380–381,
386–388, 428
state high school exit
exams, 453–454
teacher-made, 381,
389–407, 419–421
test giver's checklist,
411–412
testwise strategies,
408–409
true-false, 400–402
types of, 427–428
usability of, 377, 380
validity of, 379–380, 390
Textbook aids
common features of,
241–242
implications of cognition
and reading levels for
using, 244
Textbooks, 229–253
advantages of, 230
appraising the worth of,
252
blanding down, 231–233
comprehensibility vs.
readability in, 235
de-emphasizing in the
classroom, 239
disadvantages of, 229–230
electronic reading devices
vs., 235–237, 264–265
expository vs. narrative
structure of, 249–251
future of, 251, 253
guidelines for using, 251
information gathering for
decision making about,
246

journals, magazines, and
newspapers as alterna-
tives to, 256–257
low-level cognitive
demands of, 239–240
mentioning phenomenon
in, 230, 239
readability of, 233–235
selecting to enhance
learning, 265
stereotyping in, 230–233
structure of, 249–251
trade books/electronic
texts vs., 237–238
Textually explicit/implicit
instruction, 240
Themes/reports, 447
Thinking
cognitively, sample thought
questions for, 404
concrete vs. abstract, 523
creative, 34–36, 511–512
higher-level, 12–13, 27,
207–208
reflective/heuristic,
204–205
types of, 34–36
Thinking skills lesson plan,
156–157
Think-Pair-Share, 300
Thorndike's law of exercise,
173
Thought questions, 184
Time out, 17
Topic aims, statements of, 62
Topic approach to unit planning, 131–134
Topic objectives, 79
Topics and subtopics, 251
Tracking, deferring/limiting,
291
Trade books, 237–238
Traditional lesson plans
content/development in,
143–144
motivational devices/
activities in, 142–143
Transmission view of teaching
procedures, 145–149,
177

True-false test questions,
400–402
Trust, developing and maintaining, 360–361
Tutoring, 292, 294–296
Tyler's model for developing
goals, 74

Unit plans/unit planning
approaches to, 126–135
checklist for, 164
components of, 126–128
factors influencing, 122
guidelines for developing,
134–135
instructional resources for,
128
necessity for, 166–167
objectives, 70–73
organizing/implement-
ing, 129
presenting instructional
materials in, 225–227
taxonomic approach to,
130–131
topic/theme approach to,
131–134
Unscripted direct instruction, 175–176
Usability of tests, 377, 380

Vagueness, avoiding in lec-
tures/explanations,
203
Validity, 377, 379–380
Valuing, in affective domain,
81
Van Hiele Levels of Geometric
Reasoning, 99
Vertical relationships, 226
Virtual field trips, 259
Virtual recordkeeping,
461–463, 481

WebQuests, 259
Websites
for district-level goals and
standards, 68
goals and objectives on,
73

Wechsler Intelligence Scale
for Children (WISC), 386
Weekly planning, factors
influencing, 122
Whole-group instruction
checklist for, 316
and class size, impact on
achievement in,
280–283
classroom tasks for,
283–285

cooperative learning vs.,
318–319
criticisms of, 280
definition of, 270
guidelines for teaching
with, 287–288
instructional variables/
alterable environ-
ments in, 286–287
See also Direct instruction
Withdrawal, 342

Within-class ability group-
ing, 290, 292
Work involvement, 337
Workbooks, 253–256, 265

Yearly planning, 121–122